CORE-PLUS MATHEMATICS PROJECT

Course
Part **A** **2**

Contemporary Mathematics in Context

A Unified Approach

Arthur F. Coxford
James T. Fey
Christian R. Hirsch
Harold L. Schoen
Gail Burrill
Eric W. Hart
Ann E. Watkins
with
Mary Jo Messenger
Beth Ritsema

EVERYDAY LEARNING™

Chicago, Illinois

Photo Acknowledgments

Cover images: Images © 1997 Photodisc, Inc.

Photo credits are given on page T327 and constitute a continuation of the copyright page.
Everyday Learning Corporation would like to thank the following for providing photographs of
Core-Plus students in their schools. Many of these photographs appear throughout the text.

Janice Lee, Midland Valley High School, Langley, SC
Steve Matheos, Firestone High School, Akron, OH
Ann Post, Traverse City West Junior High School, Traverse City, MI
Alex Rachita, Ellet High School, Akron, OH
Judy Slezak, Prairie High School, Cedar Rapids, IA
The Core-Plus Mathematics Project

Everyday Learning Development Staff
Editorial: Anna Belluomini, Eric Karnowski, Steve Mico
Production/Design: Fran Brown, Hector Cuadra, Norma Underwood, Marie Walz

 This project was supported, in part, by the National Science Foundation.
The opinions expressed are those of the authors and not necessarily those of the Foundation.

ISBN 1-57039-484-9 (Part A)
ISBN 1-57039-488-1 (Part B)

About the Core-Plus Mathematics Project

The **Core-Plus Mathematics Project (CPMP)** is a multi-year project funded by the National Science Foundation to develop student and teacher materials for a complete high school mathematics curriculum. Courses 1–3 comprise a core curriculum appropriate for *all* students. The fourth-year course continues the preparation of students for college mathematics.

Development Team

Project Director

Christian R. Hirsch
Western Michigan University

Project Co-Directors

Arthur F. Coxford
University of Michigan

James T. Fey
University of Maryland

Harold L. Schoen
University of Iowa

Senior Curriculum Developers

Gail Burrill
University of Wisconsin-Madison

Eric W. Hart
Western Michigan University

Ann E. Watkins
California State University, Northridge

Professional Development Coordinator

Beth Ritsema
Western Michigan University

Advisory Board

Diane Briars
Pittsburgh Public Schools

Jeremy Kilpatrick
University of Georgia

Kenneth Ruthven
University of Cambridge

David A. Smith
Duke University

Edna Vasquez
Detroit Renaissance High School

Curriculum Development Consultants

Alverna Champion
Grand Valley State University

Cherie Cornick
Wayne County Alliance for Mathematics and Science

Edgar Edwards
(Formerly) Virginia State Department of Education

Richard Scheaffer
University of Florida

Martha Siegel
Towson University

Edward Silver
University of Pittsburgh

Lee Stiff
North Carolina State University

Technical Coordinator

Wendy Weaver
Western Michigan University

Evaluation Coordinator

Steve Ziebarth
University of Iowa

Collaborating Teachers

Emma Ames
Oakland Mills High School, Maryland

Laurie Eyre
Maharishi School, Iowa

Cheryl Girardot
Sitka High School, Alaska

Joel Goodman
North Cedar Community High School, Iowa

Michael J. Link
Central Academy, Iowa

Mary Jo Messenger
Howard County Public Schools, Maryland

Valerie Mills
Ann Arbor Public Schools, Michigan

Jacqueline Stewart
Okemos High School, Michigan

Michael Verkaik
Holland Christian High School, Michigan

Marcia Weinhold
Kalamazoo Area Mathematics and Science Center, Michigan

Graduate Assistants

Diane Bean
University of Iowa

Judy Flowers
University of Michigan

Chris Rasmussen
University of Maryland

Rebecca Walker
Western Michigan University

Production and Support Staff

James Laser

Michelle Magers

Cheryl Peters

Jennifer Rosenboom

Kathryn Wright
Western Michigan University

Software Developers

Jim Flanders
Colorado Springs, Colorado

Eric Kamischke
Interlochen, Michigan

Core-Plus Mathematics Project Field-Test Sites

Special thanks are extended to these teachers and their students who participated in the testing and evaluation of Course 1.

Ann Arbor Huron High School
Ann Arbor, Michigan
  Ginger Gajar
  Brenda Garr

Ann Arbor Pioneer High School
Ann Arbor, Michigan
  Jim Brink
  Tammy Schirmer

Arthur Hill High School
Saginaw, Michigan
  Virginia Abbott
  Felix Bosco
  David Kabobel

Battle Creek Central High School
Battle Creek, Michigan
  Teresa Ballard
  Steven Ohs

Bedford High School
Temperance, Michigan
  Ellen Bacon
  Linda Martin
  Lynn Parachek

Bloomfield Hills Andover High School
Bloomfield Hills, Michigan
  Jane Briskey
  Cathy King
  Ed Okuniewski
  Linda Robinson
  Roger Siwajek

Bloomfield Hills Middle School
Bloomfield Hills, Michigan
  Connie Kelly
  Tim Loula

Brookwood High School
Snellville, Georgia
  Ginny Hanley
  Linda Wyatt

Caledonia High School
Caledonia, Michigan
  Jenny Diekevers
  Kim Drefcenski
  Thomas Oster

Centaurus High School
Lafayette, Colorado
  Eilene Leach
  Gail Reichert

Clio High School
Clio, Michigan
  Bruce Hanson
  David Sherry
  Lee Sheridan

Davison High School
Davison, Michigan
  Evelyn Ailing
  Wayne Desjarlais
  Darlene Tomczak
  Dan Tomczak

Dexter High School
Dexter, Michigan
  Kris Chatas
  Widge Proctor

Ellet High School
Akron, Ohio
  Marcia Csipke
  Jim Fillmore
  Scott Slusser

Firestone High School
Akron, Ohio
  Barbara Adler
  Barbara Crucs
  Jennifer Walls

Flint Northern High School
Flint, Michigan
  Al Wojtowicz

Goodrich High School
Goodrich, Michigan
  Mike Coke
  John Doerr

Grand Blanc High School
Grand Blanc, Michigan
  Charles Carmody
  Linda Nielsen

Grass Lake Junior/Senior High School
Grass Lake, Michigan
  Larry Poertner

Gull Lake High School
Richland, Michigan
  Darlene Kohrman
  Dorothy Louden

Kalamazoo Central High School
Kalamazoo, Michigan
  Gloria Foster
  Bonnie Frye
  Amy Schwentor

Kelloggsville Public Schools
Wyoming, Michigan
  Jerry Czarnecki
  Steve Ramsey
  John Ritzler

Knott County Central High School
Hindman, Kentucky
  Teresa Combs
  P. Denise Gibson
  Brenda Mullins

Midland Valley High School
Langley, South Carolina
  Kim Huebner
  Janice Lee

Murray-Wright High School
Detroit, Michigan
  Jack Sada

North Lamar High School
Paris, Texas
  Tommy Eads
  Barbara Eatherly

Okemos High School
Okemos, Michigan
  Lisa Crites
  Jacqueline Stewart

Portage Northern High School
Portage, Michigan
  Pete Jarrad
  Scott Moore
  Jerry Swoboda

Prairie High School
Cedar Rapids, Iowa
  Dave LaGrange
  Jody Slezak

San Pasqual High School
Escondido, California
  Damon Blackman
  Gary Hanel
  Ron Peet
  Torril Purvis
  Becky Stephens

Sitka High School
Sitka, Alaska
  Mikolas Bekeris
  Cheryl Girardot
  Dan Langbauer
  Tom Smircich

Sturgis High School
Sturgis, Michigan
  Craig Evans
  Kathy Parkhurst
  Dale Rauh
  JoAnn Roe
  Kathy Roy

Sweetwater High School
National City, California
  Bill Bokesch
  Joe Pistone

Tecumseh High School
Tecumseh, Michigan
  Jennifer Keffer
  Elizabeth Lentz
  Carl Novak
  Eric Roberts

Traverse City High School
Traverse City, Michigan
  Diana Lyon-Schumacher
  Ken May

Vallivue High School
Caldwell, Idaho
  Scott Coulter
  Kathy Harris

Ypsilanti High School
Ypsilanti, Michigan
  Mark McClure
  Valerie Mills
  Don Peurach
  Kristen Stewart

Overview of Course 2

Part A

Unit 1 ▶ Matrix Models

Matrix Models extends student ability to use matrices and matrix operations to represent and solve problems from a variety of real-world settings while connecting important mathematical ideas from several strands.

Topics include matrix models in such areas as inventory control, social relations, archeology, recidivism, ecosystems, sports, tournament rankings, and Markov processes; matrix operations, including row sums, matrix addition, scalar multiplication, matrix multiplication, and matrix powers.

Unit 2 ▶ Patterns of Location, Shape, and Size

Patterns of Location, Shape, and Size develops student understanding of coordinate methods for representing and analyzing relations among geometric shapes, and for describing geometric change.

Topics include modeling situations with coordinates, including computer-generated graphics, distance in the coordinate plane, midpoint of a segment, slope, designing and programming algorithms, matrices, systems of equations, coordinate models of isometric transformations (reflections, rotations, translations, glide reflections) and of size transformations, and similarity.

Unit 3 ▶ Patterns of Association

Patterns of Association develops student understanding of the strength of association between two variables, how to measure the degree of the relation, and how to use this measure as a tool to create and interpret prediction lines for paired data.

Topics include rank correlation, Pearson's correlation coefficient, cause and effect related to correlation, impact of outliers on correlation, least squares linear models, the relation of correlation to linear models, and variability in prediction.

Unit 4 ▶ Power Models

Power Models develops student ability to recognize data patterns that involve both direct and inverse power variation, to construct and analyze those models and combinations such as quadratic functions, and to apply those models to a variety of practical and scientific questions.

Topics include basic power models with rules of the form $y = ax^b$ (b a positive or negative integer), combinations of power models with other simple models, and analysis of quadratic functions and equations from tabular, graphic, and symbolic viewpoints.

Overview of Course 2
Part B

Unit 5 ▶ Network Optimization

Network Optimization extends student ability to use vertex-edge graphs to represent and analyze real-world situations involving network optimization, including optimal spanning networks and shortest routes.

Topics include vertex-edge graph models, optimization, algorithmic problem solving, matrices, trees, minimal spanning trees, shortest paths, Hamiltonian circuits and paths, and Traveling Salesperson problems.

Lesson 1   *Finding the Best Networks*
Lesson 2   *Shortest Paths and Circuits*
Lesson 3   *Looking Back*

Unit 6 ▶ Geometric Form and Its Function

Geometric Form and Its Function develops student ability to model and analyze physical phenomena with triangles, quadrilaterals, and circles and to use these shapes to investigate trigonometric functions, angular velocity, and periodic change.

Topics include parallelogram linkages, pantographs, similarity, triangular linkages (with one side that can change length), sine, cosine, and tangent ratios, indirect measurement, angular velocity, transmission factor, linear velocity, periodic change, period, amplitude, and graphs of functions of the form $y = A\sin(Bx)$ or $y = A\cos(Bx)$.

Lesson 1   *Flexible Quadrilaterals*
Lesson 2   *Triangles and Trigonometric Ratios*
Lesson 3   *The Power of the Circle*
Lesson 4   *Looking Back*

Unit 7 ▶ Patterns in Chance

Patterns in Chance develops student ability to understand and visualize situations involving chance by using simulation and mathematical analysis to construct probability distributions.

Topics include probability distributions and their graphs, multiplication rule for independent events, geometric distribution, expected value, rare events, and an introduction to the binomial distribution.

Lesson 1   *Waiting Times*
Lesson 2   *The Multiplication Rule*
Lesson 3   *Probability Distributions*
Lesson 4   *Expected Value of a Probability Distribution*
Lesson 5   *Looking Back*

Capstone ▶ Looking Back at Course 2

Forests, the Environment, and Mathematics is a thematic, two-week project-oriented activity that enables students to pull together and apply the important modeling concepts and methods developed throughout the course.

Contents

Part A

Unit 1 ▶ Matrix Models

Unit 2 ▶ Patterns of Location, Shape, and Size

Correlation of Course 2 to NCTM Standards

The *Contemporary Mathematics in Context* curriculum and the instructional and assessment practices it promotes address the focal points of the National Council of Teachers of Mathematics *Curriculum Standards* for grades 9–12. By design, the **process standards** on Problems Solving, Reasoning, Communication, and Connections are an integral part of each lesson of every unit in the curriculum.

The chart below correlates Course 2 units with the **content standards** for grades 9–12 in terms of primary emphases (✓) and connections (+).

	NCTM Grades 9–12 Content Standards									
Course 2 Units	Algebra	Functions	Geometry from a Synthetic Viewpoint	Geometry from an Algebraic Viewpoint	Trigonometry	Statistics	Probability	Discrete Mathematics	Conceptual Underpinnings of Calculus	Mathematical Structure
Matrix Models	✓	✓	+			+		✓		+
Patterns of Location, Shape, and Size	✓	✓	+	✓				✓		+
Patterns of Association	✓	✓		+		✓		+		
Power Models	✓	✓	+			✓		+	✓	
Network Optimization	✓		+					✓		
Geometric Form and Its Function	✓	✓	✓	✓	✓	+			+	
Patterns in Chance	✓	✓	+	+		✓	✓	+	✓	
Capstone — Forests, the Environment, and Mathematics	✓	✓	✓	✓	✓	✓	✓	✓	✓	

Curiculum Overview

▶Introduction

Contemporary Mathematics in Context Course 2 continues a four-year integrated mathematics program developed by the **Core-Plus Mathematics Project (CPMP).** The curriculum builds upon the theme of mathematics as sense-making. Investigations of real-life contexts lead to discovery of important mathematics that make sense to students and, in turn, enable them to make sense out of new situations and problems. The curriculum materials have the following features:

■ Multiple Connected Strands

Contemporary Mathematics in Context is a comprehensive mathematical sciences curriculum. Each year the curriculum features multiple ideas from four strands: algebra and functions, geometry and trigonometry, statistics and probability, and discrete mathematics. These strands are unified by fundamental themes, by common topics, and by habits of mind or ways of thinking.

■ Mathematical Modeling

The curriculum emphasizes mathematical modeling and modeling concepts including data collection, representation, interpretation, prediction, and simulation.

■ Access

The curriculum is designed so that core topics are accessible to all students. Differences in students' performance and interest can be accommodated by the depth and level of abstraction to which topics are pursued, by the nature and degree of difficulty of applications, and by providing opportunities for student choice of homework tasks and projects.

■ Graphics Calculators

Numerical, graphics, and programming/link capabilities of graphics calculators are assumed and capitalized on. This technology permits the curriculum and instruction to emphasize multiple representations (numerical, graphical, and symbolic) and to focus on goals in which mathematical thinking is central.

■ Active Learning

Instructional practices promote mathematical thinking through the use of rich problem situations that involve students, both in collaborative groups and individually, in investigating, conjecturing, verifying, applying, evaluating, and communicating mathematical ideas.

■ Multidimensional Assessment

Comprehensive assessment of student understanding and progress through both curriculum-embedded assessment opportunities and supplementary assessment tasks enables monitoring and evaluation of each student's performance in terms of mathematical processes, content, and dispositions.

This curriculum promises to make mathematics accessible to a diverse student population. Developing mathematics along multiple strands nurtures the differing strengths and talents of students and simultaneously helps them to develop diverse mathematical insights. Developing mathematics from a modeling perspective permits students to experience mathematics as a means of making sense of data and problems that arise in diverse contexts within and across cultures. Engaging students in collaborating on tasks in small groups develops their ability to both deal with, and find commonality in, diversity of ideas. Using calculators as a means for learning and doing mathematics enables students to develop versatile ways of dealing with realistic situations and reduces the manipulative skill filter which has prevented large numbers of students from continuing their study of significant mathematics.

▶ Unified Mathematics

Each year *Contemporary Mathematics in Context* features "strands" of algebra and functions, geometry and trigonometry, statistics and probability, and discrete mathematics. These strands are unified within units by fundamental ideas such as: symmetry, function, matrices, data analysis, and curve-fitting. The strands also are connected across units by mathematical habits of mind such as visual thinking, recursive thinking, searching for and describing patterns, making and checking conjectures, reasoning with multiple representations, inventing mathematics, and providing convincing arguments. The strands are unified further by the fundamental themes of data, representation, shape, and change. Important mathematical ideas are continually revisited through this attention to connections within and across strands, enabling students to develop a robust understanding of mathematics.

■ Algebra and Functions

The algebra and functions strand develops students' ability to recognize, represent, and solve problems involving relations among quantitative variables. Central to the development is the use of functions as mathematical models. The key algebraic models in the curriculum are linear, exponential, power, and periodic functions and combinations of these basic types. Each algebraic model is investigated in at least three linked representations—graphic, numeric, and symbolic—with the aid of technology. Attention is also given to modeling with systems, both linear and nonlinear, and to symbolic reasoning.

■ Geometry and Trigonometry

The primary goal of the geometry and trigonometry strand is to develop visual thinking and students' ability to construct, reason with, interpret, and apply mathematical models of patterns in the visual world. Modeling visual patterns involves describing the patterns with regard to shape, size, and location; representing visual patterns with drawings, coordinates or vectors; and predicting changes, and invariants in visual patterns when some force is applied or action occurs to an object. Drawing, constructing, manipulating, and analyzing models of visual patterns in two and three dimensions are emphasized.

■ Statistics and Probability

The primary role of the statistics and probability strand is to develop students' ability to analyze data intelligently, to recognize and measure variation, and to understand the patterns that underlie probabilistic situations. Graphical methods of data analysis, simulations, sampling, and experience with the collection and interpretation of real data are featured.

■ Discrete Mathematics

The discrete mathematics strand develops students' ability to model and solve problems involving sequential change, decision-making in finite settings, and relationships among a finite number of elements. Topics include matrices, vertex-edge graphs, recursion, models of social decision making, and systematic counting methods. Key themes are existence (*Is there a solution?*), optimization (*What is the best solution?*), and algorithmic problem solving (*Can you efficiently construct a solution?*).

▶Instructional Model

The curriculum for Course 2 consists of seven units and a culminating capstone experience. Each of the units is comprised of four to five multi-day lessons in which major ideas are developed through investigations of rich applied problems. Units vary in length from approximately four to six weeks. The final element of Course 2, the capstone, is a thematic two-week project-oriented activity that enables students to pull together and apply the important modeling concepts and methods developed in the entire course.

The manner in which students meet mathematical ideas within lessons can be as important as the mathematics contained in those lessons. Lessons in *Contemporary Mathematics in Context* are therefore designed around a specific cycle of instructional activities intended primarily for small-group work in the classroom and for individual work outside of the classroom.

In Class The four-phase cycle of classroom activities—*Launch, Explore, Share and Summarize,* and *Apply*—is designed to actively engage students in investigating and making sense of problem situations, in constructing important mathematical concepts and methods, and in communicating their thinking and the results of their efforts. The chart on page xiv describes these phases of classroom instruction.

In-Class Instruction

LAUNCH   full-class discussion

Think About This Situation

The lesson begins with a full class discussion of a problem situation and of related questions to **think about.** This discussion sets the context for the student work to follow and helps to generate student interest; it also provides an opportunity for the teacher to assess student knowledge and to clarify directions for the group activities. *Teacher is director and moderator.*

EXPLORE   small-group investigation

INVESTIGATION 1▶

Classroom activity then shifts to having the students **investigate** focused problems and questions related to the launching situation by gathering data, looking for patterns, constructing models and meanings, and making and verifying conjectures. As students work cooperatively in small groups, the teacher circulates from group to group providing guidance and support, clarifying or asking questions, giving hints, providing encouragement, and drawing group members into the discussion to help groups work more cooperatively. The unit materials and related questions posed by students drive the learning. *Teacher is facilitator.*

Checkpoint

A full-class discussion (referred to as a *Checkpoint*) of concepts and methods developed by different small groups then provides an opportunity to **share** progress and thinking. This discussion leads to a class **summary** of important ideas or to further exploration of a topic if competing perspectives remain. Varying points of view and differing conclusions that can be justified should be encouraged. *Teacher is moderator.*

APPLY individual task

▶On Your Own

Finally, students are given a task to complete on their own to **reinforce** their initial understanding of a concept or method. The teacher circulates in the room assessing levels of understanding. *Teacher is intellectual coach.*

Out of Class In addition to the classroom investigations, *Contemporary Mathematics in Context* provides sets of MORE tasks, which are designed to engage students in *Modeling* with, *Organizing*, *Reflecting* on, and *Extending* their mathematical knowledge. MORE tasks are provided for each lesson in the CPMP materials and are central to the learning goals of each lesson. MORE tasks are intended primarily for individual work outside of class. Selection of MORE activities for use with a given class should be based on student performance and the availability of time and technology. Also, students should exercise some choice of tasks to pursue, and at times they should be given the opportunity to pose their own problems and questions to investigate. The chart below describes the types of tasks in a typical MORE set.

MORE: Out-of-Class Activities	
Modeling	*Modeling* tasks are related or new contexts to which students can apply the ideas and methods that they have developed in the lesson.
Organizing	*Organizing* tasks offer opportunities for integrating the formal mathematics underlying the mathematical models developed in the lesson and for making connections with other strands.
Reflecting	*Reflecting* tasks encourage thinking about thinking, about mathematical meanings, and about processes, and promote self-monitoring and evaluation of understanding.
Extending	*Extending* tasks permit further, deeper, or more formal study of the topics under investigation.

▶Assessment

Assessing what students know and are able to do is an integral part of *Contemporary Mathematics in Context* and the instructional model. Initially, as students pursue the investigations that make up the curriculum, the teacher is able to informally assess student performance in terms of process, content, and disposition. Then at the end of each investigation the *Checkpoint* and class discussion provide an opportunity for teachers to assess the levels of understanding that the various groups of students have reached. Finally, *On Your Own* problem situations and tasks in the MORE sets provide further opportunities to assess the level of understanding of each individual student.

A much more detailed description of the CPMP assessment program is given in *Implementing the CPMP Curriculum*.

▶Organization of the Text

The organization of the student text, like that for Course 1, differs in several other ways from traditional textbooks. There are no boxed-off definitions, "worked-out" examples, or content summaries. Students learn mathematics by doing mathematics. Concept images are developed as students complete investigations and later concept definitions may appear. Mathematical ideas are developed and then shared by groups of students at strategically placed Checkpoints in the lessons. This discussion leads to a class summary of shared understandings.

It is important that each student construct a Mathematics Toolkit consisting of mathematical concepts and methods as they are developed. By organizing important class-generated ideas from a unit, occasional summary Checkpoint responses, or a unit summary in the student's own words, the student will have a valuable set of tools that can be used throughout the course and in subsequent courses.

Implementing the Curriculum

▶Planning for Instruction

The *Contemporary Mathematics in Context* curriculum is not only changing what mathematics all students have the opportunity to learn, but also changing how that learning occurs and is assessed. Active learning is most effective when accompanied with active teaching. Just as the student text is designed to actively engage students in doing mathematics, the teacher's resource materials are designed to support teachers in planning for instruction; in observing, listening to, questioning, facilitating student work, and orchestrating classroom discussion; and in managing the classroom.

The *Teacher's Guide* provides suggestions, based on the experiences of field-test teachers, for implementing this exciting new curriculum in your classroom. You probably will find several new ideas that can be overwhelming. The developers highly recommend that teachers who are teaching *Contemporary Mathematics in Context* for the first time do so at least in pairs who share a common planning period.

Each of the items listed below are included in the *Teacher's Guide* for each unit.

- Unit Overview
- Unit Planning Guide listing objectives, suggested timeline, and materials needed
- Instructional notes and suggestions
- Suggested assignments for each MORE set
- Solutions for Investigations and MORE tasks
- Unit summary and a look ahead

Teaching Resources include blackline masters for creating transparencies and handouts. *Assessment Resources* include quizzes for individual lessons, end-of-unit exams, and take-home assessment activities. Special calculator software has been developed to support students' investigations and modeling applications. Software for the TI-82, TI-83, and (in some cases) TI-92 graphics calculators is available on disk for downloading from Macintosh and DOS- or Windows-based (PC) computers.

Each unit of *Contemporary Mathematics in Context* includes content which may be new to many teachers or new approaches to familiar content. Thus a first step toward planning the teaching of a unit is to review the scope and sequence of the unit itself. This review provides an overall feel for the goals of the unit and how it holds together. Working through the student investigations, if possible with a colleague, provides help in thinking about and understanding mathematical ideas that may be unfamiliar.

In the *Teacher's Guide* you will find teaching notes for each lesson in Course 1, including instructional suggestions and sample student responses to investigations and MORE sets. Thinking about the range of possible responses and solutions to problems in a lesson proves to be very helpful in facilitating student work.

Although not stated, it is assumed that students have access to graphics calculators at all times for in-class work and ideally for out-of-class work as well. Downloading and becoming familiar with the specially-designed calculator software will require advanced planning as will acquiring physical materials.

The developers recommend that the homework (MORE) assignment *not* be held off until the end of the lesson or the investigation just preceding the MORE set. Some teachers choose to post the MORE assignment at the beginning of a lesson along with the due date—usually a day or two following planned completion of the lesson. Other teachers prefer to assign particular Modeling and Reflecting tasks at appropriate points during the course of the multiday lesson and then assign the remaining tasks toward the end of the lesson. Note that all recommended assignments include provision for student choice of some tasks. This is but one of many ways in which this curriculum is designed to accommodate and support differences in students' interests and performance levels.

It is strongly recommended that student solutions to Organizing tasks be discussed in class. These tasks help students organize and formalize the mathematics developed in context and connect it to other mathematics they have studied. Structuring the underlying mathematics and building connections is best accomplished by comparing and discussing student work and synthesizing key ideas within the classroom.

▶Orchestrating Lessons

The *Contemporary Mathematics in Context* materials are designed to engage students actively in a four-phase cycle of classroom activities. The activities often require both students and teachers to assume roles quite different than those in more traditional mathematics classrooms. Becoming accustomed to these new roles usually takes time, perhaps a semester or more, but field-test teachers report that the time and effort required are well worth it in terms of student learning and professional fulfillment. Although realistic problem solving and investigative work by students is the heart of the curriculum, how teachers orchestrate the launching of that activity and the sharing and summarizing of results is critical to successful implementation.

Students enter the classroom with markedly different backgrounds, experience, and knowledge. These differences can be viewed as assets. Engaging the class in a free-flowing give-and-take discussion of how they think about the launch situations serves to connect lessons with the informal understandings of data, shape, change, and chance that students bring to the classroom. Try to maximize the participation of students in these discussions by emphasizing that their ideas and possible approaches are valued and important and that definitive answers are not necessarily expected at this time.

Once launched, a lesson may involve students working together collaboratively in small groups for a period of days punctuated occasionally by brief, whole-class discussion of questions students have raised. In this setting, the lesson becomes driven primarily by the instructional materials themselves. Rather than orchestrating class discussion, the teacher shifts to circulating among the groups and observing, listening, and interacting with students by asking guiding or probing questions. These small-group investigations lead to (re)invention of important mathematics that makes sense to students. Sharing and agreeing as a class on the mathematical ideas that groups are developing is the purpose of the "Checkpoints" in the instructional materials.

Class discussions at "Checkpoints" are orchestrated somewhat differently than during the launch of a lesson. At this stage, mathematical ideas and methods still may be under development and may vary for individual groups. So class discussion should involve groups comparing their methods and results, analyzing their work, and arriving at conclusions agreed upon by the class.

The investigations deepen students' understanding of mathematical ideas and extend their mathematical language in contexts. Occasionally there is a need to introduce conventional or more technical terminology and symbolism. This occurs in the student materials immediately following a "Checkpoint" and before the corresponding "On Your Own" task. These connections should be introduced by the teacher as a natural way of closing the class discussion summarizing the "Checkpoint."

Managing Classroom Activities

▶Active Learning and Collaborative Work

The *Contemporary Mathematics in Context* curriculum materials are designed to promote active, collaborative learning and group work for two important reasons. First, collaborative learning is the most effective method for engaging all the students in a class in the learning process. Second, practice in cooperative learning in the classroom is practice for real life: students develop and exercise the same skills in the classroom that they need in their lives at home, in the community, and in the workplace.

Value of Individuals

Perhaps the most fundamental belief underlying the use of cooperative learning is that every student is viewed as a valuable resource and contributor. In other words, every student participates in group work and is given the opportunity and time to voice ideas and opinions. Implementing this concept is not easy. It does not happen automatically. In order to set a tone that will promote respect for individuals and their contributions, classroom rules should be established and agreed upon by the learning community. Students should be included in the process of formulating the rules. The teacher should initiate a discussion of group rules and then post them in the classroom. The teacher should model all of the rules correctly to show that "we" begins with "me." Those who do not adhere to the rules must accept the consequences in accordance with classroom or school disciplinary procedures.

Importance of Social Connections

Even in classrooms in which the rules for showing respect have been clearly established, experience has shown that students still cannot talk with one another about mathematics (or social studies, or literature, or any other subject) if they do not first have positive social connections.

One way to develop this kind of common base is through team-building activities. These short activities (five to ten minutes) may be used at the beginning of the year to help students get acquainted with the whole class and may be used during the year whenever new groups are formed to help groupmates know one another better. Team-building activities help students learn new and positive things about classmates with whom they may have attended classes for years, but have not known in depth. The time taken for these quick team builders pays off later in helping students feel comfortable enough to work with the members of their group.

Need for Teaching Social Skills

Experience also has shown that social skills are critical to the successful functioning of any small group. Because there is no guarantee that students of any particular age will have the social skills necessary for effective group work, it often is necessary to teach these skills to build a collaborative learning environment.

These social skills are specific skills, not general goals. Examples of specific social skills that the teacher can teach in the classroom include responding to ideas respectfully, keeping track of time, disagreeing in an agreeable way, involving everyone, and following directions. Though goals such as cooperating and listening are important, they are too general to teach and practice.

One method of teaching social skills is to begin by selecting a specific skill and then having the class brainstorm to develop a script for practicing that skill. Next, the students practice that skill during their group work. Finally, in what is called the processing, the students discuss within their groups how well they performed the assigned social skill. Effective teaching of social skills requires practicing and processing; merely describing a specific social skill is not enough. Actual practice and processing are necessary for students really to learn the skill and to increase the use of appropriate behaviors during group work and other times during class.

One of the premises of cooperative learning is that by developing the appropriate skills through practice, anyone in the class can learn to work in a group with anyone else. Learning to work in groups is a continuous process, however, and the process can be helped by decisions that the teacher makes. *Implementing the Core-Plus Mathematics Curriculum* provides information and support to help teachers make decisions about group size, composition, method of selection, student reaction to working in groups, and the duration of groups. It also provides advice on dealing effectively with student absences.

The culture created within the classroom is crucial to the success of this curriculum. It is important to inculcate in students a sense of inquiry and responsibility for their own learning. Without this commitment, active, collaborative learning by students cannot be effective. In order for students to work collaboratively, they must be able to understand the value of working together. Some students seem satisfied with the rationale that it is important in the business world. Others may need to understand that the struggle of verbalizing their thinking, listening to others' thinking, questioning themselves and other group members, and coming to an agreement increases their understanding and retention of the mathematics while contributing to the formation of important thinking skills or habits of mind.

Issues of helping students to work collaboratively will become less pressing as both you and your students experience this type of learning. You may find it helpful to refer to *Implementing the Core-Plus Mathematics Curriculum* and discuss effective cooperative groups with colleagues a few weeks into the semester.

▶Assessment

Throughout the *Contemporary Mathematics in Context* curriculum, the term "assessment" is meant to include all instances of gathering information about students' levels of understanding and their disposition toward mathematics for purposes of making decisions about instruction. You may want to consult the extended section on assessment in *Implementing the Core-Plus Mathematics Curriculum.*

The dimensions of student performance that are assessed in this curriculum (see chart below) are consistent with the assessment recommendations of the National Council of Teachers of Mathematics' *Curriculum and Evaluation Standards for School Mathematics (*NCTM, 1988) and the *Assessment Standards for School Mathematics* (NCTM, 1995). They are much broader than those of a typical testing program.

Assessment Dimensions

Process	Content	Attitude
Problem Solving	Concepts	Beliefs
Reasoning	Applications	Perseverance
Communication	Representational Strategies	Confidence
Connections	Procedures	Enthusiasm

Sources of Assessment Information

Several kinds of assessment are available to teachers using *Contemporary Mathematics in Context.* Some of these sources reside within the curriculum itself; some of them are student-generated; and some are supplementary materials designed specifically for assessment. Understanding the nature of these sources is a prerequisite for establishing guidelines on how to score assessments, making judgments about what students know and are able to do, and assigning grades.

Curriculum Sources

Two features of the curriculum, questioning and observation by the teacher, provide fundamental and particularly useful ways of gathering assessment information. The student text uses questions to facilitate student understanding regarding new concepts, how these concepts fit with earlier ideas and with one another, and how they can be applied in problem situations. Whether students are working individually or in groups, the teacher is given a window to watch how the students think about and apply mathematics as they attempt to answer the questions posed by the curriculum materials. In fact, by observing how students respond to the curriculum-embedded questions, the teacher can assess student performance across all process, content, and attitude dimensions described in the chart on page xix.

Specific features in the student material that focus on different ways students respond to questions are the "Checkpoint," "On Your Own," and MORE (*Modeling, Organizing, Reflecting,* and *Extending*) sets at the end of each investigation. "Checkpoint" features are intended to bring students together, usually after they have been working in small groups, so they may share and discuss the progress each group has made during a sequence of related activities. Each "Checkpoint" is intended to be a whole-class discussion, so it should provide an opportunity for teachers to assess, informally, the levels of understanding that the various groups of students have reached.

Following each "Checkpoint," the "On Your Own" tasks are meant to be completed by students working individually. Student responses to these tasks provide an opportunity for teachers to assess the level of understanding of each student.

Activities in the MORE sets serve many purposes, including post-investigation assessment. Modeling tasks help students demonstrate how well they understand and can apply the concepts and procedures developed in an investigation. Organizing activities demonstrate how well students understand connections between the content of an investigation and other mathematical and real-world ideas. In-class discussions based on Organizing tasks are a crucial step in assisting students' development of a full understanding of the mathematical content and connections. Reflecting activities provide insights into students' beliefs, attitudes, and judgments of their own competence. Extending tasks show how well students are able to extend the present content beyond the level addressed in an investigation. The performance of students or groups of students in each of these types of activity provides the teacher with further information to help assess applicability, connectedness, and depth of the students' evolving understanding of mathematics.

Finally, an opportunity for group self-assessment is provided in the last element of each unit, the "Looking Back" lesson. These activities help students pull together and demonstrate what they have learned in the unit and at the same time provide helpful review and confidence-building for students.

Student-Generated Sources

Other possible sources of assessment information are writings and materials produced by the students in the form of student journals and portfolios. Student journals are notebooks in which students are encouraged to write (briefly, but frequently) their personal reflections concerning the class, the mathematics they are learning, and their progress. These journals are an excellent way for the teacher to gain insights into how individual students are feeling about the class, what they do and do not understand, and what some of their particular learning difficulties are. For many students, the journal is a nonthreatening way to communicate with the teacher about matters that may be too difficult or too time-consuming to talk about directly. Journals also encourage students to assess their own understanding of, and disposition toward, the mathematics they are studying. The teacher should collect, read, and respond to each journal at least once a month—more often if possible.

The *Contemporary Mathematics in Context* assessment program provides many items that would be appropriate for students' portfolios, including reports of individual and group projects, journal excerpts, teacher-completed observation checklists, end-of-unit assessments (especially the take-home activities), and the extended cumulative projects. One way students can develop a portfolio is to collect all their written work in a folder, sometimes called a working portfolio. Then at least once each semester, students go through their working portfolio and choose items that they think best represent their growth during this time period. After writing a paragraph or two explaining why each piece of work was chosen, each student puts the chosen items with the written rationales into a new folder that becomes the actual portfolio.

Assessment Resources

The *Contemporary Mathematics in Context* instructional materials include for each unit a third source of assessment information—*Assessment Resources* that contains end-of-lesson quizzes and end-of unit assessments in the form of an in-class unit exam and a take-home assessment. Calculators often are required and it is intended that they always are available to students. Since many rich opportunities for assessing students are embedded in the curriculum itself, you may choose not to use all the lesson quizzes for each unit.

End-of-Lesson Quizzes Two forms of a quiz covering the main ideas of each lesson are provided. These quizzes, which are the most traditional of all the assessment methods and instruments included with the *Contemporary Mathematics in Context* materials, are comprised of fairly straightforward problems meant to determine if students have developed understanding of the important concepts and procedures of each lesson. Thus, the quizzes focus on the content dimension of the Assessment Dimensions.

In-Class Exams Two forms of in-class exams are provided for each unit and are intended to be completed in a 50-minute class period by students working individually. Calculators are required in most cases and are intended to be available to students. It also is recommended that students have access to the textbook and to their journals and class notes. The two forms of each exam are *not* equivalent, although they assess essentially the same mathematical ideas. Teachers should preview the two versions carefully before making a choice, and they should feel free to revise or delete items and add new ones if necessary.

Take-Home Assessments Five possible take-home assessment activities are included for each unit. The students or the teacher should choose one or, at most, two of these activities. These assessments, some of which are best done by students working in pairs or small groups, provide students with the opportunity to organize the information from the completed unit, to extend the ideas of the unit into other areas of interest to them, to work with another student or group of students, and to avoid the time pressure often generated by in-class exams. Of the five activities in a take-home assessment package, the first three require a day or two for one or two students to complete. The last two activities of a take-home assessment package are extended projects that require up to a week for students, usually working in groups, to complete. It is recommended that, on one or two occasions during the time that students are working on extended projects, the teacher use some class time to check on students' progress and to give guidance and encouragement.

Extended Cumulative Projects Assessment traditionally has been based on evaluating work that students have completed in a very short time period and under restricted conditions. Some assessment, however, should involve work done over a longer time period—a week or more—and with the aid of resources. Thus an extended assessment project is included with the Unit 3 assessments. These projects are investigations that make use of some of the main ideas encountered in the curriculum up to that time. The activities, which are intended to be completed by small groups of students in a week or more, are similar to the extended take-home assessment projects at the end of each unit, except that they require understanding of mathematical content from several units.

Scoring Assessments

High expectations of the quality of students' written work will encourage students to reach their potential. Assigning scores to open-ended assessments and to observations of students' performance requires more subjective judgment by the teacher than does grading short answer or multiple-choice tests. It is therefore not possible to provide a complete set of explicit guidelines for scoring open-ended assessment items and written or oral reports. However, some general guidelines may be helpful. When scoring the student work on open-ended assessment tasks, the goal is to reward in a fair and consistent way the kinds of thinking and understanding that the task is meant to measure. Preparing to score open-ended assessment tasks is best done using a three-step process. First, teachers should have a general rubric, or scoring scheme, with several response levels in mind. The general rubric is the foundation for scoring across a wide range of types of open-ended tasks. The following general rubric can be used for most assessment tasks provided with *Contemporary Mathematics in Context*.

General Scoring Rubric

4 points	Contains complete response with clear, coherent, and unambiguous explanation; includes clear and simple diagram, if appropriate; communicates effectively to identified audience; shows understanding of question's mathematical ideas and processes; identifies all important elements of question; includes examples and counter examples; gives strong supporting arguments
3 points	Contains good solid response with some, but not all, of the characteristics above; explains less completely; may include minor error of execution but not of understanding
2 points	Contains complete response, but explanation is muddled; presents incomplete arguments; includes diagrams that are inappropriate or unclear, or fails to provide a diagram when it would be appropriate; indicates some understanding of mathematical ideas, but in an unclear way; shows clear evidence of understanding some important ideas while also making one or more fundamental, specific errors
1 point	Omits parts of question and response; has major errors; uses inappropriate strategies
0 points	No response; frivolous or irrelevant response

Assigning Grades

Because the *Contemporary Mathematics in Context* approach and materials provide a wide variety of assessment information, the teacher will be in a good position to assign a fair grade for student work. With such a wide choice for assessment, a word of caution is appropriate: *it is easy to overassess students, and care must be taken to avoid doing so.* A quiz need not be given after every lesson nor an in-class exam after every unit. The authors believe it is best to vary assessment methods from lesson to lesson, and from unit to unit. If information on what students understand and are able to do is available from their homework and in-class work, it may not be necessary to take the time for a formal quiz after each lesson. Similarly, information from project work may replace an in-class exam.

Deciding exactly how to weigh the various kinds of assessment information is a decision that the teacher will need to make and communicate clearly to the students.

Maintaining skills

The developers have identified a set of paper-and-pencil technical competencies that all students should acquire. To provide additional practice with these core competencies, a special maintenance feature is included in blackline master form in the *Teaching Resources.*

Beginning with Unit 4 of Course 1, Graph Models, and then continuing with each unit thereafter, a supplementary set of maintenance tasks provides periodic review and additional practice of basic skills. These skills will be continually revisited to ensure mastery by each student at some point in the curriculum.

Use of the maintenance material following the start of Lesson 2 of each unit will allow students time to work simultaneously on skills during the latter part of a unit without interrupting the flow of the unit. You may wish to allow a few minutes at the end of selected class periods to revisit these skills with various groups of students who need assistance while other groups choose an extending task.

The maintenance material prepared for each unit spans technical competencies across each of the strands. In each case, the first presented task is a contextual problem, but the remaining tasks are not contextualized. Students should *not* use a calculator for these tasks unless so directed.

Additional Resources

Implementing the Core-Plus Mathematics Curriculum contains expanded information on the scope and sequence of Courses 1, 2, and 3; on managing classroom activities; and on the assessment program. It also provides a list of colleges and universities to which students from pilot-test schools have been admitted. A section on communication with parents includes a template for a parent letter that overviews this curriculum and intended instructional practices. You will find it useful to have the implementation guide available for reference throughout the school year.

Unit **1** ▶ Matrix Models

UNIT OVERVIEW This unit introduces matrices as powerful mathematical models that are used throughout mathematics. This approach provides an opportunity for students to see the interconnectedness of mathematics as they use matrices to explore topics in algebra, geometry, statistics, probability, and discrete mathematics. In addition, students further develop the skill of mathematical modeling as they explicitly build matrix models, use matrix operations to form new matrices, and interpret the result in terms of the context.

Unit 1 Objectives

- To see the interconnectedness of mathematics through the use of matrices to explore topics in algebra, geometry, statistics, probability, and discrete mathematics
- To use matrices for organizing and displaying data in a variety of real-world settings like brand switching, tracking pollution through an ecosystem, and tournament rankings
- To develop further the skill of mathematical modeling by building matrix models and then operating on them to solve problems
- To learn and apply matrix operations: row sums, scalar multiplication, addition, subtraction, and matrix multiplication
- To use matrices and inverse matrices to answer questions that involve systems of linear equations

Matrix Models

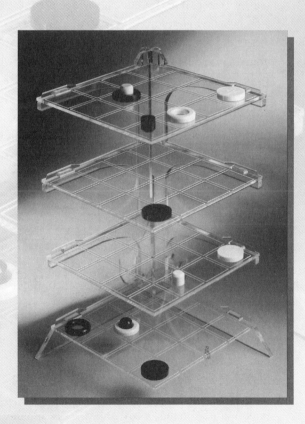

1

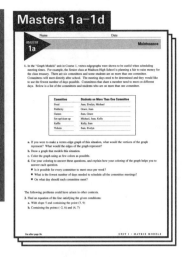

NOTE: Each matrix is read "from row to column"; that is, the element in row *i*, column *j* indicates how object *i* acts on object *j*. This is an important and recurring point about reading the matrices in this unit. The convention of reading *from* the row *to* the column will be maintained throughout the unit.

Use of Matrices Throughout the Unit

Lesson 1 introduces matrices as a tool for organizing and displaying data in a variety of real-world settings. Students informally operate on matrices in a variety of ways, and the operations of addition, subtraction, and scalar multiplication are developed. Matrix multiplication is investigated in Lesson 2, through applications like brand switching, tracking pollution through an ecosystem, and rankings from a tournament. Finally, in Lesson 3, students use matrices to represent situations and solve problems that involve systems of two linear equations in the form $ax + by = c$.

Collaborative Learning

The *Contemporary Mathematics in Context* curriculum is designed around small-group collaborative learning. Effective collaborative work requires familiarity with the factors in the composition and selection of groups as well as practice in classroom techniques for managing collaborative learning. For detailed information on these areas, please see *Implementing the CPMP Curriculum.*

Most students in this course have worked collaboratively during Course 1. However, they are now in a classroom with different students and perhaps a different teacher. You may wish to create cooperative group guidelines with the assistance of your students. During this first unit, it is important for students to focus on the guidelines that help facilitate collaborative learning and to reinforce the skills that they began developing in Course 1. A good way to do this is to incorporate group processing questions into your lessons, at least through the first unit. A good time to do this is immediately following discussion of the Checkpoints. The time you spend on this now will be returned through more efficient, smooth, and productive group work throughout the rest of the year.

Group processing questions may be open-ended or fill-in-the-blank. You will find sample questions immediately following the Checkpoint solutions throughout the teacher's notes for this unit. You may choose one or create your own to fit your particular emphasis for the day.

Maintenance Resource

The Teaching Resources for each unit begin with a series of masters entitled Maintenance. Items on the Maintenance masters reflect mathematics skills that students may need to practice periodically over the year. Concepts introduced in a unit may be included on any subsequent Maintenance pieces. The first task presented is a contextual problem, but remaining tasks are not contextualized. Students should *not* use a calculator for these tasks unless so directed.

You may wish to ask students to complete the tasks over a three-day period while they are in the process of completing a multi-day investigation. The developers recommend that Maintenance tasks be assigned at any point after students have completed Lesson 1 of a unit. This allows the students time to get accustomed to the new focus of the unit without interruption. You may wish to allow a few minutes at the end of selected class periods to revisit these skills with various groups of students who need assistance while other groups choose an Extending task.

See Masters 1a–1d for Maintenance tasks that students can work on following Lesson 1.

Unit 1 Planning Guide

Lesson Objectives	MORE Assignments	Suggested Pacing	Materials
Lesson 1 *Building and Using Matrix Models* • To use matrices as a tool for organizing and displaying data • To analyze given matrices in a variety of contexts and to appreciate their widespread use • To operate informally on matrices in a variety of ways (including summing rows and columns, comparing two rows, and finding the mean of rows or columns) and to interpret the results in terms of the context • To operate on matrices using the standard operations of addition, subtraction, and scalar multiplication and to interpret the result in terms of the context	**after page 5** Students can begin Organizing Task 2 or Reflecting Task 3 from p. 14. **after page 10** Students can begin Modeling Task 1; Organizing Task 1; or Reflecting Task 1 from p. 14. **page 14** **Modeling:** 2 and choice of one* **Organizing:** 1, 2, and 5 **Reflecting:** 1 and 3 **Extending:** Choose one*	5 days	• Teaching Resources 2–5 • Assessment Resources 1–6
Lesson 2 *Multiplying Matrices* • To use matrix multiplication, including powers of matrices, as a mathematical model that is helpful in making decisions in a variety of contexts • To investigate the properties of matrices	**after page 30** Students can complete Teaching Master 10 for decontextualized practice multiplying matrices. **after page 35** Students can begin Modeling Task 3 or Organizing Task 2 from p. 46. **after page 41** Students can begin Modeling Task 1, 2, or 4; Organizing Task 3; Reflecting Task 1; or Extending Tasks 1–4 from p. 46. **page 46** **Modeling:** 3 and choice of one* **Organizing:** 2, 3, and 4 **Reflecting:** 1 **Extending:** Choose one*	8 days	• Teaching Resources 1a–1d, 6–17 • Assessment Resources 7–12
Lesson 3 *Matrices and Systems of Linear Equations* • To represent situations involving linear relationships with systems of linear equations of the form $ax + by = c$ • To represent systems of linear equations with matrices • To solve matrix equations of the form $AX = C$ by multiplying by A^{-1} • To graph linear equations of the form $ax + by = c$, by hand and using a graphics calculator or computer software • To solve systems of linear equations by graphing	**after page 63** Students can begin Organizing Task 2 or Reflecting Task 1 from p. 66. **page 66** **Modeling:** 1 or 2 and 3* **Organizing:** 2, 3, and 4 **Reflecting:** Choose one* **Extending:** Choose one	6 days	• Graph paper • Teaching Resources 18–22 • Assessment Resources 13–18
Lesson 4 *Looking Back* • To review the major objectives of the unit		2–3 days (includes testing)	• Teaching Resources 23–24 • Assessment Resources 19–41

* When choice is indicated, it is important to leave the choice to the student.
Note: *It is best if Organizing tasks are discussed as a whole class after they have been assigned as homework.*

Lesson **1**

Building and Using Matrix Models

In Course 1, many types of mathematical models were introduced, including linear and exponential functions, vertex-edge graphs, geometric transformations, and probability simulations. These models can help you to analyze a wide range of situations, from insulin breakdown to buying a car, from assigning radio frequencies to designing tiling patterns. In this unit you will investigate another important mathematical model: a *matrix*. Matrix models are not only useful for solving a variety of problems, they also provide another link among the major strands of mathematics.

Matrix models even relate to the shoes you wear. Many people are wearing athletic shoes these days, whether on the job, at school, or on the playing field. The business of athletic shoes is big business. Nike, for instance, is building huge new stores all over the country, called Nike Town. The biggest Nike Town is in Chicago, where they get more visitors than many other tourist attractions in town. In a single day as many as 12,000 people might visit the store. Nike is not the only company with large stores. Foot Locker already has mega-stores, called World Foot Locker, in several cities around the country. Reebok also has its own giant superstores, including one in Russia.

Lesson 1 Building and Using Matrix Models

LESSON OVERVIEW This lesson introduces matrices as a tool for organizing and displaying data. The first investigation emphasizes the essential first step of mathematical modeling: building the model. In this curriculum, students should learn not only how to use and interpret models, but also how to build the model that best fits the situation. The activities in Investigation 2 help students see that a matrix model can be used to organize data in many different contexts. They will operate informally on matrices in a variety of ways before they investigate the standard matrix operations. One useful "non-standard" operation that students will use throughout the unit is summing rows or columns. Students develop the standard matrix operations of matrix addition, matrix subtraction, and multiplication of a matrix by a number (scalar multiplication) in the third investigation.

Lesson Objectives

- To use matrices as a tool for organizing and displaying data
- To analyze given matrices in a variety of contexts and to appreciate their widespread use
- To operate informally on matrices in a variety of ways (including summing rows and columns, comparing two rows, and finding the mean of rows or columns) and to interpret the result in terms of the context
- To operate on matrices using the standard operations of addition, subtraction, and scalar multiplication and to interpret the result in terms of the context

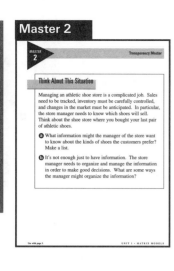

LAUNCH full-class discussion

Think About This Situation

See Teaching Master 2.

This full-class discussion should be kept brief. The goal is to get the students thinking about a situation of some interest to them, and to motivate the need for some mathematics to understand the situation.

a Students might think about shoe brands, sizes, colors, styles, men's and women's shoes, *etc*. Students will use this list later, so you may want to write the list on the board for future reference.

b Some quick brainstorming here will help students see the possibility of and need for organizing the information in a useful way. They might think about tables, lists, bar graphs, line graphs, box plots, charts like in *USA Today, etc.*

EXPLORE small-group investigation

INVESTIGATION 1 There's No Business Like Shoe Business

If you and your class spend only a brief time with the "Think About This Situation", then you should be able to do activity 1 of Investigation 1 as a large group and still have time for small groups of students to discuss adequately the ideas in activities 2, 3, and perhaps 4, even in a short class period. If you do not get as far as the Checkpoint following Investigation 1, you may want to impose a temporary closure. You could do this by asking several groups to share quickly their answers for activity 3 part c, perhaps by having a representative from each group set up their matrix on the board; or you may want to end by asking students to write, in their own words, what they think a matrix is and why it may be useful. Another option, if class time is almost over, is to have groups discuss activities 4 and 5, then ask them to identify the graph that they wish to sketch for activity 5 part c. Individually, students could analyze these items further and prepare responses for the next class period. As you observe groups at work, you can ask them to explain the meaning of a particular entry in a matrix; or you can ask them to explain their interpretations of the matrix in activity 3 using their newly acquired vocabulary.

1. The point of this activity is to generate some data. Leaving the data disorganized at this stage would be good, since one of the purposes of using matrices is to organize data. You may wish to write the list on the board or have a student do it. Encourage the class to generate a rich list, but try to keep it manageable—that is, not too many data, not too few.
2. Students probably will find this to be a natural and obvious way to organize the data. That's the point; matrices are natural and easy. It is important that all students carefully read and correctly use the terminology introduced here—matrix, row, and column. While students work on this activity, listen for incorrect use of this terminology.
    a. Responses will vary based on class data. Some classes may choose different brand names for the athletic shoes.

Think About This Situation

Managing an athletic shoe store is a complicated job. Sales need to be tracked, inventory must be controlled carefully, and changes in the market must be anticipated. In particular, the store manager needs to know which shoes will sell. Think about the shoe store where you bought your last pair of athletic shoes.

ⓐ What information might the manager of the store want to know about the kinds of shoes the customers prefer? Make a list.

ⓑ It's not enough just to have information. The manager needs to organize and manage the information in order to make good decisions. What are some ways the manager might organize the information?

INVESTIGATION 1 There's No Business Like Shoe Business

There are many different brands of athletic shoes, and each brand of shoe has many different styles and sizes. Shoe store managers need to know which shoes their customers prefer so they can have the right shoes in stock.

1. Work together with the whole class to find out about the brands of athletic shoes preferred by students in your class.

   a. Make a list of all the different brands of athletic shoes preferred by students in your class.

   b. How many males prefer each brand? How many females prefer each brand?

2. One way to organize and display these data is to use a kind of table. You can do this by listing the brands down one side, writing "Men" and "Women" across the top, and then entering the appropriate numbers.

   a. Work with your group to complete a table like the one below for your class data. Add or remove rows as needed. A rectangular array like this is called a **matrix**.

Athletic Shoe Brands

	Men	Women
Converse	___	___
Nike	___	___
Reebok	___	___

b. The matrix on the previous page has 3 *rows* and 2 *columns*. How many rows were needed in the matrix to display the class data? How many columns?

c. Could you organize the class data using a matrix with 2 rows? If so, how many columns would it have? Which display would you prefer? Why?

3. a. Knowing the brands of shoes that customers prefer certainly will help a store manager decide which shoes to stock. What other information might the manager of the store want to know about the kinds of shoes the customers prefer? Look back at the list you generated for the "Think About This Situation" on page 3. Add to your list if necessary.

b. Construct a matrix to organize some of the information from your list in part a. Don't worry about actually collecting the information; just set up the matrix, label the rows and columns, and give the matrix a title according to the information that it will show.

c. Compare your matrix with those made by other groups.

- Do all the *matrices* (plural of matrix) make sense?
- Are the row and column labels and titles appropriate?
- How many different variables can be represented in one matrix?

Suppose you were a manager of a local FleetFeet shoe store. Data on monthly sales of Converse, Nike, and Reebok shoes are shown in the matrix below. Each entry represents the number of pairs of shoes sold.

Monthly Sales

	J	F	M	A	M	J	J	A	S	O	N	D
Converse	40	35	50	55	70	60	40	40	70	35	30	80
Nike	55	55	75	70	70	65	60	60	75	55	50	75
Reebok	50	30	60	80	70	50	10	40	75	35	40	70

4. a. For each shoebrand, which month has the highest sales? What could be a reason for the high sales?

b. How many pairs of Nikes were sold over the year?

c. How many pairs of all three brands together were sold in February?

d. What was the mean number of pairs of Reeboks sold per month?

e. Which brand has more variability in its monthly sales? Explain how you determined variability.

f. What is another way that you could determine variability?

2. b. Responses will vary based on class data.

   c. The rows and columns will be switched. Students may have no preference.

3. a. Be sure that students have enough information listed so that they can have some choice in the next activity. If you feel that there isn't enough information, you may want to lead the students through some more brainstorming.

   b. The goal here is for students to build the model. That is, they should understand how a matrix is constructed using rows and columns, why it is important to label the rows and columns, and, in general, how a matrix can be used to organize data.

   c. This should be a brief but important full-class discussion.

4. The goal here is to get students to analyze and operate on the matrix. Parts b and c lead into the kind of activities coming up in the next investigation, namely, summing rows and summing columns.

   a. Converse: December

      Nike: March, September, and December

      Reebok: April

      Possible reasons for the high sales are Christmas, the start of school in September, and the beginning of spring.

   b. 765 pairs (Sum the row.)

   c. 120 pairs (Sum the column.)

   d. 50.8333 pairs (Find the mean of the row.)

   e. For these data, Reebok has the most variability. Students should determine the variability of each row and then compare the three variabilities. Possible measures: the range of values, the mean absolute deviation, the interquartile range, the five-number summary, side-by-side box plots, line plots, histograms, or stem-and-leaf plots.

   f. See part e. During the Checkpoint discussion, you may wish to have groups share their responses to this part. You also might press students to think of additional methods of comparing variability, and encourage them to think about both graphical displays and numerical measures.

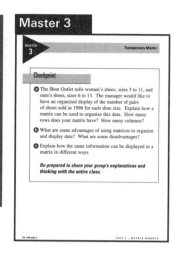

EXPLORE *continued*

5. **a.** Possible types of graphs: Stem-and-leaf plots, line plots, bar graphs, box plots, plots over time.

   b. Responses may vary. Each graph would display one brand of shoe sales or monthly sales combined for brands.

   c. ■ Possible patterns: Nike seems to have consistent sales over the year. Nike outsold both other brands in almost every month.

   ■ Trends over time: Sales are down at the beginning of the year, up during spring, down in the middle of summer, up at beginning of school in the fall, down later in the fall, up at Christmas.

   ■ The "10" in June for Reebok is much lower than might be expected. Either repeated sales are low due to some event (maybe a production or distribution problem for Reebok) or data were entered incorrectly. Students need to be aware of both possibilities when dealing with data.

SHARE AND SUMMARIZE full-class discussion

Checkpoint

See Teaching Master 3.

It is helpful to allow a different group for each part to share their response and thinking. For each part, assess the extent of agreement between groups before proceeding to the next part. Any disagreements should be resolved; you may need to facilitate that discussion.

ⓐ Responses may vary. Students may choose to display sizes from 5 to 13 which is nine different sizes (assuming no half-sizes) along the row or column. If an entry for a particular size includes both men's and women's shoes, it is not as informative for the store manager, so both men's and women's sizes must be displayed separately. This would require a 2×9 or 9×2 matrix with the two variables being size and men's or women's. If half-sizes are included, the matrix would be 2×17 or 17×2. Some students may not want to combine male and female sizes in the same matrix. If so, they should support their decision with some rationale.

ⓑ Some advantages are that they are straightforward, a natural modification of tables, useful for two variables, and easily stored in a computer. They also retain the numerical data. Some disadvantages are that they are only useful for two variables and not as visual as graphs, and quick summary data are not available visually.

> NOTE: Having groups who have thought deeply about variability in activity 4 part f share their thinking with the class will help extend everyone's understanding of this concept. Since groups will have different graphical displays for item 5, these also should be presented to the whole class at this time.

MORE
ASSIGNMENT   *pp. 14–25*

Students now can begin Organizing task 2 or Reflecting task 3 from the MORE assignment following Investigation 3.

ⓒ The same information can be represented in a matrix in different ways: (1) you might transpose rows and columns or (2) you might list the possibilities for a variable in a different order along the rows or columns.

See additional Teaching Notes on page T78C.

5. a. Identify at least two types of graphs that could be used to represent the monthly sales data.

b. Choose and sketch the type of graph you think would be most informative.

c. Using the matrix and the graph you have just sketched:
- Describe any patterns you see in the data.
- Describe any general trends over time that you observe.
- Are there any "outliers" in the data? If so, explain why you think such an outlier could have occurred.

Checkpoint

a The Shoe Outlet sells women's shoes, sizes 5 to 11, and men's shoes, sizes 6 to 13. The manager would like to have an organized display of the number of pairs sold in 1996 for each shoe size. Explain how a matrix can be used to organize this data. How many rows does your matrix have? How many columns?

b What are some advantages of using matrices to organize and display data? What are some disadvantages?

c Explain how the same information can be displayed in a matrix in different ways.

Be prepared to share your group's explanations and thinking with the entire class.

▶On Your Own

Suppose that the FleetFeet shoe chain has stores in Chicago, Atlanta, and San Diego. Their top selling brands are Nike and Reebok. In 1996 the average sales figures per month were as follows: 250 pairs of Nike and 195 pairs of Reebok in Chicago, 175 pairs of Nike and 175 pairs of Reebok in Atlanta, and 185 pairs of Nike and 275 pairs of Reebok in San Diego.

a. Organize these data using one matrix. Label the rows and columns and give the matrix a title.

b. How many pairs of Reebok shoes are sold in all three cities combined?

c. In which city were the most shoes sold?

INVESTIGATION 2 Analyzing Matrices

Matrices can be used to organize all sorts of data, not just sales data. In this investigation you will explore three different situations in which matrices are used to help make sense of data.

Archeologists study ancient people and their cultures. One way they study these people is by exploring sites where they have lived and analyzing objects which they have made. Archeologists use matrices to classify and then compare the objects they find at various archeological sites. For example, suppose that pieces of pottery are found at five different sites. The pottery has certain characteristics: it is either glazed or not glazed, ornamented or not, colored or natural, thin or thick.

1. Information about the characteristics of the pottery at all five sites is organized in the matrix below. A "1" means the pottery has the characteristic and a "0" means it does not have the characteristic.

Pottery Characteristics

	Glaze	Orn	Color	Thin
Site A	0	1	0	0
Site B	1	0	0	0
Site C	1	0	1	0
Site D	1	1	1	1
Site E	0	1	1	1

a. What does it mean for pottery to be "glazed"? "Ornamented"?

b. What does the "1" in the third row and the first column mean?

c. Is the pottery at site E thick or thin?

d. Which site has pottery that is glazed and thick, but is not ornamented or colored?

e. How many of the sites had glazed pottery? Explain how you used the rows or columns of the matrix to answer the question.

INVESTIGATION 2 Analyzing Matrices

As you listen to groups discuss these activities, it is important to remind them to use the vocabulary they are developing. By the end of the activity students should be comfortable with the terms rows and columns, the diagonal, and the row and column sums.

1. **a.** This question is to ensure that students understand the meaning of the words "glazed" and "ornamented". "Glazed" means glossy finish as opposed to dull finish. "Ornamented" means that it has designs on it as opposed to being plain.

   b. At site C the pottery was glazed.

   c. Site E had thin pottery.

   d. Site B. Examine the rows to find a 1 under the column labeled glaze and 0s in the columns under ornamented, color, and thin.

   e. Three sites had glazed pottery. You can sum the first column to obtain the total number of sites with glazed pottery.

2. **a.** By comparing the rows for A and C you can see that the entries only agree in the "thin" column.
    b. The degree of difference between D and E is 1.
3. **a.** 0, because there is no difference.
    b. The entry should be "2" because there are 2 different characteristics from site C to site D, ornamentation and thickness.
    c. ## Degree of Difference

	A	B	C	D	E
A	0	2	3	3	2
B	2	0	1	3	4
C	3	1	0	2	3
D	3	3	2	0	1
E	2	4	3	1	0

   d. Patterns include the same labels are used for rows and columns, there is the same number of rows as columns (*i.e.*, square matrix), the *n*th row is the same as *n*th column (*i.e.*, symmetric matrix), the matrix is symmetric in the main diagonal (*i.e.*, symmetric matrix), *etc*.

4. **a.** Possible response: The pottery at sites D and E differ only in the "glazed" category. The pottery at sites B and C differ in only one category, so maybe the two sites are from the same civilization. However, the category of difference is "color". How this can be explained is not clear cut. Students should see the need to support their claims as thoroughly as possible as well as the limitations of their analysis.
    b. Possible response: The pottery at sites B and E differ in each category, so maybe these sites represent two different civilizations.
    c. Possible response: The pottery at site D is glazed, ornamented, colored, and thin, all of which are "advanced" characteristics.

    Students should be aware of the assumptions they are making about what "advanced" means. They might think of "advanced" in terms of technologically advanced, in which case they might generate the possible argument stated above. On the other hand, it is certainly possible that a civilization is advanced and yet does not produce pottery that is glazed, ornamented, or colored.

2. You can use the matrix to determine how much the pottery differs between sites. For example, the pottery found at sites A and B differ on exactly two characteristics—glaze and ornamentation. So you can say that the *degree of difference* between the pottery at sites A and B is 2.

   a. Explain why the degree of difference between pottery at sites A and C is 3.

   b. Find the degree of difference between sites D and E.

3. You can build a new matrix that summarizes all the degree of difference information.

   a. What number would best describe the difference between site A and site A?

   b. What number should be placed in the third row, fourth column? What does this number tell you about the pottery at these two sites?

   c. Complete the degree of difference matrix shown below.

Degree of Difference

$$
\begin{array}{c}
 \\
A \\
B \\
C \\
D \\
E
\end{array}
\begin{array}{ccccc}
A & B & C & D & E \\
\left[\begin{array}{ccccc}
\_ & 2 & 3 & \_ & \_ \\
2 & \_ & \_ & \_ & \_ \\
3 & \_ & \_ & \_ & \_ \\
\_ & \_ & \_ & \_ & \_ \\
\_ & \_ & \_ & \_ & \_
\end{array}\right]
\end{array}
$$

   d. Describe at least one pattern you see in the degree of difference matrix.

4. Archeologists want to learn about the civilizations that existed at the sites. For instance, they would like to know whether different sites represent different civilizations and whether one civilization was more advanced than another. A lot of evidence is needed to make such decisions. However, make some conjectures based just on the pottery data in the matrices from activities 1 and 3.

   a. Find two sites that you think might be from the same civilization. Explain how the pottery evidence supports your choice.

   b. Find two sites that you think might be from different civilizations. Give an argument defending your choice.

   c. Give an argument supporting the claim that the civilization at site D was more advanced than the others. What assumptions are you making about what it means for a civilization to be "advanced"?

LESSON 1 • BUILDING AND USING MATRIX MODELS   7

Matrices also are used frequently by sociologists in their study of social relations. For example, a sociologist may be studying friendship and trust among five classmates at a certain high school. The classmates are asked to indicate with whom they would like to go to a movie and to whom they would loan $5. Their responses are summarized in the following two matrices. ("1" means "yes" and "0" means "no".) Each matrix is read from row to column. For example, the "1"in the first row and fourth column of the movie matrix means that student A would like to go to a movie with student D.

Movie Matrix

Would Like to Go to a Movie

	with				
	A	B	C	D	E
A	0	1	1	1	1
B	0	0	1	1	1
C	1	0	0	1	0
D	0	1	1	0	1
E	1	0	0	1	0

Loan Matrix

Would Loan Money

	to				
	A	B	C	D	E
A	0	0	0	1	1
B	1	0	0	1	0
C	0	0	0	1	0
D	1	1	0	0	1
E	0	1	1	0	0

5. **a.** Would student A like to go to a movie with student B? Would student B like to go to a movie with student A?

   b. With whom would student D like to go to a movie?

   c. What does the "0" in the fourth row, third column of the loan matrix mean?

   d. To whom would student A loan $5?

   e. A **square matrix** has the same number of rows and columns. The **main diagonal** of a square matrix is the diagonal line of entries running from the top left corner to the bottom right corner. Why do you think there are zeroes for each entry in the main diagonals of the matrices above?

6. **a.** Explain why the movie matrix could be used to describe *friendship*, while the loan matrix could describe *trust*.

   b. Write two interesting statements about friendship and trust among these five students, based on the information in the matrices.

7. Discuss with your group how you can use the rows or columns of the movie and loan matrices to answer the following questions.

   a. How many students does student C name as friends?

   b. How many students name student C as a friend?

   c. Who seems to be the most trustworthy student?

   d. Who seems to be the most popular student?

As indicated in the student text, sociologists use matrices to study relationships. Some students may wish to research further the ways in which sociologists use matrices.

5. **a.** Yes, student A would like to go to a movie with B, but B would not like to go to a movie with A.

    b. Student D would like to go to a movie with students B, C, and E.

    c. The "0" means that D would not loan money to C.

    d. Student A would loan money to D and E.

    e. It makes sense to decide that, *for the purpose of these data,* a student would not like to go to a movie with or loan money to himself or herself.

6. **a.** You go to movies with friends and loan money to people you trust to pay you back.

    b. The goal here is to get students to read, think about, and interpret matrices.

    Possible specific statements: (1) Student A considers everyone to be a friend, but only two people name A as a friend. (2) Student C doesn't trust many and is not trusted by many.

    Possible general statements: (1) Just because student X considers student Y to be a friend, it does not follow that Y considers X to be a friend. (2) It is possible to consider someone to be a friend and yet not trust the person enough to loan him or her $5.

7. At this point, students should start thinking explicitly in terms of summing rows and columns.

    a. Sum the third row of the movie matrix to find how many classmates student C considers a friend. (Student C names 2 friends.)

    b. Sum the third or "C" column of the movie matrix to find how many students name C as a friend. (Three students name C as a friend.)

    c. Student D seems the most trustworthy because the sum of the "D" column in the loan matrix is 3, more than any other column sum.

    d. Student D seems the most popular because the sum of the "D" column in the movie matrix is 4, more than any other column sum.

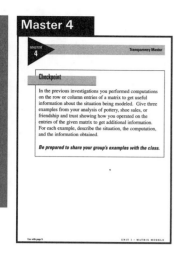

Checkpoint

See Teaching Master 4.

Examples include the following:

■ In the pottery matrix, the sum of a column tells how many sites had glazed pottery.

■ In the shoe-sales matrix, the sum of the Nike row gives the number of Nikes sold that year.

■ In the shoe-sales matrix, the mean of a row is the mean number of pairs of shoes sold per month for a particular brand.

■ In the shoe-sales matrix, summing a column results in the number of shoes sold in that month for all three brands.

■ In the movie matrix, the sum of a column tells how many people would like to go to a movie with a particular person. You then could compare these to find the most popular student.

▶Group Processing Suggestions

■ What actions helped the group to work productively?

■ What actions could be added to make the group even more productive next time?

APPLY individual task

▶On Your Own

a. Responses may vary. Other factors for which statistics are collected include the number of assists, steals, rebounds, blocked shots, turnovers, and fouls.

b. A turnover is when the player throws the ball either to the other team or out of bounds, or there is a violation that stops play and transfers possession of the ball to the other team. (Examples include traveling and 3-seconds in the lane.) Wolters had only 1 turnover.

In the previous investigations you performed computations on the row or column entries of a matrix to get useful information about the situation being modeled. Give three examples from your analysis of pottery, shoe sales, or friendship and trust showing how you operated on the entries of the given matrix to get additional information. For each example, describe the situation, the computation, and the information obtained.

Be prepared to share your group's examples with the class.

On Your Own

In 1995, the University of Connecticut won the NCAA women's basketball championship. They completed a perfect 35-0 season by defeating the University of Tennessee in the championship game.

a. Senior Rebecca Lobo was the high scorer in the championship game for the University of Connecticut, with 17 points. Teammate Nykesha Sales scored 10 points. What other factors besides points scored should be taken into account when deciding which player contributed most to the victory?

The matrix below shows some of the non-shooting performance statistics for the seven Connecticut players who played in the championship game.

Non-Shooting Performance Statistics

	Assists	Steals	Rebounds	Blocked Shots	Turn-overs	Fouls
Elliot	3	1	7	0	5	2
Lobo	2	0	8	2	2	4
Wolters	0	0	3	2	1	4
Rizzotti	3	3	3	0	4	3
Webber	2	0	1	0	0	1
Sales	3	3	6	0	1	3
Berube	2	0	3	0	3	0

Source: Statistics courtesy of University of Connecticut Athletic Communications.

b. A "turnover" is when an action (other than fouling or scoring a basket) gives the other team control of the ball. How many turnovers did Wolters have?

c. What is a "rebound"? How many rebounds were made by the Connecticut players during the game?

d. Which of the performance factors do you think are positive, that is, they contribute toward winning the game? Which performance factors do you think are negative? For the factors that are negative, change the entries in the matrix to negative numbers.

e. Which player had the largest number of positive performance actions?

f. Describe how you could give a "non-shooting performance score" to each player. The score should include both positive and negative factors. Which player do you think contributed most to the game in the area of non-shooting performance? Explain your choice.

g. How could you use row sums of the modified matrix from part d to get non-shooting performance scores?

INVESTIGATION 3 Combining Matrices

You have seen that a matrix can be used to store and organize data. You also have seen that you can operate on the numbers in the rows or columns of a matrix to get additional information and draw conclusions about the data. Sometimes it is useful to combine matrices, as you will see in the next two situations.

1. Shown below are the movie and loan matrices you analyzed in the previous investigation. Study both matrices to see how the friendship and trust they indicate are related in this group of five students.

Movie Matrix

		with			
	A	B	C	D	E
A	0	1	1	1	1
B	0	0	1	1	1
C	1	0	0	1	0
D	0	1	1	0	1
E	1	0	0	1	0

Would Like to Go to a Movie (rows A–E)

Loan Matrix

		to			
	A	B	C	D	E
A	0	0	0	1	1
B	1	0	0	1	0
C	0	0	0	1	0
D	1	1	0	0	1
E	0	1	1	0	0

Would Loan Money (rows A–E)

a. Who does student A consider friends and yet does not trust enough to loan $5?

b. Do you think it is reasonable that a student could have a friend who he or she does not trust enough to loan $5?

c. Who does student B trust and yet does not consider them to be friends? Do you know someone who you trust but who is not a friend?

d. Who does student D trust and also consider to be friends?

c. A rebound is when a player gets the ball after a missed shot. The Connecticut players got 31 rebounds during the game.

d. Assists, steals, rebounds, and blocked shots are the performance factors that contribute toward winning the game. Turnovers and fouls are the negative performance statistics. (Some students may argue that fouls are not always negative. In fact there are times when fouling is the best thing to do. If students feel strongly about this, you might suggest that they just eliminate the "foul" column from the matrix.)

e. Lobo and Sales both had 12 positive performance actions.

f. Responses may vary. A non-shooting performance score can be assigned to each player by finding the row sum of the modified matrix in part d. Some students may argue that one category is much more important than another and may want to weight the categories to reflect this.

g. Using a row sum to get a non-shooting performance score, Sales has the highest, 8, and so we could say that she contributed most to the game in terms of non-shooting performance.

ASSIGNMENT   *pp. 14–25*

Students now can begin Modeling task 1, Organizing tasks 1 or 2, or Reflecting task 1 from the MORE assignment following Investigation 3.

EXPLORE   small-group investigation

INVESTIGATION 3 Combining Matrices

As you monitor the students, remind them that it is important to properly label the rows and columns of their matrices.

1. a. Students B and C are people whom student A considers friends but does not trust enough to loan $5.

b. Students probably will agree that a person could be a friend, yet not be a person to whom you would want to loan $5. Students might answer, "No, if they are a friend they will pay you back." However, students need to at least consider the possibility of a friend that is not trusted in order to proceed.

c. Student B trusts student A, yet does not consider A to be a friend.

d. Student D trusts students B and E and considers them to be friends.

2. Responses may vary. Two possible matrices are below. They correspond to the procedures described in part b.

a.

Trustworthy Friend

	A	B	C	D	E
A	0	0	0	1	1
B	0	0	0	1	0
C	0	0	0	1	0
D	0	1	0	0	1
E	0	0	0	0	0

Trustworthy Friend

	A	B	C	D	E
A	0	1	1	2	2
B	1	0	1	2	1
C	1	0	0	2	0
D	1	2	1	0	2
E	1	1	1	1	0

b. Responses may vary. Possible responses are:

To determine an entry in the "trustworthy friend" matrix, look at the corresponding entries in the movie matrix and the loan matrix. If they are both 1s, then put a 1 in that position in the "trustworthy friend" matrix, otherwise put a 0 in that position.

Multiply the two matrices entry-by-entry (gives same matrix as in first possible response).

Sum the entries in the same positions. If there is a 2 in a position, then the "column" person is a trustworthy friend of the "row" person.

c. You may wish to have a short discussion of parts c and d once all groups complete these items. Hopefully both types of matrices described in part b will be presented by students.

d. Some possible responses are:

Nobody considers student A to be a trustworthy friend.

Everybody except student E has at least one trustworthy friend in this group of students.

Student D is considered a trustworthy friend by everybody except student E.

3. a. 400,000

   b. 80,000

   c. Ford produced 0.15 million or 150,000 small cars in 1995.

2. A friend you trust is a *trustworthy friend*.

  a. Combine the movie and loan matrices to construct a new matrix that shows who each of the five students considers to be a trustworthy friend.

  b. Write down a systematic procedure explaining how to construct the trustworthy-friend matrix.

  c. Compare your procedure with that of other groups.

  d. Write two interesting observations about the information in this new matrix.

In the next situation you will explore other ways of combining matrices and learn some of the ways in which matrix operations are used in business and industry.

As small cars have gained popularity with American consumers, the Big Three auto makers in the U.S.—General Motors, Ford, and Chrysler—have been producing more small cars. The photo above suggests that some small cars are more popular among teenagers than others. Suppose the matrices below show the production data for 1995 and 1996. Data are given in millions of small cars produced each quarter (a quarter is three months).

1995 Small Auto Production

	GM	F	C
1st Q	0.4	0.13	0.06
2nd Q	0.5	0.15	0.06
3rd Q	0.5	0.15	0.05
4th Q	0.3	0.17	0.07

1996 Small Auto Production

	GM	F	C
1st Q	0.6	0.16	0.09
2nd Q	0.6	0.18	0.08
3rd Q	0.7	0.19	0.10
4th Q	0.7	0.21	0.12

3. a. Consider the first entry in the matrix for 1995. How many cars are represented by 0.4 of a million?

  b. According to these data, how many small cars were produced by Chrysler in the second quarter of 1996?

  c. Explain the meaning of the entry in the third row and second column of the 1995 matrix.

4. a. According to these data, by how much did first-quarter, small-car production increase for GM from 1995 to 1996?

  b. Construct a new matrix with the same row and column labels that shows how much small-car production increased from 1995 to 1996 for each quarter and each manufacturer.

5. Suppose that the auto industry projected a 10% increase in small-car production from 1996 to 1997, over all quarters and all manufacturers. Construct a matrix that shows the projected 1997 production figures for each quarter and each manufacturer, based on the data given.

6. Construct a matrix with the same row and column labels as the given matrices that shows the total number of small cars produced over the two-year period 1995–96.

Checkpoint

  a Which of the activities about small-car production involved combining matrices by adding *corresponding entries*?

  b Which of the activities about small-car production involved combining matrices by subtracting corresponding entries?

  c Which of the activities about small-car production involved multiplying each entry of a matrix by a number?

  d Consider all the situations you have analyzed so far. What other operations have you performed on matrices?

  Be prepared to explain your group's selections to the entire class.

Several of the operations you have performed on matrices in this investigation are commonly used and have been given standard names. To **add matrices** means to combine them by adding *corresponding entries*. Thus, when adding two matrices you add the entry in the first row and first column from one matrix to the entry in that same position in the other matrix, and then do likewise for the entries in each of the other positions. If A represents one matrix and B represents another matrix, then $A + B$ represents the matrix found by adding the matrices entry by entry. **Subtracting matrices** $(A - B)$ is just like adding matrices, except you subtract the corresponding entries instead of adding them. **Multiplying a matrix, B, by a number, k,** means to multiply *each entry* in the matrix by that number and is represented by kB.

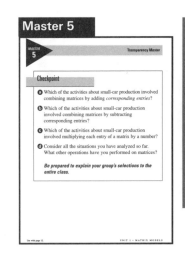

Master 5

4. **a.** 0.2 million or 200,000

    b. Subtract the 1995 matrix, entry by corresponding entry, from the 1996 matrix. See the first matrix below.

5. Multiply each entry in the 1996 matrix by 1.10 to determine a 10% increase over 1996 production. See the second matrix below.

6. Add corresponding entries to get the new matrix. See the third matrix below.

Increase from 1995–1996

	GM	F	C
1st Q	0.2	0.03	0.03
2nd Q	0.1	0.03	0.02
3rd Q	0.2	0.04	0.05
4th Q	0.4	0.04	0.05

Projected 1997 Production

	GM	F	C
1st Q	0.66	0.176	0.099
2nd Q	0.66	0.198	0.088
3rd Q	0.77	0.209	0.11
4th Q	0.77	0.231	0.132

1995-1996 Production

	GM	F	C
1st Q	1	0.29	0.15
2nd Q	1.1	0.33	0.14
3rd Q	1.2	0.34	0.15
4th Q	1	0.38	0.19

SHARE AND SUMMARIZE   full-class discussion

Checkpoint

See Teaching Master 5.

It is important that students first make sense of matrices as a representation of a real situation. However, it also is important that students transfer the information and meanings they have deduced about adding, subtracting, and multiplying by a scalar quantity to situations that do not necessarily have a supporting context. During the Checkpoint discussion, ask students to describe how to perform each of the matrix operations investigated thus far. You may wish to ask students to write in their journals, rules for when and how any two matrices can be added or subtracted. The paragraph following the Checkpoint has a description of such "rules", but students need to build understanding of these concepts before reading the formal language.

ⓐ Finding the total number of small cars produced for 1995–96 for each automaker (activity 6) involved combining matrices by adding corresponding entries.

ⓑ Determining the increase in small-car production from 1995–96 (activity 4) involved combining matrices by subtracting corresponding entries.

ⓒ Projecting the production of small cars in 1997 (activity 5) involved multiplying each entry of a matrix by a number.

ⓓ Other operations listed may include row sums, column sums, mean of row entries, multiplying entry-by-entry (trustworthy friend matrix), and row comparisons.

It is important to point out to students that there are many useful and legitimate matrix operations, including all those used so far in this unit. A few of these operations have been singled out for their particular usefulness and have been given standard names, for example, matrix addition and matrix subtraction. Another one, matrix multiplication, will be investigated in the next lesson. In the text, the term *scalar multiplication* is not used for multiplying a matrix by a number, to keep student language at this point more natural to them.

Unit 1

GROUP PROCESSING SUGGESTIONS:

■ What decisions did your group make before beginning this investigation? Which decisions helped your group operate effectively? What else might you have done to improve group work?

■ Name one thing that each person in your group did today that helped you or your group.

JOURNAL ENTRY: You may wish to use the journal suggestion in the note at the beginning of the Checkpoint. Another journal option is Reflecting task 3.

▶On Your Own

a. The result of $A + B$ tells you about the combined two-year passing performance of the three quarterbacks.

Two-year Passing Performance

	Att	Comp	TD	Int
Elway	867	522	35	27
Young	864	582	54	23
Aikman	865	573	38	20

b. The result of $A - B$ tells you about the change in passing performance from 1992 to 1993.

Change In Passing Performance

	Att	Comp	TD	Int
Elway	235	174	15	−7
Young	60	46	4	9
Aikman	−81	−31	−8	−8

c.

	Att	Comp	TD	Int
Elway	−235	−174	−15	7
Young	−60	−46	−4	−9
Aikman	81	31	8	8

- ■ The numbers in $B - A$ are the negatives of the numbers in $A - B$.
- ■ A negative number in the TD column of $A - B$ tells you that the number of touchdown passes decreased from 1992 to 1993.
- ■ A negative number in the TD column of $B - A$ tells you that the number of touchdown passes increased from 1992 to 1993.

d.

	Att	Comp	TD	Int
Elway	275.5	174	12.5	5
Young	231	157	14.5	8
Aikman	196	135.5	7.5	3

Responses may vary. Students may say that $\frac{1}{2}A$ corresponds to data for $\frac{1}{2}$ of the 1993 season. Students may say that it really does not have a legitimate interpretation for these data because it is unlikely that exactly half the data in all categories would be in each half the season.

▶ **On Your Own**

Below are two matrices showing the 1993 and 1992 passing statistics for three top NFL quarterbacks. ("Att" is an abbreviation for "passes attempted"; "Comp" refers to passes completed; "TD" refers to passes thrown for a touchdown; and "Int" refers to passes that were intercepted.)

1993 Passing Statistics

	Att	Comp	TD	Int
Elway	551	348	25	10
Young	462	314	29	16
Aikman	392	271	15	6

1992 Passing Statistics

	Att	Comp	TD	Int
Elway	316	174	10	17
Young	402	268	25	7
Aikman	473	302	23	14

Sources: *The World Almanac and Book of Facts 1994.* Mahwah, NJ: World Almanac, 1993; *The World Almanac and Book of Facts 1995.* Mahwah, NJ: World Almanac, 1994.

Let *A* represent the 1993 matrix and *B* represent the 1992 matrix.

a. Compute $A + B$. What does $A + B$ tell you about the passing performance of the three quarterbacks?

b. Compute $A - B$. What does $A - B$ tell you about the passing performance of the three quarterbacks?

c. Compute $B - A$.

■ How do the numbers in $B - A$ differ from the numbers in $A - B$?

■ What does a negative number in the TDs column of $A - B$ tell you about the trend in touchdown passes from 1992 to 1993?

■ What does a negative number in the TDs column of $B - A$ tell you about the trend in touchdown passes from 1992 to 1993?

d. Compute $\frac{1}{2} A$. What could $\frac{1}{2} A$ mean for this situation?

LESSON 1 • BUILDING AND USING MATRIX MODELS   **13**

MORE
Modeling • Organizing • Reflecting • Extending

Modeling

These tasks provide opportunities for you to use the ideas you have learned in the investigations. Each task asks you to model and solve problems in other situations.

1. The first matrix below presents combined monthly sales for three types of men's and women's jeans at JustJeans stores in three cities. The second matrix below gives the monthly sales for women's jeans.

Combined Sales

	Levi	Lee	Wrangler
Chicago	250	195	105
Atlanta	175	175	90
San Diego	185	210	275

Women's Jeans Sales

	Levi	Lee	Wrangler
Chicago	100	90	70
Atlanta	80	85	50
San Diego	105	50	150

a. Construct the matrix that shows the monthly sales for men's jeans for each brand and each city. Which matrix operation did you use to construct this matrix?

Modeling

MORE
ASSIGNMENT *pp. 14–25*

1. a.

Men's Jeans Sales

	Levi	Lee	Wrangler
Chicago	150	105	35
Atlanta	95	90	40
San Diego	80	160	125

This matrix is obtained by subtracting the women's jeans sales matrix from the combined sales matrix.

Modeling: 2 and choice of one*
Organizing: 1, 2 and 5
Reflecting: 1 and 3
Extending: Choose one*

*When choice is indicated, it is important that the choice be left to the student.
NOTE: It is best if Organizing tasks are discussed as a whole class after they have been assigned as homework.

Unit 1

1. b.

Chicago	M	W
Levi	150	100
Lee	105	90
Wrangler	35	70

Atlanta	M	W
Levi	95	80
Lee	90	85
Wrangler	40	50

San Diego	M	W
Levi	80	105
Lee	160	50
Wrangler	125	150

■ You get the following matrix by adding the three matrices above.

Jeans Sales

	M	W
Levi	325	285
Lee	355	225
Wrangler	200	270

c. ■ $3C + A + \frac{2}{3} S = T$

■ $3(300) + 270 + \frac{2}{3}(162) = 1278$

This tells us that, for these stores, a total of 1,278 pairs of women's Lee jeans were ordered during the second quarter.

b. Organizing the data in different ways can highlight different information.

- Copy and complete the matrices below to show sales of men's and women's jeans in each city, for each of the three brands. Label the rows. Use the sales information on the previous page.

Chicago

M W

$$\begin{bmatrix} \_ & \_ \\ \_ & \_ \\ \_ & \_ \end{bmatrix}$$

Atlanta

M W

$$\begin{bmatrix} \_ & \_ \\ \_ & \_ \\ \_ & \_ \end{bmatrix}$$

San Diego

M W

$$\begin{bmatrix} \_ & \_ \\ \_ & \_ \\ \_ & \_ \end{bmatrix}$$

- Construct one matrix that shows the total sales of men's and women's jeans for each of the three brands, that is, sales in all three cities combined. Label the rows of the matrix with the brands and the columns with "M" and "W". Which matrix operation did you use to construct this matrix?

c. For the first quarter, the managers of the Chicago, Atlanta, and San Diego stores have placed jeans orders with the main warehouse as indicated in the matrices below. Let *C* represent the matrix for the store in Chicago, *A* for the store in Atlanta, and *S* for the store in San Diego.

Chicago

	M	W
Levi	300	330
Lee	345	300
Wrangler	120	240

Atlanta

M	W
300	255
300	270
135	165

San Diego

M	W
252	315
513	162
405	450

For the second quarter, the managers' orders for each brand are tripled in Chicago, stay the same in Atlanta, and are $\frac{2}{3}$ as big in San Diego.

- Think about how to calculate the total orders, *T*, of men's and women's jeans in all three cities combined, for each of the three brands for the second quarter. Write an equation using *C*, *A*, and *S*.

- Compute the second row, second column entry of *T*. What does this entry tell you about jeans orders placed with the warehouse?

2. The movie matrix from Investigation 2 is reproduced below. Recall that the movie matrix can be thought of as describing friendship, and it is read from row to column. Thus, for example, student A names student B as a friend since there is a "1" in the first row and second column.

Movie Matrix

	with				
	A	B	C	D	E
A	0	1	1	1	1
B	0	0	1	1	1
C	1	0	0	1	0
D	0	1	1	0	1
E	1	0	0	1	0

Would Like to Go to a Movie

a. *Mutual friends* are two people who name each other as friends.
- Are students A and D mutual friends?
- Find at least two pairs of mutual friends.
- How do mutual friends appear in the matrix?

b. Construct a new matrix that shows mutual friends. To do this, list all five people across the top and down the side. Write a "1" or a "0" for each entry, depending on whether or not the two people corresponding to that entry are mutual friends.

c. Who has the most mutual friends?

d. Compare the first row of the mutual-friends matrix to the first column. Compare each of the other rows to its corresponding column. What relationship do you see? Explain why the mutual-friends matrix has this relationship between its rows and columns.

3. Reproduced below are the production matrices for small cars from the last investigation. The entries represent millions of cars produced in each quarter by the three auto manufacturers.

1995 Small Auto Production

	GM	F	C
1st Q	0.4	0.13	0.06
2nd Q	0.5	0.15	0.06
3rd Q	0.5	0.15	0.05
4th Q	0.3	0.17	0.07

1996 Small Auto Production

	GM	F	C
1st Q	0.6	0.16	0.09
2nd Q	0.6	0.18	0.08
3rd Q	0.7	0.19	0.10
4th Q	0.7	0.21	0.12

2. **a.** ■ No, students A and D are not mutual friends.

    ■ The following are the pairs of mutual friends: A-C, A-E, B-D, C-D, and D-E.

    ■ Each person has to have a "1" for the other person. For example, A will say C is a friend and C will say A is a friend.

    b. Mutual Friends

    $$\begin{array}{c c} & \begin{array}{c c c c c} A & B & C & D & E \end{array} \\ \begin{array}{c} A \\ B \\ C \\ D \\ E \end{array} & \left[\begin{array}{c c c c c} 0 & 0 & 1 & 0 & 1 \\ 0 & 0 & 0 & 1 & 0 \\ 1 & 0 & 0 & 1 & 0 \\ 0 & 1 & 1 & 0 & 1 \\ 1 & 0 & 0 & 1 & 0 \end{array}\right] \end{array}$$

    c. Student D has the most mutual friends.

    d. The 1s are symmetric about the main diagonal of 0s. Mutual friends each have a 1 for the other person.

3. a. ■ By summing the first column of the 1995 matrix, you obtain 1.7 million small cars produced by GM in 1995.

   ■ By summing the third row of the 1996 matrix, you obtain 0.99 million small cars produced in 1996.

   b. **Small Auto Production**

	GM	F	C
1995	1.7	0.6	0.24
1996	2.6	0.74	0.39

   ■ GM had the largest production in both 1995 and 1996.

   ■ GM had the largest increase in the number of cars produced, 0.9 million as compared to 0.14 million for Ford and 0.15 million for Chrysler.

   ■ Chrysler had the greatest percentage increase. Percentage increase is given by $\frac{\text{increase}}{\text{original amount}}$. For Chrysler, this is $\frac{0.15}{0.24}$ or 0.625, for a 62.5% increase. GM had approximately 53% increase ($\frac{0.9}{1.7}$) and Ford had approximately 23% increase ($\frac{0.14}{0.6}$).

4. a. **October**

	15	16	17
Chrome	16	24	8
Silver	8	12	4

   $= O$

   November

	15	16	17
Chrome	12	32	16
Silver	12	20	0

   $= N$

   b. The total shipped is the sum of the two matrices in part a.

   Total Shipped

	15	16	17
Chrome	28	56	24
Silver	20	32	4

   c. **December**

	15	16	17
Chrome	12	−4	12
Silver	8	0	12

   ■ The retailer has already met and exceeded the quota for ordering chrome 16-inch wheels. Thus, there is a negative value in the matrix.

a. Answer the two questions below. Explain how you used the rows or columns of the matrices to determine your responses.

- How many millions of small cars did GM produce in 1995?

- What was the total third-quarter production of small cars for these manufacturers in 1996?

b. Construct one matrix that shows the total small-car production per year for each of GM, Ford, and Chrysler for 1995 and 1996.

- Which automaker had the greatest small-car production in 1995? In 1996?

- Which automaker had the greatest increase in the number of small cars produced from 1995 to 1996?

- Which automaker had the greatest percentage increase in small-car production from 1995 to 1996?

4. An automotive manufacturer produces several styles of sport wheels. One of the styles is available in two finishes (chrome plated and silver painted) and three wheel sizes (15-inch, 16-inch, and 17-inch).

In October, a retailer in the midwest purchased sixteen 15-inch chrome wheels, twenty-four 16-inch chrome wheels, eight 17-inch chrome wheels, eight 15-inch silver wheels, twelve 16-inch silver wheels, and four 17-inch silver wheels. In November, the retailer ordered twelve 15-inch chrome wheels, thirty-two 16-inch chrome wheels, sixteen 17-inch chrome wheels, twelve 15-inch silver wheels, and twenty 16-inch silver wheels.

a. Represent the October and November wheel orders as matrices. Label the rows and columns.

b. How many of each type of wheel were ordered by the retailer during these two months combined? Represent this information in a matrix. Label the rows and columns.

c. Suppose that over the entire fourth quarter (October, November, and December) the retailer has agreed to order the number of wheels shown in the following matrix.

$$\begin{array}{c} \\ \text{Chrome} \\ \text{Silver} \end{array} \begin{array}{ccc} \text{15-in} & \text{16-in} & \text{17-in} \\ \left[\begin{array}{ccc} 40 & 52 & 36 \\ 28 & 32 & 16 \end{array}\right] \end{array}$$

- Construct a matrix that shows how many of each type of wheel must be ordered in December to meet this agreement.

- Explain any unusual entries in the matrix.

d. In October of the next year, the retailer orders twice the number of each type of wheel ordered the previous October. November's order is three times the number of each type of wheel ordered the previous November. Construct a matrix that shows the number of each type of wheel ordered in the two months combined.

5. Spreadsheets are one of the most widely-used software applications. A spreadsheet displays organized information in the same way a matrix does. One common use of spreadsheets is to itemize loans. For example, suppose that you are going to buy your first car. The one you decide to buy needs a little work, but you can get it for $500. You borrow the $500 at 9% annual interest and agree to pay it back in 12 monthly payments. The following spreadsheet summarizes all the information about this loan.

$500.00 Loan at 9% Annual Interest

Month (end)	Payment	To Interest	To Principal	Balance
1	$45.00	$3.75	$41.25	$458.75
2	$45.00	$3.44	$41.56	$417.19
3	$45.00	$3.13	$41.87	$375.32
4	$45.00	$2.81	$42.19	$333.13
5	$45.00	$2.50	$42.50	$290.63
6	$45.00	$2.18	$42.82	$247.81
7	$45.00	$1.86	$43.14	$204.67
8	$45.00	$1.54	$43.46	$161.21
9	$45.00	$1.21	$43.79	$117.42
10	$45.00	$0.88	$44.12	$73.30
11	$45.00	$0.55	$44.45	$28.85
12	$29.07	$0.22	$28.85	$0.00
Totals	**$524.07**	**$24.07**	**$500.00**	

a. How much will you still owe after the sixth payment?

b. How much interest will you pay in the fourth month?

c. In any given row, how do the entries in the "To Interest" and "To Principal" columns compare to the entry in the "Payment" column?

■ Why are the entries related in this way?

■ Does this relationship hold in the row for Month 12? What happened?

d. Why do the entries in the "To Principal" column get bigger until Month 12?

e. How can you use nearby entries to compute the entries in the Month 9 row?

f. How much money will you save if you pay for the car in cash instead of borrowing the $500 and paying off the loan over a year?

4. d. Calculate $(2 \times O) + (3 \times N)$.

$$
\begin{array}{c}
\phantom{\text{Chrome}} \begin{array}{ccc} 15 & 16 & 17 \end{array} \\
\begin{array}{c} \text{Chrome} \\ \text{Silver} \end{array}
\left[\begin{array}{ccc}
68 & 144 & 64 \\
52 & 84 & 8
\end{array} \right]
\end{array}
$$

5. a. $247.81

   b. $2.81

   c. The sum of "To Interest" and "To Principal" is the amount under "Payment."
   - The payment is split between paying off interest and paying off the principal. None of it goes to pay anything else.
   - In month 12 this does not hold because of error due to rounding the values to two decimal places. The computer does all computations and then rounds the results for the display.

   d. The interest is computed on a smaller remaining balance each month, so the interest that is added to the principal is less each month.

   e. The interest for the 9th month is $\frac{0.09}{12}$ ($161.21).
   The principal for the 9th month is $161.21 + $1.21.
   The balance for the 9th month is ($161.21 + $1.21) − $45.

   f. $524.06 − $500 = $24.06

Organizing

1. **a.** The vertices represent the people and the directed edges represent the relationship between people. A directed edge from *A* to *B* indicates that student A would like to go to a movie with student B.

   b. Friends Digraph

   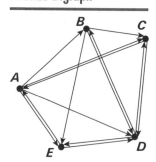

   c. Look for 2 edges between 2 vertices. Then check to be sure that an arrow is pointing to each vertex.

   d. Yes

   e. Responses may vary. Possible responses are:

   Student D has 3 mutual friends.

   Student A counts everyone as friends, but only two people count student A as a friend.

Organizing

These tasks will help you organize the mathematics you have learned in the investigations and connect it with other mathematics.

1. You may recall from Course 1 that a *digraph* is a collection of vertices and directed edges between some of those vertices. Also, an *adjacency matrix* for a digraph is a matrix where each entry of the matrix tells how many single directed edges there are from the vertex corresponding to the row to the vertex corresponding to the column. A digraph with four vertices, along with its adjacency matrix, is shown here.

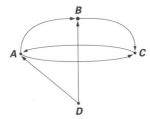

$$\begin{array}{c} \\ \text{from} \end{array} \begin{array}{cc} & \begin{array}{cccc} & \text{to} & & \\ A & B & C & D \end{array} \\ \begin{array}{c} A \\ B \\ C \\ D \end{array} & \left[\begin{array}{cccc} 0 & 1 & 1 & 0 \\ 0 & 0 & 1 & 0 \\ 1 & 0 & 0 & 0 \\ 1 & 1 & 0 & 0 \end{array}\right] \end{array}$$

Notice that the *B-C* entry is "1" because there is a directed edge from *B* to *C* in the digraph. The *C-B* entry is "0" since there is no directed edge from *C* to *B*.

The movie (friendship) matrix from Investigation 2 (reproduced below) can be thought of as an adjacency matrix for some digraph.

$$\begin{array}{c} \\ \\ \textbf{Would Like to} \\ \textbf{Go to a Movie} \end{array} \begin{array}{cc} & \begin{array}{ccccc} & & \text{with} & & \\ A & B & C & D & E \end{array} \\ \begin{array}{c} A \\ B \\ C \\ D \\ E \end{array} & \left[\begin{array}{ccccc} 0 & 1 & 1 & 1 & 1 \\ 0 & 0 & 1 & 1 & 1 \\ 1 & 0 & 0 & 1 & 0 \\ 0 & 1 & 1 & 0 & 1 \\ 1 & 0 & 0 & 1 & 0 \end{array}\right] \end{array}$$

a. What should the vertices and directed edges of the digraph represent?

b. Draw a digraph for this friendship matrix.

c. *Mutual friends* were defined in Modeling task 2 as two people who name each other as friends. How can you use the digraph for the friendship matrix to find pairs of mutual friends?

d. Does each of the five students have at least one mutual friend?

e. Write down one interesting statement about friendship among these five people that is illustrated by the friendship digraph.

2. In Investigation 1 you listed two types of graphs that could be used to represent sales data (reproduced below). You also sketched one of those graphs.

Monthly Sales

	J	F	M	A	M	J	J	A	S	O	N	D
Converse	40	35	50	55	70	60	40	40	70	35	30	80
Nike	55	55	75	70	70	65	60	60	75	55	50	75
Reebok	50	30	60	80	70	50	10	40	75	35	40	70

a. Sketch or use your graphics calculator or computer software to produce another type of graph that represents the data.

b. Compare the two graphs. Describe some information that is illustrated better in one graph than the other.

3. Symmetry is an important concept in mathematics, and one which was investigated in several units of Course 1. Symmetry also applies to matrices, but only to square matrices. A square matrix is said to be **symmetric** if it has symmetry about its main diagonal. (Recall that the main diagonal of a square matrix is the diagonal line of entries running from the top left to the bottom right corner.) That is, a square matrix is symmetric if the half of the matrix above the main diagonal is the mirror image of the half below the main diagonal. For example, consider the three matrices below. Matrices A and B are symmetric, but matrix C is not symmetric.

$$A = \begin{bmatrix} 0 & 1 & 0 & 1 \\ 1 & 0 & 1 & 1 \\ 0 & 1 & 0 & 0 \\ 1 & 1 & 0 & 0 \end{bmatrix} \qquad B = \begin{bmatrix} 25 & 3 & 4 & 5 \\ 3 & 36 & 6 & 7 \\ 4 & 6 & 9 & 8 \\ 5 & 7 & 8 & 10 \end{bmatrix} \qquad C = \begin{bmatrix} 0 & 0 & 1 & 1 \\ 1 & 0 & 1 & 0 \\ 0 & 1 & 0 & 0 \\ 1 & 1 & 1 & 0 \end{bmatrix}$$

a. Find two square matrices from Investigation 1 or 2.

b. Is the movie matrix symmetric? Explain.

c. Which of the following matrices from this lesson are symmetric?

- The pottery matrix (page 6)
- The degree-of-difference matrix (page 7)
- The loan matrix (page 8)
- The non-shooting-performance-statistics matrix (page 9)
- The mutual-friends matrix (page 16)

d. For those matrices that are symmetric, what is it about the situations that causes the matrix to be symmetric?

2. a. Possible types of graphs are: Stem-and-leaf plots, line plots, bar graphs, box plots, plots over time. Each graph will display one brand of shoe sales or monthly sales combined for brands.

   b. Descriptions will vary.

3. a. The square matrices are the movie matrix, the loan matrix, and the degree of difference matrix.

   b. No. For example, student A would like to go to a movie with student B, but B would not like to go to a movie with A.

   c. The mutual-friend matrix and the degree-of-difference matrix are symmetric.

   d. For those matrices that are symmetric:

   (1) The row and column labels are identical. The elements are being compared with other elements within the same group.

   (2) The two elements are related in both directions. There is reciprocity, i.e., if A is to B, then B is to A.

3. e. One example is

$$\begin{bmatrix} 2 & -3 & 1 & 9 \\ -3 & 0 & 8 & 7 \\ 1 & 8 & 3 & -5 \\ 9 & 7 & -5 & 4 \end{bmatrix}$$

The elements in the row are the same as the elements in the corresponding column.

f. The conjecture holds for the mutual-friend and degree-of-difference matrices.

4. a. $P = TI + TP$ or $P - TI = TP$

b. All of the equations work.

e. Create your own symmetric matrix with four rows and four columns.

- Compare the first row to the first column. Compare the second row to the second column. Do the same for the remaining two rows and columns.

- Make a conjecture about the corresponding rows and columns of a symmetric matrix.

f. Test your conjecture from part e on the symmetric matrices you identified in part c.

4. In Modeling task 5 you investigated a computer-generated spreadsheet summarizing payments on a $500 loan. Five hundred dollars was borrowed at 9% annual interest, and payments were made every month for one year. All the information about this loan was summarized in the spreadsheet, which is reproduced below. Consider how the spreadsheet entries were computed.

$500.00 Loan at 9% Annual Interest				
Month (end)	**Payment**	**To Interest**	**To Principal**	**Balance**
1	$45.00	$3.75	$41.25	$458.75
2	$45.00	$3.44	$41.56	$417.19
3	$45.00	$3.13	$41.87	$375.32
4	$45.00	$2.81	$42.19	$333.13
5	$45.00	$2.50	$42.50	$290.63
6	$45.00	$2.18	$42.82	$247.81
7	$45.00	$1.86	$43.14	$204.67
8	$45.00	$1.54	$43.46	$161.21
9	$45.00	$1.21	$43.79	$117.42
10	$45.00	$0.88	$44.12	$73.30
11	$45.00	$0.55	$44.45	$28.85
12	$29.07	$0.22	$28.85	$0.00
Totals	**$524.07**	**$24.07**	**$500.00**	

a. Let P represent the entries in the "Payment" column, TI represent the entries in the "To Interest" column, and TP represent the entries in the "To Principal" column. Write an equation that shows the relationship among P, TI, and TP.

b. If *NEXT* is the balance next month and *NOW* is the balance this month, which of the equations below show how to compute the balance next month if you know the balance this month? If an equation does not represent the *NEXT* balance, explain why it doesn't work.

- $NEXT = NOW - (45 - 0.0075\ NOW)$
- $NEXT = NOW + \frac{0.09}{12}\ NOW - 45$
- $NEXT = 1.0075\ NOW - 45$

Reflecting

These tasks will help you think about what the mathematics you have learned means to you. These tasks also will help you think about what you do and do not understand.

1. Recall that the main diagonal of a square matrix is the diagonal line of entries that runs from the top left corner of the matrix to the bottom right corner. All of the entries in the main diagonal of the movie (friendship) and loan (trust) matrices are 0s. Do you think it would make sense to have 1s in the main diagonal? Why or why not?

2. Tables are similar to matrices, and often are used in newspapers for reporting data. Find an example of a table in the newspaper. Then do the following.

   a. Briefly describe the information displayed in the table.

   b. Describe some other way that the information could have been displayed. Why do you think the newspaper editors decided to display the information using a table?

   c. How is your table similar to a matrix? How is it different?

   d. Think of the table you found as a matrix. Describe some operation on the rows, columns, or entries of the matrix that will yield additional information about the situation being modeled. Perform the operation and report the information gained.

3. Mariah claims that only two variables can be represented in a matrix. Scott claims that three variables are represented in a matrix. For each of these claims, give a supporting argument.

4. In Organizing task 1, you modeled friendship with a matrix and a digraph. What do you think are the advantages of each representation?

Extending

Tasks in this section provide opportunities for you to explore further or more deeply the mathematics you are learning.

1. One of the purposes of the penal system is to rehabilitate people in prison. Unfortunately, many people released from prison are reconvicted and return to prison within a few years after their release. Professionals working to solve this problem use data like those summarized in the matrix at the top of the next page. The entries of the matrix show the status of prisoners and released prisoners *next* year given their status *this* year. For example, look at the fourth row, fifth column. The "93%" entry means that 93% of those released from prison who are in their third year of freedom this year will remain free and be in their fourth year of freedom next year.

Reflecting

1. Either position can be supported. Some students may respond that you cannot be friends with yourself. Likewise, you cannot loan yourself $5. However, others may believe that you can be friends with yourself, or that you may go to a movie with yourself. Also, there are many ways in which one may or may not trust oneself.

   You may want to ask the students why 0 was used, especially if any students disagree. Point out that calculations such as for the mutual-friends matrix and row sums may take different, less useful meanings.

2. **a–d.** Responses will vary, depending on the students' choices of tables.

3. Mariah may be thinking the following: Matrices are two dimensional and so can only represent two variables—one across and one down. Scott may be thinking that the entries in the matrix are the third variable.

4. Possible responses may include:

   Matrix Representations
   - You quickly can sum a row or column.
   - It can be entered into a computer or calculator.
   - You easily can see symmetry or non-symmetry.

   Digraph Representations
   - You quickly can see how many people chose a particular person and how many that person chose.
   - Mutual friends are easily identified.

Extending

1. This situation may challenge some of your students. At the same time it will likely engage them in a thoughtful sense-making activity. It is important for students to be able to make sense of real data.

   Since this is an important yet potentially socially sensitive issue, it may be worthwhile to point out that it is an issue about the system, not about individual people.

1. **a.** For people in their second year of freedom, there are only two choices for the next year, (1) third year of freedom or (2) back in jail.
    b. 88%
    c. 7% of those released from prison who are in their third year of freedom this year will be back in prison next year.
    d. The rows sum to 100% because the entries in a given row account for all possibilities.
    e. The trend shown indicates that the longer it is since a person has been released the more likely it is he or she will continue to stay free. This trend could be due to the person being more completely reassimilated into society as time goes on.

2. **a.** Both the 100% entry in the sixth row and sixth column and the 0% entry in the sixth row and first column correspond to the assumption that if a person has remained out of prison for more than four years, then he or she will continue to stay out of prison.

    Given the trend shown, you would expect that after many years of freedom the percentage of people going back to jail would become very small, and virtually all would continue to stay free after that time. Certainly this is not the case after just four years, but the four-year assumption probably was made to keep the dimension of the matrix from getting too large.
    b. A released prisoner who is in the second year of freedom is more likely to go back to jail than a released prisoner who is in the fourth year of freedom.
    c. 81%
    88% of 81% = 71.3%
    93% of 88% of 81% = 66.3%
    d. (percentage that get sent back to prison within three years) =
    100% − (percentage that remain free for more than three years) =
    100% − 66.3% = 33.7%

    Another way to compute this is 19% + (12% of 81%) + (7% of 88% of 81%).

Freedom Status

This Year \ Next Year	in prison	1st yr. of freedom	2nd yr. of freedom	3rd yr. of freedom	4th yr. of freedom	> 4 yrs. of freedom
in prison	76%	24%	0%	0%	0%	0%
1st year of freedom	19%	0%	81%	0%	0%	0%
2nd year of freedom	12%	0%	0%	88%	0%	0%
3rd year of freedom	7%	0%	0%	0%	93%	0%
4th year of freedom	3%	0%	0%	0%	0%	97%
> 4 years of freedom	0%	0%	0%	0%	0%	100%

Source: Indiana State Reformatory Data from Mahoney, W.M. and C.F. Blozan, *Cost Benefit Evaluation of Welfare Demonstration Projects.* Bethesda, MD: Resources Management Corporation, 1968.

a. Most of the 0% entries refer to impossible events. For example, look at the third row, second column. Why is it impossible for a person released from prison who is in his or her second year of freedom this year to be in his or her first year of freedom next year?

b. What percentage of people released from prison who are in their second year of freedom this year will remain free and enter a third year of freedom next year?

c. Explain what the "7%" entry means.

d. What is the sum of each row of the matrix? Why does this make sense?

e. Based on your analysis of the matrix, describe at least one trend related to released prisoners returning to prison. What might explain the trend?

2. Consider the matrix from Extending task 1.

a. Often in mathematical modeling, some assumptions are made so that the situation is easier to model. In this case, it is assumed that if someone has remained out of prison for more than four years, then that person will continue to stay out of prison. Which entry or entries of the matrix correspond to this assumption? Why do you think this assumption was made? Does it seem reasonable?

b. Is a person who has been out of prison for two years more or less likely to return to prison than someone who has been out for four years?

c. What percentage of all those released from prison remain free for more than one year after release? For more than two years after release? For more than three years?

d. What percentage of people released from prison get reconvicted and sent back to prison within three years of their release? Compare your answer to the answers you found in part c.

LESSON 1 • BUILDING AND USING MATRIX MODELS 23

e. If a prison has 500 inmates, how many can be expected to be released in a given year? Of these, how many can be expected to remain out of prison for more than four years?

f. Construct a digraph that represents the matrix from Extending task 1.

3. One characteristic of spreadsheets that makes them so useful is that you can define the entries in the spreadsheet so that when you change one entry, related entries automatically change accordingly. Using spreadsheet software, create a spreadsheet that generates the loan information in Modeling task 5. Build the spreadsheet so that you can enter any loan amount, payment amount, and interest rate. Experiment with some different loan scenarios, as follows.

a. Change the annual interest rate to 19% (which could correspond to a credit card interest rate). Will a $45 payment be sufficient to pay off the loan in one year? If not, try different loan payments in the spreadsheet to find one that works.

b. Change the borrowed amount to $1000. Assuming a 9% annual interest rate, will an $85 payment be sufficient to pay off the loan in one year? If not, try different loan payments in the spreadsheet to find one that works.

c. Change the length of the loan to 24 months, but keep the loan amount at $500 and the rate at 9%. How should the payment change?

d. Compare the table and list features on a graphing calculator to a spreadsheet.

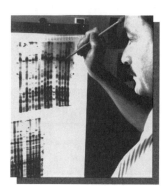

4. Did you ever stop to think about your genes? (Not the jeans you wear, but the genes that determine your physical characteristics.) Geneticists are always trying to find ways to analyze genes more precisely. One commonly-used method of analyzing genetic structure is to study *mutations*, or alterations, of a gene. One famous experiment concerned the virus called *phage T4*. The genetic structure of the virus was studied by looking at mutations of the gene which result when one segment of the gene is missing. As part of this experiment, it was possible to gather data showing how the segments of the gene overlap each other. The results were expressed in the form of a matrix, called the *overlap matrix*. One part of that matrix, showing the overlaps for nineteen segments, is shown below. The segments are labeled by the codes displayed across the top and down the side. A "1" means that there is an overlap between the two segments associated with the row and column.

2. e. 24% of the prisoners will be released. Thus, 120 people will get out of prison. Approximately 77 of these people ($500 \times 0.24 \times 0.81 \times 0.88 \times 0.93 \times 0.97 = 77$) will stay out of prison for more than four years.

f.

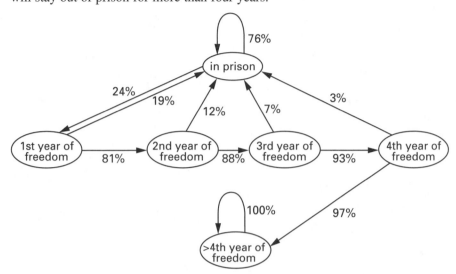

3. For most spreadsheets, build the headings as shown in Modeling task 5. The "Amount Borrowed" and "Interest" notifications might be entered in rows 1 and 2. The table headings could be entered in row 3, columns A to E. Enter 0 in cell A4 (column A, row 4) and 500 in cell E4. Set up the next row as follows: A5 = A4 + 1; B5 = min(45, E4 + C5); C5 = E4* (.09/12); D5 = B5 – C5; E5 = E4 – B5. Then, fill rows 6 to 16. In Excel, for example, select rows 5 to 16 and choose "Fill Down" from the Edit menu. The totals can be added in row 17 by setting B17 to sum(B5:B16), then selecting cells B to D in row 17 and filling right. (If you are unfamiliar with spreadsheets, you may need to consult your manual.)

a. (To change rates, modify C5 to reflect the new rate and again fill down. To change payments, modify B5 and fill down.) No, $45 is not a big enough monthly payment. The balance would be $14.13 after one year. The payment would need to be slightly more than $46.

b. No, $85 is not a big enough monthly payment. There will be a balance of $30.66 at the end of the year if $85 payments were made. However a payment of $90 would be more than enough. The minimum payment needed would be between $87 and $88.

c. The payment will decrease. The payment would be between $22 and $23.

d. Responses may vary. Possible responses are:
- The table is produced from an equation. List items can be independently entered. In a spreadsheet, the numbers located in cells depend on numbers from other cells.
- They are all charts of numbers. A list or table is like a column in the spreadsheet.

MORE *continued*

4. a. Yes, segments 882 and 221 overlap. The entry in the sixth row, tenth column means that segment 455 does not overlap with segment 761. There are seven segments that overlap with segment 749.

b. Yes, this is a symmetric matrix. If segment A overlaps segment B, then segment B must overlap segment A.

c. Segments 215 and 455 have the fewest overlaps; each overlaps two other segments.

d. Segment H23 is probably the longest because it has the most overlaps.

See Assessment Resources pages 1–6.

Gene Segments

	184	215	221	250	347	455	459	506	749	761	782	852	882	A103	B139	C4	C33	C51	H23
184	0	1	0	1	0	1	0	0	0	0	1	0	0	0	0	0	1	1	1
215	1	0	0	0	0	0	0	0	0	0	0	0	0	0	0	0	0	0	1
221	0	0	0	0	1	0	1	1	1	1	1	1	1	1	1	1	1	0	1
250	1	0	0	0	0	0	0	0	0	0	0	0	0	0	0	0	1	1	1
347	0	0	1	0	0	0	0	0	0	0	1	0	0	0	0	0	0	0	1
455	1	0	0	0	0	0	0	0	0	0	0	0	0	0	0	0	0	0	1
459	0	0	1	0	0	0	0	0	1	1	1	1	0	0	0	1	0	0	1
506	0	0	1	0	0	0	0	0	0	0	1	0	0	0	0	0	0	0	1
749	0	0	1	0	0	0	1	0	0	1	1	1	0	0	0	1	0	0	1
761	0	0	1	0	0	0	1	0	1	0	1	1	0	0	0	1	0	0	1
782	1	0	1	0	1	0	1	1	1	1	0	1	1	1	1	1	1	0	1
852	0	0	1	0	0	0	1	0	1	1	1	0	0	0	0	1	0	0	1
882	0	0	1	0	0	0	0	0	0	0	1	0	0	0	0	1	0	0	1
A103	0	0	1	0	0	0	0	0	0	0	1	0	0	0	1	0	0	0	1
B139	0	0	1	0	0	0	0	0	0	0	1	0	0	1	0	0	0	0	1
C4	0	0	1	0	0	0	1	0	1	1	1	1	1	0	0	0	0	0	1
C33	1	0	1	1	0	0	0	0	0	0	1	0	0	0	0	0	0	0	1
C51	1	0	0	1	0	0	0	0	0	0	0	0	0	0	0	0	0	0	1
H23	1	1	1	1	1	1	1	1	1	1	1	1	1	1	1	1	1	1	0

Source: Benzer, S., On the topology of the genetic fine structure, *Proc Nat Sci Acad USA* 45 (1959), 1607-1620.

a. Does segment 882 overlap segment 221? What does the entry in the sixth row and tenth column mean? How many segments overlap segment 749?

b. In Organizing task 4, a symmetric matrix was defined as a matrix that is symmetric about the main diagonal. Is the overlap matrix a symmetric matrix? If not, explain why not. If so, what is it about the situation being modeled that causes the matrix to be symmetric?

c. Which segments have the smallest number of overlaps?

d. Which segment do you think is the longest? Why?

Lesson 2

Multiplying Matrices

In Lesson 1, you operated on matrices in several different ways. In the case of a single matrix, the operations involved adding the row or column entries, multiplying all the entries by a single number, finding the mean of the row entries, or comparing two rows and counting differences. In the case of two matrices, you combined them by adding (or subtracting) entry-by-entry. These operations were seen to be particularly useful to businesses and manufacturers in tracking inventories of products. In addition to information on supply and demand, consumer-oriented companies also are interested in detecting and making forecasts based on trends.

Think About This Situation

Have you ever switched shoe brands? Maybe you bought Reebok one year and Fila the next year.

a If you have switched athletic shoe brands, what were your reasons for switching?

b Why do you think shoe stores and shoe companies would want to know about trends in brand switching?

c How do you think they could gather information and analyze trends in brand switching?

Lesson 2 *Multiplying Matrices*

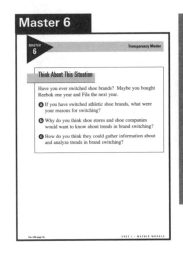
LESSON OVERVIEW In this lesson, students explore standard matrix multiplication, using the contexts of brand switching, tracking pollution through an ecosystem, and ranking players in tournaments. In the first investigation, students learn how to multiply a one-row matrix by another matrix, using the context of brand switching. This is generalized in the second investigation. Investigation 2 also helps students develop an understanding of the importance of the dimensions of matrices. Applications of matrix multiplication are explored further in Investigation 3. Once students understand multiplication of matrices, Investigation 4 helps them explore the properties of matrices and of operations on matrices, including the commutative and associative properties and existence of identity elements and inverses.

Lesson Objectives

- To use matrix multiplication, including powers of matrices, as a mathematical model that is helpful in making decisions in a variety of contexts
- To investigate the properties of matrices

LAUNCH   full-class discussion

You may wish to launch this lesson by asking the class what operations with matrices they have done so far. (You need not have students read the opening paragraph.) Terse answers such as "addition" could be followed by asking how that was done and how it could be useful. Some students may be thinking of "addition of matrices" as "finding row and column sums". Ask students to state clearly how to add matrices. Successful statements may involve students using some kind of symbols to clarify which entry from which matrix they were referring to, and where the result would be located. ("You add (1, 1) in *A* to (1, 1) in *B* to get (1, 1) in *C*.") This leads very naturally to the question of when you can add matrices and when you can not. Although students may have been successful in the previous lesson, they may not have reflected on when addition would not be possible and why. Similarly, you may wish to follow with a question about "multiplication". After getting a clear description of this process and an example of where it would be useful, indicate that the next lesson is also about "multiplication" and that students should be on the lookout for the differences between this new look at multiplication and what they already were calling multiplication.

Think About This Situation

See Teaching Master 6.

This "Think About This Situation" provides an opportunity to assess informally students' knowledge about business practices.

ⓐ A brief discussion will help engage students in the context.

ⓑ Knowing the trends in brand switching would help companies decide what kinds of shoes to order and what advertising to design, for example.

ⓒ They might gather information about brand-switching trends by in-store surveys or by hiring a market research firm, for example. They might analyze brand-switching trends using statistics, matrices, or other methods.

INVESTIGATION 1 Brand Switching

As students begin work on this investigation, it is important to let them find their answers in any way that makes sense to them. Eventually they should understand how to use matrix multiplication to formalize their procedure.

1. a. 40%

    b. 50%

    c. Fila customers are the most loyal because 70% of Fila customers do not expect to switch to Nike or Reebok, while 50% of Reebok's customers and 40% of Nike's customers do not expect to switch.

2. a. $700 \times 0.40 + 500 \times 0.20 + 400 \times 0.10 = 420$

    So, 420 people expect to buy Nike next year. Make sure students can explain how they arrived at their answers.

    b. $700 \times 0.40 + 500 \times 0.50 + 400 \times 0.20 = 610$

    So, 610 people expect to buy Reebok next year.

INVESTIGATION ▶ 1 Brand Switching

The big stores (and the big shoe companies) carry out market research to gather information about brand switching. Suppose that the results of market research on brand switching by customers of one large shoe store are shown in the following matrix.

Brand-Switching Matrix

		Next Brand		
		Nike	Reebok	Fila
Current Brand	Nike	40%	40%	20%
	Reebok	20%	50%	30%
	Fila	10%	20%	70%

This matrix summarizes the data about what percentage of people expect to buy certain brands, given the brand they now own. For example, the entry in the second row and third column is 30%. This means that 30% of the people who now own Reebok (second row) expect to buy Fila (third column) as their next pair of shoes.

1. a. What percentage of people who now own Nike expect to buy Reebok next?

   b. What percentage of people who now own Reebok expect to stay with Reebok on their next shoe purchase?

   c. Based on the data in this example, to which shoe brand do you think the customers are most loyal? Why?

2. Now assume that buyers buy a new pair of shoes every year, and suppose that this year 700 people bought Nike, 500 people bought Reebok, and 400 people bought Fila.

   a. How many people expect to buy Nike next year? Answer this question by using the brand-switching matrix and the information about how many people bought each brand this year. Explain your method.

   b. How many people expect to buy Reebok next year?

3. Shown below is a way to answer the questions in activity 2 using a new matrix operation. A one-row matrix for this year's numbers is written before the brand-switching matrix.

Buyers This Year

$$\begin{array}{ccc} N & R & F \\ [700 & 500 & 400] \end{array}$$

Brand-Switching Matrix

$$\begin{array}{c} \\ N \\ R \\ F \end{array} \begin{array}{ccc} N & R & F \\ \begin{bmatrix} 40\% & 40\% & 20\% \\ 20\% & 50\% & 30\% \\ 10\% & 20\% & 70\% \end{bmatrix} \end{array}$$

a. Complete the computation below for the number of people who expect to buy Fila next year.

Number of people
expecting to buy $= 700 \times (\underline{\hspace{0.5cm}}) + 500 \times (\underline{\hspace{0.5cm}}) + 400 \times (\underline{\hspace{0.5cm}})$
Fila next year

b. To which column of the brand-switching matrix do the numbers in the blanks correspond?

c. Which column of the brand-switching matrix can you combine with the one-row matrix to get the number of people who expect to buy Reebok next year? Explain how the row and the column are combined.

4. You have just performed a new matrix operation. This method of combining the one-row matrix with the columns of the brand-switching matrix is called **matrix multiplication**. The result can be written as another one-row matrix.

a. Using the computations you have already done, list the entries of the one-row matrix on the right below.

Buyers This Year

$$\begin{array}{ccc} N & R & F \\ [700 & 500 & 400] \end{array}$$

Brand-Switching Matrix

$$\begin{array}{c} \\ N \\ R \\ F \end{array} \begin{array}{ccc} N & R & F \\ \begin{bmatrix} 40\% & 40\% & 20\% \\ 20\% & 50\% & 30\% \\ 10\% & 20\% & 70\% \end{bmatrix} \end{array} =$$

Buyers Next Year

$$\begin{array}{ccc} N & R & F \\ [\underline{\hspace{0.3cm}} & \underline{\hspace{0.3cm}} & \underline{\hspace{0.3cm}}] \end{array}$$

We say that the one-row matrix for this year is *multiplied* by the brand-switching matrix to get the one-row matrix for next year. The term "matrix multiplication" always refers to this type of multiplication, and not to any of the other multiplications that you have done.

b. Based on the matrix multiplication in part a, describe the trend for shoe sales next year. If you were the store manager, would you adjust your shoe orders for next year from what you ordered this year? Explain.

3. **a.** $700 \times \underline{0.20} + 500 \times \underline{0.30} + 400 \times \underline{0.70}$

(This is 570 people.)

b. The numbers in the blanks correspond to the Fila column, which is the third column.

c. The Reebok column, column 2, can be combined with the one-row matrix to get the number of people who expect to buy Reebok next year.

You multiply the first entry in the row of the left matrix with the first entry in the column of the right matrix; add that to the product of the second entry of the row and the second entry of the column; *etc.*

By the end of part c, students should verbalize the row-column procedure for matrix multiplication.

4. **a.** Matrix multiplication is defined here. Students need to be clear that *matrix multiplication* is a formal expression and only applies to the row-column combination procedure, not to multiplying a matrix by a number or multiplying two matrices entry-by-entry.

```
  N    R    F
[420  610  570]
```

b. Nike sales should decrease and Reebok and Fila sales should increase. Responses about whether or not to adjust the shoe orders may vary. A sample response might be: Yes, I would adjust my shoe orders because of the expected increases and decreases. If you purchase more Nikes than suggested by the projection, you probably will lose money.

Unit 1

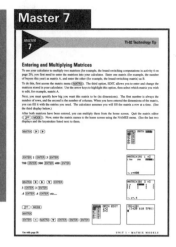

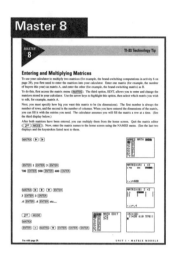

EXPLORE *continued*

5. Certainly the brand-switching matrix has limitations when used to estimate numbers far in the future. If students notice these limitations, that's great. It is brought out in the next Checkpoint for students who don't think about it now.

   a. Multiply the one-row matrix for next year's numbers by the brand-switching matrix (call it matrix *B*).

$$
\begin{array}{ccc}
\text{N} & \text{R} & \text{F}
\end{array}
\qquad\qquad
\begin{array}{ccc}
\text{N} & \text{R} & \text{F}
\end{array}
$$
$$
[420 \quad 610 \quad 570] \times B = [347 \quad 587 \quad 666]
$$

   347 people are expected to buy Nike shoes; 587 people are expected to buy Reebok shoes; 666 people are expected to buy Fila shoes.

   b. Multiply the one-row matrix for the numbers two years from now by the brand-switching matrix: 323 people are expected to buy Nike; 566 people are expected to buy Reebok; and 712 people are expected to buy Fila.

6. **See Teaching Masters 7–8.**

   This activity introduces students to using the matrix capability of their calculators or computer software. It also highlights the universality and usefulness of this seemingly strange multiplication, since it is one type of matrix multiplication that is actually built into all calculators that handle matrices. (Multiplication by a scalar can also be done with these calculators.)

   a–b. Be sure students can enter a matrix into the calculator.

   c. *NEXT = NOW ×* [*brand-switching matrix*] *= NOW × B*

   d.

$$
\begin{array}{ccc}
\text{N} & \text{R} & \text{F}
\end{array}
\qquad\qquad\qquad\qquad
\begin{array}{ccc}
\text{N} & \text{R} & \text{F}
\end{array}
$$

   in 4 years: [313   554   732]   in 5 years: [309   549   742]

$$
\begin{array}{ccc}
\text{N} & \text{R} & \text{F}
\end{array}
\qquad\qquad\qquad\qquad
\begin{array}{ccc}
\text{N} & \text{R} & \text{F}
\end{array}
$$

   in 10 years: [306   545   749]   in 20 years: [306   545   749]

   ■ After about 10 years the numbers (after rounding) become constant.

   ■ Responses will vary. One possible response is: The long-term customer buying distribution becomes constant, so order shoes according to the [306   545   749] matrix. Some students may argue that you can't plan for ordering shoes 10 years from now. Make sure they can support their reasoning.

5. The brand-switching matrix can be used to estimate how many people will buy each brand of shoe farther into the future. In the previous activity you found that:

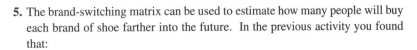

$$\begin{bmatrix} \text{The one-row matrix} \\ \text{showing how many} \\ \text{people bought each} \\ \text{brand this year} \end{bmatrix} \times \begin{bmatrix} \text{The brand-} \\ \text{switching matrix} \end{bmatrix} = \begin{bmatrix} \text{The one-row matrix} \\ \text{showing how many} \\ \text{people expect to buy} \\ \text{each brand next year} \end{bmatrix}$$

a. How many people are expected to buy each brand two years from now? Show which matrices you could multiply to get this answer.

b. Use matrix multiplication to find the number of people who are expected to buy the different brands three years from now.

You can use the matrix capability of your calculator or computer software for these computations. The way you have been multiplying matrices in this investigation is so useful that all calculators and software with matrix capability are designed with this kind of multiplication built in. All you have to do is enter the matrices and then multiply using the usual multiplication key.

6. This activity will help you become familiar with the matrix multiplication capability of your calculator or software.

a. Enter the brand-switching matrix and the matrix for the number of buyers this year. When entering a matrix, the first thing you do is enter its dimension; that is, you enter (number of rows) × (number of columns). When entering the brand-switching matrix, enter all percentages as decimals.

b. Use your calculator or software to check your computations from activities 4 and 5 for the number of people who are expected to buy each brand one, two, and three years from now.

c. Let *NOW* represent the matrix showing how many people buy each brand this year, and *NEXT* represent the matrix showing how many people are expected to buy each brand next year. Write an equation that shows how *NOW* and *NEXT* are related.

d. Use this *NOW-NEXT* equation and the last answer function on your calculator or computer software to estimate how many people will buy each brand four, five, ten, and twenty years from now. (On most calculators, the last answer function is the ANS key.)

■ Do you see a pattern? Describe the trend of sales over time.

■ If you were the shoe store manager, what would be your long-term strategy for ordering shoes? Explain.

Checkpoint

a Describe how to multiply a one-row matrix by another matrix. What must be true about the dimension of the other matrix?

b Describe any limitations you see for using the brand-switching matrix to estimate long-term shoe sales.

Be prepared to share your group's descriptions and thinking with the class.

On Your Own

a. To prepare for a dance, a school needs to rent 40 chairs, 3 large tables, and 6 punch bowls. There are two rental shops nearby that rent all these items, but they have different prices as shown in the matrix below.

Rental Prices

	U-Rent	Rent-All
Chairs	$2	$2.50
Tables	$20	$15
Bowls	$6	$4

- What is the dimension of the Rental Prices matrix?
- Put the information about how many chairs, tables, and bowls the school needs into a one-row matrix.
- Use matrix multiplication to find a matrix that shows the total cost of renting all the equipment from each of the two shops.
- From which shop should the school rent?

b. Multiply the two matrices below.

$$\begin{bmatrix} 3 & 6 & 5 & 9 \end{bmatrix} \begin{bmatrix} 3 & 5 & 2 \\ 7 & 8 & 5 \\ 3 & 9 & 7 \\ 6 & 7 & 2 \end{bmatrix}$$

SHARE AND SUMMARIZE full-class discussion

Checkpoint

See Teaching Master 9.

ⓐ Students should verbalize the row-column combination procedure. They also could be encouraged to "wave their hands" (horizontal to vertical) in the way that indicates the procedure. The number of rows in the second matrix must be equal to the number of columns in the one-row matrix. (It is not necessary for students to understand the dimensions of the resulting matrix at this point. If students themselves make conjectures or raise questions, it would be a valuable use of time to pursue their ideas immediately. Students will be more inclined to ask questions and make conjectures in the future if discussions are not always postponed.)

ⓑ The underlying assumption in the long-term brand-switching calculation is that the percentages of people switching brands stay constant and that new brands do not enter the market. This very likely will not be the case. Students may suggest researching brand-switching trends every 5 years or so.

    The sequence of matrices found in this manner is called a *Markov chain*. The limitation mentioned here is a general drawback to Markov chains. It is important that students understand it is typical of mathematical modeling to have some drawbacks. You must balance the simplicity of the model against its accuracy and make changes as needed. (However, modifying this model will not be pursued in this unit.)

▶Group Processing Suggestions

- To what group skills does your group need to pay more attention?
- I helped our group by _____ .

APPLY individual task

▶On Your Own

a. ■ 3×2
- You might need to discuss the importance of the numbers being in the correct order.

  Ch Tab Bo
$$\begin{bmatrix} 40 & 3 & 6 \end{bmatrix}$$

- The total costs are given in the calculation below.

$$\begin{bmatrix} 40 & 3 & 6 \end{bmatrix} \begin{bmatrix} \$2 & \$2.50 \\ \$20 & \$15 \\ \$6 & \$4 \end{bmatrix} = \begin{matrix} \text{U-Rent} & \text{Rent-All} \\ \begin{bmatrix} \$176 & \$169 \end{bmatrix} \end{matrix}$$

- The school should rent from Rent-All.

b. $\begin{bmatrix} 120 & 171 & 89 \end{bmatrix}$

Master 9

Master 10

ASSIGNMENT NOTE: As an extension to this "On Your Own", you may wish to have students do a little decontextualized practice. See Teaching Master 10.

INVESTIGATION ▶ 2   More Matrix Multiplication

General multiplication of matrices is studied in this investigation. Two different contexts are used. Rather than explicitly prescribe the rule for matrix multiplication, it is intended that students use their own methods. Incorrect methods will be corrected as students fill in the blanks and work through the other parts of this activity.

It is important not to let students' work with this operation degenerate into an algorithm devoid of meaning. While students should become efficient with the process, they also should be able to make sense of the outcome. As students work through parts c and d, it may help to ask how they know what the row and column labels of the answer matrix will be. Ask about the meaning of the new entries being created. Students should work hard on an explanation about why the "inner" labels seem to disappear. As one student said, "One row of entries and one column of entries are multiplied and totaled, so the answer only takes up one entry. The entry gets its meaning from the outer labels. Each entry in the answer has to mean some kind of total."

INVESTIGATION 2 More Matrix Multiplication

Matrix multiplication can be used to model many different situations. Working together as a group, explore the following two examples.

1. Suppose that three Little League baseball teams are considering two suppliers for their team uniforms: Uniforms Plus and Sporting Supplies, Inc. Since they consider the quality and delivery from each supplier to be the same, their only objective is to spend the least amount of money.

Each team will order three different sizes of uniforms, small, medium, and large. Each supplier charges different prices for these three sizes, as shown in the matrix below.

Cost per Uniform

	S	M	L
Uniforms Plus	$28	$36	$41
Sporting Supplies	$34	$35	$36

All three of the Little League teams—the Kalamazoo Zephyrs, the Fairfield Fliers, and the Prescott Pioneers—have the same number of players. However, they need different quantities of small, medium, and large size uniforms, as shown in the matrix below.

Quantity of Uniforms

	Zephyrs	Fliers	Pioneers
S	6	6	9
M	11	4	6
L	3	10	5

a. Recall how you multiplied the one-row matrix by the brand-switching matrix in Investigation 1. Use a similar method to multiply the cost matrix by the quantity matrix, without using the matrix feature of your calculator. Explain how you did the matrix multiplication.

$$
\begin{array}{c}
\\
\text{Uniforms Plus} \\
\text{Sporting Supplies}
\end{array}
\begin{array}{ccc}
S & M & L \\
\end{array}
\left[
\begin{array}{ccc}
\$28 & \$36 & \$41 \\
\$34 & \$35 & \$36
\end{array}
\right]
\times
\begin{array}{ccc}
\text{Zephyrs} & \text{Fliers} & \text{Pioneers} \\
\end{array}
\left[
\begin{array}{ccc}
6 & 6 & 9 \\
11 & 4 & 6 \\
3 & 10 & 5
\end{array}
\right]
=
\left[
\begin{array}{ccc}
— & — & — \\
— & — & —
\end{array}
\right]
$$

b. Explain what the number in the first row and second column of the answer matrix means. What does the number in the second row and third column mean?

c. Label the rows and columns of the answer matrix. What do you notice about the row and column labels of the cost-per-uniform matrix, the quantity-of-uniforms matrix, and the answer matrix?

d. Give the answer matrix a title.

e. Which supplier should each of the teams use in order to spend the least amount of money on uniforms?

f. Compare your answers and explanations in parts a–e with those of other groups. Resolve any differences.

g. Call the cost-per-uniform matrix C, and the quantity matrix Q. So far you have multiplied $C \times Q$. Try multiplying $Q \times C$. Can you do it? Explain why or why not.

2. A roofing contractor has three crews, A, B, and C, working in a large housing development of similar homes. The matrix below shows the number of houses roofed by each of the three crews during the second and third quarters of the year.

Number of Houses Roofed

$$
\begin{array}{c}
\\
\text{Apr–June} \\
\text{July–Sept}
\end{array}
\begin{array}{ccc}
A & B & C \\
\end{array}
\left[
\begin{array}{ccc}
10 & 12 & 9 \\
11 & 14 & 10
\end{array}
\right] = Q
$$

(The matrix Q could be defined $Q = \left[\begin{array}{ccc} 10 & 12 & 9 \\ 11 & 14 & 10 \end{array}\right]$ without the row and column labels. The labels are often helpful to show what the entries mean.)

1. **a.** Students should explain to each other how they did the matrix multiplication.

   ## Total Cost of Uniforms

	Zephyrs	Fliers	Pioneers
Uniforms Plus	$687	$722	$673
Sporting Supplies, Inc.	$697	$704	$696

   b. The number in the first row and second column of the answer matrix tells us that the Fliers would spend $722 if they bought their uniforms from Uniforms Plus. The $696 in the second row and third column tells us that if the Pioneers bought their uniforms from Sporting Supplies, Inc. they would spend $696.

   c. See part a for row and column labels. The column labels of the cost-per-uniform matrix are the same as the row labels of the quantity-of-uniforms matrix. The row labels of the answer matrix and the cost-per-uniform matrix are the same. The column labels of the answer matrix and the quantity-of-uniforms matrix are the same.

   NOTE: Encourage students to develop the habit of labeling the rows and columns and finding titles for matrices. Thinking about row and column labels and matrix titles will help students understand, interpret, set up, and carry out matrix multiplication.

   ---

   d. The title of the answer matrix should be "Total Cost of Uniforms."

   e. It would be less expensive for the Zephyrs to order their uniforms from Uniforms Plus. The Fliers would get a better deal if they ordered their uniforms from Sporting Supplies, Inc. and the Pioneers should order their uniforms from Uniforms Plus.

   f. Students may have been doing this comparison with each other all along. Nevertheless, it is crucial that they compare and resolve differences explicitly here so that all students are multiplying and interpreting correctly.

   g. This activity is designed to get students thinking about whether or not two matrices can be multiplied. Right now the only problem they should be expected to notice is a dimension mismatch. They should see that when they attempt the row-column combination procedure on the indicated matrices, it doesn't work. At this point, they are not expected to verbalize the precise dimension condition for matrix multiplication (see Investigation 4, activity 4). In activity 3 of this investigation, students will confront the problem that even if the dimensions allow the multiplication procedure to be carried out, doing the multiplication may not make sense in the given context.

EXPLORE *continued*

2. **a.** It took 107 days for all three crews to apply roofs from April to June. This is the first row, first column entry in the matrix $Q \times T$.

   b. Total Time

	Apply Roof	Cleanup
April–June	107	15.5
Jul–Sept	120.5	17.5

   c. $Q \times T = TT$

   d. $TT \times C = \begin{bmatrix} 107 & 15.5 \\ 120.5 & 17.5 \end{bmatrix} \begin{bmatrix} \$520 \\ \$160 \end{bmatrix} = \begin{bmatrix} \$58{,}120 \\ \$65{,}460 \end{bmatrix}$

   ■ The labels for the rows are the same as the labels for the rows of the Total Time matrix. The column label is the same as the column label for the Labor Cost per Day matrix.

Total Cost

	Cost Apply Roof
Apr–June	$58,120
Jul–Sept	$65,460

   ■ Each entry gives the total cost for application and cleaning up for the houses roofed during the indicated time period.

   e. $58,120 + $65,460 = $123,580; the grand total is $123,580.

The following matrix shows the time required (in days) for each crew to apply one roof and cleanup.

Time Required per Roof

	Apply	Cleanup
A	3.5	0.5
B	3.0	0.5
C	4.0	0.5

$= T$

Finally, this matrix shows the total crew labor cost per day to apply the roof and cleanup.

Labor per Day

	Cost
Apply	$520
Cleanup	$160

$= C$

a. What is the total time spent for all three crews combined to apply roofs from April–June?

b. Enter your answer from part a into a matrix like the one below, and then complete the rest of the entries.

Total Time

	Apply	Cleanup
Apr–June	____	____
July–Sept	____	____

$= TT$

c. What two matrices can be multiplied to give the total-time matrix above?

d. Multiply the total-time matrix (TT) by the cost matrix (C).

■ Label the rows and columns of the answer matrix. What do you notice about the labels? Compare your labeling with that of another group.

■ Explain what information the entries in the answer matrix give you. Give this matrix a title.

e. What is the grand total labor cost of all three crews, including applying the roofs and cleanup, from April–September?

3. As you may have noticed, it does not always make sense to multiply two matrices. Consider the matrices in activity 2.

   a. Can you multiply the cost-per-day matrix by the time matrix $(C \times T)$? Explain.

   b. Consider $Q \times T$.

   ■ Can you multiply $Q \times T$?

   ■ If so, does the information in the answer matrix make sense? Label the rows and columns, if possible, and describe the information contained in the answer matrix.

   c. Try multiplying in the reverse order.

   ■ Can you multiply $T \times Q$?

   ■ If so, what does the number in the first row and first column mean? Does it make sense? If possible, label the rows and columns and describe the information contained in the answer matrix.

Checkpoint

ⓐ Describe how to multiply two matrices.

ⓑ Give two reasons why it may not make sense to multiply two particular matrices.

ⓒ Does the order of matrix multiplication matter? Explain.

ⓓ If two matrices can be multiplied, what can you say about the labels on the columns of the left matrix and the labels on the rows of the right matrix? How are the labels on the answer matrix related to the labels of the matrices being multiplied?

Be prepared to share your group's descriptions and thinking with the entire class.

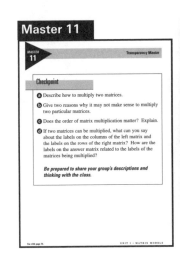

3. **a.** It is not possible to multiply $C \times T$ because of a dimension mismatch.

   b. ■ It is possible to multiply $Q \times T$. In fact, that is done in activity 2 part d to get the total-time matrix.

   ■ Row and column labels should be as in activity 2 part d. Each entry in the matrix gives the total cost for all three crews, application and cleanup, for the indicated time period.

   c. ■ It is possible to multiply $T \times Q$ just based on the dimension of the matrices.

   ■ The answer matrix does *not* make sense in this context. This becomes obvious when students try to interpret entries or label rows and columns. Students also may begin to notice that matrix multiplication is not commutative. (This fact is pursued more explicitly in Investigation 4, activity 5.)

SHARE AND SUMMARIZE   full-class discussion

Checkpoint

See Teaching Master 11.

As students share their answers to the Checkpoint questions, they should feel confident that

■ they can execute a matrix multiplication

■ they know when two matrices can be multiplied, and when they can not

■ they are able to predict the dimensions and labels of the resulting matrix

■ they can attach meaning to the resulting entries.

ⓐ Students should explain the row-column combination procedure in their own words.

ⓑ All students should be able to explain that it may not make sense to multiply two matrices for two reasons: the dimensions might not be compatible (the number of columns of the left matrix is not the same as the number of rows of the right matrix) or the answer matrix might not make sense in the context of the situation being studied. Some students may be able to state explicitly the dimension conditions for matrices to be multiplied. However, at this point it is more important that all students understand the concept that some matrices cannot be multiplied—that sometimes the row-column multiplication procedure simply doesn't work because the numbers of rows and columns of the two matrices do not "match up".

ⓒ Yes. Even if two matrices can be multiplied in either order, results may not make sense in a given context. Also, usually $A \times B \neq B \times A$ for matrices A and B. (With respect to the order of multiplication, students should have seen from activity 3 that $Q \times T \neq T \times Q$.)

CONSTRUCTING A MATH TOOLKIT: Following the full-class discussion, students should summarize these four outcomes in their Math Toolkits. In this way, individuals have the opportunity to reflect on this complicated process. See the Toolkit suggestion on page T78C.

See additional Teaching Notes on page T78C.

Unit 1

APPLY individual task

On Your Own

a. ■ The calculation is shown below.

$$\begin{array}{c} \\ \text{Elise} \\ \text{Harvey} \end{array}\begin{array}{c} \begin{array}{ccc} \text{Cr} & \text{D} & \text{Co} \end{array} \\ \begin{bmatrix} 55 & 60 & 90 \\ 80 & 50 & 100 \end{bmatrix} \end{array} \times \begin{array}{c} \text{Cr} \\ \text{D} \\ \text{Co} \end{array}\begin{array}{c} \begin{array}{cc} \text{Sept} & \text{Oct} \end{array} \\ \begin{bmatrix} 10 & 20 \\ 25 & 30 \\ 10 & 30 \end{bmatrix} \end{array} = \begin{array}{c} \\ \text{Elise} \\ \text{Harvey} \end{array}\begin{array}{c} \begin{array}{cc} \text{Sept} & \text{Oct} \end{array} \\ \begin{bmatrix} 2950 & 5600 \\ 3050 & 6100 \end{bmatrix} \end{array}$$

■ The entries in the answer matrix below are rounded to the nearest whole number.

$$\begin{bmatrix} 2950 & 5600 \\ 3050 & 6100 \end{bmatrix} \times \frac{1}{60} = \begin{bmatrix} 49 & 93 \\ 51 & 102 \end{bmatrix}$$

Converting minutes to hours is a nice example of multiplying a matrix by a number—in this case, by $\frac{1}{60}$. Calculators and mathematical software will perform this multiplication. Simply enter $\frac{1}{60} \times A$.

b. ■ $\begin{bmatrix} 2 & 3 \\ 4 & 5 \end{bmatrix} \begin{bmatrix} 6 \\ 7 \end{bmatrix} = \begin{bmatrix} 33 \\ 59 \end{bmatrix}$

■ $\begin{bmatrix} 1 & 3 \\ 6 & 5 \end{bmatrix} \begin{bmatrix} 0 & 2 \\ 3 & 3 \end{bmatrix} = \begin{bmatrix} 9 & 11 \\ 15 & 27 \end{bmatrix}$

MORE

ASSIGNMENT *pp. 46–58*

Students now can begin Modeling task 3 or Organizing task 2 from the MORE assignment following Investigation 4.

NOTE: Students may discover that implied multiplication—that is, entering two variables or matrices without entering the multiplication symbol between them—is possible with many calculators, such as the TI-82, the TI-83, and the Sharp EL-9300C.

▶**On Your Own**

a. A toy company in Seattle makes stuffed toys, including crabs, ducks, and cows. The owner designs the toys, and then they are cut out, sewn, and stuffed by independent contractors. For the months of September and October, each contractor agrees to make the number of stuffed toys shown in the following matrix.

Number of Toys Made

	Sept	Oct
Crabs	10	20
Ducks	25	30
Cows	10	30

Printed with permission of ©Ty Inc.

Two of the contractors, Elise and Harvey, know from experience how many minutes it takes them to make each type of toy, as shown in this matrix:

Time per Toy (in minutes)

	Crab	Duck	Cow
Elise	55	60	90
Harvey	80	50	100

■ Use matrix multiplication to find a matrix that shows the total number of minutes each of the two contractors will need in order to fulfill their contracts for each of the two months.

■ Convert the minute totals to hours. What matrix operation could you use to do this conversion? Does your calculator or computer software have the capability to perform this type of matrix operation?

b. Do the following matrix multiplications without a calculator, and then check your answers using your calculator.

■ $\begin{bmatrix} 2 & 3 \\ 4 & 5 \end{bmatrix} \begin{bmatrix} 6 \\ 7 \end{bmatrix}$
　　　　　■ $\begin{bmatrix} 1 & 3 \\ 6 & 5 \end{bmatrix} \begin{bmatrix} 0 & 2 \\ 3 & 3 \end{bmatrix}$

INVESTIGATION 3 The Power of a Matrix

An ecosystem is the system formed by a community of organisms and their interaction with their environments. The diagram below shows the predator-prey relationships of some organisms in a willow forest ecosystem.

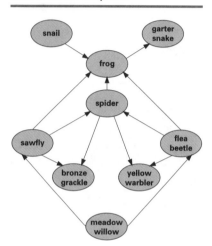

Willow Forest Ecosystem

Such a diagram is called a **food web**. An arrow goes from one species to another if one is food for the other. So, for example, the arrow from spider to yellow warbler means that spiders are food for yellow warblers.

Pollution can cause all or part of the food web to become contaminated. In this investigation you will explore how contamination of some species spreads through the rest of the food web.

1. First, think about the predator-prey relationships.

   a. Does the arrow from sawfly to spider mean that sawflies eat spiders or that sawflies are food for spiders?

   b. Spiders are food for which species? For which species are frogs food?

   c. The arrows are a very important part of this diagram. What are some ways to remember the meaning of the arrows?

2. Now think about the effects of pollution on the ecosystem.

   a. Suppose that all the frogs are contaminated by a toxic chemical that washes into the stream in which they live. Based on the predator-prey relationships shown in the food web, which other species in the ecosystem will be contaminated?

   b. If the sawflies are contaminated by a pesticide, which other species will subsequently be contaminated? Explain.

INVESTIGATION 3   The Power of a Matrix

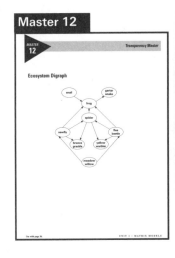

See Teaching Master 12.

This investigation is designed to meet three objectives:

■ to familiarize students with the food-chain diagram and its interpretation

■ to connect matrices to graph models

■ to introduce the square of a matrix

> NOTE: It is essential that students understand the phrase "are food for". This
> phrase is awkward, but it is needed to make it clear that the arrows point in
> the proper direction. Some students may want to read an arrow from A to B
> as "A eats B" instead of "A is food for B." Be alert for this misinterpretation.

You may wish to leave open the question for activity 4 part d, overnight. This gives students an opportunity to experiment some more. After having some time to work on their own, students could check their thinking with their group members or other groups. A class discussion may be needed to help students see that the square of the matrix, which shows one-step connections, will solve their problem.

There are two difficulties with learners in activity 4. It has been the experience of early users of this material that you should not let students avoid thinking deeply about either of these.

The first difficulty is *why* the square matrix is a model for indirect connections. If students do not ask about this then you may want to raise the question yourself. Articulating *why* the square matrix shows the total of all 2-step paths is not a simple task. It is not essential that students are able to give a complete explanation; however, they should be able to say enough to show that they do seem to understand. A complete explanation is offered in the notes for Reflecting task 1 on page T54.

The second difficulty for learners is that students already have a meaning for "square" in their vocabulary as the term relates to squaring real numbers. While the term does have the same meaning in this new context—that is, A^2 means to multiply A by itself—students may forget that the process of multiplying matrices is more complex than multiplying real numbers. The use of technology to compute the square matrix is seductively easy, and may mask the difference in procedures. It may help if you ask: Why do we not just square each of the entries in matrix A to get A^2? How is squaring a matrix like squaring a number? How is it different?

1. **a.** The arrow means that sawflys are food for spiders.

   b. Spiders are food for frogs, bronze grackles, and yellow warblers. Frogs are food for garter snakes.

   c. Responses will vary. The arrow might be thought of as indicating what "goes into" what (what is food for what). That is, the arrow from spiders to yellow warblers could be thought of as spiders going into yellow warblers. The more that students discuss the meaning of the arrows the more likely they are to interpret them correctly.

2. **a.** The species that will be contaminated are those that eat frogs. In this ecosystem only garter snakes eat frogs so only garter snakes would be contaminated.

   b. The bronze grackles, spiders, frogs, garter snakes, and yellow warblers would all be in danger of contamination. The sawflys are food for frogs, spiders, and bronze grackles. Frogs, in turn, are food for garter snakes and spiders are food for yellow warblers.

EXPLORE *continued*

c. The contamination will not spread to any other species. For this ecosystem, no species eats yellow warblers.

d. Once a species is contaminated, all other species on all paths leading away from the source species will also be contaminated. Thus, follow the paths to find the spread of contamination.

3. **Here it is especially important to emphasize the matrix-reading convention:** *from* **the row,** *to* **the column.**

   a. See Teaching Master 13 for a matrix template; without this template, your students may spend valuable time on the relatively unimportant task of drawing a grid.

	Bg	Fb	Fr	Gs	Mw	Sa	Sn	Sp	Yw
Bronze grackle	0	0	0	0	0	0	0	0	0
Flea beetle	0	0	1	0	0	0	0	1	1
Frog	0	0	0	1	0	0	0	0	0
Garter snake	0	0	0	0	0	0	0	0	0
Meadow willow	0	1	0	0	0	1	0	0	0
Sawfly	1	0	1	0	0	0	0	1	0
Snail	0	0	1	0	0	0	0	0	0
Spider	1	0	1	0	0	0	0	0	1
Yellow warbler	0	0	0	0	0	0	0	0	0

   b. Everyone needs to have identical matrices for the analysis that follows.

4. **If you have not read the notes on page T36 it may be helpful to do so now. Teaching Master 13 includes a partially-completed matrix for this activity also.**

   a. ■ There is one path of length 2 from spider to garter snake.

      ■ There is not a path of length 2 from the meadow willow to the garter snake.

      ■ There are two paths of length 2 from the meadow willow to the frog.

   b.

	Bg	Fb	Fr	Gs	Mw	Sa	Sn	Sp	Yw
Bronze grackle	0	0	0	0	0	0	0	0	0
Flea beetle	1	0	1	1	0	0	0	0	1
Frog	0	0	0	0	0	0	0	0	0
Garter snake	0	0	0	0	0	0	0	0	0
Meadow willow	1	0	2	0	0	0	0	2	1
Sawfly	1	0	1	1	0	0	0	0	1
Snail	0	0	0	1	0	0	0	0	0
Spider	0	0	0	1	0	0	0	0	0
Yellow warbler	0	0	0	0	0	0	0	0	0

   c. Everyone needs to have identical matrices for the analysis that follows.

   d. This matrix is too big to fit on one screen. Students will need to use arrow keys to be able to check that all matrix entries are correct.

   At this point students simply should observe that the squared adjacency matrix is the same as the length-two matrix from part b. They will think about why this is so in Reflecting task 1. If they do ask why at this stage, you may want to turn the question back to them and refer them to Reflecting task 1. The teacher notes for that task contain a complete explanation.

c. How far will the contamination spread if it starts with the yellow warblers?

d. Explain how the answers to parts a–c can be found by considering paths through the food web diagram.

The food web can be viewed as a *directed graph*, or *digraph*, where the vertices are the species and the edges are the arrows. You saw in part d of activity 2, above, how finding paths through the digraph helps answer questions about the spread of contamination. Using matrices can help find paths.

3. The first step to finding paths is to construct the *adjacency matrix* for the food web digraph. The adjacency matrix is constructed by listing the vertices down the side and across the top of a matrix. Then write a "1" or a "0" for each entry of the matrix depending on whether or not the vertices are *adjacent*; that is, whether or not there is a single arrow (directed edge) *from* the vertex along the side *to* the vertex along the top.

a. Construct the adjacency matrix for the food web digraph. Your teacher may have one started for you to complete.

b. Compare your matrix with the matrix constructed by other groups. Discuss and resolve any differences in your matrices so that everyone agrees upon the same matrix.

4. The adjacency matrix tells you if there is an edge from one vertex to another. An edge from one vertex to another is like a path of length one. Now think about paths of length two. A **path of length two** from one vertex to another means that you can get from one vertex to the other by moving along two directed edges.

a. Examine the partially-completed matrix provided by your teacher, which shows the number of paths of length two in the food web digraph.

■ Explain why the spider/garter-snake entry is a "1".

■ Explain why the meadow-willow/garter-snake entry is a "0".

■ Explain why the meadow-willow/frog entry is a "2".

b. Complete the matrix.

c. Compare your matrix to those constructed by other groups. Discuss and resolve any differences, so that everyone has the same matrix.

d. Enter the original adjacency matrix (which shows paths of length one) into your calculator or computer software. Check that you have entered all the numbers correctly. With your group, make and test conjectures about ways to obtain the paths-of-length-two matrix from the paths-of-length-one matrix. If you don't find a way that works, check with another group.

5. a. Propose a method for using matrix multiplication to find the matrix that shows paths of length three in the food web digraph.

b. Carry out your proposal. Check several entries in your proposed length-three matrix by examining the digraph to see if the entries really correspond to paths of length three.

c. If matrix A is the adjacency matrix from the food web digraph, what does A^3 tell you about paths in the food web digraph?

6. Suppose that the meadow willows are contaminated by polluted ground water. They in turn contaminate other species that feed directly or indirectly on them. However, at each step of the food chain the concentration of contamination decreases. Suppose that species more than two steps from the meadow willow in the food web are no longer endangered by the contamination.

a. Which species are safe?

b. How can the matrices A and A^2 be used to answer this question? Explain your reasoning.

You have seen that powers of an adjacency matrix give you information about paths of certain lengths in the associated vertex-edge graph. This connection between graphs and matrices is useful for solving a variety of problems. For example, it is often very difficult to accurately and systematically rank players or teams in a tournament. A vertex-edge graph can give you a good picture of the status of the tournament. The corresponding adjacency matrix can help determine the ranking of the players or teams. Consider the following situation.

The second round of a city tennis tournament involved six girls, each of whom was to play every other girl. However, the tournament was rained out after each girl had played only four matches. The results of play were the following:

- Emily beat Keadra.
- Anne beat Julia.
- Keadra beat Anne and Julia.
- Julia beat Emily and Maria.
- Maria beat Emily, Catherine, and Anne.
- Catherine beat Emily, Keadra, and Anne.

The problem is to rank the girls at this stage of the tournament, with no ties.

5. **a–c.** Raising the adjacency matrix to power 3 will give a matrix that shows the number of paths of length three from one vertex to another in the food web graph.

6. **a.** Snails and garter snakes are safe. All other species are one or two steps higher than the meadow willow vertex.

   b. Compute $A + A^2$. An entry of 0 in this matrix means there are no paths of length one or two between the two vertices. Thus, 0 entries in the meadow willow row correspond to safe species. This is another application of matrix powers. It also explicitly focuses on the process of mathematical modeling.

In activities 7 through 11, students are led through one sensible method for ranking players in a tournament. There is no foolproof method for finding such a ranking. In these activities (and in others in this unit), students may feel a particular ranking outcome is not quite fair. They should support any objections they feel compelled to make.

7. **a.** The matrix should have the players listed down the side and across the top in alphabetical order.

Tournament Results

	A	C	E	J	K	M
Anne	0	0	0	1	0	0
Catherine	1	0	1	0	1	0
Emily	0	0	0	0	1	0
Julia	0	0	1	0	0	1
Keadra	1	0	0	1	0	0
Maria	1	1	1	0	0	0

b. This digraph should have an arrow from one vertex to another if one player beats the other. There probably will be a lot of variation in the shapes of the graphs produced.

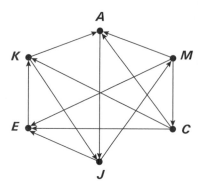

c. Students should compare matrices and digraphs to see that they all contain the same information.

d. Despite the fact that there will be different-looking graphs and matrices, all should contain the same information. It is important for students to realize that the format of matrices or graphs can differ, yet accurately model the situation.

8. This activity provides an initial examination of the graph and matrix that should generate some ambiguity and motivate the need for a deeper analysis.

a. Maria is a reasonable choice to be ranked in first place. (Catherine is another possible choice.) Students may have many different explanations.

■ Possible argument: Maria's vertex has more arrows pointing away from it, and thus more wins, than any other player except Catherine. There is an arrow from Maria to Catherine, so Maria beat Catherine. Thus, Maria should get first place.

■ Possible argument: Maria has more 1s in her row than any other player except Catherine. There is a 1 in the Maria-Catherine row, so Maria beat Catherine. Thus, Maria should get first place.

b. Julia and Keadra are tied in terms of number of wins (2 wins each), as are Emily and Anne (1 win each). However since Keadra defeated Julia it seems reasonable that Keadra will be ranked above Julia. On the other hand, Julia beat Maria and Maria seems to be the champion. So it is not clear how to rank Julia and Keadra. Emily and Ann have not played each other, so it is not clear which girl should be ranked above the other.

See additional Teaching Notes on page T78D.

7. The first step in solving this problem is to find useful mathematical representations of the situation.

   a. Represent the results of the tournament at this stage with a matrix of 0s and 1s. A "1" should show that the player represented by the row beat the player represented by the column. For convenience, list the girls alphabetically.

   b. Think of the matrix as an adjacency matrix for a digraph, and draw the digraph.

   c. Compare your matrix and digraph with those of other groups. Does everyone's matrix and digraph show that Catherine beat Keadra? That Keadra beat Julia? Make sure that your matrix and digraph contain the same information about the results of the tournament as those of your classmates.

   d. Is it possible for two matrices or two digraphs to look different, and yet both accurately represent the results of the tournament? Why or why not?

8. You now have two mathematical models of the tournament, namely, a graph and a matrix. Based on an examination of these models:

   a. If you had to rank one girl in first place right now, who would you choose? (Do not rank beyond first place.)

   ■ Give an argument based on the digraph that supports your answer.

   ■ Give an argument based on the matrix that supports your answer.

   b. Find two girls where neither one seems to be ranked clearly above the other.

9. To obtain further information about the performance of the players, sum each row of the adjacency matrix.

   a. What information does Keadra's row sum give you?

   b. Explain how you could use row sums to rank one girl over another.

   c. Based on the row sums, which girls appear tied?

   d. Give an argument for ranking Keadra above Julia.

   e. Give an argument for ranking Julia above Keadra.

10. To help resolve some of the unclear rankings, compute the square of the adjacency matrix.

   a. What do entries in the squared adjacency matrix tell you about the tennis tournament?

   b. What information does Keadra's row sum in the squared adjacency matrix give you?

   c. Investigate using row sums of the squared adjacency matrix to help rank the girls.

   ■ Have any ties or unclear rankings been resolved?

   ■ Do any ties remain?

11. Call the original adjacency matrix A.

a. Compute and record A^3, $A + A^2$, and $A + A^2 + A^3$.

b. Considering A^3, do you think that a non-zero entry that pairs a player with herself is relevant to the ranking? Explain.

c. Use the information that you now have to rank the girls, with no ties. Explain the ranking method you used.

▶ On Your Own

In any group of people, some are leaders and some are followers. This relationship of leaders and followers is called social dominance. On the next page is a digraph that shows social dominance within a group of five people. An arrow from one vertex to another means that the one person is socially dominant (is the "leader") over the other.

11. **a.**

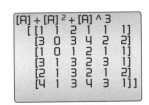

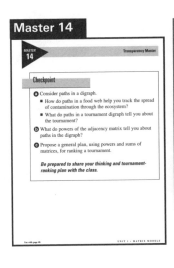

b. No, a three-stage victory of a player over herself is not relevant for ranking because players do not compete against themselves.

c. Students could use various methods. The most common probably will be checking the sums of the rows of the matrix formed by $A + A^2 + A^3$. Using this method, and probably any other the students try, yields Maria-Catherine-Julia-Keadra-Anne-Emily.

NOTE: It is worth pointing out that vertex-edge graphs give a nice picture of the situation when the problem is not too large, but in most real-world situations involving matrix methods, computers must be used to solve the problem.

SHARE AND SUMMARIZE   full-class discussion

Checkpoint

See Teaching Master 14.

ⓐ ■ The paths in the food web digraph are the paths the contamination follows.

  ■ Paths in a tournament digraph correspond to multi-stage wins.

ⓑ The entries in A^n tell how many paths of length n there are from one vertex to another.

ⓒ One plan is to sum the rows of the matrix formed by $A + A^2 + A^3$. Another plan might involve weighting the sums. (See Extending task 1.) Any thoughtful plan should be acknowledged.

▶Group Processing Suggestions

■ Name ways in which your group works better now than it did two weeks ago.

■ We included everyone today by _____.

▶**On Your Own**

a. Here are some interesting or unusual features: the A-B-E cycle (see part f); nobody dominates C, that is, C seems to be an independent thinker; D is dominated by most people, that is, D seems to be a person whose opinions are easily shaped by others; E and C have no dominance relation, that is, these two people seem to act independently of each other's opinions.

b.

$$
\begin{array}{c} \\ A \\ B \\ C \\ D \\ E \end{array}
\begin{array}{c} A \ \ B \ \ C \ \ D \ \ E \\
\begin{bmatrix}
0 & 1 & 0 & 1 & 0 \\
0 & 0 & 0 & 1 & 1 \\
1 & 1 & 0 & 1 & 0 \\
0 & 0 & 0 & 0 & 1 \\
1 & 0 & 0 & 0 & 0
\end{bmatrix} = M
\end{array}
$$

c. Responses will vary. Look at and discuss students' reasoning. Looking at row sums of M, there is no row sum of 4 (so no one directly dominates everyone else). C has the highest row sum of 3. Thus C would seem to be the most dominant. A and B have row sums of 2 and A dominates B, so A appears to be the next in rank. Then B follows A.

It is harder to determine a ranking for D and E. D dominates E but D also is dominated by more people than E is. Some students may feel certain that they are giving the most fair ranking, even if it contradicts the ranking found in part c. Remember that no ranking method is foolproof. If the students can supply reasons why they feel their rankings are better, those rankings should be acknowledged as valid.

d.

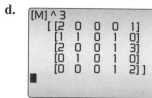

■ The A-E entry of 1 means that there is one path of length three from A to E. The path is A-B-D-E. This path means that A is dominant over B, who is dominant over D, who is dominant over E. Thus, A seems to have an indirect dominance over E. However, when paired directly with E, E is the leader over A. This shows that, in the case of social relations, direct relations can be different than indirect relations.

■ Since the entries of M^3 show the number of paths of length three, students should trace the two paths of length three from C to A. They are C-D-E-A and C-B-E-A.

MORE

ASSIGNMENT   *pp. 46–58*

Students now can begin Modeling tasks 1, 2, or 4, Organizing task 3, Reflecting task 1, or Extending tasks 1, 2, 3, or 4 from the MORE assignment following Investigation 4.

e.

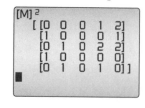   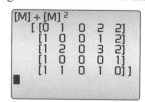

Sums of the rows of M^2 still show a tie, but sums of the rows of $M + M^2$ show a ranking of C-A-B-E-D.

See additional Teaching Notes on page T78D.

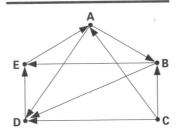

Social Dominance Graph

a. Describe and explain at least one interesting or unusual feature that you see in the dominance digraph.

b. Construct the adjacency matrix, M, for this digraph.

c. Using the adjacency matrix, identify an overall leader of this group. Can you rank, with no ties, all five people in terms of social dominance? Explain.

d. Use your calculator or computer software to compute M^3.

- Explain what the "1" for the A-E entry means in terms of social dominance.

- Trace the paths in the digraph that correspond to the "2" for the C-A entry.

e. Use powers of the adjacency matrix and sums of rows to break any ties and rank the five people in terms of social dominance.

f. What do the arrows between A, B, and E indicate about these three people? Explain how this could be possible in a social group.

INVESTIGATION ▶ 4 Properties of Matrices

Notice that in the activities of Investigation 3, with small ecosystems and small tournaments, a digraph provided a nice model of the situation. It was possible to answer most questions by examining the digraph, perhaps with some simple matrix computations. However, in many real-world settings, the digraphs become too large to draw. Then you must rely exclusively on matrix methods, often using computers, to solve the problem. In this investigation you will explore some of the properties of matrices upon which matrix methods depend.

In arithmetic, you studied numbers and operations on numbers. In algebra, you studied expressions and operations on expressions. In both settings you found that certain properties were obeyed. For example, one such property was the *distributive property for multiplication over addition*: $a(b + c) = ab + ac$.

In this unit, you have been studying matrices and matrix operations, including matrix addition and matrix multiplication. You will now investigate properties of matrices and their operations. This situation occurs frequently in mathematics: certain objects (like numbers or matrices) along with particular operations are studied, and then their properties are examined.

1. To begin this exploration of matrices, their operations, and their properties, consider matrix addition.

a. Suppose $A = \begin{bmatrix} 3 & 4 & 2 \\ 1 & 0 & 9 \end{bmatrix}$. To which of the following matrices can A be added?

$$B = \begin{bmatrix} 1 & 9 & 8 \\ 6 & 5 & 4 \end{bmatrix} \quad C = \begin{bmatrix} 2 & 3 & 4 \\ 1 & 5 & 6 \\ 8 & 5 & 6 \end{bmatrix} \quad D = \begin{bmatrix} 4 & 2 \\ 3 & 5 \\ 8 & 7 \end{bmatrix} \quad E = \begin{bmatrix} -7 & 798 & 87.9 \\ 0 & 0 & \frac{2}{3} \end{bmatrix}$$

b. Under what conditions can two matrices be added? State the conditions precisely and explain your reasoning.

2. Now, compare addition of matrices to addition of numbers.

a. When adding two numbers, does the order in which you do the addition matter? That is, is it true for all real numbers x and y that $x + y = y + x$? Give some examples of this commutative property of addition.

b. Check to see if this property is true for matrix addition.

■ Suppose $A = \begin{bmatrix} 3 & 4 & 2 \\ 1 & 0 & 9 \end{bmatrix}$ and $B = \begin{bmatrix} 1 & 9 & 8 \\ 6 & 5 & 4 \end{bmatrix}$. Is it true that $A + B = B + A$?

■ Do you think $A + B = B + A$ for *all* matrices A and B (assuming that A has the same number of rows and columns as B)? Defend your answer.

3. The number 0 has a unique property with respect to addition: adding 0 to any real number leaves the number unchanged. That is, $x + 0 = x$, for all real numbers.

a. Is there a matrix that will leave another matrix unchanged if the two are added?

■ Suppose $D = \begin{bmatrix} 4 & 2 \\ -3 & 5 \\ 8 & 0 \end{bmatrix}$. Find a matrix C so that $D + C = D$.

■ Suppose matrix A has 4 rows and 3 columns. Find a matrix E such that $A + E = A$.

■ Look at the matrices you just found. Write down a description of what you think a *zero matrix* should be.

b. Every real number has an "opposite" number. A number and its opposite sum to zero. That is, for every real number x, there is a real number $-x$, such that $x + (-x) = 0$.

■ What is the opposite of 17? Of $\frac{3}{4}$? Of -356.76?

1. **a.** Matrix A can be added to matrices B and E.

   b. Two matrices can be added together only if they have the same number of rows and the same number of columns. This is because you add the numbers from the corresponding entries.

2. **a.** Yes, it is true that for real numbers x and y, $x + y = y + x$. For example $3 + 7 = 10$ and $7 + 3 = 10$; also $-12 + 8 = -4$ and $8 + (-12) = -4$.

   b. ■ Yes, $A + B = B + A$ for these matrices A and B.

   ■ Arguments will vary. Commutativity of matrix addition (assuming the entries are real numbers) is based upon commutativity of real-number addition.

3. **a.**
$$C = \begin{bmatrix} 0 & 0 \\ 0 & 0 \\ 0 & 0 \end{bmatrix}$$

$$E = \begin{bmatrix} 0 & 0 & 0 \\ 0 & 0 & 0 \\ 0 & 0 & 0 \\ 0 & 0 & 0 \end{bmatrix}$$

   ■ A zero matrix is any matrix that has a zero in every entry.

   b. ■ The opposite of 17 is -17, of $\frac{3}{4}$ is $\frac{-3}{4}$, and of -356.76 is 356.76.

3. b. ■ The opposite of C is the matrix

$$\begin{bmatrix} -2 & -4 & 3 \\ -3 & 5 & 7 \end{bmatrix}$$

■ The opposite matrix has the same number of rows and columns as the original matrix, and each entry is the opposite of the original entry in the same position.

4. a. The entries in the matrices will vary. It is impossible to multiply $A \times B$. It is possible to multiply $B \times A$. An example follows.

$$A = \begin{bmatrix} 2 & -3 \\ 0 & 1 \\ 4 & 7 \\ 2 & 3 \end{bmatrix} \qquad B = \begin{bmatrix} -1 & 5 & 0 & 2 \\ 0 & 3 & 7 & 8 \\ 3 & -2 & 4 & 3 \end{bmatrix}$$

b. The matrix would be $n \times 3$, where n is an element of the natural numbers (a positive integer). This is because the number of columns of the first matrix and the number of rows in the second matrix must be the same if they are to be multiplied together. The dimension of the product matrix will be $n \times 2$.

c. To multiply matrix A by matrix B, the number of columns in A has to be equal to the number of rows in B.

d. For $A \times B$ to be possible, the number of columns in A must be equal to the number of rows in B; say this number is n. For $B \times A$ to be possible, the number of columns in B must equal the number of rows in A; say this number is m. Thus A will be an $m \times n$ matrix and B will be an $n \times m$ matrix. Geometrically the "shape" of the matrices are 90° rotations of each other.

5. a. Yes, it is true that multiplication of real numbers is commutative. For example, $5 \times 6 = 6 \times 5$; also $-4 \times 7 = 7 \times -4$.

b. Using almost any randomly-chosen matrices, students can verify easily that multiplication of 2×2 matrices is not commutative. You may need to remind students that in order to show something is not always true only one counterexample needs to be found.

c. Multiplication of 3×3 matrices is not commutative either. Almost any two 3×3 matrices will provide a counterexample.

6. a. The identity matrix for 2×2 matrices is the matrix $\begin{bmatrix} 1 & 0 \\ 0 & 1 \end{bmatrix}$.

- Let $C = \begin{bmatrix} 2 & 4 & -3 \\ 3 & -5 & -7 \end{bmatrix}$. Find the opposite matrix for C by solving this equation:

$$C + \begin{bmatrix} \rule{0.5cm}{0.4pt} & \rule{0.5cm}{0.4pt} & \rule{0.5cm}{0.4pt} \\ \rule{0.5cm}{0.4pt} & \rule{0.5cm}{0.4pt} & \rule{0.5cm}{0.4pt} \end{bmatrix} = \begin{bmatrix} 0 & 0 & 0 \\ 0 & 0 & 0 \end{bmatrix}$$

  - For any matrix A describe its opposite.

4. Another important matrix operation is matrix multiplication.

   a. Construct two matrices, A and B, using any numbers you like, as follows: matrix A should have 4 rows and 2 columns, and matrix B should have 3 rows and 4 columns. Is it possible to multiply $A \times B$? $B \times A$?

   b. Suppose C is a matrix that can be multiplied by a 3×2 matrix, D. That is, you can multiply $C \times D$. What could be the dimension of C? Explain. What would be the dimension of the product matrix?

   c. What are the conditions on the number of rows and columns that allow two matrices to be multiplied?

   d. What are the conditions on the dimensions of two matrices A and B so that it is possible to multiply $A \times B$ and also $B \times A$?

5. Compare multiplication of matrices to multiplication of real numbers.

   a. Is it true that the order of multiplication of real numbers does not matter? That is, is it true that $xy = yx$, for all real numbers x and y? Give several examples illustrating this *commutative property of multiplication.*

   b. Check to see if the property in part a is true for multiplication of 2×2 matrices; that is, matrices with 2 rows and 2 columns. Compare your findings with those of other groups.

   c. Is multiplication of 3×3 matrices commutative? Explain your reasoning.

Recall that a matrix with the same number of rows and columns is called a square matrix. Square matrices have several important properties with respect to matrix multiplication.

6. The number 1 has the unique property that multiplying any real number by 1 does not change the number. That is, $a \times 1 = 1 \times a = a$, for all real numbers. A square matrix that acts like the number 1 in this regard is called an **identity matrix**. Identity matrices are always square.

   a. Find the identity matrix for 2×2 square matrices by filling in the blanks for the matrix below:

$$\begin{bmatrix} 5 & 4 \\ 2 & 6 \end{bmatrix} \begin{bmatrix} \rule{0.5cm}{0.4pt} & \rule{0.5cm}{0.4pt} \\ \rule{0.5cm}{0.4pt} & \rule{0.5cm}{0.4pt} \end{bmatrix} = \begin{bmatrix} 5 & 4 \\ 2 & 6 \end{bmatrix}$$

b. Multiply $\begin{bmatrix} 5 & 4 \\ 2 & 6 \end{bmatrix}$ on the left by the identity matrix you just found.

Did you get $\begin{bmatrix} 5 & 4 \\ 2 & 6 \end{bmatrix}$ as the answer?

c. Suppose matrix A has 3 rows and 3 columns. Find the identity matrix I such that $A \times I = A$.

d. Write down a description of an identity matrix.

7. Every nonzero number has a *multiplicative inverse*. The product of a number and its multiplicative inverse is 1.

   a. What is the multiplicative inverse of 3? Of $\frac{1}{2}$? Of $\frac{5}{3}$? Of -8.6?

   b. If $D = \begin{bmatrix} 5 & 3 \\ 3 & 2 \end{bmatrix}$, then the *inverse matrix* for D, written D^{-1}, is the matrix that satisfies the equation below:

   $$\begin{bmatrix} \_ & \_ \\ \_ & \_ \end{bmatrix} \begin{bmatrix} 5 & 3 \\ 3 & 2 \end{bmatrix} = \begin{bmatrix} 1 & 0 \\ 0 & 1 \end{bmatrix}$$

   Make and test some conjectures for the entries of D^{-1}.

   c. Compute the matrix D^{-1} using your calculator or computer software. On most calculators, this can be done by entering matrix D into your calculator and then using the 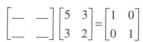 key. Check that $D^{-1} \times D$ gives the identity matrix. Check that $D \times D^{-1}$ also gives the identity matrix.

   d. Use your calculator or computer software to find A^{-1}, where

   $$A = \begin{bmatrix} -8 & -10 \\ 2 & 3 \end{bmatrix}.$$

   Check that $A^{-1} \times A$ gives the identity matrix.

8. Every real number (except 0) has a multiplicative inverse. Check to see if square matrices have this property.

   a. Enter several square matrices into your calculator or computer software and compute their inverses. Try to find a square matrix that does not have an inverse.

   b. Consider $A = \begin{bmatrix} 0 & 9 \\ 0 & 4 \end{bmatrix}$. Without using your calculator or computer software, try to find entries for the matrix in the equation below.

   $$\begin{bmatrix} \_ & \_ \\ \_ & \_ \end{bmatrix} \begin{bmatrix} 0 & 9 \\ 0 & 4 \end{bmatrix} = \begin{bmatrix} 1 & 0 \\ 0 & 1 \end{bmatrix}$$

   Does A have an inverse? That is, does the matrix A^{-1} exist?

6. **b.** Multiplying on the left by the identity matrix will give $\begin{bmatrix} 5 & 4 \\ 2 & 6 \end{bmatrix}$ as the answer.

c. The identity matrix for a 3×3 matrix is $\begin{bmatrix} 1 & 0 & 0 \\ 0 & 1 & 0 \\ 0 & 0 & 1 \end{bmatrix}$.

d. An identity matrix is a square matrix that has 1s on the diagonals from the upper left corner to the lower right corner (the main diagonal) and 0s everywhere else.

7. **a.** The multiplicative inverse of 3 is $\frac{1}{3}$, of $\frac{1}{2}$ is 2, of $\frac{5}{3}$ is $\frac{3}{5}$, and of -8.6 is $\frac{-5}{43}$ or approximately -0.116.

b. Student responses may vary. Students may guess the matrix in which each entry is the multiplicative inverse of the given matrix. When they test this conjecture they will find that it is not correct. Encourage them to use matrix multiplication to try to find the correct answer.

c. $D^{-1} = \begin{bmatrix} 2 & -3 \\ -3 & 5 \end{bmatrix}$

d. $A^{-1} = \begin{bmatrix} -0.75 & -2.5 \\ 0.5 & 2 \end{bmatrix}$

8. **a.** Not all matrices have inverses. For example $\begin{bmatrix} 3 & 6 \\ 1 & 2 \end{bmatrix}$ does not have an inverse.

If $A = \begin{bmatrix} a & b \\ c & d \end{bmatrix}$, then A will not have an inverse if and only if $ad - bc = 0$. Do not expect students to find this general rule, although they may well find a matrix that does not have an inverse. When using the calculator to find the inverse of a matrix that does not have one, an error message will be displayed.

b. Matrix A does not have an inverse. To see this, let the left-hand matrix be $\begin{bmatrix} a & b \\ c & d \end{bmatrix}$. Multiplying the matrices together, we get $a \cdot 0 + b \cdot 0$ for the first entry of the product, which must be equal to 1. But there is no solution to this equation and thus it is impossible for A^{-1} to exist.

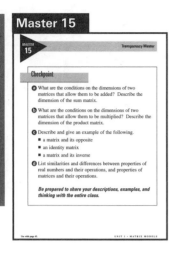

MASTER
15   Transparency Master

Checkpoint

❶ What are the conditions on the dimensions of two
  matrices that allow them to be added? Describe the
  dimension of the sum matrix.

❷ What are the conditions on the dimensions of two
  matrices that allow them to be multiplied? Describe the
  dimension of the product matrix.

❸ Describe and give an example of the following.
  ▪ a matrix and its opposite
  ▪ an identity matrix
  ▪ a matrix and its inverse

❹ List similarities and differences between properties of
  real numbers and their operations, and properties of
  matrices and their operations.

Be prepared to share your descriptions, examples, and
thinking with the entire class.

Use with page 45.   UNIT 1 • MATRIX MODELS

SHARE AND SUMMARIZE full-class discussion

Checkpoint

See Teaching Master 15.

ⓐ Two matrices can be added if and only if their dimensions are the same. The dimension of the sum matrix will be the same as the dimension of the two matrices being added.

ⓑ Matrix A can be multiplied by matrix B if the number of columns in A equals the number of rows in B.

ⓒ Examples will vary.

  ▪ The opposite of matrix A is a matrix of the same dimension, where each entry is the opposite of the corresponding entry in matrix A. One example of a matrix and its opposite is

$$\begin{bmatrix} 1 & -2 & 4.5 \\ 0 & 3 & 0.7 \end{bmatrix} \text{ and } \begin{bmatrix} -1 & 2 & -4.5 \\ 0 & -3 & 0.7 \end{bmatrix}$$

  ▪ An identity matrix is a square matrix with 1s along the main diagonal and 0s everywhere else. The 2×2 identity matrix is $\begin{bmatrix} 1 & 0 \\ 0 & 1 \end{bmatrix}$.

  ▪ The inverse of matrix A (if it exists) is the matrix such that $A \times A^{-1}$ gives the identity matrix. If $A = \begin{bmatrix} 5 & 3 \\ 4 & 2 \end{bmatrix}$ then $A^{-1} = \begin{bmatrix} -1 & 1.5 \\ 2 & -2.5 \end{bmatrix}$.

ⓓ The properties that real numbers and matrices, and their respective operations, have in common are commutativity of addition and the existence of a zero element. Multiplication of numbers is commutative, but multiplication of matrices is not. While all numbers (except 0) have multiplicative inverses, there are many matrices that do not have inverses.

CONSTRUCTING A MATH TOOLKIT: Students should summarize the properties of matrices and compare them to properties of numbers. Specific examples should be supplied so students can quickly access these ideas when needed.

APPLY individual task

▶On Your Own

a. If x and y are real numbers and $xy = 0$, then either x or y must be zero.

b. Opinions may vary.

c. $A \times B = \begin{bmatrix} 0 & 0 \\ 0 & 0 \end{bmatrix}$

The property in part a is not true for matrix multiplication. It is possible for $A \times B$ to be a zero matrix without either A or B being a zero matrix.

d. Other properties that students should be familiar with are the associative properties for addition and multiplication and the distributive property for multiplication over addition. All of these properties hold for matrices.

Checkpoint

ⓐ What are the conditions on the dimensions of two matrices that allow them to be added? Describe the dimension of the sum matrix.

ⓑ What are the conditions on the dimensions of two matrices that allow them to be multiplied? Describe the dimension of the product matrix.

ⓒ Describe and give an example of the following:

- A matrix and its opposite
- An identity matrix
- A matrix and its inverse
- A matrix that does not have an inverse

ⓓ List similarities and differences between properties of real numbers and their operations, and properties of matrices and their operations.

Be prepared to share your descriptions, examples, and thinking with the entire class.

▶ On Your Own

a. An important property of multiplication of numbers concerns products that equal zero. If x and y are real numbers and if $xy = 0$, what can you conclude about x or y? Is it possible that $xy = 0$, and yet $x \neq 0$ and $y \neq 0$?

b. Do you think the property in part a is true for matrix multiplication?

c. Suppose

$$A = \begin{bmatrix} 2 & 3 \\ 4 & 6 \end{bmatrix} \text{ and } B = \begin{bmatrix} 6 & 9 \\ -4 & -6 \end{bmatrix}.$$

Compute $A \times B$. Is it true for matrices that if $A \times B = 0$, then either $A = 0$ or $B = 0$?

d. Think of another property of addition or multiplication of real numbers, and investigate whether matrices also have this property. Prepare a brief report on your findings.

MORE
Modeling • Organizing • Reflecting • Extending

Modeling

1. Five students played in a round-robin ping-pong tournament. That is, every student played everyone else. The results were the following:

   - Anna beat Delayne.
   - Bobbie beat Anna, Chan, and Delayne.
   - Chan beat Anna, Eldin, and Delayne.
   - Delayne beat Eldin.
   - Eldin beat Anna and Bobbie.

   a. Represent the tournament results with a digraph, by letting the vertices be the players and drawing an arrow from one player to another if the one beats the other.

   b. Construct an adjacency matrix for the digraph. Remember that you write "1" for an entry if there is an arrow from the player on the row to the player on the column.

   c. Use sums and powers of the adjacency matrix to rank the five students in the tournament. Explain your method and report the rankings.

2. In Lesson 1 you investigated matrices that described friendship among a group of people. The friendship matrix below is for a different group of five people. Recall that an entry of "1" means that the person on the row names the person on the column as a friend.

Friendship Matrix

	A	B	C	D	E
A	0	1	1	1	1
B	0	0	1	1	1
C	1	0	0	1	0
D	1	1	1	0	1
E	1	0	0	1	0

Two people are mutual friends if they name each other as friends. Thus, person A and person B are not mutual friends, but C and D are. In this problem you will investigate *cliques* (pronounced "klicks"). A *clique* is a group of people who are all mutual friends of each other. (For this problem, consider only three-person cliques.)

Modeling

MORE
ASSIGNMENT   *pp. 46–58*

Modeling: 3 and choice of one*
Organizing: 2, 3 and 4
Reflecting: 1
Extending: Choose one*

When choice is indicated, it is important that the choice be left to the student.
NOTE: *It is best if Organizing tasks are discussed as a whole class after they have been assigned as homework.*

Unit 1

1. a.

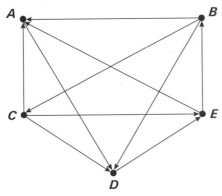

b.

$$
\begin{array}{c c} & \begin{array}{c c c c c} A & B & C & D & E \end{array} \\ \begin{array}{c} A \\ B \\ C \\ D \\ E \end{array} & \left[\begin{array}{c c c c c} 0 & 0 & 0 & 1 & 0 \\ 1 & 0 & 1 & 1 & 0 \\ 1 & 0 & 0 & 1 & 1 \\ 0 & 0 & 0 & 0 & 1 \\ 1 & 1 & 0 & 0 & 0 \end{array}\right] = M \end{array}
$$

c. The rankings (from 1st to 5th) are: Bobbie, Chan, Eldin, Delayne, and Anna. By looking individually at M, M^2, and M^3, a tie is present. $M + M^2$ has no ties, so the ranking can be made.

NOTE: $M^2 + M^3$ or $M + M^2 + M^3$ also produce matrices with no ties and the same ranking as $M + M^2$.

```
[M]²
 [[0  0  0  0  1]
  [1  0  0  2  2]
  [1  1  0  1  1]
  [1  1  0  0  0]
  [1  0  1  2  0]]
```

```
[M]^3
 [[1  1  0  0  0]
  [2  2  0  1  2]
  [2  1  1  2  1]
  [1  0  1  2  0]
  [1  0  0  2  3]]
```

```
[M]+[M]²
 [[0  0  0  1  1]
  [2  0  1  3  2]
  [2  1  0  2  2]
  [1  1  0  0  1]
  [2  1  1  2  0]]
```

```
[M]+[M]²+[M]^3
 [[1  1  0  1  1]
  [4  2  1  4  4]
  [4  2  1  4  3]
  [2  1  1  2  1]
  [3  1  1  4  3]]
```

2. **a.** Responses may vary. A-C, A-D, A-E, B-D, C-D, and D-E are the mutual-friends pairings. A-C-D and A-D-E are the only three-person cliques.

   b. This matrix (see below) is symmetric, since *x* and *y* are mutual friends if and only if *y* and *x* are mutual friends.

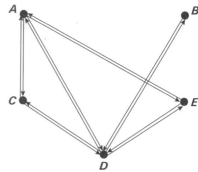

Mutual Friends

$$M = \begin{array}{c c} & \begin{array}{c c c c c} A & B & C & D & E \end{array} \\ \begin{array}{c} A \\ B \\ C \\ D \\ E \end{array} & \left[\begin{array}{c c c c c} 0 & 0 & 1 & 1 & 1 \\ 0 & 0 & 0 & 1 & 0 \\ 1 & 0 & 0 & 1 & 0 \\ 1 & 1 & 1 & 0 & 1 \\ 1 & 0 & 0 & 1 & 0 \end{array} \right] \end{array}$$

   c. See the graph above. For each arrow going one way, there is a corresponding arrow going the opposite way. That is, you can think of this as a graph with six edges, each of which is two way.

   d. In general, M^3 tells how many paths of length 3 there are between pairs of vertices. In the case of this mutual-friend digraph and matrix, M^3 tells how many mutual-friend paths of length 3 exist between any two people. A mutual-friend path of length 3 between X and Y means X is a friend of W, who is a friend of V, who is a friend of Y. For example, C is "connected" to D by mutual-friend

$$M^3 = \begin{array}{c c} & \begin{array}{c c c c c} A & B & C & D & E \end{array} \\ \begin{array}{c} A \\ B \\ C \\ D \\ E \end{array} & \left[\begin{array}{c c c c c} 4 & 2 & 5 & 6 & 5 \\ 2 & 0 & 1 & 4 & 1 \\ 5 & 1 & 2 & 6 & 2 \\ 6 & 4 & 6 & 4 & 6 \\ 5 & 1 & 2 & 6 & 2 \end{array} \right] \end{array}$$

   paths of length 3 in six different ways: C-A-C-D, C-D-C-D, C-D-E-D, C-A-E-D, C-D-B-D, C-D-A-D.

   e. Entries in the diagonal correspond to mutual-friend paths of length 3 between a person and himself or herself. That is, the paths are like X-W-V-X. But such a path indicates a group of three people, all of whom are mutual friends, that is, a clique. Thus, a main diagonal entry tells of how many three-person cliques that person is a member. (This number must be divided by two since it doesn't matter in which direction the friendships go. For example, A is in $\frac{4}{2} = 2$ cliques: C-A-D and E-A-D.)

   f. ■ Person B is in no cliques.
   ■ Person C is in one clique: A-C-D. Person A is in two cliques: A-C-D and A-D-E.
   ■ Person D is in two cliques.

3. **a.** See the Year 1 Total matrix below.

   b. The entries represent total revenue and total profit for each of the first two weeks of Year 1.

   c. See the Year 2 total matrix below.

   d. No. The first two weeks of Year 1 were better because the total profit was higher than in Year 2. If students consider total revenue they will answer that Year 2 was the better time period. You might need to discuss the ideas of profit and revenue.

Year 1 Total

	Revenue	Profit
Week 1	$5,498.80	$556.10
Week 2	$5,163.60	$521.60

Year 2 Total

Revenue	Profit
$5,587.80	$549.70
$5,296.10	$520.40

> **NOTE:** Cliques can be found easily by looking for triangles in the mutual-friend digraph.

Unit 1

a. Find one other pair of mutual friends and one clique.

There is a way to use powers of a matrix to find cliques.

b. Build a *mutual-friends matrix*, *M*, by listing the five people across the top and down the side of a new matrix and writing a "1" for each entry where the two people represented by that entry are mutual friends. If the people are not mutual friends, enter a "0".

c. Think of *M* as an adjacency matrix for a digraph, and construct the digraph. This digraph can be called the *mutual-friends digraph*.

d. What do the entries of M^3 tell you about mutual friends?

e. What do the entries in the main diagonal of M^3 tell you about cliques? Explain.

f. Consider the cliques that each person is in.

- How many cliques is B in?

- List all the cliques that C is in. List all the cliques that A is in.

- How many cliques is D in?

3. The owners of a local gas station want to evaluate their business. They decide to examine sales, prices, and gross profits for the first two weeks in each of the last two years. This information is summarized in the following matrices.

Revenue and Profit in Year 1

	Rev/gal	Profit/gal
Regular	$1.05	$0.10
Super	$1.09	$0.12
Ultimate	$1.14	$0.13

$= P1$

Number of Gallons Sold in Year 1

	Regular	Super	Ultimate
Week 1	3410	850	870
Week 2	3230	810	780

$= Q1$

Revenue and Profit in Year 2

	Rev/gal	Profit/gal
Regular	$1.07	$0.10
Super	$1.14	$0.11
Ultimate	$1.19	$0.14

$= P2$

Number of Gallons Sold in Year 2

	Regular	Super	Ultimate
Week 1	3350	870	850
Week 2	3240	780	790

$= Q2$

a. Multiply these matrices: $(Q1) \times (P1)$. Label the rows and columns of the product matrix.

b. Describe the information that is contained in the product matrix.

c. Use matrix multiplication to find the total revenue and profit for all three types of gasoline combined, for each of the two weeks in Year 2.

d. Were the first two weeks of Year 2 better than the first two weeks of Year 1? Explain.

e. Consider $(P2) \times (Q2)$. Is it possible to carry out this matrix multiplication? If so, what do the entries in the product matrix tell you, if anything, about sales, prices, and profits at the gas station?

4. For any given case which comes before the Michigan Supreme Court, one judge is designated to write an opinion on the case (although any judge can choose to write an opinion on any case). All of the judges then sit together, discuss the case, and each written opinion is passed around and signed by all who approve of it. A case is decided when a majority of judges sign one opinion. The information in the following matrix, taken from historical court records, shows how often judges on the court from 1958–60 agreed with (and signed) one another's written opinions. As usual, the matrix is read from row to column. For example, Carr agreed with 61% of Black's opinions.

Judge Agreements

	Ka	V	D	S	C	E	B	Ke
Kavanagh	—	76%	80%	85%	81%	88%	83%	77%
Voelker	81%	—	60%	90%	59%	86%	99%	63%
Dethmers	66%	65%	—	75%	99%	77%	72%	95%
Smith	78%	79%	63%	—	57%	81%	84%	64%
Carr	63%	58%	100%	66%	—	70%	61%	100%
Edwards	61%	68%	66%	76%	65%	—	70%	65%
Black	75%	84%	48%	77%	44%	68%	—	55%
Kelly	60%	53%	86%	63%	91%	61%	62%	—

Source: Ulmer, S. Sidney. Leadership in the Michigan Supreme Court. *Judicial Decision Making*, edited by Glendon Schubert. New York: Free Press of Glencoe, 1963.

There are several ways you could analyze these data. Complete the analysis which follows.

a. Examine the matrix and write down two interesting statements about this particular Michigan Supreme Court.

b. Now, convert all the entries into 0s and 1s, according to this rule:

Whenever a judge agrees with 75% or more of another judge's opinions, then say that the one judge "agrees with" the other judge, and that entry should be a "1". Otherwise, enter a "0".

c. Interpret the matrix.

- Does Kavanagh agree with Dethmers?
- Does Dethmers agree with Kavanagh?
- Which judge agrees with the most other judges?
- Which judge is agreed with by the most other judges?

3. e. Yes, it is possible to multiply the matrices in this order because the number of rows of $Q2$ is the same as the number of columns of $P2$. However, the entries in the product matrix do not convey any useful information. For example, the entry in the first row and first column is the sum of the revenue for regular gas the first week and the profit from regular gas for the second week.

4. a. Responses will vary. For example: Carr always agreed with Dethmers and Kelly; Carr and Dethmers almost always agreed with each other; any judge agreed with any other judge most (at least one half) of the time, except Black agreed with Carr only 44% of the time and Dethmers only 48% of the time.

b.

$$
\begin{array}{c c}
 & \begin{array}{c c c c c c c c} \text{Ka} & \text{V} & \text{D} & \text{S} & \text{C} & \text{E} & \text{B} & \text{Ke} \end{array} \\
\begin{array}{r} \text{Kavanagh} \\ \text{Voelker} \\ \text{Dethmers} \\ \text{Smith} \\ \text{Carr} \\ \text{Edwards} \\ \text{Black} \\ \text{Kelly} \end{array} &
\begin{bmatrix}
0 & 1 & 1 & 1 & 1 & 1 & 1 & 1 \\
1 & 0 & 0 & 1 & 0 & 1 & 1 & 0 \\
0 & 0 & 0 & 1 & 1 & 1 & 0 & 1 \\
1 & 1 & 0 & 0 & 0 & 1 & 1 & 0 \\
0 & 0 & 1 & 0 & 0 & 0 & 0 & 1 \\
0 & 0 & 0 & 1 & 0 & 0 & 0 & 0 \\
1 & 1 & 0 & 1 & 0 & 0 & 0 & 0 \\
0 & 0 & 1 & 0 & 1 & 0 & 0 & 0
\end{bmatrix}
\end{array}
$$

c. ■ Yes, Kavanagh agrees with Dethmers.

■ No, Dethmers does not agree with Kavanagh.

■ Kavanagh agrees with everyone. (Examine the Kavanagh row.)

■ Smith is the judge with whom the most other judges agree. (Examine the Smith column.)

d. **See Teaching Master 16.** All the allies are: Ka-V, Ka-S, Ka-B, V-S, V-B, D-C, D-Ke, S-E, S-B, and C-Ke.

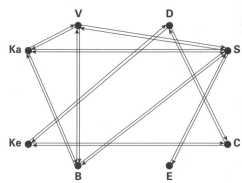

	Ka	V	D	S	C	E	B	Ke
Kavanagh	0	1	0	1	0	0	1	0
Voelker	1	0	0	1	0	0	1	0
Dethmers	0	0	0	0	1	0	0	1
Smith	1	1	0	0	0	1	1	0
Carr	0	0	1	0	0	0	0	1
Edwards	0	0	0	1	0	0	0	0
Black	1	1	0	1	0	0	0	0
Kelly	0	0	1	0	1	0	0	0

e. ■ All of the coalitions are: Ka-V-S, Ka-V-B, Ke-D-C, V-B-S, and Ka-B-S. Look for the triangles in the diagram.

■ A^3 tells how many paths of length 3 exist between any two judges. It indicates how far a judge's sphere of influence goes. If a judge is an ally, then that judge's allies might also be allies.

	Ka	V	D	S	C	E	B	Ke
Kavanagh	6	7	0	8	0	2	7	0
Voelker	7	6	0	8	0	2	7	0
Dethmers	0	0	2	0	3	0	0	3
Smith	8	8	0	6	0	4	8	0
Carr	0	0	3	0	2	0	0	3
Edwards	2	2	0	4	0	0	2	0
Black	7	7	0	8	0	2	6	0
Kelly	0	0	3	0	3	0	0	2

$= A^3$

■ If you divide the entries along the main diagonal by two, then that quotient will tell you of how many coalitions that person is a member. The entries along the main diagonal work because there must be a circuit to determine a coalition, *i.e.*, the path must start and stop with the same person (the entries on the main diagonal).

f. The digraph of allies has two detachable parts. It is reasonable that the three Republicans are Carr, Dethmers, and Kelly. Since these three are a coalition (and are members of only this coalition) it is possible that they agree on many issues. Therefore, they are "like-minded".

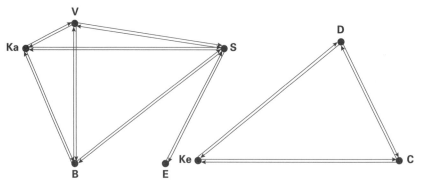

5. a.

$$[600 \quad 700 \quad 500] \begin{bmatrix} 0.4 & 0.4 & 0.2 \\ 0.2 & 0.5 & 0.3 \\ 0.1 & 0.2 & 0.7 \end{bmatrix} = [430 \quad 690 \quad 680]$$

This model projects that 430 people will buy Nike shoes, 690 will buy Reebok shoes, and 680 will buy Fila shoes next year.

d. Two judges that agree with each other are called *allies*.

  ▪ Find two allies.

  ▪ Build an *ally matrix* by listing the judges across the top and down the side of a new matrix. Write a "1" or "0" for each entry depending on whether or not the two judges corresponding to that entry are allies.

  ▪ Think of the ally matrix as an adjacency matrix for a digraph, and then construct the digraph.

e. A group of three judges who are all allies with each other is called a *coalition*.

  ▪ Find one coalition.

  ▪ Call the ally matrix A and compute A^3.

  ▪ What do the entries of A^3 tell you about allies?

  ▪ What do the entries in the main diagonal of A^3 tell you about coalitions? Explain.

  ▪ Describe some similarities and differences between coalitions and cliques. (See Modeling task 2.)

f. Three of these judges were Republicans and five were Democrats. Can you pick out the Republicans and Democrats from these data? Explain your reasoning.

5. Recall the brand-switching matrix from Investigation 1, reproduced below with decimal entries instead of percents. This matrix provides information for projecting how many people will buy certain brands of athletic shoes on their next purchase given the brand they currently own. Matrix multiplication along with its properties can help you analyze this situation.

Brand-Switching Matrix

		Next Brand	
	N	R	F
N	0.4	0.4	0.2
R	0.2	0.5	0.3
F	0.1	0.2	0.7

Current Brand $= B$

a. Assume that buyers buy a new pair of shoes every year. The following matrix shows the number of people who bought each of the three brands this year.

$$\begin{array}{ccc} N & R & F \end{array}$$
$$[600 \quad 700 \quad 500] = Q$$

How many people are projected to buy each of the brands next year? Explain how to answer this question using matrix multiplication.

b. What would the brand-switching matrix look like if there is no change in the number of people buying each brand this year and next year? What is this type of matrix called? (Refer to Investigation 4, if necessary.)

c. You may recall the *associative property of multiplication* for real numbers: $a \times (b \times c) = (a \times b) \times c$, for all real numbers a, b, and c. For example, $3 \times (5 \times 2) = (3 \times 5) \times 2 = 30$. Matrix multiplication also has this property, which can be used to project the number of people buying each brand several years into the future. From part a you know that

$$Q \times B = \begin{bmatrix} \text{The one-row matrix} \\ \text{showing how many} \\ \text{people will buy each} \\ \text{brand next year} \end{bmatrix}$$

- Compute and compare the results of $(Q \times B) \times B$ and $Q \times (B \times B)$. Explain why this is an example of the associative property for matrix multiplication. Explain the meaning of the resulting matrices.

- Describe the information obtained by computing $Q \times B^3$.

d. The following matrix shows the number of people projected to buy each brand two years from now.

$$\begin{array}{ccc} \text{N} & \text{R} & \text{F} \\ [378 & 653 & 769] \end{array}$$

Find a matrix showing how many people will buy each brand one year from now. Compare with results from parts a and c.

Organizing

1. There are at least two different types of multiplication that involve matrices:
   - multiplying two matrices using the standard row-by-column method that you learned in this lesson (matrix multiplication), and
   - multiplying each entry in a matrix by the same number (called *scalar multiplication*).

   Each method is useful in certain contexts. For each method, find one situation from this lesson where that multiplication method can be used to better understand the situation.

2. Do the following matrix multiplications without using a calculator or computer. Check your answers with a calculator or computer software.

   a. $\begin{bmatrix} 2 & 1 & 6 \end{bmatrix} \begin{bmatrix} 1 & 3 & 0 \\ 4 & -6 & 2 \\ 5 & 2 & 3 \end{bmatrix}$

   b. $\begin{bmatrix} 1 & 3 & 0 \\ 4 & -6 & 2 \\ 5 & 2 & 3 \end{bmatrix} \begin{bmatrix} 2 \\ 1 \\ 6 \end{bmatrix}$

5. b. If everybody buys the same brand of shoe each year the brand-switching matrix is

$$\begin{bmatrix} 1 & 0 & 0 \\ 0 & 1 & 0 \\ 0 & 0 & 1 \end{bmatrix}$$

This type of matrix is called an **identity** matrix.

c. ■ $(Q \times B) \times B = Q \times (B \times B) = [378 \quad 653 \quad 769]$

This is an example of the associative property for matrix multiplication since the parentheses associate different matrices. The answer matrix tells us this model projects that two years from now 378 people will buy Nike shoes, 653 will buy Reebok shoes, and 769 will buy Fila shoes.

■ $Q \times B^3 = [358.7 \quad 631.5 \quad 809.8]$

This matrix tells us that three years from now we can expect approximately 358 people to buy Nike shoes, 631 to buy Reebok shoes, and 809 to buy Fila shoes.

d.

$$[378 \quad 653 \quad 769] \begin{bmatrix} 0.4 & 0.4 & 0.2 \\ 0.2 & 0.5 & 0.3 \\ 0.1 & 0.2 & 0.7 \end{bmatrix}^{-1} = [430 \quad 690 \quad 680]$$

This product matrix is equal to the product $Q \times B$.

Organizing

1. Responses will vary. Most of the problems in this lesson use standard matrix multiplication. One example of multiplying each entry in a matrix by the same number is converting minutes to hours in the "On Your Own" part a on page 35.

2. a. $\begin{bmatrix} 36 & 12 & 20 \end{bmatrix}$ **b.** $\begin{bmatrix} 5 \\ 14 \\ 30 \end{bmatrix}$

2. c. $\begin{bmatrix} 51 & 56 \\ 23 & -6 \\ 13 & 35 \end{bmatrix}$ **d.** $\begin{bmatrix} -11 & 2 & -4 \\ 60 & 16 & 24 \\ -10 & -18 & 18 \end{bmatrix}$

3. a. Notice that S and F are presented out of alphabetical order. Students may put them in order if they so choose.

Prerequisite Tasks

	S	A	B	C	D	E	G	H	I	F
S	0	1	1	1	0	0	0	0	0	0
A	0	0	0	0	1	0	0	0	0	0
B	0	0	0	0	0	1	0	0	0	0
C	0	0	0	0	0	1	0	0	0	0
D	0	0	0	0	0	1	0	0	0	0
E	0	0	0	0	0	0	1	1	0	0
G	0	0	0	0	0	0	0	0	0	1
H	0	0	0	0	0	0	0	0	1	0
I	0	0	0	0	0	0	0	0	0	1
F	0	0	0	0	0	0	0	0	0	0

$= M$

b.

	S	A	B	C	D	E	G	H	I	F
S	0	0	0	0	1	2	0	0	0	0
A	0	0	0	0	0	1	0	0	0	0
B	0	0	0	0	0	0	1	1	0	0
C	0	0	0	0	0	0	1	1	0	0
D	0	0	0	0	0	0	1	1	0	0
E	0	0	0	0	0	0	0	0	1	1
G	0	0	0	0	0	0	0	0	0	0
H	0	0	0	0	0	0	0	0	0	1
I	0	0	0	0	0	0	0	0	0	0
F	0	0	0	0	0	0	0	0	0	0

$= M^2$

Since the *S-F* entry is zero, there is no path yet from *S* to *F*.

c. ■ The smallest power of *M* that has a nonzero *S-F* entry is 4.
■ The largest power of *M* that has a nonzero *S-F* entry is 6.
■ There are 6 paths from *S* to *F*. (2 + 3 + 1)
■ You should find the sum $M^4 + M^5 + M^6$ because these matrices are the only ones which contain a nonzero entry in the *S-F* position. This sum will tell how many 4-, 5-, and 6-link paths exist between each pair of vertices.

d. The critical path from *S* to *F* is *S-C-E-G-F*. The length is 23.

c. $\begin{bmatrix} 2 & 4 & 3 & 7 \\ 0 & 6 & 5 & 1 \\ 9 & -5 & 3 & 2 \end{bmatrix} \begin{bmatrix} 2 & 4 \\ 3 & 1 \\ 0 & -4 \\ 5 & 8 \end{bmatrix}$

d. $\begin{bmatrix} 1 & 0 & -3 \\ 2 & 5 & 6 \\ -4 & 3 & 2 \end{bmatrix} \begin{bmatrix} 7 & 5 & -1 \\ 2 & 0 & 4 \\ 6 & 1 & 1 \end{bmatrix}$

3. In Course 1 you studied *project digraphs* and *critical paths*. Consider the following project digraph. The letters designate the different tasks and the numbers tell how long it takes to complete each task. There is a directed edge from one vertex to another if the one task is a prerequisite for the other. Recall that to schedule all the tasks so that the whole project will be completed in the minimum amount of time involves finding a longest path through the digraph (called a *critical path*). The length of a critical path is the minimum time required to complete all the tasks in the project.

   Matrices can be used to find the number of paths from the starting vertex of the project digraph to the ending vertex. A critical path must be one of those paths.

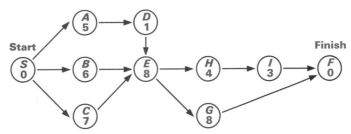

a. Construct the adjacency matrix for this digraph. Call the matrix *M*.

b. Compute M^2 using your calculator or computer software. What does each entry represent? Check the *S-F* entry. Is there a path from *S* to *F* yet?

c. Compute more powers of *M*.

   ■ What is the smallest power of *M* that has a nonzero *S-F* entry?

   ■ What is the largest power of *M* that has a nonzero *S-F* entry?

   ■ How many paths are there from *S* to *F*?

   ■ Explain how you used the powers of *M* to find the number of paths from *S* to *F*.

d. A critical path must be one of the paths from *S* to *F*. In particular, it is a path of longest length from *S* to *F*, where the length of a path is computed by summing the task times for all the tasks on the path. Note that the number of edges in the path is not important, only the sum of all the task times. Which of the paths from *S* to *F* is a critical path?

4. In Investigation 4 you reviewed some properties of real numbers and their operations and investigated corresponding properties of matrices and their operations.

a. What properties of addition and multiplication are shared by numbers and by square matrices? Which properties of numbers are not shared by square matrices?

b. The *distributive property of multiplication over addition* links multiplication and addition. That is, the distributive property states that

$$k(a + b) = ka + kb$$

■ Give two examples of the distributive property with numbers.

■ Suppose *k* is any number and *A* and *B* are any two matrices with the same dimension. Is it true that $k(A + B) = kA + kB$? Explain your reasoning.

5. Two matrix operations that you have used quite often are matrix multiplication and finding row sums. There is a connection between these two operations. Consider the following square matrix:

$$A = \begin{bmatrix} 0 & 1 & 0 & 0 \\ 0 & 0 & 1 & 0 \\ 1 & 0 & 0 & 1 \\ 1 & 1 & 0 & 0 \end{bmatrix}$$

a. Multiply *A* on the right by a one-column matrix filled with 1s.

That is, multiply:

$$\begin{bmatrix} 0 & 1 & 0 & 0 \\ 0 & 0 & 1 & 0 \\ 1 & 0 & 0 & 1 \\ 1 & 1 & 0 & 0 \end{bmatrix} \begin{bmatrix} 1 \\ 1 \\ 1 \\ 1 \end{bmatrix}$$

Compare the answer matrix to the row sums of *A*.

b. What matrix multiplication would have the same effect as summing the rows of A^2? Summing the rows of A^3?

c. Let *E* be the four-row, one-column matrix filled with 1s, and suppose that *A* represents the results of a tournament with four players. Explain the meaning of the following expression in terms of ranking the tournament:

$$AE + \frac{1}{2} A^2E + \frac{1}{3} A^3E$$

4. **a.** Commutativity of addition and the existence of additive identities, additive inverses, and multiplicative identities are properties explored in Investigation 4 that apply to both matrices and numbers. The associative properties of multiplication and addition and the distributive property of multiplication over addition also are applicable to both matrices and real numbers, but the students may not have explored this yet. At this point students may not know the formal names for all of these properties, but they still should be able to describe them adequately.

   b. ■ Examples will vary. Be sure students properly use the distributive property.

   ■ Yes, it is true that $k(A + B) = kA + kB$. Notice that an entry in $k(A + B)$ will have the form $k(a + b)$, where a and b are the entries in matrices A and B respectively. The corresponding entry in $kA + kB$ will be $ka + kb$. By the distributive property of multiplication over addition, $k(a + b) = ka + kb$, so we can see that corresponding entries in $k(A + B)$ and $kA + kB$ will be identical.

5. **a.** They are the same.

$$\begin{bmatrix} 1 \\ 1 \\ 2 \\ 2 \end{bmatrix}$$

   b. To sum the rows of A^2 (or A^3), simply multiply A^2 (or A^3) by the one-column matrix filled with 1s.

   c. This expression represents a 4×1 matrix whose entries are a weighted sum of row sums of powers of A. Thus, if A is a tournament matrix, then the entries of the 4×1 matrix $AE + \frac{1}{2} A^2E + \frac{1}{3} A^3E$ gives a ranking of the four players where direct wins are given more weight than two-stage wins, which in turn are given more weight than three-stage wins. This is, in fact, a method used to rank tournaments.

Unit 1

6. a. Using the formula we get

$$\begin{bmatrix} 6 & 8 \\ 2 & 3 \end{bmatrix}^{-1} = \frac{1}{(6)(3) - (8)(2)} \begin{bmatrix} 3 & -8 \\ -2 & 6 \end{bmatrix} = \frac{1}{2} \begin{bmatrix} 3 & -8 \\ -2 & 6 \end{bmatrix} = \begin{bmatrix} \frac{3}{2} & -4 \\ -1 & 3 \end{bmatrix}.$$

b.

$$\begin{bmatrix} 5 & 3 \\ 3 & 2 \end{bmatrix}^{-1} = \frac{1}{(5)(2) - (3)(3)} \begin{bmatrix} 2 & -3 \\ -3 & 5 \end{bmatrix} = \begin{bmatrix} 2 & -3 \\ -3 & 5 \end{bmatrix}$$

$$\begin{bmatrix} -8 & -10 \\ 2 & 3 \end{bmatrix}^{-1} = \frac{1}{(-8)(3) - (-10)(2)} \begin{bmatrix} 3 & 10 \\ -2 & -8 \end{bmatrix} = \frac{-1}{4} \begin{bmatrix} 3 & 10 \\ -2 & -8 \end{bmatrix} = \begin{bmatrix} \frac{-3}{4} & \frac{-5}{2} \\ \frac{1}{2} & 2 \end{bmatrix}$$

c. ■ Responses may vary. Whenever a 2×2 matrix does not have an inverse, the quantity $ad - bc$ will equal zero.

■ When you try to use the formula you get $(0)(4) - (9)(0) = 0$, which gives a zero in the denominator of the fraction in front of the matrix.

■ Responses will vary. Any matrix $\begin{bmatrix} a & b \\ c & d \end{bmatrix}$ where $ad - bc = 0$ will not have an inverse. Example: $\begin{bmatrix} 1 & 2 \\ 3 & 6 \end{bmatrix}$.

6. In Investigation 4, you studied multiplicative inverses of matrices. You found inverse matrices by guessing-and-testing and by using your calculator or computer software. Using technology is reliable, but it's pretty mysterious. How does a calculator or computer compute an inverse matrix? The general method works by a process called *row reduction*, which is a fairly involved procedure. (You can check out a book on *linear algebra* to find out how that method works.) But in the case of 2×2 matrices, there is a simple formula.

If $A = \begin{bmatrix} a & b \\ c & d \end{bmatrix}$ the inverse of A can be found by using the following formula.

$$A^{-1} = \frac{1}{ad - bc} \begin{bmatrix} d & -b \\ -c & a \end{bmatrix}$$

a. Use the formula to find the inverse of the following matrix.

$$\begin{bmatrix} 6 & 8 \\ 2 & 3 \end{bmatrix}$$

Use matrix multiplication to check that the product of the inverse and the original matrix is the identity matrix.

b. Use the formula to find the inverses of the following matrices.

$$\begin{bmatrix} 5 & 3 \\ 3 & 2 \end{bmatrix} \qquad\qquad \begin{bmatrix} -8 & -10 \\ 2 & 3 \end{bmatrix}$$

Compare your answers to what you found in activity 7 of Investigation 4.

c. You discovered in Investigation 4 that not all matrices have an inverse.

- Examine the formula for A^{-1} given above. What do you think will go wrong when you try to use the formula to compute the inverse of a 2×2 matrix that has no inverse?

- In activity 8 of Investigation 4, you discovered that

$$\begin{bmatrix} 0 & 9 \\ 0 & 4 \end{bmatrix}$$

  does not have an inverse. What happens when you try to use the formula?

- Use what you've discovered about limitations of the formula to construct two matrices with all nonzero entries but no inverse.

Reflecting

1. In Investigation 3, you found the number of paths of length two in the food web digraph by squaring the adjacency matrix for the digraph. Explain why multiplying the adjacency matrix by itself gives you information about the number of paths of length two.

2. Think about the ecosystem you modeled in Investigation 3.

   a. If you keep computing powers of the adjacency matrix for the food web digraph, will you eventually reach a matrix of all zeroes? What would this mean in terms of paths through the food web?

   b. What do the entries in the last matrix, before you reach all zeroes, tell you about path lengths? About the possible spread of contamination?

   c. Explain how to compute a single matrix that will show, for each species, all the species that are farther up the food chain. Compute the matrix and check it by examining the graph.

   d. Contamination of which species has the potential to impact most on the ecosystem? What matrix computation addresses this question?

   e. Do you think that the adjacency matrix for any digraph will eventually have a power for which all of its entries are 0s?

3. Describe a situation, different from those in this lesson, where matrix multiplication would be useful. Write and answer two questions about the situation which involve using matrices.

4. Think about the way matrices are added and multiplied.

   a. Why should it not be surprising that matrix addition has the same properties as addition of numbers?

   b. Why might it be reasonable to suspect that matrix multiplication would not have the same properties as multiplication of numbers?

Reflecting

1. The key to this correspondence is the row-column nature of matrix multiplication, combined with the convention of reading matrices *from* rows *to* columns. Also, keep in mind that a path of length 2 starts *from* the start, goes *to* a connecting vertex, then goes *from* the connecting vertex *to* the end.

   Imagine standing on a large copy of the food web. When multiplying the adjacency matrix by itself, you work with the *rows* of the left matrix. These rows represent where a path starts *from*. Imagine standing on the vertex for a row. As you move along that row in the matrix, an entry of 1 indicates a path *to* the vertex that column represents. You can step onto that vertex. Now the question in creating two-stage paths is whether the new vertex is a connecting vertex. That is, can you go *from* that vertex *to* somewhere else?

   As part of the multiplication process, you also are working with the *columns* of the right matrix. Since 0 times anything is 0, do nothing as long as the entries in your row are 0. (You can't step to a new vertex because you have no path.) When the entry is 1 (a "hit"), look at the corresponding entry in the column you're working with. Because of the simultaneous row-column movement of matrix multiplication, that *from* entry represents the same *to* vertex you hit in the row. So you've gone from the original (row) vertex to your new vertex, and this entry tells you if you can go from this new vertex to your final target (the column vertex).

   For example, suppose you're working with the flea-beetle row and the garter-snake column. There is a 1 in the *third* entry in the flea-beetle row; so there is a path from flea beetle to frog. But the *third* entry in the garter-snake column also concerns the frog: a 1 there indicates a path from the frog to the garter snake. So you have found a path of length 2 (that is, a path with 2 edges): flea beetle → frog → garter snake.

   Thus, whenever you find a matching pair of 1s as you do the row-column multiplication, you have found a connecting vertex. The path goes from the row vertex to the connecting vertex, and then from the connecting vertex to the column vertex.

   In summary, whenever you hit a nonzero entry simultaneously in the left and right copies of the adjacency matrix as you multiply, then you have a path of length 2. Since you multiply 1s and add the products as you go, you will get the total number of paths of length 2 as a final result.

2. **a.** Yes, eventually some power of A will be all zeros. This is because there are not any circuits in the digraph and so all paths have finite length. Eventually the lengths of the paths corresponding to some power of the matrix A will be longer than the length of any path in the digraph, so all entries will be zero. In the food web the longest paths are of length 4, so A^5 and all higher powers will contain all zeros.

   b. The power of the matrix just before you reach all zeros gives information about the length of the longest paths in the digraph. In the food web, A^4 is the highest power of A before all entries are zero, and the longest path length in the digraph is 4. In terms of possible spread of contamination, if the contamination will affect species that are 4 or fewer steps apart, then all species will be contaminated (assuming all species that do not feed on other species are contaminated directly).

See additional Teaching Notes on page T78E.

Extending

1. a. Eventually, every number in the first column is essentially the same, every number in the second column is the same, and every number in the third column is the same. Or, we could say that each row of the resulting matrix is the same. B^{20} shows the approximate percentages of shoes of each brand that will be sold 20 years later.

The matrix is: $B^{20} \approx \begin{bmatrix} 0.19 & 0.34 & 0.47 \\ 0.19 & 0.34 & 0.47 \\ 0.19 & 0.34 & 0.47 \end{bmatrix}$

The elements (*i.e.*, entries) have reached a steady state. About 19% of customers will either stay with or change to Nike; about 34% will either stay with or change to Reebok; and about 47% will either change to or stay with Fila.

NOTE: On some calculators, the last answer function works differently for matrices than usual. On the Casio CFX-9850G, for example, you must specify "Mat Ans". On *any* calculator with matrix operations, however, you should be able to simulate the "last answer" by storing the answer into a new matrix and using that new matrix. For example, "Mat A * Mat B → Mat B" calculates successive powers of *A*, if *B* is either *A* or the appropriate identity matrix before beginning.

---

b. ■ The product is approximately [313 554 732].
   ■ The product is approximately [306 545 749].
   ■ The product is approximately [306 545 749].

c. The entries in the product matrix will show how many pairs of each brand are predicted to be sold *n* years later. You may want to discuss how reliable this prediction is.

2. a. Student responses will vary. One possible digraph is shown below.

b. A digraph whose adjacency matrix has only 1s and 0s will have at most one edge from any vertex to any other vertex. These matrices can model situations where a relationship exists or does not exist. For example, an animal is food for another, or it is not.

Extending

1. Consider the brand-switching matrix from Investigation 1, reproduced below.

Brand-Switching Matrix

		Next Brand		
		Nike	Reebok	Fila
	Nike	40%	40%	20%
Current Brand	Reebok	20%	50%	30%
	Fila	10%	20%	70%

This matrix models a type of process called a *Markov process*, named after the Russian mathematician A. A. Markov. There are two key components of a Markov process: *states* and a *transition matrix*. In the brand-switching example, the states are the one-row matrices that show how many people buy each shoe brand in a given year. The transition matrix is the brand-switching matrix, which shows how the states change from year to year. Powers of this matrix give you information about the long-term behavior of the Markov process.

a. Call the brand-switching matrix B. Enter B into your calculator or computer software, entering the percents as decimals, and use the last answer function to compute all the powers of B up to B^{20}. Describe what happened. Explain the meaning of the entries of B^{20}.

b. In Investigation 1 you assumed that the numbers of people buying each brand of shoe this year were as follows: 700 people bought Nike, 500 people bought Reebok, and 400 people bought Fila. Do the following matrix multiplications using powers of B:

$$[700 \quad 500 \quad 400] \times B^4$$

$$[700 \quad 500 \quad 400] \times B^{10}$$

$$[700 \quad 500 \quad 400] \times B^{20}$$

c. Explain the meaning of $[700 \quad 500 \quad 400] \times B^n$ for a positive integer n.

2. The most general definition of an adjacency matrix for a digraph is that it is a matrix whose entries tell *how many* edges there are from the vertex on the row to the vertex on the column. In this lesson an adjacency matrix was defined as a matrix whose entries tell *if* there is an edge from the vertex on the row to the vertex on the column. Thus, the adjacency matrices in this lesson always had entries that were 1s or 0s. Using the most general definition of an adjacency matrix, an adjacency matrix can have entries that are larger than 1.

a. Draw a digraph whose adjacency matrix has some entries that are larger than 1.

b. Describe the kinds of digraphs whose adjacency matrices only have 1s and 0s as entries.

3. In music, a change of key sounds more natural if only a few notes are changed. If two keys differ by too many notes, then a change from one key to the other is "remote" and sounds "unnatural" to people in our culture. (Music from other cultures can be very different. What sounds natural to us may sound unnatural to people from another culture.) Each key has five closely-related keys, that is, keys that do not differ by very many notes. A vertex-edge graph can be used to model this situation, as follows. (The symbol ♭ is read "flat". For example, B♭ is read "B flat".)

Related Key Graph

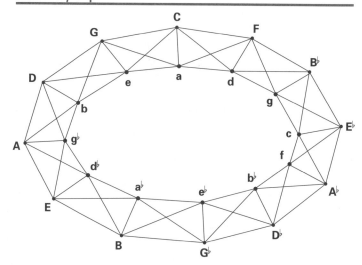

The twelve vertices in the outer circle represent the major keys: C, F, B flat, E flat, A flat, D flat, G flat, B, E, A, D, G. The vertices in the inner circle represent the twelve minor keys (written in lower-case letters): a, d, g, c, f, b flat, e flat, a flat, d flat, g flat, b, e. Each vertex is joined to the five vertices that represent the five closely-related keys.

a. Suppose that key changes between keys that are one or two edges apart on the graph are thought to sound "natural", but key changes between keys that are farther apart sound "unnatural".

  ■ Does a key change from C to g♭ sound natural? How about from G to A?

  ■ How many natural key changes are there from B?

b. What would be the dimension of an adjacency matrix for this graph?

c. How could you use operations on the adjacency matrix to answer part a? Explain your thinking.

3. a. ■ To move from C to g^b on the graph requires a path of length 3. Thus this key change does not sound natural. Since the shortest path from G to A has length 2, the key change from G to A does sound natural.

■ There are 9 natural key changes from B.

b. The adjacency matrix would have dimension 24×24.

c. You would have to find the square of the matrix and then add this to the original matrix since you are looking for the number of one-step or two-step key changes. The entries that are zero correspond to key changes that do not sound natural.

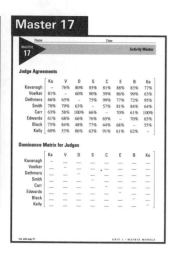

MORE *continued*

4. **a.** Kavanagh agrees with Edwards 88% of the time, while Edwards only agrees with Kavanagh 61% of the time. Edwards appears to be the dominant judge over Kavanagh.

b. **See Teaching Master 17.**

A 1 is placed in the matrix if the row judge dominates the column judge. For example, Kavanagh agrees with Voelker 76% of the time and Voelker agrees with Kavanagh 81% of the time. So Kavanagh dominates Voelker and a 1 is placed in the K-V position of the matrix.

$$
\begin{array}{c}
\begin{array}{cccccccc}
\quad\ \ \text{Ka} & \text{V} & \text{D} & \text{S} & \text{C} & \text{E} & \text{B} & \text{Ke}
\end{array}\\
\begin{array}{c}
\text{Kavanagh}\\
\text{Voelker}\\
\text{Dethmers}\\
\text{Smith}\\
\text{Carr}\\
\text{Edwards}\\
\text{Black}\\
\text{Kelly}
\end{array}
\left[
\begin{array}{cccccccc}
0 & 1 & 0 & 0 & 0 & 0 & 0 & 0\\
0 & 0 & 1 & 0 & 0 & 0 & 0 & 0\\
1 & 0 & 0 & 0 & 1 & 0 & 0 & 0\\
1 & 1 & 1 & 0 & 1 & 0 & 0 & 0\\
1 & 1 & 0 & 0 & 0 & 0 & 0 & 0\\
1 & 1 & 1 & 1 & 1 & 0 & 0 & 0\\
1 & 1 & 1 & 1 & 1 & 1 & 0 & 1\\
1 & 1 & 1 & 1 & 1 & 1 & 0 & 0
\end{array}
\right]
\end{array}
$$

4. Look back at the information on the extent of agreement among Michigan Supreme Court judges in Modeling task 4. The matrix summarizing that information is reproduced below. The modeling task involves looking for allies and coalitions among the judges. In this task you will rank the judges according to how much influence they exert upon one another.

Judge Agreements

	Ka	V	D	S	C	E	B	Ke
Kavanagh	—	76%	80%	85%	81%	88%	83%	77%
Voelker	81%	—	60%	90%	59%	86%	99%	63%
Dethmers	66%	65%	—	75%	99%	77%	72%	95%
Smith	78%	79%	63%	—	57%	81%	84%	64%
Carr	63%	58%	100%	66%	—	70%	61%	100%
Edwards	61%	68%	66%	76%	65%	—	70%	65%
Black	75%	84%	48%	77%	44%	68%	—	55%
Kelly	60%	53%	86%	63%	91%	61%	62%	—

  a. Look at the data for Kavanagh and Edwards. If you were to choose one of these judges as being dominant over the other, who would you pick as the dominant judge? Explain your reasoning.

  b. Judge X is said to *dominate* Judge Y if Y agrees with X more than X agrees with Y. The goal now is to rank the judges according to dominance. To begin, think of a way to construct a *dominance matrix* using 0s and 1s. Construct the dominance matrix.

Call the dominance matrix D. Direct dominance, as shown in D, is more powerful than the indirect dominance of second-stage, third-stage, or further removed dominance, as shown in powers of D. The powers of D can be *weighted* with an appropriate multiplier to reflect the degrees of dominance.

c. Use weighted powers of the dominance matrix, along with row sums and matrix sums, to rank the eight judges according to dominance. Give the entries in D full weight (multiply by 1) and the entries in D^2 half weight (multiply by $\frac{1}{2}$). Continue in this manner: multiply the entries in D^3 by $\frac{1}{3}$, and so on up through D^7, which would be multiplied by $\frac{1}{7}$.

(You may not need powers of D up through D^7 to get a clear ranking. A general rule, however, is to include powers up through D^{n-1}, where n is the number of vertices. The reason for stopping at $n-1$ is that the longest possible path from a vertex without returning to that vertex has length $n-1$.)

d. Use this weighted ranking method to rank the players in the tennis tournament in Investigation 3 (page 38). How does this ranking compare with your previous ranking?

5. For real numbers, finding a square root is the "reverse" of squaring. So, for example, if $x^2 = 9$ (and x is positive), then $x = \sqrt{9} = 3$. Think about reversing the process of squaring a matrix. Given the following equation, find A.

$$A^2 = \begin{bmatrix} 1 & 1 & 0 \\ 0 & 0 & 1 \\ 1 & 0 & 1 \end{bmatrix}$$

Hint: Think about what the digraph for matrix A looks like.

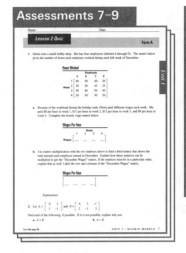

4. c. The row sums of $D + \frac{1}{2} D^2 + \frac{1}{3} D^3 + \frac{1}{4} D^4 + \frac{1}{5} D^5 + \frac{1}{6} D^6$ are shown in the table below.

Dominance Ranking

Judge	Row Sum	Ranking
Kavanagh	4.35	8
Voelker	6.08	7
Dethmers	8.85	5
Smith	19.28	4
Carr	7.78	6
Edwards	31.15	3
Black	79.05	1
Kelly	49.78	2

The ranking of the eight judges is now clear.

d. The rows of $T + \frac{1}{2} T^2 + \frac{1}{3} T^3 + \frac{1}{4} T^4 + \frac{1}{5} T^5$, along with resulting rankings, are shown in the table below:

Weighted Ranking

Player	Row Sum	Ranking
Anne	7.28	5
Catherine	15.38	2
Emily	6.7	6
Julia	13.08	3
Keadra	11.85	4
Maria	16.87	1

Tournament Results

$$\begin{bmatrix} 0 & 0 & 0 & 1 & 0 & 0 \\ 1 & 0 & 1 & 0 & 1 & 0 \\ 0 & 0 & 0 & 0 & 1 & 0 \\ 0 & 0 & 1 & 0 & 0 & 1 \\ 1 & 0 & 0 & 1 & 0 & 0 \\ 1 & 1 & 1 & 0 & 0 & 0 \end{bmatrix} = T$$

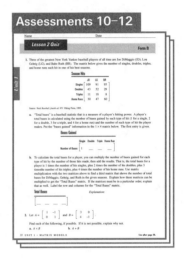

This yields the same ranking as in Investigation 3.

5. If A is an adjacency matrix, then the 1s in A^2 mean that there are paths of length two between the vertices.

$$\begin{array}{c} \\ X \\ Y \\ Z \end{array} \begin{array}{ccc} X & Y & Z \\ \begin{bmatrix} 1 & 1 & 0 \\ 0 & 0 & 1 \\ 1 & 0 & 1 \end{bmatrix} \end{array} = A^2$$

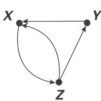

The matrix A would then be $\begin{array}{c} \\ X \\ Y \\ Z \end{array} \begin{array}{ccc} X & Y & Z \\ \begin{bmatrix} 0 & 0 & 1 \\ 1 & 0 & 0 \\ 1 & 1 & 0 \end{bmatrix} \end{array}$.

See Assessment Resources pages 7–12.

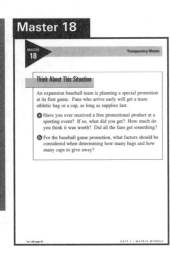

Lesson 3 *Matrices and Systems of Linear Equations*

LESSON OVERVIEW This lesson continues the study of systems of linear equations. Students first encountered linear systems in Unit 3 of Course 1, "Linear Models". In the next Unit, "Patterns of Location, Shape, and Size", students will see a more geometrical treatment of linear systems. Linear systems will be studied again in Course 3.

In Course 1, linear equations usually were investigated in the form $y = ax + b$. Based on this form, students made tables and graphs, reasoned with symbols, and solved systems of linear equations. In this lesson, students will encounter equations of the form $ax + by = c$. Although they may have some idea how to work with such equations, it is assumed that they do not already know how to graph, solve, or make tables using these equations.

In the first investigation of this lesson, students generate a system of two linear equations that models a given situation. Then they represent the system using a matrix equation. Students extend the method of solving simple linear equations that they explored in Course 1 to justify solving a matrix equation by multiplying by an inverse matrix. Based on experiences from the previous lesson, students will have the necessary understanding of inverse matrices and their properties to successfully complete this lesson. Technology will be used to find inverse matrices. (Organizing task 6 from Investigation 4 shows one way to find an inverse in the 2×2 case without using the inverse function of a calculator or computer software. Because finding inverses of larger matrices is a painstaking process easily circumvented with technology, the by-hand methods for doing so are left to more advanced courses.)

In the second investigation of this lesson, students learn how to graph equations that are not in the $y = a + bx$ form. Then they use graphs to solve linear systems, including the systems from the first investigation.

Lesson Objectives

■ To represent situations involving linear relationships with systems of linear equations of the form $ax + by = c$
■ To represent systems of linear equations with matrices
■ To solve matrix equations of the form $AX = C$ by multiplying by A^{-1}
■ To graph linear equations of the form $ax + by = c$, by hand and using a graphics calculator
■ To solve systems of linear equations by graphing

See additional Teaching Notes on page T78E.

Lesson 3

Matrices and Systems of Linear Equations

In Course 1 you used linear equations or systems of linear equations to model a wide variety of situations in which the rates of change were constant. In most of these situations, one variable could be thought of as a function of another. In this lesson, you will explore situations where there are several linear relationships between the same two variables. You also will investigate some important connections between these linear models and matrix models.

Think About This Situation

An expansion baseball team is planning a special promotion at its first game. Fans who arrive early will get a team athletic bag or a cap, as long as supplies last.

ⓐ Have you ever received a free promotional product at a sporting event? If so, what did you get? How much do you think it was worth? Did all the fans get something?

ⓑ For the baseball game promotion, what factors should be considered when determining how many bags and how many caps to give away?

LESSON 3 • MATRICES AND SYSTEMS OF LINEAR EQUATIONS   **59**

INVESTIGATION 1 Smart Promotions, Smart Solutions

Suppose the promotion manager for the expansion baseball team can buy athletic bags for $9 each and caps for $5 each. The total budget for buying bags and caps is $25,500. The team plans to give a bag or a cap, but not both, to the first 3500 fans.

1. In your group, think about and discuss how many bags and caps should be given away.

   a. Can the team give an athletic bag to all 3500 fans? Explain.

   b. Can they give a cap to all 3500 fans? Should they do so? Why or why not?

   c. How many bags and caps does your group think the team should give away?

2. Here is one method the promotion manager might use to decide how many bags and caps should be given away. Examine the partial table below.

Baseball Team Promotion

Number of Bags Given Away	Number of Caps Given Away	Total Cost of Bags and Caps Given Away	Under or Over Budget?
0	3500	$17,500	under budget
700			
1400			
2100			
2800	700	$28,700	over budget
3500			

   a. For each entry in the fifth row, explain what the entry means and how it was determined.

   b. Complete a copy of the table.

   c. The bags are more desirable to the fans. Estimate the greatest number of bags that can be given away. Explain how you found your estimate.

3. Another way the promotion manager might determine the combination of team bags and caps that can be provided for a total of 3500 fans at a cost of $25,500 is to use equations. Suppose b represents the number of bags to be given away and c represents the number of caps to be given away.

   a. In the table from activity 2, to which columns do b and c correspond?

   b. The values of b and c depend on each other. Give a general description of how c changes as b changes. Describe how b changes as c changes.

INVESTIGATION 1 Smart Promotions, Smart Solutions

Master 19

Students should be able to complete in one day the "Think About This Situation" for this lesson and, in the investigation, activities 1, 2, 3, and probably 4. There is a vital connection to solving linear equations in activity 4 that the whole class should discuss after all groups of students have thought about it. Homework this first day could be a review of solving simple linear equations of the form $ax = b$.

It works well to start the second day of Investigation 1 with a quick reprise of activity 4. In activity 5, when students enter matrix A in their calculators and produce A^{-1}, encourage them to look carefully at the entries of A^{-1}. You may wish to ask students if they expected A^{-1} to look as it does. The calculation of the inverse matrix is going to be left to the calculator for now, but it is important that students take the time to look at the inverse matrix and see what it looks like—and what it does not. A persistent misunderstanding is that the inverse matrix is simply a matrix whose entries are the reciprocals of all the entries in the original. If you do not give students time to look at the matrices involved, the process of using matrices to solve linear systems can degenerate into "magic".

You may wish to ask:

> What happens when you multiply a matrix by its inverse? What happens if you create a matrix with all the reciprocals of the original entries in matrix A; call this matrix B; and multiply $A \times B$? Why is the inverse matrix not just made of the reciprocals? Why might we want to have an inverse that, when multiplied by the original matrix, gives a matrix that has all 1s on the diagonal and 0s elsewhere? (This helps students see that the process of multiplying by the inverse matrix is parallel to the process they used in solving simple linear equations.)

1. **a.** No, because 3,500 bags cost more than $25,500.
   b. They can give a cap to all 3,500 fans, but then no fans get athletic bags, which are (presumably) the better gift. They should give away a combination of bags and caps.
   c. Student responses will vary. Responses should indicate why the group chose the combination they did. The budget should be no more than $25,500.

2. **a.** If there are 2800 bags given away, then since 3500 fans receive gifts, 700 caps must be given away. Total cost for this is (2800)($9) + (700)($5) or $28,700, and this is more than the budget of $25,500.
   b. See Teaching Master 19.

Number of Bags Given Away	Number of Caps Given Away	Total Cost of Bags and Caps Given Away	Under or Over Budget?
0	3500	$17,500	under budget
700	2800	$20,300	under budget
1400	2100	$23,100	under budget
2100	1400	$25,900	over budget
2800	700	$28,700	over budget
3500	0	$31,500	over budget

   c. Since giving away 1400 bags is under budget and giving away 2100 bags is over budget, the maximum number of bags given away must be between 1400 and 2100. It is closer to 2100 since the cost is just over budget for that amount. Any guess between 1400 and 2100 is reasonable, but students might refine their guesses to 2000.

3. **a.** The variables b and c correspond to the first two columns of the table.
   b. As b increases, c decreases. As c increases, b decreases.

3. c. Equations may vary but should be equivalent to $b + c = 3500$.

  d. $9b + 5c = 25{,}500$

  e. The number of bags and caps given away must satisfy both the requirements for number of fans and total budget. So, b and c must satisfy both equations.

4. a. $1b + 1c = 3500$
   $9b + 5c = 25{,}500$

  b.
$$\begin{bmatrix} 1 & 1 \\ 9 & 5 \end{bmatrix} \begin{bmatrix} b \\ c \end{bmatrix} = \begin{bmatrix} 3{,}500 \\ 25{,}500 \end{bmatrix}$$

  c. ■ A corresponds to $\begin{bmatrix} 1 & 1 \\ 9 & 5 \end{bmatrix}$.

   ■ X corresponds to $\begin{bmatrix} b \\ c \end{bmatrix}$.

   ■ D corresponds to $\begin{bmatrix} 3{,}500 \\ 25{,}500 \end{bmatrix}$.

  d. They have the same general form, but one has matrices and the other integers. They both will have one solution, but the solution to $AX = C$ will be a matrix and the solution to $3x = 6$ will be an integer.

5. Students who try to multiply the inverse matrix on the right, when solving the matrix equation, should see the importance of multiplication on the left because the dimensions will not be compatible. Reflecting task 1 on page 70 directs students to think more carefully about this restriction.

  a. If students solve this as suggested in the "Linear Models" unit of Course 1, they will divide both sides by 3. They might justify the method by saying that it keeps the equation in balance or that they did the same thing to both sides. Students also might solve by multiplying both sides by $\frac{1}{3}$.

  b. In order to motivate the method of solving matrix equations below, students must think about solving the linear equation here by multiplying by $\frac{1}{3}$, which is the multiplicative inverse of 3. If they did multiply by $\frac{1}{3}$ in part a, they have nothing more to do in this part. However, if they divided by 3 in part a, then they need to consider explicitly why it is also correct to multiply by $\frac{1}{3}$.

  c. Students should explain each step of the comparison to each other so that they all understand the parallel being drawn. This is essential so that they will feel comfortable with multiplying by an inverse matrix to solve the matrix equation.

c. Write an equation showing the relationship among b, c, and the total number of fans receiving a promotional gift.

d. Write an equation showing the relationship among b, c, and the total budget for the promotion.

e. Explain why the promotion manager would like to find values of b and c that satisfy both equations.

4. Equations like those in parts c and d of activity 3, which link the same variables, can be represented with matrices. The matrix representation leads to an efficient way to decide how many bags and how many caps should be given away.

a. Write the two equations, one above the other, in a form like that below.

$$\underline{\ \ } b + \underline{\ \ } c = \ \ 3{,}500$$
$$\underline{\ \ } b + \underline{\ \ } c = 25{,}500$$

b. This system of equations can be represented by a single matrix equation. Determine the entries of the matrix below so that when you do the matrix multiplication you get the two equations in part a.

$$\begin{bmatrix} \underline{\ \ } & \underline{\ \ } \\ \underline{\ \ } & \underline{\ \ } \end{bmatrix} \begin{bmatrix} b \\ c \end{bmatrix} = \begin{bmatrix} 3{,}500 \\ 25{,}500 \end{bmatrix}$$

c. Your matrix equation is of the form $AX = D$.

- Which matrix corresponds to A?
- Which matrix corresponds to X?
- Which matrix corresponds to D?

d. Compare the matrix equation $AX = D$ to the linear equation $3x = 6$. How are these equations similar? How are they different?

5. Thinking about how to solve the linear equation $3x = 6$ can help you figure out how to solve the matrix equation $AX = D$.

a. Solve the equation $3x = 6$. Explain your method and why it works.

b. One way to solve this equation is to multiply both sides by the *multiplicative inverse* of 3, that is, $\frac{1}{3}$. If this is different from the method you used, compare it to your method and explain why it works.

c. Explain or clarify each step of the following comparison so that everyone in your group understands the comparison.

Solving a Linear Equation

$3x = 6$
$x = (\text{inverse of } 3) \times 6$
$x = \frac{1}{3} \times 6$

Solving a Matrix Equation

$AX = D$
$X = (\text{inverse of } A) \times D$
$X = A^{-1} \times D$

6. Now you are ready to solve the matrix equation you completed in activity 4, part b.

   a. What matrices should you multiply to solve the matrix equation?

   b. Solve the equation. Record the matrix solution. What values for *b* and *c* do you get? How many bags and how many caps should the team give away?

   c. Compare your values for *b* and *c* with what you estimated using the table in activity 2.

   d. Use your equations in part a of activity 4 to check your solution.

   e. Use the matrix equation to check your solution.

7. The two equations below could represent the relationship between quantities of other promotional items.

$$x + \quad y = \quad 5{,}000$$

$$8x + 12y = 42{,}000$$

   a. Using the context of promotional products for a team, describe a situation that could be modeled by this system of equations.

   b. Represent the two equations with a matrix equation and then solve the matrix equation. Check that your values for *x* and *y* satisfy the original system of equations and the matrix equation.

   c. Interpret your solution in terms of the situation you described in part *a*.

   d. Suppose a situation involving promotional products was modeled by the following system of equations:

$$2x + \quad y = \quad 5{,}000$$

$$8x + 12y = 42{,}000$$

Write and solve the matrix equation that represents this new system. Check your solution.

Checkpoint

For a system of equations like the ones in this investigation:

ⓐ Describe how to represent the system with matrices.

ⓑ Describe how to solve the corresponding matrix equation $AX = C$. Explain why the method makes sense.

ⓒ Describe at least two ways to check the solution of the matrix equation that represents the system of equations.

Be prepared to share your group's descriptions and thinking with the entire class.

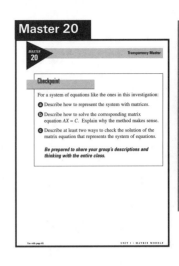

Master 20

MASTER 20   Transparency Master

Checkpoint

For a system of equations like the ones in this investigation:

ⓐ Describe how to represent the system with matrices.

ⓑ Describe how to solve the corresponding matrix equation $AX = C$. Explain why the method makes sense.

ⓒ Describe at least two ways to check the solution of the matrix equation that represents the system of equations.

Be prepared to share your group's descriptions and thinking with the entire class.

UNIT 1 • MATRIX MODELS

6. a. The solution is $A^{-1}D$ or $\begin{bmatrix} 1 & 1 \\ 9 & 5 \end{bmatrix}^{-1} \begin{bmatrix} 3,500 \\ 25,500 \end{bmatrix}$.

    b. $X = (A^{-1})C = \begin{bmatrix} -1.25 & 0.25 \\ 2.25 & -0.25 \end{bmatrix} \begin{bmatrix} 3,500 \\ 25,500 \end{bmatrix} = \begin{bmatrix} 2,000 \\ 1,500 \end{bmatrix}$.

Note that students may not calculate A^{-1} explicitly and instead do all computations on the calculator or computer. Thus they see only the final answer. This is acceptable, however, they should carefully examine the entries of an inverse matrix at least once. (See the notes in the introduction to this investigation.)

The matrix solution is $\begin{bmatrix} 2,000 \\ 1,500 \end{bmatrix}$. That is, $b = 2,000$ and $c = 1,500$. So the team should give away 2,000 bags and 1,500 caps. Note that there are three statements of the solution here: as a matrix, as values for b and c, and as quantities of bags and caps. Students should see that the solution can be stated in all ways.

    c. Students should see that the answers for b and c are close, if not identical, to what they estimated using the table in activity 2. This comparison, along with the checks below and the graphical solution in the next investigation, is important so that students will see that the "black box" solution using matrix inverses really does work.

    d. The values for b and c should satisfy both equations.

    e. The matrix solution, when substituted for X in the matrix equation, should make that equation true.

7. a. Student responses will vary. They should describe a situation where a total of 5000 items are given away. Two different items will be given away. The total budget for the promotion is $42,000. One of the items costs $8 and the other costs $12.

    b. Having stepped through the process of solving a system with matrices, now students should try it once more without all the steps laid out. The resulting matrix equation is

$$\begin{bmatrix} 1 & 1 \\ 8 & 12 \end{bmatrix} \begin{bmatrix} x \\ y \end{bmatrix} = \begin{bmatrix} 5,000 \\ 42,000 \end{bmatrix}.$$

Multiplying both sides of the equation by A^{-1} on the left gives

$$\begin{bmatrix} x \\ y \end{bmatrix} = \begin{bmatrix} 4,500 \\ 500 \end{bmatrix}.$$

So the solution, $x = 4500$ and $y = 500$, satisfies both equations.

    c. Student responses will vary. Their responses should indicate that they can connect the solution of the matrix equation with the problem situation.

    d. The matrix equation is

$$\begin{bmatrix} 2 & 1 \\ 8 & 12 \end{bmatrix} \begin{bmatrix} x \\ y \end{bmatrix} = \begin{bmatrix} 5,000 \\ 42,000 \end{bmatrix}.$$

The solution is $x = 1,125$ and $y = 2,750$.

See additional Teaching Notes on page T78F.

CONSTRUCTING A MATH TOOLKIT: Students should summarize the process of representing a system of linear equations as a matrix equation, solving the equation, and checking the solution. Summaries can be recorded under either the discrete mathematics or algebra and functions strand in their Math Toolkits. An example could be included.

Unit 1

MORE
ASSIGNMENT   *pp. 66–74*

Students now can begin
Organizing task 2 or Reflecting
task 1 from the MORE assignment following Investigation 2.

APPLY individual task

▶**On Your Own**

a. Let c represent the number of caps given away and j represent the number of jackets given away. The system of equations is

$$c + j = 4{,}500$$
$$5c + 10j = 37{,}500$$

b. $\begin{bmatrix} 1 & 1 \\ 5 & 10 \end{bmatrix}\begin{bmatrix} c \\ j \end{bmatrix} = \begin{bmatrix} 4{,}500 \\ 37{,}500 \end{bmatrix}$

c. They should give away 1,500 caps and 3,000 jackets.

d. To check their answers students may substitute the values for c and j into the original equations or the matrix equation.

EXPLORE small-group investigation

INVESTIGATION 2 Comparing Solution Methods

1. Students should draw upon the graphing work they have done previously, particularly in the Course 1 unit "Linear Models", to think about how to use graphs to solve this system. We are not assuming that students know that these graphs are lines, but nevertheless they probably will decide that they should graph the equations and see where they intersect.

2. a. Keep in mind that students probably have not seen equations in this form before; they have seen equations in the form "$y = ...$". They may come up with ideas like making a table and plotting points, solving for y to get the equation in the form "$y = ...$", or calculating some points to get a scatterplot and then using statistical curve-fitting. These are all graphing methods used in Course 1, albeit in different contexts.

b. Students should make conjectures. As the investigation proceeds, they will see that the graphs are lines.

▶ **On Your Own**

Cultivating the good will of fans is important for professional sports teams, especially after a period of bad publicity, like the prolonged 1994–95 baseball strike.

Suppose that the promotions manager of the baseball team in Investigation 1 decides to enhance the promotion by giving better prizes to more fans. The team owner agrees to increase the promotion budget to $37,500 and give a cap or jacket to the first 4500 fans. The caps still cost $5 each and the jackets cost $10 each.

a. Modify the two equations from Investigation 1 so that they model this new situation.

b. Write and solve the matrix equation representing this situation.

c. How many caps and how many jackets should be given away?

d. Show at least one way to check your answer.

INVESTIGATION ▶ 2 Comparing Solution Methods

In the last investigation you used inverse matrices to solve systems of equations. The method you used is a common one, particularly useful for large systems like those found in business and industry. However, for systems of just two equations, it may be most efficient to use other methods. In this investigation you will explore a graphical method similar to the one used in Course 1. Then you will compare the graphical method to the matrix method.

1. The system of equations that models the original promotion manager's problem from the last investigation is as follows:

$$b + c = 3{,}500$$

$$9b + 5c = 25{,}500$$

The solution you found consists of values for b and c that satisfy both equations. Suppose you had a graph for each equation. How could you use the graphs to solve the system of equations?

2. In your previous work, the equations you graphed were of the form $y = $ *some expression*.

a. With your group, brainstorm about possible ways you could graph the equations in activity 1. List all your ideas for how to graph the equations, with and without a calculator or computer software. Don't graph them yet, just list ideas.

b. What shape do you think the graphs will have? Make a conjecture now; you will check your conjecture after you have graphed the equations later in this investigation.

3. One way to graph the equations is to make a table and plot some points. Follow through with this idea now. You will get a chance to try other ways later. Copy the tables below.

$b + c = 3,500$		
b	**c**	**Point On Graph**
0	3500	(0, 3500)
500	3000	_____
_____	_____	_____
_____	_____	_____
_____	_____	_____

$9b + 5c = 25,500$		
b	**c**	**Point On Graph**
0	5100	(0, 5100)
_____	_____	(500, 4200)
1000	_____	_____
_____	_____	_____
_____	_____	_____

   a. Examine the table for the equation $9b + 5c = 25,500$.

      ■ For each entry in the first row, explain what it means and how it was determined.

      ■ How can you use the equation to verify that (500, 4200) is a point on the graph of the equation?

      ■ How can you use the equation to verify that (500, 4500) is not a point on the graph of the equation?

      ■ In the third row you are given that $b = 1000$. Find the other entries in the third row, and explain how you determined them.

   b. Now, complete both of the tables. Each group member should find at least one point (b, c) on each graph.

   c. Use the completed tables and a sheet of graph paper to sketch a graph of each equation on the same set of axes.

   d. Describe the shape of the graphs.

   e. Use the graphs to estimate the solution to the system of equations.

4. In order to use a graphing calculator or computer software to get more precise graphs, you may need to rewrite the equations in the form "$y = \ldots$".

   a. The first equation of the system is $b + c = 3,500$. Solve the equation for c; that is, complete this equation:

$$c = \underline{\qquad}$$

   b. The second equation of the system is $9b + 5c = 25,500$. Solve this equation for c, by completing the steps of the following procedure.

$$9b + 5c = 25,500$$
$$5c = \underline{\qquad}$$
$$c = \underline{\qquad}$$

3. **See Teaching Master 21.**

   a. Students need to think carefully about this table to make sure they understand how to make a table and graph for equations in this new form: $ax + by = c$. In particular, they will have to solve some linear equations to generate values in the table, and then they must remember that values satisfy the equation if and only if an ordered pair with those coordinates is a point on the graph.

   ■ If $b = 0$, then the equation becomes $5c = 25,500$, which means $c = \frac{25\,500}{5}$ or 5,100. This means that they will spend $25,500 if they give away no bags and 5,100 caps. Two values that satisfy the equation yield an ordered pair, which is a point on the graph. Thus, (0, 5100) is on the graph.

   ■ Verify that $9(500) + 5(4,200) = 25,500$. In other words, verify that the point (500, 4200) satisfies the equation.

   ■ Verify that $9(500) + 5(4,500)$ is not equal to 25,500. In other words, verify that the point (500, 4500) does not satisfy the equation.

   ■ If $b = 1000$, then the equation becomes $9,000 + 5c = 25,500$. Solving for c gives $c = 3,300$. So (1000, 3300) is a point on the graph.

   b. $b + c = 3{,}500$

b	c	Point On Graph
0	3500	(0, 3500)
500	3000	(500, 3000)
1000	2500	(1000, 2500)
1500	2000	(1500, 2000)
2000	1500	(2000, 1500)
2500	1000	(2500, 1000)
3000	500	(3000, 500)
3500	0	(3500, 0)

   $9b + 5c = 25{,}500$

b	c	Point on Graph
0	5100	(0, 5100)
500	4200	(500, 4200)
1000	3300	(1000, 3300)
1500	2400	(1500, 2400)
2000	1500	(2000, 1500)
2500	600	(2500, 600)
3000	−300	(3000, −300)
3500	−1200	(3500, −1200)

   c. Students should sketch graphs by hand on graph paper.

   d. The graphs are lines. They have negative slope and one is steeper than the other.

   e. The graphs look like they intersect at about (2000, 1500), but the approximations here could vary.

4. Before now, students have not been asked to solve linear equations with two variables. However, these equations are simple and the procedure is outlined in enough detail so that they should be able to do this, particularly if working in groups.

   a. $c = 3500 − b$

   b. $9b + 5c = 25,500$

   $$5c = 25,500 − 9b$$
   $$c = (25,500 − 9b) \div 5$$
   (or $c = \frac{25\,500}{5} − \frac{9b}{5}$ or $c = 5,100 − \frac{9}{5}b$)

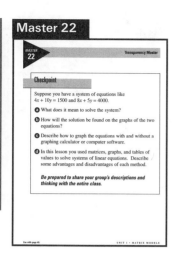

5.

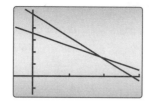

a. The solution to the system corresponds to finding the point at which the graphs intersect. Find the intersection by graphing, tracing, and zooming. The intersection point is (2000, 1500), so the solution to the system is $b = 2000$, $c = 1500$.

b. There could be some differences due to estimation and round-off between the intersection point from the sketched graphs and the intersection point from the calculator-generated graphs. The solution found by each of these methods may be slightly different than the exact solution found using the matrix method in Investigation 1.

c. Students should compare the shape of the graphs (*i.e.*, lines) to the shape they conjectured. They also should see that although the equations started out looking very different from the "$y = \ldots$" form of the linear equations in "Linear Models", after solving for c they do have the same form; that is, they look like $y = a + bx$.

6. When rewritten in the form $b = $ *some expression*, the equations are $b = 3{,}500 - c$ and $b = (25{,}500 - 5c) \div 9$ (or $b = \frac{25\,500}{9} - \frac{5}{9}c$). The solution is still $b = 2{,}000$ and $c = 1{,}500$. Students should realize that it doesn't matter which variable they solve for.

7. a. Solving for y, the equations become $y = 5{,}000 - 2x$ and $y = (42{,}000 - 8x) \div 12$ (or $y = 3{,}500 - \frac{2}{3}x$).
The graphs are as follows:

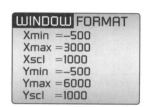

Zooming and tracing should give an intersection point of about (1125, 2750).

b. Student responses will vary. Students might solve the equations by looking at tables or by using matrices. Students who have done more exploration of their calculators may have other options, such as (on the TI-82 or TI-83) using the intersect command from the CALC menu or using the SOLVE(command from the MATH menu. Another approach is to use data lists and linear regression to get the equations, and then graph and find the point of intersection.

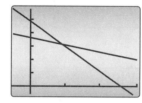

CONSTRUCTING A MATH TOOLKIT: Record at least two methods for graphing an equation given in the form $ax + by = c$.

See additional Teaching Notes on page T78G.

5. Now that you have rewritten both equations in the form $c = $ *some expression*, enter the expressions into the functions list of your calculator or computer software. Graph both equations on the same screen.

   a. Use the graphs to solve the system of equations. Explain your method.

   b. Compare your solution to the estimate from part e of activity 3 and to the matrix solution from Investigation 1. Discuss any differences.

   c. In activity 2 of this investigation, you made a conjecture about the shapes of the graphs. Was your conjecture correct? What do you observe about the equations once they are rewritten in the form "$y = \ldots$"?

6. Rewrite both equations from the original system of equations in the form $b = $ *some expression*. Solve this new system. What can you conclude?

7. The system of equations below could represent another situation involving promotional products for a team.

$$2x + y = 5,000$$
$$8x + 12y = 42,000$$

   a. Use graphs to solve this system.

   b. Describe two other methods for solving this system of equations. Use each method to solve the system of equations. Compare your solutions.

The matrix method you have been using to solve systems of linear equations is both powerful and limited. It can be generalized to solve large systems of n linear equations in n variables. In general, the matrix corresponding to the coefficients in the equations is an $n \times n$ square matrix. But for this method to work that matrix must have an inverse; as you have seen, this is not always the case.

Checkpoint

Suppose you have a system of equations like $4x + 10y = 1500$ and $8x + 5y = 4000$.

a What does it mean to solve the system?

b How will the solution be found on the graphs of the two equations?

c Describe how to graph the equations with and without a graphing calculator or computer software.

d In this lesson you used matrices, graphs, and tables of values to solve systems of linear equations. Describe some advantages and disadvantages of each method.

Be prepared to share your group's descriptions and thinking with the class.

▶ **On Your Own**

In the "On Your Own" activity on page 63 you considered a situation where a baseball team used a promotion budget of \$37,500 to give a team cap or jacket to 4500 fans. The jackets cost \$10 each and the caps cost \$5 each. In that activity you modeled the situation with the following system of linear equations.

$$j + c = 4{,}500$$

$$10j + 5c = 37{,}500$$

a. Solve this system of linear equations using graphs. How many caps and how many jackets should the team give away?

b. Check your answer using a table of values.

c. Compare your answer to what you found using matrices in the last "On Your Own".

MORE

Modeling • Organizing • Reflecting • Extending

Modeling

1. At a school basketball game, the box office sold 400 tickets for a total revenue of \$1750. Tickets cost \$6 for adults and \$4 for students. In the rush of selling tickets, the box office did not keep track of how many adult and student tickets were sold. The school would like this information for future planning.

a. Let a represent the number of adult tickets sold and s represent the number of student tickets sold.

   ■ Write an equation showing the relationship among a, s, and the number of tickets sold.

   ■ Write an equation showing the relationship among a, s, and the total revenue from ticket sales.

b. Write a matrix equation that represents the system of two linear equations from part a.

c. Solve the matrix equation. How many adult and student tickets were sold?

d. Graph the two linear equations and use the graphs to verify your solution.

e. Describe another way that you could verify your solution.

On Your Own

a. Solving for c yields these equations:

$c = 4500 - j$

$c = (37{,}500 - 10j) \div 5 = 7500 - 2j$

The graphs are shown below. The point of intersection is (3000, 1500). Thus, 3,000 jackets and 1,500 caps should be given away.

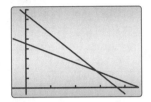

```
WINDOW FORMAT
  Xmin =−500
  Xmax =4500
  Xscl =1000
  Ymin =−500
  Ymax =8000
  Yscl =1000
```

b. Students should get a table of values for each equation. To check their answer they should see that the solution (3000, 1500) is found in both tables.

c. This answer agrees with the matrix solution from the previous "On Your Own".

MORE **independent assignment**

Modeling

1. **a.** ■ $a + s = 400$

■ $6a + 4s = 1750$

b. $\begin{bmatrix} 1 & 1 \\ 6 & 4 \end{bmatrix} \begin{bmatrix} a \\ s \end{bmatrix} = \begin{bmatrix} 400 \\ 1750 \end{bmatrix}$

c. Multiply both sides of the equation on the left by the inverse of the first (coefficient) matrix to find a and s:

$$\begin{bmatrix} a \\ s \end{bmatrix} = \begin{bmatrix} 1 & 1 \\ 6 & 4 \end{bmatrix}^{-1} \begin{bmatrix} 400 \\ 1750 \end{bmatrix} = \begin{bmatrix} -2 & 0.5 \\ 3 & -0.5 \end{bmatrix} \begin{bmatrix} 400 \\ 1750 \end{bmatrix} = \begin{bmatrix} 75 \\ 325 \end{bmatrix}$$

There were 75 adult and 325 student tickets sold.

d. **Box Office Equations**

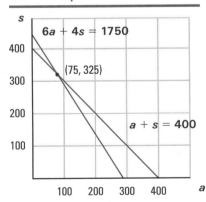

e. Students could substitute the solution into the matrix equation or system of equations.

MORE
ASSIGNMENT   *pp. 66–74*

Modeling: 1 or 2 and 3*
Organizing: 2, 3, and 4
Reflecting: Choose one*
Extending: Choose one*

When choice is indicated, it is important to leave the choice to the student.
NOTE: *It is best if Organizing tasks are discussed as a whole class after they have been assigned as homework.*

2. a. $x + y = 65$ and $20x + 25y = 1500$

b. The matrix equation is

$$\begin{bmatrix} 1 & 1 \\ 20 & 25 \end{bmatrix}\begin{bmatrix} x \\ y \end{bmatrix} = \begin{bmatrix} 65 \\ 1500 \end{bmatrix}$$

Multiplying by the inverse matrix on the left gives

$$\begin{bmatrix} x \\ y \end{bmatrix} = \begin{bmatrix} 1 & 1 \\ 20 & 25 \end{bmatrix}^{-1}\begin{bmatrix} 65 \\ 1500 \end{bmatrix} = \begin{bmatrix} 25 \\ 40 \end{bmatrix}$$

25 gift certificates will be awarded for attendance and 40 for good grades.

c. Solving the linear equations for y yields $y = 65 - x$ and $y = 60 - 0.8x$. The point of intersection of the two lines is (25, 40). Students also could look at tables of values or solve the system algebraically.

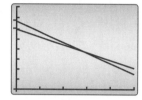
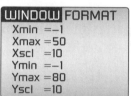

3. a.   Tourn $\begin{bmatrix} 35 \\ 50 \end{bmatrix}$
       Std

b. When we multiply the two matrices, the "Tourn" and "Std" columns in the given matrix match the "Tourn" and "Std" rows in the matrix in part a, and the product of the two matrices carries the row labels of the first matrix:

$$\begin{array}{c} \\ \text{Balls} \\ \text{Paddles} \end{array}\begin{array}{cc} \text{Tourn} & \text{Std} \\ \begin{bmatrix} 6 & 1 \\ 4 & 2 \end{bmatrix} \end{array} \times \begin{array}{c} \text{Tourn} \\ \text{Std} \end{array}\begin{bmatrix} 35 \\ 50 \end{bmatrix} = \begin{array}{c} \text{Balls} \\ \text{Paddles} \end{array}\begin{bmatrix} 260 \\ 240 \end{bmatrix}$$

So 260 balls and 240 paddles are needed.

c. The matrix equation is $\begin{bmatrix} 6 & 1 \\ 4 & 2 \end{bmatrix}\begin{bmatrix} t \\ s \end{bmatrix} = \begin{bmatrix} 110 \\ 100 \end{bmatrix}$.

d. Multiplying by the inverse of the coefficient matrix, we find

$$\begin{bmatrix} t \\ s \end{bmatrix} = \begin{bmatrix} 0.25 & -0.125 \\ -0.5 & 0.75 \end{bmatrix}\begin{bmatrix} 110 \\ 100 \end{bmatrix} = \begin{bmatrix} 15 \\ 20 \end{bmatrix}.$$

The owner can make 15 tournament sets and 20 standard sets.

e. Multiplying the matrices in part c yields $6t + s = 110$ and $4t + 2s = 100$. Solving these equations for s gives $s = 110 - 6t$ and $s = 50 - 2t$. The point of intersection of the two graphs is (15, 20).

2. A school principal and the local business community have devised an innovative plan to motivate better school attendance and achievement. They plan to give gift certificates to students who score high in each category. Students with high attendance will be awarded $20 gift certificates, and those with good grades will receive $25 gift certificates. The total budget for this plan is $1500, and the planning committee would like to award 65 certificates. The next step is to determine the number of each type of certificate to be printed.

   a. If x is the number of attendance gift certificates and y is the number of certificates for good grades, write equations that model this situation.

   b. Find and solve a matrix equation that models the system of linear equations from part a. How many of each type of certificate can be awarded?

   c. Verify your solution using an alternate method for solving a system of linear equations.

3. The Fairfield Hobbies and Games store sells two types of ping-pong sets. A Standard Set contains two paddles and one ball, and a Tournament Set contains four paddles and six balls. This information is summarized in the matrix below.

Ping-Pong Sets

	Tourn	Std
Balls	6	1
Paddles	4	2

   a. This month the store orders 35 Tournament Sets and 50 Standard Sets. Put this information into a one-column matrix. Label the rows of the matrix.

   b. Use matrix multiplication to find another matrix that shows the total number of balls and paddles in all the Tournament and Standard sets ordered this month.

   c. Later, the store receives a bulk shipment of ping-pong equipment consisting of 100 paddles and 110 balls. The owner wants to know how many of each type of ping-pong set she can make using this equipment. Let s represent the number of Standard Sets and t represent the number of Tournament Sets. Complete the following matrix equation so that it represents this situation.

$$\begin{bmatrix} 6 & 1 \\ 4 & 2 \end{bmatrix}\begin{bmatrix} — \\ — \end{bmatrix} = \begin{bmatrix} — \\ — \end{bmatrix}$$

   d. Solve the matrix equation. How many sets of each type can the owner make using the balls and paddles in the bulk shipment?

   e. Do the matrix multiplication indicated in the matrix equation from part c. Write the system of two linear equations that corresponds to the matrix equation. Solve this system by using graphs or tables and compare your solution to the answer you found in part d.

4. A new diet that Antonio is considering restricts his drinks to water, milk, and fruit juice. The matrix below shows the amount of protein and calories per cup for skim milk and fruit juice.

Protein and Calories

	Juice	Milk
Protein (g)	2	8
Calories (g)	120	85

The diet recommends that Antonio drink enough milk and juice each day to get a total of 10 grams of protein and 180 calories from those sources. He wants to know how much milk and juice he must drink to meet these recommendations.

a. Construct a one-column matrix showing the recommended daily totals for protein and calories. Label the rows of the matrix.

b. Let x represent the number of cups of juice he should drink each day and y represent the number of cups of milk he should drink. Set up a matrix multiplication equation that models this situation.

c. Solve the matrix equation. How many cups of juice and milk should Antonio drink each day to meet the recommendations of the diet?

5. The owner of two restaurants in town has decided to promote business by allocating to each restaurant a certain amount of money to spend on restaurant renovation and community service projects. He has asked the manager of each restaurant to submit a proposal stating what percentage of their money they would like to spend in each of these two categories. The matrix below shows their proposals.

Funding Requests

	Rest. A	Rest. B
Renovation	70%	45%
Community Service	30%	55%

The owner has decided to allocate a total of $16,000 to renovations and $14,000 to community projects. The managers want to know how much money each restaurant will have to spend.

a. Represent this situation with a matrix equation and with a system of two linear equations.

b. Using a method of your choice, determine how much money each restaurant should be allocated.

4. a. Protein $\begin{bmatrix} 10 \\ 180 \end{bmatrix}$
   Calories

b. The matrix equation is $\begin{bmatrix} 2 & 8 \\ 120 & 85 \end{bmatrix} \begin{bmatrix} x \\ y \end{bmatrix} = \begin{bmatrix} 10 \\ 180 \end{bmatrix}$.

c. As before, multiply the equation of part b by the inverse of the coefficient matrix:

$$\begin{bmatrix} x \\ y \end{bmatrix} \approx \begin{bmatrix} -0.1076 & 0.0101 \\ 0.1519 & -0.0025 \end{bmatrix} \begin{bmatrix} 10 \\ 180 \end{bmatrix} \approx \begin{bmatrix} 0.75 \\ 1.06 \end{bmatrix}.$$

So Antonio should drink approximately 0.75 cups of juice and approximately 1.06 cups of milk each day.

5. a. The matrix equation is $\begin{bmatrix} 0.7 & 0.45 \\ 0.3 & 0.55 \end{bmatrix} \begin{bmatrix} a \\ b \end{bmatrix} = \begin{bmatrix} 16{,}000 \\ 14{,}000 \end{bmatrix}$.

The two linear equations are $0.7a + 0.45b = 16{,}000$ and $0.3a + 0.55b = 14{,}000$.

b. One method is to multiply by the inverse of the coefficient matrix. This gives the solution

$$\begin{bmatrix} a \\ b \end{bmatrix} = \begin{bmatrix} 2.2 & -1.8 \\ -1.2 & 2.8 \end{bmatrix} \begin{bmatrix} 16{,}000 \\ 14{,}000 \end{bmatrix} = \begin{bmatrix} 10{,}000 \\ 20{,}000 \end{bmatrix}.$$

So restaurant A should get $10,000 and restaurant B should get $20,000. Students may choose a different method to solve this system of equations.

Unit 1

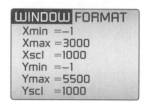

1. **a.**

x	0	500	1000	1500	2000	2500
y	5000	4000	3000	2000	1000	0

   b.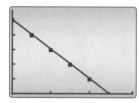

   c. The linear regression procedure gives the equation $y = 5000 - 2x$.

   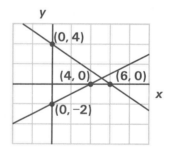

   d. $y = 5000 - 2x$, which is the same as the regression equation from part c.

2. **a.** The *y*-coordinate of the *x*-intercept will be 0. To find the *x*-intercept, substitute 0 for *y* into the equation $x + 5y = 45$ and solve the equation to get $x = 45$.

   b. The *x*-coordinate of the *y*-intercept will be 0. To find the *y*-intercept, substitute 0 for *x* into the equation $x + 5y = 45$ and solve $5y = 45$. Thus $y = 9$.

   c. The intercepts for $2x + 3y = 12$ are (0, 4) and (6, 0), and for $5x - 10y = 20$ are (0, −2) and (4, 0). By joining the intercepts for each line we get the graphs of the two lines:

   From this graph, we estimate the solution to be near (5, 0.5). Writing the equations in matrix form

   $$\begin{bmatrix} 2 & 3 \\ 5 & -10 \end{bmatrix} \begin{bmatrix} x \\ y \end{bmatrix} = \begin{bmatrix} 12 \\ 20 \end{bmatrix}$$

   we can find the inverse of the first (coefficient) matrix and multiply on the left by it to obtain the solution.

   $$\begin{bmatrix} x \\ y \end{bmatrix} \approx \begin{bmatrix} 5.14 \\ 0.57 \end{bmatrix}$$

   Comparing the graphical solution with the matrix solution, we see agreement in the whole number and, if we are careful, in the tenths.

Organizing

1. In this lesson you used your calculator or computer to graph linear equations of the form $ax + by = c$ by first solving the equation for y and then entering it into the functions list. Another way to produce a graph of the equation is to use a statistical method.

a. Complete a table of sample data pairs like the one below for the equation $2x + y = 5000$.

x	0	500	1500		
y		4000		1000	0

b. Make a scatterplot of the (x, y) data.

c. Use the linear regression procedure of your calculator or computer software to find an equation of a linear model for the data. Enter the equation in the functions list and produce its graph.

d. Solve $2x + y = 5000$ for y and compare the result with the regression equation from part c.

2. Since you now know that the graph of an equation in the form $ax + by = c$ is a line, you can quickly sketch a graph simply by plotting two points and connecting them with a line. Two points that are often easy to plot are the *intercepts*. The x-intercept is the point where the graph crosses the x-axis. The y-intercept is the point where the graph crosses the y-axis.

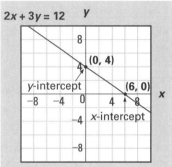

a. What is true about the coordinates of the x-intercept of any graph? How can you use this fact to find the x-intercept of $x + 5y = 45$ without graphing?

b. What is true about the coordinates of the y-intercept of any graph? How can you use this fact to find the y-intercept of $x + 5y = 45$ without graphing?

c. Find the intercepts and sketch the graph of each equation in the system below. Use the graphs to approximate the solution of the system. Then solve the system using matrices and compare the solution to your approximation.

$$2x + 3y = 12$$
$$5x - 10y = 20$$

3. In this lesson you used matrices, graphing, and tables of values to solve systems of linear equations. Course 1 presented another method for solving linear systems, which was useful as long as the equations were in the form "$y = \ldots$". That method involved reasoning with the symbolic forms themselves.

a. Solve the following system by first rewriting each equation in the form "$y = \ldots$" and then setting the expressions equal to each other.

$$6x + 4y = 12$$

$$5x - 10y = 20$$

b. Check your answer to part a by comparing it to the solution you find using matrices.

c. Choose one of the systems of linear equations from this lesson. Solve the system using the method of rewriting the equations in the form "$y = \ldots$" and then setting the expressions equal to each other.

4. Setting up a matrix equation and then multiplying by the inverse of a matrix is a very useful method for solving a system of linear equations. But there are some limitations!

a. Try the method on each of the systems below.

$$2x + 5y = 10 \qquad\qquad 6x + 4y = 12$$

$$2x + 5y = 20 \qquad\qquad 3x + 2y = 6$$

b. In each case, what happens when you try to calculate the inverse matrix?

c. For each system, sketch graphs of the equations.

- What do the graphs tell you about the solutions?

- What would the graphs look like for a system in which calculating the inverse matrix is possible?

d. What patterns in the equations of a system indicate that you will not be able to use the inverse matrix to solve the system? Check your conjecture by writing and solving systems of linear equations that exhibit these patterns.

Reflecting

1. Refer back to the comparison of methods for solving a linear equation and a matrix equation (page 61).

a. For the linear equation, the second line of the comparison could have been

$$X = 6 \times (\text{inverse of } 3)$$

but you cannot multiply $D \times A^{-1}$ to find X. Why not?

b. How do you know that D must be multiplied *on the left* by A^{-1}?

Organizing

3. a. Solving the two equations for y we find:

$$y = (12 - 6x) \div 4 = 3 - 1.5x \qquad y = (20 - 5x) \div -10 = -2 + 0.5x.$$

Setting these two expressions for y equal to each other gives an equation for x alone:

$$3 - 1.5x = -2 + 0.5x$$

From this we see that $2x = 5$, so $x = 2.5$ and $y = -0.75$.

b.
$$\begin{bmatrix} 6 & 4 \\ 5 & -10 \end{bmatrix} \begin{bmatrix} x \\ y \end{bmatrix} = \begin{bmatrix} 12 \\ 20 \end{bmatrix}$$

$$\begin{bmatrix} x \\ y \end{bmatrix} = \begin{bmatrix} 6 & 4 \\ 5 & -10 \end{bmatrix}^{-1} \begin{bmatrix} 12 \\ 20 \end{bmatrix} = \begin{bmatrix} 0.125 & 0.05 \\ 0.0625 & -0.075 \end{bmatrix} \begin{bmatrix} 12 \\ 20 \end{bmatrix} = \begin{bmatrix} 2.5 \\ -0.75 \end{bmatrix}$$

c. Responses may vary. This is an opportunity for students to practice solving systems of equations using algebraic manipulation.

4. a. Using a calculator or computer software, students should input the matrices and try to solve the systems.

b. For each system, the calculator gives an error message (there is no inverse matrix).

c. ■ In the first system, the two lines are parallel; since parallel lines never meet, there is no solution to the system. In the second system, there is only one line; all the points on the line are solutions, and so the solution is not unique.

■ When the inverse matrix exists, the system has a unique solution. In that case, the graph of the system must be two lines which intersect in a single point.

d. Answers may vary, but the essential idea is that the pair of coefficients in the first equation is proportional to the pair in the second: $ax + by = c$ and $dx + fy = g$ do not have a unique solution whenever $\frac{a}{d} = \frac{b}{f}$.

Reflecting

1. a. Responses may vary. For example, students may point out that dimensions won't "fit" or that since matrix multiplication is not commutative, you cannot change the order.

b. Students should respond with reasoning similar to the following. Two general rules for solving equations are do the same thing to both sides, and "undo" something by "doing the opposite". Applying these rules to the equation $AX = D$, we see that in order to find X (get it by itself), we have to undo the multiplication by matrix A. To do that we multiply on the left by A^{-1}, since $A^{-1} \cdot A = I$ and $I \cdot X = X$. Note that we cannot multiply on the right by A^{-1}, since then we would have $A \cdot X \cdot A^{-1}$, and this does not equal X. (Even in a situation where the dimensions are compatible, $A \cdot X \cdot A^{-1}$ does not necessarily equal X since matrix multiplication is not commutative.) Since we multiplied one side of the equation on the left by A^{-1}, we now have to do the same thing to the other side. This yields $A^{-1} \cdot D$ (and not $D \cdot A^{-1}$).

Unit 1

2. a. See Modeling task 3 parts c and e, in that order.

b. See Modeling task 3 parts e and c, in that order.

c. Responses may vary. Student preferences may depend on how comfortable the student is with matrices.

3. a. Responses may vary. To solve using the matrix method developed in this lesson, set up a matrix equation and then multiply both sides of the equation on the left by the inverse of the first (coefficient) matrix. The graphical method finds the solution by graphing both lines and finding the point of intersection. One way to solve using equations is to solve each equation for y, set the two resulting expressions in x equal to each other, and solve. Solving by using a table involves making a table for each equation, or one table for both equations, and looking for x values that yield the same y value.

b. Responses may vary. The matrix method is generally the most efficient, but it is a bit mysterious at this point since finding the inverse matrix is done solely by using technology. Compared to solving by using the two equations, the matrix method requires solving only one equation. Compared to the graphical solution, the matrix solution is faster and gives a more accurate answer.

c. Responses may vary. The choice of which method to use depends on how accurate the solution needs to be (graphing the equations and using a table of values may not be exact), the form of the original equation in the system, one's access to technology, and personal preference.

Unit 1

2. Consider Modeling task 3, restated below.

The Fairfield Hobbies and Games store sells two types of ping-pong sets. A Standard Set contains two paddles and one ball, and a Tournament Set contains four paddles and six balls. This information is summarized in the matrix below.

Ping-Pong Sets

	Tourn	Std
Balls	6	1
Paddles	4	2

The store receives a bulk shipment of ping-pong equipment consisting of 100 paddles and 110 balls. The owner wants to know how many of each type of ping-pong set she can make using this equipment. Let s be the number of Standard Sets and t be the number of Tournament Sets.

This situation can be modeled with a matrix equation or a system of two linear equations. Think about the following ways to construct these models, outlined in parts a and b.

a. Proceed in the manner outlined in Modeling task 3; that is, first find the matrix multiplication model that represents this situation. Then multiply the matrices to produce the system of linear equations (see details in Modeling task 3).

b. Now, proceed in the reverse order. Write an equation that shows the relationship among s, t, and the total number of balls. Write another equation that shows the relationship among s, t, and the total number of paddles. Then represent this system of two linear equations with a matrix equation.

c. You get the same matrix equations and linear systems in parts a and b. But in part a, you find the matrix equation first and then use it to get the linear system, while in part b you find the linear system first and then use the system to get the matrix equation. Which sequence for finding these models do you prefer? Why?

3. You have solved systems of linear equations using matrices, graphs, and tables of values. In Organizing task 3 you solved linear systems by reasoning with the symbolic forms themselves.

a. Briefly describe how each method works.

b. Compare the matrix method to each of the others in terms of which was easier to learn and which is easier to use.

c. When solving a system of linear equations, how do you decide which method to use?

4. If you were advising a friend who is about to learn the matrix method for solving systems of linear equations, what would you tell your friend about things to watch out for, easy parts, shortcuts, or other tips?

5. When a linear model is expressed by an equation of the form $y = a + bx$, you can immediately tell what its slope and y-intercept are. As seen in this lesson, sometimes linear models are written in the form $ax + by = c$. Find a way to think about this form so that you can calculate mentally the slope, y-intercept, and x-intercept.

Extending

1. A designer plans to inlay the brick design below into a concrete patio.

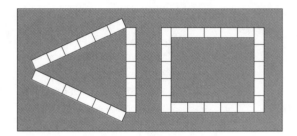

The design must meet the following specifications.

- The figures are bordered by a strip of bricks, one brick wide.
- The perimeter of the rectangle must be 50 bricks.
- The perimeter of the isosceles triangle must be 40 bricks.
- The "inside length" of the long sides of the rectangle are the same length as the long sides of the triangle, and the short sides of the rectangle are the same length as the short side of the triangle.

Find the number of bricks needed for each side of each figure by setting up and solving a system of linear equations.

2. You have seen how to use matrices to solve a system of linear equations in the form $ax + by = c$. This method also will work for systems of linear equations given in the form "$y = \ldots$", but first you have to rewrite the equations into the form $ax + by = c$. Solve the system below by setting up and solving a matrix equation. Verify your answer by solving the system with another method.

$$y = 5.5 + 3x$$
$$y = -11 - 4x$$

4. Responses may vary. Examples may include the following points: Be sure the equations are in the right form, with the variables in the same order, and with the equations neatly arranged on top of each other so the matrix form can be seen readily.

5. If the linear model has the form $ax + by = c$, then the slope is $\frac{-a}{b}$, the y-intercept is $\frac{c}{b}$, and the x-intercept is $\frac{c}{a}$.

Extending

1. Let s represent the number of bricks in the short sides of the rectangle and triangle, and let l represent the number in the long sides. Then the system of equations is

$$2s + 2l = 50$$
$$s + 2l = 40$$

The matrix equation is $\begin{bmatrix} 2 & 2 \\ 1 & 2 \end{bmatrix}\begin{bmatrix} s \\ l \end{bmatrix} = \begin{bmatrix} 50 \\ 40 \end{bmatrix}$. The inverse matrix is $\begin{bmatrix} 1 & -1 \\ -0.5 & 1 \end{bmatrix}$, and so the

solution is given by: $\begin{bmatrix} s \\ l \end{bmatrix} = \begin{bmatrix} 1 & -1 \\ -0.5 & 1 \end{bmatrix}\begin{bmatrix} 50 \\ 40 \end{bmatrix} = \begin{bmatrix} 10 \\ 15 \end{bmatrix}$.

Each short side requires 10 bricks and each long side requires 15 bricks.

2. To solve this system, first find the equivalent linear equations $-3x + y = 5.5$ and $4x + y = -11$. Solving with matrices in the usual way, we have

$$\begin{bmatrix} -3 & 1 \\ 4 & 1 \end{bmatrix}\begin{bmatrix} x \\ y \end{bmatrix} = \begin{bmatrix} 5.5 \\ -11 \end{bmatrix}.$$

$$\begin{bmatrix} x \\ y \end{bmatrix} = \begin{bmatrix} -3 & 1 \\ 4 & 1 \end{bmatrix}^{-1}\begin{bmatrix} 5.5 \\ -11 \end{bmatrix} = \begin{bmatrix} -0.143 & 0.143 \\ 0.571 & 0.429 \end{bmatrix}\begin{bmatrix} 5.5 \\ -11 \end{bmatrix} \approx \begin{bmatrix} -2.36 \\ -1.58 \end{bmatrix}.$$

To verify this answer, set the two values of y equal in the original equations to obtain $5.5 + 3x = -11 - 4x$, so $7x = -16.5$. Thus $x \approx -2.36$ and $y \approx 5.5 + 3x$, or -1.58 as before.

In both solution methods, rounding causes a small failure to satisfy the second equation: $-4(-2.36) - 11 = -1.56$, which is 0.02 less than our value of y.

Unit 1

3. **a.** Amy is substituting the expression for *y*, from the first equation, into the second equation. She then solves that equation by algebraic methods. This gives Amy the value for *x*. She then substitutes *x* back into the first equation and determines the value for *y*.

    b. Yes, this method would work also, as long as she substitutes the expression for *x* into the second equation for *x*.

    c. System on the left: Solve the first equation for *x*, which results in $x = -2y + 2$. Substitute this into the second equation.

    $$5[-2y + 2] - 3y = -29$$
    $$-10y + 10 - 3y = -29$$
    $$-13y = -39$$
    $$y = 3$$
    $$x = -2(3) + 2$$
    $$= -4$$

    So the solution to the system of equations on the left is $x = -4$ and $y = 3$.

    System on the right: Solve the second equation for *y* and get $y = -3x + 3.1$. Substitute this into the first equation.

    $$3x + 5[-3x + 3.1] = 4.7$$
    $$3x - 15x + 15.5 = 4.7$$
    $$-12x = -10.8$$
    $$x = 0.9$$
    $$y = -3(0.9) + 3.1$$
    $$= 0.4$$

    So the solution to this system is $x = 0.9$ and $y = 0.4$.

    d. Rewriting each system in the form $y = a + bx$ and then setting the expressions equal to each other is a special case of the substitution method where one side of the equation is what is being substituted into the other equation for *y*.

4. **a.** The matrix equation is

    $$\begin{bmatrix} 2 & 2 & 8 \\ 10 & 29 & 12 \\ 45 & 120 & 85 \end{bmatrix} \begin{bmatrix} T \\ O \\ M \end{bmatrix} = \begin{bmatrix} 15 \\ 46 \\ 246 \end{bmatrix}$$

    Isabelle must drink approximately 0.93 cups of tomato juice, 0.65 cups of orange juice, and 1.48 cups of skim milk.

Unit 1

3. In Organizing task 3 you solved the system $6x + 4y = 12$ and $5x - 10y = 20$ by rewriting each equation in the form "$y = \ldots$" and then setting the expressions equal to each other. When Amy reflected back on her solution process, she invented a new method. She rewrote only the first equation in the form "$y = \ldots$". She then reasoned as follows.

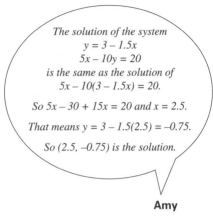

The solution of the system
$$y = 3 - 1.5x$$
$$5x - 10y = 20$$
is the same as the solution of
$$5x - 10(3 - 1.5x) = 20.$$

So $5x - 30 + 15x = 20$ and $x = 2.5$.

That means $y = 3 - 1.5(2.5) = -0.75$.

So $(2.5, -0.75)$ is the solution.

Amy

a. Analyze Amy's reasoning and explain why it works.

b. Could Amy have rewritten the first equation in the form $x = some\ expression$ and then substituted into the second equation? Would this method also work? Why or why not?

c. Solve each of the following systems of linear equations using a *substitution method* similar to Amy's.

$$x + 2y = 2 \qquad\qquad 3x + 5y = 4.7$$
$$5x - 3y = -29 \qquad\qquad 6x + 2y = 6.2$$

d. Think about the symbolic reasoning method for solving a system of linear equations outlined in Organizing task 3. In what sense can that method be thought of as a special case of the substitution method used by Amy?

4. Matrix equations and inverse matrices can be useful for solving systems of more than two "linear" equations.

a. Isabelle is considering a diet that restricts her drinks to skim milk, orange juice, tomato juice, and water. On the following page is a matrix that shows the amount of protein, carbohydrate, and calories per cup for each beverage except water.

Protein, Carbohydrate, and Calories

	TJ	OJ	M
Protein (g)	2	2	8
Carbohydrate (g)	10	29	12
Calories	45	120	85

The diet recommends that Isabelle drink enough milk and juice each day to get a total of 15 grams of protein, 46 grams of carbohydrate, and 246 calories from these sources. She wants to know how much of each beverage she must drink to meet these recommendations exactly. Set up a matrix equation that models this situation. Use multiplication by an inverse matrix to solve this equation. How much milk, orange juice, and tomato juice must Isabelle drink each day?

b. In Organizing task 4 you may have discovered some limitations to using inverse matrices to solve systems of two linear equations. From a geometric perspective, how are two lines related when the corresponding system of equations does not have a solution?

c. Just as with systems of two linear equations, there are limitations to using inverse matrices to solve larger systems. To see why, try thinking graphically. The graph of an equation in the form $ax + by + cz = d$ is a plane in 3-dimensional space. Consider a system of three such equations, such as the one in part a.

■ In what ways can three planes intersect?

■ Suppose you solve a system of three linear equations and you find a single solution: (x, y, z), with specific values of x, y, and z. How would this situation be represented by the graphs of the three linear equations?

d. Try using an inverse matrix to solve the following linear system.

$$x - y + 2z = 1$$
$$2x + y + z = 1$$
$$4x - y + 5z = 5$$

Do these three planes intersect in a single point? (You may wish to use graphing software that can graph the three planes, if available.)

e. Solve the linear system below using matrix methods.

$$-5x + y + 7z + 12w = 8$$
$$-3x + 2y + 7z + 8w = 3$$
$$-2x + 2y + 7z + 10w = 7$$
$$x + 2y + 8z + 13w = 13$$

MORE *continued*

4. **b.** A system of two linear equations does not have a solution when the equations represent parallel lines.

 c. ■ Three planes could intersect in the following ways: not at all (the planes are parallel); two at a time, forming three lines that will not intersect; or all three together, forming a point, a single line, or a plane (if the three planes are identical).

 ■ If by solving you find a single solution (x, y, z), then the planes all must intersect in a single point.

 d. When we try to solve this system by using an inverse matrix, we get an error message: the matrix of coefficients does not have an inverse. This indicates that these planes do not have a unique point as their intersection. (In fact, they intersect two at a time, forming three lines.)

 e. The solution to the linear system is $(0.745, 0.020, -1.118, 1.627)$.

See Assessment Resources pages 13–18.

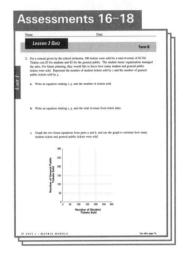

Lesson 4 *Looking Back*

SYNTHESIZE UNIT IDEAS   small-group activity

1. Because the distances ran by the youngest students are shorter than the distances run by the others, care must be taken when working with these matrices. For example, notice that in part d of this activity the distance run by the youngest age group is not the same as those of the others.

    a. Responses will vary. Some possible trends are: Times increase from 1980 to 1989. Older kids run faster (except for the 14–17 year-old girls in 1989). The average time for boys is less than the average time for girls. Any of the trends above are acceptable responses, if explanation is given. One other surprise is that in 1989 the 14–17 year-old girls were slower than the 12–13 year-old girls.

    b.

    $$
    \begin{array}{cc}
    \textbf{1980} & \\
    \begin{array}{cc} \text{B} & \text{G} \end{array} & \\
    \begin{bmatrix} 6.5 & 7.4 \\ 8.4 & 9.8 \\ 7.5 & 9.6 \end{bmatrix}
    \begin{array}{l} \text{10–11 year olds} \\ \text{12–13 year olds} \\ \text{14–17 year olds} \end{array}
    \end{array}
    \qquad
    \begin{array}{cc}
    \textbf{1989} & \\
    \begin{array}{cc} \text{B} & \text{G} \end{array} \\
    \begin{bmatrix} 7.3 & 8.0 \\ 9.1 & 10.5 \\ 8.6 & 10.7 \end{bmatrix}
    \end{array}
    $$

Lesson 4 · Looking Back

The process of mathematical modeling involves constructing a mathematical model to represent a situation, operating on the model, and then interpreting the results of the operations in terms of the situation. In this unit you have used matrix models to represent a wide variety of situations. You have operated on matrices in many different ways to help analyze the situations. You also have extended your understanding of ways in which situations can be modeled with systems of linear equations and with vertex-edge graphs.

The activities in this final lesson of the unit give you an opportunity to pull together the ideas you have developed and to strengthen your skills in modeling with matrices, linear systems, and graphs.

1. The U.S. Department of Education collected data on the physical fitness of American youths in the 1980s. Some of the data, summarized below, show the average time, in minutes, for students 10–11 years old to run three-quarters of a mile and for students 12–17 years old to run one mile.

Boys

	1980	1989	
	6.5	7.3	10–11 year olds
	8.4	9.1	12–13 year olds
	7.5	8.6	14–17 year olds

Girls

	1980	1989	
	7.4	8.0	10–11 year olds
	9.8	10.5	12–13 year olds
	9.6	10.7	14–17 year olds

Source: U.S. Department of Education. *Youth Indicators 1991: Trends in the Well-being of American Youth.* Washington, DC: U.S. Government Printing Office, 1991.

   a. Write down two trends you see in the data. Write down one fact that you find surprising and explain why it surprises you.

   b. The data as given are organized in two matrices titled "Boys" and "Girls". Reorganize the data into two different matrices titled "1980" and "1989". Don't change the row labels.

c. Combine the 1980 matrix and the 1989 matrix, from part b, to construct a single matrix that shows the change in average times from 1980 to 1989.

- What matrix operation did you use to combine the 1980 and 1989 matrices into this new matrix?

- What are the row labels of this new matrix?

d. Think about the average time for three-person relay races, where the first leg is three-quarters of a mile run by 10–11 year olds, the second leg is one mile run by 12–13 year olds, and the third leg is one mile run by 14–17 year olds.

- What do you think would have been the average time for such a relay race in 1989 if all three legs were run by girls?

- What matrix operation did you use to answer this question?

e. Jeremy claimed that in 1980 the 10–11 year-old boys ran faster than the 14–17 year-old boys, since 6.5 is less than 7.5. Do you agree? Explain. If you disagree, describe a method for making a more accurate comparison between the younger and older boys.

2. The vertex-edge graph below shows the direct flights between seven cities for a major airline.

Direct Flights

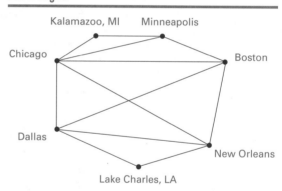

a. Construct the adjacency matrix for the graph. (List the vertices in alphabetical order.)

b. How many cities can be flown to directly from Chicago? What matrix operation can be used to answer this question?

c. What is the fewest number of stopovers needed to fly from Kalamazoo to Lake Charles?

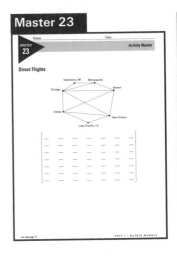

1. **c.** The "change" matrix is found by subtracting the 1980 matrix from the 1989 matrix.

   Change in Times

	B	G
10–11 year olds	0.8	0.6
12–13 year olds	0.7	0.7
14–17 year olds	1.1	1.1

   - ■ Matrix subtraction was used.
   - ■ See the matrix above.

   d. ■ 29.2 minutes
   - ■ Find the column sum of the 1989 girls' column.

   e. Jeremy is incorrect because the distance for the youngest group was less than that for the others. A more accurate comparison could be made by scaling one group; for example, by multiplying the times for the 14–17 year-old boys by 0.75.

2. **See Teaching Master 23.**

   a. You may want to check that everyone lists the vertices in alphabetical order. This will avoid unnecessary confusion as students analyze the problem and compare responses.

   $$
   \begin{array}{c c}
   & \begin{array}{ccccccc} B & C & D & K & LC & M & NO \end{array} \\
   \begin{array}{c} B \\ C \\ D \\ K \\ LC \\ M \\ NO \end{array} &
   \left[\begin{array}{ccccccc}
   0 & 1 & 1 & 0 & 0 & 1 & 1 \\
   1 & 0 & 1 & 1 & 0 & 1 & 1 \\
   1 & 1 & 0 & 0 & 0 & 1 & 0 \\
   0 & 1 & 0 & 0 & 0 & 1 & 0 \\
   0 & 0 & 1 & 0 & 0 & 0 & 1 \\
   1 & 1 & 0 & 1 & 0 & 0 & 0 \\
   1 & 1 & 1 & 0 & 1 & 0 & 0
   \end{array} \right] = A
   \end{array}
   $$

   b. 5; compute the row (or column) sum for Chicago in the matrix.

   c. The minimum number of stopovers needed to fly from Kalamazoo to Lake Charles is 2. The route would be Kalamazoo-Chicago-Dallas (or New Orleans)-Lake Charles.

2. d. ■ Construct $A + A^2$ and look for all nonzero entries. This task is to reinforce the concept of powers of the adjacency matrix yielding information about paths of certain lengths in the corresponding graph.

■ Two cities are connected by a flight with no more than one stopover if the corresponding entry in $A + A^2$ is not a zero.

$$\begin{array}{c} \\ B \\ C \\ D \\ K \\ LC \\ M \\ NO \end{array} \begin{array}{c} \begin{array}{ccccccc} B & C & D & K & LC & M & NO \end{array} \\ \left[\begin{array}{ccccccc} 4 & 4 & 3 & 2 & 2 & 2 & 3 \\ 4 & 5 & 3 & 2 & 2 & 3 & 3 \\ 3 & 3 & 4 & 1 & 2 & 2 & 4 \\ 2 & 2 & 1 & 2 & 0 & 2 & 1 \\ 2 & 2 & 2 & 0 & 2 & 0 & 2 \\ 2 & 3 & 2 & 2 & 0 & 3 & 2 \\ 3 & 3 & 4 & 1 & 2 & 2 & 4 \end{array}\right] \end{array} = A + A^2$$

3. a. Let s be the number of start-up guides completed and r be the number of reference manuals completed.

■ $30s + 45r = 64{,}800$ seconds
$15s + 30r = 36{,}000$ seconds

■ $\begin{bmatrix} 30 & 45 \\ 15 & 30 \end{bmatrix} \begin{bmatrix} s \\ r \end{bmatrix} = \begin{bmatrix} 64{,}800 \\ 36{,}000 \end{bmatrix}$

■ This table is constructed so that the shrink-wrap time used is always 36,000 seconds.

Production Time Requirements

Number of Start-up Guides	Number of Reference Guides	Shrink-wrap Time (sec)	Binding Time (sec)	Over or Under Binding Time
0	1200	36,000	54,000	Under
400	1000	36,000	57,000	Under
800	800	36,000	60,000	Under
1200	600	36,000	63,000	Under
1600	400	36,000	66,000	Over
2000	200	36,000	69,000	Over
2400	0	36,000	72,000	Over

■ Graphs of $r = (64{,}800 - 30s) \div 45$ and $r = (36{,}000 - 15s) \div 30$ are shown at the left, above.

b. 1440 start-up guides and 480 reference manuals will be ready to ship in two days.

c. Look at students' work and verify that they know how to find the solution using any one of the four representations.

d. $\begin{bmatrix} 30 & 45 \\ 15 & 30 \end{bmatrix} \begin{bmatrix} 2000 \\ 800 \end{bmatrix} = \begin{bmatrix} 96{,}000 \\ 54{,}000 \end{bmatrix}$

Making 2000 start-up guides and 800 reference guides will require 96,000 seconds on the binding machine and 54,000 seconds on the shrink-wrap machine. Scalar multiplication can be used to change these times into hours.

$$\frac{1}{3600} \begin{bmatrix} 96{,}000 \\ 54{,}000 \end{bmatrix} = \begin{bmatrix} 26.67 \\ 15 \end{bmatrix}$$

So this job will require $26\frac{2}{3}$ hours to bind and 15 hours to shrink-wrap.

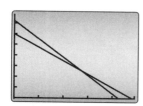

```
WINDOW FORMAT
Xmin =-1
Xmax =2500
Xscl =500
Ymin =-1
Ymax =1500
Yscl =200
```

d. It is tiring and expensive to have more than one stopover, that is, more than two segments, on a flight. Use the adjacency matrix to construct a new matrix that shows which pairs of cities can be connected with a flight of two segments or less.

- What operations did you perform on the adjacency matrix to get the new matrix?

- How can you use the new matrix to identify cities connected by a flight with no more than one stopover?

3. Marcus, the owner of a small software company, is producing two manuals for his new software product. One manual is a brief start-up guide and the other is a larger reference guide.

He contracts to have the manuals bound and shrink-wrapped at a local printer. However, he is on a deadline to ship the manuals in two days, and the machines that do the jobs are only available to him for a limited time. For the next two days, the binding machine is available for a total of 18 hours and the shrink-wrap machine is available for 10 hours. The matrix below shows how many seconds each machine requires for each manual.

Time Required

	Start-up Guide	Reference Guide
Bind	30	45
Shrink-Wrap	15	30

Marcus wants to know how many of each type of manual will be ready to ship in two days, if he uses all the available time on each machine.

a. Represent this situation in four ways:

- using a system of linear equations
- using a matrix equation
- using tables
- using graphs

b. Using one of the representations from part a, determine how many of each type of manual will be ready to ship in two days.

c. Verify your answer using each of the other representations in part a.

d. The next week Marcus receives an unexpectedly large order. He needs 2000 start-up guides and 800 reference guides bound and shrink-wrapped. How many hours will this require on each of the machines? Use matrix multiplication to determine how many hours will be needed on each of the machines.

Checkpoint

a In order for information to be useful, it must be organized.

- Describe how matrices can be used to organize information.
- Can the same information be displayed in a matrix in different ways? Explain.
- What are some advantages of using matrices to organize and display information? What are some disadvantages?

b Sometimes a situation involves two variables that are linked by two or more conditions. These situations often can be modeled by a system of two linear equations of the form $ax + by = c$. Describe at least three different methods for solving such a system of linear equations.

c List all the different operations on matrices that you have investigated in this unit.

d For each operation that you listed in part c:

- Describe how to perform the operation using paper-and-pencil.
- Describe how to perform the operation using your calculator or computer software.
- Give at least one example showing how the operation can be used to help you analyze some situation.

Be prepared to share your descriptions and examples with the entire class.

SHARE AND SUMMARIZE   full-class discussion

Checkpoint

See Teaching Master 24.

You may want to have a different group share their response and thinking for each part. You can assess the extent of agreement of other groups by their responses to a part. You may need to facilitate resolutions of disagreements before proceeding to the next part.

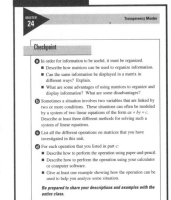

Master 24

ⓐ It is particularly necessary in this information age to have effective ways to organize and analyze information.

- Student explanations could include a discussion of rows and columns, displaying information in a rectangular array, or organizing information related to two variables where the dimensions of one variable are in the rows and the dimensions of a second variable are in the columns (*e.g.*, information about running time depending on gender and age).

- Yes. You might transpose rows and columns (that is, "rotate" the matrix 90°), list the dimensions of a variable in a different order along the rows or columns, or combine matrices *via* some operation.

- Advantages include the following: Matrices are a straightforward, natural modification of tables, usable for data that depend on two variables, and easily stored in a computer. Matrices also can be operated on in a variety of ways, allowing you to analyze the information.

  Disadvantages include the following: Matrices are only usable for two variables and are not as visual as graphs.

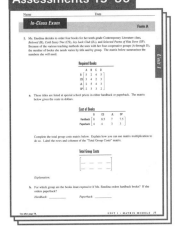

Assessments 19–35

ⓑ Students have several different methods available to them:

  Setting up the matrix equation and multiplying by the inverse matrix

  Graphing the equations and finding the point of intersection

  Rewriting the system using only one variable

  Making tables of values and looking for the solution

ⓒ Possible responses are: row or column sums, multiplying a matrix by a single number, multiplying two matrices using the row-column procedure, multiplying two matrices entry by entry, taking powers of matrices, adding matrices, and subtracting matrices. Students might even list things like finding the mean of a row, the mean absolute deviation of a column, or other variations.

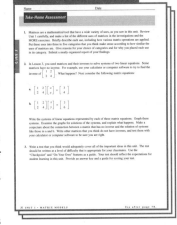

Assessments 36–41

ⓓ Students should be able to explain how to perform each operation by hand and on the calculator. They should be able to find an example, from this unit or another source, of how that operation is used in a particular situation to yield additional information or a deeper analysis.

It is worthwhile to conclude this unit by asking students to think about what it means to make a mathematical model. You might ask students the following questions:

We know that a graph is a mathematical model for a situation. It shows us patterns or trends and we can use it to make predictions. In what way is a matrix a mathematical model? (Students probably will say it lets us organize information.) And what can we use it for? (Students probably will talk about such operations as row sums or addition of matrices. Push them to give an example of how this is useful.)

See additional Teaching Notes on page T78H.

Looking Back, Looking Ahead

▶Reflecting on Mathematical Content

Matrices were encountered briefly in Course 1 in the form of adjacency matrices in the Graph Models chapter. However, the first systematic study of matrices is in this unit. Students will continue to study and apply matrices in future units.

This unit had three major outcomes: (1) Students learned to construct, analyze, operate on, and apply matrices. They learned and applied matrix operations, such as row sums, matrix addition, scalar multiplication, and matrix multiplication. They also studied properties of matrices, including inverses and identities. (2) Students experienced the interconnectedness of mathematics as they explored matrices in the context of different strands of mathematics. For example, they used matrices to organize data (statistics), to solve systems of linear equations (algebra), and to model Markov processes (discrete mathematics and algebra). (3) Students further developed their skill of mathematical modeling. They used matrices to model and solve problems in a variety of real-world settings, including inventory control, social relations, archeology, ecosystems, tournament rankings, political coalitions, genetics, and product promotions.

The study and application of matrices will continue in future chapters. For example, in the next unit, "Patterns of Location, Shape, and Size", students will use matrices to represent polygons and geometric transformations and to produce computer graphics; in Unit 3, "Patterns of Association", students will study correlation matrices and scatterplot matrices; in Unit 5, "Network Optimization", distance matrices will be used to find shortest paths through networks; and in the Capstone, "Forests, the Environment, and Mathematics", students will explore the use of matrices in geographic information systems. Matrices are powerful mathematical models that contribute significantly to students' mathematical power.

▶Reflecting on Instruction

Now that students are in the second course of the *Contemporary Mathematics in Context* curriculum, you probably will find that classes run more smoothly. After a year in Course 1, students should have settled into the classroom climate of cooperative work, individual responsibility, student-centered investigations, writing, explaining, discussing, and thinking! Building on the solid mathematical foundation of Course 1, students in Course 2 will extend their understanding in all four mathematical strands—algebra and functions, geometry and trigonometry, statistics and probability, and discrete mathematics. They will hone their skills of mathematical modeling, problem solving, and reasoning. They also will continue the multiple-representation approach to understanding and applying mathematics, by using verbal descriptions, graphs, tables, and symbols. Teachers who have taught Course 2 of this curriculum indicate that even though the mathematics is advanced, most students are learning the concepts successfully.

Unit 1 Assessment

Teaching Notes continued

Unit 1

Notes continued
from page T5

Group Processing Suggestions

■ How did your group include everyone?

■ How did someone in your group help you or how did you help someone in your group?

JOURNAL ENTRY: Following the discussion of Checkpoint items, students can make individual journal entries. This gives them the opportunity to reflect on the discussion and organize or record their own thoughts. You will find journal suggestions after some Checkpoints in the teacher's notes. The Reflecting tasks in each MORE set also make good entries. Reflecting task 3 from the set following Investigation 3 is appropriate at this time.

APPLY individual task

On Your Own

a. One possible matrix is a 3×2 matrix:

Shoe Sales per Month

	Nike	Reebok
Chicago	250	195
Atlanta	175	175
San Diego	185	275

b. 645 pairs of Reebok

c. San Diego

Notes continued
from page T34

d Thinking about the labels on the rows and columns can help students find the correct matrices to multiply and correctly carry out the multiplication. They should notice that if two matrices can be multiplied, then the labels on the columns of the left matrix must be the same as the labels on the rows of the right matrix. Encourage students to look back at their multiplications if they have not observed this. The row labels on the answer matrix are the same as the row labels of the matrix on the left. The column labels on the answer matrix are the same as the column labels of the matrix on the right.

NOTE: This is the first Math Toolkit entry for Course 2. Students should have retained their Toolkit from Course 1. That Toolkit should contain the important mathematical ideas from the first year of this curriculum.

CONSTRUCTING A MATH TOOLKIT: After the full-class discussion has enabled students to clarify and extend their understandings of matrix multiplication, students should summarize the four outcomes described at the beginning of the Checkpoint notes. They can record their summaries in their Math Toolkits under the discrete mathematics strand. You also may have students provide an example of two matrices A and B, with row and column labels, such that $A \times B$ is possible and makes sense but $B \times A$ is not possible.

Group Processing Suggestions

■ How does your group help someone when they don't understand?

■ We did well on checking for understanding by _____ .

Teaching Notes *continued*

▶ Notes continued
from page T39

9. **a.** The row sums tell you the number of players Keadra beat.

   b. A higher row sum would indicate a higher ranking.

   c. Based on the row sums, there appear to be the following ties: Maria-Catherine, Julia-Keadra, and Emily-Anne.

   d. Rank Keadra above Julia because Keadra beat Julia.

   e. Rank Julia above Keadra because Julia beat Maria, who seems to be the champion. A deeper analysis is needed to decide between Julia and Keadra.

10. **a.** Entries of the squared adjacency matrix tell how many paths of length two there are from one vertex to another. In the context of tournaments, the entries tell how many stage-two wins one player has over another. For example, there is one path of length two from Catherine to Keadra, passing through Emily. Thus, Catherine beat Emily who beat Keadra, and so Catherine has one stage-two victory over Keadra. Another example: Catherine has two stage-two wins over Julia, and so the Catherine-Julia entry of the squared adjacency matrix is 2.

$$\begin{array}{c} \\ \text{Anne} \\ \text{Catherine} \\ \text{Emily} \\ \text{Julia} \\ \text{Keadra} \\ \text{Maria} \end{array} \begin{array}{c} \begin{array}{cccccc} \text{A} & \text{C} & \text{E} & \text{J} & \text{K} & \text{M} \end{array} \\ \left[\begin{array}{cccccc} 0 & 0 & 1 & 0 & 0 & 1 \\ 1 & 0 & 0 & 2 & 1 & 0 \\ 1 & 0 & 0 & 1 & 0 & 0 \\ 1 & 1 & 1 & 0 & 1 & 0 \\ 0 & 0 & 1 & 1 & 0 & 1 \\ 1 & 0 & 1 & 1 & 2 & 0 \end{array} \right] = A^2 \end{array}$$

   b. Keadra had three stage-two wins in the tournament.

   c. ■ The Maria-Catherine tie seems to be resolved because Maria has five stage-two wins while Catherine has only four stage-two wins.

   ■ Students might use A^2 alone to do the ranking, or they might try to factor in the information from A in some way as well. However students do it, there still will be some ties. For example, using A^2 alone there are ties between Emily and Anne and between Catherine and Julia. If they use the information from A to conclude that Catherine should have at least second place, then the tie between Emily and Anne still exists.

▶ Notes continued
from page T41

   f. The arrow from A to B means that A dominates B. The one from B to E indicates that B dominates E. The arrow from E to A means that E dominates A. The puzzling thing about this situation is that since A dominates B, who in turn dominates E, we might expect A to dominate E. But this is not true. This shows that in the case of social relations, direct relations are different from indirect relations. Mathematically this says that social dominance is not transitive.

   > NOTE: You may wish to discuss with students what a matrix or digraph would look like for a group of 4 students who are truly cooperating.

EXPLORE small-group investigation

INVESTIGATION 4 ▶ Properties of Matrices

In this investigation, students begin exploring the abstract properties of matrices and of operations on matrices. Beginning with activity 2, comparisons are made between matrices and real numbers. You may need to review what is meant by the term *real number*.

**Notes continued
from page T54**

2. c. Compute $A + A^2 + A^3 + A^4$. Compute up to the fourth power because 4 is the longest path length in the digraph. Thus, entries in $A + A^2 + A^3 + A^4$ show the number of paths of all possible lengths from one vertex to any other. For each species, look at the non-zero entries in the row corresponding to the species. The species corresponding to the column of the nonzero entry is higher than the species represented by the row.

d. Contamination of the meadow willows will have the most impact on the ecosystem because there is a path of some length from the meadow willow to every other vertex except snails. Thus, all species except snails could become contaminated either directly or indirectly from the meadow willows. You can see this in the matrix $A + A^2 + A^3 + A^4$. This matrix shows existence of any path from one vertex to another, and the meadow-willow row of that matrix has the most nonzero entries (all nonzero except meadow-willow/snail).

e. No, the adjacency matrix A for a digraph that contains circuits will never have a power that is all zeros. This is because by going around the circuit over and over you can get paths of any length. Thus A^n, whose entries give the number of paths of length n, will always have some non-zero entries.

3. Student responses will vary. Students should select situations from their own experiences.

4. a. Since matrices are added just by adding the corresponding entries, it seems reasonable that the same properties will be applicable in matrix addition as for addition of numbers.

b. To multiply two matrices you do not just multiply corresponding entries. Rather, you multiply the entries in one row by corresponding entries in a column and then find the sum of those products. If the order of the matrix multiplication is reversed, it is likely that the resulting matrix multiplication will not give the same result.

**Notes continued
from page T59**

LAUNCH full-class discussion

Think About This Situation

See Teaching Master 18.
   Newly formed teams often are called expansion teams. It is likely some of your students will be able to tell this to the rest of the class, if the question is asked.

a These questions are included in order to engage students in the context. At least some students probably will have been to a sporting event where promotional items were given away. Regardless, students will need to start thinking about the cost of such items and how many may have been given away.

b Factors include: cost of the bags and jackets, budget allocated for the promotion, expected number of fans, and the perceived need to cultivate the good will of fans. (For example, maybe there has been a recent downturn in public opinion or attendance and it is felt that fans need to be courted.)

Teaching Notes *continued*

Notes continued from page T62

SHARE AND SUMMARIZE **full-class discussion**

Checkpoint

See Teaching Master 20.

ⓐ If you have a system of equations

$$ax + by = c$$
$$dx + ey = f$$

then you can represent the system by the matrix equation

$$\begin{bmatrix} a & b \\ d & e \end{bmatrix} \begin{bmatrix} x \\ y \end{bmatrix} = \begin{bmatrix} c \\ f \end{bmatrix}.$$

(If students do not mention it themselves, you may want to point out that this matrix equation is of the general form $AX = C$. You then can ask, "How can you describe the entries of A? of X? of C?")

ⓑ You can solve a matrix equation $AX = C$ by multiplying both sides by A^{-1}. That is, the solution is $X = A^{-1}C$. This works because, analogous to solving simple linear equations, you multiply both sides of the equation by the same thing; in this case, by the inverse of matrix A.

Since the product of a matrix and its inverse is the identity matrix I, on the left side of the equation you simply have the variable matrix X, whose entries are equal to those of the matrix on the right side of the equation. (**Note:** There are, of course, limitations to this method, such as when A does not have an inverse. This is explored in Organizing task 4 following Investigation 2.)

ⓒ ■ To check using the original two equations, substitute the values for the variables into each equation to see if both equations are satisfied.

■ To check using a table as in activity 2, see if the entries yield a cost that is right on, not over or under, the budget amount.

■ To check using the matrix equation, substitute the matrix solution for X and see if the matrix equation is satisfied.

▶Group Processing Suggestions

■ How did your group make sure everyone understood?

■ I really felt good when others in my group _____ .

_____

JOURNAL ENTRY: Discuss the role of the inverse matrix in solving a system of linear equations.

_____

Notes continued from page T65

SHARE AND SUMMARIZE full-class discussion

Checkpoint

See Teaching Master 22.

ⓐ Solving a system means finding values for x and y that satisfy both equations.

ⓑ The values of x and y that are the solution will be the coordinates of the point of intersection of the two lines.

ⓒ To graph these equations with a graphing calculator or some computer software, you first need to convert the equations into the form "$y = \ldots$". Then they can be entered into the functions list and graphed. To graph them without technology, you need to make a table, plot some points, and then draw the lines.

ⓓ **Graphical method:** Advantages are it's visual, so you can see what's happening, and it's quick, once you get the equations into the functions list. Disadvantages are it can be slow and algebraically complicated, if the equations are not in the form "$y = \ldots$"; you generally only get an approximate answer.

Matrix method: Advantages are it's quick and exact (and very slick). Disadvantages are it's more abstract; you can't easily see what the entries of the inverse matrix should be; it's not so easy if the equations are not in the form $ax + by = c$; and it may not work in all cases (see Organizing task 4, page 70).

Table method: Advantages are by comparing the y values, you can get a good numerical sense for where they are equal. Disadvantages are it's not exact and can be time consuming.

A good follow-up to part d is to ask students what clues they would use to decide which method to use to solve a system of linear equations.

▶Group Processing Suggestions

- What actions helped the group work productively?
- What actions could be added to make the group even more productive next time?
- I contributed to my group today by _____ .

Teaching Notes *continued*

Notes continued from page T78

The kinds of problems students solved in this unit were connected in some ways to problems students had solved before, and to mathematical models they had used before. In other ways the situations modeled and the methods were quite different. One way to stimulate further discussion follows.

In Course 1 you used statistical graphs as models, algebraic equations showing a relationship between two variables (often x and y), vertex-edge graphs to show circuits, and geometric shapes as models. What connections can you observe among these models you have already seen and this new model? (Students probably will point out that algebraic equations were solved graphically and using matrices, and perhaps that the ecological contamination problem was modeled with a vertex-edge graph as well as with a matrix.) What advantages did the matrix model have? (In the contamination problem, square matrices made indirect contamination clear. Students also may say that they prefer the use of matrices over graphical methods to solve a system of equations, since it involves little or no algebraic manipulation.)

See Assessment Resources pages 19–41.

Unit 2 ▶ Patterns of Location, Shape, and Size

UNIT OVERVIEW This unit focuses on coordinate geometry. Just as Rene Descartes' (1596–1650) work in coordinate geometry permitted both algebra and geometry to move forward, the introduction of coordinate geometry in Course 2 of the *Contemporary Mathematics in Context* curriculum advances the algebra and geometry concepts begun in Course 1. The representations of shapes in the plane and of transformations in the plane now are explored systematically using coordinate geometry. Coordinate models also lead to a simple, yet powerful, base for computer animations. In the case of algebra, coordinate geometry permits a closer look at linear models and their properties. Systems of linear equations are revisited from an algebraic point of view, and the geometry of systems of linear equations is studied, leading to the linear combination method of solving systems. The use of matrices as a representation tool is extended to describing shapes and transformations, thereby underscoring the connectedness of strands within the curriculum and the utility of matrices as a connector.

Unit 2 Objectives

- To use coordinates to model points, lines, and geometric shapes in the plane and to analyze the properties of lines and shapes
- To write systems of linear equations that model real-life situations, to solve systems using linear combinations, and to explain the geometry behind this method
- To use coordinate geometry and programming techniques as a tool to implement computational algorithms, model transformations, and investigate the properties of shapes that are preserved under transformations
- To build and use matrix representations to model polygons, transformations, and computer animations

Patterns of Location, Shape, and Size

79

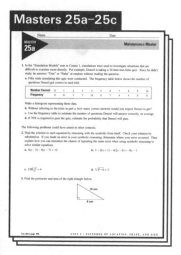

The Importance of Coordinate Systems

To motivate an appreciation for the topics in this unit, it will be helpful for students to reflect briefly on the importance of coordinate systems in our world, particularly for computer graphics. One possibility is to ask students to cite an example of a coordinate system, then briefly discuss the enormous variety of ways in which we use coordinates to locate points in everyday life. For example, on a trip in which a student flies from his or her home to Washington, D.C., how many times might the student encounter a coordinate system? The home might be located by a coordinate, (*house number, street name*); the airport might be located on a map by coordinates; the student might need to remember a parking place at the airport with a coordinate (*area, row*); the student might find the departure gate by a coordinate (*concourse, gate*) and his or her seat on the airplane by a coordinate (*row, seat*); and so on.

Once you have discussed the broad applications of coordinate systems, focus attention on computer graphics as an important application that depends on the use of a coordinate system. Software packages that allow us to draw and to manipulate lines and shapes also use coordinate systems. To generate enthusiasm about geometric transformations, you may wish to demonstrate the calculator program GEOXPLOR on the overhead and ask students to react to its capabilities: What are some of the features displayed in this program? Following the calculator demonstration, you also may ask if students have seen computer software packages that have similar capabilities. Regardless of the environment, these features and many others can be implemented using coordinates to describe points, lines, and shapes. Let students know that in this unit they will learn how to use a coordinate system to recreate several of the software features just demonstrated, and they will explore the application of coordinates to quadrilaterals.

> NOTE: When demonstrating the GEOXPLOR program, it may be helpful to select "COORDINATES ON" and "INTEGER" during program execution. Also, creating a relatively simple figure such as a right triangle or a rectangle will make it easier to focus classroom discussion on the coordinate geometry aspects of the demonstration.

See Masters 25a–25c for Maintenance tasks that students can work after Lesson 1.

Planning Guide

Lesson Objectives	MORE Assignments	Suggested Pacing	Materials
Lesson 1 *A Coordinate Model of a Plane* • To use coordinates to model points, lines, and geometric shapes in the plane and to analyze the properties of lines and shapes • To use coordinate representations of geometric ideas, such as distance, slope, and midpoint, to design planning algorithms for programs that perform routine geometry-related computations • To investigate the geometry of a system of two linear equations and any linear combination of the equations, in order to understand and to be able to use the method of linear combinations to solve systems of equations	**after page 87** Students can begin Modeling Task 6; Organizing Tasks 1–3; Reflecting Task 1 or 4; or Extending Task 1 or 2 from p. 90. **page 90** **Modeling:** 1, 5 and 6 **Organizing:** 2, 5, and choice of one* **Reflecting:** 1 and 4 **Extending:** Choose one* **page 102** **Modeling:** 3 and choice of one* **Organizing:** 1 and 2 **Reflecting:** 2 and 3 **Extending:** Choose one*	8 days	• Graph paper • Transformation geometry software (GEOXPLOR) • Teaching Resources 26–37 • Assessment Resources 42–47
Lesson 2 *Coordinate Models of Transformations* • To use coordinate geometry and planning algorithms as a tool to model translations, line reflections, and rotations and size transformations centered at the origin • To use coordinate geometry to investigate properties of shapes under the given transformations, individually and in combinations • To explore the concept of function composition using successive transformations	See assignment note on page T110. **after page 116** Students can begin Modeling Task 2; Organizing Task 4; or Extending Task 3 or 4 from p. 125 **page 120** **Modeling:** 1 and choice of 2, 3, or 4* **Organizing:** 2, 5, and choice of 1 or 4* **Reflecting:** 3 **Extending:** Choose one* **after page 130** Students could begin Organizing Task 3 or 4; Reflecting Task 2; or Extending Task 1, 2, 4, or 5 from p. 137. **page 133** **Modeling:** 1 or 2 and 4* **Organizing:** 1, 3, or 4* **Reflecting:** 2 **Extending:** 3 and choice of one* **after page 141** Students can begin Modeling Tasks 1–4; Reflecting Task 3 or 4; or Extending Task 1 from p. 147. **page 144** **Modeling:** 1 and choice of one* **Organizing:** 2 and 3 **Reflecting:** Choose one* **Extending:** 1	12 days	• Graph paper • Transformation geometry software (GEOXPLOR) • Teaching Resources 25a–25c, 38–49 • Assessment Resources 48–53
Lesson 3 *Transformations, Matrices, and Animation* • To use the coordinate rules for rotations about the origin to get the corresponding matrix representations • To use the coordinate rule for a size transformation centered at the origin to get the corresponding matrix representation • To use the matrix representations to write planning algorithms for animations involving rotations and size transformations	**after page 154** Students can begin Modeling Tasks 1–3; Organizing Tasks 1–3; or Extending Task 2, 4, or 6 from pp. 163,164. **page 157** **Modeling:** 2 and choice of one* **Organizing:** 3 and choice of one* **Reflecting:** Choose one* **Extending:** Choose one*	6 days	• Transformation geometry software (GEOXPLOR) • Teaching Resources 50–53 • Assessment Resources 54–57
Lesson 4 *Looking Back* • To review the major objectives of the unit		4 days (includes testing)	• Transformation geometry software (GEOXPLOR) • Teaching Resource 54 • Assessment Resources 58–75

* When choice is indicated, it is important to leave the choice to the student.
Note: *It is best if Organizing tasks are discussed as a whole class after they have been assigned as homework.*

Lesson 1

A Coordinate Model of a Plane

Computer-generated graphics influences your world almost daily. It has become an important feature of the computer/human interface. Computer graphics is the key element of video games and animated and special-effects films. Computer graphics is now a commonly-used tool in the design of automobiles and buildings. And of course, computer or calculator graphics has been an important tool in your study of mathematics. It has helped you produce, trace, and analyze graphs of data and functions.

In this unit, you will explore some of the mathematics behind computer graphics as it relates to geometric shapes.

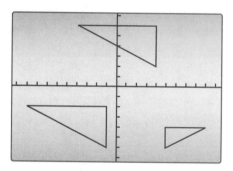

Think About This Situation

Examine the calculator graphics display above.

a How do you think such graphics displays are produced?

b How could you describe the locations of the three triangles?

c Describe how you could transform the *leftmost* triangle so that it will coincide with the *upper* triangle.

d Describe how you might transform the *rightmost* triangle so that it will coincide with the *leftmost* triangle.

Lesson 1 A Coordinate Model of a Plane

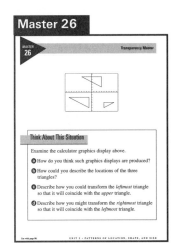

LESSON OVERVIEW Lesson 1 focuses students' thoughts on uses of coordinates to model two-dimensional space. Applications of coordinate models are investigated; in particular students discover how to compute distances, slopes, and midpoints as well as how to use those calculations for identifying quadrilaterals.

During Investigation 1, students will develop formulas to find the distance between two points and the midpoint of a line segment. They will review slope and its computation. They will explore writing algorithms that can be used to guide development of a calculator or computer program. In the process, the Pythagorean Theorem is reviewed.

In Investigation 2, students will use the tools developed in Investigation 1 to further review the slope of a line and to discover the relationship between the slopes of perpendicular lines. Students will use distance between two points, the midpoint of a line segment, and the slope of a line to explore the characteristics of various quadrilaterals. In the process, students are introduced to a matrix representation for polygons.

In the third investigation of this lesson, students should observe that the graphs of the sums of any multiples of two linear equations contain the same point of intersection. Students then develop the algebraic technique of linear combinations to determine the coordinates of that point.

In this lesson, planning algorithms are introduced. They are simply a sequence of steps that would need to be performed in order for a computer or calculator to do a task. Students are asked periodically to write such algorithms as new ideas arise. These algorithms may be translated into calculator programs by using the built-in commands on a programmable calculator. Many students enjoy programming and should be given the opportunity to do so. Some Extending tasks ask for calculator programs corresponding to the various planning algorithms. If students are using programmable calculators with computer links, a display capture (or "screen dump") is one way to obtain a quick copy for their Math Toolkits. Some students may wish to make a special section in their ring binders for programming notes.

Lesson Objectives

- To use coordinates to model points, lines, and geometric shapes in the plane and to analyze the properties of lines and shapes
- To use coordinate representations of geometric ideas, such as distance, slope, and midpoint, to design planning algorithms for programs that perform routine geometry-related computations
- To investigate the geometry of a system of two linear equations and any linear combination of the equations, in order to understand and to be able to use the method of linear combinations to solve systems of equations

See additional Teaching Notes on page T168C.

INVESTIGATION 1 ▸ Plotting Polygons and Computing Distances

Activities 1 and 2 are intended to familiarize students with the geometry software (references are to the calculator software GEOXPLOR) and to have them consider how coordinates are used to get slope and distance. It may be appropriate to demonstrate the software on the overhead projector before students begin to investigate more completely how it works. Notice that activity 1 part c asks students to compute slope using two points. As you circulate among groups, be sure that students are calculating the slope of the diagonals correctly. Part d gives students an opportunity to check their own work.

1. As you listen to groups discuss the way the program works and how to decide if a shape is a square or a rectangle, push them to be as specific as possible about the characteristics they are using as identifiers. If they do not mention lengths of sides, slopes, or perpendicular sides, you may want to mention those characteristics yourself, but you also may choose to postpone this review since it is dealt with more specifically in Investigation 2.

    a. Responses will vary. Most students probably will draw rectangles with sides that are parallel to the axes. One such rectangle has its vertices at (5, 5), (5, 15), (30, 15), and (30, 5). Notice that the opposite sides are equal in length. Also adjacent sides are perpendicular since they are horizontal and vertical line segments. Thus the figure is a rectangle.

    b. Responses will vary. One square has its vertices at (0, 0), (10, 0), (10, 10), and (0, 10). In general the coordinates will have the form (0, 0), $(a, 0)$, (a, a), and $(0, a)$ where a is positive. This is a square since all sides have length a and adjacent sides are clearly perpendicular.

    c. Responses will vary. If students orient the rectangle either horizontally or vertically then the slopes of the lines containing the sides will be zero and undefined. The slopes of the lines containing the diagonals depend on the lengths of the sides of the rectangle. For the square, the slopes of the lines containing the sides will be zero and undefined, and the slopes of the lines containing the diagonals will be 1 and –1.

INVESTIGATION 1 Plotting Polygons and Computing Distances

Graphics calculators are named as they are because, among other capabilities, they can display "pictures" or "graphics". These graphics are composed of a set of lighted *pixels* (screen points) whose coordinates satisfy specified conditions. Useful geometry drawing programs have been developed for computers and for some graphics calculators. These programs produce shapes by using algorithms based on a mathematical model of the displayed object. In this investigation, instructions are given for a program called GEOXPLOR. Other software may work differently.

1. First, use your calculator or computer software to draw a rectangle. If you wish to do this with the program GEOXPLOR, you should see a series of beginning screens like those below. Choose "DRAW" from the main menu. Then Choose the "INTEGER" scale and enter vertices "FROM SCREEN".

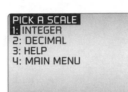 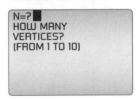

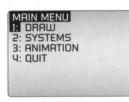 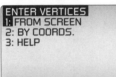

a. Select four vertices so that the figure displayed is a rectangle. Record the coordinates of the vertices in the order in which you selected them. Discuss how you know that the displayed figure is, in fact, a rectangle.

b. Next, draw a square that has one side on the positive *x*-axis and one side on the positive *y*-axis. Record the vertices. Explain how you know the displayed figure is a square.

c. Working in pairs, choose the rectangle or the square. (Each pair should choose a different figure.) Then use the coordinates of the vertices of the chosen quadrilateral to calculate the slopes of the lines containing each side and the diagonals. Compare your findings. Make notes of any interesting observations.

d. Now use the program to calculate the slope. Choose the "CALCULATE" option in the main menu and then choose "SLOPE". Use the software to calculate the slopes of the same lines from part c. Compare the results to those in part c. Explain any differences.

e. Use the software to compute the lengths of each pair of opposite sides and of the diagonals of your quadrilateral.

2. Think about how the software GEOXPLOR might perform the calculations in activity 1.

   a. Explain how the program could use the coordinates of two points to calculate the slope of the line through those points.

   b. As a group, try to determine how the program could calculate the length of a segment by using the coordinates of the endpoints.

   c. Test your conjecture from part b on these pairs of points: (−1, 3) and (2, −1); (−8, −11) and (5, −3). You should get 5 and 15.264 (to 3 decimal places). If your group did not get these results, check to be sure you did not make a computational error. If your arithmetic is correct but you still did not get these answers, don't worry: activities 3 and 4 will help you discover how to calculate distances in a *coordinate plane*.

3. Examine the coordinate grid below.

   a. The line that goes through the points (1, 3) and (5, 3) is a horizontal line. What is the distance between these points? How did you find it?

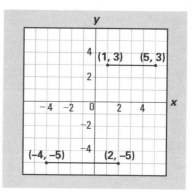

   b. The points (−4, −5) and (2, −5) are on the same horizontal line. What is the distance between these points? How did you find it? How can the coordinates of the points be used to determine this distance?

   c. Suppose two points have coordinates (*a*, *b*) and (*c*, *b*) with $a < c$.

     ■ Explain how you know that the points (*a*, *b*) and (*c*, *b*) are on the same horizontal line.

     ■ Write an expression for the distance between the points.

     ■ How would you modify your distance expression if $a > c$?

1. **d.** Responses will vary.

   e. Responses will vary depending on the students' figures.

2. In this activity students are challenged to determine a way coordinates are used to calculate distance (length). Encourage groups to draw pictures and seek ways that coordinates can help. It is not expected that all groups discover the Euclidean distance formula, $d = \sqrt{(x_1 - x_2)^2 + (y_1 - y_2)^2}$. Unique ways may be shared with the entire class. Groups that find the distance between specific points may need encouragment to generalize.

   a. The software could compute the change in the *y*-coordinates, Δy, and the change in the *x*-coordinates, Δx. Then it would need to find the quotient $\frac{\Delta y}{\Delta x}$.

   b. Responses will vary. See the note at the beginning of this activity.

   c. Students who found (or already know) the distance formula or otherwise can calculate the correct lengths for the given segments should be allowed to skip activities 3 and 4.

3. **a.** Because the *y*-coordinates do not change, the distance between (1, 3) and (5, 3) is the same as the distance between 1 and 5 on the number line, namely 4.

   b. By the same reasoning, the distance is 6. Students could subtract the *x*-coordinates and find the absolute value of the answer.

   c. ■ Any two points with the same *y*-coordinate are on a horizontal line.
   ■ Acceptable expressions include $c - a$, $|a - c|$, or $|c - a|$.
   ■ If students use an absolute value expression, then no modification is necessary; otherwise the expression should be $a - c$.

3. d. ■ All points lying on the same vertical line have the same *x*-coordinate.

 ■ Any point lying on the same vertical line as (*a, b*) will have coordinates (*a, y*) for some number *y*.

 ■ The distance between (*a, b*) and (*a, y*) is $|b - y|$.

4. Students may need to be asked to recall the distinction between a line, which extends infinitely, and a segment, which is bounded (has finite length). Most students will have studied these terms in earlier years.

a. Since neither the *x*- nor the *y*-coordinates of the two points are identical, the line through both points is neither vertical nor horizontal.

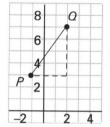

b. ■ Vertically, *P* is 4 units from *Q*.

 ■ Horizontally, *P* is 3 units from *Q*.

 ■ A right triangle is formed.

 ■ The coordinates for the third vertex are (2, 3).

c. Students' procedures should be described clearly and correctly. For example: The distance between *P* and *Q* is the length of the segment *PQ*. This may be determined by using the Pythagorean Theorem to compute the hypotenuse of the newly formed triangle. Let the third vertex in the above triangle be *C*.

$$(PQ)^2 = (PC)^2 + (QC)^2$$
$$= 3^2 + 4^2$$
$$= 25$$

so *PQ* = 5.

That is, *P* and *Q* are 5 units apart.

d. $ST = \sqrt{(-5 - 3)^2 + [4 - (-2)]^2}$
$= \sqrt{64 + 36}$
$= \sqrt{100}$
$= 10$

S and *T* are 10 units apart.

e. 15.264

NOTE: As groups complete activity 4, you might ask each group (or the whole class) to state in their own words the *strategy* for finding the distance between two points. This description helps students make the transition to writing the instructions with general coordinates. It is not necessary for them to *write* such a description until Checkpoint part b.

---

5. This activity is intended to reinforce the use of the Pythagorean Theorem.

a. Check to be sure that students are able to find the coordinates for the third vertex (*a, d*) of the triangle.

b. Horizontal distance: $|a - c|$ or $|c - a|$ (or *a* − *c*, since we know that *a* > *c*)

 Vertical distance: $|b - d|$ or $|d - b|$ (or *b* − *d*, since we know that *b* > *d*)

c. The length of *RS* is precisely the length of the hypotenuse of the right triangle the student just created. The Pythagorean Theorem often is used for computing such lengths.

$$(RS)^2 = (|a - c|)^2 + (|b - d|)^2$$
$$(RS)^2 = (a - c)^2 + (b - d)^2$$
$$RS = \sqrt{(a - c)^2 + (b - d)^2}$$

d. Experiment with finding distances between pairs of points on vertical lines.

- What is true of the coordinates of all points that are on the same vertical line?

- Using variables, write coordinates for a point on the same vertical line as the point with coordinates (a, b).

- Write an expression for the distance between the points.

4. a. Explain how you know that the line that goes through the points $P(-1, 3)$ and $Q(2, 7)$ is neither a horizontal nor a vertical line. Make a sketch on graph paper showing points P and Q, and segment PQ.

b. ■ Draw a vertical segment that extends down from point Q. The other endpoint should be on the same horizontal line as point P. What is the *vertical distance* between P and Q?

- Draw a horizontal segment to the right from point P. The other endpoint should be on the same vertical line as point Q. What is the *horizontal distance* between P and Q?

- What type of triangle is formed?

- Write the coordinates of the third vertex of the triangle.

c. Find the distance between points P and Q. Compare your procedure with that of other groups.

d. Find the distance between points $S(-5, 4)$ and $T(3, -2)$.

e. Now try again to find the distance between the pair of points $(-8, -11)$ and $(5, -3)$ in part c of activity 2.

5. Points $R(a, b)$ and $S(c, d)$ are graphed below.

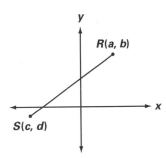

a. Complete a copy of the diagram to show the horizontal and vertical distances between the points.

b. Find expressions for the horizontal and vertical distances.

c. Recall the Pythagorean Theorem, which was introduced in Course 1. How could the Pythagorean Theorem be used to find an expression for the distance between points R and S?

Checkpoint

a Write a formula for calculating the distance, D, between any two points $P(x_1, y_1)$ and $Q(x_2, y_2)$.

$$D = \underline{\hspace{3cm}}$$

b Explain in words how this formula determines the distance.

Be prepared to explain your formula and why it works to the entire class.

▶ On Your Own

Use graph paper to plot each pair of points below. Draw a line segment between them, then use your formula to compute the distance between the points in each pair. Which segment is the longest? The shortest?

a. (3, –2) and (5, –1)   **b.** (2, –1) and (–4, 3)

c. (–1, –3) and (4, 1)   **d.** (0.5, 2.1) and (4, 2.1)

```
CALCULATE
1: SLOPE
2: LENGTH
3: LAST MENU
```

The calculator program GEOXPLOR uses a formula equivalent to yours to calculate distance between two points. In order to calculate distance (or slope) the calculator needs information or *input* (in this case, coordinates of two points); instructions for *processing* the information (in this case, a formula); and then instructions on what to do with the results or *output* (in this case, it displays the distance or slope). Specifying such instructions is called **programming** the calculator. Before writing a program, it is helpful to prepare a **program planning algorithm**. The planning algorithm lists the major sequence of steps needed to accomplish the task. The *Distance Algorithm* below illustrates a planning algorithm that could be used to guide program writing for any calculator or computer.

Distance Algorithm

Step 1: Get the coordinates of one point.
Step 2: Get the coordinates of the other point.   } input

Step 3: Use the coordinates and the distance formula to compute the desired distance.   } processing

Step 4: Display and label the distance.   } output

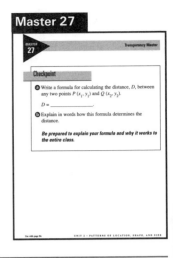

Checkpoint

See Teaching Master 27.

While a correctly-stated formula for the distance between two points is important, students also should understand how the formula was developed and how it is used. Putting into their own words that the process starts with the known coordinates, and uses sensible arithmetic operations to calculate lengths, greatly aids understanding and remembering the process. In addition to checking that students do understand, you might want to discuss ways in which computation errors using the distance formula may occur, such as errors with $+/-$ signs.

ⓐ $D = \sqrt{(a-c)^2 + (b-d)^2}$

ⓑ The formula gives the distance because $|a - c|$ and $|b - d|$ are the legs of a right triangle and D is the hypotenuse.

NOTE: If students do not raise the issue of whether they should use $a - c$ or $c - a$, and whether the order of subtracting for both the x- and y-coordinates must be consistent, you may wish to bring it up yourself. (Of course, because the quantities are squared, the order doesn't matter. However, students should be aware that order of subtraction usually does matter, and they must be careful in general.)

CONSTRUCTING A MATH TOOLKIT: Following a discussion of the Checkpoint items, ask students to enter the distance formula and a summary of its development in their math toolkits.

Unit 2

APPLY individual task

▶On Your Own

The length of each segment is given to the nearest hundredth.
a. 2.24   **b.** 7.21
c. 6.40   **d.** 3.5

EXPLORE small-group investigation

As a launch for the remainder of the investigation, you could sketch 4 or 5 points on coordinate axes on the chalkboard, and ask students what they can currently tell about these points and related points. One suggestion is to ask, "What else might you want to do with these points?" Students may suggest finding what different shapes can be created by joining the points in different orders, or finding where lines that join the points will intersect. The point of the discussion is to get students into the habit of being active in posing the next question, rather than waiting for a question to be asked of them. Even if no one suggests finding a midpoint, you may tell them that finding the coordinates of the midpoint of a segment and writing planning algorithms to do so are the focus of the remainder of the investigation.

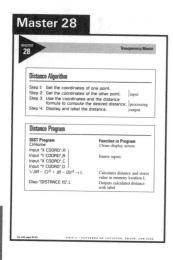

EXPLORE *continued*

See Teaching Master 28.

6. A full-class discussion of the Distance Algorithm and DIST program may be valuable and help understanding. The best way to approach the Distance Algorithm is probably from a common-sense point of view; *i.e.*, if you wanted to calculate the distance between two points, what information would you need? (The coordinates and a computational procedure.) Which do you need first? (The coordinates, since the formula is of no use without them.) Then ask the groups to speculate on the program itself.

    You may want to talk about the "store" command included in line 6 of the DIST program. The value of the radical is stored in variable L. Students need to realize that each variable holds only one value, so the old value is lost when a new value is stored.

    You also may want to ask your students how each line of the program relates to the verbal description of their strategy for finding a distance. (See activity 5.) Learning to program is not the focus of this lesson, but some students may enjoy entering programs for slope and distance into their calculators. You may wish to assign some practice finding the distance between two points, with and without GEOXPLOR.

    a. The program has the fundamental parts of the Distance Algorithm in the same order.

    b. The points have coordinates (A, B) and (C, D).

    c. The processing portion uses the coordinates of the points and substitutes them into the distance formula. The distance is then stored in L.

    d. Replace the present processing portion (line 6 in the DIST program) with
    $$(B - D)/(A - C) \to L.$$

    e. Step 1: Get the coordinates of one point.
        Step 2: Get the coordinates of the other point.
        Step 3: Use the coordinates and the slope formula to calculate the slope of the segment. (If A = C this will not work.)
        Step 4: Display and label the slope.

7. As you listen to groups discuss their conjectures for finding a midpoint from given endpoints, you may want to ask them why their strategy makes sense geometrically. (Students may say they need to find coordinates of a point that is further than one endpoint from the origin, but not so far as the other endpoint; an average makes sense.) The focus is on making sense of the algorithm for finding a midpoint and being able to do simple examples by hand.

    a. Students' estimates may vary but should be close to the actual midpoint coordinates.

Point 1	Point 2	Midpoint
(−3, 2)	(1, 2)	(−1, 2)
(−4, 1)	(−2, 1)	(−3, 1)
(3, 3)	(3, −2)	(3, 0.5)
(1, −3)	(1, 2)	(1, −0.5)
(3, 2)	(1, 1)	(2, 1.5)
(−3, −1)	(2, 3)	(−0.5, 1)
(4, −2)	(−3, 3)	(0.5, 0.5)

    b. Measure the distances from each endpoint to the estimated midpoint. The two distances should be equal. Alternatively, measure the distance between the endpoints and halve it. The half should be the length of the segment from either endpoint to the midpoint.

    c. GEOXPLOR will not calculate midpoints. To check their estimates, students must input the midpoint estimate and either point 1 or point 2. The result of calculating the length of this segment should be half the distance from point 1 to point 2.

For one graphics calculator, the Distance Algorithm was used for the following program, which computes distance between two points. The left-hand column is the program; the right-hand column describes the function of the commands.

DIST Program

Program	Function in Program
ClrHome	Clears display screen
Input "X COORD",A	
Input "Y COORD",B	Enters inputs
Input "X COORD",C	
Input "Y COORD",D	
$\sqrt{((A-C)^2 + (B-D)^2)} \rightarrow L$	Calculates distance and stores value in memory location L
Disp "DISTANCE IS",L	Outputs calculated distance with label

6. Analyze the DIST program.

   a. Describe how this program uses the distance algorithm.

   b. What does the program call the coordinates of the two points?

   c. Explain why the processing portion actually calculates the distance.

   d. How would you change the processing portion so that this program computes the slope of the line containing the two points, rather than the distance between them?

   e. Write a Slope Algorithm similar to the Distance Algorithm. Compare your algorithm to that of other groups.

You now have a formula for calculating the slope of a line and a formula for calculating the distance between two points. Thus, you can compute the length and slope of a segment in the coordinate plane. Coordinates also can be used by a graphics program to find the *midpoint* of a segment.

7. In the table on the next page, pairs of points are given which determine two horizontal line segments, two vertical line segments, and three *oblique* (neither horizontal nor vertical) line segments.

   a. The point on a segment that is the same distance from each endpoint is called the **midpoint**. Use graph paper to estimate the coordinates of the midpoint for each segment.

   b. Explain how a ruler could be used to check your estimates.

   c. Use software such as the program GEOXPLOR to check your estimates. Correct any inaccurate estimates. Divide the workload among members of your group.

Point 1	Point 2	Midpoint Estimate with Graph Paper
(−3, 2)	(1, 2)	
(−4, 1)	(−2, 1)	
(3, 3)	(3, −2)	
(1, −3)	(1, 2)	
(3, 2)	(1, 1)	
(−3, −1)	(2, 3)	
(4, −2)	(−3, 3)	

d. Using the data in the table, search for a pattern that would allow you to predict the coordinates of the midpoints. Test your conjecture about midpoint coordinates with the following pairs: (−800, 41) and (−23, 700); (1.3, 2.1) and (−2.4, 3.8). You should get (−411.5, 370.5) and (−0.55, 2.95). Did you?

e. Find an expression for the coordinates of the midpoint of a segment with endpoints (a, b) and (c, d).

f. Find the midpoint of each segment in the "On Your Own" on page 84.

8. a. Write a Midpoint Algorithm that could be used by a calculator programmer to calculate and display the coordinates of the midpoint of a segment.

b. How much information would you need to input?

c. How will the processing portion of your algorithm differ from the algorithms you used to calculate distance and slope?

d. What formula or formulas will be used in the processing portion?

Checkpoint

a Suppose $P(x_1, y_1)$ and $Q(x_2, y_2)$ are two points. Write a formula for the midpoint of segment PQ. Explain why this formula makes sense.

b Describe the importance of the input, processing, and output parts of the algorithms developed in this investigation.

c Describe an algorithm that could be used to write a program that would draw a segment on a graphics screen.

Be prepared to explain your formula, algorithm, and thinking to the class.

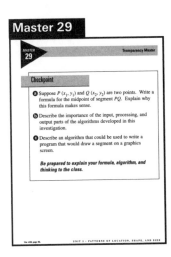

7. d. Students should discover that the *x*-coordinate (*y*-coordinate) of the midpoint is the mean of the *x*-coordinates (*y*-coordinates) of the endpoints.

e. The midpoint of the segment with endpoints (a, b) and (c, d) is $(\frac{a+c}{2}, \frac{b+d}{2})$.

f. The midpoints for parts a–d are $(4, -1.5)$, $(-1, 1)$, $(1.5, -1)$, and $(2.25, 2.1)$, respectively.

8. a. Step 1: Get the coordinates of one point.
Step 2: Get the coordinates of the other point.
Step 3: Calculate the *x*-coordinate of the midpoint.
Step 4: Calculate the *y*-coordinate of the midpoint.
Step 5: Display and label the coordinates of the midpoint.

b. The coordinates of the two endpoints must be input.

c. The processing portion results in two values that are reported rather than one. Also, addition of coordinates is used rather than subtraction.

d. $\frac{A+C}{2}$ and $\frac{B+D}{2}$ are the formulas that will need to be used in the processing portion.

SHARE AND SUMMARIZE full-class discussion

Checkpoint

See Teaching Master 29.

ⓐ The midpoint of segment *PQ* has coordinates $(\frac{x_1+x_2}{2}, \frac{y_1+y_2}{2})$. It makes sense because it is the average of the appropriate coordinates and the average lies exactly midway between the two numbers averaged.

ⓑ The input part is needed because the program needs to get the information to manipulate. The processing part is important because it is here that the new information is produced. The output part is needed in order to communicate the results of the processing that occurred.

ⓒ Step 1: Input the coordinates of two points.
Step 2: Draw the segment joining the points.
Step 3: Display the result of the drawing.

CONSTRUCTING A MATH TOOLKIT: Students should record the formula for the midpoint of a segment in their math toolkits.

▶**On Your Own**

a.

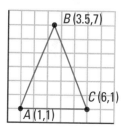

$$AB = \sqrt{(3.5 - 1)^2 + (7 - 1)^2}$$
$$= \sqrt{42.25}$$
$$= 6.5$$
$$BC = \sqrt{(6 - 3.5)^2 + (1 - 7)^2}$$
$$= \sqrt{42.25}$$
$$= 6.5$$
$$AC = 5$$

b. $\triangle ABC$ is isosceles since $AB = BC$.

c.   (3.5, 1) is the midpoint of segment AC. (4.75, 4) is the midpoint of segment BC.

d.   The slope of side AB is $\frac{7-1}{3.5-1} = \frac{6}{2.5} = 2.4$.
The slope of the segment joining the midpoints of sides AC and BC is $\frac{4-1}{4.75-3.5} = \frac{3}{1.25} = 2.4$.
Since the segments have the same slope they are parallel.

e.   Many student questions could be generated. Students might find the slopes of the other sides of the triangle; they might find the length of the segment joining the midpoints of sides AC and BC; or they might redo parts c and d using a different pair of sides of the triangle. Students also might wish to investigate whether the segment joining the midpoints of two sides is parallel to the third side of a triangle even if the triangle is not isosceles.

See additional Teaching Notes on page T168D.

MORE

ASSIGNMENT   *pp. 90–96*

Students now can begin Modeling task 6, Organizing tasks 1, 2, or 3, Reflecting tasks 1 or 4, or Extending tasks 1 or 2 from the MORE assignment following Investigation 2.

▶**On Your Own**

△*ABC* has vertices *A*(1, 1), *B*(3.5, 7), and *C*(6, 1).

a. Make a drawing of △*ABC* on a coordinate grid. Then find the length of each side.

b. What kind of triangle is △*ABC*? Explain your reasoning.

c. Find the coordinates of the midpoints of sides *AC* and *BC*.

d. Find the slope of side *AB* and of the segment joining the midpoints found in part b. How are these segments related?

e. What other questions related to your work in parts a–d might be investigated? Pick one question to investigate and write a report of your findings.

INVESTIGATION ▶2 Things Are Not Always What They Seem to Be

1. Below are three quadrilaterals displayed on graphics calculator screens. Examine the shape in each display.

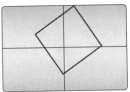 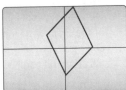 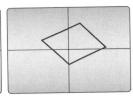

a. What kind of quadrilateral does each appear to be? Explain your choices.

b. The coordinates of the vertices of the three shapes are identical. Why might the displays appear so different?

c. The coordinates of the entered vertices are (3, 0), (1, 3), (–2, 1) and (0, –2). What type of quadrilateral is this?

d. Which display most closely resembles the true nature of the shape?

Graphics displays do not always show shapes as they are expected to appear. A square can look like a rhombus or a general parallelogram; a right triangle can appear to be otherwise; a circle can look like an oval. However, if you know the coordinates of key points such as vertices, you can calculate slopes, distances, and midpoints to determine the precise nature of the shape.

2. The shape in activity 1 is, in fact, a square. To verify this, you could establish that all sides have the same length, opposite sides are parallel, and adjacent sides are perpendicular.

a. Sharing the computational workload within your group, find the length of each side. Are they equal?

b. Continuing to share the workload, compute the slope of each side. Are opposite sides parallel? Explain how you use the slopes to decide.

c. Compare the slopes of adjacent sides. What pattern do you notice?

d. The diagonals of a square are known to be perpendicular. Compare the slopes of the diagonals of this square. What do you notice about these two slopes?

e. On graph paper, draw a segment with endpoints $(-1, 2)$ and $(2, 3)$. Draw lines through these points perpendicular to the segment. Compare the slopes of these lines. What pattern is evident in these cases?

f. Based on your group work in parts c–e, make a conjecture of the form:

If two lines are perpendicular, then their slopes…

Compare your conjectures with those of other groups. Resolve any differences there may be.

3. Recall that the calculator software GEOXPLOR allows you to draw polygons with any number of sides. For efficiency, the program stores the coordinates of the vertices of a polygon in a matrix. For example, quadrilateral *PQRS* is determined by the points $P(0, 0)$, $Q(10, -2)$, $R(14, 18)$, and $S(4, 20)$. This quadrilateral can be represented by the matrix below.

$$PQRS = \begin{bmatrix} \overset{P}{0} & \overset{Q}{10} & \overset{R}{14} & \overset{S}{4} \\ 0 & -2 & 18 & 20 \end{bmatrix} \begin{matrix} \text{\textit{x}-coordinates} \\ \text{\textit{y}-coordinates} \end{matrix}$$

a. Use graph paper to make a sketch of *PQRS*. Compare your sketch with the shape produced by GEOXPLOR.

b. If you used GEOXPLOR for part a, examine the entries of matrix A in your calculator. What are these entries?

c. Find the lengths and slopes of the sides of *PQRS*. (If you are using the program GEOXPLOR, select "CALCULATE" from the main menu.) Make a table of these values.

d. How are the lengths and the slopes of the opposite sides of *PQRS* related? What kind of quadrilateral is *PQRS*? Explain your conclusion.

e. How are the slopes of the adjacent sides of *PQRS* related? What special quadrilateral is *PQRS*? Explain how you know.

2. In order to see the relationship between the slopes of perpendicular lines, students may need to represent all slopes as fractions.

   a. Each side has length $\sqrt{13}$.

   b. For one pair of sides, each has slope $\frac{-3}{2}$, and for the other pair, each has slope $\frac{2}{3}$. The opposite sides are parallel because they have the same slope or rate of change.

   c. The slopes of adjacent sides are negative reciprocals of each other, or the product of the slopes of adjacent sides is -1.

   d. The slopes of the diagonals are $\frac{-1}{5}$ and 5. The product is -1 and they are negative reciprocals of each other.

   e. The slopes of the drawn segments will be -3. The slope of the segment is $\frac{1}{3}$. Some of the following observations may be made: The slopes of the two lines perpendicular to the segment are the same, indicating these two lines are parallel. Their slopes are the negative reciprocals of the slope of the segment; that is, the product of the slope of the segment and the slope of a line perpendicular to the segment is -1.

   f. The sentence can be completed with either "are negative reciprocals" or "have a product of -1".

NOTE: If not already done, a review of properties of polygons may be appropriate before students work on activity 3. You may wish to have students compile a list of properties for their math toolkits.

---

3. a. See grid below.

   b. The matrix [A] now contains the matrix $PQRS = \begin{bmatrix} 0 & 10 & 14 & 4 \\ 0 & -2 & 18 & 20 \end{bmatrix}$.

   c.

Segment	Length	Slope
PQ	10.2	−0.2
QR	20.4	5
RS	10.2	−0.2
SP	20.4	5

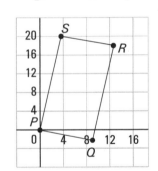

   d. The lengths of opposite sides of *PQRS* are equal. Opposite sides have identical slopes. Thus, the quadrilateral is a parallelogram. (Some students may say correctly that *PQRS* is a rectangle. If so, they should explain how they know that adjacent sides are perpendicular.)

   e. Slopes of adjacent sides of *PQRS* are negative reciprocals of one another. This means each pair of adjacent sides forms a 90° angle. Thus, the figure is a rectangle.

4. Students may prefer to use graph paper or their calculators or computer software to complete this activity. If students choose to use GEOXPLOR to help them with this activity, they will need to choose the decimal scale rather than the integer scale. This choice will allow the polygons to be large enough to give reasonable visual clues.

   As you circulate among the groups, encourage them to explain why they think a particular polygon is a rectangle or a parallelogram. They might not recall some definitions of special quadrilaterals. When someone remembers correctly you might want to write an informal definition on the board for reference. (For example: A rectangle has opposite sides equal. It has to have a right angle at each vertex.) Formal vocabulary is not necessary. Push students to be clear, and supply the vocabulary only as needed.

   a. Isosceles triangle—two sides are equal in length
   b. Parallelogram—opposite sides are parallel (same slopes)
   c. Isosceles right triangle—two sides are perpendicular and equal in length
   d. Kite—two pairs of adjacent sides (but not all four sides) are equal in length
   e. Rectangle—opposite sides are parallel, and adjacent sides are perpendicular, but not equal in length

5. a. Encourage students to graph the given points to determine the missing coordinates. See the second graph below. The fourth vertex has coordinates (5, 12).

   b.

   Responses will vary, depending on accuracy of students' displays or sketches. From the calculator screen above, it is not clear if the figure is a rectangle.

   c. Slope of segment $XW = -\frac{2}{5} = -0.4 = $ slope of segment YZ

   Slope of segment $WZ = \frac{10}{4} = 2.5 = $ slope of segment XY

   Since the slopes of adjacent sides are negative reciprocals of one another, each pair of adjacent sides forms a 90° angle.

6. a. The slope is 3. It is determined by the coefficient of the x term.

   b. Responses will vary. Any equation of the form $y = 3x + b$ will have the same slope as $y = 3x - 2$.

   c. Responses will vary. Any equation of the form $y = \frac{-1}{3}x + b$ will be perpendicular to $y = 3x - 2$. These lines will be perpendicular to the given line since their slopes are $\frac{-1}{3}$, which is the negative reciprocal of 3.

   d. Responses will vary, but all should have slopes of $\frac{-1}{3}$. The lines are parallel to each other and perpendicular to those in part b.

   e. The shapes formed by the four lines will be rectangles or squares with extended sides.

   f. The rates of change are negative reciprocals of each other.

4. Below are the coordinates of the vertices of different polygons. In each case, determine as precisely as possible the nature of the polygon. If it is a triangle, is it right, isosceles, or equilateral? If it is a quadrilateral, is it a square, rectangle, rhombus, parallelogram, kite, or trapezoid? Identify the properties used to determine your classifications. (Saying *It looks like a ...* is not sufficient. You must give confirming data about the polygon.)

   a. (−1, 1), (4, 3), (2, −2)

   b. (2, 1), (−1, 3), (−2, 1), (1, −1)

   c. (2, −1), (1, 3), (−2, −2)

   d. (−1, 0), (2, 0), (1, 2), (−1, 3)

   e. (0, 1), (2, 2), (4, −2), (2, −3)

5. Quadrilateral *WXYZ* is a rectangle.

$$WXYZ = \begin{bmatrix} 1 & 6 & 10 & ? \\ 2 & 0 & 10 & ? \end{bmatrix}$$

   a. Find the coordinates of the fourth vertex.

   b. Sketch quadrilateral *WXYZ* on graph paper or display it on your calculator or a computer. Does *WXYZ* appear to be a rectangle?

   c. Verify that *WXYZ* is a rectangle by giving evidence pertaining to its sides and angles.

6. In your previous work, you have seen that slope is an important descriptor of graphs of linear models.

   a. What is the slope of the line with equation $y = -2 + 3x$?

   b. Write the equations of three other lines with the same slope as the line in part a. How are the four lines related?

   c. Write an equation of a line perpendicular to $y = -2 + 3x$. Explain how you know this second line is perpendicular to the line $y = -2 + 3x$.

   d. Write equations of three more lines, each of which is perpendicular to $y = -2 + 3x$. How are these three lines related? How are these lines related to the lines in part b?

   e. What geometric shapes are determined by pairs of lines in part b together with pairs of lines in part d?

   f. The slope of a linear model $y = a + bx$ gives the rate of change of y with respect to x. Explain how the rates of change of linear models of two perpendicular lines are related.

Unit 2

Checkpoint

a Suppose a line l in a coordinate plane has slope $\frac{p}{q}$.

- What is the slope of a line parallel to l? Why must this be the case?
- What is the slope of a line perpendicular to l? Why does this seem reasonable?

b Given quadrilateral $QUAD$ with vertex matrix

$$QUAD = \begin{bmatrix} -6 & 6 & 0 & -12 \\ -3 & 3 & 15 & 9 \end{bmatrix},$$

determine specifically what shape $QUAD$ is. Explain how you can be sure.

Be prepared to discuss your ideas with the class.

▶**On Your Own**

Consider quadrilateral $PQRS$.

$$PQRS = \begin{bmatrix} 8 & 28 & 24 & 4 \\ 4 & 12 & 28 & 20 \end{bmatrix}$$

What special kind of quadrilateral is $PQRS$? Explain your reasoning.

MORE
Modeling • Organizing • Reflecting • Extending

Modeling

1. Geometry helps us to model the physical world. In Course 1, for example, you used geometry to represent and help analyze space structures and decorative patterns. Similarly, coordinates can be used to represent and help analyze geometric shapes. Complete a table like the one at the top of the next page, which summarizes key features of a two-dimensional **coordinate model** of geometry. Then give a specific example of each idea from the coordinate model.

SHARE AND SUMMARIZE full-class discussion

Checkpoint

See Teaching Master 30.

ⓐ ■ Every line parallel to l also has slope $\frac{p}{q}$. Students may think of the slope as the rate of change and the parallel line as a translation of the given line. This does not affect "rate of change" so the slopes are identical.

■ The slope of any line perpendicular to l is $\frac{-q}{p}$.

Student comments on the reasonableness may vary. The change in sign seems reasonable because there is a 90° angle involved. So if one line has positive slope, then the perpendicular line would have negative slope.

The relationship between the sizes of the slopes is more difficult to understand. Consider the intersection point of the perpendicular lines. When one line has small, positive slope, the other has a negative slope which is large in absolute value. Rotate both lines slowly counterclockwise about the intersection point to see that, as the positive one increases, the absolute value of the negative one decreases.

Another way to think about the sizes of the slopes is to visualize on a grid: if the slope of one line is over a and up b, then the line perpendicular to it would have a corresponding change of over $-b$ and up a.

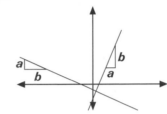

ⓑ The shape is a square. Slopes of adjacent sides are $\frac{1}{2}$ and -2 and each side has length $6\sqrt{5}$ or $\sqrt{180}$.

CONSTRUCTING A MATH TOOLKIT: Students should record in their math toolkit the relationship they discovered for the slope of parallel and perpendicular lines.

APPLY individual task

▶ On Your Own

PQRS is a parallelogram; both pairs of opposite sides are parallel and equal in length.

$PQ = RS = 21.54$

$QR = PS = 16.49$

slope of segment PQ = slope of segment RS = 0.4

slope of segment PS = slope of segment QR = −4

See additional Teaching Notes on page T168E.

MORE
ASSIGNMENT   pp. 90–96

Modeling: 1, 5, and 6
Organizing: 2, 5, and choice of one*
Reflecting: 1 and 4
Extending: Choose one*

*When choice is indicated, it is important to leave the choice to the student.
NOTE: It is best if Organizing tasks are discussed as a whole class after they have been assigned as homework.

2. **a.**

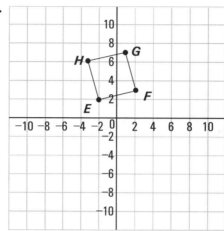

b. Quadrilateral *EFGH* is a square. All four sides are the same length, and opposite sides have identical slopes while adjacent sides have slopes which are negative reciprocals of each other.

c. Midpoint of segment *EF*: (0, 2.5)
Midpoint of segment *FG*: (1.5, 5)
Midpoint of segment *GH*: (−1, 6.5)
Midpoint of segment *HE*: (−2.5, 4)

d. The quadrilateral formed by the midpoints is also a square. All four sides are the same length, and opposite sides have identical slopes while adjacent sides have slopes which are negative reciprocals of each other.

3.

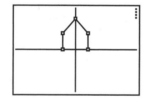

a. Responses will vary. One example is (10, 0), (10, 8), (0, 14), (−10, 8), and (−10, 0).

b. Responses will vary. Using the coordinates in part a the length of the bottom is 20; the upright (vertical) sides have length 8 and the remaining two sides have length $2\sqrt{34}$.

c. The upright sides are parallel and equal in length. The adjacent sides meeting on the *y*-axis are equal in length. The upright sides are perpendicular to the bottom side.

Geometric Idea	Coordinate Model	Example
Point	Ordered pair (x, y) of real numbers	
Plane	All possible ordered pairs (x, y) of real numbers	(No example needed.)
Line	All ordered pairs (x, y) satisfying $y = a + bx$ or $x = c$	$y = -4 + 2x$
Parallel lines		
Perpendicular lines		
Distance		
Midpoint		

2. Quadrilateral *EFGH* has vertices $E(-2, 2)$, $F(2, 3)$, $G(1, 7)$, and $H(-3, 6)$.

   a. Sketch quadrilateral *EFGH* on a coordinate grid.

   b. What kind of quadrilateral is *EFGH*? What reasons can you give to support your response?

   c. Find the midpoint of each side of the quadrilateral.

   d. Connecting the midpoints of adjacent sides determines a quadrilateral. What type of quadrilateral is this? Explain your reasoning.

3. Use software such as the GEOXPLOR program (the "DRAW" option) to draw a model of a school crossing sign. Locate the shape on the coordinate axes so that one side of the shape is on the *x*-axis and the *y*-axis is a line of symmetry.

   a. Give the coordinates of each vertex.

   b. Determine the length of each side.

   c. Identify sides that are parallel, perpendicular, or equal in length.

4. An engineering school offers a special reading and writing course for all entering students. Students are assigned to one of two sections based on performance on a placement test. Section A emphasizes reading skills; Section B stresses writing skills. The mean test scores for Section A are 64.2 (reading) and 73.8 (writing). For Section B, the mean reading and writing scores are 74.4 and 57.6, respectively. Shown on the following page are placement test scores of five students.

LESSON 1 • A COORDINATE MODEL OF A PLANE   **91**

Placement Test Scores		
	Reading Score	Writing Score
Jim	68	64
Emily	67	67
Anne	70	62
Juan	66	69
Gloria	60	60

a. Represent the reading and writing scores of each student listed in the table above as a point on a coordinate grid. Plot and label the points. On the same grid, also plot and label the points corresponding to the mean scores for Sections A and B.

b. Using only the visual display, assign students to Section A or B. What influenced your choices?

c. Suppose distance from the point corresponding to the section mean point is the criterion to use. Assign each student to a section. Compare your assignments for parts b and c.

d. Are there any students for whom neither section appears appropriate? Explain your response.

5. A quadrilateral has vertices at (2, 1), (7, 1), (5, 9), and (4, 9).

a. What type of quadrilateral is this?

b. Find the midpoints of the two sides that aren't parallel.

c. Draw the line segment determined by these midpoints. How is this line segment related to the other two sides?

d. How is the length of the middle segment related to the lengths of the two shorter sides of the quadrilateral?

e. On a coordinate grid, draw another quadrilateral of the type in part a. Do the relationships you discovered in parts c and d also hold for this quadrilateral?

6. Drilling teams from oil companies search around the world for new sites to place oil wells. Increasingly, oil reserves are being discovered in offshore waters.

The Gulf Oil Company has drilled two high-capacity wells in the Gulf of Mexico 5 km and 9 km from shore, as shown in the diagram at the top of the next page. The 20 km of

4. a.

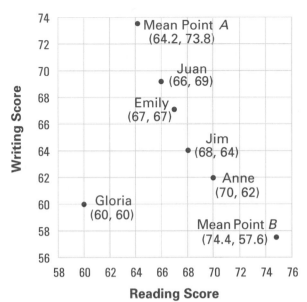

b. Visually, Emily and Juan have scores closer to Section A's mean scores, whereas Jim and Anne have scores closer to Section B's mean scores. Students may choose to assign Gloria to either section since visually there seems to be little difference in the distances from her ordered pair to the mean points for Sections A and B.

c. The following table summarizes the pertinent calculations:

Student	Distance From A's Mean	Distance From B's Mean
Jim	10.51	9.05
Emily	7.35	11.96
Anne	13.15	6.22
Juan	5.13	14.16
Gloria	14.42	14.60

To assign a student to one section or the other, simply choose the section whose ordered pair of mean placement test scores is closer to the student's own scores. Then Emily, Juan, and Gloria would be in Section A, with Jim and Anne in Section B.

d. Since Gloria's test score ordered pair is almost equidistant from both A and B, and this distance is relatively large, neither section seems particularly appropriate for her.

5. a. This quadrilateral is an isosceles trapezoid.

b. The midpoints are (3, 5) and (6, 5).

c. This line segment is parallel to both the top and the base of the trapezoid.

d. The length of the top is 1 unit, the length of the middle segment is 3 units, and the length of the base is 5 units. Note the length of the middle segment is the mean of the lengths of the top and the base.

e. Responses will vary. The relationships described in parts c and d above will hold for any trapezoid.

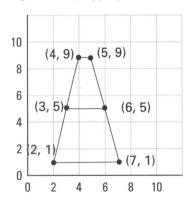

6. **a.** Student responses may vary. Each point on the model may be represented by an ordered pair. For example, if *A* is (0, 0), then *B* is (20, 0), Well #1 is (0, 5), and Well #2 is (20, 9). Students may choose other locations for the origin.

   b. The refinery should be closer to *A*. (Students' reasoning for this may vary, but should address the issue of minimizing the sum of the lengths of the two hypotenuses that will represent the pipeline connecting the wells and the refinery on shore.)

   c. To minimize pipeline used, the best location for the refinery is represented by the ordered pair $(\frac{50}{7}, 0)$, or approximately (7.14, 0). Students probably will use a guess-and-check method. (To find the exact point, reflect Well #1 over the line *AB* and draw the line connecting Well #2 to the reflection of Well #1. The point at which this line intersects segment *AB* is the best location for the refinery.)

shoreline is nearly straight, and the company wants to build a refinery on shore between the two wells. Since pipe and labor cost money, the company wants to find the location that will serve both wells and uses the least amount of pipe when it is laid in lines from each well to the refinery.

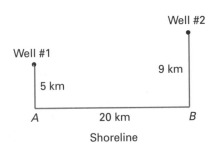

a. How can coordinates be used to investigate this situation?

b. Do you think the refinery should be closer to *A*, to *B*, or at the midpoint? Explain your reasoning.

c. What is your best estimate for the location of the refinery? How did you decide on that location?

Organizing

1. In Investigation 1, you wrote program planning algorithms for calculating slope (activity 6, part e), calculating midpoint (activity 8, part a), and drawing a segment (Checkpoint, page 86, part c). These algorithms can be used to write computer or calculator programs. Below is a program for a graphics calculator that will compute the midpoint of a segment.

MIDPT Program

Program	Function in Program
ClrHome	1. Clears display screen
Input"X COORD",A	2.
Input"Y COORD",B	3.
Input"X COORD",C	4.
Input"Y COORD",D	5.
(A+C)/2 →X	6.
(B+D)/2 →Y	7.
Disp"MIDPOINT COORDS"	8. Displays words, MIDPOINT COORDS
Disp X	9.
Disp Y	10.
Stop	11.

LESSON 1 • A COORDINATE MODEL OF A PLANE   93

a. Analyze this program and explain the purpose of each command line as was done for lines 1 and 8.

b. Obtain a copy of MIDPT from your teacher or enter it into your calculator or computer. (You may need to modify the commands slightly.) Test the program on pairs of points of your choosing.

2. How do you use the concept of mean in your procedure to calculate the coordinates of the midpoint of a segment?

3. Suppose (x_1, y_1) and (x_2, y_2) are given points with $x_2 > x_1$. Then the x-coordinate of the midpoint is half the distance from x_1 to x_2 added to x_1.

a. Show that the above statement is true when $x_1 = 6$ and $x_2 = 11$.

b. Explain why the above statement makes sense.

c. Rewrite the expression $x_1 + \dfrac{x_2 - x_1}{2}$ in a simpler equivalent form. Is this the x-coordinate of the midpoint?

4. An equilateral triangle has two vertices at $(0, 0)$ and $(0, 8)$. What are the possible coordinates of the third vertex?

5. Quadrilateral $ABCD$ has vertex A at the origin, and adjacent sides of length 13 and 5 units.

a. If $ABCD$ is a rectangle, what coordinates may B, C, and D have?

b. If $ABCD$ is a parallelogram (but not a rectangle), what coordinates may B, C, and D have?

c. How many different parallelograms can be drawn with adjacent sides of length 13 and 5 units? Explain.

Reflecting

1. Rectangles and squares often are displayed so that sides are parallel to the coordinate axes of a graphics screen.

a. Why do you think these figures are positioned this way?

b. A horizontal line has 0 slope. Explain the zero slope in terms of rate of change.

c. A vertical line has no slope. Explain the lack of slope in terms of rate of change.

2. In the first investigation, you invented formulas for calculating the distance between two points in a coordinate plane and the midpoint of the segment determined by those points. You were asked to write your formulas for general points (x_1, y_1) and (x_2, y_2), that is, using *subscript notation*. What advantages or disadvantages do you see in using subscript notation in these cases?

Organizing

Masters 32a–32b

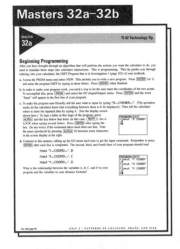

1. a. **Function in Program**
    1. Clears display screen.
    2. Get x-coordinate of the first point.
    3. Get y-coordinate of the first point.
    4. Get x-coordinate of the second point.
    5. Get y-coordinate of the second point.
    6. Calculate x-coordinate of the midpoint and store in X.
    7. Calculate y-coordinate of the midpoint and store in Y.
    8. Displays words, MIDPOINT COORDS.
    9. Display x-coordinate of the midpoint.
    10. Display y-coordinate of the midpoint.
    11. Stop the program.

    b. Students should use the MIDPT program so they can see that it actually works.

2. The midpoint of two ordered pairs (a, b) and (c, d) is
    (the mean of a and c, the mean of b and d).

Masters 33a–33b

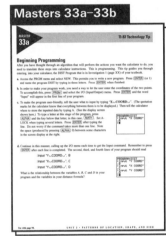

3. a. Using the indicated procedure, the x-coordinate of the midpoint is $\frac{11 - 6}{2} + 6 = \frac{5}{2} + 6 = 8\frac{1}{2}$.
    Using the midpoint formula, the x-coordinate of the midpoint is $\frac{11 + 6}{2} = \frac{17}{2} = 8\frac{1}{2}$.
    Since the given procedure produces the correct x-coordinate for the midpoint, the statement is true, at least in this case.

    b. It makes sense since the midpoint is halfway between the two endpoints.

    c. $x_1 + \dfrac{x_2 - x_1}{2} = \dfrac{2x_1}{2} + \dfrac{x_2}{2} - \dfrac{x_1}{2} = \dfrac{x_1}{2} + \dfrac{x_2}{2} = \dfrac{x_1 + x_2}{2}$

    It is the coordinate of the midpoint. (This shows the statement before part a in the student text is true in all cases where $x_2 > x_1$.)

4. There are two possible coordinates for the third vertex: $(6.93, 4)$ and $(-6.93, 4)$, approximately. If students are having difficulty, encourage them to draw a diagram. They should be able to see that the y-coordinate of the third point must be 4.

Using the Pythagorean Theorem,
$$4^2 + x^2 = 8^2$$
$$x^2 = \sqrt{48}$$
$$x \approx \pm 6.93$$

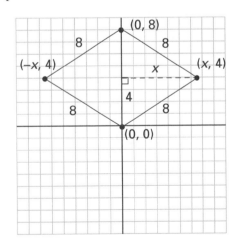

See additional Teaching Notes on page T168F.

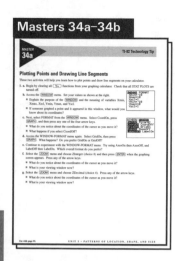

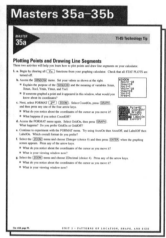

MORE *continued*

3. The phrase "on a segment" is included to insure there is only 1 possible midpoint. Given any two points *A* and *B*, there exist infinitely many points which are equidistant from *A* and *B* (namely, all points lying on the perpendicular bisector of *AB*). However, if we require the midpoint to lie on the segment, the midpoint is a unique ordered pair.

4. For the distance formula, it makes no difference whether you evaluate $x_1 - x_2$ or $x_2 - x_1$ since the square of each is the same. The same can be said for the *y* values.

   For the slope, the order in which you subtract makes no difference as long as the first coordinate in each difference comes from the same point. If you mix points, the slopes computed are not correct.

5. Responses may vary. Some possibilities are as follows:
   - Finding the length of the hypotenuse of a right triangle.
   - Determining which of two segments is longer.
   - Finding the perimeter of a given triangle.
   - Evaluating an expression.

Extending

1. **See Teaching Masters 34a–35b.**

   Using options from the DRAW menu, students can plot points and draw line segments. A good reference for students is their calculator manual. You may wish to have them store their pictures and then download them (through a linking program) to a computer for printing.

2. **a.** The taxi-distance between points *O* and *P* is 8.
   The taxi-distance between points *T* and *Q* is 11.

   b. The closer van, at point $B(-11, -7)$, should make the pickup: taxi-distance from *A* to *X* is 32 and from *B* to *X* is 30.

   c. Since taxi-distance is the sum of the horizontal distance and the vertical distance between two points, a possible formula is $TD = |a - c| + |b - d|$.

3. In the definition of the midpoint of a segment, the phrase "on the segment" is included. Why is that phrase needed?

4. For points $P(x_1, y_1)$ and $Q(x_2, y_2)$ in a coordinate plane:

■ the slope of line PQ is $\frac{\Delta y}{\Delta x}$ or $\frac{y_1 - y_2}{x_1 - x_2}$

■ the distance PQ is $\sqrt{(\Delta x)^2 + (\Delta y)^2}$ or $\sqrt{(x_1 - x_2)^2 + (y_1 - y_2)^2}$

In each case, the differences of coordinates are calculated. When calculating either the slope or the distance, does the order in which you subtract the coordinates make any difference? Illustrate and explain your reasoning.

5. What other procedures from your mathematics or science courses could be programmed on the calculator?

Extending

1. The program GEOXPLOR plots points and connects them to form polygons. Learn how to plot and connect points using the built-in feature of your calculator. Test your understanding by producing a graphics display of a star or a logo.

2. Streets in a city or neighborhood often are built in a rectangular grid. These systems may be represented by a rectangular coordinate system. In this situation, distances can be measured along streets, as a car would drive, not diagonally across blocks. (Of course, there are no one-way streets!) The shortest street distance between two locations is called the **taxi-distance**. For example, on the coordinate grid at the right, the taxi-distance between points P and Q is 5.

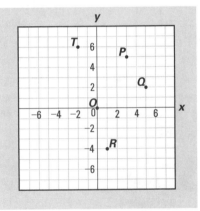

a. Find the taxi-distance between the given points O and P, and between points T and Q.

b. A Dial-a-Ride dispatcher receives a request for a pickup at point $X(-8, 20)$. Vans are stationed at point $A(12, 8)$ and at point $B(-11, -7)$. Which van should make the pickup? Why?

c. Write a formula for computing the taxi-distance between points $P(a, b)$ and $Q(c, d)$.

d. Draw a graph of all points in the plane whose taxi-distance from (0, 0) is 1. Do the same for all points whose taxi-distance from (0, 0) is 2, and again for a taxi-distance of 4.

e. What would be a reasonable name for the figures you graphed in part d?

f. The taxi-perimeter of a figure is the taxi-distance around the figure. That is, add the taxi-distances between each pair of vertices. Find the ratio of the taxi-perimeter to the taxi-distance across each figure in part d. What appears to be true?

3. Quadrilateral *STAY* has vertices *S*(1, −1), *T*(7, 6), *A*(3, 3), and *Y*(−3, −4).

a. What type of quadrilateral is *STAY*?

b. How long is diagonal *SA*?

c. At what point do the two diagonals intersect?

d. What, if anything, is special about this point?

4. Two points, *A*(0, −4) and *B*(2, −1), determine line *AB*.

a. What is the slope of line *AB*?

b. What is the equation of line *AB*?

c. What is the midpoint of segment *AB*?

d. What is the slope of a line perpendicular to line *AB*?

e. What is the equation of the line perpendicular to line *AB* and containing the midpoint of segment *AB*?

f. Use your calculator or computer software to graph the equations in parts b and e. In what viewing window do the lines look perpendicular?

5. Many graphics calculators can be programmed to have additional capabilities. For example, GEOXPLOR computes distances, slopes, and coordinates of midpoints because it is programmed to do those specific computations. It is not difficult to program your graphics calculator when you know a few basic instructions.

a. Research information on how to program your calculator.

b. Obtain a copy of the program DIST from your teacher or enter it in your calculator or computer yourself. (The *listing* for the program appears on page 85. You may need to modify the commands.) Modify this program so that it will compute the slope of the line determined by two points. (The two points cannot be on the same vertical line.) Call your new program SLOPE2PT. Check your program for accuracy by testing it with several pairs of points.

c. Write a program that will let you input the coordinates of two points and then will display the slope of the line determined by the points and the slope of the line perpendicular to that line. Call the program SLOLAR. Check your program for accuracy by testing it with several pairs of points.

2. d. If students continue to think contextually, they may graph only the vertices of the squares. Encourage them to move out of context but keep the idea of moving only in horizontal or vertical directions.

Taxi distance from (0, 0) is 1.   Taxi distance from (0, 0) is 2.   Taxi distance from (0, 0) is 4.

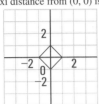 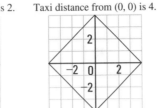

  e. The figures are all squares whose diagonals intersect at the origin (or whose vertices lie on the axes).

  f. The ratios are $\frac{8}{2}$, $\frac{16}{4}$, and $\frac{32}{8}$ for the three squares. The ratios are equivalent to $\frac{4}{1}$.

3. a. *STAY* is a parallelogram. The slopes of segments *ST* and *AY* are both $\frac{7}{6}$ and the slopes of segments *AT* and *YS* are both $\frac{3}{4}$.

  b. *SA* is $\sqrt{(1 - 3)^2 + (-1 - 3)^2} = \sqrt{20} \approx 4.47$.

  c. The diagonals intersect at (2, 1).

  d. This point is the midpoint of both diagonals.

4. a. The slope of line *AB* is $\frac{3}{2}$.

  b. The equation of line *AB* is $y = \frac{3}{2}x - 4$.

  c. The midpoint of segment *AB* is (1, −2.5).

  d. The slope of a line perpendicular to line *AB* is $\frac{-2}{3}$.

  e. The equation of the perpendicular bisector of segment *AB* is $y = \frac{-2}{3}x - \frac{11}{6}$.

  f. These lines will look perpendicular in the ZSquare, ZInteger, or ZDecimal viewing windows. (Actually on the TI-82 or TI-83, any window that has a ratio of 47:31 for (Xmax − Xmin): (Ymax − Ymin) will make the lines look perpendicular.) If students are not aware of these Zoom options, this may be a particularly difficult task.

5. This task has students writing simple programs for their calculator. This is the first of several opportunities for students to write their own programs. You may wish to lead a discussion of programming to make sure all students get some exposure to simple programming ideas. Then those that are more interested can pursue these ideas further as they progress through the unit.

  a. One source for information is the manual that comes with the calculator.

  b. The code for DIST is given on page 85 of the student text. To get a program that will find the slope, replace the last two lines in that code as follows.

Original

```
√((A−C)² + (B−D)²) → L
Disp "DISTANCE IS", L
```

Modified

```
(B − D)/(A − C) → L
Disp "SLOPE IS", L
```

  c. Typical code for SLOLAR follows.

```
ClrHome
Input "X COORD", A
Input "Y COORD", B
Input "X COORD", C
Input "Y COORD", D
(B − D)/(A − C) → L
Disp "SLOPE IS", L
Disp "PERP SLOPE IS", −1/L
Stop
```

Unit 2

EXPLORE small-group investigation

INVESTIGATION 3 ▶ Families of Lines

During this investigation, students will observe that the sum of multiples of two linear equations contains their point of intersection. Students also will develop graphical and algebraic techniques to determine the coordinates of that point.

The "SYSTEMS" option of GEOXPLOR can save students time and effort in graphing systems and sums of multiples of equations. This software will graph any two linear equations and a linear combination of those equations on the same display. This is done so that the students can concentrate on the geometry without needing to do the manipulation and graphing associated with the activities.

As a brief introduction, you might display several linear and non-linear equations in the form $y = ax^n + b$ and some in the form $ax^m + by^n = c$. Ask: Which of these are linear? How do you know? (Students should be able to spot terms that involve powers or exponents, and recognize that these give non-linear graphs.)

1. **See Teaching Master 36.**

   You may wish to pull the groups together to discuss their work following activity 1. In order to decide which equation was appropriate for each line, some students will rewrite the equation in the form $y = a + bx$. (They may not always do this successfully so some common difficulties in this process can be discussed briefly.) Some may find the x- and y-intercepts and check them against what they can see on the graph. Some will try to identify points on the graph and substitute the coordinates into the equations. It is worthwhile for everyone to see a variety of approaches.

   a. Students may use slopes and y-intercepts to help them match each equation to the appropriate line. Alternatively, they could solve the equations for y and have their calculator draw the graphs.

   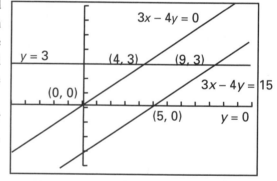

   b. The coordinates of the three other vertices of the rhombus are $(5, 0)$, $(9, 3)$, and $(4, 3)$.

   c. ■ The x-coordinates of the points on that side of the rhombus are all between 0 and 4, inclusive, while the y-coordinates are between 0 and 3, inclusive. This gives $0 \leq x \leq 4$ and $0 \leq y \leq 3$.

      ■ $4 \leq x \leq 9$ and $y = 3$ for the side determined by $(4, 3)$ and $(9, 3)$.

      $5 \leq x \leq 9$ and $0 \leq y \leq 3$ for the side determined by $(5, 0)$ and $(9, 3)$.

      $0 \leq x \leq 5$ and $y = 0$ for the side determined by $(0, 0)$ and $(5, 0)$.

   d. Diagonal containing $(4, 3)$ and $(5, 0)$:

      $y = -3x + 15$ or $3x + y = 15$, with $4 \leq x \leq 5$ and $0 \leq y \leq 3$

      Diagonal containing $(0, 0)$ and $(9, 3)$:

      $y = \frac{1}{3}x$ or $x - 3y = 0$, with $0 \leq x \leq 9$ and $0 \leq y \leq 3$

INVESTIGATION 3 Families of Lines

In the previous two investigations, you saw how polygons could be modeled and analyzed by using the coordinates of their vertices. The "DRAW" option of the GEOXPLOR program displayed polygons by plotting and connecting the vertices in order. You were able to use the coordinates of the vertices to calculate lengths, slopes, and midpoints of the sides of these polygons.

1. You also can think of polygons as being enveloped by a *family of lines*. Examine this graphics display of lines and the rhombus that is enveloped by them. The scale on both axes is 1 unit for each mark.

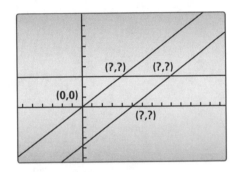

a. On a copy of this display, match each equation given below with the corresponding side of the rhombus. Describe clues you used to determine the matches.

i. $y = 0$ **ii.** $3x - 4y = 15$ **iii.** $y = 3$ **iv.** $3x - 4y = 0$

b. Determine the coordinates of the vertices of the rhombus.

c. The equations in part a describe lines that contain the sides of the rhombus. The equations will describe only the points on the sides if you restrict the input values for x and y.

■ In the case of the equation for the side determined by the vertices $(0, 0)$ and $(4, 3)$, explain why $0 \leq x \leq 4$ ($x \geq 0$ and $x \leq 4$) and $0 \leq y \leq 3$.

■ For each of the remaining equations in part a, describe the restrictions on x and y so that the equation describes just the side of the rhombus.

d. Write equations for the lines containing the diagonals of the rhombus. Describe restrictions on the input values for x and y so that each equation will represent only the points on the corresponding diagonals.

When modeling polygons or investigating geometric relationships in a coordinate plane, it is common to use linear equations in the form $ax + by = c$ rather than $y = \ldots$. This is because the variables x and y vary jointly; one is not viewed as a function of the other.

2. Now examine the family of lines displayed below.

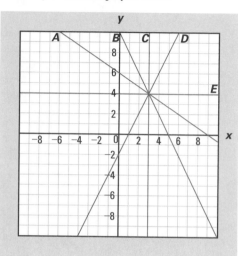

a. Match each line with the corresponding equation given below.

    i. $2x - y = 2$ **ii.** $4x + 2y = 20$ **iii.** $y = 4$

    iv. $x = 3$ **v.** $2x + 3y = 18$

b. Explain how you could match these lines with their equations by examining the x- and y-intercepts.

c. Describe any interesting features of these linear equations and their graphs.

d. Explain how you could quickly sketch the graph of $2x - 3y = -6$ by using x- and y-intercepts. How is this line related to the given family of lines?

In the following activities you will explore families of lines generated by a system of linear equations. Begin by considering the following system of equations.

$$x + 2y = 8$$
$$4x - y = 5$$

Various operations can be performed on one or more of the equations in a system. For example, you can multiply each term in $x + 2y = 8$ by a constant such as 2, or you may combine the two equations in the system.

3. With your group, investigate the effects of multiplying each term of a linear equation by a constant.

a. On a coordinate grid, draw the graphs of $x + 2y = 8$ and $2(x + 2y = 8)$, that is, $2x + 4y = 16$. Compare the graphs of $x + 2y = 8$ and $2x + 4y = 16$.

b. Draw the graphs of $x + 2y = 8$ and $4(x + 2y = 8)$ on a coordinate grid.

c. What do you think is true about the graphs of $k(x + 2y = 8)$ for each nonzero integer k? Check your conjecture.

d. What do you think is true about the graphs of $k(4x - y = 5)$ for each nonzero integer k? Check your conjecture and revise it if necessary.

2. a. i. *D* ii. *B* iii. *E*

    iv. *C* v. *A*

  b. The *y*-intercept of each equation can be determined by substituting 0 for *x* and solving for *y*. Since all of the *y*-intercepts are distinct, this allows all equations to be matched to the appropriate graph. This process also could be applied to the *x*-intercepts.

  c. All five of the equations contain the point (3, 4).

  d. The *x*-intercept is the point $(-3, 0)$ and the *y*-intercept is the point (0, 2). Plotting these two points and then drawing the line containing them allows one to sketch quickly the graph of $2x - 3y = -6$. This line also contains the point (3, 4).

As students work on activities 3–5, and you are circulating among the groups, you might want to ask them why it makes sense that any multiple of a linear equation will give the same line. Students may have ingenious explanations. ("It's the same relationship between *x*'s and *y*'s, just disguised." "It's like the cost of *x* tickets at \$1 each and *y* tickets at \$2 each is \$8. So, if you buy twice as many of each ticket at the same prices you pay 2 · \$8, but the combinations (proportions) of tickets are the same.")

Sometimes students expect that a sum of lines will make a triangle with the given two lines; they may be surprised that the sum gives a line that goes through the intersection point. Students tend to over-generalize and say that the new line is "halfway" between the original lines. As you circulate, push them to be clear with their descriptions of what they observe. For example, you might want to follow up on the language they are using by asking:

So, geometrically a multiple of a line is ....

Geometrically, the sum of two linear equations is ....

What does it mean that the point of intersection "fits" the original equations? (Students may use something similar to "fit".) And why does it have to fit the combination equations also?

3. a. The graphs are the same line.

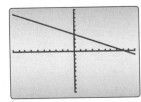 

  b. There is only one line. The graphs are identical to the graph in part a.

  c. The graphs are the same line as the graph of the equation $x + 2y = 8$.

  d. The graph is always the same line as the graph of the equation $4x - y = 5$.

4. a. The sum equation is a line also.

    b.

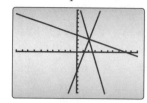

```
WINDOW FORMAT
 Xmin =-10
 Xmax=10
 Xscl =1
 Ymin =-10
 Ymax=10
 Yscl =1
```

    c. The three lines have a common point.

    d. $4(x + 2y = 8) + (-2)(4x - y = 5)$ gives a sum equation of $-4x + 10y = 22$.

    e. This line also contains the point at which the other three lines intersect.

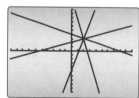

```
WINDOW FORMAT
 Xmin =-10
 Xmax=10
 Xscl =1
 Ymin =-10
 Ymax=10
 Yscl =1
```

    f. The four lines all intersect at the same point.

5. a. ■ $E_1 + E_2$: $6x + 5y = -3$

      ■ $E_1 + 5E_2$: $10x + 17y = -31$

      ■ $E_1 + (-5)E_2$: $-13y = 39$

    b. The scale on both axes of the following graphs is 1.

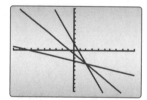 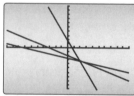 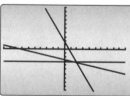

    c. They all contain the point of intersection of equations E_1 and E_2.

    d. $(2, -3)$ is the solution.

    e. The combination $E_1 + (-5)E_2$, which gives the equation $-13y = 39$, is most help-ful because it is horizontal. It is easy to find the y-coordinate of the solution.

6. a. ■ $E_1 + E_2$: $5x + 5y = 5$

      ■ $E_1 + (-1)E_2$: $-x - 3y = -11$

      ■ $3E_1 + 2E_2$: $12x + 11y = 7$

      ■ $3E_1 + (-2)E_2$: $-5y = -25$

    b. The scale on both axes of the following graphs is 1.

■ 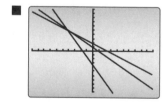 ■ 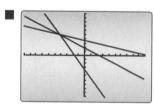 ■ 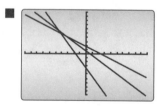 ■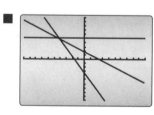

4. Investigate what happens when you add the two equations of a linear system.

a. Add the two equations of the system above activity 3 on the previous page. That is:

$$\begin{array}{r} x + 2y = 8 \\ \underline{4x - y = 5} \\ 5x + y = 13 \end{array}$$

What geometric figure is described by the "sum" equation?

b. Graph the original equations and the sum equation on the same coordinate grid.

c. What, if anything, is special about these three lines?

d. Multiply both sides of $x + 2y = 8$ by 4 and both sides of $4x - y = 5$ by -2. Add the resulting equations.

e. What do you think is true about the graph of this sum equation? Check your conjecture by graphing the sum equation on the coordinate grid you prepared in part b.

f. What is special about the four graphs?

5. Let E_1 be the equation: $5x + 2y = 4$.

Let E_2 be the equation: $x + 3y = -7$.

a. Write each sum equation.

- $E_1 + E_2$
- $E_1 + 5E_2$
- $E_1 + (-5)E_2$

b. Use the "SYSTEMS" option of GEOXPLOR or similar computer software to graph the original system of equations and each sum equation in part a.

c. What appears to be true about each of these lines?

d. What is the solution to the system of equations E_1 and E_2?

e. Which of the lines in part b is most helpful in finding the solution? Why? To which equation in part a does this line correspond?

6. Next consider the following system of equations.

E_1: $2x + y = -3$

E_2: $3x + 4y = 8$

Complete parts a and b by dividing up the work among members of your group. Then share your results and thinking to complete parts c–e.

a. Write each sum equation.

- $E_1 + E_2$
- $E_1 + (-1)E_2$
- $3E_1 + 2E_2$
- $3E_1 + (-2)E_2$

b. Use "SYSTEMS" to graph the original system of equations E_1 and E_2 and each sum equation in part a.

c. What is the solution of the original system?

d. Which of the lines in part b is the most helpful in finding the solution? Explain. To which equation in part a does the line correspond?

e. What relationship, if any, do you see between the original system and the choice of multipliers that produced the equation in part d?

7. Finally, consider this system of linear equations.

$$E_1: 3x - y = 2$$
$$E_2: x + 2y = 10$$

Complete parts a and b by dividing the workload among members of your group. Then share your results and thinking to complete parts c–e.

a. Write each sum equation.

- $E_1 + E_2$
- $E_1 + 3E_2$
- $2E_1 + E_2$
- $E_1 + (-3)E_2$

```
6X  +  −2Y  =   4
1X  +   2Y  =  10
7X  +   0Y  =  14
```

b. Graph the original system of equations and each sum equation in part a.

c. What is the solution of the original system?

d. Which of the lines and corresponding equations in part a are the most helpful in finding the solution? Explain.

e. What relationship do you see between the original system and the choice of multipliers that produced the equations in part d? Compare the pattern seen by your group with that found by other groups.

8. E_1 and E_2 are equations of lines intersecting at point (a, b). What do you think is true about each **linear combination** $m \cdot E_1 + n \cdot E_2$, when m and n are nonzero numbers?

9. Use an appropriate linear combination of the following equations to find the coordinates of the point of intersection for the corresponding pair of lines. Check each solution by solving the system of equations using another method.

a. $2x + y = 4$
$x - y = 5$

b. $2x + 3y = 6$
$2x + y = -4$

c. $x + 3y = -1$
$2x - y = 12$

d. $3x + 4y = -2$
$-2x - 3y = 1$

e. The modeling equations you wrote for the diagonals of the rhombus in activity 1 (page 97).

10. Consider the following system of equations.

$$x - y = 7$$
$$2x - 2y = 5$$

a. Try to solve this system using a linear combination of the equations.

b. What difficulties did you encounter in part a?

6. **c.** $(-4, 5)$ is the solution.

    d. The horizontal line is the most helpful. The equation of the line is $-5y = -25$ and it corresponds to $3E_1 + (-2)E_2$.

    e. The multipliers were chosen so that the x-coefficients in the two equations were additive inverses of each other. Thus, when added, they eliminated the x variable. There was no special relationship between the multipliers and the y-coefficients.

7. **a.** ■ $E_1 + E_2$: $4x + y = 12$
      ■ $2E_1 + E_2$: $7x = 14$
      ■ $E_1 + 3E_2$: $6x + 5y = 32$
      ■ $E_1 + (-3)E_2$: $-7y = -28$

    b. The scale on both axes of the following graphs is 1.

■ 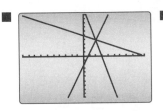 ■ 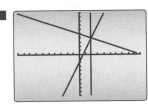 ■ 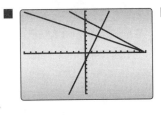 ■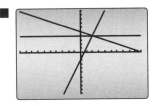

    c. The solution of the original system is $(2, 4)$.

    d. The vertical line with equation $7x = 14$, and the horizontal line with equation $-7y = -28$, are the most helpful in solving this system.

    e. The multipliers produced additive inverses for either the x- or y-coefficients.

8. Each sum is again a line, and that line contains the intersection of the original two lines.

9. **a.** $(3, -2)$

    b. $(-4.5, 5)$

    c. $(5, -2)$

    d. $(-2, 1)$

    e. The equations for the diagonals are $3x + y = 15$ and $x - 3y = 0$. The solution to this system is $(4.5, 1.5)$.

10. **a.** The procedure leads to the statement that $0 = -9$.

    b. The difficulty that arose was that both the x and y terms vanished and the remaining expression said that 0 was equal to another number.

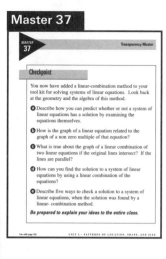

Master 37

10. c. The difficulties indicate that the lines have no point of intersection. This situation can be predicted from the equations, since the coefficients of *x* and *y* of one equation are proportional to those of the other and the constant terms are not equal.

d. The graph of the sum line is always parallel to the two given lines. If students choose a linear combination that makes both the *x* and *y* terms drop out, they will not get an equation of a line at all. Encourage them to explore another linear combination of the equations.

SHARE AND SUMMARIZE   full-class discussion

Checkpoint

See Teaching Master 37.

ⓐ To predict whether or not a system of linear equations has a solution, examine the ratio formed by coefficients of *x* and *y* in each equation. If the ratios are equal (that is, the coefficients are proportional), then the system has no unique solution since the lines are either parallel (no solutions) or identical (many solutions).

ⓑ The graph of a linear equation and the graph of any nonzero multiple of the equation are the same.

ⓒ The sum is a line containing the intersection of the other two lines if they intersect and parallel to the other two lines if they do not intersect.

ⓓ You can eliminate one of the variables by adding multiples of the equations of the lines. Use the resulting equation to determine precisely the value of one of the coordinates of the point of intersection. Then substitute that value into one of the original equations and solve for the remaining variable.

ⓔ Five ways to check the solution are: substitute the solution back into the original equations, solve the system using matrices, use a table of values, solve each equation for *y* and then solve the system, and graph the system and find the point of intersection of the two lines.

CONSTRUCTING A MATH TOOLKIT: You may wish to assign Reflecting task 3 as a math toolkit entry. This task encourages students to think about the variety of methods available for solving a system of equations. It also encourages them to reflect on when one method might be more appropriate than others.

APPLY   individual task

▶On Your Own

a. Since the coefficients are not proportional, the system will have a solution.

b. The solution is (40, 80). There are many different sets of multipliers that can be used to solve the system.

c. Students may choose any method they wish to check their solution. This is a good place to stress the importance of always checking that the solution is correct.

d. Responses will vary. Students should explain why one method is easier for them than another.

c. What do those difficulties tell you about the lines? Can the difficulties be predicted by examining the equations before you begin combining the equations? If so, how?

d. How is the graph of a linear combination of these equations related to the graphs of the equations themselves?

Checkpoint

You now have added a linear-combination method to your toolkit for solving systems of linear equations. Look back at the geometry and the algebra of this method.

a Describe how you can predict whether or not a system of linear equations has a solution by examining the equations themselves.

b How is the graph of a linear equation related to the graph of a nonzero multiple of that equation?

c What is true about the graph of a linear combination of two linear equations if the original lines intersect? If the lines are parallel?

d How can you find the solution to a system of linear equations by using a linear combination of the equations?

e Describe five ways to check a solution to a system of linear equations, when the solution was found by a linear-combination method.

Be prepared to explain your ideas to the entire class.

On Your Own

Consider the following system of linear equations.

$$2x - 2y = -80$$
$$6x - \ y = 160$$

a. Explain, in terms of the equations themselves, why you know this system has a solution.

b. Solve this system using a linear combination. Explain how you chose the multipliers you used to find this solution.

c. Check your solution using another method.

d. Which of the two methods was easiest to use? Why?

MORE
Modeling • Organizing • Reflecting • Extending

Modeling

1. The four lines with equations $x + y = 2$, $y = 1$, $x + y = -2$, and $x - 3y = 2$ determine a quadrilateral.

   a. Find the coordinates of its vertices.

   b. Sketch the quadrilateral.
   - For each modeling equation, what restrictions on the input values for x and y are needed so the equation describes only the side of the figure?
   - What kind of quadrilateral is it? How do you know?

   c. Find equations for the lines containing the diagonals of the quadrilateral. What restrictions on the input values for x and y confine the lines to the diagonals?

   d. What are the coordinates of the point of intersection of the diagonals?

   e. Verify your answer in part d using a different method than the one you used to find that answer.

2. Triangle ABC is enveloped by three lines as shown here.

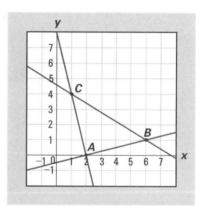

   a. Write modeling equations for the sides of $\triangle ABC$.

   b. For each equation, what restrictions on the input values for x and y confine the lines to the sides of the triangle?

   c. Is $\triangle ABC$ a special kind of triangle? Explain your reasoning.

   d. Find the area of $\triangle ABC$.

Modeling

MORE
ASSIGNMENT *pp. 102–108*

Modeling: 3 and choice of one*
Organizing: 1 and 2
Reflecting: 2 and 3
Extending: Choose one*

*When choice is indicated, it is important to leave the choice to the student.
NOTE: It is best if Organizing tasks are discussed as a whole class after they have been assigned as homework.

1. a. The vertices are $A(1, 1)$, $B(2, 0)$, $C(-1, -1)$, and $D(-3, 1)$.

b.

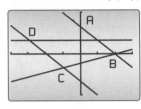

```
WINDOW FORMAT
 Xmin =-4
 Xmax= 3
 Xscl = 1
 Ymin =-3
 Ymax= 3
 Yscl = 1
```

■ For the equation $x + y = 2$, the restrictions are $1 \le x \le 2$ and $0 \le y \le 1$.
For the equation $y = 1$, the restrictions are $-3 \le x \le 1$ and $y = 1$.
For the equation $x + y = -2$, the restrictions are $-3 \le x \le -1$ and $-1 \le y \le 1$.
For the equation $x - 3y = 2$, the restrictions are $-1 \le x \le 2$ and $-1 \le y \le 0$.

■ $ABCD$ is a trapezoid because two sides are parallel. Segments AB and CD are parallel; the slopes of lines AB and CD are both -1.

c. The equation of the diagonal joining $(-1, -1)$ and $(1, 1)$ is $y = x$ or $x - y = 0$, and the restrictions are $-1 \le x \le 1$ and $-1 \le y \le 1$. The equation of the diagonal joining $(-3, 1)$ and $(2, 0)$ is $x + 5y = 2$, and the restrictions are $-3 \le x \le 2$ and $0 \le y \le 1$.

d. The diagonals intersect at the point $(\frac{1}{3}, \frac{1}{3})$.

e. Student responses will vary. Students should use a method other than the one used in part d.

2. a. The equation for the line containing side AB is $x - 4y = 2$.
The equation for the line containing side BC is $3x + 5y = 23$.
The equation for the line containing side AC is $4x + y = 8$.

b. For the equation $x - 4y = 2$, the restrictions are $2 \le x \le 6$ and $0 \le y \le 1$.
For the equation $3x + 5y = 23$, the restrictions are $1 \le x \le 6$ and $1 \le y \le 4$.
For the equation $4x + y = 8$, the restrictions are $1 \le x \le 2$ and $0 \le y \le 4$.

c. Since the slope of the line containing side AC is -4 and the slope of the line containing side AB is $\frac{1}{4}$, side AC is perpendicular to side AB and $\triangle ABC$ is a right triangle. Since $AC = AB$, $\triangle ABC$ is also isosceles.

d. The length of side AC is $\sqrt{(2 - 1)^2 + (0 - 4)^2}$ or $\sqrt{17}$.
The length of side AB is $\sqrt{(6 - 2)^2 + (1 - 0)^2}$ or $\sqrt{17}$.
So the area of $\triangle ABC$ is $\frac{1}{2}(\sqrt{17})(\sqrt{17})$ or 8.5 square units.

3. **a.** The line *PR* is $2x + y = 7$. The line *QS* is $4x - 3y = -6$.

   b. The point of intersection is (1.5, 4).

   c. Responses will vary. One example is $6x - 2y = 1$, which is the sum of the given equations. All lines should contain the point of intersection of the two given lines.

   d. One possibility is: $-2(2x + y = 7) + (4x - 3y = -6)$, which yields $-5y = -20$, or $y = 4$.

   e. From part d we know the *y*-coordinate of the point of intersection is 4. We can substitute 4 for *y* in either of the given equations to find the corresponding *x* value. The *x* value corresponding to $y = 4$ is $x = 1.5$. The estimate in part c should be close to this solution of (1.5, 4).

4. **a.** Let *x* be the number of adults and *y* the number of children. Then $8x + 3y = 1900$ is the model.

   b. With the same meanings for variables as in part a, the modeling equation is $x + y = 300$.

   c. Responses may vary. The students know at least the following five methods.
   - Graph the two equations and find the point of intersection by tracing or using the intersect command on the calculator.
   - Use tables of values to find the solution.
   - Set up and solve a matrix equation.
   - Use linear combinations.
   - Put each equation in the form "$y = \ldots$" and set them equal. Solve the equations for the *x* value, then substitute the value for *x* into an original equation and solve for *y*.

   d. 200 adults and 100 children are needed to assure the estimates are met exactly.

3. In the diagram below are shown two lines and two points on each line. The equations of these lines are $2x + y = 7$ and $4x - 3y = -6$.

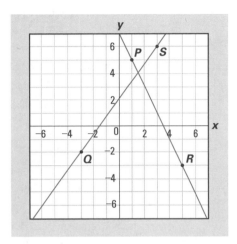

a. Make a copy of this diagram. Label each line with the equation that corresponds to it.

b. Estimate the coordinates of the point of intersection using the diagram.

c. Use linear combinations to find equations of three different lines that contain the point of intersection of the given lines. Sketch their graphs on the diagram in part a.

d. Find a linear combination of the original equations whose graph is a horizontal line containing the point of intersection.

e. Explain how to use the horizontal line in part d and one of the original equations to find the coordinates of the point of intersection. Compare these values to those estimated in part c.

4. The Middletown Boosters Club is planning a community event to raise money for the school theater program. Based on previous fund-raising events, they estimate that about 300 adults and children will attend. Plans are to charge adults $8 and children $3 admission. The club estimates that they will receive $1900 from admission charges.

a. Write an equation that models the relationship among adult attendance, child attendance, and estimated income from admission charges. Describe what the variables represent.

b. Write an equation that models the expected adult and child attendance. Describe what the variables represent.

c. Describe four different ways you could determine the number of adults and children that must attend in order for the booster club to meet both estimates exactly.

d. Find the solution using a method of your choice. Check your solution.

LESSON 1 • A COORDINATE MODEL OF A PLANE   **103**

Organizing

1. In order to graph linear equations on a graphing calculator, they must be written in a "$y = \ldots$" form. The equation then can be entered in the functions list.

   a. For $y = a + bx$, what do the values of a and b tell you about the graph?

   b. Rewrite each equation below in the form $y = a + bx$.

   ■ What are the slope and y-intercept of each line?

   ■ Match each equation with its graph.

   i. $y + x = 7$

   ii. $5 - 2x = 3y$

   iii. $4y - 2x = -7$

   iv. $3x - 4y = 5$

   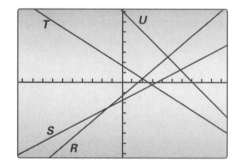

   c. Rewrite $Ax + By = C$ (A and B nonzero) in the form $y = a + bx$. What are the slope and y-intercept in terms of A, B, and C?

   d. Find the slope and y-intercept of $-2x + 5y = 15$.

2. Given lines l_1 and l_2 in a plane, they either are the same line, intersect in a point, or are parallel. Visually it is easy to see which situation is the case. In a coordinate model, these lines are represented algebraically as a system of linear equations.

   a. For each system below, determine if the lines represented are the same, are different and intersect in a point, or are different and parallel.

   i. $y = -4x + 5$ **ii.** $y = 6x - 2$ **iii.** $y = 1.5x + 9$

       $y = -4x - 2$ $y = 3x - 2$ $y = \frac{3}{2}x + 9$

   b. Explain how you can arrive at your conclusion in part a just by examining the equations in each system.

   c. Determine if the lines represented in each system below are the same, different and intersect in a point, or different and parallel.

   i. $x + 2y = 8$ **ii.** $x - 3y = 6$ **iii.** $3x - 2y = 1$

       $2x + y = 4$ $3x - 9y = 18$ $6x - 4y = 10$

   d. Search for a way to predict when a system of equations of the form in part c represents lines that are the same, are different and intersect in a point, or are parallel. Test your conjectures by writing and checking other systems of linear equations.

Organizing

1. a. The slope of the line is b. The y-intercept is a.

b. Have students list the steps they performed to arrive at the following responses.

    i. $y = 7 - x$

      ■ Slope: -1; y-intercept: 7

      ■ Line U

    ii. $y = \frac{5}{3} - \frac{2}{3}x$

      ■ Slope: $\frac{-2}{3}$; y-intercept: $\frac{5}{3}$

      ■ Line T

    iii. $y = \frac{-7}{4} + \frac{1}{2}x$

      ■ Slope: $\frac{1}{2}$; y-intercept: $\frac{-7}{4}$

      ■ Line S

    iv. $y = \frac{-5}{4} + \frac{3}{4}x$

      ■ Slope: $\frac{3}{4}$; y-intercept: $\frac{-5}{4}$

      ■ Line R

c. $y = \frac{-A}{B}x + \frac{C}{B}$; the slope is $\frac{-A}{B}$ and the y-intercept is $\frac{C}{B}$.

d. The slope is $\frac{2}{5}$ and the y-intercept is 3.

2. a. i. Different and parallel

    ii. Different and intersect in a point

    iii. The same line

b. One method is to look at the slopes. If the slopes are different, then the lines must intersect in a point. If the slopes are the same, then the lines are parallel if the y-intercepts are different. If both the slopes and the y-intercepts are the same, then the equations are the same line.

c. i. Different and intersect in a point

    ii. The same line

    iii. Different and parallel

d. Students may have different ways of explaining this, but their answers should convey the same general thinking as the following one. Try to get students to find a way to predict the relationship between the lines without graphing them or putting the equations into the form "$y = \ldots$".

Consider the following system:

$$Ax + By = C$$
$$Dx + Ey = F$$

The two lines will be the same if $\frac{A}{D} = \frac{B}{E} = \frac{C}{F}$.

They will be different and parallel if $\frac{A}{D} = \frac{B}{E}$ and $\frac{B}{E} \neq \frac{C}{F}$.

They will be different and intersect at a point if $\frac{A}{D} \neq \frac{B}{E}$.

Unit 2

3. **a.** If the given directions are followed, the result is the equation $x = -6$. This says the vertical line modeled by $x = -6$ passes through the solution of the linear system. In other words, the x-coordinate of the point of intersection is -6.

   b. The graphics display shows a vertical line for the sum. The table of values for the sum equation will indicate an error. This is due to division by zero. Many graphing calculators will not give an error message when the graphics involve division by zero as happens in this case.

4. **a.** Substitute the points into the equations and verify that each point satisfies the appropriate equation.

   b. The lines are perpendicular; the slopes are $\frac{1}{3}$ and -3, negative reciprocals of each other.

   c. The point of intersection is $(-0.5, 1.5)$.

   d. The midpoint of segment AB is $(-0.5, 1.5)$. The midpoint of segment CD is $(0, 0)$. The segments intersect at the midpoint of segment AB.

   e. *ACBD* is a kite. The diagonals are perpendicular, but since both diagonals do not bisect each other it is not a rhombus or square. Students may use other reasoning to justify their answers. As you go over this task in class, it is important to draw on the variety of student responses. This will help students extend their understanding of how diagonals can determine a figure.

Reflecting

1. Responses may vary. Possible advantages are: concise representation, the way such expressions may be manipulated algebraically, and the ease with which students may check to see if a point lies on a given line or polygon.

2. **a.** Yes, Daryl's solution method is correct. There is no solution to the original system of equations because the two equations represent parallel lines.

   b. Yes, Candra's solution method is correct. There are an infinite number of solutions to the original system because the two equations represent the same line. Any ordered pair that satisfies $4x - y = 2$ will satisfy $12x - 3y = 6$ as well.

3. Suppose you have the system $-3x + 4y = -2$ and $x - 2y = 4$.

   a. What added information is provided about the system if you multiply the equation $x - 2y = 4$ by 2 and add it to $-3x + 4y = -2$? Explain your response.

   b. Use the "SYSTEMS" option of GEOXPLOR or similar software to graph the system and the sum equation you found in part a. What is unusual about the graphics display? Create a table of values for the system equations and the sum equation. What is unusual about the table? Why does this happen?

4. Segment AB has endpoints $A(-2, 1)$ and $B(1, 2)$. Segment CD has endpoints $C(-1, 3)$ and $D(1, -3)$. The equations of the lines containing segments AB and CD are $x - 3y = -5$ and $3x + y = 0$, respectively.

   a. How could you quickly check that these modeling equations are correct?

   b. How are the lines related? How do you know?

   c. Find the point of intersection of segments AB and CD using a linear combination of the equations.

   d. Find the midpoints of segments AB and CD. Compare your results with part c.

   e. What kind of quadrilateral is $ACBD$? Explain your reasoning.

Reflecting

1. In Lesson 1, geometric objects such as points, lines, and polygons were modeled algebraically using coordinates and equations. What do you see as some advantages of these models?

2. Study the methods used by Daryl and Candra as they began to solve these systems of equations.

   Daryl's method:

$$\left. \begin{array}{r} 2x + 3y = 1 \\ 6x + 9y = -4 \end{array} \right\} \qquad \begin{array}{r} -6x - 9y = -3 \\ \underline{6x + 9y = -4} \\ 0 = -7 \quad \text{Always False!} \end{array}$$

   Candra's method:

$$\left. \begin{array}{r} 4x - y = 2 \\ 12x - 3y = 6 \end{array} \right\} \qquad \begin{array}{r} -12x + 3y = -6 \\ \underline{12x - 3y = 6} \\ 0 = 0 \quad \text{Always True!} \end{array}$$

   a. Is Daryl's solution method correct? What is the solution of the original system? Explain.

   b. Is Candra's solution method correct? What is the solution of the original system? Explain.

LESSON 1 • A COORDINATE MODEL OF A PLANE   **105**

3. You now have several methods for solving a system of linear equations: linear combinations, matrices, graphs, tables of values, and substitution (rewriting the system as a single equation). Some of these methods are done more easily using technology; others are done more easily with paper and pencil. Sometimes you even can solve a system simply by examining the equations themselves. (See Organizing task 2.)

For each system of equations below, identify the solution method you would use and the reasons for your choice.

a. $y = x - 4$
$2x - y = -2.5$

b. $s + p = 5$
$2s - p = 4$

c. $x + 3y = 12$
$4x + 12y = 48$

d. $a = 5b + 40$
$a = 9b$

e. $y = 0.85 + 0.10x$
$y = 0.50 + 0.15x$

f. $6x + 8y = 22$
$40x + 30y = 100$

4. In mathematics as well as in daily life, the words *and* and *or* must be used carefully. For example, "Hattie and Lorena went to the store" is different from "Hattie or Lorena went to the store." Why? In a coordinate plane, the solution to the system of linear equations

$$Ax + By = C$$
$$Dx + Ey = F$$

is the solution to the statement $Ax + By = C$ **and** $Dx + Ey = F$. What is the solution to the statement $Ax + By = C$ **or** $Dx + Ey = F$? Draw a sketch illustrating your response.

Using the word *or* instead of *and* changes the relationship significantly.

Extending

1. Given the linear equations $Ax + By = C$ and $Dx + Ey = F$ and nonzero numbers m and n, the equation $m(Ax + By) + n(Dx + Ey) = mC + nF$ is a linear combination of the two equations.

   a. What is the slope of the linear combination above?

   b. What is the y-intercept?

   c. If (h, k) is a solution of the system $Ax + By = C$ and $Dx + Ey = F$, is (h, k) also a solution to the linear combination of the equations? Explain your reasoning.

   d. How must A, D, m, and n be related in order to eliminate the x term from the linear combination?

3. Student responses may vary. Encourage students to consider which method would be the easiest in each case. For some systems there is not a clear-cut easiest method, but often there are one or two methods that make more sense to use. Give students latitude with their responses here, but responses should indicate consideration of more than one method.

4. All points on both lines satisfy the disjunction. That is, for a graph of both lines, the entire graph is the solution.

Extending

1. **a.** The slope of the linear combination is $\frac{-(mA + nD)}{(mB + nE)}$.

    b. The y-intercept is $\frac{(mC + nF)}{(mB + nE)}$.

    c. Yes. If a point satisfies the two separate equations, it also satisfies their sum. That is, if (h, k) satisfies the original system, then $Ah + Bk = C$ and $Dh + Ek = F$. So $m(Ah + Bk) + n(Dh + Ek) = m(C) + n(F) = mC + nF$. Thus (h, k) also satisfies the linear combinations.

    d. $mA = -nD$

Unit 2

1. e. $mB = -nE$

f. The m and n that eliminate x would also eliminate y.

2. This task gives students a glimpse of the row-reduction method of solving linear equations.

a.
$$\begin{bmatrix} 2 & -1 \\ 3 & 4 \end{bmatrix}\begin{bmatrix} x \\ y \end{bmatrix} = \begin{bmatrix} 7 \\ -6 \end{bmatrix}; \begin{bmatrix} x \\ y \end{bmatrix} = \begin{bmatrix} 2 \\ -3 \end{bmatrix}$$

b. ■ $\begin{bmatrix} 6 & -3 & 21 \\ 3 & 4 & -6 \end{bmatrix}$

■ $\begin{bmatrix} 6 & -3 & 21 \\ -6 & -8 & 12 \end{bmatrix}$

■ $\begin{bmatrix} 6 & -3 & 21 \\ 0 & -11 & 33 \end{bmatrix}$

c. $6x - 3y = 21$
$0x - 11y = 33$

d. The solution is $(2, -3)$.

e. The solution should be $(2, -3)$ regardless of the method used.

f. i. The solution is $(0, -1)$.

ii. The solution is $(7, 4)$.

iii. The solution is $(0.5, -2.5)$.

iv. The solution is $(\frac{10}{9}, \frac{20}{9})$.

e. How must B, E, m, and n be related in order to eliminate the y term from the linear combination?

f. If the original linear equations represent parallel lines, what happens when you try to choose m and n so that x is eliminated from the sum equation?

2. Consider the following system of linear equations.

$$2x - y = 7$$
$$3x + 4y = -6$$

a. Write the matrix equation that corresponds to this system. Solve the matrix equation.

b. When you multiply an equation by a nonzero number k, you multiply the *coefficient* of each of the variables and the constant by k. Similarly, when you add two equations, you add the coefficients of variables which are alike and you add the constants. This suggests that these operations could be done just as well on a matrix whose entries are the coefficients and constants. One way to represent the above system is as follows:

$$A = \begin{bmatrix} 2 & -1 & 7 \\ 3 & 4 & -6 \end{bmatrix}$$

where the entries in the last column are the constants.

■ Rewrite the first row of matrix A so that it represents the system with the first equation replaced by 3 times the first equation.

■ Rewrite this modified matrix so that it represents the system with the second equation replaced by −2 times the second equation.

■ Finally, rewrite the modified matrix so that row 2 is replaced by the sum of modified rows 1 and 2.

c. Write the system of equations represented by the final matrix in part b.

d. Use the results of part c to solve the original system of equations.

e. Compare your solution in part d with that in part a.

f. Use matrix row operations similar to those described in part b to solve each of the following systems of equations.

i. $-2x + y = -1$
$\quad 3x - y = \ 1$

ii. $x - y = \ 3$
$\quad 4x + y = 32$

iii. $x + y = \ -2$
$\quad 6x + y = \ 0.5$

iv. $3x - 6y = -10$
$\quad 6x - 3y = \ 0$

3. The three lines $4x - 3y = 0$, $2x - 5y = 0$, and $x + y = 7$ determine a triangle.

   a. Find the coordinates of the vertices.

   b. Each segment perpendicular to a side from the vertex opposite that side is called an **altitude** of the triangle. Write equations of the lines containing the altitudes for this triangle.

   c. Draw and label a diagram showing the triangle and its altitudes.

   d. Find the coordinates of the points of intersection of each pair of altitudes.

   e. Based on the results in part d, what do you think is true about the altitudes of a triangle?

   f. Explain how you could test your conjecture in part e.

4. Triangle ABC has vertices $A(2, -1)$, $B(-2, 1)$, and $C(1, 4)$.

   a. What kind of triangle is $\triangle ABC$?

   b. Find the midpoints of each side of $\triangle ABC$.

   c. Write equations of the lines containing the segments connecting each vertex to the midpoint of the opposite side (connecting C to the midpoint of segment AB, for example). The segments are called **medians**.

   d. Find the point of intersection for each pair of medians in part c.

   e. For one median, compute the distances from a point of intersection found in part d to the endpoints of the median. Compare the distances.

   f. Repeat part e for one of the other medians. Does the same relationship seem to hold?

   g. Compare your findings with those of a classmate who also has investigated this situation. On the basis of your combined results, what do you think is true about the medians of a triangle?

Assessments 42–44

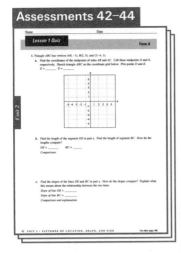

3. a. The coordinates are $A(0, 0)$, $B(5, 2)$, and $C(3, 4)$.

b. The equations of the lines containing the altitudes of the triangle are $x - y = 0$, $3x + 4y = 23$, and $5x + 2y = 23$.

c.

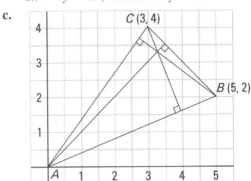

d. The coordinates of the point of intersection of each pair of equations is $\left(\frac{23}{7}, \frac{23}{7}\right)$.

e. The altitudes of a triangle intersect in a common point. (This point is called the *orthocenter*.)

f. Student responses may vary. One way they can test their conjecture is to pick three other lines and go through the same process. Students also could use geometry software (such as that found on the TI-92) to construct triangles and altitudes. While the existence of a single intersection also can be verified algebraically, the manipulations required can be very involved, so this method is not recommended for students at this point.

Assessments 45–47

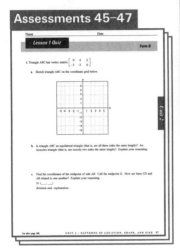

4. a. $\triangle ABC$ is a scalene triangle. The approximate lengths are: $AB \approx 4.47$; $BC \approx 4.24$; and $AC \approx 5.1$.

b. The midpoints of the three sides are $(0, 0)$, $\left(-\frac{1}{2}, \frac{5}{2}\right)$, and $\left(\frac{3}{2}, \frac{3}{2}\right)$.

c. $y = 4x$ or $4x - y = 0$

$y = \frac{-7}{5}x + \frac{9}{5}$ or $7x + 5y = 9$

$y = \frac{1}{7}x + \frac{9}{7}$ or $-x + 7y = 9$

d. $\left(\frac{1}{3}, \frac{4}{3}\right)$ is the intersection of any two medians.

e. Responses will vary. If the student chooses the median connecting C with the midpoint of AB (namely, $y = 4x$), the distance from $C(1, 4)$ to $\left(\frac{1}{3}, \frac{4}{3}\right)$ is approximately 2.75 and from the midpoint of AB $(0, 0)$ to $\left(\frac{1}{3}, \frac{4}{3}\right)$ is approximately 1.37. Regardless of which distance they find and use the longer distance should be twice the shorter one.

f. Consider the median connecting A with the midpoint of BC: the distance from A to $\left(\frac{1}{3}, \frac{4}{3}\right)$ is approximately 2.87 while the distance from $\left(-\frac{1}{2}, \frac{5}{2}\right)$ to $\left(\frac{1}{3}, \frac{4}{3}\right)$ is approximately 1.43. The same relationship holds here.

g. The medians always intersect in a common point. This point divides each median into two segments that have a 2 to 1 ratio. (The point is sometimes called the *centroid* of the triangle and it is the *center of gravity* for the triangle.)

See Assessment Resource pages 42–47.

Unit 2

Lesson 2 Coordinate Models of Transformations

LESSON OVERVIEW In Lesson 2, students are engaged in modeling transformations using coordinates and algebraic rules. Students examine specific points under transformations and generalize a coordinate rule for the transformation. From specific cases, students generalize the effects of transformations on distance, angle measure, and area. In some cases they may verify their conjectures algebraically. Students also investigate composition of transformations, again making generalizations. In the Organizing task 2 on page 146, students investigate composition of translations and size transformations to see an instance of the importance of order (non-commutativity) in composition.

Lesson Objectives

- To use coordinate geometry and planning algorithms as a tool to model translations, line reflections, and rotations and size transformations centered at the origin
- To use coordinate geometry to investigate properties of shapes under transformations, individually and in combinations
- To explore the concept of function composition using successive transformations

Lesson 2

Coordinate Models of Transformations

In Course 1, the idea of symmetry was used to analyze shapes. For example, the shape may have illustrated a distribution of data. The symmetry or nonsymmetry of that shape would have told you something about the relationship between the mean and median of the distribution. The shape also might have been that of a geometric model of something you see often. The Chrysler Corporation logo, for example, is based on a regular pentagon. The visual appeal of the logo is due, in part, to the symmetry of its form.

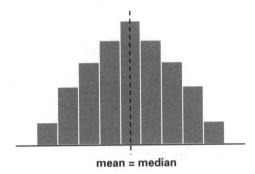

mean = median

The PENTASTAR logo is used with permission from Chrysler Corporation.

Recall that shapes such as the regular pentagon have two kinds of symmetry: reflection and rotational.

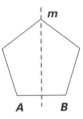

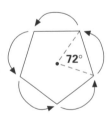

Reflection symmetry for regular pentagon: reflection across line *m* maps the pentagon onto itself. Two points, *A* and *B*, are symmetric when *m* is the perpendicular bisector of segment *AB*.

Rotational symmetry for regular pentagon: rotations of 72°, 144°, 216°, 288°, and 360° map the pentagon onto itself.

LESSON 2 · COORDINATE MODELS OF TRANSFORMATIONS **109**

Translational symmetry was seen to be the key idea in the design of ornamental strip patterns. A horizontal translation maps the strip onto itself. Strip patterns, such as that below, also may exhibit reflection and rotational symmetry.

In this lesson, you will investigate how coordinates can be used to model the transformations underlying these symmetries: reflections, translations, and rotations. Such transformations are called **rigid transformations**. They provide a way to move figures in a plane without changing the shape or the size of the figures.

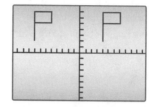 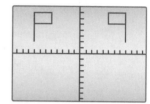

Think About This Situation

The calculator screens above show two flag patterns. The scale on both axes is 1.

a Examine the first display.

- What single transformation will map the left flag onto the right flag?
- How do you think coordinates might be used to create the appearance of moving the left flag to the position of the right flag?
- Suppose you want to produce a flag in each of the remaining quadrants so that the resulting flag patterns will have the *x*-axis as a line of symmetry. What steps would a calculator program need to follow, in order to do this?

b Now examine the second display.

- Suppose you want to produce a flag in each of the remaining quadrants so that the resulting flag pattern is symmetric with respect to both the *x*-axis and the *y*-axis. What steps would a calculator program need to follow, in order to do this?
- Will this pattern have any other symmetry? Explain.

LAUNCH full-class discussion

As an introduction to this lesson, let students know that they are going to use coordinate geometry to help them explore and learn more about transformations. Students need only prior familiarity with the concepts of coordinate representation and symmetry, and an understanding of what transformations do to shapes. You may need to remind them of vocabulary learned in Course 1, such as translation, reflection, and rotation, and to ask them to give examples where possible. Then facilitate a class discussion of the "Think About This Situation" questions, helping students to link what they know about transformations, coordinate geometry, and graphing. (There are several classroom posters available from commercial publishers that illustrate transformations in creative and colorful ways.)

NOTE: When work begins on the first MORE set for this lesson, it is important that some students in your class choose M2, M3, M4, O1, and O4. The ideas on preservation of distance, parallelism, perpendicularity, and area under the rigid transformations appear in these items. It would benefit the entire class if you pull all this together with a class discussion following the assignment.

Think About This Situation

See Teaching Master 38.

ⓐ ■ A translation with components 12 and 0 maps the left flag onto the right flag.

■ Add an appropriate constant (12) to each of the *x*-coordinates for each of the defining points of the flag.

■ First, input the coordinates for the endpoints of the four segments of the flag; then draw the flag.

For each quadrant, calculate the coordinates for a new flag:

The flag in quadrant I will be a translation image of the original.

The flag in quadrant III will be the image of the original reflected across the *x*-axis.

The flag in quadrant IV will be either a translation of the flag in quadrant III, or a reflection across the *x*-axis of the flag in quadrant I.

NOTE: The important idea here is how to translate or reflect a line or a point. Students should not write the program at this time. If you wish, let them know that by the end of this set of activities, they will be able to produce translations, reflections, and rotations on a graphics calculator if they choose to do so.

ⓑ ■ Input the coordinates for both flags; find the coordinates for the reflection across the *x*-axis of the two flags; and use the calculated coordinates to draw the image flags.

■ Yes, the new pattern also has 180° rotational symmetry.

Unit 2

INVESTIGATION 1 Modeling Rigid Transformations

This investigation asks students to develop general rules and a program planning algorithm for three of the four rigid transformations: translation, reflection, and rotation. (The fourth, glide reflection, is examined in Extending task 6 on page 125 in the student text.) In most cases, students should be able to complete these activities by working in small groups. If classroom discussion about the "Think About This Situation" questions leads you to believe your class may need more support, an alternative approach would be to work through the translation activities 1–3 as a whole class, and then move into small groups for the rest of the investigation.

As you move from group to group, you can check to be sure students are using the language of transformations so that they will become familiar with the standard terminology. In addition, you may want to check that each student, not just the recorder, is keeping careful and complete notes as new rules and planning algorithms are developed. These notes will be helpful in completing Modeling task 1 on page 120 in the student text. If you notice some groups moving faster than others, you may ask them extra questions, such as: "What happens to the slope of a line segment when it is translated? What is there about the slope calculation that makes your answer sensible?"

1.

Pre-Image	Translation Image
$A(-8, 2)$	$A'(4, 2)$
$B(-8, 5)$	$B'(4, 5)$
$C(-8, 7)$	$C'(4, 7)$
$D(-5, 7)$	$D'(7, 7)$
$E(-5, 5)$	$E'(7, 5)$

a. If we know the translation images of points A, B, C, D, and E, then we can draw the image flag by connecting the image points in the same order as the corresponding pre-image points. This is true since the image of a line segment is another line segment.

b.

Pre-Image	Translation Image
$(0, 0)$	$(12, 0)$
$(1, -5)$	$(13, -5)$
$(-5, -4)$	$(7, -4)$
$(-2.4, 1.3)$	$(9.6, 1.3)$
(a, b)	$(a + 12, b)$

c. To get the x-coordinate of the image of any point, add 12 to the x-coordinate of the point. The y-coordinate of the image is the same as the y-coordinate of the point. In symbols, this is $(x, y) \rightarrow (x + 12, y)$.

INVESTIGATION 1 Modeling Rigid Transformations

The first calculator display on the previous page was produced by translating the left flag horizontally to the right. The display is reproduced below on a coordinate grid. The scale on both axes is 1.

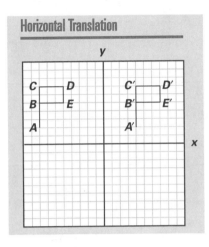

Horizontal Translation

Pre-image	Translation Image
A(?, ?)	A'(?, ?)
B(?, ?)	B'(?, ?)
C(?, ?)	C'(?, ?)
D(?, ?)	D'(?, ?)
E(?, ?)	E'(?, ?)

1. Complete a copy of the table above.

   a. Explain why the translation image of the flag could be produced using only the translation images of points A, B, C, D, and E.

   b. Under this translation, what would be the image of (0, 0)? Of (1, −5)? Of (−5, −4)? Of (−2.4, 1.3)? Of (a, b)?

   c. Describe a rule you can use to obtain the image of any point (x, y) under this translation. State it in words and in symbolic form $(x, y) \rightarrow (\_, \_)$.

2. Shown below are two more graphics displays. Each is a flag and its image under other translations.

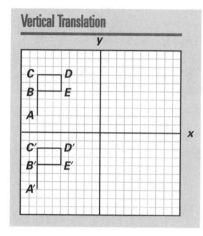 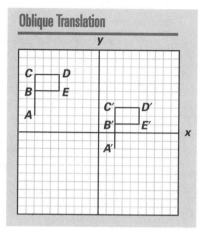

a. For each translation, complete a table similar to the one for activity 1.

b. Under the vertical translation, what would be the image of (0, 0)? Of (2, 5)? Of (−10, −4)? Of (4.1, −2)? Of (*a*, *b*)?

c. Write a rule you can use to obtain the image of any point (*x*, *y*) under the vertical translation. State it in words and in symbolic form.

d. Under the oblique translation, what would be the image of (0, 0)? Of (2, 5)? Of (−10, −4)? Of (4.1, −2)? Of (*a*, *b*)?

e. Write a rule you can use to obtain the image of any point (*x*, *y*) under the oblique translation. State it in words and in symbolic form.

f. Compare the transformation rules you developed for part c of activity 1 and for parts c and e of this activity. Write a general rule which tells how to take any point (*x*, *y*) and find its translation image if the pre-image is moved horizontally *h* units and vertically *k* units.

You now have a rule you can use to find the translation image of any point when you know the **components** of the translation: the horizontal and vertical distances and directions moved. This is exactly the information a calculator or computer program needs in order to display a set of points and their translation images.

3. a. Write an algorithm that would guide a programmer in the development of a program. The program would allow the user to enter coordinates of a point and the horizontal and vertical components of a translation. Then the program would display the point and its image along with their coordinates. Identify the input, processing, and output portions of your algorithm.

2. a.

Vertical Translation

Pre-Image	Translation Image
$A(-8, 2)$	$A'(-8, 7)$
$B(-8, 5)$	$B'(-8, -4)$
$C(-8, 7)$	$C'(-8, -2)$
$D(-5, 7)$	$D'(-5, -2)$
$E(-5, 5)$	$E'(-5, -4)$

Oblique Translation

Pre-Image	Translation Image
$A(-8, 2)$	$A'(2, -2)$
$B(-8, 5)$	$B'(2, 1)$
$C(-8, 7)$	$C'(2, 3)$
$D(-5, 7)$	$D'(5, 3)$
$E(-5, 5)$	$E'(5, 1)$

b. Vertical Translation

Pre-Image	Translation Image
$(0, 0)$	$(0, -9)$
$(2, 5)$	$(2, -4)$
$(-10, -4)$	$(-10, -13)$
$(4.1, -2)$	$(4.1, -11)$
(a, b)	$(a, b - 9)$

c. To find the image of any point (x, y) under the vertical translation, leave the x-coordinate as it is and subtract 9 from the y-coordinate. Symbolically this is written $(x, y) \rightarrow (x, y - 9)$.

d. Oblique Translation

Pre-Image	Translation Image
$(0, 0)$	$(10, -4)$
$(2, 5)$	$(12, 1)$
$(-10, -4)$	$(0, -8)$
$(4.1, -2)$	$(14.1, -6)$
(a, b)	$(a + 10, b - 4)$

e. To obtain the coordinates of any point (x, y) under the oblique translation, add 10 to the x-coordinate of the point and subtract 4 from the y-coordinate of the point. Symbolically this is $(x, y) \rightarrow (x + 10, y - 4)$.

f. The general rule which tells how to take any point (x, y) and find its translation image if the pre-image is moved horizontally h units and vertically k units is $(x, y) \rightarrow (x + h, y + k)$.

3. Student algorithms may be less well-defined than the one given below. At this point students will use the words *input, output,* and *processing* intuitively. When they refer back to the program in the student text, while answering part c, the meaning of the terms should become clearer to them.

a. Step 1: Get the coordinates of a point.

Step 2: Get the horizontal and vertical components of the translation.

Step 3: Compute the translation image.

Step 4: Display the coordinates of the point.

Step 5: Display the coordinates of the image point.

Step 6: Display the plots of the two points.

Steps 1 and 2 are the input portion of the algorithm. Step 3 is the processing portion, and Steps 4, 5, and 6 are the output portion.

Unit 2

EXPLORE *continued*

3. **See Teaching Master 39**.

   b. **Some students may find the language of programming intimidating and may need help to make sense of what the program instructions actually cause the calculator to do.**

   Line 2 allows input of the *y*-coordinate of the pre-image point.

   Line 3 allows input of the horizontal component of the translation.

   Line 6 displays the graph of the image point.

   Lines 9–11 display the coordinates of the pre-image, the word IMAGE, and then the coordinates of the image.

   c. Lines 1–4 are the input portion.

   Lines 6 and 11 are part of both the processing and the output portion of the program.

   Lines 5, 6, and 8–11 are the display portion.

   d. Students should run the program. They should verify that the coordinates of the image point output by the calculator are the same as what they would get if they found them without using the program.

   e. If "Pause" were not inserted, you would not be able to see the graphs of the points, because the calculator would continue the program and immediately display the other information.

The following is one program that works as described in part a. It is called TRANSL.

TRANSL Program

Program	Function in Program
Input "X⌣COORD-PRE⌣",A	Requests input for *x*-coordinate of the initial point. Stores the value in variable named A.
Input "Y⌣COORD-PRE⌣",B	
Input "X⌣COMP-TRANS⌣",H	
Input "Y⌣COMP-TRANS⌣",K	Requests input for *y*-component of translation. Stores value in variable named K.
ClrDraw	Clears all drawings.
Pt-On (A,B)	Illuminates point with coordinates (A, B).
Pt-On (A+H,B+K)	_____
Pause	Pause stops a program from continuing until ENTER is pressed.
Disp "PRE-IMAGE"	Displays word PRE-IMAGE.
Disp A,B	_____
Disp "IMAGE"	_____
Disp A+H,B+K	_____

b. Analyze this program and explain the purpose of each command line not already described.

c. Identify the input, processing, and output portions of TRANSL.

d. Get a copy of TRANSL from your teacher or enter it in your calculator or computer. (You may have to modify some commands.) Run the program for translations having different horizontal and vertical components. Be sure all equations and statistical plots are turned off. You will need to set your viewing window so that both the pre-image and image points will be displayed.

e. Why, in TRANSL, is there the "Pause" instruction?

Coordinates also provide simple models for *line reflections*. Geometry drawing programs use coordinates to create reflections across horizontal and vertical lines, as well as across the lines $y = x$ and $y = -x$. In the following activities you will build coordinate models for reflections across each of these lines.

4. The table below shows six pre-image points and a general point. Plot each point and its reflection image across the *x*-axis. Connect pre-image/image pairs with a dashed segment.

   a. Record the coordinates of the image points in a table like the one below.

Pre-image	Reflection Image across *x*-axis
(−4, 1)	(−4, −1)
(3, −2)	
(−2, −5)	
(4, 5)	
(0, 1)	
(−3, 0)	
(*a*, *b*)	

   b. What pattern relating coordinates of pre-image points to image points do you observe?

   c. Write a rule which tells how to take any point (*x*, *y*) and find its reflection image across the *x*-axis. State your rule in words and in symbols.

   d. How is the *x*-axis related to the segment determined by a point and its reflection image?

5. Draw the graph of $y = -x$. Plot each pre-image point in the table below and its reflection image across that line. Connect each pre-image/image pair with a dashed segment.

   a. Record the coordinates of the image points in a copy of the table.

Pre-image	Reflection Image across $y = -x$
(−4, 1)	(−1, 4)
(3, −2)	
(−2, −5)	
(4, 5)	
(1, −2)	
(−4, 4)	
(*a*, *b*)	

4. Students should be plotting points (not just looking for numerical patterns) so they can relate the coordinate model to what they see is happening on the graph.

   The pre-image points are indicated by * and the image points are indicated by •.

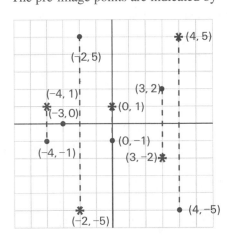

a.

Pre-Image	Reflection Image across *x*-axis
(−4, 1)	(−4, −1)
(3, −2)	(3, 2)
(−2, −5)	(−2, 5)
(4, 5)	(4, −5)
(0, 1)	(0, −1)
(−3, 0)	(−3, 0)
(a, b)	(a, −b)

b. The *x*-coordinates are the same and the *y*-coordinates are opposites.

c. The *x*-coordinates of the pre-image and image are the same. The *y*-coordinate of the image is −1 times the *y*-coordinate of the pre-image. In symbols, the rule is $(x, y) \rightarrow (x, -y)$.

d. The *x*-axis is perpendicular to and bisects the segment determined by each point and its reflection image.

5. The pre-image points are indicated by * and the image points are indicated by •.

a.

Pre-Image	Reflection Image across *y* = −*x*
(−4, 1)	(−1, 4)
(3, −2)	(2, −3)
(−2, −5)	(5, 2)
(4, 5)	(−5, −4)
(1, −2)	(2, −1)
(−4, 4)	(−4, 4)
(a, b)	(−b, −a)

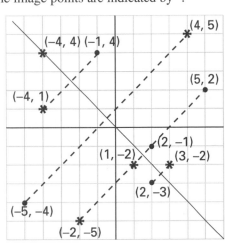

5. b. The *x*-coordinate of the image is the opposite of the *y*-coordinate of the pre-image. The *y*-coordinate of the image is the opposite of the *x*-coordinate of the pre-image.

c. $(x, y) \rightarrow (-y, -x)$

d. The slope of each pre-image/image segment is 1 and the slope of $y = -x$ is -1. This indicates that the reflection line is perpendicular to each of the segments. Students also should find that the midpoint of each segment lies on the line $y = -x$.

6. a. The *x*-coordinate for the image of a point reflected across the *y*-axis is the opposite of the pre-image *x*-coordinate. The *y*-coordinates are the same.

b. $(x, y) \rightarrow (-x, y)$

7. a. The *x*-coordinate of the image is the *y*-coordinate of the pre-image. The *y*-coordinate of the image is the *x*-coordinate of the pre-image. Symbolically this can be written $(x, y) \rightarrow (y, x)$.

b. The line $y = x$ is the perpendicular bisector of the segment.

8. Step 1: Get *x*- and *y*-coordinates of point.

Step 2: Calculate the coordinates of the image point using the appropriate rule.

Step 3: Display the graphs of the points.

Step 4: Display the coordinates of the points.

This algorithm works for each transformation. The planning programs would differ only in the formula used for calculating the coordinates of the image point:

■ reflection across *x*-axis: $(x, y) \rightarrow (x, -y)$

■ reflection across *y*-axis: $(x, y) \rightarrow (-x, y)$

■ reflection across the line $y = x$: $(x, y) \rightarrow (y, x)$

■ reflection across the line $y = -x$: $(x, y) \rightarrow (-y, -x)$

Step 1 is the input portion of the algorithm.

Step 2 is the processing portion of the algorithm.

Steps 3 and 4 are the output portion of the algorithm.

NOTE: Groups finishing quickly could begin working on Modeling task 2, Organizing task 4, or Extending tasks 3 or 4.

---

b. Describe a pattern relating coordinates of pre-image points to image points.

c. What are the coordinates of the reflection image of any point (x, y) across the line $y = -x$?

d. Investigate the relationship between the line of reflection, $y = -x$, and the segment determined by a point (x, y) and its image. Use the ideas of distance, midpoint, and slope.

6. The second calculator display for the "Think About This Situation" on page 110 was produced by reflecting the left flag across the y-axis. The display is reproduced here on a coordinate grid.

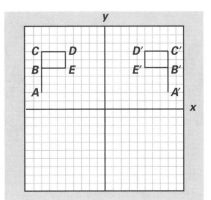

a. Investigate patterns in the coordinates of pre-image and image pairs when points are reflected across the y-axis.

b. Write a general rule which tells how to take any point (x, y) and find its reflection image across the y-axis.

7. Next, investigate patterns in the coordinates of the pre-image and image pairs when points are reflected across the line $y = x$.

a. What are the coordinates of the image of any point (x, y) when reflected across the line $y = x$?

b. How is the segment determined by a point and its reflection image related to the line $y = x$?

8. You now have coordinate models for the following line reflections:

- reflection across x-axis
- reflection across y-axis
- reflection across $y = x$
- reflection across $y = -x$

Sharing the workload among your group members, develop planning algorithms for line reflection programs. The programs should accept the coordinates of a point and do the necessary processing. Then they should display the graph of the point and its reflection image, and then the coordinates of those points. Label the input, processing, and output portions of your algorithms.

Checkpoint

You now have developed coordinate models for translations and certain line reflections.

ⓐ How do the rules relating coordinates for line reflections differ from the rules for translations?

ⓑ How do the rules for reflecting across the lines $y = x$ and $y = -x$ differ from rules for reflecting across an axis?

ⓒ Suppose the reflection image of a point A across a line m is A'. Describe how segment AA' and m are related.

Be prepared to explain your group's ideas to the class.

▶ On Your Own

On graph paper, sketch triangle ABC on three separate coordinate grids.

$$ABC = \begin{bmatrix} -1 & 4 & 3 \\ 2 & -3 & 5 \end{bmatrix}$$

Sketch and label the image of triangle ABC under each transformation below.

a. Reflection across the y-axis

b. Translation with components -3 and 2

c. Reflection across the line $y = x$

The use of coordinates resulted in easily-applied models for translations and for some line reflections. *Rotations* about the origin have similar coordinate models. Recall that the angle of the rotation is given as the measure of an angle at the center of rotation.

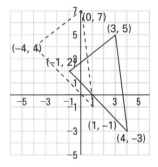
SHARE AND SUMMARIZE   full-class discussion

Checkpoint

See Teaching Master 40.

ⓐ When a point (x, y) is reflected, the image point is found by some combination of $\pm x$ and $\pm y$. Thus the absolute values of the coordinates of the two points are the same, although possibly reversed. In the case of a translation, values are added to the x- and y- coordinates to give the new point.

ⓑ When points are reflected over the x- or y-axis, the x- and y-coordinates of the images differ from the x- and y- coordinates of the pre-images only in the sign (if that). However, when points are reflected over the 45° lines, the coordinates of the images switch: the x-coordinate of the image is the y-coordinate of the pre-image (possibly with a sign change) and similarly for the y-coordinate.

ⓒ The line m is the perpendicular bisector of segment AA'.

APPLY   individual task

▶On Your Own

In each sketch below, $\triangle ABC$ is drawn with solid segments and $\triangle A'B'C'$ with dashed segments.

a. Reflection across y-axis:

$$\triangle A'B'C' = \begin{bmatrix} 1 & -4 & -3 \\ 2 & -3 & 5 \end{bmatrix}$$

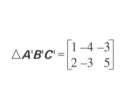

b. Translation with components -3 and 2:

$$\triangle A'B'C' = \begin{bmatrix} -4 & 1 & 0 \\ 4 & -1 & 7 \end{bmatrix}$$

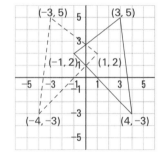

c. Reflection across the line $y = x$:

$$\triangle A'B'C' = \begin{bmatrix} 2 & -3 & 5 \\ -1 & 4 & 3 \end{bmatrix}$$

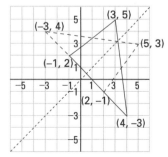

MORE
ASSIGNMENT   *pp. 120–126*

Students now can begin Modeling task 2, Organizing task 4, or Extending tasks 3 or 4 from the MORE assignment following Investigation 1.

EXPLORE small-group investigation

As you listen to groups discuss rotations, you might find it appropriate to ask how rotations are different from translations and reflections. (For example, a 90° rotation does not retain the absolute value of either coordinate.) Students need to be comfortable with the ideas and language of all three transformations and be able to make sense of them visually and symbolically. If you see an able group completing activity 10 more quickly than the rest of the class, then you might want to ask if the result of the 180° rotation of the flag is the same as a reflection over the line $y = x$, or over any other line. (The result of a 180° rotation cannot be obtained by a single reflection.)

9. See Teaching Master 41.

a.

Pre-image	90° Counterclockwise Rotation Image
A (0, 0)	A' (0, 0)
B (3, 3)	B' (−3, 3)
C (5, 5)	C' (−5, 5)
D (7, 3)	D' (−3, 7)
E (5, 1)	E' (−1, 5)
(−2, −5)	(5, −2)
(−4, 1)	(−1, −4)
(5, −3)	(3, 5)

b.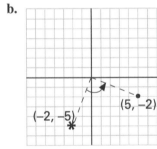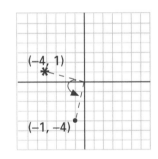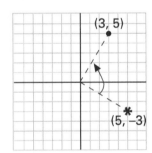

c. $(x, y) \rightarrow (-y, x)$

d. The image of (0, 0) is (0, 0). This makes sense because (0, 0) is the center of rotation and the center does not move in a rotation.

9. Examine these images of a flag under counterclockwise rotations of 90°, 180°, and 270° about the origin.

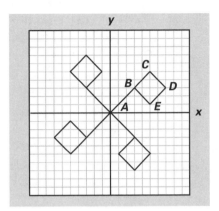

The table below shows the coordinates of five points on the flag in the first quadrant. Also shown are coordinates of other points in the coordinate plane.

Pre-image	90° Counterclockwise Rotation Image	180° Counterclockwise Rotation Image	270° Counterclockwise Rotation Image
A(0, 0)	A′(,)		
B(3, 3)	B′(,)		
C(5, 5)	C′(,)		
D(7, 3)	D′(,)		
E(5, 1)	E′(,)		
(−2, −5)			
(−4, 1)			
(5, −3)			

a. On a copy of this table, record the images of the five points on the flag under a 90° counterclockwise rotation about the origin.

b. Use any patterns you see between pre-image and image points to help plot the remaining points and their images on a new coordinate grid. For each pre-image point, use dashed segments to connect the pre-image to the origin and the origin to the image. Then draw a "turn" arrow that connects the pre-image and image segments and shows the direction of rotation.

c. Write a rule relating the coordinates of any pre-image point (x, y) and its image point.

d. According to your rule, what is the image of (0, 0)? Why does this image make sense?

e. How should the slope of the line through a pre-image point and the origin be related to the slope of the line through the origin and the image point? Verify your idea by computing and comparing slopes.

f. Write an algorithm to guide the development of a program that would take a point, rotate it 90° counterclockwise about the origin, and then display the point and its image along with their coordinates.

10. As you probably expect, rotations of 180° and 270° about the origin have nice coordinate patterns also.

a. Complete the remaining columns in your copy of the table from activity 9.

b. What pattern do you see among the coordinates of the pre-images and the rotation images for 180°? For 270°?

c. Summarize your patterns symbolically.

- What is the image of the point (x, y) under a 180° rotation about the origin?

- What is the image of the point (x, y) under a 270° counterclockwise rotation about the origin?

d. Describe how you could modify the algorithm in part f of activity 9 so that it would outline a program to rotate a point 180° or 270° counterclockwise about the origin instead of 90°.

M.C. Escher's "Path of Life II" ©1997 Cordon Art-Baarn-Holland. All rights reserved.

11. A triangle, $\triangle ABC$, has vertices as follows: $A(4, -2)$, $B(7, 9)$, and $C(-8, 4)$.

a. Draw $\triangle ABC$ on a coordinate grid. Then perform each of the following transformations on $\triangle ABC$ and draw the resulting image. Label each image for easy reference.

- Rotation of 180° counterclockwise about the origin

- Rotation of 90° counterclockwise about the origin

- Rotation of 90° clockwise about the origin

b. Compare the length of segment AB to the length of its image under each transformation.

9. e. These lines should be perpendicular, so their slopes should be negative reciprocals of one another.

f. One possible rotation algorithm:

Step 1. Get coordinates of the pre-image point.

Step 2. Calculate the coordinates of the image point.

Step 3. Display the graphs of the two points.

Step 4. Display the coordinates of each point.

10. a.

Pre-image	90° Counterclockwise Rotation Image	180° Counterclockwise Rotation Image	270° Counterclockwise Rotation Image
A (0, 0)	A' (0, 0)	(0, 0)	(0, 0)
B (3, 3)	B' (−3, 3)	(−3, −3)	(3, −3)
C (5, 5)	C' (−5, 5)	(−5, −5)	(5, −5)
D (7, 3)	D' (−3, 7)	(−7, −3)	(3, −7)
E (5, 1)	E' (−1, 5)	(−5, −1)	(1, −5)
(−2, −5)	(5, −2)	(2, 5)	(−5, 2)
(−4, 1)	(−1, −4)	(4, −1)	(1, 4)
(5, −3)	(3, 5)	(−5, 3)	(−3, −5)

b. The x- and y-coordinates of the image of a point under a 180° counterclockwise rotation are the opposites of the x- and y-coordinates of the pre-image.

Under a 270° counterclockwise rotation, the x-coordinate of the image is equal to the y-coordinate of the pre-image and the y-coordinate of the image is the opposite of the x-coordinate of the pre-image.

c. ■ For 180° rotation, the general transformation rule is $(x, y) \rightarrow (-x, -y)$.

■ For 270° counterclockwise rotation, the general transformation rule is
$(x, y) \rightarrow (y, -x)$.

d. The algorithm given for activity 9 part f (above) does not need to be changed at all. If a student included more detail for the processing portion, that part would be different in each program because the mapping rules are different for each rotation.

See additional Teaching Notes on page T168G.

Unit 2

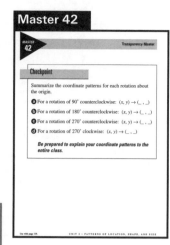

Checkpoint

See Teaching Master 42.

ⓐ For a 90° counterclockwise rotation: $(x, y) \rightarrow (-y, x)$.

ⓑ For a 180° counterclockwise rotation: $(x, y) \rightarrow (-x, -y)$.

ⓒ For a 270° counterclockwise rotation: $(x, y) \rightarrow (y, -x)$.

ⓓ For a 270° clockwise rotation: $(x, y) \rightarrow (-y, x)$.

Notice that parts a and d are identical. You may wish to prompt students to notice that a counterclockwise rotation of $x°$ is equivalent to a clockwise rotation of $360° - x°$.

CONSTRUCTING A MATH TOOLKIT: Following the discussion on properties preserved under rigid transformations (see the note beginning the following MORE set), you may wish to have students summarize the discussion in their math toolkits.

APPLY individual task

▶**On Your Own**

a. $A'(-2, -3)$; $B'(6, 2)$

b. The midpoint of segment AB is $(-0.5, -2)$.

c. The midpoint of segment $A'B'$ is $(2, -0.5)$.

d. The midpoint of $A'B'$ is a 90° counterclockwise rotation of the midpoint of segment AB.

Checkpoint

Summarize the coordinate patterns for each rotation about the origin.

a For a rotation of 90° counterclockwise: $(x, y) \rightarrow (\_\_ , \_\_)$

b For a rotation of 180° counterclockwise: $(x, y) \rightarrow (\_\_ , \_\_)$

c For a rotation of 270° counterclockwise: $(x, y) \rightarrow (\_\_ , \_\_)$

d For a rotation of 270° clockwise: $(x, y) \rightarrow (\_\_ , \_\_)$

Be prepared to explain your coordinate patterns to the entire class.

On Your Own

Find the images of $A(-3, 2)$ and $B(2, -6)$ under a 90° counterclockwise rotation about the origin. Call the images A' and B'.

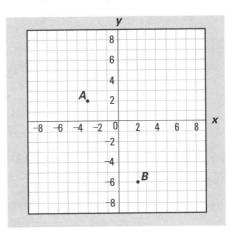

a. What are the coordinates of A' and B'?

b. Find the midpoint of segment AB.

c. Find the midpoint of segment $A'B'$.

d. How are the midpoints in parts b and c related?

Unit 2

MORE
Modeling • Organizing • Reflecting • Extending

Modeling

1. Refer to the table you completed for Modeling task 1 in Lesson 1 (page 90). Extend that table to include the coordinate models of rigid transformations you developed in this investigation.

Geometric Idea	Coordinate Model	Example
Translation	$(x, y) \rightarrow (x + h, y + k)$	
Reflection across x-axis	$(x, y) \rightarrow (?, ?)$	
Reflection across y-axis	$(x, y) \rightarrow (?, ?)$	
Reflection across line $y = x$		
Reflection across line $y = -x$		
90° counterclockwise rotation		
180° rotation		
270° counterclockwise rotation		$(2, 5) \rightarrow (5, -2)$

2. On a coordinate grid, draw the segment AB determined by $A(-3, 2)$ and $B(4, -3)$.

   a. Find the image of segment AB under a translation with horizontal and vertical components of -2 and 4 respectively. Draw the image segment $A'B'$ on the same coordinate grid.

   b. Compare the lengths of segments AB and $A'B'$.

   c. Compare the slopes of the lines through A and B and through A' and B'.

   d. What kind of quadrilateral is formed by connecting A to A' and B to B'? Explain your conclusion.

   e. Investigate whether the relationships in parts b, c, and d hold for other segments and their images under this translation. Write a summary of your findings.

3. The image of a polygon is found by locating the images of the vertices and connecting them in order. For this task, use the triangle

$$ABC = \begin{bmatrix} 2 & 5 & -1 \\ 4 & -2 & -1 \end{bmatrix}$$

When work begins on this MORE set, it is important that some students in your class choose M2, M3, M4, O1, and O4. The ideas on preservation of distance, parallelism, perpendicularity, and area under the rigid transformations appear in these items. It would benefit the entire class if you pull all this together with a class discussion following the assignment.

Master 43

Name _____ Date _____

MASTER 43 | Activity Master

Coordinate Models II

Geometric Idea	Coordinate Model	Example
Translation	$(x, y) \to (x + h, y + k)$	
Reflection across x-axis	$(x, y) \to (\ ,\ )$	
Reflection across y-axis	$(x, y) \to (\ ,\ )$	
Reflection across line y = x		
Reflection across line y = -x		
90° counterclockwise rotation		
180° rotation		
270° counterclockwise rotation		$(2, 5) \to (5, -2)$

Use with page 126.   UNIT 2 • PATTERNS OF LOCATION, SHAPE, AND SIZE

Modeling

1. **See Teaching Master 43.**

   You may wish to have students add this table to their math toolkits.

Geometric Idea	Coordinate Model	Example
Translation	$(x, y) \to (x + h, y + k)$	$(3, 4) \to (8, 1)$ $(h = 5, k = -3)$
Reflection across x-axis	$(x, y) \to (x, -y)$	$(1, -3) \to (1, 3)$
Reflection across y-axis	$(x, y) \to (-x, y)$	$(2, 5) \to (-2, 5)$
Reflection across line $y = x$	$(x, y) \to (y, x)$	$(3, 6) \to (6, 3)$
Reflection across line $y = -x$	$(x, y) \to (-y, -x)$	$(-2, 5) \to (-5, 2)$
90° counterclockwise rotation	$(x, y) \to (-y, x)$	$(6, -1) \to (1, 6)$
180° rotation	$(x, y) \to (-x, -y)$	$(3, -2) \to (-3, 2)$
270° counterclockwise rotation	$(x, y) \to (y, -x)$	$(2, 5) \to (5, -2)$

**MORE
ASSIGNMENT** *pp. 120–126*

Modeling: 1 and choice of
2, 3, or 4*

Organizing: 2, 5, and choice of
1 or 4*

Reflecting: 3

Extending: Choose one*

*When choice is indicated, it is important to leave the choice to the student.
NOTE: It is best if Organizing tasks are discussed as a whole class after they have been assigned as homework.

2. **a.**

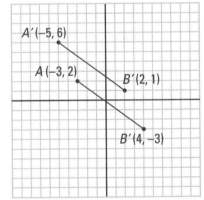

   b. The lengths of the two segments are the same. Both segments are approximately 8.6 units long.

   c. The two lines both have slope of $\frac{-5}{7}$ or -0.71.

   d. The quadrilateral $ABB'A'$ is a parallelogram because the opposite sides are parallel. The lines through AA' and BB' have slope of -2. Students may provide other reasoning to justify that the quadrilateral is a parallelogram. One alternative justification is that sides AB and $A'B'$ are both parallel and equal in length.

   e. The relationships of parts b, c, and d will hold for any translation. These activities can be summarized by saying that lengths and slopes are preserved under translations.

Unit 2

3. a.

■ 180° rotation about the origin   ■ Reflection across $y = -x$ ■ Vertical translation of −4 units

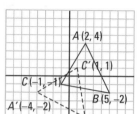

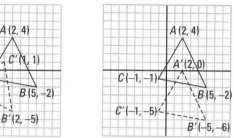

b.

Segment	Pre-Image Image	Image, 180° Rotation	Image, Reflection Across $y = x$	Image, Vertical Trans. of −4 units
AB	6.71	6.71	6.71	6.71
BC	6.08	6.08	6.08	6.08
AC	5.83	5.83	5.83	5.83

It appears that the four triangles have the same shape and size. The lengths of the sides remain unchanged under the transformations.

4. a. See the graph below. The slope of both lines is 0.5, therefore, the lines are parallel.

b. See the graph below. The images of lines *m* and *n* can be determined by reflecting points *A*, *B*, *C*, and *D* across the line $y = x$ as shown in the graph.
The images of lines *m* and *n* are parallel lines. The slope of each image line is 2.

c. See the graph below. The images of lines *m* and *n* can be determined by reflecting points *A*, *B*, *C*, and *D* across the *x*-axis. The image lines are parallel. The slope of each image line is −0.5.

d. See the graph below. The images of lines *m* and *n* can be determined by rotating points *A*, *B*, *C*, and *D* 180° about the origin. The images are parallel lines. Each image line has slope 0.5.

e. It would appear that parallel lines remain parallel under translations, reflections, and rotations. The conjectures could be further explored using different lines and different transformations. This exploration may be easier for students to do if they use GEOXPLOR or similar software.

Graph for 4a.

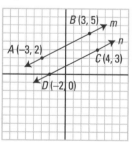

Graph for 4b.

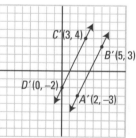

Graph for 4c.

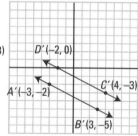

Graph for 4d.

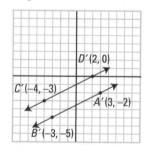

See additional Teaching Notes on page T168H.

Unit 2

a. On separate coordinate grids, sketch triangle *ABC* and its image under each of the following transformations.

- 180° rotation about the origin
- Reflection across the line $y = -x$
- A vertical translation of 4 units in the negative direction

Label the vertices of each image triangle.

b. Compare the lengths of the sides of △*ABC* with those of the corresponding sides of the images. What can you conclude about the four triangles?

4. Line *m* contains $A(-3, 2)$ and $B(3, 5)$; line *n* contains $C(4, 3)$ and $D(-2, 0)$. Sketch these lines. Use a coordinate model to help answer the following.

a. How is line *m* related to line *n*?

b. Find the images of *m* and *n* when reflected across the line $y = x$. Are the images lines? How are the images related?

c. Find the images of *m* and *n* when reflected across the *x*-axis. How are the images related?

d. Find the images of *m* and *n* when rotated 180° about the origin. Are the images lines? How are the images related?

e. Write a conjecture about the images of parallel lines under the transformations in parts b, c, and d. How could you check your conjecture?

Organizing

1. Triangle $ABC = \begin{bmatrix} -2 & 2 & 0 \\ -1 & 1 & 5 \end{bmatrix}$.

a. What kind of triangle is △*ABC*? How do you know?

b. What is the area of △*ABC*?

c. Sketch △*ABC* and its image under each of the following transformations.

- Reflection across the *y*-axis
- Counterclockwise rotation of 270° about the origin
- Reflection across the *x*-axis

d. What kind of triangle is each of the three image triangles in part c? How do you know?

e. Find the area of each of the three image triangles in part c. What do you notice?

2. In this unit you have seen that a matrix is a useful way of recording the vertices of a polygon. For example, the matrix in Organizing task 1 represents the triangle with vertices $A(-2, -1)$, $B(2, 1)$, and $C(0, 5)$. In this task you will explore how polygons can be represented and transformed using the List and Line Plot (plot over time) features of a calculator.

L1	L2	L3
-2	-1	-----
2	1	
0	5	
-----	-----	

L2 (4)=

  a. Enter in List 1 the *x*-coordinates of the vertices of triangle *ABC* in the order given above. Similarly, enter the *y*-coordinates in List 2.

  b. Produce a line plot of this data. Add coordinates of a fourth point to List 1 and List 2 so that when replotted, triangle *ABC* will be displayed.

  c. Transform the data in List 1 by adding 6 to each value, and store the new data in List 3. Similarly, transform the data in List 2 by adding 4 to each value and store the new data in List 4.

  d. Produce a line plot of the transformed data. Maintain the display of triangle *ABC*. Use a rigid transformation to describe as completely as possible how the two displayed triangles are related.

  e. Use lists and line plots to display triangle *PQR* with vertices $P(-8, 0)$, $Q(-5, 7)$, and $R(-2, 3)$ and its image under each of the following rigid transformations.

  ■ Reflection across the *x*-axis

  ■ Reflection across the *y*-axis

  ■ Rotation of 90° counterclockwise about the origin

3. For all the rigid transformations examined in Investigation 1, the image of a line is a line.

  a. For one type of these transformations, the image of a line is always *parallel* to the pre-image line. For another type, the image of a line is sometimes parallel to the pre-image line. What are these transformations? Verify your choices by showing that the image of the line containing $(-1, 3)$ and $(2, 5)$ is parallel to the pre-image line for each transformation.

  b. Which of the rigid transformations examined in Investigation 1 map a line onto an image line which is *perpendicular* to the initial line? Illustrate your choice or choices using the line containing $(-1, 3)$ and $(2, 5)$ and its image.

© Mondrian Estate/Holtzman Trust

2. **a.** Students must enter the coordinates in the same order and in the order in which the points should be connected.

    b. The coordinates of point *A* must be entered again, as a fourth point. This produces the third side of the triangle from *C* to *A*.

    c–d. A translation with components 6 and 4 maps $\triangle ABC$ onto the triangle whose coordinates are in List 3 and List 4 .

    e. Students should enter the coordinates of *P, Q,* and *R* into Lists 1 (L_1) and 2 (L_2) as they did in parts a and b. They must remember to repeat the coordinates of point *P* as the last entries in the lists. For each transformation, Lists 3 (L_3) and 4 (L_4) should be defined as indicated below. Then a line plot using L_3 and L_4 will draw the indicated triangle.

    - Let $L_3 = L_1$ and $L_4 = -1 * L_2$.
    - Let $L_3 = -1 * L_1$ and $L_4 = L_2$.
    - Let $L_3 = -1 * L2$ and $L_4 = L_1$.

3. **a.** Under any translation, the image of a line is parallel to the pre-image line. The slope of the line given is $\frac{2}{3}$ or 0.67. For any components students select, the slope of the image line also will be 0.67. That is, for components *h* and *k*, the slope will be $\frac{(5 + k) - (3 + k)}{(2 + h) - (-1 + h)}$ which equals 0.67.

    Under a 180° rotation about the origin, pre-image and image lines remain parallel. The image points of the given line are $(1, -3)$ and $(-2, -5)$. The slope of the image line is 0.67.

    b. Rotations of 90° or 270° map a line onto an image line that is perpendicular to the pre-image line. The slope of the given line is $\frac{2}{3}$ or 0.67.

    A 90° counterclockwise rotation maps the points $(-1, 3)$ and $(2, 5)$ onto the points $(-3, -1)$ and $(-5, 2)$. The slope of the image line is $\frac{-3}{2}$ or -1.5. The product of the slopes is -1; therefore the image and pre-image lines are perpendicular.

    Under a rotation of 270°, the pre-image points map onto the points $(3, 1)$ and $(5, -2)$. The slope of the image segment is -1.5. Again the product of the slopes of the pre-image and image lines is -1; therefore the lines are perpendicular.

4. **a.** The slope of the line *BC* is -2 and the slope of the line *BD* (or line *CD*) is -2; therefore the points must lie on the same line. (Alternatively, students could write the equation for line *BC* and check that the coordinates for *D* satisfy the equation.) The slope of the line *AD* is 0.5. Since the product of the slopes of the segments *BC* and *AD* is -1, the segments must be perpendicular.

b. The area of $\triangle ABC = \frac{1}{2}(AD)(BC)$
$$= \frac{1}{2}\sqrt{20}\sqrt{45} = 15 \text{ square units}$$

c.

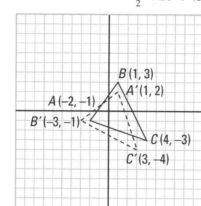

d. The area of the image triangle is 15 square units. Students should use a method similar to that used in parts a and b to verify this.

e.

f. The area of the image triangle is 15 square units. Students should use a method similar to that used in parts a and b to verify this.

5. **a.** 2. Get the *x*-coordinate of the pre-image.
   3. Get the *y*-coordinate of the pre-image.
   5. Calculates the *y*-coordinate of the image.
   7. Plots the pre-image point.
   8. Plots the image point.
   10. Displays the words PRE-IMAGE POINT.
   11. Displays the coordinates of the pre-image.
   12. Displays the words IMAGE POINT.
   13. Displays the coordinates of the image.

b. Students should obtain and run the program.

4. Triangle $ABC = \begin{bmatrix} -2 & 1 & 4 \\ -1 & 3 & -3 \end{bmatrix}$.

   a. Verify that $D(2, 1)$ is a point on line BC. Also, verify that segment AD is perpendicular to segment BC.

   b. Find the area of $\triangle ABC$. Use the results in part a to help you.

   c. Find the image of $\triangle ABC$ when reflected across the line $y = -x$.

   d. Find the area of the image triangle in part c.

   e. Find the image of $\triangle ABC$ when translated with components 2 and –3.

   f. Find the area of the image triangle of part e.

5. Below is a calculator program. When the program is executed, the calculator will display a point and the point's image under a 90° counterclockwise rotation about the origin. Then it displays the coordinates of both points.

ROT90 Program

Program	Function in Program
ClrHome	1. Clears the home screen.
Input "PRE-IMAGE X",A	2.
Input "PRE-IMAGE Y",B	3.
–B → C	4. Calculates the x-coordinate of image.
A → D	5.
ClrDraw	6. Clears Graphics screen.
Pt-On (A,B)	7.
Pt-On (C,D)	8.
Pause	9. Waits for ENTER to be pressed.
Disp "PRE-IMAGE POINT"	10.
Disp A,B	11.
Disp "IMAGE POINT"	12.
Disp C,D	13.
Stop	14. Stops program.

---

   a. Analyze the ROT90 program and explain the purpose of each of the lines not already annotated.

   b. Obtain a copy of ROT90 from your teacher. Run it to observe the pre-image and image graphs of several points.

Reflecting

1. Compare the planning algorithms you wrote in Investigation 1. How are they similar? How do they differ? (See activities 3 part a, 8, 9 part f, and 10 part d.)

2. In Course 1, line reflections, rotations, translations, and glide reflections were investigated in the context of strip patterns and tiling patterns of the plane. The descriptions and analyses were visual and did not depend upon coordinates. In Investigation 1, you built coordinate representations of most of these rigid transformations. Which way of thinking about and describing transformations seems to be most understandable and useful for you?

3. In Investigation 1, you and your groupmates developed symbolic rules for describing various transformations of a coordinate plane. If you forget one of these rules, how would you go about reconstructing it? Illustrate with a rule for a specific transformation.

4. Which clockwise rotation will be the same as a 270° counterclockwise rotation? Why? Which will be the same as a 90° counterclockwise rotation? Why?

5. Refer back to the rigid transformations you examined in Investigation 1.

   a. In which cases were distances between pairs of pre-image points the same as the distances between their images?

   b. If two lines are perpendicular, how are their images related under rigid transformations?

Extending

1. In Investigation 1, you prepared planning algorithms for programs that would translate, reflect, or rotate a point. Examples of such programs appear in activity 3 of the investigation (page 113) and in Organizing task 5.

   a. Write separate programs that will display the pre-image point and its image for the four reflections for which you developed coordinate models. Call them RXAXIS, RYAXIS, RYEX, RYENX.

   b. Write separate programs that will rotate a point about the origin through 180° and 270° (clockwise).

2. a. Modify TRANSL (activity 3 of Investigation 1) and your programs from Extending task 1 that transform individual points, so that they do the following: accept three points, display the triangle determined, and then display the image triangle under the transformation.

   b. Further modify your new TRANSL program so that it creates an animation of the triangle moving horizontally across the display screen.

Reflecting

1. Responses may vary. Some students may have included more calculational detail in their algorithms, making them different. However, they should be similar: get coordinates, calculate images, and plot them.

2. Responses may vary. Some students more easily understand visual descriptions and analysis. Others prefer the coordinate rules that can be associated with rigid transformations and find this representation easier to understand.

3. Responses may vary. Most students probably will suggest choosing several points and performing the indicated transformation, based upon what they know about the transformation. Then, by examining the coordinates of the pre-image points and the image points, they should be able to reconstruct the symbolic rule.

4. A clockwise rotation of 90° will be the same as a 270° counterclockwise rotation. Likewise, a 270° clockwise rotation will be the same as a counterclockwise rotation of 90°. This is because a circle has 360°, and $270 + 90 = 360$. So 90° in one direction brings you to the same place as 270° in the opposite direction.

5. **a.** Distance is preserved (remains the same) under all the rigid transformations.

   b. Under rigid transformations, perpendicular pre-image lines have perpendicular images.

Extending

1. **a.** The programs written below will work on a TI-82 or TI-83 graphics calculator.

```
PROGRAM: RXAXIS
Input "X COORD-PRE", A
Input "Y COORD-PRE", B
Pt-On (A, B)
Pt-On (A, -B)
Pause
Disp "PRE-IMAGE"
Disp A, B
Disp "IMAGE"
Disp A, -B
```

```
PROGRAM: RYAXIS
Input "X COORD-PRE", A
Input "Y COORD-PRE", B
Pt-On (A, B)
Pt-On (-A, B)
Pause
Disp "PRE-IMAGE"
Disp A, B
Disp "IMAGE"
Disp -A, B
```

```
PROGRAM: RYEX
Input "X COORD-PRE", A
Input "Y COORD-PRE", B
Pt-On (A, B)
Pt-On (B, A)
Pause
Disp "PRE-IMAGE"
Disp A, B
Disp "IMAGE"
Disp B, A
```

```
PROGRAM: RYENX
Input "X COORD-PRE", A
Input "Y COORD-PRE", B
Pt-On (A, B)
Pt-On (-B, -A)
Pause
Disp "PRE-IMAGE"
Disp A, B
Disp "IMAGE"
Disp -B, -A
```

See additional Teaching Notes on page T168I.

3. a. Students may observe that the *y*-coordinate remains unchanged and the *x*-coordinate changes. The *x*-coordinate of the image is obtained by adding $2(5 - x)$ to the *x*-coordinate of the pre-image. The pre-image (a, b) has reflection image $(10 - a, b)$.

   b. The image of (a, b), when reflected across $x = h$, is $(2h - a, b)$.

4. a. Students may observe that the *x*-coordinate remains unchanged and the *y*-coordinate changes. The *y*-coordinate of the image is obtained by adding $2(-6 - y)$ to the *y*-coordinate of the pre-image. The pre-image (a, b) has reflection image $(a, -12 - b)$.

   b. The image of (a, b), when reflected across $y = k$, is $(a, 2k - b)$.

5. a. The slope of the line containing pre-image points (a, b) and (c, d) is $\frac{d - b}{c - a}$. The coordinates of the image points under a 180° rotation are $(-a, -b)$ and $(-c, -d)$. The slope of the line containing the image points is $\frac{-d + b}{-c + a} = \frac{-1(d - b)}{-1(c - a)} = \frac{d - b}{c - a}$. The image and pre-image lines have equal slopes and so they must be parallel.

   b. The slope of the line containing pre-image points (a, b) and (c, d) is $\frac{d - b}{c - a}$. The coordinates of the image points under a translation with components (h, k) are $(a + h, b + k)$ and $(c + h, d + k)$. The slope of the line containing the image points is $\frac{(d + k) - (b + k)}{(c + h) - (a + h)}$ or $\frac{d - b}{c - a}$. The image and pre-image lines have equal slopes and so they must be parallel.

6. a. The coordinates of the image are $(8, 4)$.

   b. $(x, y) \rightarrow (x + h, -y)$

Unit 2

3. Recall your rule for predicting the coordinates of images for points reflected across the *y*-axis.

   a. Explore patterns in the coordinates of the pre-image and image points in the case of a reflection across the vertical line *x* = 5. What are the coordinates of the reflection image of point (*a*, *b*) across this line?

   b. Write a rule that gives the coordinates of the image of any point (*x*, *y*) when reflected across the vertical line *x* = *h*.

4. Recall your rule for predicting the coordinates of images for points reflected across the *x*-axis.

   a. Explore patterns in the coordinates of the pre-image and image points in the case of a reflection across the horizontal line *y* = −6. What are the coordinates of the reflection image of point (*a*, *b*) across this line?

   b. Write a rule that gives the coordinates of the image of any point (*x*, *y*) when reflected across the horizontal line *y* = *k*.

5. Suppose a line contains points with coordinates (*a*, *b*) and (*c*, *d*). Use these general coordinates to justify each following statement.

   a. Under a 180° rotation, the image of a line is a line parallel to the pre-image line.

   b. Under a translation with components *h* and *k*, the image of a line is a line parallel to the pre-image line.

6. The fourth rigid transformation in the Course 1 unit, "Patterns in Space and Visualization", was the **glide reflection**. Recall that a glide reflection translates a point parallel to a line and then reflects the translated image across the line (or vice versa). Below, point *A* translates to *B* and *B* reflects across line *l* to give the image point *C*. Check that the glide reflection image of *A* also can be found by reflecting across *l* first and then translating the distance and direction of segment *AB*.

   a. Suppose the glide reflection image of point (3, −4) is found by translating it 5 units parallel to the *x*-axis and then reflecting across the *x*-axis. (Translate in the positive direction.) What are the coordinates of the image?

   b. Suppose a point (*x*, *y*) is translated *h* units parallel to the *x*-axis, then the image is reflected across the *x*-axis. What are the coordinates of the glide reflection image point?

LESSON 2 • COORDINATE MODELS OF TRANSFORMATIONS   125

c. Investigate glide reflections using the *y*-axis. If a point (*x*, *y*) is translated *k* units parallel to the *y*-axis and then reflected across the *y*-axis, what are the coordinates of the image point?

d. Choose one of the coordinate patterns you found in part b or c and design a graphics calculator program that will perform the glide reflection. The program should allow the user to enter the distance of translation. Call the program GLIDEX or GLIDEY. Test the program.

INVESTIGATION 2 Modeling Size Transformations

In the previous investigation, you found patterns in the coordinates of pre-image/image pairs for transformations with which you were familiar. For those transformations, the distances between pairs of pre-image points and between their images were the same. As a result, under these rigid transformations, a polygon and its image had the same size and shape.

In this investigation, you will reverse the procedure. You will start with a rule relating coordinates of any pre-image and its image, and you will explore what the transformation does to familiar shapes.

1. The first transformation to be considered is defined by the following rule.

pre-image		image
(*x*, *y*)	$\longrightarrow$	(3*x*, *y*)

This rule is read "the *x*-coordinate of the image is 3 times the *x*-coordinate of the pre-image; the *y*-coordinate of the image is the same as the *y*-coordinate of the pre-image."

a. Using graph paper, plot *A*(4, 4) and *B*(−2, 1). Predict how the lengths of segment *AB* and its image *A'B'* will compare. Check your prediction by computing the coordinates for *A'* and *B'* and comparing lengths. How good was your prediction?

b. Find *M*, the midpoint of segment *AB*, and its image, *M'*. Is *M'* on the line determined by *A'* and *B'*? Is *M'* the midpoint of segment *A'B'*? What does this transformation seem to do to midpoints?

c. Are *C*(0, 2) and *D*(2, 3) on the line determined by points *A* and *B*? Find the images of points *C* and *D*. Are they on the line determined by *A'* and *B'*? What evidence supports your position? Does this evidence support the conjecture that the image of a line is again a line? Explain your reasoning.

d. Where does the line *AB* intersect its image? Where does the line through (3, −1) and (−2, −6) intersect its image? Do you think this will happen for any line and its image under this transformation? Explain.

6. **c.** $(x, y) \rightarrow (-x, y + k)$

   d. The programs below will run on a TI-82 or TI-83 graphics calculator. Slight modification may be necessary for them to run on other graphics calculators.

```
PROGRAM: GLIDEX
Input "A COORD-PRE ", A
Input "B COORD-PRE ", B
Input "TRANS DIST ", H
Pt-On (A, B)
Pt-On (A + H, -B)
Pause
Disp "PRE-IMAGE"
Disp A, B
Disp "IMAGE"
Disp A + H, -B
```

```
PROGRAM: GLIDEY
Input "A COORD-PRE ", A
Input "B COORD-PRE ", B
Input "TRANS DIST ", K
Pt-On (A, B)
Pt-On (-A, B + K))
Pause
Disp "PRE-IMAGE"
Disp A, B
Disp "IMAGE"
Disp -A, B + K
```

EXPLORE small-group investigation

INVESTIGATION 2 Modeling Size Transformations

During this investigation students will use coordinate geometry techniques to discover several aspects of size transformations. These include:

■ The effects of size transformations on length, slope, and area for various shapes.

■ The concepts associated with size transformations and similarity for plane shapes and how to apply these concepts in real-world situations.

To introduce this investigation you might want to refer students back to the "Think About This Situation" questions on the first page of the unit. Ask them to describe in words, using appropriate vocabulary (or in symbols), how one triangle was transformed onto another. Other questions to ask are, "Which triangle can not be rotated, reflected, or translated to transform it into either of the other two? Why not?"

A good way to begin the investigation itself is to start a discussion of the transformation represented by $(x, y) \rightarrow (3x, y)$. Ask students to give image points for specific pre-image points. Reverse this process also. Instruct students to predict the effects of the transformations throughout this investigation, before doing the graphing and computing.

As you circulate among groups, you can caution students that it will be helpful for them to make careful graphs for each of the figures in these activities, before they try to generalize ideas about size transformations. However, on some occasions you might want to push able students not to rely solely on their drawings. For example, activities 1, 2, and 3 are rich in connections to prior units, and students should discuss how to tell if a point is a midpoint or if a point lies on a line. Some students will say that they can see (without verification) that a point lies on a line.

See additional Teaching Notes on page T168J.

Unit 2

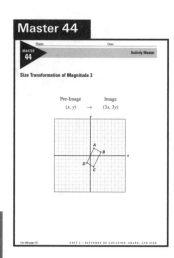

1. e.

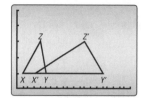 

The vertices of the image triangle are X' (3, 1), Y' (15, 1), and Z' (12, 3). Students may estimate the areas by measuring the altitude of their triangle or by counting the squares enclosed by the triangle. For these two triangles it is also easy to use the formula $A = \frac{b \times h}{2}$. The height of the triangle is 1 less than the y-coordinate of Z or Z' and the length of the base is the length of the horizontal segment XY or $X'Y'$. The area of the pre-image triangle is 4 square units and the area of the image triangle is 12 square units. The area of triangle $X'Y'Z'$ is three times the area of the original triangle.

2. **See Teaching Master 44.**

a. The coordinates of the image are A' (3, 6), B' (9, 3), C' (3, −9), and D' (−3, −6).

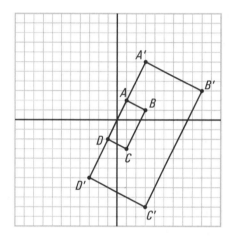

b. *ABCD* and *A'B'C'D'* each have 4 sides and 4 angles. Angles in the image quadrilateral appear to have equal measure to corresponding angles in the pre-image. Corresponding sides appear parallel, and the two figures have the same shape.
ABCD and *A'B'C'D'* seem to differ in that they are of different size (the corresponding sides are different lengths).

3. a. ■ The length of segment *AB* is $\sqrt{5}$ or approximately 2.24 units, and the length of segment *A'B'* is $\sqrt{45}$ or approximately 6.71 units. The length of the image segment is three times the length of the pre-image segment.

■ This relationship holds for each of the other pairs of line segments. The image length is three times the length of the pre-image.

b. Lines *AB* and *AD* are perpendicular. (The slope of *AB* is $\frac{1}{2}$ and the slope of *AD* is −2.) Yes, the same relationship holds for the image lines, *A'B'* and *A'D'*. (The slope of *A'B'* is $\frac{1}{2}$ and the slope of *A'D'* is −2.) The slopes of both sets of lines are negative reciprocals of one another.

c. The slope of *BC* and the slope of *AD* are both −2 so they are parallel. *B'C'* and *A'D'* are also parallel, with slopes of −2.

e. Consider the points $X(1, 1)$, $Y(5, 1)$, and $Z(4, 3)$. How do you think the area of $\triangle XYZ$ will compare to the area of the image triangle? Draw $\triangle XYZ$ and its image $\triangle X'Y'Z'$ under the transformation. Compute the areas and evaluate your conjecture.

Your investigation has shown that even a simple transformation like the one in activity 1 might not preserve all characteristics of pre-image shapes. By modifying the transformation rule slightly, you can create a transformation which has many interesting and useful characteristics.

2. A **size transformation of magnitude 3** is defined by the following rule.

pre-image   image

$(x, y) \qquad \longrightarrow \qquad (3x, 3y)$

a. On a copy of the diagram shown here, draw the size transformation image of quadrilateral $ABCD$. Label image vertices A', B', C', and D'.

b. Examine your pre-image and image shapes. Make a list of all the properties of quadrilateral $ABCD$ that seem also to be properties of quadrilateral $A'B'C'D'$. Also describe how the two shapes seem to differ.

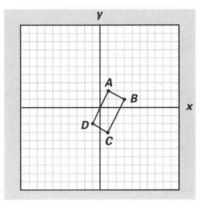

Making visual comparisons, as you did in activity 2, is useful; but such comparisons should be made with some skepticism. You always should seek additional evidence to verify or refute your visual conjectures. This is where coordinate representations and formulas for distance and slope can be very helpful.

3. Examine more carefully quadrilateral $ABCD$ and its size transformation image $A'B'C'D'$.

a. What appears to be true about the length of corresponding sides of the two shapes?

- Compare the length of segment AB with the length of segment $A'B'$.

- Does the same relation hold for other pre-image/image pairs of segments? Explain.

b. How are lines AB and AD related? Does the same relationship hold for their images? Give evidence to refute or support your claim.

c. How are lines BC and AD related? Is this relationship true for their images? Justify your conclusion.

d. What kind of quadrilateral is *ABCD*? Is the image quadrilateral *A'B'C'D'* the same kind of quadrilateral? Explain your reasoning.

e. How do the areas of quadrilaterals *ABCD* and *A'B'C'D'* appear to be related? State a conjecture. Test your conjecture by computing the areas. How does the magnitude of the size transformation come into play here?

f. Use a ruler to draw lines through *A* and *A'*, *B* and *B'*, *C* and *C'*, and *D* and *D'*. Extend the lines to intersect the axes. What do you notice about the intersection of these four lines?

g. This size transformation with magnitude 3 has its **center at the origin** since the lines in part f intersect at the origin.

- Compare the distances from the center, *O*, to a point and to the image of that point. State a conjecture.

- Compare the distance from *O* to *A* and from *O* to *A'*. From *O* to *B* and from *O* to *B'*. Do these distances confirm your conjecture?

- Make similar comparisons for points *C* and *D* and their images. What seems to be true? Modify your original conjecture, if necessary, based on the evidence.

- Based on your conjecture, how would the distances from the origin, *O*, to (x, y) and from *O* to $(3x, 3y)$ be related?

- Complete the following statement:

    If *O* is the center of a size transformation with magnitude *k* and the image of *P* is *P'*, then distance *OP'* = _____ and $\frac{\text{distance } OP'}{\text{distance } OP}$ = _____.

    Compare your general statement with that of other groups. Resolve any differences.

4. a. Write a rule for a size transformation with magnitude 0.5 and center at the origin.

b. Re-draw quadrilateral *ABCD*, given in activity 2 part a and repeated here. Plot and label its image under your new size transformation. How do you think quadrilateral *ABCD* and its image are related in terms of shape? How do you think the quadrilateral *ABCD* and its image are related in terms of size?

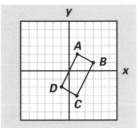

c. Compare segment lengths in the image with corresponding lengths in quadrilateral *ABCD*.

d. Find the area of the image quadrilateral. Compare it to the area of quadrilateral *ABCD*. How does the magnitude 0.5 affect the relation between areas?

3. d. *ABCD* is a rectangle. *A'B'C'D'* is also a rectangle. Both quadrilaterals have two pairs of opposite sides that are parallel and adjacent sides that are perpendicular.

e. The area of *ABCD* = $(AB)(BC) = (\sqrt{5})(\sqrt{20}) = 10$ square units. The area of *A'B'C'D'* = $(A'B')(A'D') = (\sqrt{45})(\sqrt{180}) = 90$ square units. The area of the image is 9 times the area of the pre-image. This change is the magnitude of the transformation squared.

f. When the lines are extended, they all intersect at the origin. (This characteristic always holds for size transformations centered at the origin. For any size transformation, the intersection point of these lines is the center of the transformation.)

g. This activity is central to the concept of a size transformation. You might want to draw groups together to discuss their answers. Students easily will see the true, but somewhat superficial, idea that a size transformation makes each side of a shape get bigger. Through this activity, students should progress beyond that idea to the more important, core idea: what is causing this expansion is that the distances from the origin are all increased by a certain factor. Having students talk about a size transformation with its center at the origin should help to keep the issue in focus. This core idea gets formalized after the Checkpoint. In particular, the magnification factor is given as a ratio of two distances from the origin.

■ The distance appears to be multiplied by 3.

■ $OA = \sqrt{5} \approx 2.236$ units and $OA' = \sqrt{45} \approx 6.708$ units; $OB = \sqrt{10} \approx 3.162$ units and $OB = \sqrt{90} \approx 9.486$ units. This confirms the conjecture given above.

■ $OC = \sqrt{10} \approx 3.162$ units and $OC' = \sqrt{90} \approx 9.486$ units. $OD = \sqrt{5} \approx 2.236$ units and $OD' = \sqrt{45} \approx 6.708$ units.

In each case the length of the image segment is three times the length of the pre-image segment.

■ The length of the image segment would be 3 times as long as the length of the pre-image segment. The two distances are $\sqrt{x^2 + y^2}$ and $\sqrt{9x^2 + 9y^2}$ (that is, $3\sqrt{x^2 + y^2}$). This last distance is 3 times the first. This proves the conjecture. It is not expected that students supply this algebraic proof. Rather, they should generalize from the observations that have preceded this question.

■ distance $OP' = k \cdot$ distance OP and $\frac{\text{distance } OP'}{\text{distance } OP} = k$

4. a. $(x, y) \rightarrow (0.5x, 0.5y)$

b. The image quadrilateral has vertices *A'* (0.5, 1), *B'* (1.5, 0.5), *C'* (0.5, −1.5), and *D'* (−0.5, −1). It is shown in the plot at the right. Conjectures may vary. The length of each segment in the image is half the length of its pre-image segment. The quadrilaterals are the same shape. The size is one-fourth the size of the original when area is considered; it is one-half when lengths are considered.

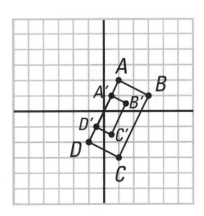

See additional Teaching Notes on page T173L.

Unit 2

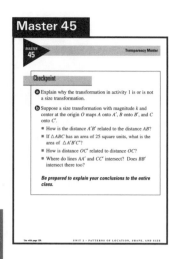

5. **a–b.** The image rectangle has vertices A' (7.5, 10), B' (−7.5, 5), C' (−5, −2.5), and D' (17.5, 5). The scale on both axes below is 2.

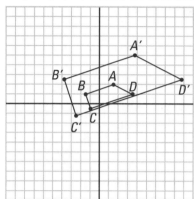

c. Image segments are 2.5 times the length of pre-image segments. For example, $AB = \sqrt{40} \approx 6.32$ while $A'B' = \sqrt{250} \approx 15.81$.

d. The slope of line AB is $\frac{1}{3}$ and the slope of line BC is -3, therefore line AB is perpendicular to line BC. The same is true for lines $A'B'$ and $B'C'$.

e. Since line AB is parallel to line CD, the shape is a trapezoid. The area of trapezoid $ABCD$ is $\frac{1}{2} \cdot BC(BA + CD)$.

$$\text{Area } ABCD = 0.5\sqrt{10}\,(\sqrt{40} + \sqrt{90})$$
$$= 0.5 \cdot 50 = 25 \text{ square units}$$

The area of trapezoid $A'B'C'D'$ can be determined in the same manner. The area of $A'B'C'D'$ is 2.5^2 or 6.25 times the area of $ABCD$.

$$\text{Area } A'B'C'D' = 0.5(B'C')(B'A' + C'D')$$
$$= 0.5\sqrt{62.5}\,(\sqrt{250} + \sqrt{562.5})$$
$$= 156.25 \text{ square units}$$

6. **a.** Students should draw $\triangle XYZ$ using GEOXPLOR or similar software.

b. The triangle, $\triangle XYZ$, is a right triangle since line XY is perpendicular to line XZ. (Slopes are $\frac{1}{2}$ and -2.) The triangle has area $\frac{1}{2} \cdot \sqrt{125} \cdot \sqrt{500}$ or 125 square units. The areas of the image triangles are as follows:

$(0.75)^2 \cdot 125 \approx 70.31$
$(1.5)^2 \cdot 125 \approx 281.25$
$(2.5)^2 \cdot 125 \approx 781.25$
$(3)^2 \cdot 125 \approx 1125$

All image lengths are the magnitude of the transformation times the length of the pre-image.

SHARE AND SUMMARIZE   full-class discussion

Checkpoint

JOURNAL ENTRY: Following a discussion of the Checkpoint items, ask students to summarize what they have learned about size transformations and how are they alike and different from the rigid transformations they examined in the previous investigation.

See Teaching Master 45.

ⓐ The transformation is not a size transformation because the definition states that both the x- and the y-coordinates must be multiplied by the same constant. In activity 1 only the x-coordinate was multiplied by a factor of 3.

ⓑ ■ The distance $A'B'$ will be k times the distance AB.

■ The area of $\triangle A'B'C'$ is $25k^2$ square units.

■ The distance OC' is k times the distance OC.

■ Lines AA' and CC' intersect at the center of the transformation (in this case O). Yes, line BB' intersects there also because O is the center.

5. Now consider quadrilateral $ABCD = \begin{bmatrix} 3 & -3 & -2 & 7 \\ 4 & 2 & -1 & 2 \end{bmatrix}$.

   a. Sketch $ABCD$ on graph paper.

   b. Sketch the image quadrilateral, $A'B'C'D'$, resulting from transforming $ABCD$ with a size transformation of magnitude 2.5 and center at the origin.

   c. Compare lengths of corresponding pre-image and image sides.

   d. How are lines AB and BC related? Lines $A'B'$ and $B'C'$?

   e. Use the information in parts c and d to help you determine the area of $ABCD$ and $A'B'C'D'$. Compare the areas and relate them to the magnitude 2.5.

6. The program GEOXPLOR can draw shapes and their images under size transformations with center at the origin. Use GEOXPLOR or similar software to complete this activity.

   a. Let $\triangle XYZ = \begin{bmatrix} 5 & 15 & -5 \\ 10 & 5 & -10 \end{bmatrix}$. Draw $\triangle XYZ$ using GEOXPLOR.

   b. Use the "SIZE CHANGE" option from the "TRANSFORM" menu to find images of $\triangle XYZ$ when transformed with magnitudes 0.75, 1.5, 2.5, and 3. Share the workload among your group. In each case, compare corresponding pre-image/image lengths and compare areas of pre-image and image. Are the results of your comparisons consistent with what you would have predicted? Explain.

Checkpoint

ⓐ Explain why the transformation in activity 1 is or is not a size transformation.

ⓑ Suppose a size transformation with magnitude k and center at the origin O maps A onto A', B onto B', and C onto C'.

   ■ How is the distance $A'B'$ related to the distance AB?

   ■ If $\triangle ABC$ has an area of 25 square units, what is the area of $\triangle A'B'C'$?

   ■ How is distance OC' related to distance OC?

   ■ Where do lines AA' and CC' intersect? Does BB' intersect there too?

   Be prepared to explain your conclusions to the entire class.

LESSON 2 • COORDINATE MODELS OF TRANSFORMATIONS   **129**

The size transformations examined in activities 2 through 6 had magnitudes ranging from 0.5 to 3. The magnitude can be any number other than zero. A **size transformation with magnitude $k \neq 0$ and center at the origin** is given by

$$\begin{array}{ccc} \text{pre-image} & & \text{image} \\ (x, y) & \longrightarrow & (kx, ky) \end{array}$$

The transformation with magnitude $k > 1$ can be visualized as shown below.

Transformation of Magnitiude $k > 1$

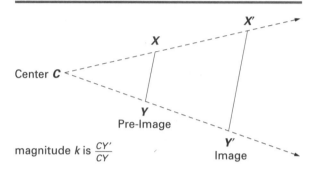

magnitude k is $\dfrac{CY'}{CY}$

You could think of the center as a flashlight, $\overline{XY}$ as a ruler, and $\overline{X'Y'}$ as its shadow.

▶ On Your Own

a. A size transformation with magnitude 3.5 and center at the origin transforms a right triangle with legs of 4 cm and 5 cm.

■ What are the lengths of the three sides of the image triangle?

■ What is the area of the given triangle and of its image?

b. Write an algorithm for a program that will accept the coordinates of a point and the magnitude of a size transformation (with center at the origin). The program then should display the point, its image, and their coordinates.

Size transformations are important in producing computer graphics images that are the same shape, but differ in size. Principles of size transformations are also applied in many other situations.

7. Examine how a photographic enlarger uses the principles of size transformations. The light source is the center, a photographic negative or slide is the pre-image, and the photographic paper is the image. On one brand of enlarger, the distance between the light source and film negative is fixed at 5 cm. The distance between the paper and the negative adjusts to distances between 5 cm and 30 cm.

▶On Your Own

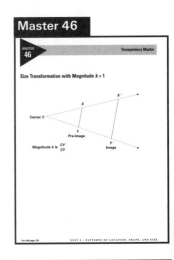

Master 46

a. ■ The length of the third side of the original triangle is $\sqrt{41}$, which is approximately 6.4 units. The lengths of the sides of the image triangle are 14 units, 17.5 units, and approximately 22.4 units.

   ■ The area of the original triangle is 10 square units. The area of the image triangle is $10(3.5)^2$ or 122.5 square units.

b. Step 1: Get the coordinates of a point.

Step 2: Get the magnitude of the size transformation.

Step 3: Compute the coordinates of the image point.

Step 4: Display the graphs of the points.

Step 5: Display the coordinates of the points.

7. See Teaching Master 46.

In parts a and b of this activity, students need to use distances to calculate magnification factors. If they do not understand this process, they may be confused about which distance they are trying to find in part f. As they begin part f, you may want to prompt them by asking, "What magnification factor did you need? How does that relate to distances?"

MORE
ASSIGNMENT   *pp. 133–138*

Students now can begin Organizing tasks 3 or 4, Reflecting task 2, or Extending tasks 1, 2, 4, or 5 from the MORE assignment following Investigation 2.

Unit 2

7. **a.** The magnitude of the size transformation is the ratio of the distance between the light source and the paper to the distance between the light source and the negative. In this case, it is $\frac{20}{5}$ or 4.

   b. The ratio we are looking for is $\frac{\text{light source to paper}}{\text{light source to negative}}$. In this case, we are told the distance from negative to paper. The distance from light source to negative is fixed at 5 cm. Adding 5 to this gives the distance from light source to paper. Thus the ratio is $\frac{15 + 5}{5}$, or 4. So the magnitude of the size transformation is 4.

   c. ■ The paper is 5 cm below the negative, or 10 cm from the light source, and so the magnitude of the size transformation is $\frac{10}{5}$ or 2. Thus the size of the original picture is doubled from 35 mm by 23 mm to 70 mm by 46 mm.

   ■ When the paper is 10 cm from the negative, it is 15 cm from the light source. So the magnitude of the size transformation will be $\frac{15}{5}$ or 3. Therefore the image or print will have dimensions 3 times the dimensions of the original.

   ■ The magnitudes are 2 and 3, respectively. These are the ratios of distances, $\frac{\text{light source to paper}}{\text{light source to negative}}$.

   d. The closest the paper tray can be to the light source is 10 cm. This gives a size transformation of magnitude $\frac{10}{5}$ or 2. The dimensions of the smallest print are therefore 7.0 cm by 4.6 cm, twice the original dimensions. At the maximum setting of 30 cm from the negative, the paper is 35 cm from the light source. So the magnitude of the size transformation is $\frac{35}{5}$ or 7. Thus, the dimensions of the largest print are 24.5 cm by 16.1 cm, 7 times the dimensions of the original print.

   e. At 20 cm from the negative, the paper is 25 cm from the light source, so the magnitude of the size transformation is $\frac{25}{5}$ or 5. The dimensions of the print will be 17.5 cm by 11.5 cm, 5 times the original dimensions.

   f. To produce a print whose longest side is 12 cm, we need a size transformation of magnitude $\frac{12}{3.5}$ or approximately 3.43. So

   $$3.43 = \frac{\text{distance from light source to paper}}{5}.$$

   Thus the distance from the light source to the paper should be approximately $5 \cdot 3.43$ or 17.14 cm.

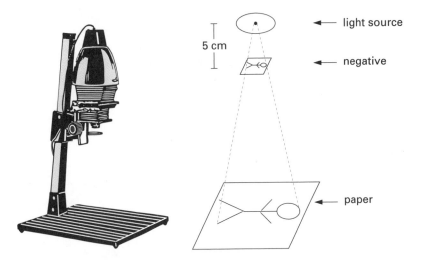

light source

5 cm

negative

paper

a. If the distance from the light source to the paper is 20 cm, what ratio gives the magnitude of the size transformation represented?

b. If the distance between the negative and the paper is 15 cm, what is the magnitude of the size transformation?

c. Deonna uses 35 mm film in her camera, so her negatives measure 35 mm by 23 mm.

- When the paper is 5 cm from the negative, her prints are 70 mm by 46 mm (7.0 cm by 4.6 cm). Use a diagram and your understanding of size transformations to explain why this is the case.

- When she adjusts the distance between the paper and the negative to 10 cm, her prints are 105 mm by 69 mm (10.5 cm by 6.9 cm). Explain why this is the case.

- What is the magnitude of the enlargement in each of the two settings above? How does this relate to the distances involving the light source, negative, and photographic paper?

d. Recall that the distance between the paper and the negative can be adjusted to distances from 5 cm to 30 cm. What are the dimensions of the *smallest* print that Deonna can make from a negative using this brand of enlarger? What are the dimensions of the *largest* print?

e. Suppose the paper is 20 cm from the negative. What size print is produced?

f. How far should the paper be from the negative to produce a print whose longest side is 12 cm?

8. In the definition of a size transformation, the magnitude was specified as any *nonzero* number. Thus, negative numbers may be used as magnitudes. Investigate the effects of a size transformation with a magnitude of –2 and center at the origin defined by the rule:

$$(x, y) \longrightarrow (-2x, -2y)$$

a. Each group member should plot on graph paper a pre-image polygon of his or her choice, but one for which the origin is *not inside* the polygon. Then find the coordinates of the images of the vertices and plot the image polygon.

b. For each polygon:

- Compare the lengths of line segments in the pre-image with the lengths of corresponding segments in the image.

- What else can you say about pre-image and image segments and the lines containing them?

- Compare the shape of your pre-image polygon to its image.

- Compare the area of your pre-image polygon to its image.

c. Draw the lines determined by each pre-image/image pair of points. What point is on each of these lines? How is that point related to the size transformation?

d. Share and compare your results from part b. Write a summary about the effects on shapes of size transformations with negative magnitudes.

9. In a slide projector, light passes through a slide, is collected in the lens, and then is projected onto a screen. In one model, the slide is 10 cm from the lens.

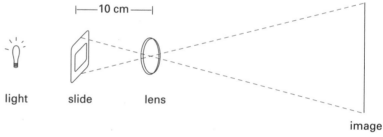

a. In this case, what would be considered the center of the size transformation? What is the pre-image?

b. Why are slides put in the projector upside down?

c. A slide made from 35 mm film is the same size as the negative. (See activity 7.) Using such a slide, what is the magnitude of the size transformation that projects an image for which the longest side is 3.5 meters?

d. If the screen is 6 meters away from the projector lens, how large is the image of the 35 mm slide?

8. **a.** Students' polygons will vary. Allow students to choose the tool of their choice for this activity. They could use graph paper (which is the most flexible tool), GEOXPLOR, or lists and lineplots. Students need to be able to find the area of their polygons.

    b. ■ The lengths of the line segments in the image will be changed by a factor of 2. That is, they will be twice as long as the segments in the pre-image.

    ■ The line segments are in different quadrants. They are parallel to the pre-image segments. The line segments have been rotated 180° about the origin.

    ■ The shapes are the same, but the length of each side of the image is twice the length of the corresponding side of the pre-image.

    ■ The area of the image figure is $(-2)^2$ or 4 times the area of the pre-image figure.

    c. Each of these lines contains the origin. The origin is the center of the size transformation.

    d. A size transformation with a negative magnitude k causes the following:

    The lengths of sides change by a factor of k.

    The area of the figure changes by a factor of k^2.

    The figure is rotated 180° about the origin.

9. **a.** The lens is the center of the size transformation and the slide is the pre-image.

    b. Because the lens rotates the pre-image 180°; that is, it reverses the picture. This is an example of a size transformation of negative magnitude.

    c. The magnitude of the size transformation is -100. ($\frac{-3.5 \text{ m}}{35 \text{ mm}} = \frac{-3500 \text{ mm}}{35 \text{ mm}} = -100$)

    d. The magnitude of the size transformation is $\frac{-600 \text{ cm}}{10 \text{ cm}}$ or -60. So the dimensions of the image are 60×35 or 2100 mm (2.1 meters) by 60×23 or 1380 mm (1.38 m).

Unit 2

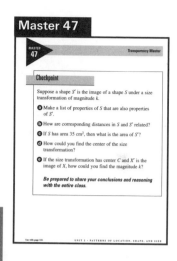
SHARE AND SUMMARIZE   full-class discussion

Checkpoint

See Teaching Master 47.

ⓐ S and S' have the same shape. Distances in S can be multiplied by $|k|$ to get corresponding distances in S'. Segments in S are parallel to corresponding segments in S'.

ⓑ For a distance d in S and the corresponding distance d' in S', $d' = k \cdot d$.

ⓒ Area of $S' = k^2 \cdot 35$.

ⓓ To find the center of the size transformation, find the point of intersection of two lines, each determined by an image point and its pre-image.

ⓔ The magnitude, k, is equal to the ratio $\frac{CX'}{CX}$. The magnitude k is negative if the center is between the image and pre-image.

APPLY   individual task

▶ On Your Own

You should place the paper tray 8 cm from the slide or 12 cm from the light.

Since we want the print to be 105 mm by 69 mm or 3 times larger than the original, the paper tray needs to be 3 times 4 cm from the light source. Therefore, the paper tray needs to be placed 12 cm from the light source or 8 cm from the slide.

MORE   independent assignment

ASSIGNMENT   *pp. 133–138*

Modeling: 1 or 2, and 4*
Organizing: 1, 3, or 4*
Reflecting: 2
Extending: 3 and choice of one*

*When choice is indicated, it is important to leave the choice to the student.
NOTE: It is best if Organizing tasks are discussed as a whole class after they have been assigned as homework.

Modeling

1. **a.** The center is the pinhole. The pre-image is what you are taking a picture of and the image will be captured on the film.

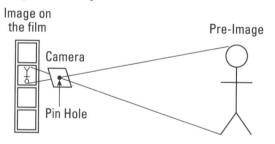

Image on the film
Camera
Pin Hole
Pre-Image

b. The magnitude of the size change is $\frac{-2}{50}$ or $\frac{-1}{25}$. The height of the object could be $25 \cdot 23$ or 575 mm (57.5 cm). A horizontal distance of $25 \cdot 35$ or 875 mm (87.5 cm) could be captured.

Checkpoint

Suppose a shape S' is the image of a shape S under a size transformation of magnitude k.

a Make a list of properties of S that are also properties of S'.

b How are corresponding distances in S and S' related?

c If S has area 35 cm^2, then what is the area of S'?

d How could you find the center of the size transformation?

e If the size transformation has center C and X' is the image of X, how could you find the magnitude k?

Be prepared to share your conclusions and reasoning with the entire class.

▶ On Your Own

A photographic enlarger has a 35 mm by 23 mm negative positioned 4 cm from the light. How far from the negative should the paper be placed to produce a print that measures 10.5 cm by 6.9 cm? Explain your reasoning.

MORE
Modeling • Organizing • Reflecting • Extending

Modeling

1. A pinhole camera is a simple device to expose film to light. Light passes through a pinhole and exposes the film in its path. Suppose you have 35 mm film centered 2 cm from the hole.

   a. Draw a diagram illustrating how a size transformation can model this situation. Where is the center of the transformation? What is the pre-image? Where will the image be?

   b. The film measures 23 mm vertically. What height object could be photographed if it were 50 cm from the pinhole? The film measures 35 mm horizontally. How much of the object (horizontally) could be captured?

c. Suppose you want to photograph a person 1.6 meters in height. How far from the pinhole should the person stand to ensure a full-height image?

d. When sighting an object 100 cm from the pinhole, you realize that you can not see all of the object. If your camera has an adjustable film holder, should you move it closer or further away from the pinhole to capture more of the object on the film? Explain your reasoning.

2. A *camera obscura* is a device similar to a pinhole camera except that you can view the image rather than photograph it. You can make a model of a camera obscura: Put a pinhole in the bottom of a cereal box. Tape a translucent waxed paper strip inside the box, parallel to the bottom of the box and 1 to 5 cm from the pinhole. Cut off the opposite end. When you look into the box through the open end, keeping the inside as dark as possible, you will see the image of a scene on the wax paper.

a. Make a sketch of the interior of the camera obscura. Label the parts. What point serves as the center of the size transformation?

b. How will the scene you observe on the wax paper appear to you? Explain.

c. If the wax paper is 3 cm from the pinhole and the base of the box measures 15 cm × 6 cm, what is the tallest building that would be visible 50 meters away?

d. Suppose the base of the box is 12 cm × 5 cm. Where should you place the wax paper in order to view an entire 40-meter building that is 30 meters away?

e. **Optional:** Make a model of a camera obscura. Demonstrate it to your classmates. Compare the view through your model with views through other models made by your classmates.

3. You can use the ideas of size transformations to measure lengths or distances indirectly. For example, suppose that when you stand 3 yards away from a friend, you can line up the top of a yardstick with the top of your friend's head. Keeping the yardstick parallel to your friend, you line up the feet of your friend with the mark 1 foot below the top of the yardstick.

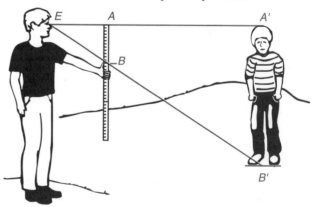

1. c. The magnitude of the size change needs to be $-23 \div 1600$ or approximately -0.014. Since the film (the image) is 2 cm from the pinhole (the center), we have the following:

$$\frac{\text{center to image}}{\text{center to pre-image}} = \text{magnitude}$$

$$\frac{-2}{\text{center to pre-image}} = \frac{-23}{1600}$$

$$\text{center to pre-image} = \frac{-2 \cdot 1600}{-23} \approx 139.13$$

So the camera needs to be approximately 139 cm from the person.

d. Move the film holder closer to the pinhole to capture a larger image. As the distance (in absolute value) between the film holder and the pinhole decreases, the magnitude of the size transformation increases.

2. a. The pinhole is the center of the size transformation.

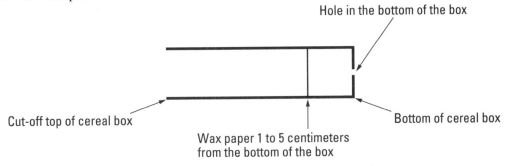

Hole in the bottom of the box

Cut-off top of cereal box

Bottom of cereal box

Wax paper 1 to 5 centimeters
from the bottom of the box

b. The image is inverted. The top of the pre-image is projected to the bottom of the image and vice versa. This is always the case when the center is between the image and pre-image, *i.e.,* the transformation has a negative magnitude.

c. In this situation, the magnitude of the size change, k, will be $-3 \div 5000$, or -6×10^{-4}. Assuming the cereal box is turned so that the longer side of the base corresponds to the height of the building, the building could have a height up to $1.5 \div k$ or 25,000 cm (250 m).

d. The magnitude of the size change needs to be $-12 \div 4000$, or -0.003. Thus the absolute value of the distance from the pinhole to the wax paper should be given by 3000 cm $\times$ 0.003, or 9 cm.

e. Another option for creating a camera obscura uses an oatmeal canister (or any cardboard cylinder with a plastic lid), as shown here.

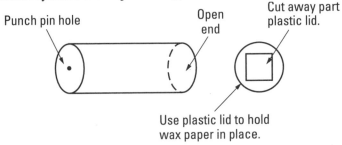

Punch pin hole

Open
end

Cut away part
plastic lid.

Use plastic lid to hold
wax paper in place.

Unit 2

3. **a.** Considering the yardstick to be the "pre-image" and the friend to be the "image" as shown in the diagram, the magnitude of the size change is $9 \div 2$ or 4.5. So the friend's height is 4.5 feet.

  b. The scale factor needs to be 15. The person is 30 feet from the tree so the ruler would need to be 2 feet from the eyes.

4. The height of the tree is 7 times the distance from the person's eyes to the ground. So the height is 12.6 m.

Organizing

1. **a.** The *x*- and *y*-coordinates of the image are 1 times the *x*- and *y*-coordinates of the pre-image; therefore the pre-image and image figures are identical.

  b. A size transformation about the origin of magnitude -1 is the same as a rotation of 180° about the origin.

2. **a.** Line *n* may appear curved to some students.

  b. Yes; point *O* and any point on *n* determine a line, and that line must intersect *m*. That point of intersection is the pre-image.

a. If the yardstick is 2 feet from your eyes, how tall is your friend?

b. Suppose 1 foot of the yardstick covered a 15-foot tall tree that is 10 yards away. How far is the yardstick held from your eyes?

4. A method for measuring heights indirectly is shown below. It is based on the physics principle that light reflects at equal angles (see diagram). A mirror is placed on the ground 7 meters from the base of a tree. When a person whose eyes are 180 cm from the ground stands 1 meter behind the mirror, the person can see the top of the tree in the mirror. How tall is the tree?

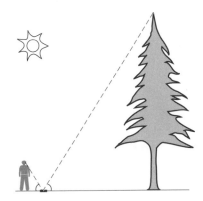

Organizing

1. You have now studied rigid transformations and size transformations. Examine possible connections between these sets of transformations.

a. What is the size transformation image of a figure, if the magnitude of the transformation is 1? Explain your reasoning.

b. What size transformation is the same as the 180° rotation about the origin?

2. In the diagram below, O is the center of a size transformation and m is a line. The size transformation image of the points on m are the corresponding points on n.

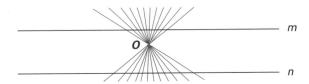

a. Does n appear to be a line or does it appear to be curved?

b. Does every point on n have a pre-image on m? Explain your reasoning.

LESSON 2 • COORDINATE MODELS OF TRANSFORMATIONS   135

c. If a point on m is between two other points, where is the image in relation to the images of the two other points? Give evidence supporting your view.

d. Is n a line? Justify your view using your knowledge of coordinates and transformations.

3. Suppose a size transformation with magnitude k and center at the origin maps $A(x_1, y_1)$ and $B(x_2, y_2)$ onto A' and B' respectively.

a. What are the coordinates of A' and B'?

b. Nathan provided the following general argument to show that
$$\text{distance } A'B' = k \cdot (\text{distance } AB).$$
Check the correctness of Nathan's work. Correct any errors that you find.

$$\text{distance } A'B' = \sqrt{(kx_1 - kx_2)^2 + (ky_1 - ky_2)^2}$$
$$\text{distance } A'B' = k\sqrt{(x_1 - x_2)^2 + (y_1 - y_2)^2}$$
$$\text{distance } A'B' = k \cdot (\text{distance } AB)$$

4. A line l contains points $A(a, b)$ and $B(c, d)$. Line m is the image of line l under a size transformation with magnitude k and center at the origin. Use the definition of slope to show that m is parallel to l.

Reflecting

1. The coordinate models of size transformations you investigated had their centers at the origin of a coordinate plane. Draw a triangle and a point on a plain sheet of paper. How could you find the image of the triangle under a size transformation with the given point as center and magnitude 3? Write an explanation of your method that could be used by a classmate.

2. How is the Zoom feature on your graphing calculator or computer software like a size transformation?

a. What determines the center?

b. What determines the magnitude?

3. What are other situations, such as the photographic enlarger, slide projector, or pinhole camera, in which principles of size transformations are involved?

4. What was the most difficult aspect of the concept of size transformation for you to understand? What caused you the difficulty? How did you overcome the difficulty?

2. c. The image point is between the images of the other two points. To give evidence supporting this view, students may show that this is true from the illustration in the student text.

d. In the investigation, image points of collinear pre-image points maintained collinearity, therefore, *n* must be a line. The coordinate definition also could be used to make the argument more concrete. Let *m* be the line with equation $y = a$, and let *O* be the origin of the coordinate system. Let the magnitude of the size transformation be $-k$ (*k* is positive). If $(0, a)$, $(1, a)$, $(2, a)$, and (x, a) are on *m*, then the images are $(0, -ka)$, $(-k, -ka)$, $(-2k, -ka)$, and $(-kx, -ka)$. These are all on the line $y = -ka$.

3. a. $A' = (kx_1, ky_1)$ and $B' = (kx_2, ky_2)$

b. Nathan is correct. (This may be a good time to discuss properties of powers, specifically in regard to squares and square roots.)

4. Slope of line $l = \frac{b-d}{a-c}$

$A' = (ka, kb)$ and $B' = (kc, kd)$

Slope of line $m = \frac{kb-kd}{ka-kc} = \frac{k(b-d)}{k(a-c)} = \frac{b-d}{a-c}$

Since the slope of line *l* is equal to the slope of line *m*, the two lines are parallel.

Reflecting

1. Responses may vary, but the general idea should be the same as the following. From the center point *O*, draw rays through the vertices of $\triangle ABC$. Measure the segment *OA*. Extend the ray *OA* to create a segment three times the length of *OA*, and mark the endpoint *A'*. Find *B'* and *C'* by repeating the procedure. $\triangle A'B'C'$ is the image triangle.

2. ■ The location of the cursor determines the center.
   ■ Zoom factors define the magnification factor.

3. Movie projectors, overhead projectors, magnifying glasses, and telescopes all involve size transformations.

4. Responses may vary. Some students find the relationship between size transformation and area difficult to understand.

Unit 2

Extending

1. Programs may vary. The program here will run on a TI-82 or TI-83 graphics calculator.

```
Input "X1", A
Input "Y1", B
Input "X2", C
Input "Y2", D
Input "X3", E
Input "Y3", F
Input "Scale Fact", K
Line (A, B, C, D)
Line (C, D, E, F)
Line (E, F, A, B)
Pause
Line (KA, KB, KC, KD)
Line (KC, KD, KE, KF)
Line (KE, KF, KA, KB)
Pause
```

2. The area of a triangle is found by evaluating $\frac{1}{2}bh$ where b is a base and h is the corresponding height. Under a size transformation of magnitude k, the length of the image's base is kb, and the height of the image is kh. Thus the area of the image is $\frac{1}{2}(kb)(kh)$ or $\frac{1}{2}bh(k^2)$.

3. **a.** The cross section whose area is M has dimensions one-half times the dimensions of the base. Thus M is $\frac{1}{4}B$. So,

$$V = \frac{B + 4\left(\frac{1}{4}B\right) + 0}{6} \times h = \frac{2B}{6} \times h = \frac{Bh}{3} = \frac{1}{3}Bh.$$

   b. No. The value of M always will be $\frac{1}{4}$ the area of the base. Thus $V = \frac{1}{3}Bh$ will be true for any pyramid whose base has area B.

   c. $V = \frac{1}{3}(60)(12) = 20(12) = 240 \text{ cm}^3$

   d. $V = \frac{1}{3}(415)^2(120) = \frac{1}{3}(20,667,000) = 6,889,000$ cubic feet

Extending

1. Write a graphics calculator program for size transformations on a triangle. The user should input the coordinates of three points and a magnitude. The program then should compute the images under a size transformation with center at the origin. Finally, the program should draw the two triangles determined by the three points and their images.

2. Using the fact that a size transformation of magnitude k multiplies distances by k, show that the same transformation multiplies the area of a triangle by k^2.

3. The formulas for volumes of space-shapes developed in Course 1 can be viewed as special cases of the *prismoidal formula*:

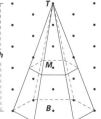

$$V = \frac{B + 4M + T}{6} \cdot h$$

where B is the area of the cross section at the base;
M is the area of the cross section at the "middle";
T is the area of the cross section at the top; and
h is the height of the solid.

a. Consider the hexagonal pyramid above. Suppose the area of the base is B square units. Use the prismoidal formula and your understanding of size transformations to help find a formula for the volume of the pyramid in terms of B and height h.

b. Is your formula affected at all by the shape of the base whose area is B? Explain your reasoning.

c. What is the volume of an octagonal pyramid whose base has area 60 cm^2, and whose height is 12 cm?

d. The Corporate Development Center of Steelcase Inc. in Grand Rapids, Michigan is the company's furniture Research and Development facility. The building is a square pyramid, approximately 120 feet tall, whose base is 415 feet on each side. Estimate the volume of air that must be heated or cooled to keep the workers comfortable.

4. Investigate the effects of the transformation described by the following rule.

$$(x, y) \rightarrow (2x, 3y)$$

a. Are any points their own images?

b. Consider points on a line. Are their images also on a line?

c. Consider midpoints of segments. Are their images the midpoints of the image segments?

d. What is the effect of this transformation on the length of line segments?

e. What is the effect of this transformation on areas?

5. Investigate the effects of the transformation described below.

$$(x, y) \rightarrow (x + y, x)$$

a. Are any points their own images?

b. When you transform points on a line, are the images also on a line?

c. When you transform midpoints of segments, are the images also midpoints of the image segments?

d. What is the effect of this transformation on the length of line segments?

e. What is the effect of this transformation on areas?

INVESTIGATION ▶3 Modeling Combinations of Transformations

Computer graphics includes the creation, storage, and manipulation of shapes both simple and complex. Translations, rotations, and size transformations are essential to many graphics applications to change the position, tilt, and size of shapes. You now have the basic tools for constructing computer graphics, because you know the coordinate patterns defining these key transformations.

Computer scientists enjoy the challenge of thinking through algorithms and designing programs for computers and calculators. These people seek new and better ways to accomplish tasks through computing. Software, based on algorithms they developed, can be used to produce and manipulate computer graphics representations of three-dimensional *surfaces*, as shown below.

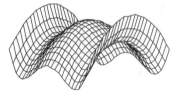 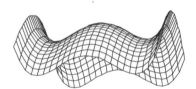

4. Since this is an Extending task, you may wish to encourage students to reason abstractly, as done in the solutions below. Students should explain their responses to each part.

   a. Only the point $(0, 0)$ is its own image.

   b. Yes. If the collinear pre-image points are (a, b), (c, d), and (e, f), the image points are $(2a, 3b)$, $(2c, 3d)$, and $(2e, 3f)$. The slopes of the line segments containing the image points can be represented by $\frac{3(b-d)}{2(a-c)}$, $\frac{3(d-f)}{2(c-e)}$ or $\frac{3(a-e)}{2(b-f)}$. Since the pre-image points are collinear and $\frac{b-d}{a-c}$, $\frac{d-f}{c-e}$, and $\frac{a-e}{b-f}$ are therefore equal, the image points are collinear.

   c. Yes. The midpoint of the pre-image segment with endpoints (a, b) and (c, d) is $(\frac{a+c}{2}, \frac{b+d}{2})$. The image segment has endpoints $(2a, 3b)$ and $(2c, 3d)$. The midpoint is $(\frac{2a+2c}{2}, \frac{3b+3d}{2})$ which simplifies to $(\frac{2}{2}(a+c), \frac{3}{2}(b+d))$. Using the transformation rule, the coordinates of the image of the pre-image midpoint are $(\frac{2}{2}(a+c), \frac{3}{2}(b+d))$. So the image of the midpoint of the original segment is the same point as the midpoint of the image segment.

   d. The size transformation on the length of a horizontal line segment is 2, but the size transformation on the length of a vertical line segment is 3. For oblique line segments the length of the image segment will be between 2 and 3 times the length of the pre-image segment.

   e. The ratio of the area of the image to the area of the pre-image will be 6. Students should use some examples to help them draw their conclusion. One way to see why the ratio is always 6 is to begin with an arbitrary triangle. First translate the triangle so that one vertex is at the origin. Then rotate the triangle so one edge is coincident with the x-axis. Apply the transformation, and it is easy to see that the ratio of the areas is 6. Although it is not easy to prove that this is always true, this translate-rotate-expand process will help develop some understanding of this transformation.

5. Since this is an Extending task, you may wish to encourage students to reason abstractly, as done in the solutions below. Students should explain their responses to each part of the question.

   a. The origin is the only point that is its own image.

   b. Yes. If three collinear pre-image points have coordinates (x_1, y_1), (x_2, y_2), and (x_3, y_3), and the points are not on the same vertical line, the slope m equals $\frac{y_3 - y_2}{x_3 - x_2}$ which is equal to $\frac{y_2 - y_1}{x_2 - x_1}$. The equation for the line can be written as $y_3 - y_2 = m(x_3 - x_2)$ and as $y_2 - y_1 = m(x_2 - x_1)$. The coordinates of the image points are $(x_1 + y_1, x_1)$, $(x_2 + y_2, x_2)$, and $(x_3 + y_3, x_3)$. The slope of the line containing the first two image points is $\frac{(x_2 - x_1)}{(x_2 - x_1) + (y_2 - y_1)}$ which is equivalent to $\frac{(x_2 - x_1)}{(x_2 - x_1) + m(x_2 - x_1)}$ and simplifies to $\frac{1}{(1 + m)}$. Finding the slope of the line containing another pair of image points also yields a slope of $\frac{1}{(1 + m)}$. Thus the image points are collinear.

   If the pre-image points are on the same vertical line, their slopes are undefined. However, it is easy to see that the image points will have the same y-coordinates, and so they will be collinear on the same horizontal line.

See additional Teaching Notes on pages T168K–168L.

1. **a.** ■ $B'(-27, 9)$; $A'(-9, 18)$; $C'(-18, -9)$
   ■ $B''(-9, -27)$; $A''(-18, -9)$; $C''(9, -18)$
   b. ■ Yes, they are all the same size and shape.
   ■ Angle B is a right angle because the slopes of the line segments that form angle B are negative reciprocals of one another. The measure of angle B'' is 90°.

2. **a.** Responses will vary. Call the components of the translation h and k.
   b. Responses will vary. Call the components of the translation h_1 and k_1.
   c. The size and shape of the original figure and the final image should be the same.
   d. Responses will vary but students should note that each original point will be translated as follows:
   $$(x, y) \rightarrow (x + h + h_1, y + k + k_1).$$
   e. Students should find the same pattern for each pair of translations.
   f. The x- and y-coordinates for the image can be obtained by adding both translation components to the corresponding coordinates for the pre-image:
   $$(x, y) \rightarrow (x + h + h_1, y + k + k_1)$$

Although your graphing calculator probably is not as powerful as the computer that produced these graphic displays, it can be programmed to perform rather complex tasks. You have used the "TRANSFORM" option of the GEOXPLOR software or similar software to transform the sizes of shapes. That software also can be used to investigate what happens when you combine in succession two or more rigid transformations or size transformations.

If you prefer, you may use other computer drawing software or graph paper in completing the following activities. You should focus your attention on (i) what pre-image/image point coordinate patterns result, and (ii) how the pre-image shape and its image are related.

1. This first activity will help you and your group experiment with combinations of transformations.

   a. Using GEOXPLOR, draw $\triangle ABC = \begin{bmatrix} 9 & 27 & 18 \\ 18 & 9 & -9 \end{bmatrix}$.

   - Reflect $\triangle ABC$ across the y-axis. Use the program to find the coordinates of B', the image of B. Similarly, find the coordinates of A' and C'.
   - Now rotate the image, $\triangle A'B'C'$, 90° counterclockwise about the origin. Find the coordinates of B'', which is the image of B'. What are the coordinates of A'' and C''?

   b. Examine triangles ABC, $A'B'C'$, and $A''B''C''$.

   - Are they the same size and shape?
   - What is the measure of angle B? Explain. What is the measure of angle B''?

In the following activities you will investigate more systematically the effects of various combinations of transformations.

2. Examine first the effects of one translation followed by another. Draw a triangle or a quadrilateral of your choice. Keep a record of the coordinates of your shape's vertices.

   a. Translate your figure using any translation you like. What components did you use? That is, over what horizontal and vertical distances did you translate the figure, and in which directions?

   b. Translate the image figure. What components did you use?

   c. Compare the size and shape of the original figure and the final image.

   d. Compare the coordinates of the vertices of the initial figure with those of the final image. What patterns do you observe?

   e. Repeat parts a–d for a new figure and two new translations.

   f. Describe the relationship between pre-image and final image coordinates resulting from two translations applied in succession.

g. Suppose the following two translations are applied in succession.

$$(x, y) \rightarrow (x + a, y + b)$$

$$(x, y) \rightarrow (x + h, y + k)$$

Write a symbolic rule $(x, y) \rightarrow (\_\,, \_)$ which describes the new combined transformation.

```
TRANSFORM MENU
1: TRANSLATION
2: SIZE CHANGE
3: ROTATION
4: REFLECTION
5: CLEAN SKETCH
6: CALCULATE
7: MAIN MENU
```

3. Now investigate the effects of successively applying two size transformations with center at the origin. First, draw a triangle or a quadrilateral.

a. Choose a magnitude and find the image of the figure.

b. Choose another magnitude and find the image of the first image.

c. Compare the size and shape of the original figure and the final image.

d. Compare the coordinates of the vertices of the final image with those of the original pre-image. What patterns do you observe?

e. Make a conjecture about the effects of applying two size transformations in succession. Choose several more points to test your conjecture.

f. Suppose the following two size transformations are applied in succession.

$$(x, y) \rightarrow (hx, hy)$$

$$(x, y) \rightarrow (mx, my)$$

Write a symbolic rule which describes the new combined transformation.

4. The process of successively applying transformations is called **composing** transformations. The transformation that maps the *original* pre-images to the *final* images is called the **composite transformation**. Investigate the effects of composing two rotations about the origin. Develop an investigative procedure based on your work in activities 2 and 3 and write a statement summarizing your findings.

5. Investigate the effects of composing two line reflections. Choose a triangle or a quadrilateral, then reflect and reflect again. Compare the pre-image coordinates with those of the final image. What patterns do you observe? Write a summary of your findings. Consider two cases:

a. A different line is used for each reflection. (Consider pairs of lines that intersect or are parallel. Divide the workload among members of your group.)

b. The same line is used twice.

2. g. $(x, y) \rightarrow (x + a + h, y + b + k)$

3. a. Responses will vary depending on the figure and magnitude selected. In general, for a size transformation of magnitude s: $(x, y) \rightarrow (sx, sy)$.

b. Again, responses will vary. In general, given a second size transformation of magnitude k: $(sx, sy) \rightarrow (ksx, ksy)$.

c. The original and final image have the same shape but are probably different sizes. They will be the same size only if k and s are reciprocals of each other.

d. The x- and y-coordinates for the final image can be obtained by multiplying each pair of coordinates of the pre-image by the product of the two magnitudes.

e. The image of a figure that has undergone two size transformations will be the same shape as the original figure, but may not be the same size. The length of a side will change by a factor equal to the product of the magnitudes of the two size transformations.

f. $(x, y) \rightarrow (hmx, hmy)$

4. In general, students should select several points and perform a series of successive rotations. Next they should review the results and make a conjecture concerning a general rule. Students should test their conjecture using new points and then finalize their findings. They should find that the composite of two rotations, say of magnitude a and b, will be a rotation of magnitude $a + b$.

Students should discover that they can perform one composite rotation that will result in the same final image as if they had performed two successive rotations. If the sum of the magnitudes of the two rotations is greater than 360°, then they may want to subtract a multiple of 360°, to make the magnitude of the single composite rotation between 0° and 360°.

5. This activity is rather open-ended. Students should follow a procedure similar to the one established in activities 2 and 3. You may wish to start this as a large-group activity, to help students focus on what is meant by investigating lines that are related to each other in a different way. Once students have articulated that lines might be parallel, perpendicular, or intersecting but non-perpendicular, then you might ask each person in a group to choose one case with which to investigate several examples. Alternatively, you may ask each group to choose 2 cases to investigate. This activity is easier to talk about with pictures for reference, and your students may need pictures to help them get started. You may wish to have groups share their findings by showing sketches of the compositions on transparent grids or on large sheets of paper.

a. If they do not use the same reflection line twice, then the composite transformation will vary. Since the GEOXPLOR software reflects only over a small set of lines, the resulting composites will be rotations, some of which will be recognized as the rotations already known. Some students may notice that the order in which reflections are performed will affect the result.

If some groups finish early, you may wish to ask them to think about the "size" of the composite rotation. In general, if the lines of reflection are parallel, the composite transformation will be a translation that slides the figure two times the distance between the two lines, and in a direction perpendicular to the lines. If the lines of reflection intersect, the composite transformation will be a rotation about the point of intersection. The magnitude of the rotation is equal to twice the measure of the non-obtuse angle formed by the two lines.

b. Students should discover that if they use the same reflection line twice, a figure will be mapped back onto itself.

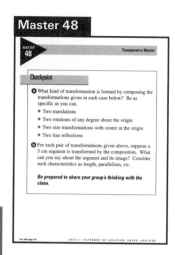

Master 48

MASTER 48
Transparency Master

Checkpoint

ⓐ What kind of transformation is formed by composing the transformations given in each case below? Be as specific as you can.
■ Two translations
■ Two rotations of any degree about the origin
■ Two size transformations with center at the origin
■ Two line reflections

ⓑ For each pair of transformations given above, suppose a 5 cm segment is transformed by the composition. What can you say about the segment and its image? Consider such characteristics as length, parallelism, *etc.*

Be prepared to share your group's thinking with the class.

Use with page 141.   UNIT 2 • PATTERNS OF LOCATION, SHAPE, AND SIZE

SHARE AND SUMMARIZE   full-class discussion

Checkpoint

See Teaching Master 48.

ⓐ ■ The resulting transformation will be a translation with components that are the sum of the components of the individual translations.

■ The composition of two rotations about the origin is a rotation about the origin with a magnitude that equals the sum of the magnitudes of the individual rotations.

■ The composition of two size transformations with center at the origin is a size transformation, with center at the origin, of magnitude equal to the product of the magnitudes of the individual size transformations.

■ See answer to activity 5 above. Encourage various groups to share their findings. You may wish to extend students' thinking by asking about the angle of rotation and the distance of the composite translation.

ⓑ Under all of the transformations the image will be a line segment. The translations would move the position of the line segment (unless the components are additive inverses of one another) and the image would be parallel (or identical) to the pre-image. The rotations would alter the tilt of the line segment (unless the sum of the magnitudes of the rotations is a multiple of 360°). The size transformations would change the length of the segment (unless one magnitude is the reciprocal of the other) and the image would be parallel to the pre-image. And finally, the reflections would result in a translation or rotation of the line segment (unless the same reflecting line is used both times).

MORE

ASSIGNMENT   *pp. 144–148*

Students now can begin Modeling tasks 1, 2, 3, or 4, Reflecting tasks 3 or 4, or Extending task 1 from the MORE assignment following Investigation 3.

APPLY   individual task

▶On Your Own

a. The triangle is a right triangle. The area is $\frac{\sqrt{288}\ \sqrt{72}}{2}$ or 72 square units.

b. The area of the transformed figure is the same as the original; 72 square units.

c. The area of the composite image is 128 square units. Students may find the image ordered pairs and then calculate the area of the image triangle, or they may multiply the pre-image area of 72 square units by $\left(\frac{4}{3}\right)^2$ (or by 16 and then by $\frac{1}{9}$).

Checkpoint

ⓐ What kind of transformation is formed by composing the transformations given in each case below? Be as specific as you can.

- Two translations
- Two rotations (of any degree) about the origin
- Two size transformations with center at the origin
- Two line reflections

ⓑ For each pair of transformations given above, suppose a 5-cm segment is transformed by the composition. What can you say about the segment and its image? Consider such characteristics as parallelism, length, and so on.

Be prepared to share your group's thinking with the class.

▶ **On Your Own**

$$\triangle ABC = \begin{bmatrix} 6 & 18 & 12 \\ 12 & 0 & -6 \end{bmatrix}$$

a. Find the area of $\triangle ABC$.

b. Predict the effect on area of the image triangle under successive application of two translations, one with components 2 (horizontal) and 3 (vertical), and the other with components −1 and 2. Then compute the area of the final image triangle and compare it to the area of $\triangle ABC$.

c. Predict the area of the image triangle when $\triangle ABC$ is transformed successively by size transformations centered at the origin with magnitudes of 4 and $\frac{1}{3}$. Then compute the area of the final image triangle and compare it to the original area. Explain the result.

The two transformations composed do not have to be two of the same kind. In the activities that follow, you will explore compositions involving size transformations and rigid transformations (translations, rotations, and reflections). Such composite transformations allow shapes, for example, to be rotated and enlarged or reduced in computer graphics applications.

LESSON 2 • COORDINATE MODELS OF TRANSFORMATIONS   **141**

6. Investigate the effects of composing size transformations with counterclockwise rotations about the origin. Choose three points that form the vertices of a triangle whose area you can calculate.

a. Use the "TRANSFORM" option to rotate the triangle 90° counterclockwise about the origin. Then apply a size transformation to the image triangle.

■ Predict how the coordinates of the pre-image are related to those of the image. Check your predictions.

■ Predict how the lengths of corresponding sides are related. Check your predictions.

■ Predict how the areas of the pre-image and image triangles are related. Check your predictions.

b. Reverse the order in which the transformations are applied—the size transformation first, then the rotation. How are the pre-image and the image related this time?

c. On the basis of parts a and b, what would you predict would happen if you used a different rotation? Would the order in which you applied the transformations lead to different final images? Test your conjectures.

7. Make a conjecture about the effects on shapes of composing size transformations and translations. Use a procedure similar to the one used in activity 6 to test your conjecture.

a. How are distances affected by composing size transformations with translations?

b. How are areas affected by composing size transformations with translations?

c. Does the order in which you apply the transformations lead to different final images? If it does, are the effects on distances and areas different also? Give evidence supporting your views.

Shapes that are related by a size transformation, or by a composite of a size transformation with a rigid transformation, are called **similar**. In activities 6 and 7, all the pre-image/image pairs are examples of similar shapes. The magnitude of the size transformation is the **scale factor**. It is the multiplier you use to convert lengths in one figure to those in the similar figure. For the next activity, think about how you find the scale factor if you compose two size transformations.

In activities 6 through 8, students can use GEOXPLOR to check conjectures about compositions of transformations. However, it is important that they also write either their examples or general examples in symbolic form. This will help them see why some compositions give different results when the order is reversed.

6. **a.** Responses will vary; however, in general, for a 90° counterclockwise rotation about the origin and a size transformation of magnitude k:

    ▪ $(x, y) \rightarrow (-y, x) \rightarrow (-ky, kx)$ so the coordinate rule for the composition is $(x, y) \rightarrow (-ky, kx)$.

    ▪ The length of the image sides are changed by a factor of $|k|$.

    ▪ The area of the image triangle is changed by a factor of k^2.

    b. The relationship between the pre-image and the image does not change because of the order in which the transformations are applied.

    c. For all rotations, it does not make a difference in which order the transformations are applied.

7. **a.** Conjectures may vary. However, students should discover that for a size transformation of magnitude k, the length of the image sides are changed by a factor of $|k|$.

    b. The area of the image triangle is changed by a factor of k^2.

    c. With these two transformations the order of application does make a difference. Sketches will show this clearly. For example, use a translation with the components $(3, 1)$ and size transformation with magnitude 2. The algebraic representation is:

    $$(x, y) \rightarrow (x + 3, y + 1) \rightarrow (2x + 6, 2y + 2)$$
    $$(x, y) \rightarrow (2x, 2y) \rightarrow (2x + 3, 2y + 1)$$

    The final image will not be the same point. However, the effects on distances and areas are the same when the order of composition is reversed. Students may justify this by looking at a particular figure, or by arguing that only the size transformation affects distances and area, so it doesn't matter in which order the transformations are applied.

Before proceeding to activity 8, you might want to check that students understood activities 6 and 7 by asking about one or two cases.

$(2, 3) \rightarrow$ size transformation, magnitude 2 $\rightarrow$ (,) $\rightarrow$ rotation, 90° $\rightarrow$ (,)

$(2, 3) \rightarrow$ rotation 90° $\rightarrow$ (,) $\rightarrow$ size transformation, magnitude 2 $\rightarrow$ (,)

Be sure to ask where the center of the rotation is, and where the center of the size transformation is. These may seem to be superfluous concepts to students because we always seem to use the origin to make the symbolic representations easier to understand. However, any point can be a center, as is seen in the next activity.

NOTE: Recall that congruent figures are also similar figures, so a scale factor of 1 still produces similar figures.

Unit 2

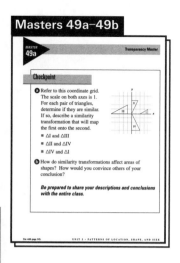

8. This activity permits students to select the center of the size transformation. Since different strategies can be used to complete a mapping, students need to explain their transformations very carefully, including what centers they used and what order.

    a. The scale factor is 1.5 since $\frac{XY}{AB} = \frac{7.5 \text{ units}}{5 \text{ units}} = 1.5$.

    b. Responses may vary. For example, a size transformation with a magnitude of 1.5 and a translation with an x-component of h and a y-component of 0; or the translation could be done by mapping A to X first, then applying a size transformation to the small triangle to expand it to the size of triangle XYZ. If the translation is applied first, then the most likely choice for the center of the size transformation is the point X. (Any other point on $\triangle XYZ$ also could be used.) If the size transformation is done first, the most likely choice would be A. (Any point on $\triangle ABC$ could be used.)

    c. $XZ = 10.05$ units

    d. $BC \approx 4.87$ units

    e. The area of triangle XYZ is $(1.5)^2(20)$ or 45 square units.

    f. The area of triangle ABC is $90 \div (1.5)^2$ or 40 square units.

SHARE AND SUMMARIZE   full-class discussion

Checkpoint

See Teaching Masters 49a–49b.

Students may continue to size transform incorrectly, by enlarging the figure by the required factor, but not attending to the center of the transformation.

For example, a size transformation with center at the origin and magnitude 2 will transform the first figure below into the second figure—not the third.

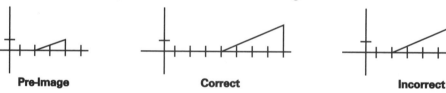

Pre-Image   Correct   Incorrect

It is worth taking time to have students demonstrate their similarity transformations for part a, giving them an opportunity to question and correct each other.

ⓐ All of the indicated pairs of triangles are similar. The similarity transformations that students give may differ. One possible response for each part is given.

  ■ A size transformation of magnitude 2 centered at the origin, then a translation with components -9 and 0.

  ■ Reflection across the x-axis, then a size transformation of magnitude $\frac{4}{3}$ centered at the origin.

  ■ 90° counterclockwise rotation centered at the origin, then a size transfor-mation of magnitude 0.5 centered at the origin, then a translation with components 2 and 0.

ⓑ A size transformation with magnitude $k \neq 0$ will change the area of a shape by a factor of k^2. Translations and rotations do not affect the area of a shape. Students could demonstrate this using several different examples. Alternatively they could reason that for a triangle with area $A = \frac{1}{2}bh$, the area of the image would be $A' = \frac{1}{2}(kb)(kh)$. Thus, $A' = k^2(\frac{1}{2}bh) = k^2A$.

JOURNAL ENTRY: Following a discussion of the Checkpoint items, ask students to summarize what they have learned about composite transformations.

Unit 2

8. In the figure below, △ABC is similar to △XYZ.

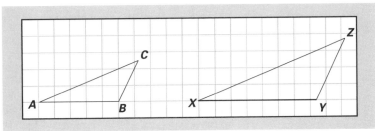

a. Explain why the scale factor is 1.5.

b. Describe a **similarity transformation** (a size transformation or a size transformation composed with one or more rigid transformations) that will map △ABC onto △XYZ. What is the center of your size transformation?

c. If AC = 6.7, how long is segment XZ?

d. If YZ = 7.3, how long is segment BC?

e. If the area of △ABC is 20 square units, what is the area of △XYZ?

f. If the area of △XYZ is 90 square units, what is the area of △ABC?

Checkpoint

a Refer to this coordinate grid. The scale on both axes is 1. For each pair of triangles, determine if they are similar. If so, describe a similarity transformation that will map the first onto the second.

- △I and △III
- △II and △IV
- △IV and △I

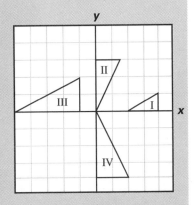

b How do similarity transformations affect areas of shapes? How would you convince others of your conclusion?

Be prepared to share your descriptions and conclusions with the entire class.

> **On Your Own**

a. Consider the similarity transformation that is a composite of these two transformations in the order given:

   i. $(x, y) \rightarrow (\frac{2}{3}x, \frac{2}{3}y)$

   ii. $(x, y) \rightarrow (x, -y)$

- Identify each type of transformation as completely as possible.
- What is the image of the point $P(-2, 6)$ under the similarity transformation?
- Write a statement of the form $(x, y) \rightarrow (\_ , \_)$ which describes the similarity transformation.

b. Examine the two triangles on the coordinate grid at the right. Are triangles *ABC* and *DCE* similar? Use your understanding of transformations to explain why or why not.

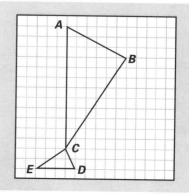

MORE
Modeling • Organizing • Reflecting • Extending

Modeling

1. A photograph that is 12.5 cm in length by 7.5 cm in width is enlarged to a width of 10 cm.

  a. What is the scale factor for the enlargement?

  b. What is the length of the enlargement?

  c. What are the areas of the picture and its enlargement? Explain how these areas are related and why the relationship exists.

  d. How are the perimeters related? Explain why the relationship exists.

On Your Own

a. ■ Transformation i is a size transformation with magnitude $\frac{2}{3}$ and center at the origin. Transformation ii is a reflection over the *x*-axis.

 ■ $(-2, 6) \rightarrow (-\frac{4}{3}, 4) \rightarrow (-\frac{4}{3}, -4)$

 ■ $(x, y) \rightarrow (\frac{2}{3}x, \frac{-2}{3}y)$

b. The lengths of the sides of the small triangle are approximately 2.2, 3.6, and 4 units. The lengths of the corresponding sides of the large triangle are approximately 6.7, 10.8, and 12 units. Under a size transformation of magnitude 3, the lengths of the sides of the small triangle can be converted to the lengths of the sides of the large triangle; therefore, the triangles are similar.

MORE | independent assignment

Modeling

1. **a.** The scale factor is $\frac{10}{7.5}$ or $\frac{4}{3}$, or approximately 1.333.
 b. The length of the enlargement is $\frac{25}{2} \cdot \frac{4}{3}$ or $16\frac{2}{3}$ cm.
 c. The area of the picture is 93.75 square cm and the area of the enlargement is approximately $10 \cdot 16.667$ or 166.67 square cm. The enlargement's area is larger than the original by a factor of the square of the scale factor. This is because both of the original's dimensions are multiplied by the scale factor.
 d. The ratio of the perimeter of the enlargement to the perimeter of the photograph is approximately 1.333.
 Original perimeter $= (12.5 \times 2) + (7.5 \times 2) = 40$
 Enlarged perimeter $\approx (16.667 \times 2) + (10 \times 2) \approx 53.33$
 Ratio $\approx \frac{53.33}{40} \approx 1.333$

MORE
ASSIGNMENT *pp. 144–148*

Modeling: 1 and choice of one*
Organizing: 2 and 3
Reflecting: Choose one*
Extending: 1

*When choice is indicated, it is important to leave the choice to the student.
NOTE: *It is best if Organizing tasks are discussed as a whole class after they have been assigned as homework.*

Unit 2

2. The area ratio is 2.25 because the scale factor is 1.5. A fair price for the cost of the new pizza is $9.98 $\times$ 2.25 or $22.46 since the new pizza is 2.25 times larger than the original. Some students may find the area of each pizza to determine the area ratio.

3. **a.** $0.70 \cdot 30$ by $0.70 \cdot 5$, or 21 cm by 31.5 cm
   b. $\frac{30}{0.7}$ by $\frac{45}{0.7}$, or 42.9 cm by 64.3 cm

4. **a.** The dimensions of the floor of the doll house are 3.5 feet by 2 feet:
   $70 \times 0.05 = 3.5$, $40 \times 0.05 = 2$.
   b. The floor space of the doll house is 7 square feet: $2800 \times 0.05^2 = 7$.
   So 7 square feet or 1,008 square inches (7×144) of carpeting will be needed for the doll house. Some students may find the area of the doll house by multiplying the dimensions ($3.5 \cdot 2$).

Organizing

1. **a.** Distances remain unchanged under a line reflection but are affected by a size transformation. Multiplying the length of the pre-image by the scale factor will give the length of the image.
   b. Areas are affected only by the size transformation. Multiplying the area of the pre-image by the square of the scale factor will give the area of the image.
   c. The order in which a size transformation and a reflection are applied does not affect the image. Students may give specific examples to support their claims, or they may use an argument employing general coordinates similar to the following:

	Reflect over the x-axis		Size transformation
$(x, y) \rightarrow$	$(x, -y)$	$\rightarrow$	$(kx, -ky)$

	Size transformation		Reflect over the x-axis
$(x, y) \rightarrow$	(kx, ky)	$\rightarrow$	$(kx, -ky)$

2. At one time, a pizza delivery chain sold rectangular pizzas that measured 10 inches by 30 inches. The store charged $9.98 (plus tax). A competitor planned to sell pizzas measuring 15 inches by 45 inches. What is a comparable price for this pizza? Why?

3. When clay pottery is fired, its linear dimensions shrink about 30%.

    a. If you started with a tray 30 cm by 45 cm, what would be the size of the finished tray?

    b. How big should you initially make a rectangular tray so that you end up with a 30 cm by 45 cm tray?

4. A doll house is a scale model of a full-size house. The linear scale on one particular doll house is 5%.

    a. The floor of the house measures 70 feet by 40 feet. What are the dimensions of the doll house?

    b. About how many square inches of carpet would you need to decorate the doll house with wall-to-wall carpeting? Explain your reasoning.

Organizing

1. Investigate the effects of composing size transformations and line reflections on shapes. Use a procedure similar to the one used in activity 6 of Investigation 3 (page 142).

    a. How are distances affected by this composition of transformations?

    b. How are areas affected by this composition of transformations?

    c. Does the order in which you apply the transformations lead to different images? If it does, are the effects on distances and areas different also? Give evidence supporting your views.

2. **a.** In the investigation, you found that the order in which you applied a size transformation and a rotation made no difference. Use the symbolic representations for a size transformation, $(x, y) \rightarrow (kx, ky)$, and a 90° rotation, $(x, y) \rightarrow (-y, x)$, to justify this observation for a rotation of 90° and a size transformation of magnitude k with center at the origin.

   b. Order did make a difference in composing size transformations and translations. Explain why and how the positions of the images differ.

3. How would you respond to the following assertions? In each case, explain the reasoning behind your response.

   a. Composing two rotations with the same center always results in a rotation.

   b. Composing two size transformations with the same center always results in a size transformation.

   c. Composing two line reflections always results in a line reflection.

4. If you reflect a point (x, y) across the y-axis, its image is $(-x, y)$. If you then reflect the image point $(-x, y)$ across the y-axis, the final image is (x, y), your original point.

   a. For each rigid transformation, describe a transformation with which it can be composed so that for any point, the pre-image and the final image are the same.

   b. For a size transformation with magnitude k and center at the origin, describe a transformation with which it can be composed so that for any point, the pre-image and the final image are the same.

   c. How is your work in parts a and b related to the concept of multiplicative *inverses* for real numbers and for matrices?

5. Write a program planning algorithm for a program that accepts three points, draws the triangle determined, then displays a size transformation image of the triangle and a half-turn image of the transformed triangle.

Reflecting

1. What are examples of the use of similar shapes that you see in your other courses in school?

2. Describe what the idea of *composing transformations* means to you. How would you explain it to a friend?

3. Think about a size transformation, or a composite of size transformations, that has magnitude 1.

   a. How does a size transformation of magnitude 1 affect a shape?

2. a.

		Rotation of 90°		Size transformation
(x, y)	$\rightarrow$	$(-y, x)$	$\rightarrow$	$(-ky, kx)$

		Size transformation		Rotation of 90°
(x, y)	$\rightarrow$	(kx, ky)	$\rightarrow$	$(-ky, kx)$

b.

		Size transformation		Translation (a, b)
(x, y)	$\rightarrow$	(kx, ky)	$\rightarrow$	$(kx + a, ky + b)$

		Translation (a, b)		Size transformation
(x, y)	$\rightarrow$	$(x + a, y + b)$	$\rightarrow$	$(kx + ka, ky + kb)$

When the size transformation is applied first, the translation components are not multiplied by a factor of k, as they are when the translation is applied first. The images differ by a translation with components $(k - 1)a$ and $(k - 1)b$.

3. a. This is true. The special case of rotations with magnitudes that are additive inverses results in a rotation with magnitudes that are 0.

b. This is true. The magnitude of the new size transformation is the product of the magnitudes of the two transformations.

c. This is never true. Composites of two reflections are always rotations or translations.

4. a. It is not expected that students will include glide reflection, especially if they have not completed Extending task 6 on page 125 in the student text. However, a sample response is provided here for those students who do include it.

Translation	A translation with components (h, k) followed by a translation with components $(-h, -k)$. $(x, y) \rightarrow (x + h, y + k) \rightarrow (x + h - h, y + k - k) \rightarrow (x, y)$
Reflection	A reflection across a line followed by a reflection across the same line. For example, across the line $y = -x$: $(x, y) \rightarrow (-y, -x) \rightarrow (-(-x), -(-y)) \rightarrow (x, y)$
Rotation	A rotation of $n°$ followed by a rotation of $(360 - n)°$. For example, a rotation of 270° followed by a rotation of 90°: $(x, y) \rightarrow (y, -x) \rightarrow (-(-x), y) \rightarrow (x, y)$
Glide reflection	A glide reflection with components (h, k) and across a line with slope $\frac{k}{h}$, followed by a glide reflection across the same line and with components $(-h, -k)$. For example, across the line $y = x$ (so $h = k$): $(x,y) \rightarrow (x + h - h, y + h - h) \rightarrow (x, y)$

b. Compose a size transformation of magnitude k with a size transformation of magnitude $\frac{1}{k}$ centered at the same point.

c. The product of a number and its multiplicative inverse is 1, and 1 times any number is that number. So, $x \cdot a \cdot \frac{1}{a} = x$. This is the same type of process that students were exploring with transformations in parts a and b. They were finding inverse transformations.

See additional Teaching Notes on page T168M.

Unit 2

3. **b.** If the magnitudes are reciprocals, the composite is a size transformation of magnitude 1.

    c. The identity element 1 ($1 \cdot x = x$ for all x), and the product of reciprocals (multiplicative inverses) equals 1.

4. Composing transformations is similar to adding real numbers in the following ways:

    Composing is associative as is addition.

    Composing always gives a transformation just as addition always gives a number.

    Just as adding a number can be "undone" by adding the opposite number, transformations can be "undone".

    Composing transformations is different from adding numbers, because composing is not always commutative whereas addition is.

Extending

1. **a.** Yes, because any circle can be mapped onto any other by a size transformation and a translation. The scale factor is the ratio of the radii.

    b. Yes, because the length of a side completely determines the square. The scale factor is the ratio of the sides of the two squares.

    c. Regular polygons with the same number of sides are always similar because the length of one side determines the lengths of all sides. The scale factor will be the ratio of the sides.

2. **a.** A size transformation using a factor less than 1 would give the appearance of walking away.

    b. The center of the body should stay in the same location on the screen.

    c. The size transformation must be centered at the center of the character's body.

    d. If the character is centered at the origin, the coordinates of points only need to be multiplied by the scale factor. If the character is not at the origin, the size transformation will involve some addition as well.

    e. Student responses will vary.

3. **a.** On a separate strip of paper, mark off the length OA to use as a unit of measure; alternatively, use a ruler to measure the length OA. On the paper where you draw O and A, draw a segment connecting the two points and extend it through point A. From point A and in the opposite direction from point O, mark off a distance equal to OA and label the image point A'. The length of the segment OA' is twice the length of the segment OA.

    b. On the strip, mark off lengths equal to OA and OB. Extend two rays, one from point O through A and the other from point O through B. On the ray OA, mark off two lengths equal to OA in the opposite direction from O, and label the last mark as image point A'. Repeat the procedure on ray OB using the length OB and label the image point B'. Connect A' and B'. The length of $A'B'$ is 3 times as long as AB.

b. What composites of two size transformations are equivalent to the size transformation with magnitude 1?

c. To what characteristics of real numbers and multiplication are the ideas in parts a and b similar?

4. Which characteristics of composing transformations are similar to characteristics of adding real numbers or adding matrices? Which are different?

Extending

1. Investigate the following classes of shapes in terms of similarity.

   a. Are any two circles similar? Explain your reasoning.

   b. Are any two squares similar? Explain.

   c. What types of polygons are always similar to each other? Why?

2. Suppose you wanted to create a computer graphics display of a cartoon character walking away from the viewer and "into" the screen.

   a. What transformation would you use to accomplish this animation?

   b. Would it look best to have the character's head, feet, or some other part of the body stay in the same location on the screen?

   c. How would you accomplish part b with transformations?

   d. How does the location of the character with respect to the origin affect the ease of this task?

   e. Illustrate your answers to parts a–d with a triangle.

3. For this task, you will investigate how to apply size transformations to figures, without the use of coordinates. A ruler or strip of paper may be helpful in your work.

   a. Sketch two separate points on paper. Label one O and one A. Using point O as the center and a magnitude of 2, find the size transformation image of point A. Label the image A'. Explain your procedure.

   b. Sketch a segment and a point not on the segment. Label the segment AB and the point O. With O as the center and a magnitude of 3, find the size transformation image of segment AB. Label the image $A'B'$. Is the new segment 3 times as long as the original?

c. Repeat part b using $\frac{1}{2}$ as the magnitude of the size transformation. Is the length of segment $A'B'$ half the length of segment AB?

d. Now draw a triangle ABC.

- Choose a point O as the center and a magnitude for a size transformation. Find the size transformation image of $\triangle ABC$ and label it $\triangle A'B'C'$.

- Choose another point P and another magnitude. Find the size transformation image of $\triangle A'B'C'$ and label it $\triangle A''B''C''$.

- Are $\triangle ABC$ and $\triangle A''B''C''$ related by a size transformation? If so, find its center and magnitude. Explain your procedure.

4. Determine whether the following procedure will apply a size transformation on a figure correctly when the center of the size transformation is $A(2, 1)$ and the magnitude is 3.

a. Draw a triangle on a coordinate grid and label it $\triangle PQR$. Plot point A.

b. Translate $A(2, 1)$ to the origin. Use the same translation to find the image of $\triangle PQR$. Label the image $\triangle P'Q'R'$.

c. Apply a size transformation to $\triangle P'Q'R'$ using the origin as center and 3 as the magnitude. Label the image $\triangle P''Q''R''$.

d. Translate $\triangle P''Q''R''$ by the translation that maps the origin back to $A(2, 1)$.

5. Write a program for your graphics calculator that conforms to the planning algorithm written in Organizing task 5.

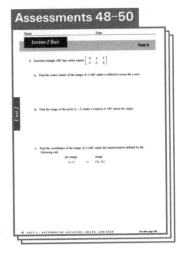

3. **c.** Yes, the length of $A'B'$ is half of the length of AB.

   d. ■ Draw 3 rays from point O through points A, B, and C respectively. Mark off a point A' on ray OA that is k times the length of OA, where k is the magnitude for the size transformation. Repeat the procedure using the length of the segment OB to determine the point B' on ray OB and the length of OC to find point C' on ray OC. Draw $\triangle A'B'C'$.

   ■ Repeat the above procedure.

   ■ It appears that the triangles are related by a size transformation. The pre-image and the image appear to be similar, and pre-image line segments appear to be parallel to image line segments. The center O'' of the size transformation is determined by the intersection of the lines AA'', BB'', and CC''. The magnitude is the ratio of $O''A''$ to $O''A$ which is equal to the product of the two size transformations used.

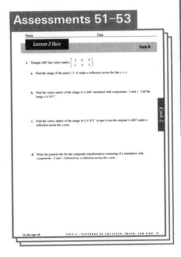

4. **a–b.** A translation with components -2 and 1 translates point A to the origin. For any triangle chosen, the pre-image points $P\,(a, b)$, $Q\,(c, d)$, and $R\,(e, f)$ translate to

   $P\,(a, b) \rightarrow P'\,(a - 2, b - 1)$,
   $Q\,(c, d) \rightarrow Q'\,(c - 2, d - 1)$, and
   $R\,(e, f) \rightarrow R'\,(e - 2, f - 1)$.

   c. The image points under the size transformation are

   $P' \rightarrow P''\,(3a - 6, 3b - 3)$,
   $Q' \rightarrow Q''\,(3c - 6, 3d - 3)$, and
   $R' \rightarrow R''\,(3e - 6, 3f - 3)$.

   d. For a translation with components 2 and 1 the image points are

   $P'' \rightarrow P'''\,(3a - 4, 3b - 2)$,
   $Q'' \rightarrow Q'''\,(3c - 4, 3d - 2)$ and
   $R'' \rightarrow R'''\,(3e - 4, 3f - 2)$.

   Notice that the length of PQ is $\sqrt{(a - c)^2 + (b - d)^2}$ and the length of $P'''Q'''$ is $\sqrt{[3a - 4 - (3c - 4)]^2 + [3b - 2 - (3d - 2)]^2}$ or $\sqrt{9(a - c)^2 + 9(b - d)^2}$ or $3\sqrt{(a - c)^2 + (b - d)^2}$. Similar computations can be done for the other line segments. Thus the ratio of the length of each image segment to the length of each pre-image is 3. Also the intersection of the lines through each pre-image point and its image determines the center of the size transformation and coincides with point A. Thus this algorithm correctly performs a size transformation centered at $A(2, 1)$ with a magnitude of 3.

5. The program below will run on a TI-82 or TI-83 graphics calculators. If students are using other calculators their programs may be different.

```
ClrHome
Input "X COORD #1", A        Line (A, B, C, D)
Input "Y COORD #1", B        Line (C, D, E, F)
Input "X COORD #2", C        Line (E, F, A, B)
Input "Y COORD #2", D        Line (KA, KB, KC, KD)
Input "X COORD #3", E        Line (KC, KD, KE, KF)
Input "Y COORD #3", F        Line (KE, KF, KA, KB)
Input "Magnitude", K         Line (-KA, -KB, -KC, -KD)
ClrDraw                      Line (-KC, -KD, -KE, -KF)
                             Line (-KE, -KF, -KA, -KB)
                             Stop
```

See Assessment Resource pages 48–53.

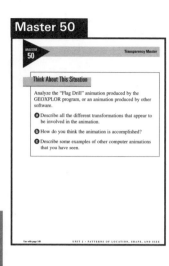

Lesson 3 *Transformations, Matrices, and Animation*

LESSON OVERVIEW In this lesson, students discover how to model computer animations by using matrix representations of transformations of the plane. The lesson builds on the coordinate work with transformations that students did in the previous two lessons. In particular, they use the coordinate rules for rotations and size transformations centered at the origin to get the matrix representations. Other transformations are investigated in the MORE tasks.

Lesson Objectives

- ■ To use the coordinate rules for rotations about the origin to get the corresponding matrix representations
- ■ To use the coordinate rule for a size transformation centered at the origin to get the corresponding matrix representation
- ■ To use the matrix representations to write planning algorithms for animations involving rotations and size transformations

LAUNCH full-class discussion

Think About This Situation

See Teaching Master 50.

ⓐ The intent of the demonstration is to get students thinking about geometric transformations. Formal discussion about and terminology for transformations is not necessary here. However, the students should see that the flag seems to be rotating about its shaft endpoint. The flag is rotated, reflected, translated, and enlarged.

ⓑ Students with some experience with programming might mention the technique of sequentially drawing and erasing points, or they might even mention matrices. Other students might say just that it is done by some kind of program or that it is built into the calculator. This brief discussion is meant to get students thinking about how to do the animation.

ⓒ Special effects in movies and video games are two such examples. Each investigation of this lesson concludes by having students use what they have learned to write a planning algorithm for an animation similar to a small piece of the "Flag Drill" demonstration.

Lesson 3

Transformations, Matrices, and Animation

In the first two lessons of this unit, you used coordinates to model geometric ideas such as distance in a plane, lines, and transformations. The coordinate models provided ways to describe familiar and not-so-familiar ideas numerically and algebraically. You saw how coordinate representations can be used to create computer or calculator graphics displays. In this lesson you will investigate how matrices, together with the geometric ideas studied in the first two lessons, can be used to produce computer animations.

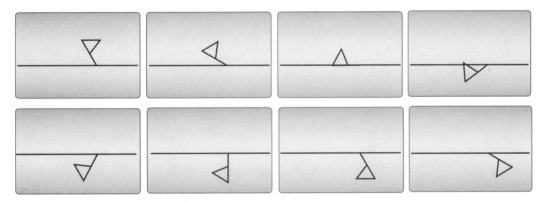

Think About This Situation

Shown above are sample displays from software developed for a graphics calculator. Analyze the "Flag Drill" animation produced by the GEOXPLOR program, or an animation produced by other software.

a Describe all the different transformations that appear to be involved in the animation.

b How do you think the animation is accomplished?

c Describe some examples of other computer animations that you have seen.

INVESTIGATION 1 ▶ Spinning Flags

In the Flag Drill animation, the flag moves above and below a horizontal line. Think about how the flag could be transformed from a straight-up position to a straight-down position, as shown in the figure below.

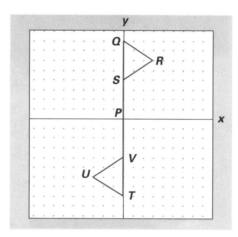

1. In your group, discuss at least two ways to transform the up-flag into the down-flag using one or more transformations.

   a. Did you, or could you, transform the up-flag into the down-flag by using a 180° rotation?

   ■ Which of the labeled points is the center of such a rotation?

   ■ Which point is the image of point *S*?

   ■ What is the pre-image of segment *UV*?

   b. What is the image of a point (*x*, *y*) under a 180° rotation about the origin? Assuming point *P* is located at the origin, verify your rule using points P, *Q*, *R*, and *S* as pre-images.

2. Using matrix multiplication and the general coordinate rule for a 180° rotation about the origin, you can find a matrix that represents the rotation. First, you will need to represent points as one-column matrices. So, (*x*, *y*) looks like

   $\begin{bmatrix} x \\ y \end{bmatrix}$ and its image under a 180° rotation, (−*x*, −*y*), looks like $\begin{bmatrix} -x \\ -y \end{bmatrix}$.

   a. Recall that matrices may be multiplied when the number of columns in the first matrix equals the number of rows in the second. Now, consider the following matrix multiplication. Determine the entries of the 2 × 2 matrix.

   $$\begin{bmatrix} \rule{1em}{0.4pt} & \rule{1em}{0.4pt} \\ \rule{1em}{0.4pt} & \rule{1em}{0.4pt} \end{bmatrix} \begin{bmatrix} x \\ y \end{bmatrix} = \begin{bmatrix} -x \\ -y \end{bmatrix}$$

INVESTIGATION 1 Spinning Flags

In this investigation, students will use the coordinate rules for 180° and 90° counterclockwise rotations about the origin to find the matrix representation of such rotations. In addition, to allow for more interesting animations, students are given the matrix for a 45° counterclockwise rotation centered at the origin.

You may wish to introduce this investigation by rerunning the "Flag Drill" demonstration. The "Think About This Situation" questions are closely connected to activity 1.

In anticipation of activities 2 through 5, you can let students know that they are going to use matrices to model the transformations they have learned about in the previous lessons. Remind them that they already have symbolic models for transformations. You might ask, "What transformation does $(x, y) \rightarrow (x, -y)$ model?" (Reflection across the x-axis.) "What transformation does $(x, y) \rightarrow (-y, -x)$ model?" (Reflection across the line $y = -x$.) "What could the matrix $\begin{bmatrix} 2 \\ 3 \end{bmatrix}$ model?" (A point.) What could $\begin{bmatrix} 2 & 0 & 5 \\ 3 & 1 & 5 \end{bmatrix}$ model?" (3 points or a triangle.)

You also might also tell students that they are going to have to use matrix multiplication to do some transformations, then review matrix multiplication using a specific example such as $\begin{bmatrix} 1 & 2 \\ 2 & 3 \end{bmatrix} \begin{bmatrix} 3 & 4 & 2 \\ 1 & 5 & 0 \end{bmatrix}$.

As students think about the multiplication procedure, draw out how the dimensions of the first and second matrix must be related.

1. The down-flag could be produced by a 180° rotation in either direction or by horizontal and vertical reflections.

   a. Yes, a 180° rotation would produce this figure.
      - P is the center of the rotation.
      - V is the image of S.
      - Segment RS is the pre-image of segment UV.

   b. The general coordinate rule for a 180° rotation about the origin is $(x, y) \rightarrow (-x, -y)$.

If students seem to be having difficulty with activity 1, bring the whole class together for a discussion before moving on to activities 2 through 5. As students work on activities 2 through 5, you may find it worthwhile to ask why a matrix is a good model for a polygon. (Students may say that it stores the pairs of coordinates in the correct order.) You also may want the students to think about why multiplying by a matrix is a good model for a rotation. This second question is more sophisticated, and students do not really have the experience to answer it, but they can at least begin to think about what we mean by a model in this case. (To be a good model, the multiplication would have to preserve important aspects of the geometric representation. For example, the model must continue to give correct geometric results if you continue to apply several rotation matrices for 90°, or if you apply the rotation matrix for 90° and then the matrix for 180°. If you reverse the order of the multiplication, the geometric result also must be the same. These issues are returned to in future courses.)

2. a. $\begin{bmatrix} -1 & 0 \\ 0 & -1 \end{bmatrix}$

2. **b.** All students should have found this matrix.

    c. Students need to remember that the matrix representing the pre-image always should be on the right of the transformation matrix. Students should get the image points as shown in the picture at the beginning of this investigation; if not, you may want to check that they are multiplying matrices properly.

3. **a.**

Point	Image
(2, 0)	(0, 2)
(2, 3)	(−3, 2)
(8, −5)	(5, 8)

b. $(x, y) \rightarrow (-y, x)$

c.
$$\begin{bmatrix} 0 & -1 \\ 1 & 0 \end{bmatrix}$$

d. Students should get the same image points as in part a.

4. **a.** Students sketch the image triangle (dotted edges) in part c.

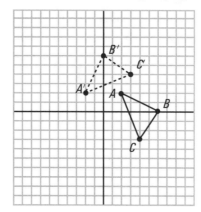

b. Students may choose to use their calculators for the matrix multiplication.

$$\begin{bmatrix} 0 & -1 \\ 1 & 0 \end{bmatrix}\begin{bmatrix} 2 & 6 & 4 \\ 2 & 0 & -3 \end{bmatrix} = \begin{bmatrix} -2 & 0 & 3 \\ 2 & 6 & 4 \end{bmatrix} = \triangle A'B'C'$$

c. See diagram in part a. The sketches of the triangle and its image under the rotation should help students see that the matrix multiplication really does provide the correct coordinates for the rotation. This also reinforces one important connection between geometry and matrices.

d. The dimension of the transformation matrix is 2 × 2, and the dimension of the polygon matrix is 2 × *n* where *n* is the number of sides in the polygon. The matrix multiplication will be possible only if the matrix representing the polygon is the factor on the right.

b. Compare your answer for part a with that of other groups. Resolve any differences.

c. The matrix you agreed upon in part b is a representation of a 180° rotation about the origin. When you multiply a point by the matrix you get its image under the rotation. Check this using the labeled points on the flag in activity 1. Be sure to represent the points as one-column matrices and multiply with the point matrix on the right of the transformation matrix.

3. In a similar way, you can construct a matrix representation of a 90° counterclockwise rotation centered at the origin.

a. Find the image of (2, 0) under a 90° counterclockwise rotation centered at the origin. Do the same for the points (2, 3) and (8, –5).

b. What is the coordinate rule for a 90° counterclockwise rotation? Write your answer in the following form: $(x, y) \rightarrow (\_ , \_)$.

c. Build a matrix representation for this 90° rotation by determining the entries of the 2×2 matrix below.

$$\begin{bmatrix} \_\_ & \_\_ \\ \_\_ & \_\_ \end{bmatrix} \begin{bmatrix} x \\ y \end{bmatrix} = \begin{bmatrix} -y \\ x \end{bmatrix}$$

d. Now you have a matrix that models a 90° counterclockwise rotation about the origin. Multiply the matrix by the one-column matrices for the points (2, 3) and (8, –5). Check to see that you get the same answers as in part a.

4. One advantage of a matrix representation of a transformation is that you can use it quickly to transform an entire polygon. Consider $\triangle ABC = \begin{bmatrix} 2 & 6 & 4 \\ 2 & 0 & -3 \end{bmatrix}$.

a. Sketch this triangle in a coordinate plane.

b. Multiply the matrix representation of $\triangle ABC$ by the 90° transformation matrix. The result gives the image of $\triangle ABC$ under a 90° counterclockwise rotation centered at the origin. When multiplying the two matrices, the matrix representation of $\triangle ABC$ should be on the right of the rotation matrix.

c. Sketch the image triangle, $\triangle A'B'C'$.

d. When transforming a polygon using matrices, why should the matrix representation of the polygon be the factor on the right?

5. You have found matrices that represent 90° counterclockwise and 180° rotations about the origin. The matrix below represents another transformation.

$$A = \begin{bmatrix} 0.707 & -0.707 \\ 0.707 & 0.707 \end{bmatrix}$$

Unit 2

a. Investigate the effect of this transformation.

- Represent the flag shown below with a 2 × 4 matrix.
- Multiply the given transformation matrix by the matrix representation of the flag.
- Sketch the flag and its image in a coordinate plane.

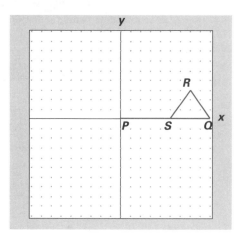

b. Describe as completely as you can the transformation that is represented by the matrix. Compare your description to that of other groups.

c. Now consider a vertical flag pole, with no banner, that is 10 units long. Using your description of the transformation in part b, sketch the image of the vertical flag pole. Check your image by representing the vertical flag pole as a matrix and using matrix multiplication to find the image.

6. A computer or calculator program can be written that will rotate a flag about the origin using steps of 45°. A planning algorithm is given below.

Flag Turn Algorithm

Step 1. Set up the 45° rotation matrix.

Step 2. Input the matrix representing the flag.

Step 3. Compute the coordinates of a flag rotated 45°.

Step 4. Store the coordinates in the flag matrix.

Step 5. Draw the flag.

Step 6. Erase the flag.

Step 7. Repeat steps 3–6.

a. Identify the input, processing, and output parts of the Flag Turn Algorithm.

5. Since there is no quick, easy way to get the coordinate rule for a 45° rotation, it is not possible to build the matrix as in the previous problems. But students need this rotation to do reasonable computer animations. Here, they are given the matrix without being told what it represents, and then they investigate the effect of multiplying by the matrix. They should conclude that it represents a 45° rotation. (See Extending task 2 on page 163 in the student text for a way to build this transformation matrix.)

a. ■ $\begin{bmatrix} 0 & 9 & 7 & 5 \\ 0 & 0 & 3 & 0 \end{bmatrix}$

> NOTE: When the matrix representation is used in the FLAGTURN program in activity 6, the order of the columns is important because of the drawing command. Points need to be connected in a particular order so that the entire flag is drawn.

■ $\begin{bmatrix} 0.707 & -0.707 \\ 0.707 & 0.707 \end{bmatrix} \begin{bmatrix} 0 & 9 & 7 & 5 \\ 0 & 0 & 3 & 0 \end{bmatrix} = \begin{bmatrix} 0 & 6.363 & 2.828 & 3.535 \\ 0 & 6.363 & 7.07 & 3.535 \end{bmatrix}$

■ The sketch will help students determine the motion represented by the matrix.

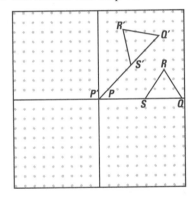

b. The matrix represents a 45° counterclockwise rotation centered at the origin.

c. Focusing on the flag pole, without a banner, will eliminate the technicalities of dealing with the exact coordinates of the banner. The image of (0, 10) will be (−7.07, 7.07).

6. **The FLAGTURN program is an important outcome of the lesson, since it allows students to apply their new knowledge to create some elementary computer graphics. However, the important mathematical component is using matrices to represent the flag and the rotation.**

   If your students are interested in embellishing or writing programs for the graphics calculator, you may wish to ask them to work on Extending task 3, page 163 in the student text. If you do this, it might be wise to suggest that they write programs that do not include matrix and window set-up in the programs themselves, especially for a first attempt at programming. Those students who would like to write more self-sufficient and elaborate programs certainly should be encouraged to do so.

   a. Input: steps 1 and 2
      Processing: steps 3 and 4
      Output: steps 5 and 6

6. b. **Step 7 is a loop control. It is an essential tool in programming. For those students who are interested in programming, refer them to information on For loops and, perhaps, Repeat and While loops also.**

The steps will need to be performed 8 times, since $\frac{360}{45}$ is 8.

c. $B = \begin{bmatrix} 0 & 0 & 3 & 0 \\ 0 & 8 & 6 & 4 \end{bmatrix}$ $A = \begin{bmatrix} 0.707 & -0.707 \\ 0.707 & 0.707 \end{bmatrix}$

The matrices and drawings for the image flags are given below. (Matrix entries are approximate.)

First image: $\begin{bmatrix} 0 & -5.65 & -2.12 & -2.83 \\ 0 & 5.65 & 6.36 & 2.83 \end{bmatrix}$

Second image: $\begin{bmatrix} 0 & -8 & -6 & -4 \\ 0 & 0 & 3 & 0 \end{bmatrix}$

Third image: $\begin{bmatrix} 0 & -5.65 & -6.36 & -2.83 \\ 0 & -5.65 & -2.12 & -2.83 \end{bmatrix}$

Fourth image: $\begin{bmatrix} 0 & 0 & -3 & 0 \\ 0 & 8 & -6 & -4 \end{bmatrix}$

Fifth image: $\begin{bmatrix} 0 & 5.65 & 2.12 & 2.83 \\ 0 & -5.65 & -6.36 & -2.83 \end{bmatrix}$

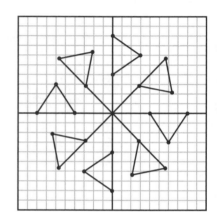

Sixth image: $\begin{bmatrix} 0 & 8 & 6 & 4 \\ 0 & 0 & -3 & 0 \end{bmatrix}$

Seventh image: $\begin{bmatrix} 0 & 5.65 & 6.36 & 2.83 \\ 0 & 5.65 & 2.12 & 2.83 \end{bmatrix}$

Eighth image: $\begin{bmatrix} 0 & 0 & 3 & 0 \\ 0 & 8 & 6 & 4 \end{bmatrix}$

d. **See Teaching Master 51.**

The input portion is done before the program is executed. The processing portion is line 3: [A] ∗ [B] → [B]. The 3 "Line" commands and the "ClrDraw" command make up the output portion. The control part is "For (N, 1, 8, 1)" and the final "End". The pause loop consisting of the lines "For (K, 1, 25, 1)" and "End" are inserted into the program so that you have time to see each flag before it is erased. You may wish to point this out to your students.

b. Step 7 is a new kind of instruction in an algorithm. It is a *control* command because it controls the action of the algorithm. To make the flag rotate all the way around once, how many times should steps 3–6 be performed?

c. Simulate the Flag Turn Algorithm. Let A be the 45° rotation matrix and let B be the Flag matrix for the up-flag in activity 1 (page 150). Place the coordinates for point P in column 1, for point Q in column 2, for point R in column 3, and for point S in column 4.

- Draw the flag on graph paper using present coordinates.
- Calculate new coordinates.
- Repeat the above steps eight times using the last answer function of your calculator.

d. For one popular graphics calculator, the Flag Turn Algorithm has been converted into a program called FLAGTURN. For this program to work, matrices A and B must be entered into the calculator before the program is run. Match parts of this program with the corresponding steps in the Flag Turn Algorithm.

FLAGTURN Program

Program	Comments
ClrDraw	Clears all drawings.
For(N,1,8,1)	Beginning of loop. Transforms the flag in 8 steps.
[A]*[B]→[B]	Stores the product of the transformation matrix A and matrix B in matrix B.
Line ([B](1,1),[B](2,1),[B](1,2),[B](2,2))	Draws a line segment from the point whose coordinates are in the 1st column of the shape matrix B to the point whose coordinates are in the 2nd column.
Line ([B](1,2),[B](2,2),[B](1,3),[B](2,3))	Draws a line segment from the point whose coordinates are in the 2nd column of B to the point whose coordinates are in the 3rd column of B.
Line ([B](1,3),[B](2,3),[B](1,4),[B](2,4))	Draws a line segment from 3rd column point to 4th column point.
For(K,1,25,1)	Beginning of pause loop. This loop causes the program to wait a moment before changing the drawing.
End	End of pause loop.
ClrDraw	Clears all drawings.
End	End of loop (N, 1, 8, 1).
Stop	End of program.

e. How could this program be modified to completely match the Flag Turn Algorithm? (You can answer with general instructions. Specific commands for the calculator are not necessary.)

f. Optional: Obtain a copy of FLAGTURN from your teacher and run it to view the animation. You may need to reset your window in order to view the animation.

Checkpoint

ⓐ Explain how to use the coordinate representation of a 90° clockwise rotation about the origin to find the matrix representation for that rotation. Find the matrix.

ⓑ Describe how to change the Flag Turn Algorithm to rotate the flag clockwise about the origin using steps of 90°.

ⓒ Describe how matrices can be used to create an animation of a flag spinning around the origin.

Be prepared to share your group's matrix and descriptions with the class.

▶ On Your Own

a. Build a matrix representing a 270° counterclockwise rotation about the origin.

b. Use the matrix to find the image of the point (–2, 5).

c. Use the matrix to find the image of $\triangle HJK = \begin{bmatrix} -1 & 4 & 3 \\ 2 & -3 & 5 \end{bmatrix}$.

d. Sketch the triangle and its image on a coordinate system.

INVESTIGATION 2 Stretching and Shrinking

At the end of the Flag Drill animation, the flag grew in size. This was accomplished by using a size transformation with center at the origin. Altering the magnitude of the size transformation created this growing effect. In this investigation all size transformations will be centered at the origin.

6. e. Input parts would need to be added to simulate the complete algorithm. We do not expect students to be specific about the actual code that would need to be included, although you may have some students who enjoy programming and would like to provide the programming code. (See Extending task 3, page 163 in the student text.)

f. At the very least, all students should see a demonstration of this program. Seeing the program run will help them believe that their interpretation of the program is correct.

SHARE AND SUMMARIZE full-class discussion

Checkpoint

See Teaching Master 52.

ⓐ The matrix representation for a 90° clockwise rotation about the origin is

$$\begin{bmatrix} 0 & 1 \\ -1 & 0 \end{bmatrix}.$$

Explanations will vary, but should involve using matrix multiplication to obtain an image of $(y, -x)$ for any point (x, y).

ⓑ In step 1, set up the matrix for a 90° clockwise rotation. You may wish to discuss how many times you would need to repeat steps 3–6 in order for the flag to go around exactly one time.

ⓒ Represent the flag and the rotation with matrices. Then repeatedly rotate the flag by using a "For" loop to repeat the following: multiply the image's matrix by the rotation matrix to compute the next image, erase the old image, and draw the new image.

APPLY individual task

▶ On Your Own

a. $\begin{bmatrix} 0 & 1 \\ -1 & 0 \end{bmatrix}$

b. $\begin{bmatrix} 0 & 1 \\ -1 & 0 \end{bmatrix}\begin{bmatrix} -2 \\ 5 \end{bmatrix} = \begin{bmatrix} 5 \\ 2 \end{bmatrix}$

The image of $(-2, 5)$ is $(5, 2)$.

c. $\begin{bmatrix} 0 & 1 \\ -1 & 0 \end{bmatrix}\begin{bmatrix} -1 & 4 & 3 \\ 2 & -3 & 5 \end{bmatrix} = \begin{bmatrix} 2 & -3 & 5 \\ 1 & -4 & -3 \end{bmatrix} = \triangle H'J'K'$

d. See the graph at the right.

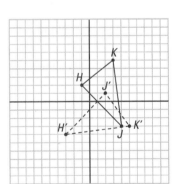

See additional Teaching Notes on page T168N.

Master 52

MORE
ASSIGNMENT *pp. 157–164*

Students now can begin Modeling tasks 1, 2, or 3, Organizing tasks 1, 2, or 3, or Extending tasks 2, 4, or 6 from the MORE assignment following Investigation 2.

1. a. The magnitude of the size transformation is 3 (for example, $\frac{\text{length of } UT}{\text{length of } QP} = \frac{12}{4} = 3$).

b. $(x, y) \rightarrow (3x, 3y)$

c–d.

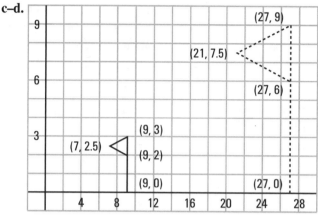

e. Each segment in the image flag is three times the length of the corresponding segment of the pre-image flag. The flags are the same shape but different sizes. Thus, the flags are similar.

2. a. The transformation matrix is $\begin{bmatrix} 3 & 0 \\ 0 & 3 \end{bmatrix}$.

b. $(-2, 3)$ has image $(-6, 9)$. Students should check that matrix multiplication produces the same points. They may choose to compute by hand or by calculator.

c. Students should get the same image coordinates as they did in Activity 1.

$$\begin{bmatrix} 3 & 0 \\ 0 & 3 \end{bmatrix} \begin{bmatrix} 9 & 9 & 7 & 9 \\ 0 & 3 & 2.5 & 2 \end{bmatrix} = \begin{bmatrix} 27 & 27 & 21 & 27 \\ 0 & 9 & 7.5 & 6 \end{bmatrix}$$

3. a. The matrix representation for a size transformation of magnitude $\frac{1}{2}$ is

$$\begin{bmatrix} 0.5 & 0 \\ 0 & 0.5 \end{bmatrix}$$

b. $\begin{bmatrix} 0.5 & 0 \\ 0 & 0.5 \end{bmatrix} \begin{bmatrix} 15 & 15 & 9 & 15 \\ 0 & 12 & 9 & 6 \end{bmatrix} = \begin{bmatrix} 7.5 & 7.5 & 4.5 & 7.5 \\ 0 & 6 & 4.5 & 3 \end{bmatrix}$

c. Students should sketch both flags to verify the size change.

d. The length of a segment in the image flag should be one-half the length of the corresponding segment in the pre-image flag. Students should check several segments.

1. Examine the flags in the figure below.

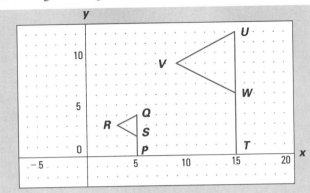

a. What is the magnitude of the size transformation that transforms the small flag into the large flag?

b. Write a coordinate rule for this transformation: $(x, y) \rightarrow (\_, \_)$.

c. Consider a flag represented by this matrix: $\begin{bmatrix} 9 & 9 & 7 & 9 \\ 0 & 3 & 2.5 & 2 \end{bmatrix}$. Sketch this flag in a coordinate plane.

d. Sketch the image of the flag under the size transformation in part b. Be sure to use the origin as the center.

e. How are the two flags related?

2. Matrix representations for size transformations can be found using the same technique as in Investigation 1.

a. Determine the entries of the 2×2 transformation matrix below.

$$\begin{bmatrix} \_ & \_ \\ \_ & \_ \end{bmatrix} \begin{bmatrix} x \\ y \end{bmatrix} = \begin{bmatrix} 3x \\ 3y \end{bmatrix}$$

b. What should the image of $(-2, 3)$ be? Multiply the transformation matrix by the one-column matrix for the point $(-2, 3)$ and check to see that you get the correct image.

c. Multiply the transformation matrix by the matrix for the flag in part c of activity 1. Compare this result with what you got for part d of that activity.

3. Next consider a size transformation of magnitude $\frac{1}{2}$ centered at the origin.

a. Find the matrix representation for this size transformation.

b. Using matrix multiplication, find the size transformation image of the large flag in activity 1.

c. Sketch the original flag and its image in a coordinate plane.

d. Predict how corresponding lengths should be related in the flag and its image. Check your prediction by calculating a few corresponding distances and lengths.

Unit 2

4. Now consider the matrix $A = \begin{bmatrix} 5 & 0 \\ 0 & 5 \end{bmatrix}$.

  a. Does this matrix represent a size transformation? If so, what is the magnitude of the size transformation? What is the center?

  b. What is the coordinate rule for this transformation?

  c. Describe the effect of this transformation on lengths.

5. Write a planning algorithm for an animation program that depicts a flag that enlarges. It should meet the following specifications.

  ■ Begin with the small flag shown in activity 1.

  ■ Use successive size transformations of magnitude 1.1 to create an animation that shows the flag growing and moving away from the origin until its pole is beyond (20, 0).

  a. Identify the input, processing, output, and control parts in your algorithm.

  b. In the control step, how many times should the program repeat to get the pole first beyond (20, 0)?

Checkpoint

ⓐ Explain how to use the coordinate rule for a transformation to find the matrix representation of the transformation.

ⓑ Write the matrix that represents a size transformation of magnitude k.

ⓒ Explain how your matrix in part b can be used to find the image of a point and the image of a polygon.

Be prepared to explain your matrix and methods to the entire class.

▶**On Your Own**

Choose a magnitude for a size transformation (different from any magnitude used so far in this investigation), and choose some figure to be transformed. Then do the following.

a. Represent the transformation and the figure with matrices.

b. Use matrix multiplication to find the image of the figure under the transformation.

EXPLORE *continued*

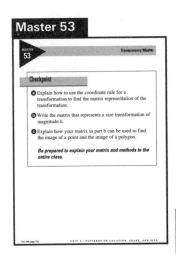

4. a. Yes, it represents a size transformation of magnitude 5 with center at the origin.

   b. $(x, y) \rightarrow (5x, 5y)$

   c. Lengths will be multiplied by 5.

5. One planning algorithm for this animation is provided below. Students' algorithms may differ slightly from this one.

   Step 1: Define the matrix for the size transformation with magnitude 1.1.

   Step 2: Define the matrix for the flag.

   Step 3: Draw the flag.

   Step 4: Erase the flag.

   Step 5: Multiply the matrices to compute the coordinates of the transformed flag.

   Step 6: Store the new coordinates in the flag matrix.

   Step 7: Repeat steps 3–6.

   a. For the planning algorithm above:

      Input Portion: steps 1 and 2   Processing Portion: steps 5 and 6

      Output Portion: steps 3 and 4   Control Portion: step 7

   b. The program should loop 15 times. Students may have difficulty with this question. Ask them to recall how the coordinates of a point change if the same size transformation is applied repeatedly. The first time $(5, 0) \rightarrow (1.1 \cdot 5, 0)$ or $(5.5, 0)$. The second time through the program $(5.5, 0) \rightarrow (1.1 \cdot 5.5, 0)$ or $((1.1)^2 \cdot 5, 0)$.

     In general the nth application of steps 3–6 maps $(1.1^{n-1} \cdot 5, 0)$ to $(1.1^n \cdot 5, 0)$. Thus we seek n so that $(1.1)^n \cdot 5 > 20$. This can be accomplished using the calculator and counting or trial and error. When n is 15, then $(1.1)^n \cdot 5 \approx 20.89$.

SHARE AND SUMMARIZE full-class discussion

Checkpoint

See Teaching Master 53.

ⓐ The coordinate rule gives the general formula for each coordinate of the image point. Change each coordinate formula into an equation using x and y. Then "pull out" the coefficients of x and y, and that's the transformation matrix.

ⓑ $\begin{bmatrix} k & 0 \\ 0 & k \end{bmatrix}$

ⓒ To obtain the image point, multiply the matrix in part b by the matrix representing the point. To find the image of a polygon, multiply the matrix in part b by the matrix representing the polygon.

CONSTRUCTING A MATH TOOLKIT: You may wish to have students add a column to their table from Modeling task 1 (page 120 in the student text) for the matrix representations.

APPLY individual task

▶On Your Own

a. The transformation matrix should be of the form $\begin{bmatrix} k & 0 \\ 0 & k \end{bmatrix}$.

b. The figure matrices will vary.

          [Transformation] [Coordinates] = [Image]

Unit 2

APPLY *continued*

   c. Sketching the figure and its image will help students check their work.

   d. Students will need only to alter the input steps of the algorithm developed in activity 5. You might want to have some students write the program and share their animations with others in their group or with the class by using the overhead calculator.

MORE
ASSIGNMENT   *pp. 157–164*

Modeling: 2 and choice of one*
Organizing: 3 and choice of one*
Reflecting: Choose one*
Extending: Choose one*

When choice is indicated, it is important to leave the choice to the student.
NOTE: *It is best if Organizing tasks are discussed as a whole class after they have been assigned as homework.*

MORE   independent assignment

Modeling

1. a. A reflection across a vertical line will create the effect of the banner flipping back and forth.

   b. The image of (2, 3) is (−2, 3). The image of (3, −4) is (−3, −4).

   c. $(x, y) \rightarrow (−x, y)$

   d. The matrix representation for a reflection across the y-axis is $\begin{bmatrix} -1 & 0 \\ 0 & 1 \end{bmatrix}$.

   e. Students may interpret "flip the banner back and forth" to mean the banner should come back to its original position 10 times. In that case, Steps 3–6 must be repeated a total of 20 times.

   Reflection Algorithm
   Step 1: Define the matrix that represents a reflection across the y-axis.
   Step 2: Define the matrix representing the flag.
   Step 3: Draw the flag.
   Step 4: Erase the flag.
   Step 5: Compute the coordinates of the reflection image of the flag.
   Step 6: Store the new coordinates in the flag matrix.
   Step 7: Repeat steps 3–6, 10 times.

2. a. The matrix representation for a reflection across the x-axis is $\begin{bmatrix} 1 & 0 \\ 0 & -1 \end{bmatrix}$.

   b. The matrix representation of a reflection across the line $y = x$ is $\begin{bmatrix} 0 & 1 \\ 1 & 0 \end{bmatrix}$.

   c. The composite transformation can be found by multiplying the matrices from parts a and b.

   $$\begin{bmatrix} 0 & 1 \\ 1 & 0 \end{bmatrix} \begin{bmatrix} 1 & 0 \\ 0 & -1 \end{bmatrix} = \begin{bmatrix} 0 & -1 \\ 1 & 0 \end{bmatrix}$$

   The matrix representing the composite transformation is $\begin{bmatrix} 0 & -1 \\ 1 & 0 \end{bmatrix}$.

   d. The matrix $\begin{bmatrix} 0 & -1 \\ 1 & 0 \end{bmatrix}$ is the matrix representing a 90° counterclockwise rotation with center at the origin.

c. Sketch the figure and its image in a coordinate plane.

d. Create an algorithm for a size-changing animation of this figure to guide programming of your calculator.

MORE
Modeling • Organizing • Reflecting • Extending

Modeling

1. At places in the Flag Drill animation, the banner on the flag flips back and forth.

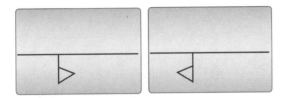

a. What kind of transformation can create this effect?

b. Consider a reflection across the y-axis. What is the image of (2, 3) under this reflection? The image of (3, −4)?

c. Write a coordinate rule for reflection across the y-axis.

d. Use the coordinate rule to find the matrix representation of this reflection.

e. Write a Reflection Algorithm that outlines a reflection animation according to the following specifications.

- Begin with a vertical flag that has its pole along the y-axis.
- Use matrix multiplication to flip the banner back and forth ten times.

2. In addition to reflection across the y-axis as investigated in Modeling task 1, two other important line reflections are reflection across the x-axis and reflection across the line $y = x$.

a. Find the matrix representation of a reflection across the x-axis.

b. Find the matrix representation of a reflection across the line $y = x$.

c. Investigate how you could use these two matrix representations to model composing the two line reflections, first reflecting over the x-axis. Write a matrix representation for the composite transformation.

d. What special transformation is represented by the matrix in part c? Explain your reasoning.

3. You previously saw that to translate a shape in the coordinate plane, you add the same horizontal component, h, and the same vertical component, k, to the coordinates of each point comprising the shape. This suggests how translations might be modeled with matrices.

a. In the figure below, what is the coordinate rule for the translation that transforms the triangle on the left into the triangle on the right?

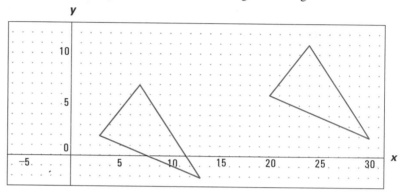

b. Consider this translation in terms of matrices.

■ Represent the translation using matrix addition by finding the missing entries of the second matrix below.

$$\begin{bmatrix} 3 & 7 & 13 \\ 2 & 7 & -2 \end{bmatrix} + \begin{bmatrix} \text{—} & \text{—} & \text{—} \\ \text{—} & \text{—} & \text{—} \end{bmatrix} = \begin{bmatrix} 20 & 24 & 30 \\ 6 & 11 & 2 \end{bmatrix}$$

■ What does the first matrix represent? The second matrix? The third matrix?

c. Use matrix addition to find the image of $\triangle ABC = \begin{bmatrix} 5 & -3 & 0 \\ 2 & 8 & 12 \end{bmatrix}$ under this translation. Sketch the triangle and its image.

d. Describe an algorithm that would outline an animation of a flag moving horizontally to the right. Begin with a vertical flag that has its pole along the y-axis.

4. The matrix $T = \begin{bmatrix} 3 & 0 \\ 0 & 1 \end{bmatrix}$ is an example of another basic type of transformation of the plane. Investigate this transformation by completing the following tasks.

a. Write a 2×4 matrix R that represents the rectangle shown on the right.

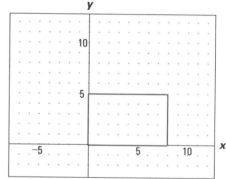

3. **a.** $(x, y) \rightarrow (x + 17, y + 4)$

   b. ■ $\begin{bmatrix} 17 & 17 & 17 \\ 4 & 4 & 4 \end{bmatrix}$

   ■ The first matrix represents the original coordinates of the triangle. The second matrix represents the translation. The third matrix represents the coordinates of the image triangle.

   c. $\begin{bmatrix} 22 & 14 & 17 \\ 6 & 12 & 16 \end{bmatrix}$

   Students should sketch the triangles so that they can see the translation.

   d. **Translation Algorithm**
   Step 1: Define the matrix representing the translation.
   Step 2: Define the matrix representing the flag.
   Step 3: Draw the flag.
   Step 4: Erase the flag.
   Step 5: Add the matrices to compute the coordinates of the translated flag.
   Step 6: Store the coordinates in the flag matrix.
   Step 7: Repeat steps 3–6.

4. **a.** $R = \begin{bmatrix} 0 & 0 & 8 & 8 \\ 0 & 5 & 5 & 0 \end{bmatrix}$

Unit 2

4. **b.** $\begin{bmatrix} 3 & 0 \\ 0 & 1 \end{bmatrix} \begin{bmatrix} 0 & 0 & 8 & 8 \\ 0 & 5 & 5 & 0 \end{bmatrix} = \begin{bmatrix} 0 & 0 & 24 & 24 \\ 0 & 5 & 5 & 0 \end{bmatrix}$

c.

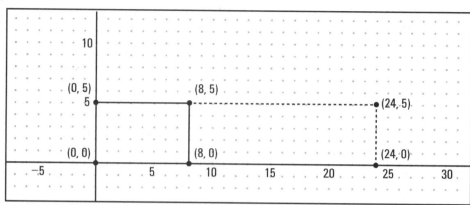

d. Descriptions will vary. One possible description is that the new figure is three times as long as the original, but the same height.

e. $(x, y) \rightarrow (3x, y)$

5. **a.** $\begin{bmatrix} 0 & 0 & 8 & 8 \\ 0 & 5 & 5 & 0 \end{bmatrix} \rightarrow \begin{bmatrix} 1 & 1 \\ 0 & 1 \end{bmatrix} \begin{bmatrix} 0 & 0 & 8 & 8 \\ 0 & 5 & 5 & 0 \end{bmatrix} = \begin{bmatrix} 0 & 5 & 13 & 8 \\ 0 & 5 & 5 & 0 \end{bmatrix}$

b.

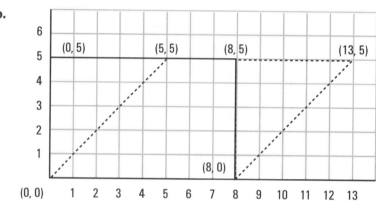

c. Descriptions will vary. The points on the *x*-axis remain the same while all other points shift *y* units to the right, where *y* is the *y*-coordinate of the pre-image point.

d. $(x, y) \rightarrow (x + y, y)$

This may not be easy for students to identify since it is a variable pattern based on *y*. It may be easier to identify from the matrix than the graph. To find the coordinate rule from the matrix, multiply the transformation matrix by the matrix for the point (x, y).

$$\begin{bmatrix} 1 & 1 \\ 0 & 1 \end{bmatrix} \begin{bmatrix} x \\ y \end{bmatrix} = \begin{bmatrix} x + y \\ y \end{bmatrix}$$

So the transformation sends the point (x, y) to the point $(x + y, y)$.

See additional Teaching Notes on page T168N.

b. Use matrix multiplication to find the image of the rectangle under the transformation.

c. Sketch the rectangle and its image on a coordinate plane.

d. Describe the transformation that T represents as completely as you can.

e. Write the coordinate rule for the transformation.

5. Consider the transformation of the plane represented by this matrix:

$$S = \begin{bmatrix} 1 & 1 \\ 0 & 1 \end{bmatrix}$$

a. Find the image of the rectangle in Modeling task 4 under the transformation represented by S.

b. Sketch the rectangle and its image in a coordinate plane.

c. Describe the transformation that S represents as completely as you can. This transformation is called a **shear**.

d. Find the coordinate rule for the transformation.

Organizing

1. Using the Flag Turn Algorithm, you outlined other animations that worked by successively computing the images of a flag figure. In each case, if matrix *NOW* represents the current image and matrix *NEXT* represents the next image in the animation sequence, write an equation showing how *NOW* and *NEXT* are related.

2. In Unit 1, "Matrix Models", you found many useful interpretations of powers of matrices. When matrices are used to represent transformations, their powers have a special interpretation. The matrix

$$R = \begin{bmatrix} 0.707 & -0.707 \\ 0.707 & 0.707 \end{bmatrix}$$

is the matrix approximation for a 45° counterclockwise rotation about the origin.

a. Compute R^2 and R^4, and compare your results to the other matrices you constructed in Investigation 1.

b. What rotation do you think R^6 represents? R^3? Explain your reasoning.

c. Represent a 270° counterclockwise rotation about the origin as a power of the matrix for a 90° counterclockwise rotation.

3. All the transformations you have seen in this lesson, except translations, can be represented by a 2×2 matrix. You typically found the matrix representation by finding the coordinate representation of the transformation first. Another way of finding the matrix representation for a transformation is to

look at the connection between two fundamental points, (1, 0) and (0, 1), and their images. For example, under a 90° clockwise rotation about the origin, the image of (1, 0) is (0, –1) and the image of (0, 1) is (1, 0). You can write the equations:

$$\begin{bmatrix} a & b \\ c & d \end{bmatrix} \begin{bmatrix} 1 \\ 0 \end{bmatrix} = \begin{bmatrix} 0 \\ -1 \end{bmatrix} \text{ and } \begin{bmatrix} a & b \\ c & d \end{bmatrix} \begin{bmatrix} 0 \\ 1 \end{bmatrix} = \begin{bmatrix} 1 \\ 0 \end{bmatrix}$$

where $\begin{bmatrix} a & b \\ c & d \end{bmatrix}$ is the transformation matrix.

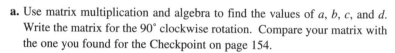

a. Use matrix multiplication and algebra to find the values of a, b, c, and d. Write the matrix for the 90° clockwise rotation. Compare your matrix with the one you found for the Checkpoint on page 154.

b. Using the method in part a, find the matrix representation for a 270° clockwise rotation about the origin.

c. Using the method in part a, find the matrix representation for a size transformation of magnitude 10 centered at the origin.

d. In parts a–c, compare the columns of the matrix representation of the transformation to the images of (1, 0) and (0, 1). Describe how to find the matrix representation of a transformation quickly, once you know the images of (1, 0) and (0, 1).

e. Check if your discovery in part d also applies to the matrix representation for a line reflection.

4. In Investigation 2 you found that a size transformation of magnitude k can be modeled using the matrix $\begin{bmatrix} k & 0 \\ 0 & k \end{bmatrix}$. To find an alternative way to model a size transformation, consider the size transformation of magnitude 3 and its effect on rectangle $PQRS = \begin{bmatrix} 1 & 1 & 6 & 6 \\ 2 & 5 & 2 & 5 \end{bmatrix}$.

a. Sketch the rectangle and its image on a coordinate plane.

b. Multiply these two matrices: $\begin{bmatrix} 3 & 0 \\ 0 & 3 \end{bmatrix} \begin{bmatrix} 1 & 1 & 6 & 6 \\ 2 & 5 & 2 & 5 \end{bmatrix}$.

c. What other matrix operations could be used to find the image of rectangle $PQRS$ under this size transformation?

d. Describe two ways of using matrices to find the image of the rectangle under a size transformation of magnitude 7.

e. Find a single matrix that will represent the composite of a 180° rotation with center at the origin, followed by a size transformation of magnitude 2 with center at the origin.

3. a.

$$\begin{bmatrix} a & b \\ c & d \end{bmatrix}\begin{bmatrix} 1 \\ 0 \end{bmatrix}=\begin{bmatrix} 0 \\ -1 \end{bmatrix}$$

$1a + 0b = 0$, so $a = 0$.
$1c + 0d = -1$, so $c = -1$.

$$\begin{bmatrix} a & b \\ c & d \end{bmatrix}\begin{bmatrix} 0 \\ 1 \end{bmatrix}=\begin{bmatrix} 1 \\ 0 \end{bmatrix}$$

$0a + 1b = 1$, so $b = 1$.
$0c + 1d = 0$, so $d = 0$.

Therefore, the matrix is $\begin{bmatrix} 0 & 1 \\ -1 & 0 \end{bmatrix}$.

b. The matrix is $\begin{bmatrix} 0 & -1 \\ 1 & 0 \end{bmatrix}$.

c. The matrix is $\begin{bmatrix} 10 & 0 \\ 0 & 10 \end{bmatrix}$.

d. The image of (1, 0) becomes the first column of the transformation matrix and the image of (0, 1) is the second column of the transformation matrix.

e. The same method will work.

4. a.

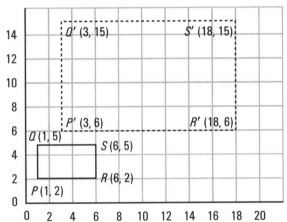

b. $\begin{bmatrix} 3 & 3 & 18 & 18 \\ 6 & 15 & 6 & 15 \end{bmatrix}$

c. Multiplying each entry by 3 (*i.e.*, scalar multiplication) also could be used to find the matrix representing the image rectangle.

d. ■ Use matrix multiplication and the transformation matrix $\begin{bmatrix} 7 & 0 \\ 0 & 7 \end{bmatrix}$.

■ Multiply each entry in the matrix representing the rectangle by 7.

e. $2\begin{bmatrix} -1 & 0 \\ 0 & -1 \end{bmatrix}=\begin{bmatrix} -2 & 0 \\ 0 & -2 \end{bmatrix}$

Unit 2

Reflecting

1. **a.** Responses will vary. The columns of the matrix are the coordinates of the images of (1, 0) and (0, 1) respectively.

   b. Responses will vary. The use of matrices to represent transformations allows a quick way for using technology to help with calculations and graphic manipulations. However, the matrix representation may be harder to understand than the coordinate representation.

   c. Opinions will vary. Be sure students explain why they prefer one representation over the others.

2. **a.** By using matrices, a verbal description of a transformation can be replaced with an algebraic representation. This representation allows the transformations to be performed mechanically.

   b. Examples will vary. Students have seen matrices that model rotations with center at the origin, translations, reflections, and size changes.

   c. Responses will vary. Matrices are multiplied to get a composite transformation. The transformation being applied first will be the factor on the right:

   [Composite] = [Second Transformation] [First Transformation].

   d. Composition of transformations is not commutative, in general, although many compositions are unaffected by order. If a reflection is involved, order often makes a difference.

3. **a.** ■ $(x, y) \rightarrow (-y, x)$ is a 90° counterclockwise rotation with center at the origin. $(x, y) \rightarrow (y, -x)$ is a 90° clockwise (or 270° counterclockwise) rotation with center at the origin.

   ■ $(x, y) \rightarrow (x, y)$

   b. $\begin{bmatrix} 0 & -1 \\ 1 & 0 \end{bmatrix}$ and $\begin{bmatrix} 0 & 1 \\ -1 & 0 \end{bmatrix}$ are the matrix representations for these transformations. The composite of the two transformations is found by multiplying these matrices. The product is $\begin{bmatrix} 1 & 0 \\ 0 & 1 \end{bmatrix}$. This is the identity matrix.

   c. ■ $(x, y) \rightarrow (4x, 4y)$ is a size change with a magnitude of 4.

   $(x, y) \rightarrow (\frac{1}{4}x, \frac{1}{4}y)$ is a size change with a magnitude of $\frac{1}{4}$.

   ■ $(x, y) \rightarrow (x, y)$

   d. $\begin{bmatrix} 4 & 0 \\ 0 & 4 \end{bmatrix}$ and $\begin{bmatrix} \frac{1}{4} & 0 \\ 0 & \frac{1}{4} \end{bmatrix}$

   Multiplying these two matrices produces the matrix $\begin{bmatrix} 1 & 0 \\ 0 & 1 \end{bmatrix}$ which is the matrix representing the composite transformation. This is the identity matrix.

   e. The matrices are inverses of each other. When multiplied together they produce the identity matrix. The transformations are also inverses of each other. One transformation undoes what the other does. The composite is called the identity transformation.

4. Examples and descriptions will vary.

Reflecting

1. You now know how to represent transformations using coordinates, using matrices, and using geometric descriptions with no reference to coordinates.

   a. How are these three representations connected?

   b. What are some advantages and disadvantages of each representation?

   c. Which representation do you prefer? Why?

2. The title of this lesson is "Transformations, Matrices, and Animation".

   a. What does it mean to say that a matrix is a mathematical model of a transformation?

   b. Give three examples from this lesson of matrices that model transformations.

   c. Using two of your examples from part b, show how to form the composite of the two transformations.

   d. Recall that multiplication of matrices is not commutative. Is composition of transformations commutative? Explain.

3. Think about how composition of transformations is similar to multiplication of real numbers.

   a. Find the composite of the transformation $(x, y) \rightarrow (-y, x)$ followed by the transformation $(x, y) \rightarrow (y, -x)$.

   ■ Identify each transformation as completely as you can.

   ■ Write a rule for the composite transformation: $(x, y) \rightarrow (\_\_ , \_\_)$.

   b. Find the matrix representation of each transformation in part a. Use a matrix operation to find the composite of the two transformations. What do you notice?

   c. Find the composite of the transformation $(x, y) \rightarrow (4x, 4y)$ followed by the transformation $(x, y) \rightarrow (\frac{1}{4}x, \frac{1}{4}y)$.

   ■ Identify each transformation as completely as you can.

   ■ Write a rule for the composite transformation: $(x, y) \rightarrow (\_\_, \_\_)$.

   d. Find the matrix representation of each transformation in part c. Use a matrix operation to find the composite of the two transformations. What do you notice?

   e. How are the pairs of matrices in parts b and d related? How are the pairs of transformations in parts a and c related? What name would you give to the composite transformations in parts a and c?

4. In this lesson you learned some of the mathematics behind computer animation, and you applied that knowledge to create several simple animations of your own. One common use of computer animation today is for logos and advertisements on TV. Of course, these are much more complex animations

than those you studied in this lesson, but they use the same basic ideas. The next time you are watching TV, look for examples of computer animations, particularly in network logos and commercials. Find and briefly describe (in writing) two examples of computer animations on TV that involve rotations or size transformations.

Extending

1. In addition to rigid transformations and size transformations, there are many other transformations of the plane. Consider the transformation that has this coordinate rule:

$$(x, y) \rightarrow (2x + y, x + 2y)$$

   a. Find the matrix representation of this transformation.

   b. Use matrix multiplication to find the image under this transformation of the rectangle in Modeling task 4.

   c. Sketch the rectangle and its image in a coordinate plane.

   d. Which of the following statements are true about the transformation of the rectangle into its image?

   - Lengths do not change.

   - Angle sizes do not change.

   - Pairs of parallel sides are transformed into pairs of parallel sides.

   - Area does not change.

Extending

1. a. $\begin{bmatrix} 2 & 1 \\ 1 & 2 \end{bmatrix}$

b. $\begin{bmatrix} 2 & 1 \\ 1 & 2 \end{bmatrix}\begin{bmatrix} 0 & 0 & 8 & 8 \\ 0 & 5 & 5 & 0 \end{bmatrix} = \begin{bmatrix} 0 & 5 & 21 & 16 \\ 0 & 10 & 18 & 8 \end{bmatrix}$

c.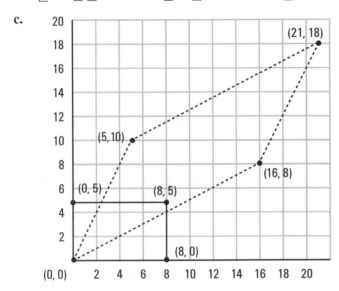

d. ■ False; length does change, but if two sides are equal in length in the pre-image, they will be equal in length in the image.

■ False; angle sizes change.

■ True; pairs of parallel sides are transformed into pairs of parallel sides.

■ False; area of the image is not necessarily the same as the area of the pre-image.

2. **a.** The image of (1, 0) is ($\sqrt{0.5}$, $\sqrt{0.5}$) or approximately (0.707, 0.707). Students may see this by recognizing that the 90-45-45 triangle is isosceles, then applying the Pythagorean Theorem to find the length of the legs.

   b. The image of (0, 1) is ($-\sqrt{0.5}$, $\sqrt{0.5}$) or approximately (−0.707, 0.707).

   c. $$\begin{bmatrix} \sqrt{0.5} & -\sqrt{0.5} \\ \sqrt{0.5} & \sqrt{0.5} \end{bmatrix} \approx \begin{bmatrix} 0.707 & -0.707 \\ 0.707 & 0.707 \end{bmatrix}$$

3. All of these programs are obtained by making small changes to the FLAGTURN program provided in the text. Many of them only require that matrices A and B be changed.

   a. The program is given in the text.

   b. The FLAGTURN program can be used if the matrices A and B are changed as follows:

   $$A = \begin{bmatrix} 1.1 & 0 \\ 0 & 1.1 \end{bmatrix} \qquad B = \begin{bmatrix} 5 & 5 & 3 & 5 \\ 0 & 4 & 3 & 2 \end{bmatrix}$$

   Matrix B can be different than the one above, but the points must be entered in an order that allows the flag to be drawn properly. Since the program replaces matrix B, students cannot run it more than once without re-entering matrix B into the calculator. Also, the window may need to be adjusted. Some students may want to incorporate matrix and window setups into their programs. They also may wish to change the number of times the loop repeats.

   c. Students will need to alter matrices A and B and the window setting, and then run FLAGTURN. You might want to have students share their animations with others in their group or with the class by using the overhead calculator.

   d. The program FLAGTURN itself does not require modifying. Simply change the matrices A and B. Students may modify the number of flips by changing the 8 in the "For (N, 1, 8, 1)" command. Students enter the coordinates of their flag into matrix B. Matrix A should be

   $$\begin{bmatrix} -1 & 0 \\ 0 & 1 \end{bmatrix}$$

   e. Students need to enter the coordinates of their flag into matrix B and the coordinates of their translation into matrix A. Additionally, the third line of FLAGTURN should be changed from multiplication to addition. You may want to have students demonstrate their animations.

2. Recall that a 45° counterclockwise rotation about the origin can be approximated by the matrix

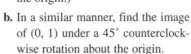

$$\begin{bmatrix} 0.707 & -0.707 \\ 0.707 & 0.707 \end{bmatrix}$$

Where do the 0.707s come from? Using the images of (1, 0) and (0, 1) and the method outlined in Organizing task 3, you can construct the matrix for the 45° rotation.

a. Find the image of (1, 0) under a 45° counterclockwise rotation about the origin. (**Hint:** Study the diagram at the right. The right triangle inside the circle has a 45° angle at the origin.)

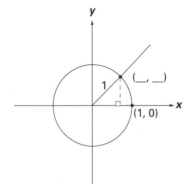

b. In a similar manner, find the image of (0, 1) under a 45° counterclockwise rotation about the origin.

c. Use your answers from parts a and b to build the matrix for this 45° rotation. Compare the matrix you built to the one given above.

3. You have written several algorithms that set up the framework for programming a calculator or computer to do various animations. In this task you are given the opportunity to translate those algorithms into calculator programs for your graphics calculator.

a. Write and run a calculator program based on the Flag Turn Algorithm from activity 6, Investigation 1 (page 152).

b. Write and run a calculator program based on the planning algorithm from activity 5, Investigation 2 (page 156).

c. Write and run a calculator program performing the animation suggested in "On Your Own", Investigation 2 (page 156).

d. Write and run a calculator program based on the Reflection Algorithm written for Modeling Task 1 part e (page 157).

e. Write and run a calculator program based on the planning algorithm written in Modeling Task 3 part d (page 158).

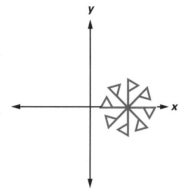

4. All the rotations and size transformations that you have worked with in this lesson have been centered at the origin. To spin a flag around a point other than the origin as in the Flag Drill animation, you can translate the point to the origin, do the rotation at the origin, and then translate back out to the original center point. Use this method to write a program, using matrices, that will rotate a flag figure around the point (5, 0). Follow these guidelines:

- Translate the flag and its images to the origin, rotate in steps of 45°, and then translate back out. Use matrix addition for the translation as in Modeling task 3.

- Base your program on the FLAGTURN program (page 153).

5. a. Describe the type of motion that you think successive application of a size transformation followed by a rotation will produce.

b. The Spiral animation in GEOXPLOR is done using this combined transformation. Run GEOXPLOR and choose ANIMATION. Select the "SPIRAL" animation. Did you predict this type of motion in part a?

c. Write your own calculator program that produces a spiral-type animation, according to these specifications:

- Start with the triangle $\begin{bmatrix} 0 & 2 & 2 \\ 0 & 0.5 & -0.5 \end{bmatrix}$.

- Successively transform the triangle using the composite of a size transformation of magnitude 1.1, followed by a 45° counterclockwise rotation. Both transformations should be centered at the origin.

- Set up the viewing window so that you can see at least 30 steps.

6. Homogeneous coordinates of a point (x, y) are $(x, y, 1)$. When plotting the point $(x, y, 1)$, the "1" is ignored. But writing a point in homogeneous coordinates allows matrix multiplication to be used to translate points.

a. $A = \begin{bmatrix} 1 & 0 & h \\ 0 & 1 & k \\ 0 & 0 & 1 \end{bmatrix}$. What is the effect of multiplying $\begin{bmatrix} x \\ y \\ 1 \end{bmatrix}$ on the left by A?

b. Construct a matrix that will translate a point 2 units to the right and 3 units down.

c. Use homogeneous coordinates to construct an animation showing a flag moving across the calculator screen from left to right.

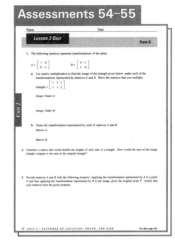

4. Before running the program define matrices A and C as follows:

$$A = \begin{bmatrix} 0.707 & -0.707 \\ 0.707 & 0.707 \end{bmatrix} \qquad C = \begin{bmatrix} 5 & 5 & 5 & 5 \\ 0 & 0 & 0 & 0 \end{bmatrix}$$

Matrix B should be a matrix representing a flag. One possible matrix follows:

$$\begin{bmatrix} 5 & 13 & 11 & 10 \\ 0 & 0 & 3 & 0 \end{bmatrix}$$

To help students to see that the flag is rotating about (5, 0), they could make the end of the flagpole be at the point (5, 0).

Using the flag given by the matrix above, a reasonable viewing window is shown below.

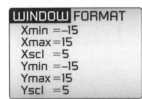

The following program will run on a TI-82 or TI-83 graphics calculator. Slight modifications may be necessary if students are using other technology.

```
PROGRAM: FLAGSPIN
For (N,1,8)
[B] – [C] → [B]
[A] * [B] → [B]
[B] + [C] → [B]
Line ([B](1,1),[B](2,1),[B](1,2), [B](2,2))
Line ([B](1,2),[B](2,2),[B](1,3), [B](2,3))
Line ([B](1,3),[B](2,3),[B](1,4), [B](2,4))
For (K,1,50)
End
ClrDraw
End
Stop
```

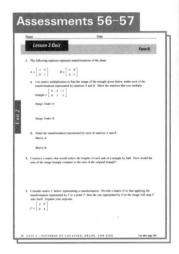

See additional Teaching Notes on page T1680.

SYNTHESIZE UNIT IDEAS small-group activity

1. a.

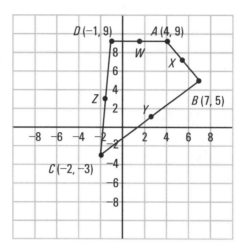

b. $AB = 5$ $BC \approx 12.04$ $CD \approx 12.04$ $AD = 5$
The quadrilateral is a kite because it has two pairs of adjacent equal sides.

c. The diagonals are perpendicular because the slopes of those segments are negative reciprocals of each other. The slope of line segment AC is 2, and the slope of line segment BD is -0.5. The diagonal AC bisects the diagonal BD. The measure of BD is 8.94.

d. The coordinates of the midpoints (as labeled in the diagram in part a) are $X(5.5, 7)$, $Y(2.5, 1)$, $Z(-1.5, 3)$, and $W(1.5, 9)$. The slopes of the sides are -0.5 and 2; therefore the sides are perpendicular and the polygon is a rectangle. Some students may justify their conjecture that the figure is a rectangle because the opposite sides are parallel and it contains one right angle.

Looking Back

The three-dimensional computer graphics display, below, shows the amount of carbon dioxide in the atmosphere over time. Note the patterns of linear change across the years and the periodic change with the seasons of each year. Also notice the exponential change in the highest levels (the "hills") with the change in latitude (90°S to 90°N of the equator).

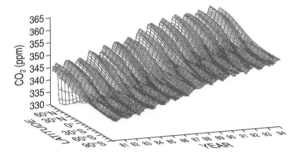

Climate Monitoring and Diagnostics Laboratory, National Oceanic and Atmospheric Administration

   Even though software such as the one used to produce this display is complex, many of the algorithm planning ideas you used in this chapter also are used in planning such software.

   The activities in this final lesson give you the opportunity to pull together ideas you have developed. Review the different ways coordinates are used to model geometric ideas as you work.

1. A quadrilateral *ABCD* has the following coordinates: *A*(4, 9), *B*(7, 5), *C*(−2, −3), and *D*(−1, 9).

   a. Sketch this quadrilateral on a coordinate plane or display it on your calculator.

   b. Determine the lengths of the sides of quadrilateral *ABCD*. Does this quadrilateral have a more specific name? If so, what is the name?

   c. How are the diagonals related?

   d. Find the midpoints of each side and connect them in order. What kind of polygon is formed? (Be as specific as possible.) Justify your answer.

2. Computer graphics often use transformations to move shapes on the computer screen. In this unit you found ways to do rigid transformations and size transformations using your graphics calculator. Reproduced below is the calculator graphics display from the "Think About This Situation" on page 80.

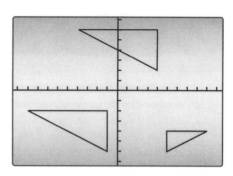

a. Describe a transformation or sequence of transformations that maps the lower left triangle onto the upper triangle. Write a rule $(x, y) \rightarrow (\_, \_)$ that relates pre-image and image.

b. Describe a transformation or sequence of transformations that maps the lower left triangle onto the lower right triangle. Write a rule $(x, y) \rightarrow (\_, \_)$ that relates pre-image and image.

c. Describe a sequence of transformations to transform the lower left triangle according to the following specifications:

■ The image is a right triangle of the same size.

■ The longest leg of the image lies along the positive y-axis.

3. Use graph paper or your graphics calculator to display $\triangle ABC$, where

$$\triangle ABC = \begin{bmatrix} 1 & 9 & 1 \\ 7 & 2 & 2 \end{bmatrix}.$$

a. Find the image of $\triangle ABC$ under each transformation below. Draw the image and write its matrix representation.

■ 90° counterclockwise rotation about the origin

■ Reflection across the x-axis

■ Translation with components –2 and 3

■ Size transformation with center at the origin and magnitude 3

b. Which of the images of $\triangle ABC$ in part a are congruent to (have the same size and shape as) $\triangle ABC$? Which are similar (same shape)? Which are neither?

c. What is the area of $\triangle ABC$? What is the area of each image of $\triangle ABC$ in part a? How did you determine the area of each image?

2. The solutions provided here assume that the scales on both axes are 1.

   a. A translation with horizontal component 5 and vertical component 8 will map the lower left triangle to the upper right triangle. $(x, y) \rightarrow (x + 5, y + 8)$

   You might suggest to students that they choose points on the lower left triangle and see if their transformation rule does produce the correct image point.

   b. Responses may vary. A sequence of transformations is (1) a reflection over the y-axis, (2) a size transformation of magnitude 0.5, and (3) a translation with components 4.5 and -3.

   Rule: $(x, y) \rightarrow (-x, y) \rightarrow (-0.5x, 0.5y) \rightarrow (-0.5x + 4.5, 0.5y - 3)$

   Interchanging steps 1 and 2 provides an alternative sequence, that is, do a size transformation of magnitude 0.5 followed by a reflection over the y-axis before translating with components 4.5 and -3. Again, you might suggest that students test their rules by trying points.

   NOTE: Expect errors to be made. These errors can be used by the students to deepen their understanding.

   ---

   c. Responses may vary. One sequence of transformations is a 90° clockwise rotation centered at the origin followed by a translation 2 units to the right.

   Rule: $(x, y) \rightarrow (y, -x) \rightarrow (y + 2, -x)$

3.

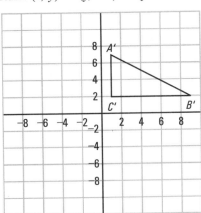

   a. ■ 90° counterclockwise about the origin:

   $$\begin{bmatrix} -7 & -2 & -2 \\ 1 & 9 & 1 \end{bmatrix}$$

   ■ Reflection across the x-axis:

   $$\begin{bmatrix} 1 & 9 & 1 \\ -7 & -2 & -2 \end{bmatrix}$$

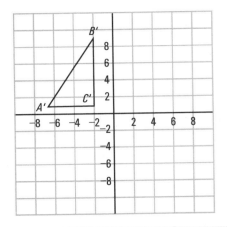

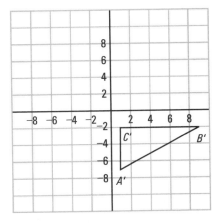

   See additional Teaching Notes on page T168P.

Unit 2

4. **a.** A composition of a reflection across the *y*-axis and a translation with components 0 and −5 maps rectangle *PQRS* onto rectangle *P′Q′R′S′*.
       Rule: $(x, y) \rightarrow (-x, y - 5)$

    b. A composition of a 90° counterclockwise rotation with center at the origin and a size transformation of magnitude 3 maps rectangle *PQRS* onto rectangle *P′Q′R′S′*.
       Rule: $(x, y) \rightarrow (-3y, 3x)$

5. Note the sequence of this task and how it illustrates the process of mathematical modeling: Given a situation, get some additional information if needed, represent the situation with a matrix model, and operate on the matrix to analyze the situation.

    a. ■ Stretch the rectangle vertically by a factor of three to get the image rectangle.

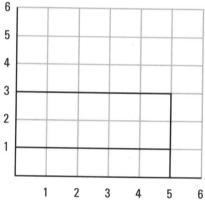

    ■ The original rectangle can be represented by the matrix $\begin{bmatrix} 0 & 0 & 5 & 5 \\ 0 & 1 & 1 & 0 \end{bmatrix}$.

    The image rectangle then would be represented by this matrix: $\begin{bmatrix} 0 & 0 & 5 & 5 \\ 0 & 3 & 3 & 0 \end{bmatrix}$.

■ Original Point	Image Point
(8, 4)	(8, 12)
(0, 2)	(0, 6)
(−3, 7)	(−3, 21)
(−5, −6)	(−5, −18)

    b. $(x, y) \rightarrow (x, 3y)$

    c. $T = \begin{bmatrix} 1 & 0 \\ 0 & 3 \end{bmatrix}$

    d. The transformation matrix should be on the left. The multiplication should produce the same points as in part a.

4. Give a sequence of transformations that will transform the rectangle with vertices $P(1, 1)$, $Q(2, 1)$, $R(2, 3)$, and $S(1, 3)$ into

   a. the rectangle with vertices $P'(-1, -4)$, $Q'(-2, -4)$, $R'(-2, -2)$, $S'(-1, -2)$.

   b. the rectangle with vertices $P'(-3, 3)$, $Q'(-3, 6)$, $R'(-9, 6)$, $S'(-9, 3)$.

5. Consider the transformation that stretches figures vertically by a factor of 3 but does not change them in any other way.

   a. Gather some data about how this transformation affects shapes, as follows.

     ■ Sketch the rectangle below and its image under the transformation.

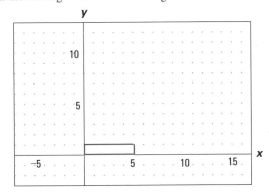

     ■ Write 2×4 matrices that represent the rectangle and its image.

     ■ Complete a table like the one below, showing the images of the given points under the transformation.

Original Point	Image Point
(8, 4)	
(0, 2)	
(–3, 7)	
(–5, –6)	

   b. Construct a coordinate model for this transformation. That is, write a symbolic rule that relates the coordinates of any point (x, y) and its image.

   c. Construct a matrix model for the transformation. Call the matrix T.

   d. When you multiply a matrix of points and a transformation matrix, on which side should the transformation matrix appear? Why?

     ■ Multiply T by the matrix for the rectangle in part a.

     ■ Multiply T by the matrix of the original points from the table in part a.

     ■ Compare these images to those you found in part a.

e. Now consider powers of the matrix T.

- Using matrix multiplication, find the image of the rectangle in part a under the transformation represented by T^2. Sketch the rectangle and its image under this composite transformation.
- Describe the transformation represented by T^2.
- Without computing, describe the transformation represented by T^3.

f. Consider the matrix $S = \begin{bmatrix} 2 & 0 \\ 0 & 1 \end{bmatrix}$.

- Make a conjecture about the effect on shapes of the transformation represented by S. Defend your conjecture.
- Make a conjecture about the effect of the transformation represented by $T \times S$. Defend your conjecture.

Checkpoint

a Describe several different ways that coordinates are used to model geometric ideas. Illustrate with examples.

b Describe how to solve a system of two linear equations using a linear combination method. How can this method be interpreted geometrically? Illustrate with an example.

c Describe several different ways that matrices are used to model geometric ideas. Illustrate with examples.

d How do rigid transformations affect distance? Angle measure? Parallelism of lines? Areas of plane shapes?

e How do size transformations affect distance? Angle measure? Parallelism of lines? Areas of plane shapes? Distances of a point and its image from the center of the transformation?

f Describe how animation effects can be produced by a graphing calculator.

Be prepared to share your descriptions, illustrations, and summaries with the class.

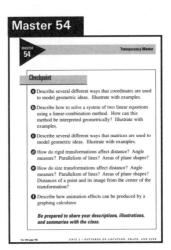

5. e. Students should see that powers of the matrix represent repeating the transformation.

- $T^2 = \begin{bmatrix} 1 & 0 \\ 0 & 9 \end{bmatrix}$

$$\begin{bmatrix} 1 & 0 \\ 0 & 9 \end{bmatrix} \begin{bmatrix} 0 & 0 & 5 & 5 \\ 0 & 1 & 1 & 0 \end{bmatrix} = \begin{bmatrix} 0 & 0 & 5 & 5 \\ 0 & 9 & 9 & 0 \end{bmatrix}$$

- T^2 stretches the figure vertically by a factor of 3^2 or 9.
- T^3 stretches the figure vertically by a factor of 3^3 or 27.

f. ■ S stretches figures horizontally by a factor of 2. Students should defend their conjectures. They might do this by relating it to previous situations or by showing examples.

- $T \times S = \begin{bmatrix} 2 & 0 \\ 0 & 3 \end{bmatrix}$

TS stretches figures both vertically and horizontally—vertically by a factor of 3 and horizontally by a factor of 2. Again, students should defend their conjectures.

SHARE AND SUMMARIZE   full-class discussion

Checkpoint

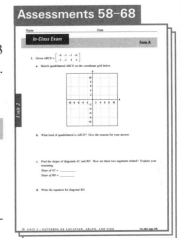

See Teaching Master 54.

ⓐ Coordinates can be used to model points, lines, shapes, distance, slope, and transformations. Examples will vary.

ⓑ To solve a system of equations, multiply each equation in such a way that either the x terms or the y terms add to 0. Add the equations, and the resulting equation will be easy to solve for the remaining variable. Use the value for that variable (assuming there was one) and one of the original equations to solve for the other variable.

Geometrically, such a linear combination gives a horizontal or vertical line (or a statement that is always true if the original equations give the same line, or always false if the original equations give parallel lines). That line intersects the original lines in the same place those lines intersect each other.

Students should include an example.

ⓒ Matrices may represent the coordinates of vertices of a polygon, a transformation, or a linear system of equations. Examples will vary.

ⓓ The rigid transformations are: rotation, reflection, and translation. They preserve distance, angle measure, parallelism of lines, and area of plane shapes.

See additional Teaching Notes on page T168Q.

Looking Back, Looking Ahead

▶Reflecting on Mathematical Content

The geometry strand began in Course 1, when students observed, built, and drew objects seen in the world. Those shapes were examined for patterns that were characteristic of a single class of shapes (*e.g.,* parallelograms) or other patterns that were characteristic of two shapes in the class (*e.g.,* congruent shapes). Symmetry was extended to infinite patterns of shapes (strip patterns). Methods of describing the size of shapes—using length, area, volume—were developed and applied in realistic contexts.

In this unit, coordinates for points were introduced and shapes were modeled using a coordinate plane. The Pythagorean Theorem was used to develop a way of computing the distance between two points using their coordinates. A formula for computing midpoints of segments also was developed. Coordinate models for lines and relationships between lines (such as parallelism and perpendicularity) were developed. When combined, these ideas provided a useful way for analyzing and characterizing polygons, quadrilaterals in particular.

Algorithmic thinking was extended in this unit to include the development of algorithms (and calculator-based programs) for computing measures in a coordinate plane and for simulating motions in a plane. Systems of linear equations were examined from a geometric perspective, and the method of finding solutions using linear combinations was developed. Upon completion of this unit, students have at least five different ways to solve systems of two linear equations.

Coordinates were also used for a new look at rigid transformations, which led eventually to matrix representations of selected transformations. Similar figures were introduced by examining the results of applying a certain transformation rule, such as $(x, y) \rightarrow (2x, 2y)$, to a shape and comparing the image shape and its preimage. Matrix representations for selected transformations were used to understand computer graphics better. Combining transformations represented by coordinate rules and by matrices foreshadows the idea of function composition, which is developed more fully in Course 4.

The use of coordinates to represent points, and the rules relating certain sets of points, will be important in all the work that follows in this course, both algebraic and geometric. Geometric ideas also will continue to be examined from a coordinate synthetic (coordinate) perspective.

In Unit 6, "Geometric Form and Its Function", the emphasis returns to geometric settings without coordinates. Students will examine these settings to understand more fully how shape and shape properties allow or disallow motion to occur. The concept of similarity is used to introduce trigonometric ratios. Many of the intuitively accepted properties of shapes that are used in this unit are developed within a deductive system in Course 3.

Unit 2 Assessment

Teaching Notes continued

Notes continued
from page T80

LAUNCH   full-class discussion

To launch this lesson in an interesting way, you might want to ask if any students play computer or video games. Of course, many of them do, and you can extend the conversation with questions such as the following:

Do any of the games involve guessing at the position of a hidden obstacle? Hitting a target? (Many involve avoiding pitfalls, or aiming at moving targets.) Are there animations to keep the visual display interesting? (Creative graphics are a major factor in keeping the player interested.) Do the obstacles or graphics stay in the same position for each game? (This depends somewhat on the game. Some follow patterns that will not change from game to game, but many will change.) How does the game know where "you" are on the screen and where the target is? How are the graphics created?

You will have many students who have played such games without ever thinking about the instructions that have to be in place to create graphics. You also may want to ask them how the instructions decide whether the point you aim at is close enough to the target to be considered a hit. The "Think About This Situation" will follow this discussion well, as it asks about placing and moving specific graphics.

Think About This Situation

See Teacher Master 26.

When facilitating the full-class discussion, you should have the opportunity to draw in a variety of student ideas, or at least to confirm that more than one idea is valid.

ⓐ Students who have explored graphics calculators such as the TI-82 or TI-83 may have found options such as Line and Point under the DRAW menu. Other students may speculate on the presence of these calculator functions. In either case, students may mention the need to supply the coordinates for the vertices of the triangles.

ⓑ One could describe the locations of the three triangles by listing coordinates for their three vertices. A more general way is to describe the location to the right or left, and above or below, the axes.

ⓒ Since the two triangles are already "facing" the same way and are the same size, all that is necessary is a shift to the right and up (or up and to the right). Since the scales for the axes are not provided we can not say how far up and to the right the triangle should be shifted.

ⓓ Responses may vary. One possible response is: first the triangle would be reflected vertically (or just flipped over), then "stretched" so each edge would be twice as long, and finally moved up and to the left.

Teaching Notes continued

Notes continued
from page T87

INVESTIGATION 2 Things Are Not Always What They Seem To Be

As an introduction to this investigation you may wish to review very briefly what students know about squares and rectangles. One suggestion is to draw a square, a nonsquare rectangle, and a nonsquare rhombus on the board and ask students to brainstorm about all the characteristics of each, noticing which they share and which are specific to each shape. This should bring out comments about parallel and perpendicular sides, equal and perpendicular diagonals, and so on. Students probably do not know the minimum conditions to make a square, for example, but this review may help to put everyone on a level field. During this investigation, students will review the slope of a line and discover the relationship between the slopes of perpendicular lines. GEOXPLOR permits easy graphing and exploration of the characteristics of various polygons. You will want to have grid paper available for activity 2.

1. At the end of this activity, you may wish to point out special zoom options on your calculator or computer software. For example, the Casio CFX-9850G has a "SQR" option that scales the axes to show true shape. On the TI-82 or -83, this is accomplished using either ZSquare, ZDecimal, or ZInteger.

    a. The first looks like a square; the second and third look like parallelograms or rhombi.

    b. The scales on the axes are different so the shapes do not clearly display all the characteristics of the quadrilateral.

    c. The shape is a square. The sides are equal in length ($\sqrt{13} \approx 3.6$) and they "look" perpendicular if the figure is drawn using the same scale on both axes.

    d. Since the shape is known to be a square, the first diagram best resembles the true nature of the shape.

Teaching Notes continued

Unit 2

Notes continued
from page T80

CONSTRUCTING A MATH
TOOLKIT: You may wish to
have students place this item
in their math toolkits for future
reference.

MORE independent assignment

Modeling

1. **See Teaching Master 31.**

Geometric Idea	Coordinate Model	Example
Point	Ordered pair (x, y) of real numbers	$(3, -2)$
Plane	All possible ordered pairs (x, y) of real numbers	(No example needed.)
Line	All ordered pairs (x, y) satisfying $y = a + bx$ or $x = c$	$y = -4 + 2x$
Parallel lines	Any two lines of the form $y = mx + b$ and $y = mx + c$, where m, b, and c are real numbers and $b \neq c$	$y = 3x + 1$ and $y = 3x - 5$
Perpendicular lines	Any two lines of the form $y = mx + b$ and $y = \frac{-1}{m} x + c$	$y = 2x - 7$ and $y = \frac{-1}{2} x + 2$
Distance	Given two points (a, b) and (c, d), the distance between them is the real number $D = \sqrt{(a - c)^2 + (b - d)^2}$.	Distance between $(3, 4)$ and $(6, 0)$ is $\sqrt{(3 - 6)^2 + (4 - 0)^2}$ $= \sqrt{9 + 16} = \sqrt{25} = 5$.
Midpoint	Given two points (a, b) and (c, d), the midpoint of the segment is the ordered pair $M = (\frac{a + c}{2}, \frac{b + d}{2})$	Midpoint of $(3, 4)$ and $(6, 0)$ is $(4.5, 2)$.

T168E   UNIT 2 • PATTERNS OF LOCATION, SHAPE, AND SIZE

Teaching Notes continued

Notes continued from page T94

5. **a.** Responses will vary. Since the orientation of rectangle *ABCD* is not specified, there are infinitely many possibilities for the coordinates of *B, C,* and *D*. A natural choice would be *B*(13, 0), *C*(13, 5), and *D*(0, 5). However, acceptable answers are any coordinates for *B, C,* and *D* which define a quadrilateral with opposite sides parallel, adjacent sides perpendicular, and of the specified dimensions.

b. Responses will vary. *B, C,* and *D* may have any coordinates which insure that a parallelogram of the required dimensions will be constructed, but the parallelogram is not a rectangle. One example is *B*(3, 4), *C*(16, 4), and *D*(13, 0).

c. Infinitely many parallelograms may be constructed. Some students may think of a parallelogram with sides 13 and 5 units and realize that it is not rigid. Others may think of rotating the parallelogram from part b and getting infinitely many different locations.

Reflecting

1. **a.** When the figure is displayed with sides parallel to the coordinate axes, it is clear that adjacent sides are perpendicular.

b. Since a horizontal line is modeled by the equation $y = c$, no matter how much x changes, y stays the same. Rate of change is calculated (change in y) divided by (change in x). Since y never changes, the rate of change will be 0.

c. Since a vertical line is modeled by the equation $x = c$, no matter how much y changes, x stays the same. Thus the rate of change will have a denominator of 0, and so it will be undefined.

2. Responses may vary. One advantage of using the subscript notation is that it is clear which variables refer to the x-coordinate and which refer to the y-coordinate. It is also clear to which point the coordinate refers. Until students get used to using the subscript notation they may find it cumbersome.

Teaching Notes continued

**Notes continued
from page T118** ▶

11. a. ■ Rotation of 180° counterclockwise about the origin:

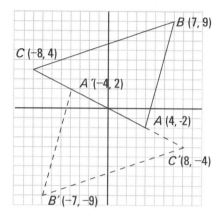

■ Rotation of 90° counterclockwise about the origin:

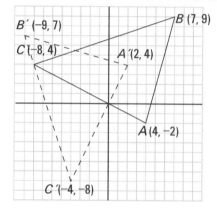

■ Rotation of 90° clockwise about the origin:

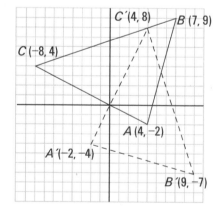

b. $AB = \sqrt{(4-7)^2 + (-2-9)^2} = \sqrt{9+121} = \sqrt{130}$

180° rotation: $A'B' = \sqrt{(-4+7)^2 + (2+9)^2} = \sqrt{9+121} = \sqrt{130}$

90° counterclockwise rotation: $A'B' = \sqrt{(2+9)^2 + (4-7)^2} = \sqrt{121+9} = \sqrt{130}$

90° clockwise rotation: $A'B' = \sqrt{(-2-9)^2 + (-4+7)^2} = \sqrt{121+9} = \sqrt{130}$

All lengths are identical.

Teaching Notes *continued*

Notes continued
from page T121

Organizing

1. **a.** Triangle *ABC* is an isosceles right triangle. The slope of the line *AB* is 0.5 and the slope of the line *BC* is −2. Since the slope of the line *BC* is the negative reciprocal of the slope of the line *AB*, the lines are perpendicular. Also, *AB* = *BC* since the length of both line segments is $\sqrt{20}$ or approximately 4.47 units.

    b. The area of $\triangle ABC$ is 10 square units: $\frac{\sqrt{20}\ \sqrt{20}}{2} = \frac{20}{2} = 10$.

    c. ■ Reflection across the *y*-axis ■ 270° rotation counterclockwise about the origin

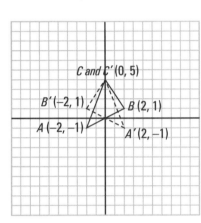 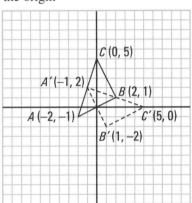

   ■ Reflection across the *x*-axis

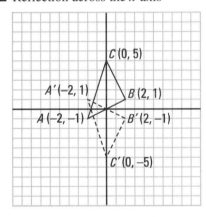

    d. For each of the transformations, the lengths of the image of segment *AB* and segment *BC* are unchanged from the lengths of the original segments. The slopes of the images of segment *AB* and segment *BC* are negative reciprocals of each other. Under a reflection across the *y*-axis the slopes are −0.5 and 2; under a rotation of 270° the slopes are −2 and 0.5; and under a reflection across the *x*-axis the slopes are −0.5 and 2. Each image triangle is an isosceles right triangle.

    e. The area of each of the three image triangles is 10 square units. Areas are not changed by rotations or reflections.

Teaching Notes continued

Notes continued from page T124

1. **b.** Only two lines differ from one of these programs to the next. Begin with the program RXAXIS in part b and make the changes in italic below.

PROGRAM: ROT180

Input "X COORD-PRE ", A
Input "Y COORD-PRE ", B
Pt-On (A, B)
Pt-On (–A, –B)
Pause
Disp "PRE-IMAGE"
Disp A, B
Disp "IMAGE"
Disp –A, –B

PROGRAM: ROT270

Input "A COORD-PRE ", A
Input "B COORD-PRE ", B
Pt-On (A, B)
Pt-On (B, –A)
Pause
Disp "PRE-IMAGE"
Disp A, B
Disp "IMAGE"
Disp B, –A

2. **a.** Here is a modified TI-82 or TI-83 program for a translation with H and K.

Input "X1", A
Input "Y1", B
Input "X2", C
Input "Y2", D
Input "X3", E
Input "Y3", F
Input "HORIZONTAL CHANGE", H
Input "VERTICAL CHANGE", K

Line (A, B, C, D)
Line (C, D, E, F)
Line (E, F, A, B)
Pause
Line (A + H, B + K, C + H, D + K)
Line (C + H, D + K, E + H, F + K)
Line (E + H, F + K, A + H, B + K)

The lines in italic type will differ depending on the transformation used.

b. Student programs may vary. This is a first attempt at animation and is much more complicated than the programs they wrote above. One possible program is below. Students may repeat some lines if they do not know about loops.

Input "X1", A
Input "Y1", B
Input "X2", C
Input "Y2", D
Input "X3", E
Input "Y3", F

For (N, 0, 15)
ClrDraw
Line (A + N, B, C + N, D)
Line (C + N, D, E + N, F)
Line (E + N, F, A + N, B)
For (K, 1, 50)
End
End

Unit 2

Teaching Notes continued

Notes continued
from page T126

In general, try to ask questions that push the student to offer a more rigorous explanation. One helpful question is simply, "How do you know that is so?" For example, when asked if (2, 3) lies on the line joining (4, 4) and (−2, 1), a student might say that if the point was not on the line then there would appear to be two segments meeting at an angle, not 180°. You might then ask if these segments would have the same slope. (If the point is not on the line, the two segments will not have the same slope.)

1. **a.** The image points are A' (12, 4) and B' (−6, 1).
   Segment AB is approximately 6.7 units. Segment $A'B'$ is approximately 18 units long. The lengths of the two segments are not equal.

   b. The midpoint of segment AB is M (1, 2.5). The image of M is M' (3, 2.5). The equation of the line through $A'B'$ is $y = \frac{1}{6}x + 2$ and M' satisfies this equation. So, M' is on line $A'B'$. This transformation seems to map the midpoint of a pre-image segment onto the midpoint of the image segment.

   c. The equation of the line through points A and B is $y = \frac{1}{2}x + 2$. Since points C and D both satisfy this equation, they are both on the line. The images of points C and D are C' (0, 2) and D' (6, 3). Both C' and D' are on line $A'B'$; they both satisfy the equation of the line through $A'B'$, $y = \frac{1}{6}x + 2$. This example supports the conjecture because if a point (x, y) is on a given line AB, then (x', y') also seems to be on line $A'B'$. It looks like it should work for any point (x, y) on line AB.

   d. Line AB intersects its image, line $A'B'$, at the point (0, 2). The line through (3, −1) and (−2, −6) intersects its image at (0, −4). Under this transformation the image of a line and its pre-image will always intersect at the y-intercept. If the pre-image point is (0, y) then the image point is (0, y) because (0, y) → (3 · 0, y), which is (0, y).

Notes continued
from page T128

c. Each image length is half the length of the pre-image segment.

Segment	Approximate Length
AB	$\sqrt{5} \approx 2.236$
$A'B'$	$\sqrt{1.25} \approx 1.118$
BC	$\sqrt{20} \approx 4.472$
$B'C'$	$\sqrt{5} \approx 2.236$
CD	$\sqrt{5} \approx 2.236$
$C'D'$	$\sqrt{1.25} \approx 1.118$
AD	$\sqrt{20} \approx 4.472$
$A'D'$	$\sqrt{5} \approx 2.236$

Each image length is half the length of the pre-image segment.

d. The area of $ABCD$ is 10. The area of $A'B'C'D'$ is approximately 2.5 square units. The area of the image rectangle is one-fourth the area of the pre-image rectangle. This proportion is the magnitude of the transformation squared: $0.5^2 = 0.25$.

Unit 2

Notes continued from page T138

5. **c.** Yes. The midpoint of the pre-image segment with endpoints (a, b) and (c, d) is the point $(\frac{a+c}{2}, \frac{b+d}{2})$. The transformation of the pre-image midpoint yields the point $(\frac{a+b+c+d}{2}, \frac{a+c}{2})$. The image segment has endpoints $(a + b, a)$ and $(c + d, c)$. The midpoint is $(\frac{a+b+c+d}{2}, \frac{a+c}{2})$. From this we see that the image of the midpoint of a segment is the midpoint of the image segment.

d. The length of the pre-image segment with endpoints (a, b) and (c, d) is
$$D_p = \sqrt{(c-a)^2 + (d-b)^2}$$
The length of the image segment with endpoints $(a + b, a)$ and $(c + d, c)$ is
$$D_i = \sqrt{[(c+d)-(a+b)]^2 + (c-a)^2}$$
$$= \sqrt{[(c-a)+(d-b)]^2 + (c-a)^2}$$
$$= \sqrt{(c-a)^2 + [(c-a)+(d-b)]^2}$$

Compare the expression for D_p to the last expression for D_i. From this we can see that if $c - a$ and $d - b$ are both negative or both positive, the length of the image segment will be greater, because then $|(c-a)+(d-b)| > |d-b|$. If $c - a$ and $d - b$ are opposite signs, the image length will be smaller, because then $|(c-a)+(d-b)| < |d-b|$.

Another way to say this is:

If the pre-image line is vertical ($a = c$), the length of the image segment will be the same as the length of the pre-image. If $a \neq c$, the length of the image segment will be longer than the pre-image if the line containing the pre-image points has positive slope. The length of the image segment will be shorter if the line containing the pre-image points has negative slope.

e. The area remains unchanged. Any triangle can be transformed under rigid motions so that its vertices are given by $(0, 0)$, (a, b), and $(c, 0)$. This triangle will be congruent (identical in size and shape) to the original triangle. The area of the pre-image triangle is $\frac{1}{2}bc$.

The coordinates of the image vertices under the transformation given in this task are $(0, 0)$, $(a + b, a)$ and (c, c). Finding the area of this triangle is more difficult. Using the side with vertices $(0, 0)$ and (c, c) as the base, the base length is $c\sqrt{2}$. The altitude to this base is on the line perpendicular to the line $y = x$ and goes through $(a + b, a)$. This line is $y = -x + 2a + b$, and the intersection of these two lines is $(a + \frac{b}{2}, a + \frac{b}{2})$. The height of the triangle is the distance from the intersection to $(a + b, a)$, which is $\frac{b}{\sqrt{2}}$. The area of the image triangle is therefore $\frac{1}{2}bc$.

Page T138 Teaching Notes continued on next page

Teaching Notes continued

Notes continued
from page T138

INVESTIGATION 3 Modeling Combinations of Transformations

Now that students have looked at several different transformations individually, this investigation asks them to explore combinations of transformations. It provides a good opportunity to cement understanding of the basic transformations from a coordinate geometry perspective and to relate transformations to ideas of similarity.

Students will use coordinate geometry techniques to explore the effects of various composite transformations on position, length, slope, and area. Finding the end result of a composition of transformations can be accomplished by applying the transformations, each on the image of the previous transformation, or by determining the single transformation (if one exists) that is equivalent to the composition, then applying that single transformation.

You may wish to introduce this investigation by using a TI-92 calculator or other computer software to show changing 3D graphs. The graphs shown in the student text are the same surface ($z = -x^2 + y^4 - 5y^2 + 4$), shown from different viewing perspectives. Some software programs will allow you to "animate" a graph, rotating or tilting it automatically. For others, you may need to show the orginal graph, then alter the perspective. The second graph should be drawn faster, as the software will transform the original rather than completely reconstructing the graph. (Check your manual for specific instructions.) It only takes a moment to show the images and to comment that this kind of animation (or change of perspective) is made possible because programmers are able to combine transformations. This sets up an air of anticipation for the investigation.

Working in groups, students should be able to accomplish activities 1, 2, and 3 with minimal assistance from the teacher. As you circulate among the groups, you can ask them questions that require them to use the new vocabulary they are acquiring. For example, ask: "What is the difference between the two types of transformations in activities 2 and 3?" (Geometrically they have different effects; translations are achieved symbolically by adding components to the original, while size transformations work by multiplying.)

Activity 4 might be more challenging than the first three activities. You might wish to choose a successful group to demonstrate activity 4. This makes a good summary activity on the subject of simple compositions. Before they proceed, all students should understand what "rotation about the origin" means and what does and does not move in a rotation. All students should be able to demonstrate, both geometrically and symbolically, a rotation of 90° followed by another rotation of 180°.

Unit 2

Teaching Notes *continued*

Notes continued from page T146

5. Step 1: Get the three sets of coordinates for the vertices of the triangle.
   Step 2: Compute the coordinates of the vertices of the image triangle from the size transformation.
   Step 3: Display the original triangle.
   Step 4: Display the image triangle from the size transformation.
   Step 5: Compute the coordinates of the vertices of the rotated triangle using the image vertices of the size transformation as pre-image points.
   Step 6: Display the rotated triangle.

Reflecting

1. Responses may vary. In biology, students use microscopes to examine specimens. Teachers use overhead projectors to enlarge images. Drafting and art classes require students to make scale drawings. In social studies, a globe represents the earth.

2. Responses will vary. Composing transformations is the successive application of transformations, each to the image of the previous transformation. Students may explain compositions in terms of specific transformations, such as a reflection followed by a translation. It also could be described as a mapping of an image of a given pre-image onto a new image using more than one transformation.

3. **a.** It maps the shape onto itself (leaves the shape unchanged).

Teaching Notes *continued*

Notes continued
from page T154

EXPLORE small-group investigation

INVESTIGATION 2 Stretching and Shrinking

In this investigation, students will use the coordinate rule for a size transformation centered at the origin to get the matrix representation. Then they will edit the Flag Turn Algorithm to create a planning algorithm for a size-changing animation.

A short and motivating introduction to this investigation can be achieved by showing the Flag Drill demo again. You might have students call out (this is noisy but fun) whenever they observe a rotation. At the end of the demo, ask if every move of the flag was created by a rotation. (Obviously not.) Then tell them they are going to find out how to use matrix multiplication to model size transformations. (Run the demo again if you like, maybe having students call out whenever they see a size transformation.)

While you circulate among the groups you may want to check specifically that students are reading the instructions carefully, using the origin as the center and using the correct flag for the original to be transformed. Activity 5 would be a good summary activity. By that time everyone should have discovered how to use a matrix multiplication to model size transformations. You might wish to have successful groups post their algorithms on large sheets of paper around the classroom.

Organizing

Notes continued
from page T159

1. $NEXT = [\text{TRANSFORMATION}] \times NOW$

2. **a.** $R^2 = \begin{bmatrix} 0 & -0.999698 \\ 0.999698 & 0 \end{bmatrix}$; $R^4 = \begin{bmatrix} -0.9993960912 & 0 \\ 0 & -0.9993960912 \end{bmatrix}$

   They are the same matrices (when rounded) as those previously identified with 90° counterclockwise and 180° rotations with center at the origin.

   b. R^6 represents a rotation of 270°. R^3 represents a rotation of 135°. The power of the matrix represents the number of 45° rotations.

   c. The matrix representing a 90° counterclockwise rotation is $\begin{bmatrix} 0 & -1 \\ 1 & 0 \end{bmatrix}$. So the matrix representing a 270° counterclockwise rotation is $\begin{bmatrix} 0 & -1 \\ 1 & 0 \end{bmatrix}^3$.

Teaching Notes continued

Notes continued from page T164

5. **a.** The object will grow as it spins (rotates).

b. Responses may vary.

c. This is a program which defines the matrices within the program. It will run on a TI-82 or TI-83 calculator. If your students are using different technology, some modifications may be required.

```
[[1.1, 0][0,1.1]] → [A]
[[0, 2, 2] [0, 0.5, −0.5]] → [B]
[[√2/2, −√2/2] [√2/2, √2/2]] → [C]
[A]*[C] → [D]
For(N,1,35,1)
ClrDraw
Line([B](1,1),[B](2,1),[B](1,2),[B](2,2))
Line([B](1,2),[B](2,2),[B](1,3),[B](2,3))
Line([B](1,3),[B](2,3),[B](1,1),[B](2,1))
[D]*[B] → [B]
For(K,1,10,1)
End
End
Stop
```

6. **a.** The product is $\begin{bmatrix} x + h \\ y + k \\ 1 \end{bmatrix}$. This is a translation of (x, y) with components of h and k.

b. $\begin{bmatrix} 1 & 0 & 2 \\ 0 & 1 & -3 \\ 0 & 0 & 1 \end{bmatrix}$ is a matrix that represents a translation with components of 2 and -3.

c. Let $A = \begin{bmatrix} 1 & 0 & 2 \\ 0 & 1 & 0 \\ 0 & 0 & 1 \end{bmatrix}$ which translates a point two units to the right.

Let $B = \begin{bmatrix} 0 & 0 & -3 & 0 \\ 0 & 8 & 6 & 4 \\ 1 & 1 & 1 & 1 \end{bmatrix}$ which will represent a flag using homogeneous coordinates.

Then use FLAGTURN (with the above matrices) to do the animation.

See Assessment Resource pages 54–57.

Teaching Notes *continued*

Notes continued
from page T166

■ Translation with components
−2 and 3:

$$\begin{bmatrix} -1 & 7 & -1 \\ 10 & 5 & 5 \end{bmatrix}$$

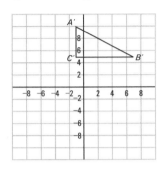

■ Size transformation with center
at the origin and magnitude 3:

$$\begin{bmatrix} 3 & 27 & 3 \\ 21 & 6 & 6 \end{bmatrix}$$

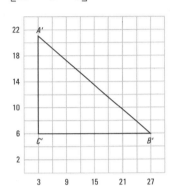

b. The rotation, reflection, and translation images are congruent to $\triangle ABC$. All of the transformations result in an image similar to the pre-image.

c. The area of $\triangle ABC$ is $\frac{1}{2}(5 \times 8)$ or 20 square units. Rotating, reflecting, or translating a figure does not affect the area of the figure, so the areas of the first three image triangles in part a are 20 square units. The area of the image triangle under a size transformation of magnitude 3 is 9×20 or 180 square units.

Unit 2

Teaching Notes continued

**Notes continued
from page T168** ▶

e Size transformations preserve angle measure and parallelism of lines. Under a size transformation of magnitude 1, distance does not change. Under size transformations of magnitude $k \neq 0$, image lengths are k times pre-image lengths, and area of each image is k^2 times the area of the pre-image. The distances of a point and its image from the center of a size transformation are related by the multiplicative factor of the magnitude. Thus if the center is C, the magnitude is k, and A has image A', then we get $CA' = k \cdot CA$ or $k = \frac{CA'}{CA}$. Help students see that this is a special case of the effect of the size transformation on length: the image of C is itself, so CA has as image CA', thus $CA' = k \cdot CA$. (When the center is between the image and pre-image, k will be negative.)

f Animation effects can be produced on a graphing calculator by first representing a figure and a transformation using matrices. Then using the appropriate matrix operation (usually multiplication) the image matrix can be computed. The calculator can then draw the image and use the image matrix to find a new image. Repeating this procedure (calculate, draw, and erase) will produce animation effects. This is done most easily by writing a program for the calculator.

CONSTRUCTING A MATH TOOLKIT: If students did not include a response to Reflecting task 3 from the MORE set (page 161) in their math toolkits, they could do so at this point. An alternative toolkit addition could be a response to Checkpoint part b above.

See Assessment Resource pages 58–75.

Unit 2

Unit 3 ▶ Patterns of Association

UNIT OVERVIEW In this unit, students explore the concept of association between pairs of variables. Your students may ask why the unit "Patterns of Association" sometimes uses the word *association* and sometimes uses the word *correlation* to mean what they perceive as the same thing. The distinction is that the word *correlation* is reserved by statisticians for when there is a linear relationship between two variables. When the ordered pairs appear to cluster about a line, even if the cluster isn't tight, we can say the variables are *correlated. Association* is a much more general term. For example, two variables might follow a relationship that is quadratic or exponential or some other discernible pattern. In those cases, we would say the variables are *associated* and we would not use the word *correlated*. (It is also okay to say two variables are associated when they have a linear relationship. In fact, correlation is linear association.)

Unit 3 Objectives

- To describe the association between two variables by interpreting a scatterplot
- To interpret correlation coefficients
- To understand that just because two variables are correlated, it does not mean that one directly causes the other
- To know when it is appropriate to make predictions from the least squares regression line or its equation
- To understand the effects of outliers on correlation coefficients, on the equation of the least squares regression line, and on the interpretations of correlation coefficients and regression lines in real-world contexts

Patterns of Association

Unit **3**

Unit 3

169

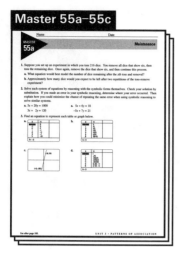

Master 55a–55c

▶Development of Association Throughout Unit

Lesson 1 introduces association from an intuitive standpoint, with activities that have students rank their music preferences and then compare their own rankings with those of their classmates. Later, a numerical measurement of association, Spearman's rank correlation coefficient r_s, is developed. Students investigate the relationship between r_s and the scatterplot. They develop an understanding of strong versus weak correlation and positive versus negative correlation for ranked data. Interpretation of scatterplots and the necessary accompanying critical thinking is crucial to the students' success.

Once correlation for pairs of ranked data has been investigated, students begin an exploration of pairs of unranked data in Lesson 2. Another numerical measurement of the strength of a linear relationship, Pearson's correlation coefficient r, is developed and used in several practical applications. Students are shown the importance of looking at the plot of the data as they complete activities with data that has outliers and with nonlinear data that has a high correlation. As students see more and more examples of strongly correlated data, many interesting questions are posed asking students whether a strong correlation between two variables necessarily implies a cause-and-effect relationship.

In Lesson 3, students explore some characteristics of the least squares regression line, including the fact that it is the unique line that minimizes the sum of the squared errors (residuals). They discover that the line is sensitive to outliers and so must always be interpreted in conjunction with the scatterplot. The question of when it may be appropriate to model an association with a line underlies much of the work in the unit. As the students discover, there is no simple answer to this question. They must combine information from their real-world experience with the techniques they learn in this unit.

See Teaching Masters 55a–55c for Maintenance tasks that students can work on after Lesson 1.

Unit 3 Planning Guide

Lesson Objectives	MORE Assignments	Suggested Pacing	Materials
Lesson 1 *Seeing and Measuring Association* • To explore association through the interpretation of scatterplots and the scatterplot matrix • To investigate and create a numerical measure to describe the degree of association between two sets of ranks • To calculate and interpret Spearman's rank correlation coefficient	**page 179** **Modeling:** 1 and 3 **Organizing:** 1 and choice of one* **Reflecting:** 2 and choice of one* **Extending:** 1	4 days	• Graph paper • Teaching Resources 56–62 • Assessment Resources 76–81
Lesson 2 *Correlation* • To interpret Pearson's correlation coefficient as a measure of how closely points cluster about a line • To explore the effects of influential points on the correlation coefficient • To understand that correlation between two variables does not necessarily mean that one of the variables *causes* the other • To understand that a set of points may not follow a linear model even if the correlation is strong, and that a linear model may be appropriate even if the correlation is weak	**after page 196** Students can begin Modeling Task 1 or 4; Organizing Tasks 1 or 3–5; Reflecting Task 2; or Extending Task 1 from p. 200<hr>**page 200** **Modeling:** Choice of two* **Organizing:** 1 and choice of one* **Reflecting:** 2 and 1 or 4* **Extending:** 1	6 days	• Graph paper • Teaching Resources 55a–55c, 63–70 • Assessment Resources 82–87
Lesson 3 *Least Squares Regression* • To use the least squares regression line for prediction and understand when that is appropriate • To understand the meaning of a residual • To understand that the least squares regression line minimizes the sum of the squared errors	**after page 216** Students can begin Organizing Task 3 or Reflecting Task 4 from p. 220.<hr>**page 220** **Modeling:** 1 and choice of one* **Organizing:** 3 and 1 or 2* **Reflecting:** 4 **Extending:** 2 or 5*	6 days	• Graph paper • Teaching Resources 71–78 • Assessment Resources 88–93
Lesson 4 *Looking Back* • To review the major objectives of the unit		3 days (includes testing)	• Graph paper • Teaching Resource 79 • Assessment Resources 94–126

* When choice is indicated, it is important to leave the choice to the student.
Note: *It is best if Organizing tasks are discussed as a whole class after they have been assigned as homework.*

Lesson 1 Seeing and Measuring Association

Did you ever notice how some things just seem to go together? For example, there seems to be an association between each of the following pairs of variables: time spent studying for an exam and score on the exam, age of a car and its value, height and age of a child, amount of sugar eaten and number of decayed teeth, or playing time and points scored in basketball. In each case, an increase in the value of one variable tends to be associated with an increase (or decrease) in the value of the second variable. Detecting, measuring, and explaining patterns of association between pairs of variables help in making decisions and predictions.

The table below gives a university's overall score (a rating of how good the university is, based on several factors) and education expenditure per student (the average amount the university spends per year to educate one student) for the top 24 universities in the United States.

University Ratings

University	Expenditure per Student	Overall Score	University	Expenditure per Student	Overall Score
Yale	$45,507	100.0	Pennsylvania	32,022	95.2
Princeton	32,417	99.8	Cornell	22,285	94.8
Harvard	42,902	99.6	Johns Hopkins	61,704	94.6
Duke	31,652	98.7	Rice	25,878	94.1
MIT	37,376	98.3	Notre Dame	15,874	93.0
Stanford	36,643	96.8	Washington	54,020	93.0
Dartmouth	31,491	96.5	Emory	30,163	92.9
Brown	23,889	96.2	Vanderbilt	25,490	90.6
Caltech	73,967	95.5	Virginia	14,142	89.2
Northwestern	29,760	95.5	Tufts	20,226	89.1
Columbia	32,738	95.4	Georgetown	20,924	88.5
Chicago	40,686	95.3	Michigan	16,293	87.7

Source: Copyright September 18, 1996 *U.S. News & World Report*. Reprinted with permission.

Lesson 1 Seeing and Measuring Association

LESSON OVERVIEW Prior to this unit, students have graphed paired variables on a scatterplot and modeled a linear relationship with a regression line. In this lesson, the association between two variables is further quantified with the introduction of rank correlation. The purpose of this lesson is to introduce students to the concept of finding a numerical measure to describe the degree of linear association for ranked data. Students first make statements about the association that can be observed from graphs, and then explore their own methods of finding a numerical measure.

Lesson Objectives

- To explore association through the interpretation of scatterplots and the scatterplot matrix
- To investigate and create a numerical measure to describe the degree of association between two sets of ranks
- To calculate and interpret Spearman's rank correlation coefficient

LAUNCH full-class discussion

By discussing the "Think About This Situation" questions with your students, you should be able to assess how well they remember how to interpret a scatterplot and how much they remember about the concept of a regression line.

Unit 3

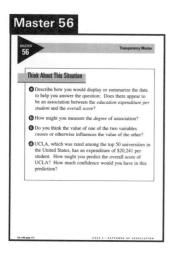

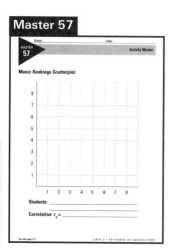

Think About This Situation

See Teaching Master 56.

The total education expenditure per student is the amount per full-time equivalent student that the school spent during the 1994 academic year for instruction, student services, administration, and academic support, including computers and libraries. The overall score was determined from reputation, how selective the university is in admitting students, faculty resources, financial resources, retention rates, and alumni satisfaction.

ⓐ A scatterplot best shows the extent of association between education expenditures per student and overall score. The scatterplot is shown at the right. In general, as the overall score increases the expenditure also tends to increase.

Students may note that the association would be much stronger except for the three schools that have the highest expenses. These three universities—Caltech, Washington, and Johns Hopkins—are what we later will call influential points.

University Ratings

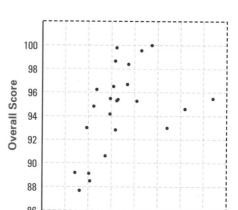

ⓑ Responses about how to measure the strength of association will vary. Some students may remember that a regression line can be used to summarize linear relationships. They may talk about using how well a line fits as a way to measure an association. If they do, you can ask if there is a way to give a numerical value to the goodness of fit. In this case they may suggest the slope, or number of points on the line, or some other way they can see that a value could be assigned. It is unlikely students will agree on a way to measure the association, but you can use this as an opportunity to tell them they will learn one way to compute just such a measure. (The numerical measure they will learn is called Pearson's correlation coefficient. For these data, the value is 0.46.)

ⓒ Student responses will vary. To help them think about the issues you might ask students, "If a college increases tuition by $10,000 a year and spends it on instruction, will the overall score go up?" If so, then there is a cause-and-effect relationship. One of the goals of this unit is to get students to understand that a strong association does not necessarily mean there is a cause-and-effect relationship between the two variables.

ⓓ Students may say that a line that seems to fit the data for the first 24 schools could be extended for other levels of expenditures, both higher and lower. Most students will realize that they can't be very sure of predictions from such extrapolation.

See additional Teaching Notes on pages T231C.

Unit 3

a Describe how you would display or summarize the data to help you answer the question: Does there appear to be an association between the *education expenditure per student* and the *overall score*?

b How might you measure the *strength* of association?

c Do you think the value of one of the two variables causes or otherwise influences the value of the other?

d UCLA, which was rated among the top 50 universities in the United States, has an expenditure of $21,500 per student. How might you predict the overall score of UCLA? How much confidence would you have in this prediction?

INVESTIGATION 1 Rank Correlation

In the United States we seem to be "rank-happy." In addition to ranking sports teams, motion pictures are ranked weekly by viewer preference or gross revenue; video tapes are ranked on the number of rentals; automobiles are ranked by their safety; and colleges are ranked on their quality. Music preferences also can be ranked. Different kinds of music are listed below.

Alternative Rock	Hip-Hop	Classical
Jazz	Country	Latino
Rhythm and Blues	Easy Listening	

1. Using the types of music listed above, rank your favorite type of music with a 1. Continue ranking with a 2 for your second favorite and an 8 for your least favorite. Ties are not allowed!

   a. Working with a partner, compare your rankings on a scatterplot. Plot one point (*your ranking, partner's ranking*) for each of the eight types of music. For example, in the figure at the right, Gail ranked Hip-Hop music seventh and Kuong ranked it second. Using a full sheet of paper, make your scatterplot as large as possible, then display it on the wall of your classroom.

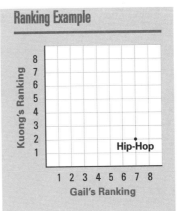

Ranking Example

LESSON 1 • SEEING AND MEASURING ASSOCIATION   171

b. Does there seem to be an association between your rankings and your partner's rankings? Explain your reasoning.

c. Examine the large scatterplots from the pairs of students around the classroom. Which plots show strong **positive association** between the pairs, that is, the rankings are similar? Describe these plots.

d. Which plots show strong **negative association** between the pairs, that is, the rankings tend to be opposite? Describe these plots.

e. Which plots show **little association**?

f. For which of the plots would you feel confident in predicting the musical taste of one person from that of the other? Explain your reasoning.

2. By looking at the scatterplots, you have made decisions about the *direction* (positive, negative, or none) of the association of two variables. As is often the case in mathematics, it is helpful to have a numerical measure to aid your visual perception of the *strength* of association.

   a. Use the music rankings to help your group brainstorm about ways to assign a number to each scatterplot. The number should represent the direction and the strength or weakness of the association. Describe your ideas.

   b. Use your preferred method to assign a number to three of the scatterplots. Do the results make sense? If not, revise your method.

   c. One way to test a method is to use it on extreme cases. What numerical value does your method give you for a *perfect positive association*—two sets of rankings that are identical? For a *perfect negative association*— two sets of rankings that are opposite of each other? Do the results make sense? If not, revise your method.

   d. The following pairs of rankings were given by Tmeka and Paula:

   (1, 4), (2, 5), (3, 3), (4, 7), (5, 2), (6, 6), (7, 8), (8, 1).

   ■ Is there a strong or weak association between the two rankings?

   ■ What numerical value would you assign to this association?

   ■ How does your numerical value indicate that this is a strong or weak association?

1. b. Students should look for similar rankings or opposite rankings. It is important for students to see that having opposite rankings is a form of association and that a pattern does exist when the rankings are opposite.

c. Each pair of students should post their plot, so everyone can see all the plots. Graphs that show strong positive association have points that cluster closely about a line with slope of 1. Generally the points move upward and to the right.

d. Negative association means a high ranking by one partner tends to be paired with a low ranking by another and vice versa. The points generally fall from the upper left corner to the lower right corner of the scatterplot.

e. In plots that show no association, we wouldn't be able to predict one person's rankings from the other person's. That is, we wouldn't be able to say that types of music ranked higher by one person tend to be ranked higher (or lower) by the other.

f. Those plots that show strong positive or negative association can help in predicting the musical taste of one person from that of the other. (Students may not realize that predictions can be made confidently for plots with strong negative association as well as for those with strong positive association.) For other plots, there is no way to tell where a corresponding ranking will be because the points are too scattered.

2. a. Responses will vary. Students should work in groups to find a measure and then be ready to share their thoughts with the class. Their methods do not have to be sophisticated. Encourage students to discuss how well their method will work for a variety of cases.

Methods often suggested by students include finding the sum of the differences between the rankings (not a good method as the sum is always 0!), finding the sum of the absolute differences, and finding the average absolute difference. One method almost invariably suggested is to find the number of exact matches. You can help students understand why this method is inadequate by giving them these examples:

Music Rankings

Mary	1	2	3	4	5	6	7	8
Steve	2	1	4	3	6	5	8	7

Jason	1	2	3	4	5	6	7	8
Alka	8	7	6	4	5	23	2	1

Mary and Steve agree very closely, but they have no exact matches. Jason and Alka disagree almost totally, but they have two exact matches.

b. Responses will vary depending on the method.

c. Responses will vary depending on the method.

d. ■ The association between the rankings is so weak, it is almost nonexistent.

■ Answers will depend on the students' method. The correlation coefficient is about 0.

■ There is no association, and student methods should show that fact as well.

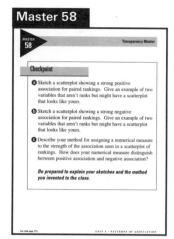

SHARE AND SUMMARIZE full-class discussion

Checkpoint

See Teaching Master 58.

ⓐ Responses will vary. The scatterplot should have data that clusters around a line with a slope of 1. One possible pair of variables is number of years of school completed and annual salary at age 40.

ⓑ Responses will vary. Data points should cluster around a line with a slope of -1. A possible pair of variables is the age of a car and its value.

ⓒ Responses will vary. Have students share their methods, so that multiple methods can be analyzed by the class. This also gives them options to use for the following "On Your Own" questions.

APPLY individual task

On Your Own

a. Student rankings will vary.

b. Students should look for positive, negative, or no association.

c. Responses will vary. Students probably will use one of the methods discussed during part c of the "Checkpoint".

EXPLORE small-group investigation

After the "On Your Own", the text presents a formula for calculating a rank correlation coefficient. Before launching into applying the formula, it would be helpful to take the time to be sure students understand the symbols. In a whole-class discussion, you might want to bring out the meaning of d and the fact that r_s depends on d and n. Asking questions about extreme cases will help students understand the formula: "If the rankings are very similar, how will this show up in the formula? What part of the formula will reflect this? What if the rankings are exactly alike? How will this influence the value of r_s? What is the smallest value that Σd^2 can take? Is there a largest value that Σd^2 can take? (This largest value is the subject of Extending task 2.) Is there a largest value for r_s? Is there a smallest value for r_s?" Students will not have all the answers for these questions at this point, but they can begin to think about how various values of r_s come about. You can revisit this discussion after activity 3.

The formula is Spearman's rank correlation coefficient, which can be used on ranked data when there are no or very few ties in each person's rankings. In the following activities students should become very familiar with the formula. There is no need to emphasize memorizing the formula. It is more important to encourage students to describe the procedure in activity 3. Help them connect what they did in the table to what the unfamiliar symbols say.

Checkpoint

a Sketch a scatterplot showing a strong positive association for paired rankings. Give an example of two variables that aren't ranks but might have a scatterplot that looks like yours.

b Sketch a scatterplot showing a strong negative association for paired rankings. Give an example of two variables that aren't ranks but might have a scatterplot that looks like yours.

c Describe your method for assigning a numerical measure to the strength of the association seen in a scatterplot of rankings. How does your numerical measure distinguish between positive association and negative association?

Be prepared to explain your sketches and the method you invented to the class.

▶ On Your Own

There are many brands of low-cut athletic shoes, including Adidas, Avia, Converse, Fila, New Balance, Nike, Puma, and Reebok.

a. Rank the brands listed here from 1 to 8, with 1 being your first choice and 8 being your last choice.

b. Aaron ranked Reebok - 1, Fila - 2, New Balance - 3, Adidas - 4, Puma - 5, Nike - 6, Avia - 7, and Converse - 8. Compare your ranking with Aaron's on a scatterplot. Is there positive, negative, or no association?

c. Calculate a measure of the strength of the association between your ranking and Aaron's.

Charles Spearman

Charles Spearman, a British statistician who lived from 1863 to 1945, invented a simple measure for the strength of the linear association between two rankings (that is, the degree to which the pairs cluster about a line). The measure is called a *rank correlation coefficient*. **Spearman's rank correlation coefficient**, denoted by r_s, is given by the formula

$$r_s = 1 - \frac{6\sum d^2}{n(n^2-1)} \ .$$

Here, n represents the number of items ranked and $\sum d^2$ represents the sum of the squared differences between the rankings.

The meaning and use of rank correlation is explored below in terms of rankings of kinds of music.

3. Working with your partner, make a table (like the one below) to help you compute r_s. Correlation coefficients usually are rounded to the nearest thousandth, although some statistical software rounds to more decimal places.

Type of Music	Your Ranking	Partner's Ranking	Difference of Rankings (d)	Squared Difference (d^2)
Alternative Rock				
Classical				
Country				
Easy Listening				
Hip-Hop				
Jazz				
Latino				
Rhythm and Blues				
$n = 8$				$\sum d^2 =$

a. Label your large scatterplot displayed in the classroom (see activity 1) with the rank correlation coefficient for your rankings.

b. How could you use a calculator to help you compute r_s?

c. Exchange rankings with another pair of students. Check their work by computing r_s for their rankings.

4. Study the scatterplots and rank correlations displayed in your classroom.

a. What patterns do you observe?

b. Suppose you ranked the kinds of music in exactly the same way as your partner did.

- Describe the scatterplot of identical rankings.
- What would the rank correlation be? Explain your response based on the formula for r_s.

c. Suppose you ranked the kinds of music exactly opposite of the way your partner ranked the music.

- Describe the scatterplot of opposite rankings.
- What would the rank correlation be? Verify by computing r_s.

d. Which scatterplot in your classroom has a rank correlation closest to 0? What can you say about the taste in music of those two classmates?

3. **See Teaching Master 59.**

   a. Each table will be different. Partners should have the same Σd^2 when they complete the table.

   b. Students should write the value of r_s they found in part a on their scatterplot.

   c. Make sure students are using the correct procedures in their descriptions. Students can use data lists as follows:

L_1 Type of Music	L_2 Your Ranking	$L_3 = L_1 - L_2$ Partner's Ranking	$L_4 = L_3{}^2$ Difference of Rankings (*d*)	Squared Difference (*d²*)
_____	_____	_____	_____	_____
_____	_____	_____	_____	_____
_____	_____	_____	_____	_____
_____	_____	_____	_____	_____

Then Σd^2 can be found by calculating the sum of L_4.

4. **This activity offers a good opportunity to draw the whole class together for a discussion of the patterns observed on the scatterplots and their correlations. To facilitate the discussions, you may want to ask, "Why can't we get a rank correlation coefficient greater than 1? Does the formula help us to see why this would be so? (This is easier to see than why we do not get a rank correlation coefficient less than -1.) Which scatterplot had the strongest correlation? Which seemed to have no correlation? Is there a pattern in the values of r_s that are associated with strong positive correlations? (Students should infer from their experiences that strong correlation has a coefficient close to 1 if a positive linear association exists or -1 if a negative linear association exists, and that weak or no association gives a rank correlation coefficient near to 0.)**

   a. Rank correlation coefficients close to 1 or -1 will correspond to narrow, almost linear plots. Low rank correlation coefficients, $-0.5 \le r \le 0.5$ will correspond to points that aren't clustered close to a line.

   b. ■ The points on the scatterplot would fall on a line with slope 1.
      ■ The rank correlation coefficient would be 1. $\Sigma d^2 = 0$ so $r_s = 1$.

   c. ■ The points would fall on a line with slope -1.
      ■ The rank correlation coefficient would be -1. The sum of the squared differences would be $7^2 + 5^2 + 3^2 + 1^2 + 1^2 + 3^2 + 5^2 + 7^2$ or 168. So
      $$r_s = 1 - \frac{6(168)}{8(8^2 - 1)} = 1 - \frac{1008}{504} = 1 - 2 = -1.$$

   d. Responses will vary. If the rank correlation coefficient is close to zero, it is impossible to predict one partner's ranking by knowing the other's ranking. Their tastes in music are independent of each other.

5. ■ A is -0.9.   ■ B is 0.5.
   ■ C is 0.1.   ■ D is 0.8.

6. **a.** Applying this formula to Tmeka and Paula's rankings from activity 2 part d, for example, we get the following:

Tmeka's Ranking	Paula's Ranking	d
1	4	-3
2	5	-3
3	3	0
4	7	-3
5	2	3
6	6	0
7	8	-1
8	1	7

Here $\Sigma d = 0$. This should be the case no matter what the students' rankings are.

   b. Σd will be 0.

   c. One thing squaring does is eliminate negative signs so the resulting sum is always positive. Squaring does other things as well. For example, a big difference, say 8, between two ranks is weighed more heavily than two smaller differences, say 4 and 4: $8^2 = 64$ but $4^2 + 4^2 = 32$. Later in this unit, students will relate this sum of squared differences to the formula for Euclidean distance.

5. Examine the plots below, showing paired rankings of favorite movies. Match each rank correlation coefficient below with the most appropriate scatterplot. The scales on each scatterplot are the same.

0.1   0.8   −0.9   0.5

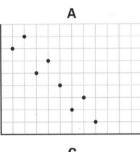

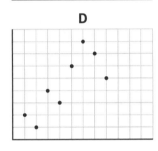

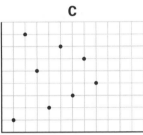

6. In this activity you will investigate why, in Spearman's formula for the rank correlation coefficient, the differences d are squared before they are summed. If the differences weren't squared, then the formula would be

$$1 - \frac{\sum d}{n(n^2 - 1)}.$$

  a. Apply the formula above to your and your partner's music rankings from activity 3. To find the values of d, always subtract in the same order: either (*your ranking – partner's ranking*) or (*partner's ranking – your ranking*). This will cause some of the values of d to be negative.

  b. Try this formula again on a different set of rankings.

  c. What does squaring the values of d in Spearman's formula accomplish?

The formula for Spearman's rank correlation coefficient r_s includes the sum of the squared differences. (Such a sum typically is used in statistics to measure how much *variation* exists.) The closer r_s is to 1, the more alike the rankings are. The closer r_s is to –1, the more different the rankings are.

Unit 3

7. The *Places Rated Almanac* ranks metropolitan areas according to a variety of categories including

- education—the number of available educational opportunities beyond high school
- crime—violent crime and property crime rates
- health care—the supply of health care services (such as number of specialists or breadth of hospital services)

Philadelphia

Los Angeles

Boston

Some characteristics of the fifteen largest metropolitan areas in the United States are ranked in the table below. For crime, health care, and education, a rank of 1 is best.

Rankings of Metropolitan Areas

Metro Area	Population	Crime	Health Care	Education
Los Angeles CA	1	14	2	4
New York NY	2	15	1	2
Chicago IL	3	13	3	3
Philadelphia PA	4	4	4	8
Washington DC	5	5	5	7
Detroit MI	6	9	7	9
Houston TX	7	7	6	15
Atlanta GA	8	10	11	14
Boston MA	9	6	10	1
Riverside CA	10	11	15	13
Dallas TX	11	12	14	11
San Diego CA	12	8	13	12
Minneapolis MN	13	2	8	10
Orange County CA	14	3	12	5
Long Island NY	15	1	9	6

Source: Savageau, David and Geoffery Loftus. *Places Rated Almanac*, 5th ed. New York: Macmillan, 1997.

7. See Teaching Master 60.

   The scatterplot matrix is a recent invention. The first written discussion of the idea appeared in the early 1980s. For a longer discussion of the scatterplot matrix see William S. Cleveland, *The Elements of Graphing Data* (Monterey, CA: Wadsworth, 1985). A revised edition was published by Hobart Press of Summit, NJ in 1994.

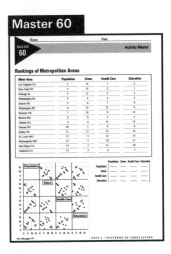

a. Students should expect to spend some time studying a scatterplot matrix. In this 4-by-4 scatterplot matrix, four variables are graphed; there are 12 scatterplots; each scatterplot has 15 points on it; and each point represents 2 numbers. This is a tremendous amount of information displayed in a small area.

- The first scatterplot has the health care ranking on the *x*-axis and the crime ranking on the *y*-axis. There is almost no correlation between the two. The second scatterplot has education on the *x*-axis and crime on the *y*-axis. Again there is almost no correlation.

- *Health care* is the variable on the *x*-axis for all scatterplots in the third column and on the *y*-axis for all scatterplots in the third row.

- In each case a category would be plotted against itself. The points would be (1, 1), (2, 2), ..., (15, 15). This doesn't give us any information about the cities.

- Riverside, CA is the highlighted city.

- *Population* and *health care* seem to have the greatest (positive) correlation.

- *Crime* is negatively correlated with all other variables. The correlation with *education* is so close to zero, however, students may not mention it.

b. Responses will vary. For actual correlation coefficients see part c on page T178.

a. The plot below is called a **scatterplot matrix**.

- Describe what is shown by the scatterplot entry in the second row and third column of the matrix. Do the same for the entry in the second row and fourth column.

- Where are all the scatterplots for which *health care* is the variable graphed on the *x*-axis? On the *y*-axis?

- Why are the scatterplots down the main diagonal of the matrix not included? What would they look like if they were included?

- For each scatterplot, does the highlighted city (represented by the open circle) tend to be ranked towards the best or towards the worst? Which city is the one that is highlighted in each case?

- Which pair of variables with a positive correlation appears to have the greatest correlation?

- Which pairs of variables appear to have negative correlation?

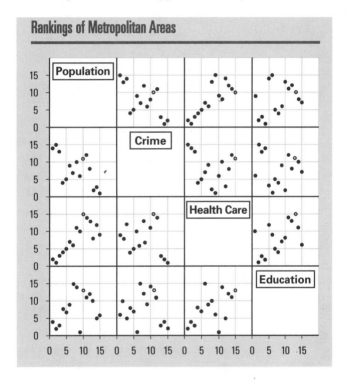

Rankings of Metropolitan Areas

b. Each member of your group should select one pair of rankings and then do the following.

- Locate the two scatterplots of your pair of rankings in the scatterplot matrix.

Unit 3

■ Estimate the rank correlation coefficient, using −1 for a negative, perfectly linear correlation and 1 for a positive, perfectly linear correlation.

■ Compute Spearman's rank correlation coefficient, r_s. How close was your estimate?

c. Working with other groups, fill in a copy of the following matrix. Place the rank correlation coefficient r_s between two variables in the appropriate entry. This matrix is called a **rank correlation matrix**.

$$
\begin{array}{c}
 \\
\text{Population} \\
\text{Crime} \\
\text{Health Care} \\
\text{Education}
\end{array}
\begin{array}{cccc}
\text{Population} & \text{Crime} & \text{Health Care} & \text{Education} \\
\left[\rule{0pt}{2.5em}\right. \text{———} & \text{———} & \text{———} & \text{———} \\
\text{———} & \text{———} & \text{———} & \text{———} \\
\text{———} & \text{———} & \text{———} & \text{———} \\
\text{———} & \text{———} & \text{———} & \text{———} \left.\rule{0pt}{2.5em}\right]
\end{array}
$$

d. Use your correlation matrix to answer the following questions.

■ Which pair of variables has the strongest positive rank correlation? Give some reasons why you think this correlation is so strong.

■ Which entries could you fill in by knowing the value of r_s used for another entry?

■ Which pair of variables has the weakest correlation? Give some reasons why you think there was so little association between the rankings in this case.

■ Which variable is most highly correlated with *crime*?

■ Why should the entries along the diagonal be 1?

■ How is this correlation matrix related to the scatterplot matrix on the previous page?

e. State in words what the correlation between *population* and *crime* indicates.

Checkpoint

ⓐ How can positive rank correlation be seen in a list of paired rankings? In a scatterplot? In the value of r_s?

ⓑ How can negative rank correlation be seen in a list of paired rankings? In a scatterplot? In the value of r_s?

ⓒ What information can you get from a scatterplot matrix that is difficult to see in the table of data?

Be prepared to explain your thinking to the entire class.

7. c.

	Population	Crime	Health	Education
Population	1.000	−0.636	0.796	0.318
Crime	−0.636	1.000	−0.229	0.086
Health	0.796	−0.229	1.000	0.507
Education	0.318	−0.086	0.507	1.000

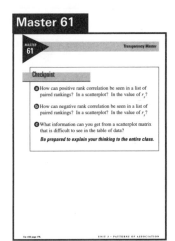

d. ■ The strongest positive rank correlation is between population and health care. Reasons for the high correlation may vary. Larger cities may operate more hospitals and clinics.

■ You can fill in the xth row, yth column, if you know the yth row, xth column. Entries symmetrically placed across the main diagonal are equal.

■ The weakest correlation was between education and crime. Reasons given may vary.

■ Population is most highly correlated with crime. This correlation is negative, which means the larger the city is, the worse the crime rate tends to be.

■ The entries along the diagonal are all 1 because Σd^2 will be 0.

■ The entry in row i and column j of the correlation matrix gives the rank correlation between the two variables graphed in the scatterplot in row i and column j of the scatterplot matrix.

e. The larger the city, the higher the crime rate. Be sure students understand that although a low population ranking indicates a larger population, a low crime ranking indicates fewer crimes per person. The rank correlation coefficient of $−0.636$ indicates that for metro areas with larger populations (a rank with a small number), the rank for crime tended to be a larger number (that area had more crime than the others). Finally, be sure students understand that this isn't just the number of crimes that is higher, but the crime *rate* (number of crimes per 1,000 people).

Students need practice in interpreting what negative correlation indicates. Too often people confuse zero correlation and negative correlation. Be sure students understand that a negative correlation means there is a pattern, but as one variable's value increases the other decreases, and that zero correlation indicates we can make no such general statement. You might refer to the rank scatterplots around the room for negative and near zero correlation.

SHARE AND SUMMARIZE full-class discussion

Checkpoint

See Teaching Master 61.

At this point, students should understand that a strong rank correlation has a coefficient near 1 or −1 and a weak rank correlation has a coefficient near 0. They also need to know what the corresponding plots might look like. They should understand what is happening from the table of differences, the scatterplot, and the numerical value of r_s.

CONSTRUCTING A MATH TOOLKIT: Students should summarize the concepts of strong, weak, positive, and negative rank correlations in their Math Toolkits. They may wish to include sample scatterplots with their summary.

See additional Teaching Notes on page T231D.

▶**On Your Own**

a. Scatterplots may vary some. Points should cluster around a straight line from the top left to the bottom right.

b. If Joshua liked a movie, Daliea would tend to dislike it; the other way around also would be true.

c. You wouldn't know anything about how Joshua felt about a movie that Sterling ranked first. It's possible that they both ranked the same movie first. For example, the pair of rankings below has a rank correlation coefficient of 0.2.

Sterling	1	2	3	4	5	6	7	8	9	10
Joshua	1	7	8	4	5	10	2	3	9	6

It's also possible that Joshua gave a last place ranking to the movie Sterling ranked first. For example, the pair of rankings below also has a correlation coefficient of 0.2.

Sterling	1	2	3	4	5	6	7	8	9	10
Joshua	10	2	3	4	5	6	7	1	8	9

MORE

ASSIGNMENT *pp. 179–185*

Modeling: 1 and 3
Organizing: 1 and choice of one*
Reflecting: 2 and choice of one*
Extending: 1

*When choice is indicated, it is important that the choice be left to the student.
NOTE: *It is best if Organizing tasks are discussed as a whole class after they have been assigned as homework.*

MORE independent assignment

We recommend that students rarely be required to copy calculator-produced scatterplots onto their papers since it is very time-consuming.

Unit 3

Suppose Joshua and two friends ranked ten recent movies. The rank correlation between the rankings of Joshua and Daliea was –0.8, and the rank correlation between the rankings of Joshua and Sterling was 0.2.

a. Make a scatterplot that might have a correlation of –0.8. Find r_s for your scatterplot. How close were you to –0.8?

b. Suppose Joshua and Daliea were going to a movie. Describe what might happen when they started looking through the list of movies.

c. If Sterling gave a rank of 1 to a certain movie, how do you think Joshua ranked the movie? Explain your response by giving several examples.

MORE
Modeling • Organizing • Reflecting • Extending

Modeling

1. Which are the best roller coasters in the United States? It's impossible to tell, really, but the rankings below are from an annual survey of the readers of *Inside Track*, a magazine for roller-coaster enthusiasts. Fifty roller coasters were ranked in the survey. The table gives only the top eight, which happened to include the same eight roller coasters in both 1992 and 1993.

BATMAN and all related characters, names and indicia are trademarks of DC comics © 1997
SIX FLAGS and all related indicia are trademarks of Six Flags Theme Parks Inc. ©1997

Roller Coaster Rankings		
Roller Coaster	**1992 Rank**	**1993 Rank**
Magnum XL-200, Cedar Point, OH	2	1
Texas Giant®, Six Flags Over Texas, TX	1	2
The Beast, Kings Island, OH	3	3
Phoenix, Knoebel's, PA	5	4
Timber Wolf, Worlds of Fun, MO	4	5
Batman The Ride®, Six Flags Great America, IL	6	6
Cyclone, Coney Island, NY	7	7
Thunderbolt, Kennywood, PA	8	8

Source: *http://www.cis.ohio-state.edu/hypertext/faq/usenet/roller-coaster-faq/part3/faq.html*

a. Make a scatterplot of the ordered pairs (*1992 Rank*, *1993 Rank*). Estimate the rank correlation coefficient by examining the plot. Is it strong or weak? Positive or negative?

b. Calculate the rank correlation coefficient. Compare it to your estimate.

c. How might these rankings have been determined from a survey?

2. Select a category from the following list, or choose a category of your own. Decide on at least seven items for the category, and have two people rank the items. Make a scatterplot of the pairs of rankings. Find the rank correlation coefficient between the two sets of rankings. Write a summary of what you did and what the results were.

Ice Cream Flavors	Movie Actresses	Restaurants
Movies	Clothing Stores	Movie Actors
Sports Teams	TV Shows	Musical Groups

3. The population rankings for the ten largest cities in the world for the years 1985 and 1991 are given in the chart below. Also given are the projected population and projected relative rank for the year 2000.

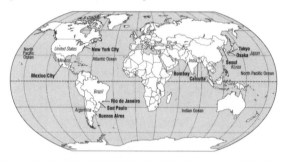

Population Ranks, World Cities

City	Population Projected for 2000 (millions)	Projected Relative Rank for 2000	Rank 1985	Rank 1991
Bombay, India	15.63	5	9	7
Buenos Aires, Argentina	12.91	10	7	10
Calcutta, India	14.09	9	8	8
Mexico City, Mexico	27.87	2	2	2
New York, U.S.	14.65	6	4	5
Osaka, Japan	14.33	7	6	6
Rio de Janeiro, Brazil	14.17	8	10	9
Sao Paolo, Brazil	25.35	3	3	3
Seoul, Korea	21.98	4	5	4
Tokyo, Japan	29.97	1	1	1

Source: *The World Almanac and Book of Facts 1994, 1988.* Mahwah, NJ: World Almanac, 1993, 1987.

Modeling

1. **a.** The rank correlation is strong and positive. Estimates for the coefficient should be close to 1, but not 1. A good estimate would be 0.9.

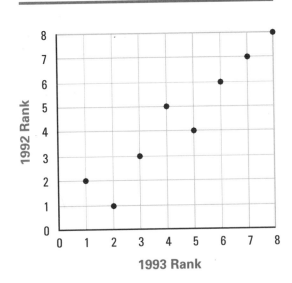

Roller Coaster Rankings

b. $r_s = 0.952$. Comparisons to estimates will vary.

c. It is unlikely that very many people have ridden all 50 roller coasters, so each person in the survey must have been asked to rate only those he or she has ridden. If this is the case, the ratings would have been combined. There are several possibilities for such a combination.

2. Student work will vary. This task can be used as an assessment by having students write their results in a report or by giving an oral report to the class. Grades can be given on the basis of topic presentation, graphical representation, calculation and interpretation of r_s, conclusions, and rationale for conclusions.

Unit 3

3. **a.** The complete scatterplot matrix is shown below. Students should notice that the two missing plots are related by a reflection over the line $y = x$. (This is another informal introduction to the concept of an inverse relation.)

Possible observations: All of the correlations are strong and positive. The highest correlation is between 1991 and 2000 and the lowest correlation is between 1985 and 2000. The three largest cities maintained the same ranking in all three years. All of the variation occurs in ranks 4 through 10. To get the plot in position (i, j), reflect the points in the plot in position (j, i) over the line $y = x$.

Population Ranks, World Cities

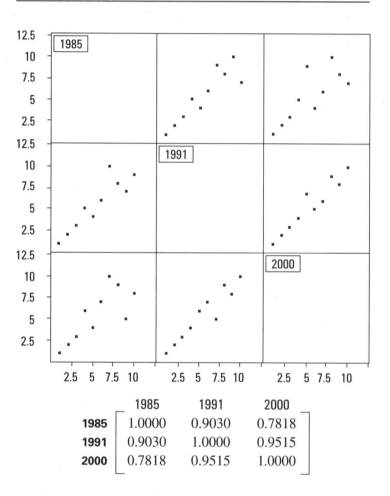

	1985	1991	2000
1985	1.0000	0.9030	0.7818
1991	0.9030	1.0000	0.9515
2000	0.7818	0.9515	1.0000

b. The complete correlation matrix is shown above.

- The 1985 and 1991 rankings have a correlation coefficient of 0.9030. The 2000 and 1991 rankings have a correlation coefficient of 0.9515.
- The rank correlation coefficients for two of the missing entries are the same because both are based on the 1985 and 1991 rankings. Order doesn't matter in computing a correlation coefficient (but it does when computing the regression line).
- The correlations are all strongly positive, which means that the ranking of the cities hasn't changed much over the years.

c. The highest correlation is between 1991 and 2000, then 1991 and 1985, and the lowest correlation is between 1985 and 2000. The farther apart two years are, the lower the correlation. That makes sense as there is more time for population patterns to change.

a. Examine the following scatterplot matrix for these rankings. Produce a scatterplot for the (*1985*, *1991*) and (*1991*, *1985*) entries. Write two observations that you can make from looking at the complete scatterplot matrix.

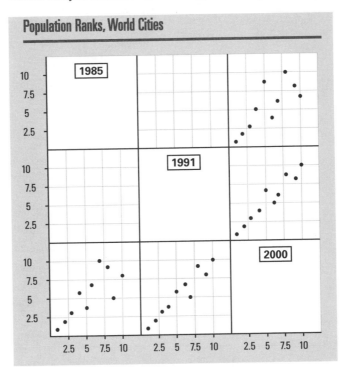

Population Ranks, World Cities

b. The rank correlation matrix for the population rankings is given below.

$$\begin{array}{c} & 1985 & 1991 & 2000 \\ 1985 & \begin{bmatrix} 1.0000 & & 0.7818 \\ & 1.0000 & 0.9515 \\ 0.7818 & & 1.0000 \end{bmatrix} \\ 1991 & \\ 2000 & \end{array}$$

- Calculate the missing rank correlation coefficients.
- What do you notice about this correlation matrix?
- Explain what these correlation coefficients indicate about the association between the rankings for the largest cities.

c. Compare the correlation between the 1985 and 1991 rankings with the correlation between the 1985 ranking and the 2000 projected ranking. What might explain the difference?

Unit 3

4. The ten products that patients in the United States most often said were related to their injuries are listed below, in alphabetical order.

> Bathtubs and showers
> Bicycles and accessories
> Chairs
> Drinking glasses
> Fences and fence posts
> Knives
> Ladders
> Nails, screws, and tacks
> Stairs and steps
> Tables

a. Rank the products from 1 to 10, assigning 1 to the product you think causes the most injuries, 2 to the product that causes the second largest number of injuries, and so on.

b. Obtain the actual rankings from your teacher. Compute the rank correlation coefficient between your rankings and the actual rankings.

c. Compare your rank correlation coefficient with those of your classmates.

■ Which member of your class did the best job of predicting the rankings? How did you determine this?

■ How could you have determined who did the best job from (*student ranking*, *actual ranking*) scatterplots?

Organizing

1. Are the two expressions $\sum d^2$ and $(\sum d)^2$ equivalent? Give an example to support your answer.

2. If $r_s = 1$ or $r_s = -1$, all points fall on a line. Write equations for these two lines.

3. Ann and Bill each throw a dart at a larger version of the grid shown here. Ann's dart lands at the point with coordinates (3, 4). Bill's dart lands at the point (–5, 1).

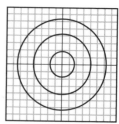

a. How far is Ann's dart from Bill's dart?

b. Whose dart is farther from the center?

c. How is the distance formula like the formula for Spearman's rank correlation coefficient?

MORE *continued*

4. a. Rankings will vary.
b. The actual rankings are given below. See Teaching Master 62. The students' rank correlation coefficients will vary.

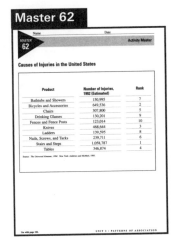

Number of Injuries, 1992

Product	Estimated	Rank
Bathtubs and Showers	150,995	7
Bicycles and Accessories	649,536	2
Chairs	307,800	5
Drinking Glasses	130,201	9
Fences and Fence Posts	123,014	10
Knives	468,644	3
Ladders	139,595	8
Nails, Screws, and Tacks	239,711	6
Stairs and Steps	1,058,787	1
Tables	346,874	4

Source: *The Universal Almanac 1994,* NY: Andrews and McMeel, 1993.

c. Responses will vary.
- Students probably will just compare the rank correlation coefficients and find the value of r_s closest to 1.
- This could be determined from scatterplots by looking for the scatterplot that is clustered most closely around a line with slope 1.

Organizing
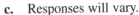

1. Σd^2 is not the same as $(\Sigma d)^2$. To compute Σd^2, the numbers are squared and then added; to compute $(\Sigma d)^2$, the numbers are added first, then the sum is squared.

For example, $(1 + 2 + 3)^2 = 36$ but $1^2 + 2^2 + 3^2 = 13$. An explanation might show students that $(1 + 2 + 3)^2 = (1 + 2 + 3)(1 + 2 + 3)$ and in the multiplication process, the 2 from the first parentheses is multiplied by every element in the second parentheses, not just itself. The same is true of 1 and 3. In the second quantity, $1^2 + 2^2 + 3^2$, each number is multiplied only by itself. You might tie this into the relation between $(x + y)^2$ and $x^2 + y^2$.

2. $y = x$ and $y = -x + (n + 1)$, where n is the number of items being ranked.
3. a. $\sqrt{8^2 + 3^2} = \sqrt{73} \approx 8.54$ units
b. Ann's dart is $\sqrt{3^2 + 4^2}$ or 5 units from the center. Bill's dart is $\sqrt{(-5)^2 + 1^2}$ or approximately 5.1 units from the center. Bill's is farther from the center.
c. Both involve a sum of squared differences.

Unit 3

4. There are $3 + 2 + 1$ or 6 possible ways to pair four things. Students might count, or use the scatterplot matrix. There are $6 + 5 + 4 + 3 + 2 + 1$ or 21 ways to pair rankings of seven categories.

   There are $\frac{(k^2 - k)}{2}$ ways to pair the rankings of k categories. Students can visualize this using the scatterplot matrix. The number of unordered pairings is equal to the number of plots above the main diagonal. There are k^2 scatterplots in the matrix. Subtracting the number, k, on the main diagonal gives $k^2 - k$; half of those is $\frac{(k^2 - k)}{2}$.

Reflecting

1. Typical student responses might include ranking the schools in your athletic conference on two different sports; ranking a class of students on their grade point average and their PSAT score; or ranking a group of students for most popular and for most likely to succeed.

2. This item is an informal introduction to the concept of inverse relation.

   a. The scatterplots will not be the same (unless the rankings are exactly the same). The x- and y-coordinates will be reversed in the two scatterplots. Michael's scatterplot will be the reflection over $y = x$ of Tina's scatterplot.

   b. The correlation coefficients will be the same. You can see this by looking at the formula. Although a given value of d for (*set A, set B*) will have the opposite sign of that of (*set B, set A*), the value of d^2 will be the same.

3. a. The two reporters felt almost the same way about the order the candidates would finish in the election.

   b. The judges not only didn't have agreement in their rankings, they disagreed slightly.

   c. The managers were somewhat alike in how they ranked the employees.

   d. The managers were almost opposite in how they ranked the employees. Those employees one manager ranked high for efficiency, the other manager tended to rank low.

4. Responses will vary.

4. In activity 7 of Investigation 1, you examined ratings of metropolitan areas. How many possible **unordered pairings** of the four categories are there? (Don't include pairing a ranking with itself.) Unordered means that the pair (*crime, health care*) is the same as (*health care, crime*). Explain how you determined your answer. If there were seven categories in a ranking, how many unordered pairs of rankings would there be? If there were k categories, how many unordered pairs of rankings would there be?

Reflecting

1. Describe a situation in school where you might be interested in a rank correlation.

2. Tina made a scatterplot of two sets of rankings, (*set A*, *set B*), and calculated the correlation between them. Michael made a scatterplot of (*set B*, *set A*) rankings and calculated the correlation between them.

   a. Will the scatterplots be the same? Explain.

   b. Will the correlations Tina and Michael found be the same? Explain why or why not.

3. Write a conclusion that can be drawn from each of the following situations.

   a. Two reporters from opposite political parties ranked the seven candidates for state representative according to the number of votes they thought the candidates would get in the primary election. The correlation between the rankings of the two reporters was 0.8.

   b. Two judges ranked ten skaters according to their performance. The correlation between the rankings of the two judges was –0.2.

   c. Two managers ranked a set of employees on job effectiveness. The correlation between their rankings was 0.5.

   d. The two managers in part c ranked the same employees on efficiency. The correlation between their rankings was –0.7.

4. Compare Spearman's rank correlation coefficient formula with the ones invented by you and your classmates in activity 2 of Investigation 1. What are the advantages and disadvantages of each?

Unit 3

Extending

1. Twelve people applied for part-time jobs at a local grocery store. They were interviewed and given a test on their ability to make proper change for a purchase. Their rankings on the basis of the interview (1 is the highest and 12 the lowest) and their test scores are shown in the table below.

Job Candidates Summary

Person	Interview Rank	Test Score
Ann	8	80
Bryan	5	84
Claudio	3	88
Denise	6	81
Ella	12	60
Frank	1	94
Gino	10	72
Howie	7	77
Ingrid	2	93
Jed	11	66
Keisha	9	68
Lynn	4	92

a. Make a scatterplot, noting any unusual features. Calculate the rank correlation coefficient.

b. Is there enough evidence to indicate that the tests alone could be used for hiring purposes? How did you determine your answer?

c. What information is lost when scores are transformed into ranks?

2. Give an example to show that, for a given number n of items ranked, the largest possible value of $\sum d^2$ is $\frac{n(n^2 - 1)}{3}$. What does this imply about the rank correlation coefficient?

Extending

1. **a.** Students first must rank the test scores from 1 to 12, then calculate the correlation coefficient which is 0.98. The scatterplot shows a linear relationship with no influential points. (See the discussion of influential points on page 193 in the student text.)

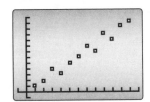
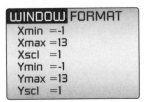

```
WINDOW FORMAT
Xmin =-1
Xmax =13
Xscl  =1
Ymin =-1
Ymax =13
Yscl  =1
```

   b. It would seem that the correlation is strong enough to allow the company to rely on the tests. Those who ranked high on the tests also tended to rank high in the interview; the other way around is also true.

   c. The actual values of the test scores tell us more than the ranks do about how well the applicants scored in relation to each other. In fact, when the actual scores are used with an analogous formula that allows unranked data, the correlation is not quite as high.

2. Oppositely ranked data pairs will give the maximum value of Σd^2. For example, if the paired ranks are (1, 5), (2, 4), (3, 3), (4, 2), and (5, 1), then
$$\Sigma d^2 = (-4)^2 + (-2)^2 + (0)^2 + (2)^2 + (4)^2 = 40.$$
Notice that in this case, $\quad \dfrac{n(n^2 - 1)}{3} = \dfrac{5(25 - 1)}{3} = 40.$

This implies that the rank correlation coefficient is always greater than or equal to -1:

$$\Sigma d^2 \leq \frac{n(n^2 - 1)}{3}$$

$$3\Sigma d^2 \leq n(n^2 - 1)$$

$$\frac{3\Sigma d^2}{n(n^2 - 1)} \leq 1$$

$$-\frac{6\Sigma d^2}{n(n^2 - 1)} \geq -2$$

$$1 - \frac{6\Sigma d^2}{n(n^2 - 1)} \geq 1 - 2$$

The expression on the left is the definition of r_s, so $r_s \geq -1$. This means that when ranks are opposite, the rank correlation is -1.

Unit 3

MORE *continued*

3. a. Each case is the sum of the five rankings 1 through 5, and $1 + 2 + 3 + 4 + 5 = 15$.

b.

$$\Sigma d = (a - v) + (b - w) + (c - x) + (d - y) + (e - z) \quad \text{Definition of } \Sigma d$$
$$= a - v + b - w + c - x + d - y + c - z \quad \text{Associativity of addition}$$
$$= a + b + c + d + e - v - w - x - y - z \quad \text{Commutativity of addition}$$
$$= (a + b + c + d + e) - (v + w + x + y + z) \quad \text{Associativity of addition}$$

Associativity of addition (and Distributive property of multiplication over addition)

$$= 15 - 15 \quad \text{Substitution}$$
$$= 0 \quad \text{Subtraction}$$

c. Yes. The argument is similar. For ten items, the sum of the ranks is 55. The proof for the general case of n ranks is parallel.

4. a.

Here, there are two crossings or $c = 2$, so $r_k = 1 - \dfrac{2(2)}{\frac{8}{2}(7)} = \dfrac{6}{7} \approx 0.857$.

b. For perfect agreement, there are no crossings or $c = 0$, so $r_k = 1 - \dfrac{2(0)}{\frac{5}{2}(4)} = 1$.

For perfect disagreement, there are 10 crossings or $c = 10$, so $r_k = 1 - \dfrac{2(10)}{\frac{5}{2}(4)} = 1 - 2 = -1$.

c. No. For example, for the roller coaster data, $r_s = 0.952$, while $r_k = 0.857$.

d. If the rankings are identical, there are no crossings, and so

$$r_k = 1 - \frac{2(0)}{\frac{n}{2}(n-1)} = 1$$

for $n > 1$. If the rankings are opposite, there are $1 + 2 + \ldots + (n-1) = \dfrac{n(n-1)}{2}$ crossings and so

$$r_k = 1 - \frac{2\left(\frac{n(n-1)}{2}\right)}{\frac{n}{2}(n-1)} = -1$$

for $n > 1$.

See Assessment Resource pages 76–81.

3. Suppose you are given two general sets of rankings of five items as shown below. It always will be the case that $\sum d = 0$ no matter what the rankings are.

	First Ranking	Second Ranking
Item 1	a	v
Item 2	b	w
Item 3	c	x
Item 4	d	y
Item 5	e	z

   a. Why is it true that $a + b + c + d + e = 15$ and $v + w + x + y + z = 15$?

   b. Explain why each of the following equalities holds.

   $$\sum d = (a - v) + (b - w) + (c - x) + (d - y) + (e - z)$$
   $$= a - v + b - w + c - x + d - y + e - z$$
   $$= a + b + c + d + e - v - w - x - y - z$$
   $$= (a + b + c + d + e) - (v + w + x + y + z)$$
   $$= 15 - 15$$
   $$= 0$$

   c. Do you think a similar argument could be given to show that for two sets of rankings of 10 items, $\sum d = 0$? Why or why not?

4. Kendall's rank correlation coefficient, r_k, is given by the formula

   $$r_k = 1 - \frac{2c}{\frac{n}{2}(n - 1)}$$

   where n is the number of items being ranked. To find c, write the ranks for each item side-by-side and connect the ranks as shown below.

   The number of crossings of the lines is c. Here, $c = 4$.

   a. Find Kendall's correlation coefficient for the roller coaster data in Modeling task 1.

   b. Compute Kendall's correlation coefficient when there is perfect agreement between the ranks 1 to 5. Compute Kendall's correlation coefficient when there is completely opposite ranking of five items.

   c. Are Spearman's and Kendall's rank correlation coefficients **equivalent**? That is, do they always give the same value? Explain your answer.

   d. Investigate whether r_k always lies between –1 and 1.

Lesson 2 ▸ *Correlation*

As you observed in Lesson 1, the rank correlation coefficient, r_s, is a measure of the strength of the linear association between a pair of rankings. But usually when you are studying a possible association between two variables, the variables are not ranks. You could be investigating the association between age and the number of hours of sleep, or between income and number of years of education, or between schools' graduation rates and the amount of money spent per student. Shown in the chart below is nutritional information on chicken fast-food entrees.

How Fast Foods Compare

Company	Entree	Total Calories	Fat (grams)	Cholesterol (mg)	Sodium (mg)
Hardee's	Grilled Chicken	290	9	65	860
	Chicken Fillet	420	15	50	1190
Wendy's	Grilled Chicken	290	7	55	720
	Chicken (regular)	450	20	60	740
Burger King	BK Broiler Chicken	550	29	80	480
	Chicken Sandwich	710	43	60	1400
McDonald's	McChicken	510	30	50	820
	Chicken McNuggets (6)	300	18	65	530
Kentucky Fried Chicken	Lite'n Crispy (4 pieces)	198	12	60	354
	Original Recipe (4 pieces)	248	15	90	575
	Extra Crispy (4 pieces)	324	21	99	638

Source: *McDonald's Nutrition Facts,* McDonald's Corporation, 1995; *Good Nutrition News from Wendy's,* Wendy's International, Inc., 1994; *Nutritional Information,* Burger King Corp., 1996; *Nutritional Information,* Hardee's, 1996; *KFC Nutrition Facts,* KFC, 1995.

Lesson 2 *Correlation*

LESSON OVERVIEW The primary objective of this lesson is to develop students' ability to interpret Pearson's correlation coefficient for variables that aren't necessarily ranked. The Spearman rank correlation coefficient is actually a special version of the more general Pearson's correlation coefficient. Rank correlation was investigated in Lesson 1 so that students will have a sense of the meaning of correlation. Pearson's r is the correlation coefficient commonly used for either ranked or unranked data.

The correlation coefficient is a measure of the degree of linear association between any two variables. However, as students begin to work with a numerical measure of r, they need to develop an understanding of the importance of combining critical analysis of scatterplots with numerical results. Students should begin each exploration of a data set with a scatterplot of the variables. Outliers or influential points can affect the results and create a data set for which r is close to 1 or -1, but in which the linear pattern does not appear strong. Conversely, data that otherwise have a strong correlation can have a small value of r because of one influential point.

After some initial investigation of scatterplots and the formula for Pearson's correlation coefficient, students are directed to the value of r under linear regression on a calculator or computer software. They should notice again that it is always the case that $-1 \le r \le 1$. A coefficient is 1 for perfect positive correlation and -1 for perfect negative correlation. If the correlation is weak, r is close to 0.

In the second investigation, students should think carefully about the fact that a high correlation does not mean that one variable necessarily causes the other.

Lesson Objectives

- To interpret Pearson's correlation coefficient as a measure of how closely points cluster about a line
- To explore the effects of influential points on the correlation coefficient
- To understand that correlation between two variables does not necessarily mean that one of the variables causes the other
- To understand that a set of points may not follow a linear model even if the correlation is strong, and that a linear model may be appropriate even if the correlation is weak

Unit 3

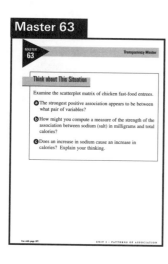

MASTER
63   Transparency Master

Think about This Situation

Examine the scatterplot matrix of chicken fast-food entrees.

ⓐ The strongest positive association appears to be between
what pair of variables?

ⓑ How might you compute a measure of the strength of the
association between sodium (salt) in milligrams and total
calories?

ⓒ Does an increase in sodium cause an increase in
calories? Explain your thinking.

Use with page 187.   UNIT 3 • PATTERNS OF ASSOCIATION

LAUNCH full-class discussion

The lesson may be launched by examination of the fast-food data shown in the table. Ask students whether they think there is an association between the various variables, and, if so, whether it is strong or weak and whether it is positive or negative.

Think About This Situation

See Teaching Master 63.

ⓐ Only calories and fat have an obviously strong positive (linear) association.

ⓑ The *sodium* and *calories* data each could be ranked and the correlation between ranks measured using Spearman's rank correlation coefficient from Lesson 1. Encourage students to offer other ideas.

ⓒ Since salt has no calories, an increase in salt cannot cause an increase in calories. However, it does seem that when the sodium level increases, the calories increase. The positive correlation is probably because both calories and sodium are strongly related to serving size. Generally, the larger the serving, the more sodium and calories it has. (Later in this lesson, students will learn that variables such as sandwich size are called lurking variables. Further, the appearance of a positive association in this case is due largely to the single point at the upper right. One rule of thumb is that if you think you see a strong linear association, but can change this impression by covering up only one or two points, then it's wise to delay judgment.)

A scatterplot matrix of these data is shown below.

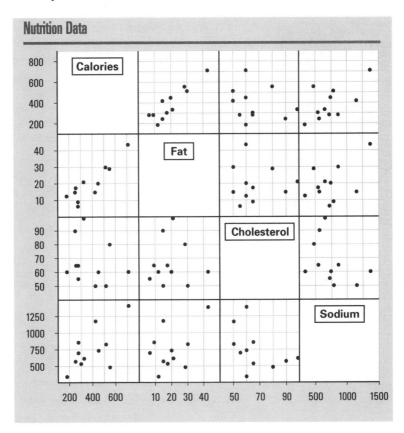

Nutrition Data

Think About This Situation

Examine the scatterplot matrix above of chicken fast-food entrees.

a The strongest positive association appears to be between what pair of variables?

b How might you compute a measure of the strength of the association between sodium (salt) in milligrams and total calories?

c Does an increase in sodium cause an increase in calories? Explain your thinking.

INVESTIGATION 1 Pearson's Correlation Coefficient

Karl Pearson

A formula for calculating a measure of linear association between pairs of values (x, y) that are ranked or unranked was developed by the British statistician Karl Pearson (1857–1936). The resulting correlation coefficient, called **Pearson's r**, can be interpreted in the same way as Spearman's correlation coefficient, r_s. The correlation coefficient indicates the direction (positive or negative) and strength (near 1 or −1 versus near 0) of the association between the two variables. Spearman's formula is a special case of Pearson's. For ranked data with no ties, Pearson's and Spearman's formulas give the same value.

1. Since Pearson's formula can be used with either ranked (with no ties) or unranked data, you might expect the formula to be more complex than Spearman's formula. You would be right! The formula for **Pearson's correlation coefficient r** is

$$r = \frac{\sum (x - \bar{x})(y - \bar{y})}{\sqrt{\sum(x - \bar{x})^2} \ \sqrt{\sum(y - \bar{y})^2}}$$

where $\bar{x}$ is the mean of the x values and $\bar{y}$ is the mean of the y values.

   a. With your group, examine the formula and then share your interpretations with the class. To use the formula:

   ■ Where would you begin?

   ■ How would you compute the numerator of the formula?

   ■ How would you compute the denominator?

   b. Now examine the plot shown at the right. What value of r would you expect for these data? Explain your reasoning.

   c. When using complex formulas, it is often helpful to organize intermediate calculations in a table.

   ■ Complete a copy of the following table.

   ■ Calculate r by substituting the appropriate sums in the formula. Compare your calculated value for r with your prediction in part b.

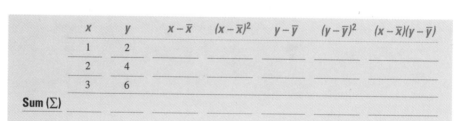

x	y	$x - \bar{x}$	$(x - \bar{x})^2$	$y - \bar{y}$	$(y - \bar{y})^2$	$(x - \bar{x})(y - \bar{y})$
1	2					
2	4					
3	6					
Sum ($\sum$)						

Master 64

INVESTIGATION 1 Pearson's Correlation Coefficient

In the first part of this investigation, students learn to use the formula for Pearson's correlation coefficient r, and then find it on their calculators or using computer software. The important ideas here are that another formula becomes necessary for unranked data, the new formula also measures differences and results in numbers between 1 and -1, and because this formula is so widely used, many calculators will calculate it.

1. The formula for Pearson's correlation coefficient can be daunting at first. Emphasize to students that they do not need to memorize this; rather, what they should concentrate on is making sense of the symbols. You may wish to ask questions such as the following ones. "In what way is this formula similar to Spearman's formula?" (Students may say that it involves adding some values in the numerator, as indicated by the Σ.) "In what ways is it different?" (Students may say that instead of a "difference^2" there is an expression with x's and y's, and instead of the number of rankings appearing in the denominator there is now another complicated expression.)

As you share interpretations with the class for part a, help students see that since the data are no longer ranked, the x and y variables will take a different range of values. The formula takes this into account by measuring how far x varies from the mean of all the x values and how far y varies from the mean of all the y values. Most students have seen this notation for the mean x value before, and they have measured the deviation from the mean when they calculated mean absolute deviation (MAD).

a. ■ The first thing that should be done is compute $\bar{x}$ and $\bar{y}$.
   ■ Subtract the mean from each value, multiply the paired differences, and then add the products.
   ■ Subtract $\bar{x}$ from each value of x, square the result, add these squares, and take the square root of the sum. Repeat for y and the values of y. Finally, multiply the two square roots.

b. The value of r should be 1 because the points all fall on a line with positive slope. While circulating among the groups, you may wish to connect students' results to their work in Lesson 1 by asking, "What correlation would we have expected from a graph with ranked data where the points are collinear?"

c. **See Teaching Master 64.**

■
x	y	$x - \bar{x}$	$(x - \bar{x})^2$	$y - \bar{y}$	$(y - \bar{y})^2$	$(x - \bar{x})(y - \bar{y})$
1	2	-1	1	-2	4	2
2	4	0	0	0	0	0
3	6	1	1	2	4	2
Sum 6	12	0	2	0	8	4

■ $r = \dfrac{4}{\sqrt{2}\sqrt{8}} = \dfrac{4}{\sqrt{16}} = \dfrac{4}{4} = 1$

Unit 3

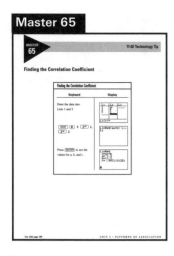
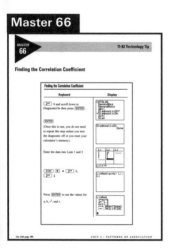
EXPLORE *continued*

2. a. About −0.9 would be a good estimate.

b. Again, see Teaching Master 64.

x	y	x − x̄	(x − x̄)²	y − ȳ	(y − ȳ)²	(x − x̄) (y − ȳ)
1	10	−3	9	4	16	−12
3	8	−1	1	2	4	−2
5	3	1	1	−3	9	−3
7	3	3	9	−3	9	−9
Sum	12	24	0	20	0	38	−26

$$r = \frac{-26,}{\sqrt{20}\ \sqrt{38}} \approx -0.943$$

c. Comparisons will vary according to the student's estimate.

3. See Teaching Masters 65 and 66 for Technology Tips.

a. Using a calculator, $r \approx -0.943$ which is what we got by using the formula.

b. The transformed points are (1.3, 4), (3.9, 3.2), (6.5, 1.2), and (9.1, 1.2). The correlation coefficient remains –0.943, the same as for the data before the transformations. This makes sense because if you look at the graph of the transformed points their relative positions haven't changed.

4. a. The points fall on a straight line. (See the diagram shown here.)

b. The correlation coefficient is 1.

c. When points fall on a line with positive slope, the correlation coefficient between the variables is 1.

d. Answers will vary. Students may discover that the correlation coefficient for points that lie on a line with negative slope is –1. The correlation for points that lie on a horizontal line is undefined, although some calculators (such as the TI-82) give a value of zero.

2. Now examine the scatterplot at the right. All coordinates of the plotted points are integers.

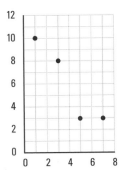

   a. Estimate the value of r.

   b. Compute the value of r by making a table like the one in activity 1.

   c. Compare your calculated value of r with your estimate in part a.

3. For most sets of real data, step-by-step calculation of Pearson's r is tedious and prone to error. In the remainder of this unit, you will calculate r using your graphing calculator or computer software.

   a. Use your calculator or computer software to verify the value of r that you computed in activity 2.

   b. Refer back to the data in activity 2. *Transform* the data using the following rule: $(x, y) \rightarrow (1.3x, 0.4y)$. Find r for the transformed values. What do you notice? Explain why your observation makes sense.

4. Jenny, Nicole, and Mike performed an experiment to determine how far a rubber band would stretch when different weights were attached to the end of the band. Shown below is their data set.

Rubber Band Length						
Weight (oz)	0	2	4	7	9	12
Length (cm)	3	4	5	6.5	7.5	9

   a. Produce a scatterplot of these data and describe the relation between weight and length of the rubber band.

   b. Calculate the correlation between weight and length of the rubber band.

   c. What conjecture can you make about the pattern of data and the correlation?

   d. Test your conjecture using another set of data. Choose the set from among the sets in this unit, or one you find or create yourself.

5. Examine each of the following plots.

   a. Match each correlation coefficient with the appropriate plot.

$$-0.4 \qquad 0.5 \qquad -0.8 \qquad 0.94$$

   b. Write a sentence that describes the association between the two variables in each plot.

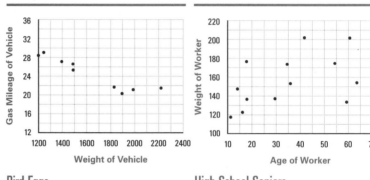

Vehicles

Office Workers

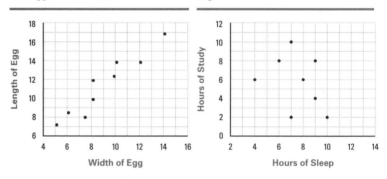

Bird Eggs

High School Seniors

Checkpoint

a Describe how to use Pearson's formula for a correlation coefficient.

b If the correlation coefficient is 1, what does that tell you about the points on the scatterplot? If the correlation coefficient is -1, what does that tell you?

c For what kinds of data is it appropriate to compute Pearson's correlation coefficient?

Be prepared to share your description and thinking with the class.

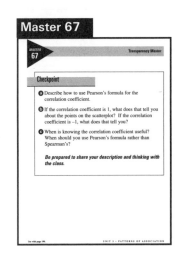

Master 67

5. a. −0.4:   (*hours of sleep, hours of study*)

     0.5:   (*age of worker, weight of worker*)

   −0.8:   (*weight of vehicle, gas mileage of vehicle*)

   0.94:   (*width of egg, length of egg*)

b. Student responses will vary. Examples might be as follows:

- Weight of vehicles has a strong negative correlation with gas mileage. The heavier the vehicle, the worse the gas mileage tends to be.
- There is a weak positive correlation between the age and weight of the office workers. The older the office worker, the more he or she tends to weigh.
- There is a strong positive correlation between the width and length of bird eggs. The wider the egg, the longer it tends to be.
- There is a weak negative correlation between the number of hours seniors sleep and the number of hours they study. Students who sleep more tend to study less.

SHARE AND SUMMARIZE   full-class discussion

Checkpoint

See Teaching Master 67.

ⓐ Students probably will describe how to make a table such as the one in activity 1 part c, since a table is the best way to keep the work organized.

ⓑ If the correlation coefficient is 1, the points fall on a straight line that has positive slope. If the correlation coefficient is −1, the points fall on a straight line that has negative slope.

ⓒ You should use Pearson's correlation coefficient when you want to measure the strength of the linear association between two variables. The variables may be ranked or unranked.

After students have reached agreement on the "Checkpoint" responses, and you are sure that everyone is able to attach a meaning to Pearson's correlation, you may want to revisit, if time allows, the whole idea of linear regression that students first saw when they studied linear models. To get students thinking, you may ask, "What is the calculator doing when it produces a line that is a good fit?" (Students may say that the line hits as many points as possible, or gets close to as many points as possible.) "What does the calculator do when finding a linear regression on paired data where at least one of the pairs does not seem to fit the linear pattern that the rest of the data shows?" (It finds a line to try to include the outlying point, but then the line does not fit the other points so well.)

To give everyone an opportunity to remember a prior skill and relate it to correlation coefficients, try this: Have student groups sketch a scatterplot of a data set and draw an estimation of the line of best fit. They should give their best guess for the correlation coefficient. Allow the groups to trade their work; each group should critique the estimates given by their partner group. Then they can use their calculators or computer software to find the line of best fit and correlation coefficient, and then compare those to the estimates.

▶On Your Own

a. Burger King's Fried Chicken Sandwich is the highest in both fat and calories. It is located in the upper right hand corner of the scatterplot.

b. The correlation appears to be about 0.8 or 0.9.

c. The correlation is about 0.89. As the fat content increases, items tend strongly to have more calories also (and vice versa).

▶ **On Your Own**

The following data about "lite" fast food came from a poster sponsored by *Health & Healing*.

Lite Fast Food

Fast-Food Restaurant	Food	Fat (gm)	Calories
McDonald's	McLean Deluxe Sandwich	10	320
	Fillet O'Fish	18	370
	McLean Deluxe and Fries	22	540
Burger King	Fettuccine Broiled Chicken	11	298
	Fried Chicken Sandwich	40	685
Wendy's	Chicken Sandwich	20	450
	Baked Potato, Broccoli & Cheese	24	550
	Taco Salad	23	530
KFC	Skinfree Crispy Breast	17	293
	Chicken Sandwich	27	482
Hardee's	Lean Deluxe & Small Fries	18	440
	Oat Bran Muffin	24	570

Source: *Health and Healing*

a. A plot of the data is at the right. Which item is highest in fat content? Where is this item on the plot?

b. Estimate the correlation coefficient for fat and calories from the plot.

c. Calculate the correlation coefficient. What does it tell you about the association between the amount of fat and calories in these fast-food items?

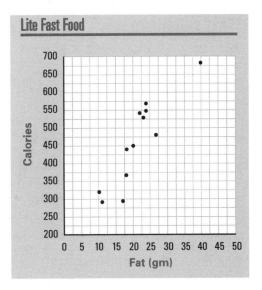

Lite Fast Food

Unit 3

6. In this activity you will explore possible connections between correlation coefficients and linear data patterns.

   a. Find the correlation coefficient for the following data. From your calculated value, would you expect the data to have a linear pattern?

x	0	8	1	7	3	6	5	4	2	−2	−1
y	0	65	2	50	8	35	25	15	4	3	1

   b. Produce the scatterplot on your calculator. Are the data linear?

   c. How well does $y = 0.97x^2 + 0.2x + 0.5$ model the data?

   d. Create another set of data that is highly correlated, but not modeled well by a line.

   e. Write a summary of what you can conclude from this activity.

7. At a local used car lot, Marta examined several cars, all her favorite model. They had similar options, such as air conditioning and a radio, but were manufactured in different years. To help her decide which car to buy, Marta noted their ages and prices, and then she also noted how many scratches were on each car. The following scatterplots show her results.

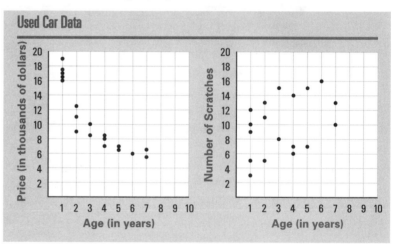

Used Car Data

   a. Estimate the value of the correlation coefficient for each of the scatterplots above.

   b. What kind of equation would best model each set of data?

   c. The correlation coefficient tells you how closely a set of points cluster about a line. For the (*age*, *price*) data, the correlation coefficient is −0.880. For the (*age*, *scratches*) data, the correlation is 0.390. Does a high correlation mean that the points cluster more closely about a linear function than about any other function? Does a low correlation mean that a linear function isn't the most appropriate model for the data? Explain.

On page T190, following the Checkpoint, are some ideas for launching the rest of this investigation. That discussion and activity sets the stage for the main event in the next few activities, where students find out that the value of *r* should be interpreted cautiously. They see that data can have a very strong association that is not linear, and therefore may have a low *r* value; they also see that a single point can have a large influence on the correlation coefficient and regression equation. As you circulate among groups working on these activities, you can help the students relate the graph to the value of *r* by asking questions such as, "What did the value of *r* lead you to expect? Is this justified by the graph?"

6. **a.** $r \approx 0.90$

Most students will say at this point that this indicates the data are linear.

    b. It is clear that the relationship is not a linear one.

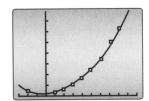

WINDOW	FORMAT
Xmin	=−3
Xmax	=10
Xscl	=1
Ymin	=0
Ymax	=75
Yscl	=10

    c. The equation $y = 0.97x^2 + 0.2x + 0.5$ models the data very well, as may be seen on the above graph.

    d. Responses will vary. For example, the points in the following table all lie on the graph of $y = x^2 - 1$ and thus are not modeled well by a line. (The residuals have a distinct pattern.) However, for this data set, Pearson's $r = 0.98$.

x	1	2	3	4	5	6
y	0	3	8	15	24	32

    e. Given a high value of *r*, it might appear at first that the data could be modeled well with a line. But as we have seen, the relationship may actually be quadratic or some other nonlinear function. A high correlation does not necessarily indicate that a linear relationship is the best model to use.

7. **a.** The correlation coefficients for the two plots are about −0.9 for the (*age, price*) data and about 0.4 for the (*age, scratches*) data.

    b. The (*age, price*) data is modeled well by the equation $y = \frac{15000}{x} + 4000$. Students should realize this is not a linear function, although they may believe it is exponential. In Unit 4, "Power Models", students will explore inverse power models. At that time you may wish to return to these data to encourage students to view this as a translation of the inverse power model $y = \frac{a}{x}$. The (*age, scratches*) data is best modeled by a linear function.

    c. These examples should show students that a high correlation does not necessarily mean a linear function is the best type of equation to model the data. Although the points cluster somewhat closely to a line, there is a pronounced curve that indicates a nonlinear equation might be more appropriate. Similarly, a low correlation does not necessarily mean that a linear function is *not* the best type of equation to use. Although the points do not cluster closely about a line, the general pattern in the data is linear.

8. a. The correlation coefficient is approximately 0.5, not especially strong.

   b. No, a linear model is a good one for these data. Even though there would be a lot of error in predicting the son's height from that of the father, the cloud of points definitely follows a linear trend.

9. a. $r \approx 0.644$, which indicates a fairly strong, positive correlation.

   b. The data point (1400, 710), representing Burger King's Chicken Sandwich, is an influential point. Without this point, $r \approx 0.318$, which is quite a bit smaller than the correlation coefficient with this point.

   c. Burger King's Chicken Sandwich is also an influential point in the (*fat, sodium*) data. The correlation coefficient for (*fat, sodium*) with the Chicken Sandwich is 0.446 and without it is -0.111.

10. a. There does not appear to be much of an association between amount of fiber and number of calories in a serving of cereal. The data point (1, 50), Puffed Wheat, is an influential point. It has far fewer calories than the other cereals but its amount of fiber isn't unusual. We would expect the correlation to be closer to zero with Puffed Wheat included than if it weren't.

   b. Since the scatterplot looks as though it could be modeled with a line with negative slope, the data have a weak negative association. Therefore a good guess is -0.2.

Unit 3

8. The scatterplot at the right shows the heights of 1078 fathers and their sons. The data were collected by Karl Pearson around 1900.

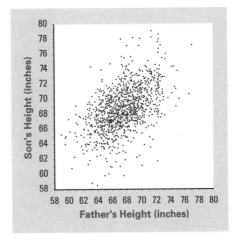

a. Make an estimate of the correlation coefficient. Would you say this is a strong correlation?

b. Does this correlation coefficient mean that a linear model is not appropriate for these data? Explain your reasoning.

9. Refer to the table and scatterplot matrix for fast-food chicken items at the beginning of this lesson (pages 186 and 187).

a. What is the correlation coefficient between amount of sodium and calories?

b. An **influential point** is a point that strongly influences the value of the correlation coefficient. That is, if the point is removed from the data set, the value of the correlation coefficient changes quite a bit. (The definition of "quite a bit" depends on the specific situation.) Are there any influential points in the (*sodium, calories*) data set? Explain.

c. Examine the other scatterplots in the scatterplot matrix of the fast-food chicken data. Which of these plots contain an influential point?

10. A plot of the relation between the amount of fiber and the number of calories in a serving of various kinds of cereal is shown at the right. A number by a point indicates how many cereals that point represents.

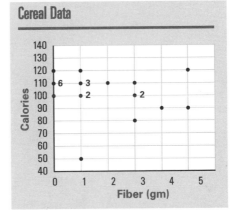

a. Describe the relationship between the grams of fiber and the calories in a serving of cereal. Include any observations about influential points.

b. Which of the following seems likely to be the correlation coefficient?

    −0.8   −0.2   0.5   0.9

c. Use the following data to calculate the correlation coefficient. Compare the calculated value with what you predicted in part b.

d. Calculate the correlation coefficient without Puffed Wheat. Explain what happened.

Cereal Nutrition Information

Cereal	Calories	Fiber (gm)	Cereal	Calories	Fiber (gm)
Apple Jacks	110	1	Honey Graham Oh's	120	1
Bran Chex	90	4	Kix	110	0
Bran Flakes	90	5	Lucky Charms	110	0
Cap'n Crunch	120	0	Product 19	100	1
Cheerios	110	2	Puffed Wheat	50	1
Cocoa Puffs	110	0	Raisin Bran	120	5
Corn Flakes	100	1	Rice Krispies	110	0
Froot Loops	110	1	Shredded Wheat	80	3
Golden Crisp	100	0	Smacks	110	1
Golden Grahams	110	0	Trix	110	0
Grape Nuts Flakes	100	3	Wheaties	100	3
Grape Nuts	110	3			

Source: The Data and Story Library. *http://lib.stat.cmu.edu/DASL/*

Checkpoint

a Explain why it is important to examine a scatterplot of a set of data even though you have found the correlation coefficient.

b For each of the plots below, identify and describe the effect of the influential point on the correlation coefficient.

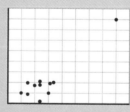 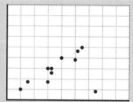

c Does a high correlation indicate a linear relationship? Does a low correlation indicate that the relationship is not linear?

Be prepared to defend your views to your classmates.

c. The correlation coefficient is approximately −0.220.

d. The correlation without Puffed Wheat is −0.424. Puffed Wheat is an influential point. Taking the outlier Puffed Wheat out of the data set yields a scatterplot that is slightly more linear.

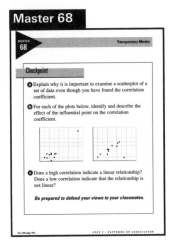

SHARE AND SUMMARIZE full-class discussion

Checkpoint

See Teaching Master 68.

a Scatterplots should be examined carefully for linearity. A high correlation does not mean the data necessarily follow a linear model. A low correlation does not mean the basic model can't be linear. We also need to look at a scatterplot to make sure an influential point is not affecting the correlation.

b In the plot on the left, the outlier seems to "pull" the cloud of data points into a vaguely linear shape, strengthening the correlation.

In the plot on the right, the outlier makes an otherwise linear scatterplot look less linear and weakens the correlation.

c No, a set of points can have a high correlation, but follow a curved line. Similarly, a low correlation tells us nothing about whether or not the data follow a linear model.

CONSTRUCTING A MATH TOOLKIT: Students should draw scatterplots which illustrate Pearson's correlation coefficient, effects of influential points, and how to determine when a linear model is appropriate for a set of data. Students may wish to refer to examples from Investigation 1.

Unit 3

▶On Your Own

Sometimes a student will replace an "NA" entry with a zero when considering the questions posed. The NA means either not applicable to that university or not available for that university. In either case, substituting a zero value is misleading.

You may want to point out to your students that we cannot take inferences from such small data sets too far. The conclusions they will be tempted to draw may not be correct for all universities beyond our sample.

a.   There appears to be some positive correlation between average entrance scores for football players and for all students at these universities.

▶On Your Own

Shown below are average SAT and ACT scores of entering students at the Big Ten universities.

Big Ten Average Scores

School	Football Players' SAT	All Students' SAT	Football Players' ACT	All Students' ACT
Illinois	872	1140	21	27
Indiana	841	1007	21	24
Iowa	814	NA	21	24
Michigan	826	1190	20	27
Michigan State	788	998	19	23
Minnesota	838	1050	21	24
Northwestern	1034	1250	23	28
Ohio State	820	986	20	23
Penn State	897	1083	20	NA
Purdue	881	1009	20	24
Wisconsin	825	1090	22	26

Copyright 1993, *USA Today*. Reprinted with permission.

a. Does there appear to be any connection between the average scores for football players and the average scores for all students at these universities?

A correlation matrix for these data appears below. A scatterplot matrix is shown on the following page.

	Football Players' SAT	All SAT	Football Players' ACT	All ACT
Football Players' SAT	1.0000	0.6740	0.7375	0.6340
All SAT	0.6740	1.0000	0.6259	0.9642
Football Players' ACT	0.7375	0.6259	1.0000	0.6689
All ACT	0.6340	0.9642	0.6689	1.0000

Unit 3

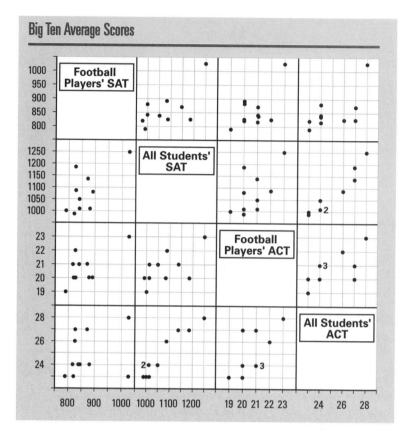

Big Ten Average Scores

b. Examine the scatterplot of (*football players' SAT*, *all SAT*) data for the schools with complete data. Explain how the influential point affects the correlation coefficient.

c. Which association is stronger between football players and all students: ACT scores or SAT scores? List two ways that you could decide.

d. Find a pair of variables data with a correlation between 0.6 and 0.75 that does *not* seem to follow a linear model. Find a pair of variables with a correlation between 0.6 and 0.75 that *does* seem to follow a linear model.

b. Northwestern, in the upper right-hand corner of the scatterplot, is the influential point. It will make the correlation much stronger than it would be otherwise. In fact, the correlation with Northwestern is approximately 0.665 and the correlation without Northwestern is approximately 0.215.

c. The first way is to check the correlation matrix. The correlation is slightly larger between SAT scores than between ACT scores, but, as we saw, that is due to Northwestern. If we check only the correlation matrix, we lose the important fact that Northwestern is an influential point. We also should compare the scatterplots (*football players' SAT, all SAT*) and (*football players' ACT, all ACT*) in the scatterplot matrix. In spite of the fact that it has a slightly smaller correlation, the linear trend looks stronger for (*football players' ACT, all ACT*).

d. ■ None of the pairs (*football players' SAT, all SAT*), (*football players' SAT, football players' ACT*), nor (*football players' SAT, all ACT*) seem to follow a linear model.

   ■ The plot of (*football players' ACT, all ACT*) seems to follow a linear model.

MORE

ASSIGNMENT   *pp. 200–211*

Students now can begin Modeling tasks 1 or 4; Organizing tasks 1, 3, 4, or 5; Reflecting task 2; or Extending task 1 from the MORE assignment following Investigation 2.

Unit 3

INVESTIGATION 2 Association and Causation

In this investigation students explore what factors might cause an association to occur. Students may find it difficult to understand that if there is a high correlation, it does not mean that one of the variables causes the other. Remind students about the initial activity in the unit when they found the rank correlation between two people's music preference. Even though there was a strong correlation between some partners, there probably was no direct cause-and-effect relation involved at all. However, there probably were hidden or lurking variables that account some-what for the high correlation. For example, all of the students are about the same age and so are more likely to prefer music identified with teenagers than, say, classical music.

The activities in this investigation ask students to think about many different contexts. As you circulate among the groups you may hear some common misconceptions that students have, as well as some sophisticated thinking. They can reasonably hypothesize about the nature of the relationship between the variables, but a definitive conclusion about cause-and-effect can come only from a well-designed experiment. Encourage students to explain their thinking clearly to each other and to follow up on disagreements. When you hear students disagree about a relationship, you might mention that the issue of whether a cause is present is an issue that absorbs researchers, instead of taking one position or another. Ask them how they could design an experiment in such a way that no one could dispute that a causal relationship is or is not present. The link between tobacco smoking and lung cancer has been extensively researched from many different viewpoints. You might suggest this as an extra credit report to interested students. (See a similar task in Reflecting task 4 on page 207.)

Throughout this lesson and the ones that follow, it will help students see the importance of this topic if they are on the lookout for articles and claims about correlation or causation. Students can bring such articles or claims to class, and the class can discuss how the authors might have reached their conclusions and whether there really is a cause-and-effect relationship.

1. The last sentence says "The new study … suggests that a … rise in the unemployment rate lowers the total death rate …"

   a. Students may feel the link is justified, others may feel there is no real relationship at all. While there are issues such as job-related stress and injuries, as well as traffic fatalities as people travel to and from work, these may be balanced by other issues, such as the stress of finding the means to live from day to day.

   b. It is possible that a lurking variable might explain the relationship. For example, a slow economy causes both unemployment and higher prices; many people may choose their food more carefully, fixing their lunches themselves (which saves money) instead of buying less healthy fast-food or deli sandwiches. Higher gas prices also may encourage people to drive less, or more slowly, to conserve gas; this may result in fewer traffic accidents as well as less air pollution. It is also possible that there is no link. For example, as the population has been rising over the years and more people are entering the work force, medical advances in the past few decades are prolonging lives for many Americans.

Unit 3

INVESTIGATION 2 Association and Causation

Reports in the media often suggest that research has found a cause-and-effect relationship between two variables. Read the article reproduced below.

> ## Study Links Job Loss, Longer Life
>
> As the economy enters another year of expansion and low unemployment, new research suggests that loss of a job may actually contribute to a healthier, longer life for at least some Americans. Christopher Ruhm, a professor of eco- nomics at the University of North Carolina at Greensboro, has concluded in a study that higher unem- ployment may lead to lower overall mortality rates and reduce fatalities from sever- al major causes of death. The new study, which looks at state-level data compiled between 1972 and 1992, suggests that a 1 percentage point rise in the unemploy- ment rate lowers the total death rate by 0.5 percent.
>
> *San Diego Union-Tribune*, January 27, 1997.

Reprinted by permission of Reuters.

1. Find a sentence in the above article that claims that unemployment allows people to live longer.

   a. Do you think there is a cause-and-effect relationship between unemploy- ment and longer life? Why or why not?

   b. A **lurking variable** is a variable that lurks in the background and affects both of the original variables. Do you think a lurking variable might explain the relationship between higher unemployment rates and longer lifespans?

For people in the United States, there is a high correlation between number of years of schooling S and total lifetime earnings E. One theory is that the corre- lation is high because jobs that pay well tend to require many years of schooling. This theory can be modeled by the directed graph below. The graph illustrates the idea that more years of schooling qualifies a person for better-paying jobs, and so more schooling directly causes total lifetime earnings to increase.

But some people have suggested that there is a lurking variable P, which is the economic status of the person's parents. That is, a person whose parents have more money tends to have the opportunities to earn more money. He or she also tends to go to school longer. The directed graph at the right models this theory.

2. The correlation for each pair of variables below is strong. Identify the most likely reason for the large correlation, which might be a lurking variable in some cases. Then draw a directed graph to indicate the cause-and-effect relationship between the two variables, or among the three variables (if there is a lurking variable).

a. Calories burned by a person and the number of hours of exercise

b. The U.S. national deficit and cancer rates over the years

c. Age of a car this year and its value

d. Student's test score in mathematics and the number of hours studied

e. Reading ability of a child and his or her shoe size

f. Number of people attending a concert and ticket income

3. Read each of the following two newspaper articles and then answer these questions:

a. What variables are said to be correlated in each article?

b. Determine if there is a cause-and-effect relationship assumed by each author, and if so, do you think it is a reasonable assumption? Why or why not?

Schooling Pays Off on Payday

Workers earn more from their investment in education than had been thought, a new study says. Students can increase their future income by an average of 16% for each year they stay in school, the study reports. Researchers Alan Krueger and Orley Ashenfelter, both of Princeton, based their estimate on interviews with 250 sets of twins. They correlated differences in wages and years of schooling within sets of twins.

Source: Todd Wallack, *USA Today*, September 1993.

Study Finds Waist-Hip Ratio Is a Useful Index of Health

People who want to know how risky it is to carry extra pounds should compare waist circumference to that of the hips, a study suggests. The bigger the waist in comparison with the hips, they found, the higher the risk of death, regardless of the weight of the people in the study. In the study, researchers found that an increase of 0.15 in the waist-hip ratio—for example, a 6-inch increase in waist size for a woman with 40-inch hips—increased the risk of death by 60 percent. [The researcher says the ratio should be less than 0.8 for women and less than 0.95 for men.]

New York Times, January 27, 1993. Reprinted by permission of AP.

2. a. Exercise causes calories to be burned.

$$E \bullet \longrightarrow \bullet\, C$$

b. Although the national deficit and cancer rates are both increasing, students may indicate no cause-and-effect relation whatsoever between the two. In this case a digraph is not a good model for their relationship. Some students may suggest that the lurking variable is time. As we become more "modernized" over the years, both cancer rates and the national deficit increase.

c. As a car's age increases, the value of the car will decrease.

$$A \bullet \longrightarrow \bullet\, V$$

d. Usually, the more studies, the better his or her tests scores will be.

$$S \bullet \longrightarrow \bullet\, T$$

e. The lurking variable is age. A child's reading ability and shoe size both increase with age.

f. The number of people attending a concert directly corresponds to the number of gate receipts.

$$P \bullet \longrightarrow \triangleright \bullet\, R$$

3. a. According to the first article, researchers found a positive correlation for (*schooling, wage*). The more schooling a worker had, the higher the wages earned.

The researchers, mentioned in the second article, found a positive correlation between the ratio $\frac{\text{waist circumference}}{\text{hip circumference}}$ and risk of death.

b. The headline of the first article states a cause-and-effect relationship between schooling and pay. It is reasonable to assume that schooling does have some causal role in how much money people earn. The higher-paying jobs usually require more education and skills. (Note: This might be a time to discuss the relatively large sample size and the choice of twins for the study. Also, to circumvent the lurking parental economic status, the twins chosen probably grew up in the same household and were not separated.)

The author in the first sentence of the second article assumes that location of extra weight causes an increased risk of death. Responses will vary as to whether this assumption is reasonable.

Unit 3

EXPLORE *continued*

4. a. Cause-and-Effect Relationships

Variable Pair	Explanatory Variable
calories burned, hours of exercise	hours of exercise
age of car, car's value	age of car
test score, hours of study	hours of study
number of attendees, ticket income	number of attendees

b. When a scatterplot is made, the explanatory variable should go on the horizontal or
x-axis.

SHARE AND SUMMARIZE full-class discussion

Checkpoint

See Teaching Master 69.

ⓐ Lurking variables of time and age are likely in parts b and e, respectively. The remaining situations all seem to have causal relationships.

ⓑ **Correlation Category**   **Directed Graph**
another lurking variable causes each
of the two to change

one variable causes the other to change
purely coincidental   not modeled well by
                                                 a directed graph
                                                 or

ⓒ There is only one tried-and-true way to tell whether a nonzero correlation means that
there is a cause-and-effect relationship between two variables: run an experiment. Such
an experiment should be controlled and randomized. "Controlled" means that, for example, to determine if studying increases test scores, there should be a group that studies
and a control group that doesn't. "Randomized" means that whether a person goes into
the studying group or the control group is determined by chance.

If two variables are related in such a way that a change in one variable tends to cause a change in the other variable, the relationship is said to be a **cause-and-effect relationship**. In activity 2, you modeled cause-and-effect relationships by directed graphs. The **explanatory** (or **independent**) **variable** is the one that causes a change in the **response** (or **dependent**) **variable**.

4. a. Refer back to the pairs of variables in activity 2. Identify the pairs that seem to have a cause-and-effect relationship. For each pair, identify the explanatory variable.

   b. When you make a scatterplot, on which axis should you put the explanatory variable?

Checkpoint

There are several reasons why two variables may be correlated, including the following.

- The two variables have a cause-and-effect relationship. That is, an increase in the value of one variable tends to cause an increase (or decrease) in the value of the other variable.

- The two variables have nothing directly to do with each other, however an increase in the value of a third (lurking) variable tends to cause the values of each of the two variables to increase together, to decrease together, or one to increase and the other to decrease.

- Even though the correlation between the two variables is actually zero or close to zero, you get a non-zero correlation just by chance when you take a sample of values.

a Look back at activity 2. Which situations seem to fit each category above?

b What type of directed graph best models each category above?

c How can you be certain whether a nonzero correlation coefficient means that there is a cause-and-effect relationship between two variables?

Be prepared to share your responses with the entire class.

▶On Your Own

a. Describe a situation involving two variables for which the correlation is strong, but there is no cause-and-effect relationship.

b. Describe a situation involving two variables for which the correlation is strong, and where a change in one variable causes a change in the other variable.

c. By listening to your family and friends or reading the newspaper, bring an example to class where someone said that there is a cause-and-effect relationship between two variables. For example, if someone says, "It's sure humid today, no wonder I feel wiped out," they probably believe that the more humid it is, the more tired they feel. Do you agree with your family member's or friend's reasoning? Why or why not?

MORE
Modeling • Organizing • Reflecting • Extending

Modeling

1. Seals live in the water and are thought to have adapted themselves from being on the land millions of years ago. The average length and weight of five different kinds of seals are given below.

Seal Sizes

Seals	Length	Weight
Ribbon Seal	4.8 ft.	176 lbs.
Bearded Seal	7.0 ft.	660 lbs.
Hooded Seal	8.0 ft.	880 lbs.
Common Seal	5.2 ft.	220 lbs.
Baikal Seal	4.2 ft.	187 lbs.

Source: *Grzimek's Encyclopedia, Mammals v4*. New York: McGraw-Hill, 1990.

a. Produce a scatterplot of the data in the table, and then estimate the correlation you would expect between the length and weight of the seals.

b. Calculate the correlation coefficient. How does the calculated value match your expectations?

c. If you include the Northern Elephant seal at 14.4 feet long and 5500 pounds, how do you think the correlation coefficient will be affected? Check your conjecture.

▶ **On Your Own**

a. Student responses will vary. Some possible examples are the relation between tests in different courses (the lurking variable is the student's ability and study habits), or the number of CDs a person has and the number of hours spent listening to them (the lurking variable is the student's interest in music).

b. Student responses will vary. One variable might directly cause the other in situations such as the number of hours spent practicing free throws and a free throw shooting average, or the number of people who eat in your house and the amount of money spent on food.

c. Responses will vary. Many students will bring in examples of categorical variables. For example, "men are taller than women" as an example of gender correlating to height. Accept these, but point out to students that we are dealing in this unit with numerical variables. That is, variables you can plot on a scatterplot. (Male/female is generally considered to be a categorical variable.)

MORE   independent assignment

Modeling

1. a. The estimates should indicate a strong positive correlation. See the scatterplot below.
b. $r \approx 0.981$
c. The elephant seal data does not lie on the line that the other points cluster around (see part d) so we might suspect that the correlation will be smaller. On the other hand, we have seen that an influential point such as the data for the elephant seal can often increase the correlation. In fact, the new value of r is 0.968; not as much lower as you might expect.

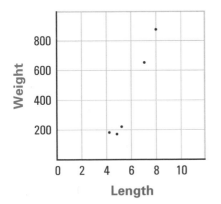

MORE
ASSIGNMENT   *pp. 200–211*

Modeling: Choice of two*
Organizing: 1 and choice of one*
Reflecting: 2 and 1 or 4*
Extending: 1

When choice is indicated, it is important to leave the choice to the student.
NOTE: *It is best if Organizing tasks are discussed as a whole class after they have been assigned as homework.*

Unit 3

   d. See the scatterplot below. A line is a good model for these data if the Northern
   Elephant seal is not included. If it is included, a curve such as a cubic equation would
   be a better fit.

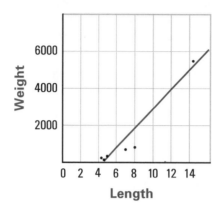

   e. Yes, as most things grow longer or taller, they also gain weight.

d. Do you think a line is a good model of the data? Why or why not?

e. Do you think that there is a cause-and-effect relationship between length and weight of seals? Explain your response.

2. The following table gives the percentage of women, men, teens, and children who watched America's favorite prime-time network television programs in 1992–93 according to Nielsen Media Research.

Television Program Audience

Rank	Program	% Women	% Men	% Teens	% Children
1	60 Minutes	16.5	16.1	2.8	2.9
2	Roseanne	15.3	10.6	15.3	12.2
3	Home Improvement	14.1	12.0	13.4	11.8
4	Murphy Brown	14.7	9.6	6.6	4.9
5	Murder She Wrote	16.0	10.1	2.6	2.4
6	Coach	13.1	10.7	10.4	8.4
7	NFL Monday Nite Football	7.6	15.3	7.5	4.1
8	CBS Sunday Movie	14.3	8.4	3.9	2.6
9	Cheers	11.6	10.4	7.0	5.1
10	Full House	10.7	6.4	13.0	16.9
11	Northern Exposure	11.8	9.0	3.9	2.0
12	Rescue 911	11.7	9.2	6.4	7.2
12	20/20	11.6	9.0	4.6	4.8
14	CBS Tuesday Movie	11.8	8.3	5.9	4.2
15	Love and War	11.9	7.7	4.5	3.1
16	Prince of Bel Air	9.5	6.6	17.1	12.4
16	Hangin' With Mr. Cooper	9.9	6.1	13.2	14.0
16	Jackie Thomas Show	10.5	7.8	10.3	7.0
19	Evening Shade	12.4	8.2	3.6	3.7
20	Hearts Afire	12.1	7.7	3.8	3.6
20	Unsolved Mysteries	11.2	8.8	4.7	4.5
22	Prime TIME Live	10.7	9.1	2.5	1.6
23	NBC Monday Nite Movie	11.2	6.4	7.6	4.6
24	Dr. Quinn Medicine Woman	12.3	8.0	5.3	5.0
25	Seinfeld	9.9	8.7	5.0	3.2
26	Blossom	8.7	5.6	17.1	11.5
26	48 Hours	10.2	8.4	3.0	2.0
28	ABC Sunday Night Movie	10.2	8.2	6.9	4.9
29	Matlock	11.6	7.8	2.5	2.2
30	Simpsons	6.3	7.2	15.5	16.2
30	Wings	9.5	8.1	5.3	4.0

Source: *The World Almanac and Book of Facts 1994.* Mahwah, NJ: World Almanac, 1993.

Unit 3

LESSON 2 • CORRELATION   **201**

a. Examine the scatterplot matrix below. What can you say about the program that is highlighted (indicated by the open circle in each plot)? Which program is this?

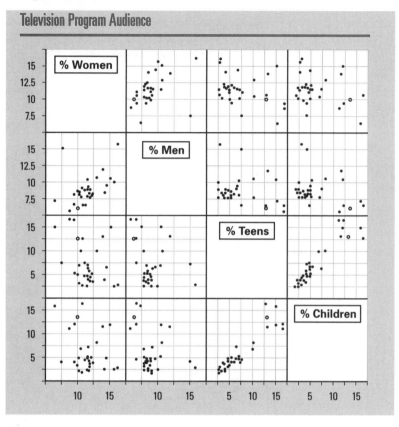

b. Now examine this correlation matrix for the audience data. What is the correlation between percentage of men and percentage of women viewers?

	% Women	% Men	% Teens	% Children
% Women	1.0000	0.4167	−0.3276	−0.2868
% Men	0.4167	1.0000	−0.2508	−0.2790
% Teens	−0.3276	−0.2508	1.0000	0.9204
% Children	−0.2868	−0.2790	0.9204	1.0000

■ Two points on the scatterplot of (*percentage men, percentage women*) are influential. Which programs are represented by these points?

■ Which influential point do you think affects the correlation the most? Test your conjecture by eliminating the points one at a time and recalculating the correlation.

2. a. A relatively large percentage of both teens and children watch this show. It is one of the least popular shows among women and is even less popular among men. The show is *Hangin' With Mr. Cooper.*

b. $r = 0.4167$

■ The influential points are *Monday Night Football*, which is much more popular with men than with women, and *60 Minutes*, which is most popular with both groups.

■ The influential point will make the correlation smaller or larger than it would be otherwise. The correlation without *Monday Night Football* is 0.72, a big increase from 0.42. The correlation without *60 Minutes* is 0.25. Clearly, *Monday Night Football* affects the correlation more.

Unit 3

    c. Teens and children seem to be most alike in the programs they watch, $r \approx 0.92$. This might surprise your students.

    d. Answers here will vary! The strong correlation between the viewing habits of children and teens could be the result of the fact each group watches earlier in the evening, younger children try to copy the older ones, younger ones have control of the television, *etc.*

    e. The negative sign means that if a large percentage of one group watches a program, we would expect a small percentage of the other group to watch that program.

3. a. Glendale spends the most per person on police, $222.25, yet their suburban crime rate is the highest at 74.39 per 1,000 residents. Students may mention other communities that are at the top of the cloud of points, such as West Allis. Of course, it may be the case that if those communities didn't spend so much, the crime rates might be higher.

c. Which two groups of people are most alike in the programs they watch?

d. Discuss the viewing habits of children and teens in terms of possible types of cause-and-effect relationships.

e. Write a sentence that explains what the negative sign means in front of several of the correlation coefficients.

3. The following appeared in a suburban Milwaukee newspaper article.

Spending More On Police Doesn't Reduce Crime

A CNI study of crime statistics and police department budgets over the last four years reveals there really is no correlation between what a community spends on law enforcement and its crime rate. In fact some of the suburbs that increased spending the most over the last four years also have seen the highest increases in crime during that period. And some communities that spent the least on law enforcement witnessed the slowest growth in crime during that time.

Hub, November 4, 1993.

Reprinted courtesy of CNI newspapers.

a. Using the data below and the scatterplot on the next page, find a community that spends a lot on police and doesn't have a low crime rate.

Law Enforcement and Crime Rate

Community	Per Capita Spending on Police	Suburban Crime Rate per 1,000 Residents
Glendale	$222.25	74.39
West Allis	164.47	50.43
Greendale	123.43	50.25
Greenfield	143.59	48.68
Wauwatosa	150.34	48.52
South Milwaukee	110.64	43.20
Brookfield	131.42	42.16
Cudahy	137.12	41.47
St. Francis	144.84	41.32
Shorewood	156.39	40.84
Oak Creek	160.41	40.84
Brown Deer	150.57	37.09
Germantown	125.86	31.16
Menomonee Falls	159.28	29.73
Hales Corners	155.40	27.04
New Berlin	125.33	25.45
Franklin	94.92	23.09
Elm Grove	191.64	21.86
Whitefish Bay	120.34	21.28
Muskego	105.35	17.00
Fox Point	132.85	15.07
Mequon	136.39	11.31

Source: *Hub*, November 4, 1993.

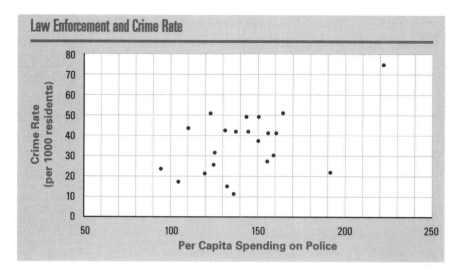

Law Enforcement and Crime Rate

b. Calculate the correlation coefficient between per capita spending on police and suburban crime rate.

c. Do the correlation coefficient and scatterplot support the newspaper's conclusion?

d. Do you think that there is a cause-and-effect relationship between per capita spending and crime rate? Explain your thinking.

4. The College Board reports statistics about the students who take the SAT. Among the information given is student-provided data about family income. Use the data below to investigate the correlation between income and SAT scores and write a summary of what you found. (Find some way to describe the income by a single number.) Give reasons for your conclusions.

Family Income	Percent Taking Test	SAT Verbal Mean	SAT Math Mean
Less than $10,000	4	429	444
$10,000–$20,000	8	456	464
$20,000–$30,000	10	482	482
$30,000–$40,000	12	497	495
$40,000–$50,000	10	509	507
$50,000–$60,000	9	517	517
$60,000–$70,000	7	524	525
$70,000–$80,000	6	531	533
$80,000–$100,000	7	541	544
$100,000 or more	9	560	569

Source: College Board Online. *The SAT Summary Reporting Service.* The College Board, 1997.
http://www.collegeboard.org/

3. b. $r = 0.50$

    c. The correlation is a moderate 0.50. When Glendale, an influential point, is excluded, the correlation drops to 0.20. Even so, the newspaper's statement that "there really is no correlation" doesn't seem reasonable. In fact, the more a community spends, the more crime there tends to be. If there is a cause-and-effect relationship, however, it is probably that more crime results in more spending on police. The newspaper's headline can't be evaluated from these data. For example, if Glendale spent even more, its crime rate might go down.

    d. Student responses will vary. Look for good explanations. (Even experts don't seem to agree on this one.)

4. Students should include plots to support their conclusions. Before they can work with the data they will have to find some way to organize the information about income. One method is to use the midpoint of each interval and assume some reasonable average amount for those over $100,000. Another method is to use the upper and lower bound for each interval and look at a band rather than a point. Allow students the opportunity to discover their own method. Using the upper bounds (and 120,000 for the upper income bracket), the correlation coefficient for (*income, math*) is 0.982 and for (*income, verbal*) is 0.951. Both the plots and the numbers indicate a correlation between income and SAT scores; the higher the income, the higher the scores. The correlation between income and the percent taking the test is 0.019 which is not strong; the plot reveals the relationship is not linear. It is not necessarily true that the more income a family earns, a larger percent of students from those families will take the SAT.

    You may want to mention the fact that the SAT scores given are averages (means) for each income level and so do not reflect the variability that exists among individuals in each income level. There are many students with high SAT scores who come from families with low incomes. There are also students with low SAT scores who come from families with high incomes.

	Family Income	% Taking Test	SAT Verbal Mean	SAT Math Mean
Family Income	1.000	0.236	0.149	0.019
% Taking Test	0.236	1.000	0.991	0.951
SAT Verbal Mean	0.149	0.991	1.000	0.982
SAT Math Mean	0.019	0.951	0.982	1.000

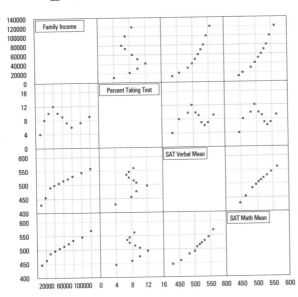

Organizing

1. Student responses will vary. Examples are given.
   a. (1, 0), (2, 5), (3, 10), (4, 15), (5, 20); $r = 1.0$
   b. (1, 10), (2, 0), (3, 20), (4, 15), (5, 5); $r = 0.1$
   c. (1, 20), (2, 0), (3, 10), (4, 5), (5, 15); $r = -0.1$
   d. (1, 20), (2, 15), (3, 10), (4, 5), (5, 0); $r = -1.0$

2. a. As time increases, the height increases, reaches a maximum, then decreases. The points do not follow a linear model.

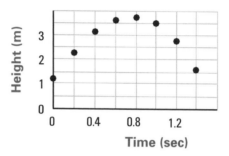

   b. $r \approx 0.19$
   c. The correlation coefficient only indicates the degree to which points cluster about a line; it gives no indication of the degree to which they follow another relationship.
   d. The height of the ball is not caused by the time that has elapsed. We wouldn't refer to this as a cause-and-effect relationship.

3. a.

x	1	2	7	10	15
y	3	6	21	30	45

   b. The regression line for ranked data with a correlation of 1 has slope of 1. The slope for unranked data may be any positive number. For ranked data with a correlation of 1, a change of 1 in a ranking corresponds to a change of 1 in the other ranking, so the slope is $\frac{1}{1}$ or 1. For unranked data, a change of 1 in a variable may be associated with a change of any positive amount in the other.

4. Yes it does. In the denominator there is a sum of squared differences from the mean $\bar{x}$, $\Sigma(x - \bar{x})^2$, and from the mean $\bar{y}$, $\Sigma(y - \bar{y})^2$.

Organizing

1. Let *A* be the set of numbers 1, 2, 3, 4, and 5. Let *B* be the set of numbers 0, 5, 10, 15, and 20. Create a set of ordered pairs, using the numbers in set *A* as the first coordinates and the numbers in set *B* as the second coordinates, so that

   a. the correlation is very strong and positive.

   b. the correlation is weak and positive.

   c. the correlation is weak and negative.

   d. the correlation is very strong and negative.

2. The following data were collected in a physics experiment in which students threw a ball straight up in the air and measured the height of the ball over a series of time intervals.

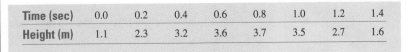

Time (sec)	0.0	0.2	0.4	0.6	0.8	1.0	1.2	1.4
Height (m)	1.1	2.3	3.2	3.6	3.7	3.5	2.7	1.6

   a. Produce a scatterplot of the (*time, height*) data. Describe the pattern in the scatterplot relating time and height. Would a linear model provide a good fit for the pattern in this data?

   b. Calculate the correlation coefficient.

   c. What do you know about correlation that explains this situation?

   d. Discuss a possible cause-and-effect relationship for elapsed time and height of the ball.

3. **a.** Find the missing values in the table if the correlation coefficient is to equal 1.

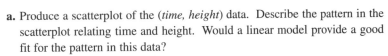

x	1	2	7	10	?
y	3	6	21	?	45

   b. If ranked data have a correlation coefficient of 1, what is the slope of the linear model with the best fit? Is the same true for unranked data with a correlation coefficient of 1? Why or why not?

4. Spearman's correlation coefficient r_s involved a sum of squared differences. Does the formula for Pearson's correlation coefficient include any sums of squared differences? Explain.

Unit 3

5. In this task you will compare Pearson's correlation coefficient and Spearman's rank correlation coefficient for two sets of data.

a. Use your calculator to compute Pearson's correlation coefficient for the 1985 and 2000 population rankings of the cities in Modeling task 3 on page 180. Spearman's rank correlation coefficient was 0.7818. Compare the two coefficients.

b. Refer to the chicken fast-food data given at the beginning of Lesson 2. Rank the fast foods in terms of total number of calories. Rank the fast foods in terms of total grams of fat. Compute Spearman's rank correlation coefficient. Pearson's correlation coefficient was 0.8983. Compare the two coefficients.

c. Examine the data sets used in parts a and b. Try to figure out why the relationships between the coefficients were different in these cases. Write a summary of what you discover.

d. When might you want to rank data before computing a correlation coefficient? When wouldn't you want to rank data before computing a correlation coefficient?

Reflecting

1. Find an article in a newspaper or magazine that uses the concept of correlation. Examine the article carefully for the way correlation is mentioned or implied. Write a paragraph describing the article. Include whether there is any suggestion of cause-and-effect and, if so, whether you think it is reasonable. What additional information about the situation would help you to understand better the correlation and its causes?

2. Discuss whether the following statements are true. Give examples to support your conclusions.

a. If the correlation between two variables is strong, the relationship is linear.

b. If the relationship between two variables is linear, the correlation will be strong.

3. In each of the following news clips, a study is reported that revealed a correlation between two variables. Comment on the validity of the conclusion and whether or not you think there is a cause-and-effect relationship between the two variables.

a. *USA Today* (Nov. 12, 1991) reported a study by researcher Patricia Hebert of Brigham and Women's Hospital, Boston, that being short raises heart attack risk. "Being short may raise heart attack risk because small people's narrower arteries might clog more quickly. The taller you are, the lower the risk. But Hebert cautions that height is not as strong a risk factor as smoking, high blood pressure, obesity or diabetes."

5. **a.** Pearson's correlation coefficient is the same as Spearman's, 0.7818. This is always the case in rankings where there are no ties.

   b. Note that two items have the same number of grams of fat. They either can be ranked 5 and 6 or both can be given rank 5.5 (or 5). Spearman's rank correlation coefficient is about 0.82. In this case, Spearman's is close to Pearson's.

   c. When there are no ties with ranked data, Spearman's correlation coefficient will be equal to Pearson's. If there are ties in the ranking they will not be the same.

   d. Responses may vary. You might want to rank the data if the numerical values had been approximated in the first place and you didn't have much faith in them. You might want to rank the data if there is an outlier in the data set that would be too influential. You wouldn't want to rank the data if you didn't want to lose the extra information that you get from the actual values.

Reflecting

1. Encourage students to share their results. They can report on the article, or they can produce an overhead highlighting the main points. To make the reporting more efficient, each student in a group can bring an article, then the group can determine which of the articles they would like to present to the class.

2. **a.** This is not necessarily true. One outlier can make the correlation seem strong even though the rest of the points are clustered in a circle. Examples from this unit include the SAT scores for football players versus for all students, and crime rate versus spending on police. Nonlinear data also may have a high correlation.

   b. This is not necessarily true. The correlation coefficient may have a small value and the data still may follow a (widespread) linear trend. In other cases, the points on the plot can cluster very closely to a line, but one outlier can decrease the correlation significantly. Examples from this unit include fat versus calories, and the percent of women versus the percent of men watching television shows.

3. **a.** Student comments will vary. They might observe that the correlation between height and heart attack risk is probably smaller than that between some of the other factors mentioned.

Unit 3

3. **b.** The article implies that a greater frequency of abduction reports is due to a greater emphasis in the media and entertainment industry on such phenomena. Students might prefer to argue that the causation relationship could go the other direction: because of a greater frequency in abduction reports, the media and entertainment industry has focused more on the subject. However, it's also possible that the general rise in population, or greater stress and irrational fear of technological advances, has caused a greater rise in the frequency of abduction reports. Students should support their conclusions.

4. **a.** There are many variables that affect voter turnout, such as educational attainment. Racial balance is another factor that is traditionally considered to affect voter turnout.

   b. You would need to have a large number of communities. Communities would be selected at random and placed into one of three groups; required high voter turnout, required low voter turnout, and a control group (no requirement). In each community (except the control group), each citizen would be required either to vote or not to vote. (Voting status would be determined at random.) Quality of life must be measured before the experiment and after. The experiment must be prolonged over several years, perhaps decades, to give the communities the opportunity to make any adjustments that may occur. The changes in quality of life for each community must be compared to determine if there was a significant difference between the three groups.

   c. Constitutionality, as well as cost and other factors, make such an experiment unrealistic.

Unit 3

b. An article in the Akron (Ohio) *Beacon Journal* on April 4, 1996, reported the unusual rise in popularity of the television show *The X-Files*. With a focus on alien abductions, conspiracies, and strange occurrences, the show was initially of interest only to fans of science fiction. Eventually, it began to enjoy a more widespread audience. Many "knock-off" shows have tried to cash in on the popularity of *The X-Files* with a similar focus on bizarre happenings.

The article also reported that some people question whether the show has had an effect on popular culture, beyond pure entertainment. Since *The X-Files* debuted in 1993, there has been an increase in interest in paranormal events, from extraterrestrials and ghosts to strange, unexplained disappearances.

According to the article, the PBS television show *Nova* tracked both the frequency of abduction reports and the frequency with which the topic is portrayed in the media. Some such reports date back to 1961, over three decades before *The X-Files* was first broadcast. Comparing these two variables, *Nova* reported a correlation between them.

4. The following is another article reporting an association.

Voter Turnout Correlates to Quality of Life

A new study suggests that your vote may count after all, even if every candidate you favor goes down to defeat on Election Day.

A study by the Durham-based Institute for Southern Studies reveals that states with the highest rates of voter turnout also have higher rates of employment and a smaller gap in incomes between the rich and poor.

"Very clearly, it pays to vote," said study author Bob Hall. "There's more reasons to vote than you may think. It may actually influence the quality of life in a broad way."

Source: *The Charlotte Observer,* October 29, 1996.

a. The article then says that some people believe the study may not consider enough variables that determine whether voters go to the polls. What are some variables that might affect voter turnout? Do you think any of those variables might be lurking variables in this situation?

b. The study compared state voter turnout data to twelve social, economic, and government policy indicators. Describe an experiment that would determine if higher voter turnout improves the quality of life.

c. Since lurking variables are always a concern, why wasn't such an experiment done?

5. Examine the reasoning in each case below. Do the conclusions given make sense in each case? Why or why not?

a. The correlation between Aleita's and Sue's preferences in music is −0.9. Therefore, Sue influenced how Aleita feels about music.

b. The correlation between the rankings of metropolitan areas in health care and the arts is a high positive number. Thus, if you would like to increase the number of hospitals and health care specialists in a city, first build some museums and increase the number of theaters.

c. The correlation between the rankings of metropolitan areas in population and per capita incidence of crime is −0.64. Therefore, large populations cause crime to increase.

Extending

1. In this task you will explore how Pearson's formula works. Examine the formula for the correlation coefficient *r*, reproduced below.

$$r = \frac{\sum (x - \bar{x})(y - \bar{y})}{\sqrt{\sum(x - \bar{x})^2} \ \sqrt{\sum(y - \bar{y})^2}}$$

a. As long as the values of *x* aren't all the same and the values of *y* aren't all the same, the denominator of the formula gives a positive number. Explain why this is true.

On the scatterplot below are graphed some points (*x*, *y*) and the point ($\bar{x}$, $\bar{y}$). Horizontal and vertical lines are drawn through ($\bar{x}$, $\bar{y}$).

b. For the points in region A, is (*x* − $\bar{x}$) positive or negative? Is (*y* − $\bar{y}$) positive or negative? Is (*x* − $\bar{x}$)(*y* − $\bar{y}$) positive or negative?

c. Fill in each space on a copy of the table below with the word "positive" or the word "negative".

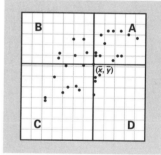

Region	Value of (*x* − $\bar{x}$)	Value of (*y* − $\bar{y}$)	Value of (*x* − $\bar{x}$)(*y* − $\bar{y}$)
A			
B			
C			
D			

5. Student responses may vary considerably. Look for careful thought in the explanations given. Possible directions of thought are given below as sample responses.

   a. We would have to know more about the situation here. It is possible that the two don't even know each other, they are from different cultures, or they are of different ages so their taste in music is independently quite different. If this is the case, Sue did not influence how Aleita feels about music. It also is possible that Aleita and Sue know each other and that Aleita deliberately ranked the music pretty much the opposite of Sue. For example, Aleita may be a younger sister who wants to stake out her own identity. In this case, Sue did influence how Aleita feels.

   b. This conclusion seems reasonable. The high correlation is most likely due to the fact that some cities are nicer places to live than others and one of the things that goes into making a city a nice place to live is the opportunity to attend cultural events. Health care specialists in the United States are in demand and can choose their place of residence. They are likely to choose these nice cities. If a city would like more health care specialists, it might well attract them by building museums and theaters. On the other hand, educational facilities or population could be lurking variables.

   c. This conclusion seems reasonable. Larger populations give more opportunities for crime, and they may well result in more crime per capita.

Extending

1. **See Teaching Master 70.**

   a. This is true as long as all of the values of x aren't the same and all of the values of y aren't the same. The square of a number is zero or positive. Each factor of the denominator thus involves the sum of positive numbers (and perhaps some zeros). The square roots of these positive sums are also positive, as is their product.

   b. Positive; positive; positive

   c.

Region	Value of $(x - \bar{x})$	Value of $(y - \bar{y})$	Value of $(x - \bar{x})(y - \bar{y})$
A	Positive	Positive	Positive
B	Negative	Positive	Negative
C	Negative	Negative	Positive
D	Positive	Negative	Negative

1. d. The points in regions A and C will contribute positive values to the sum in the numerator of the formula for r. The points in regions B and D will contribute negative values. There are more points in regions A and C than in B and D and the values of $(x - \bar{x})$ and $(y - \bar{y})$ tend to be larger in regions A and C. Thus the sum in the numerator will be positive. Since the denominator is always positive, the value of r will be positive. Note also that points close to $(\bar{x}, \bar{y})$ or to the lines $x = \bar{x}$ or $y = \bar{y}$ will contribute a smaller product than a point farther away.

e. The points in regions A and C will contribute positive values to the sum in the numerator of the formula for r. The points in regions B and D will contribute negative values. There are more points in regions B and D than in A and C and the values of $(x - \bar{x})$ and $(y - \bar{y})$ tend to be larger in regions B and D. Thus the sum in the numerator will be negative. Since the denominator is always positive, the value of r will be negative.

2. ■ For Kerrigan, the correlation was 0.716. For Baiul, the correlation was 0.468. If the required elements were scored high, in general, so was the presentation. This was true for both skaters but much stronger for Kerrigan. In fact, for Baiul, there was an influential judge, Czechoslovakia.

■ No. The judge from Czechoslovakia was hard on Baiul, but also relatively hard on Kerrigan. The judge from the U.S. gave high scores to Kerrigan, but also gave relatively good scores to Baiul.

Unit 3

d. Explain why the formula will give a positive value of *r* for the points on the scatterplot at the bottom of page 208.

e. Use a copy of the scatterplot below to explain why the formula will give a negative value of *r*.

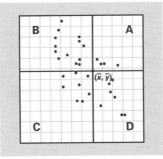

2. Nancy Kerrigan and Oksana Baiul both won medals in the 1994 Winter Olympics women's figure skating competition. The scores given by the judges for their first-round technical programs are presented in the table below. Each skater was judged on inclusion of the required elements and on presentation.

Explore these data, making appropriate plots and computations. Write a report that gives your answers to these questions.

- Does a judge who grades higher on required elements also tend to grade higher on presentation? Is this true for both skaters?

- Compared to other judges, do any judges stand out as favoring one skater over the other?

Figure Skating Scores

		Gr. Brit.	Pol.	Czec.	Ukr.	China	USA	Japan	Can.	Germ.
Kerrigan	**Req.**	5.6	5.8	5.6	5.8	5.8	5.9	5.8	5.8	5.9
	Pres.	5.6	5.9	5.7	5.7	5.9	5.9	5.9	5.8	5.8
Baiul	**Req.**	5.7	5.8	5.4	5.7	5.7	5.6	5.7	5.6	5.5
	Pres.	5.9	5.8	5.7	5.9	5.9	5.8	5.9	5.9	5.9

Source: *USA Today*, Feb. 24, 1994.

Unit 3

3. The academic requirements to participate in sports for men and women athletes entering college were raised in 1986. The graduation percentage rates for colleges in the Big Ten and the Pac Ten Conferences for those students entering school in 1985 and 1986 are given in the table below. Explore these data and write a report of what you found.

Percentage Graduation Rates

School	Students Entering In 1986	Athletes Entering In 1985	Athletes Entering In 1986	Football Players Entering in 1985	Football Players Entering in 1986
Illinois	78	64	74	71	75
Indiana	65	66	62	72	50
Iowa	59	64	63	58	63
Michigan	85	63	79	61	80
Michigan State	69	65	62	48	56
Minnesota	42	53	53	42	32
Northwestern	89	82	77	75	62
Ohio State	54	67	69	63	72
Penn State	77	75	78	81	78
Purdue	70	61	65	47	55
Wisconsin	70	64	69	63	81
Arizona	49	50	54	53	57
Arizona State	45	40	52	24	30
California	77	62	61	57	44
Oregon	54	57	66	60	63
Oregon State	52	49	47	52	70
Southern Cal	66	53	69	60	71
Stanford	92	89	86	84	79
UCLA	74	58	60	55	42
Washington	63	56	61	35	54
Washington State	55	53	49	38	50

Source: Copyright 1993, *USA* TODAY. Reprinted with permission.

MORE *continued*

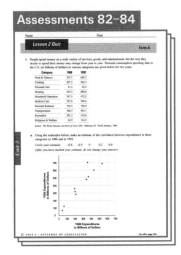

3. Student responses may include observations such as the following: the correlation between the number of students who graduated and the number of athletes who graduated, 0.81, was quite strong after the requirements were raised. For schools in which a large percentage of the students graduated, so did a large percentage of the athletes. The correlation between all students and football players, 0.50, was not as strong. If Minnesota and Arizona were removed from the plot, the correlation would be even smaller. The correlation between the number of football players who graduated from the class of 1985 and those who graduated from the class of 1986 was 0.69 which indicated that if a school had a large percentage of football players who graduated before the requirements were raised, they also had a large percentage of football players who graduated after the requirements were raised. More significant, however, is the $y = x$ line on the plot of (*football players entering in 1985, football players entering in 1986*), which shows that a majority of the schools lie above the line. These schools increased their graduation rate for football players after the requirements were raised, which was the desired outcome.

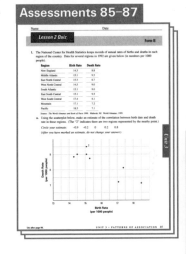

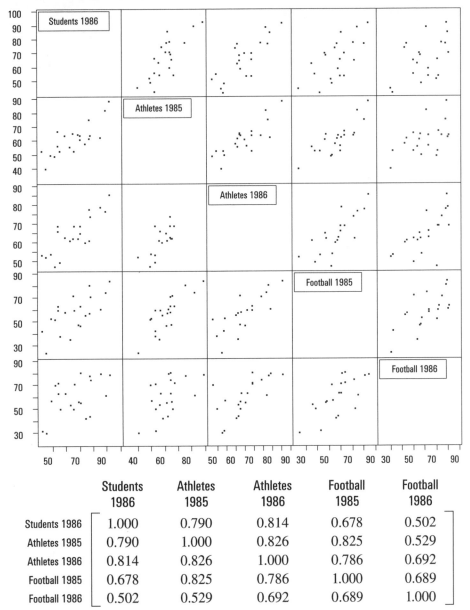

	Students 1986	Athletes 1985	Athletes 1986	Football 1985	Football 1986
Students 1986	1.000	0.790	0.814	0.678	0.502
Athletes 1985	0.790	1.000	0.826	0.825	0.529
Athletes 1986	0.814	0.826	1.000	0.786	0.692
Football 1985	0.678	0.825	0.786	1.000	0.689
Football 1986	0.502	0.529	0.692	0.689	1.000

See Assessment Resource pages 82–87.

Unit 3

Lesson 3 Least Squares Regression

LESSON OVERVIEW In this lesson, students will use the least squares regression line to model bivariate data that follows a linear pattern. In much the same way that the mean is a summary of single-variable data, the regression line is a summary of bivariate data. Residuals indicate how closely the line fits the points. By the time students complete Investigation 2, they will understand that the least squares regression line is the line that minimizes the sum of the squared residuals.

Lesson Objectives

- To use the least squares regression line for prediction and understand when that is appropriate
- To understand the meaning of a residual
- To understand that the least squares regression line minimizes the sum of the squared errors

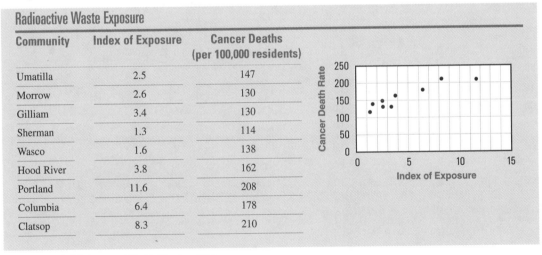

Least Squares Regression

The correlation coefficient is a measure of the strength of the linear association between two variables. You have seen that the correlation can be affected by an influential point. That is, one point may substantially decrease the correlation coefficient of data that are otherwise strongly linear or may increase the correlation coefficient of data that are not otherwise linear. Thus, you always should look at the scatterplot when interpreting the correlation coefficient.

Even if the correlation is not strong, if the scatterplot reveals a linear pattern, a linear model should be considered as a way to describe and summarize the relationship. In the "Linear Models" unit of Course 1, two ways to produce a linear model were developed: estimating the model by eye and finding the equation of the regression line. In this lesson you will investigate some properties of the regression line and how your calculator or computer software computes it.

Examine the data below from a study of nine Oregon communities in the 1960s, when nuclear power was relatively new. The study compared exposure to radioactive waste from a nuclear reactor in Hanford, Washington, and the rate of deaths due to cancer in these communities.

Radioactive Waste Exposure

Community	Index of Exposure	Cancer Deaths (per 100,000 residents)
Umatilla	2.5	147
Morrow	2.6	130
Gilliam	3.4	130
Sherman	1.3	114
Wasco	1.6	138
Hood River	3.8	162
Portland	11.6	208
Columbia	6.4	178
Clatsop	8.3	210

Source: *Journal of Environmental Health,* May–June 1965.

INVESTIGATION 1 How Good is the Fit?

1. The grade point averages (GPAs) for a sample of twenty-five students are given in the table below. The line on the scatterplot, shown on the next page, is the least squares regression line. Its equation is $y = 0.58x + 1.33$. The correlation coefficient is 0.702.

Grade Point Averages

	Eighth-Grade GPA	Ninth-Grade GPA		Eighth-Grade GPA	Ninth-Grade GPA
Andy	1.9	2.9	Missy	3.2	3.6
Betina	3.0	3.3	Monica	2.9	3.5
Bhvana	1.8	2.5	Paul	2.6	3.1
Bill	2.8	2.5	Peggy	2.8	3.1
Dan	2.8	3.0	Raquel	3.1	3.6
Grant	3.4	3.0	Reggie	2.8	2.4
Kara	3.3	3.0	Roberon	2.9	2.6
Kisha	1.9	3.1	Sandra	3.8	3.4
Kristen	1.6	2.0	Shiomo	2.9	3.0
Liliana	2.5	2.8	Sterling	2.3	2.3
Luann	2.4	2.2	Stu	1.6	1.9
Maya	3.2	2.9	Tony	3.4	3.6
Michael	3.6	3.5			

Think About This Situation

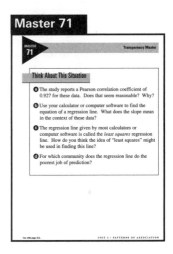

See Teaching Master 71.

ⓐ A Pearson correlation coefficient of 0.927 seems reasonable for two reasons. It is believable that exposure to radioactive waste would correlate strongly with cancer deaths. Also, if one looks at the scatterplot, it is evident that the points fall close to a line. Students may think that 0.927 is slightly high.

ⓑ The equation of the least squares regression line is $y = 9.27x + 114.68$. The slope of 9.27 tells you that 9.27 more cancer deaths per 100,000 residents can be expected for an increase of 1 unit in the index of exposure.

ⓒ Student responses will vary. They may recall their early efforts to draw lines which fit and suggest that the line may be calculated to hit as many points as possible. In that case, you may want to sketch quickly a scatterplot and a line that hits many points but for which all remaining points lie above the line. Students probably will suggest that a compromise be made between hitting points and getting close to many points. Ask how the calculator might determine if it is "getting close" to the points. Students will not think of calculating a *mean square error*, but they may suggest making the average error or the sum of all errors as low as possible. It's not so important that they reach a conclusion now as that they make sense of the question. The calculator or computer software must make some numerical determination of the best fit.

ⓓ Students probably will choose Portland, Clatsop, or Gilliam. Encourage them to articulate why they made their choices.

INVESTIGATION 1 How Good is the Fit?

In this investigation, students first will learn how to use a regression line to make a prediction and how to compute the error in that prediction. (Usually it is impossible to find the error in prediction because we don't know the true *y* value.) Then students will practice finding residuals both graphically and using the regression equation. Residuals are the difference between the actual *y* value of a point used to find the regression equation and the *y* value predicted by that equation. (We can always compute the residuals.)

As you circulate among the working groups, you can help them stay focused on the meaning of the model by engaging in short dialogues such as, "Which students did better than expected in 9th grade? How do you know this?" Encourage students to move back and forth between the scatterplot and the context by asking often what the points on the line represent, and what the vertical segments represent. Push students to state clearly which element of the model relates to which element in the real situation. Questions to ask might include: "If a point representing a student is below the line, what does that mean? If one vertical line segment is longer than another, what does that mean? How many points are there on the line? Suppose we picked a point on the line not directly above or below a point representing a student in the list. What would that point represent?"

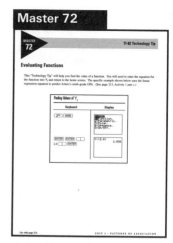

See Teaching Masters 72 and 73 for Technology Tips.

1. **a.** Yes, the points cluster loosely about the regression line.

    b. In this equation, x is the eighth-grade GPA and y is the ninth-grade GPA. The slope of 0.58 means that if one student has an eighth-grade GPA one point higher than another student, he or she will tend to have a ninth-grade GPA 0.58 points higher than the other student. Be sure students understand the importance of the phrase "will tend to have" (which could be replaced with "will have, on the average,"). The regression line provides a summary; it does not predict exactly.

    Many students will say that since the slope is less than 1, ninth-grade GPA's tend to be less than eighth-grade GPA's. This isn't the case! Students who say this are forgetting the effect of the y-intercept, 1.33.

    c. ■ The prediction could be obtained graphically by looking at the regression line at $x = 2.6$ and estimating the y value.

    ■ Using the equation of the regression line, let $x = 2.6$ and evaluate:
    $y = 0.58(2.6) + 1.33 = 2.838$.

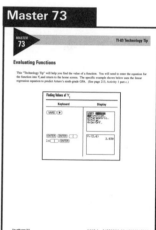

    d. 0.462, or about 0.5

    e. Elisa's predicted GPA was 2.664, or about 2.7. The error in prediction is -0.364, or about -0.4. The regression equation was a better predictor for Elisa (predicting 0.4 points too high) than for Arturo (predicting 0.5 points too low).

Unit 3

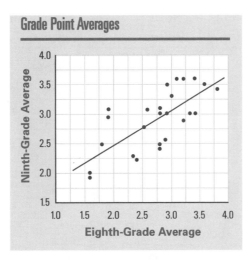

Grade Point Averages

Ninth-Grade Average vs *Eighth-Grade Average*

a. Does a line appear to be an appropriate model for these data?

b. What is the meaning of the slope of the regression line in the context of these data?

c. A different student, Arturo, has an eighth-grade GPA of 2.6. Explain how to use each of the following to predict Arturo's ninth-grade GPA.

- The regression line on the scatterplot
- The equation of the regression line

d. The difference between the actual (observed) value and the value predicted by the regression equation is called the **error in prediction**. Arturo eventually had a ninth-grade GPA of 3.3. What was the error in prediction for Arturo?

e. Elisa had an eighth-grade GPA of 2.3. Use the regression equation to predict the ninth-grade GPA for Elisa. Elisa eventually had a ninth-grade GPA of 2.3. What is the error in prediction for Elisa? Did the regression equation give a better prediction for Arturo or for Elisa?

Unit 3

2. Now think about the geometry involved in the regression line.

a. Examine the scatterplot shown here. Two students and two corresponding points on the regression line are identified.

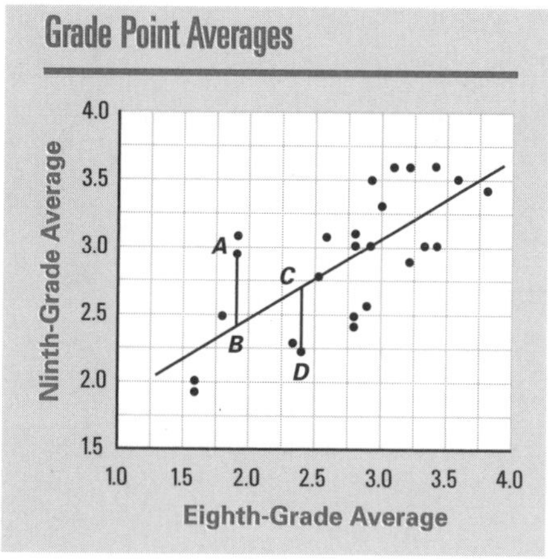

Grade Point Averages
Ninth-Grade Average
Eighth-Grade Average
4.0
3.5
3.0
2.5
2.0
1.5
1.0
1.5
2.0
2.5
3.0
3.5
4.0
A
B
C
D

- Which student is represented by point *A*?
- Estimate the coordinates of point *B* and indicate what they represent.
- What does the *length* of segment *AB* represent?
- Which student is represented by point *D*?
- How is point *C* related to point *D*?

b. How do segments *AB* and *CD* compare? What do they tell you about how well the line fits these points?

c. Draw several more segments between actual GPAs and predicted GPAs and indicate what they represent.

d. Describe how you could use the equation of the regression line to calculate the lengths of segments *AB* and *CD*.

3. For the points that were used to find the regression line, the difference (*observed value – predicted value*) is called the **residual**.

a. Compute the residuals for Andy, Liliana, and Reggie.

b. Find a student for whom the residual is negative. What does that residual tell you about where the point lies with respect to the regression line?

c. Find a student for whom the residual is close to zero. What does that residual tell you about where the point lies with respect to the regression line?

Checkpoint

ⓐ Describe two ways in which you can use a linear model to make a prediction.

ⓑ How can you find the difference between an observed value and the predicted value from the scatterplot? From the equation?

Be prepared to share your descriptions with the class.

Unit 3

214 UNIT 3 • PATTERNS OF ASSOCIATION

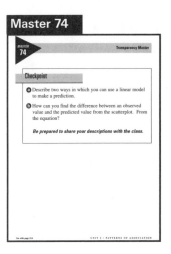

2. **a.** ■ Andy is represented by point *A* at (1.9, 2.9).

   ■ The coordinates of *B* are approximately (1.9, 2.4). For a student who earned an eighth-grade GPA of 1.9, the regression line predicts a ninth-grade GPA of 2.4.

   ■ The length of segment *AB* represents the absolute value of the difference between Andy's actual ninth-grade GPA and the GPA predicted by the regression line.

   ■ Luann is represented by point *D* at (2.4, 2.2).

   ■ The *y*-coordinate of point *C* gives Luann's predicted ninth-grade GPA. The *y*-coordinate of point *D* gives Luann's actual ninth-grade GPA.

   b. Segment *CD* is a bit longer than segment *AB*, which means that the absolute value of the difference between the actual and predicted values was a bit larger for Luann than for Andy. Since point *A* is above the line, Andy's actual ninth-grade GPA was higher than predicted. The fact that Luann's actual GPA is below the line indicates that her GPA was less than predicted.

   c. Responses will vary.

   d. Find the *y* value of point *B* on the regression line using the equation where *x* represents Andy's eighth-grade average. Subtract this predicted *y* from the *y* value at *A*, which is Andy's actual ninth-grade GPA. A similar process yields the length of segment *CD*, except the absolute value of the difference must be found.

3. The difference between residual and error in prediction is simple: If the observed value was used in the calculation of the regression equation, then the difference is a residual. If the observed value was not used, the difference is an error of prediction. Depending on the level of your students, you should decide how much emphasis you wish to place on this distinction. Note that we rarely are able to compute errors of prediction. To compute the error of prediction, we need to know the actual value of *y*. If we know the actual value, then we wouldn't need to predict it. However, errors of prediction eventually can be found in cases such as predicting a person's adult height from height as a six-year-old.

   a. Andy: 2.9 – 2.43 = 0.47   Liliana: 2.8 – 2.78 = 0.02   Reggie: 2.4 – 2.95 = –0.55 (Answers may vary slightly because of rounding.)

   b. Students could select any student whose GPA falls below the line. For example, the residual is negative for Sandra, Kristen, Reggie, and Stu. A negative residual means that the actual GPA was lower than the equation would have predicted.

   c. Liliana and Shiomo had residuals very close to zero. This tells us that the predicted ninth-grade GPA's and their actual ninth-grade GPA's were almost the same.

SHARE AND SUMMARIZE   **full-class discussion**

Checkpoint

See Teaching Master 74.

ⓐ A linear model may be used for prediction by finding and interpreting the *y* value for a given value of *x*. This may be done using the equation or the graph.

ⓑ The residual or error of prediction is the vertical distance on the scatterplot from the point to the line, given a positive sign if the point is above the line and a negative sign if the point is below the line. You can use the equation by subtracting the value of *y* predicted from the equation from the *y* value of the observed point.

CONSTRUCTING A MATH TOOLKIT: Students should write definitions of the error in prediction and the residual in their Math Toolkits and describe how to find them from the scatterplot and equation.

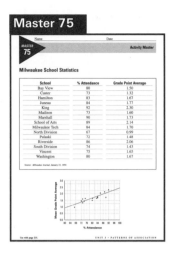

On Your Own

See Teaching Master 75.

a. $r \approx 0.87$

The association between attendance and grade point average is strong; the higher the attendance rate is, the higher the grade point average tends to be.

On Your Own

The table below gives the 1992–93 attendance and mean GPA for students at high schools in Milwaukee, Wisconsin.

Milwaukee School Statistics

School	% Attendance	Mean Grade Point Average
Bay View	80	1.50
Custer	73	1.32
Hamilton	83	1.67
Juneau	84	1.77
King	92	2.30
Madison	73	1.60
Marshall	90	1.73
School of Arts	89	2.14
Milwaukee Tech	84	1.70
North Division	67	0.99
Pulaski	72	1.48
Riverside	86	2.06
South Division	74	1.43
Vincent	75	1.65
Washington	80	1.67

Source: *Milwaukee Journal,* January 23, 1994.

a. A scatterplot of (*% attendance, mean grade point average*) follows. Find the correlation coefficient. What does this number tell you?

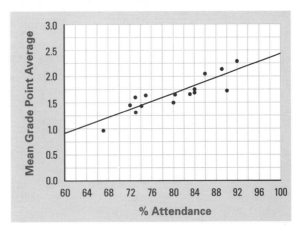

b. List some possible reasons for the positive correlation between attendance and mean GPA.

c. The equation graphed is the regression line. What is the slope and what does it indicate in the context of these data?

d. Use the equation of the regression line to predict the mean grade point average for students at Bay View. What is the residual for Bay View? Draw a line segment on a copy of the scatterplot to represent this residual.

INVESTIGATION 2 The "Best-Fitting" Line

There are several possible criteria you could use to determine which line through a cloud of points is the "best-fitting" linear model. You might choose the line passing through the most points, or you might choose the one with the smallest average distance from the points. In this investigation, you will explore the method used by most calculators—the *method of least squares*.

1. Refer back to the data on grade point averages (page 212) in Investigation 1. The mean eighth-grade GPA is 2.74 and the mean ninth-grade GPA is 2.912. Is the point (*mean eighth-grade GPA, mean ninth-grade GPA*) on the regression line? Give two ways to find the answer to this question.

The point (*mean eighth-grade GPA, mean ninth-grade GPA*) or $(\bar{x}, \bar{y})$ can be thought of as the balance point for the data. This point is called the **centroid**. The regression line always goes through the centroid. You will explore another characteristic of the regression line in the following activities.

2. Consider the three data points in the table below.

x	1	2	3
y	1	2	5

a. The equation of the regression line is $y = 2x - \frac{4}{3}$.

- Graph this line on a scatterplot showing the three points. Draw in the residuals.

- Verify that the regression line contains the centroid $(\bar{x}, \bar{y})$.

- Complete a copy of the table below using the equation of the regression line.

x	y	Predicted y	Error	Squared Error
1	1			
2	2			
3	5			
		Total		

b. Student responses will vary. The most obvious reason is if students aren't in school it is harder for them to learn the material covered in class, and so their grades are lower.

c. Slopes may vary slightly if students estimate it from the graph. The slope is about 0.04. The slope indicates that a school that has an attendance rate 1% higher than another school tends to have a mean GPA 0.04 higher.

d. Predictions may vary slightly if students estimate from the graph. The equation of the regression line is $y = 0.038x - 1.37$. The predicted GPA for Bay View would be 1.67. The residual for Bay View is -0.17. This error is represented by the length of the vertical segment between the point $(80, 1.50)$ and the regression line.

EXPLORE   small-group investigation

INVESTIGATION 2   The "Best-Fitting" Line

There are several techniques that can be used to fit a line to data. However, the least squares regression line is the one most commonly used. It is the line that minimizes the sum of the squared errors, hence the name *least squares*. It also has another important characteristic: it contains the point $(\bar{x}, \bar{y})$.

If students ask why the errors are squared, you might explain that the sum of squared errors is a measure of the "difference" between the points and the line. Statisticians have chosen this measure over others because of its relationship to the Euclidean distance formula, which uses a sum of squared differences. The sum of squared errors is used throughout statistics as a measure of distance. Students will meet this idea again when they study standard deviation in Course 3.

1. The point appears to be on the regression line. This can be determined by looking at the graph or by using the equation of the regression line, $y = 0.58x + 1.33$. If $x = 2.74$, then $y = 2.9192$. (The predicted value is not exactly $\bar{y}$ because of rounding.)

2. See Teaching Master 76.

This activity encourages students to experiment a little with the idea of minimizing the squared error. Because it would be easy for students to lose the big picture in the technicalities of using the equation (either a provided equation or their own) to make predictions, then calculating errors and squaring them and finally summing the squares, it would be helpful to draw the class together after groups have finished with this activity, to show a few of the lines that were tried. After this experimentation the calculator output for the real data in activities 3 and 4 should be more easily understood.

Actually sketching the "square errors", squares which touch the line, with side length equal to the residual, helps students to see the purpose in adjusting the line to make the total area of these squares as small as possible. This idea is investigated further in Extending task 2 on page 226.

a. ■ See the graph at the right.
  ■ $(\bar{x}, \bar{y}) = (2, \frac{8}{3})$ which does fit the regression equation $y = 2x - \frac{4}{3}$.

■ x	y	Predicted y	Error	Squared Error
1	1	$\frac{2}{3}$	$\frac{1}{3}$	$\frac{1}{9}$
2	2	$\frac{8}{3}$	$\frac{-2}{3}$	$\frac{4}{9}$
3	5	$\frac{14}{3}$	$\frac{1}{3}$	$\frac{1}{9}$
		Total	0	$\frac{6}{9} = \frac{2}{3}$

Master 76

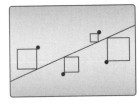

MORE
ASSIGNMENT *pp. 221–227*

Students now can begin Organizing task 3 or Reflecting task 4 from the MORE assignment following Investigation 2.

Unit 3

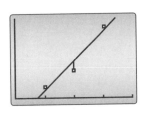

2. **b.** The equation of the line containing the points (1, 1) and (2, 2) is $y = x$.

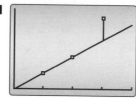

■ No, $y = x$ does not contain the point $(\bar{x}, \bar{y}) = (2, \frac{8}{3})$.

x	y	Predicted y	Error	Squared Error
1	1	1	0	0
2	2	2	0	0
3	5	3	2	4
		Total	2	4

c. Responses will vary depending on the students' equations. One example of a line that fits the points fairly well and that goes through the centroid is the line through (1, 1) and $(2, \frac{8}{3})$. This line has equation $y = \frac{5}{3}x - \frac{2}{3}$. The sum of the squared errors is $0.\overline{8}$. Notice that this is larger than the sum of squared errors for the regression line, which was $\frac{2}{3}$. No line will have a smaller sum of squared errors than $\frac{2}{3}$.

d. The regression line with equation $y = 2x - \frac{4}{3}$ gave the smallest sum of squared errors. For any set of data points, the regression line always gives the smallest sum of squared errors.

e. Students should find that any line will produce a greater sum of squared errors than the least squares regression line does.

b. Write the equation of the line that goes through the points (1, 1) and (2, 2).

- Graph this line on a scatterplot showing the three points. Draw in the residuals.

- Does this line contain the point $(\bar{x}, \bar{y})$?

- Complete a copy of the table below using this new equation to predict values of y.

x	y	Predicted y	Error	Squared Error
1	1			
2	2			
3	5			
		Total		

c. Find the equation of a third line that fits these three points reasonably well and contains the centroid $(\bar{x}, \bar{y})$. Complete another copy of the table using your new equation to predict values of y. Graph this line on a scatterplot showing the three points. Draw in the residuals.

d. Which of the three equations gave the smallest sum of squared errors?

e. Compare your answer with that of other groups who may have used a different third line and equation.

The **least squares regression line** is the line that gives the smallest **sum of squared errors (SSE)** for a set of points.

3. The following table gives the federal minimum wage in the United States for the years when Congress passed an increase in the minimum wage.

Year	Federal Minimum Wage	Year	Federal Minimum Wage
1955	0.75	1978	2.65
1956	1.00	1979	2.90
1961	1.15	1980	3.10
1963	1.25	1981	3.35
1967	1.40	1990	3.80
1968	1.60	1991	4.25
1974	2.00	1996	4.75
1975	2.10	1997	5.15

a. Find the equation of the least squares regression line to model the (*year*, *minimum wage*) data. Find the sum of the squared errors. Is this line a reasonable model for these data?

b. Verify that the regression line contains the centroid $(\bar{x}, \bar{y})$.

c. What is the slope of the regression line? What does it mean in the context of these data?

d. Use the regression line to predict the minimum wage for the current year. What was your error in prediction?

4. Refer to the data and scatterplot for the number of milligrams of sodium and number of calories in fast-food chicken items at the beginning of Lesson 2, page 186.

a. Compute the equation of the regression line for the (*number of calories*, *milligrams of sodium*) data.

b. This data set contains one influential point. Which item corresponds to the influential point? Predict how the regression line will change if the influential point is removed from the data set.

c. Compute the equation of the regression line after removing the influential point. How close was your prediction?

Checkpoint

ⓐ How is the idea of a sum of squared differences important to least squares regression?

ⓑ Describe two characteristics of the least squares regression line.

ⓒ Give an example to show that a low correlation doesn't always indicate that a line is not a good model for the data. Give an example to show that a high correlation doesn't always indicate that a line is a good model for the data.

Be prepared to discuss your group's responses with the entire class.

218 UNIT 3 • PATTERNS OF ASSOCIATION

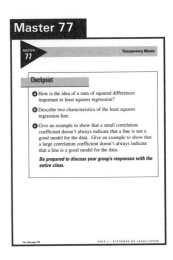

3. **a.** The scatterplot with the regression line appears in the margin below. Although the points appear to follow a pattern that is concave upward and a non-linear model might be best, the points do cluster closely about a line, and so using a line for prediction may be reasonable. There do not appear to be outliers to investigate. If the rate of inflation stayed constant from year to year and the minimum wage was adjusted each year for inflation, the data would fit an exponential model. An exponential model does appear to be more appropriate for the years before 1981.

   The equation of the regression line is approximately $y = 0.102x - 198.969$.

   The sum of the squared errors is about 1.048. (Answers will vary because of rounding.)

   b. The mean year is 1975.6875 and the mean federal minimum wage is 2.575. Using the equation of the regression line when $x = 1975.6875$ we get $y = 2.551$.

   The centroid is on the regression line. The value of 2.551 varies slightly from 2.575 because the coefficients of the regression equation were rounded.

   c. The slope of the regression line is 0.102. This means that the federal minimum wage has tended to increase by $0.102 per year.

   d. Answers will vary based upon the current year and minimum wage.

4. **a.** $y = 1.29x + 250.53$

   b. Burger King's Chicken Sandwich is the influential point (the point in the upper right corner of the plot at the left). Removing it from the data set makes the regression line much more horizontal.

   c. With Burger King's Chicken Sandwich removed, the equation of the regression line is $y = 0.638x + 462.44$.

Graph for 3a.

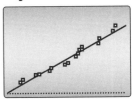

Graph for 4b.

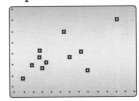

SHARE AND SUMMARIZE   full-class discussion

Checkpoint

See Teaching Master 77.

ⓐ When fitting a line to data, for some of the points, there probably will be some error. This error is the difference between the actual y value of the point and the value given by the equation of the line. The least squares regression line is the line where the total squared error (the sum of squared differences) is a minimum (as small as possible).

ⓑ The least squares regression line passes through the centroid. It also minimizes the sum of the squared errors. Students also may say that the slope of the regression line tells you something about the relationship between the variables. (For example, minimum wage tends to increase at a rate of 10¢ per year.)

ⓒ Responses will vary. For example, the correlation between fathers' and sons' heights in activity 7 of Investigation 1 in Lesson 2 was not especially strong, only 0.5. However, the points clearly cluster, loosely, about a straight line. On the other hand, in activity 3 of Investigation 2 in this lesson, the correlation between year and federal minimum wage is a very high 0.976. However, we have evidence both from the scatterplot and from our knowledge of inflation and exponential growth that a linear model may not be the most appropriate one.

CONSTRUCTING A MATH TOOLKIT: Following a whole-class discussion of the "Checkpoint", students should summarize these important concepts in their Math Toolkits.

Unit 3

▶**On Your Own**

a.

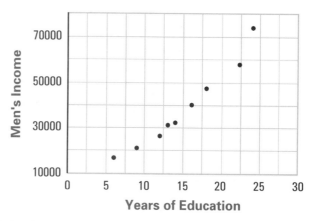

■ The correlation is 0.97.

■ The plot indicates that the data are not linear. The points follow an upward curve. A straight line would not capture the relationship as well as another model might.

b.

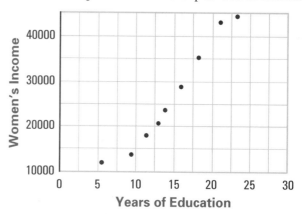

The correlation between years of education and women's income is 0.98.

These data are not linear either. The rate of increase is slower when x is small and when x is large. The points with years of education between 12 and 21 seem to be linear but the others don't seem to fit the pattern.

c. The regression line is $y = 2150.58x - 4449.80$.

■ The slope is 2150.58 and it means that for one year more of education a woman can expect to earn an additional $2150.58 per year.

■ The largest error of prediction is for 6 years of education. The error of prediction for this number of years of education is $3722.32.

■ 35,790,893.5. Note how large this SSE is even though $r = 0.984$, which is very high.

d. Responses will vary. Possible response: People who have more education tend to get jobs that require more training. These jobs pay more than jobs requiring less education because not just anyone can do them.

e. Possibly. At the higher education levels, women's income doesn't increase as fast as men's income.

Again, you may want to point out to your students that the incomes given are averages (medians in this case) and so do not reflect the variability in individual incomes at a given number of years of education. Some people with few years of education have a high income, and some people with many years of education have a small income. Using averages for groups, as is done here, inflates the correlation.

On Your Own

The amount of money a person earns is strongly correlated with the number of years of education the person has completed. The following data show recent median incomes and years of education for men and women who are year-round full-time workers 25 years and older.

Years of Education	Men's Income ($)	Women's Income ($)
6	16,980	12,176
9	21,179	13,760
12	26,766	18,648
13	31,413	21,987
14	32,349	24,849
16	40,381	29,287
18	47,260	35,018
21	58,590	43,699
23	73,942	44,405

Source: *Money Income of Households, Families and Persons in the United States: 1992,* U.S. Bureau of the Census.

a. Construct a scatterplot of the (*years of education, men's income*) data.

- Find the correlation coefficient between these two variables.

- George wrote the following conclusion: "There is a high degree of correlation between education and men's income so the regression line is a good model for these data." What would you say to George?

b. Construct a scatterplot of the (*years of education, women's income*) data and find the correlation coefficient between these two variables. Does it appear that a line is a reasonable model of these data?

c. Find the equation of the regression line for the (*years of education, women's income*) data.

- What is the slope of this regression line and what does it mean in the context of these data?

- For which year is the residual the largest?

- What is the sum of the squared errors for this regression line?

d. Discuss a possible cause-and-effect relationship between education and income.

e. It has been suggested that there is a "glass ceiling", a level beyond which it is difficult for a woman to be promoted. Is there any evidence of such a "glass ceiling" in these 1992 data?

Unit 3

MORE
Modeling • Organizing • Reflecting • Extending

Modeling

1. A study was conducted to determine if babies bundled in warm clothing learn to crawl later than babies dressed more lightly. The parents of 414 babies were asked the month their child was born and the age that the child learned to crawl. The table below and the scatterplot on the next page give the average daily outside temperature when the babies were six months old and the average age in weeks at which those babies began to crawl.

Crawling Age

Birth Month	Temperature (°F) at Age 6 Months	Age Began to Crawl (weeks)
January	66	29.84
February	73	30.52
March	72	29.70
April	63	31.84
May	52	28.58
June	39	31.44
July	33	33.64
August	30	32.82
September	33	33.83
October	37	33.35
November	48	33.38
December	57	32.32

Source: Benson, Janette. *Infant Behavior and Development.* 1993.

Modeling

1.   See Teaching Master 78 for an Activity Master.

Master 78

MORE
ASSIGNMENT   *pp. 220–226*

Modeling: 1 and choice of one*
Organizing: 3 and 1 or 2*
Reflecting: 4
Extending: 2 or 5*

*When choice is indicated, it is important
to leave the choice to the student.
NOTE: *It is best if Organizing tasks are
discussed as a whole class after they
have been assigned as homework.*

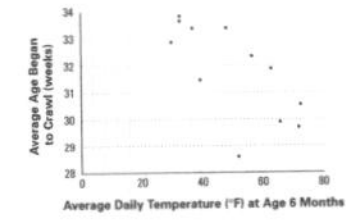

Unit 3

1. **a.** Yes. The only month that doesn't follow this trend is May.
   b. About $\frac{414}{12}$ or 34.5 babies are represented, assuming the births were evenly distributed throughout the year.
   c. $y = -0.078x + 35.7$
   d. Every degree increase in average temperature tends to reduce the average time to learn to crawl by 0.078 weeks.
   e. The residual with largest absolute value is -3.056, for May.
2. A power model, quadratic model, or cubic model would be a better fit for parts a and b. Students may connect this to the work they did in Unit 2, "Patterns of Location, Shape, and Size". The relationship between linear dimensions and volume will be investigated further in Unit 4, "Power Models".

Unit 3

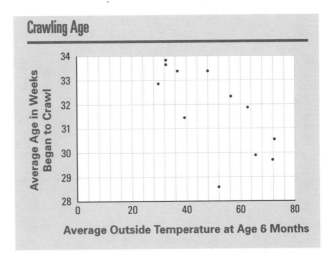

Crawling Age

(y-axis: Average Age in Weeks Began to Crawl, 28–34)
(x-axis: Average Outside Temperature at Age 6 Months, 0–80)

a. Does it appear from the scatterplot that babies who are six months old during the cold months of the year learn to crawl at a later age than babies who are six months old during warmer months?

b. Each point on the scatterplot represents approximately how many babies?

c. Find the least squares regression line and graph it on a copy of the scatterplot.

d. Interpret the slope of the regression line in the context of these data.

e. What point has the largest residual (in absolute value)? Find the residual for that point.

2. To help hunters estimate how much edible meat they should expect from their hunting, a meat processor wrote an article about a model relating the size of a deer to the amount of meat. The table below gives the *girth* (the measure around the chest just behind the front legs), the *weight* before processing, and the weight of the *edible meat* from a deer.

Deer Measurements

Girth (in.)	Weight (lbs.)	Edible Meat (lbs.)	Girth (in.)	Weight (lbs.)	Edible Meat (lbs.)
22	56	26	36	145	65
24	65	30	38	166	74
26	74	34	40	191	85
28	85	38	42	218	97
30	97	44	44	250	110
32	111	50	46	286	126
34	127	57			

Source: *Milwaukee Journal,* November, 1993.

LESSON 3 • LEAST SQUARES REGRESSION   221

a. Make a scatterplot of the (*girth, weight*) data. Is a linear model appropriate? If so, find the least squares regression line. If not, what kind of equation gives a better fit?

b. Plot the (*girth, edible meat*) data. Is a linear model appropriate? If so, find the least squares regression line. If not, what kind of equation gives a better fit?

c. Plot the (*weight, edible meat*) data. Is a linear model appropriate? If so, find the least squares regression line. Use it to predict the edible meat from a deer that weighs 200 pounds. What does the slope of the regression line mean in the context of these data?

3. The *Runzheimer Guide to Daily Prices* contained the following data on the average cost of a meal and one night's lodging in selected major United States cities for 1996–1997.

Meals and Lodging Costs

City	Lodging	Dining	City	Lodging	Dining
Atlanta	$161	$25.05	New York	$227	$40.75
Boston	194	28.20	Orlando	101	21.80
Chicago	217	29.05	Philadelphia	171	24.60
Denver	116	23.25	San Antonio	131	19.45
Houston	127	24.65	San Diego	122	24.25
Los Angeles	138	26.00	San Francisco	178	28.45
Memphis	95	16.90	Seattle	166	25.20
Miami	122	26.25	St. Louis	115	27.05
Minneapolis	132	22.00	Tampa	115	23.90
New Orleans	133	25.85	Washington, D.C.	145	32.25

Source: *Runzheimer Guide to Daily Prices.* Rochester, Wisconsin: Runzheimer International, 1997.

a. Estimate the correlation coefficient you would expect between lodging and dining costs. Find the correlation and see how it matches your expectation.

b. Make a scatterplot of (*lodging costs*, *dining costs*). Does the pattern of the plot seem consistent with the correlation coefficient you calculated?

c. Use the least squares regression line to predict the cost of dining in a city where lodging costs $100 per night. How much faith would you have in this prediction?

d. What does the slope of the regression line mean in the context of these data?

2. a.

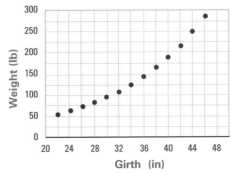

The pattern is not linear. A least squares regression line would not be a good way to make a prediction about the weight of a deer from its girth.

From the geometry of the situation, we suspect the relationship might be cubic since deer are (somewhat) similar in shape and linear measures are related by a cubic equation to measures dependent on volume (*i.e.* weight).

b. The relationship is not modeled well by a line. See the first graph below.

c. The least squares regression line is $y = 0.44x + 1.67$. See the second graph below. A 200 pound deer will yield about 90 pounds of edible meat. The slope of the regression line, 0.44, tells us that for every additional pound a deer weighs, there tends to be 0.44 more pounds of edible meat.

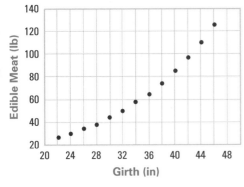

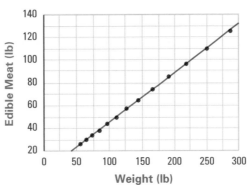

3. a. Students probably will expect r to be strong and positive. $r = 0.92$.

b. The plot looks somewhat linear although New York is rather influential, affecting both the correlation and the least squares line. (Without New York, $r = 0.87$.)

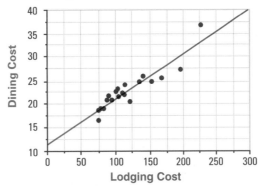

c. The equation of the least squares regression line is $y = 0.095x + 11.7$. Students might make their prediction from the line on the scatterplot or from the equation of the regression line. Using the equation of the regression line, the estimate of the cost of dining would be $21.20. A prediction using the graph of the line will vary slightly from the prediction using the equation.

d. The slope of the regression line, 0.095, means that in a city where the cost of lodging is $1 more than in another city, the cost of dining tends to be 9.5¢ more.

4. a.

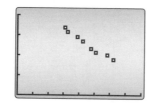 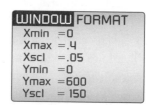

$r = -0.986$

The value of r tells you that the variables are strongly, negatively correlated. That is, as the length of the tube increases, its frequency tends to decrease. However, it is clear from the scatterplot that this relationship is not a linear one.

b. $y = -1570.5x + 735$

The plot containing the regression line appears below. Now we can see clearly that a linear model is not the best one because the points tend to be above the line at the ends and below the line in the middle.

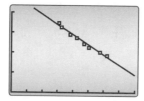

WINDOW FORMAT
Xmin =0
Xmax =.4
Xscl =.05
Ymin =0
Ymax =600
Yscl = 150

Even though a linear equation does not model the data very well, the centroid (0.2286, 376) is still on the regression line.

$$y = -1570.5\bar{x} + 735$$
$$= -1570.5(0.2286) + 735$$
$$\approx 376$$

c. $y = -1570.5(0.2) + 735 \approx 421$, which is a reasonable estimate, but not the best. It is probably a bit high as the points for nearby values of x fall under the regression line.

d. The frequency becomes negative. This is additional evidence that a line is not the best model for this situation.

Organizing

1. a. Responses will vary depending on the data set.

b. Responses will vary depending on the data set.

c. All of the coefficients in the least squares regression line will be cut in half. (The slope will be half as large and the y-intercept will be half as large.) The sum of the squared errors will be one-fourth as large. The correlation coefficient remains the same.

d. All distances in the y direction have been halved, so coefficients of the regression equation also will be halved (every point is half as high as it was before). Each error also is halved. Squaring these errors makes the sum of the squared errors one-fourth as large as before. The correlation is the same, which is not obvious without looking at the formula for r.

4. A science class conducted the following experiment on the speed of sound. One person placed a plastic tube in a beaker of water. Another person held a vibrating tuning fork over the tube, and the first person adjusted the length of the tube that was in the water until the sound of the vibrating fork became louder. The pair measured the length of the part of the tube that was out of the water and recorded that length with the frequency of vibration of the tuning fork. Data collected by Nancy and Marcus are shown below.

Length (m)	0.318	0.287	0.255	0.154	0.239	0.168	0.190	0.218
Frequency	256	288	320	512	341.3	480	426.7	384

a. Plot the (*length*, *frequency*) data. Find the correlation coefficient. What does it tell you about the relationship?

b. Find the equation of the least squares linear regression line and graph it on your plot. Does a linear equation appear to model the relationship well? Verify that the least squares regression line contains the centroid for these data.

c. Use your equation to predict the frequency for a tube of length 0.200 meters. Is this a reasonable estimate?

d. What will happen if you use your equation to predict the frequency associated with a very long tube? What conclusions can you draw from this task?

Organizing

1. Make up a data set containing five (*x*, *y*) pairs for which the *y* values are all even, positive integers.

a. Make a scatterplot of your data.

b. Find the correlation coefficient, the least squares regression line, and the sum of the squared errors for these data.

c. Transform the data using the rule (*x*, *y*) → (*x*, 0.5*y*). Make a scatterplot of the transformed data. Then find the least squares regression line for these data and recalculate the correlation coefficient and the sum of the squared errors.

d. Compare and explain the results of parts b and c.

Unit 3

2. For a project, Talar is examining the question of whether she can use linear regression to predict the height of a daughter from the height of the mother. She did all of her measurements in inches and has computed the mean height of the mothers, the mean height of the daughters, the value of r, and the equation of the regression line. Her science teacher suggested that she report her results in centimeters rather than in inches. There are approximately 2.54 centimeters in an inch.

   a. How can Talar most easily find the mean height in centimeters of the mothers? Of the daughters?

   b. How is the value of r affected, if Talar reports her results in centimeters rather than in inches?

   c. How does the equation of the regression line change, if Talar reports her results in centimeters rather than in inches?

   d. How is the value of r affected, if the heights of the mothers are left in inches but the heights of their daughters are reported in centimeters?

3. Imagine a scatterplot of points (x, y) and a second scatterplot of the same points reflected across the y-axis.

   a. How do the plots of (x, y) and $(-x, y)$ differ?

   b. How do you think the correlation coefficients of these data sets are related?

   c. How do you think the least squares regression lines for these data sets are related?

   d. Test your conjectures with a data set (x, y) and a transformed set $(-x, y)$.

4. a. Find the equations of three different lines that go through the centroid of the points below.

x	y
0	0
0	1
1	0
1	1

   b. What is the sum of the errors for each line? What is the sum of the absolute values of the errors? The sum of squared errors?

   c. Which of your three lines has the smallest sum of errors? Sum of absolute errors? Sum of squared errors?

   d. What is one helpful result of squaring the errors when finding the least squares regression line?

2. In this Organizing task, students discover the important fact that the value of the correlation coefficient doesn't depend on the units of measurement. The correlation coefficient wouldn't be a very useful measure if its value changed depending on whether we measured the heights in inches or in centimeters or if we reported value in cents rather than in dollars.

    Encourage students to make up a small data set of sample heights of mothers and daughters measured in inches. Then they can transform the data to centimeters and see how the values change.

    a. Multiply each mean height by 2.54, since there are 2.54 centimeters per inch.

    b. The value of r does not change if the units of measurement are changed. In fact, the value of r does not change if either or both variables are subjected to any linear transformation.

    c. Each coefficient is multiplied by 2.54.

    d. The value of r does not change if the units of measurement are changed, even if the unit of measurement on the x-axis and the unit of measurement on the y-axis are different.

3. a. Each plot is a reflection over the y-axis of the other.

    b. The correlations should be the same in absolute value but with opposite signs.

    c. The least squares regression lines have the same y-intercept but opposite slopes. $y = ax + b$ for (x, y) data becomes $y = -ax + b$ for $(-x, y)$ data.

    d. Student work will vary.

4. a. Answers will vary. The centroid is $(0.5, 0.5)$. Several such lines are $y = x$, $y = 0.5$, $y = 1 - x$, $y = \frac{3}{4} - \frac{1}{2}x$.

    b. Any line that goes through the centroid has the sum of the errors equal to zero. The sums of the absolute errors and the squared errors will vary.

    c. Answers will vary depending on the line the students choose. The line with the smallest SSE is $y = 0.5$, the regression line.

    d. As students see in this task, minimizing the sum of the squared errors gives a horizontal line. On the other hand, each line through the centroid has the same sum of errors and many of these are not reasonable summary lines. It is also interesting that the equations $y = x$, $y = 1 - x$, and $y = \frac{1}{2}$ each have the same sum of absolute errors. In each case $\Sigma | y - \bar{y} | = 2$, yet $y = \frac{1}{2}$ is clearly the best summary line.

Unit 3

1. The slope tells you the sign of the correlation, whether it is zero, positive, or negative. (If the variables are standardized, which students will learn about in Course 3, then the slope of the regression line is the same as the correlation coefficient.) Be sure students don't think that the slope alone tells them the strength of the association.

2. Student responses will vary. Many experiments in both biological and physical sciences involve finding a line of best fit. In the social sciences they may be looking at experiments in psychology or at population trends in history.

3. An outlier can dramatically affect the least squares regression line. An outlier tends to pull the regression line towards it, especially if its x value is far away from those of the other points. The impact is less dramatic if the outlier lies directly above or below the rest of the points.

4. This task should firmly convince students that it is always important to examine the plot for a data set.

   Each of the four data sets has the same correlation coefficient, $r = 0.816$ and the same regression equation, $y = 3.0 + 0.5x$. However, examining the scatterplots makes it clear that this model can be appropriate only for the first data set. The second data set looks quadratic, concave down. The third data set has an influential point, which should be examined and possibly discarded as the remaining 10 points are collinear. The fourth data set is different from the remaining three as there are only two different values of x. There isn't enough information to speculate on a model. The single point $(19, 12.5)$ determines the slope of the regression line.

Data Set 1

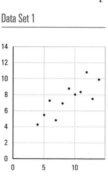

Data Set 2

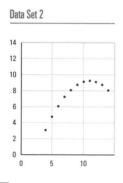

Data Set 3

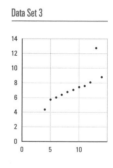

Data Set 4

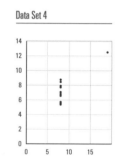

Extending

1. **a.** $b = \dfrac{\frac{5}{3} + 0 + \frac{7}{3}}{1 + 0 + 1} = \dfrac{4}{2} = 2;\ a = \dfrac{8}{3} - 2(2) = \dfrac{-4}{3};\ y = 2x - \dfrac{4}{3}$

   b. They are exactly alike except the formula for r has an extra factor in the denominator $\sqrt{\Sigma(y - \bar{y})^2}$ and the square root of $\Sigma(x - \bar{x})^2$ is taken.

   c. The centroid lies on the regression line.

Reflecting

1. What does the slope of the least squares regression line tell you about the correlation coefficient between the two variables?

2. Describe an experiment from a science class or any other class where you might be interested in using a least squares regression line.

3. How will an outlier affect the least squares regression line?

4. What can you illustrate about correlation and regression using the four data sets below?

Data Set 1		Data Set 2		Data Set 3		Data Set 4	
x	y	x	y	x	y	x	y
10	8.04	10	9.14	10	7.46	8	6.58
8	6.95	8	8.14	8	6.77	8	5.76
13	7.58	13	8.74	13	12.74	8	7.71
9	8.81	9	8.77	9	7.11	8	8.84
11	8.33	11	9.26	11	7.81	8	8.47
14	9.96	14	8.10	14	8.84	8	7.04
6	7.24	6	6.13	6	6.08	8	5.25
4	4.26	4	3.10	4	5.39	19	12.50
12	10.84	12	9.13	12	8.15	8	5.56
7	4.82	7	7.26	7	6.42	8	7.91
5	5.68	5	4.74	5	5.73	8	6.89

Extending

1. The formulas for the slope b and y-intercept a of the least squares regression line $y = a + bx$ are

$$b = \frac{\sum(x - \overline{x})(y - \overline{y})}{\sum(x - \overline{x})^2} \qquad a = \overline{y} - b\overline{x}$$

   a. Use these formulas to find the equation of the regression line for the points (1, 1), (2, 2), and (3, 5).

   b. How is the formula for the slope of the regression line similar to the formula for Pearson's correlation coefficient?

   c. What fact is reflected in the formula for a?

Unit 3

2. Make a scatterplot of the points (1, 1), (2, 2), and (3, 5). Plot the regression line $y = 2x - \frac{4}{3}$.

   a. Draw lines on your graph to show the errors for each data point. Illustrate the geometry of the term *squared errors* by drawing on the graph an appropriate square for each error.

   b. How would you show geometrically the effect of an influential point on the sum of the squared errors?

3. There is a relationship between *r* and the sum of the squared errors (SSE). The following equation can be used to find *r* if you know the SSE and the values of *y*:

$$r^2 = 1 - \frac{\text{SSE}}{\sum(y - \overline{y})^2}$$

   Refer to your work for part a of activity 2 in Investigation 2. Verify that this equation works with the points (1, 1), (2, 2), and (3, 5) and the least squares regression line $y = 2x - \frac{4}{3}$.

4. a. Find the centroid of the four points (1, 1), (2, 3), (3, 4), and (6, 8).

   b. Find the equation of the line that goes through the centroid and has a slope of 0. Compute the sum of squared errors (SSE) for that line.

   c. Repeat part b using the slopes in the table below. Fill in the values of the SSE.

Slope	0	0.5	1	1.5	2	2.5
SSE						

   d. Plot the pairs (*slope*, *SSE*). What do you observe?

   e. Estimate the slope that will give the smallest SSE.

   f. Check your answer to part e by finding the equation of the regression line.

5. This task is a sample item for the Advanced Placement Statistics exam.

The regression line $y = 1.6 + 2.2x$ for the five points on the scatterplot on the right was computed using the method of least squares. Make a copy of the scatterplot and graph the regression line on it. Use your plot and graph to demonstrate the meaning of the term "least squares".

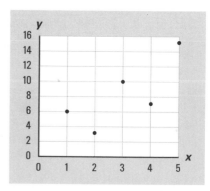

Source: *Advanced Placement Course Description: Statistics.* College Entrance Examination Board, 1996.

2. **a.** The sum of the areas of the squares is the SSE. See the illustration below.

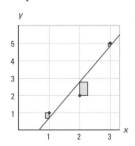

b. Perhaps the best way to illustrate the effect of an influential point would be a two-step process. First calculate the regression line with the influential point as one of the points, and show the "error square" for the influential point. Next calculate the regression line for the data excluding the influential point, and again show the error square for the influential point. The difference in the lines should be apparent from the difference in this square.

3. $(0.961)^2 = 1 - \left(\dfrac{\frac{1}{9} + \frac{4}{9} + \frac{1}{9}}{\frac{25}{9} + \frac{4}{9} + \frac{49}{9}} \right)$

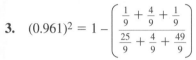

4. **a.** (3, 4)

b. $y = 4$; SSE = 26

c.

Slope	Equation	SSE
0	$y = 4$	26
0.5	$y = 0.5x + 2.5$	10.5
1	$y = x + 1$	2
1.5	$y = 1.5x - 0.5$	0.5
2	$y = 2x - 2$	6
2.5	$y = 2.5x - 3.5$	18.5

d. The points follow a parabola.

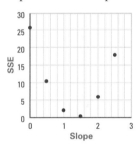

e. Students should realize that the equation of the regression line is the one that goes through the centroid and has the smallest SSE. That is, the slope of the regression line would be the x value at the vertex of the parabola. This appears to be at approximately 1.4.

f. The equation of the regression line is $y = 1.36x - 0.07$. The slope of the regression line is 1.36, close to the approximation found using the graph.

5. The regression line is used as a model that predicts the value of y when x is given. Since we think of x as being fixed, we measure the residual of y as the vertical distance from the point to the regression line. The heavy vertical lines on the plot at the right represent the residuals. To get the value for a residual, we compute (*observed y – expected y*). These residuals are $(6 - 3.8)$, $(3 - 6)$, $(10 - 8.2)$, $(7 - 10.4)$, and $(15 - 12.6)$. Squaring these residuals and adding we get $4.84 + 9 + 3.24 + 11.56 + 5.76$ or 34.4. No other line would give a smaller sum.

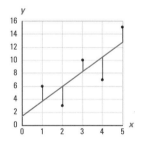

Alternatively, students could make squares of the residuals on the plot, as in the diagram at the right, and say that the regression line makes the total area of these squares smaller than any other line does.

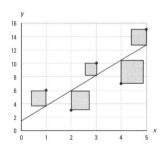

See Assessment Resource pages 88–93.

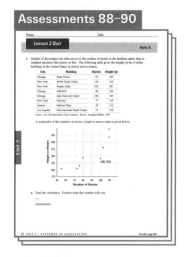

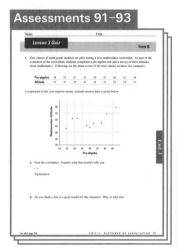

Unit 3

Lesson 4 *Looking Back*

SYNTHESIZE UNIT IDEAS   small-group activity

Before embarking on this section, you might wish to give your students an opportunity to list, individually at first, and then as a large group, all the new ideas they learned about in this unit. As individuals offer their contributions you can list these on the board and, once the class is satisfied the list is complete, you can ask students to give a brief explanation of each idea or explain how ideas are connected. This should serve the dual purpose of focusing students on the review section and giving them a sense of accomplishment as they recall ideas which were unfamiliar at the beginning of this unit.

You may wish to have students do task 1 and choose either task 2 or 3 to complete. A class discussion around tasks 2 and 3 should be sufficient to bring closure to students' understandings of the major objectives of this unit.

Looking Back

In this unit, you investigated both visually and numerically the strength of the association between paired variables. You used patterns in scatterplots and Spearman's and Pearson's correlation coefficients to estimate the strength of association between variables. You discovered that influential points, which can be detected visually on a scatterplot, can have a marked influence on the correlation coefficient and the regression line. You also examined cause-and-effect relationships for highly-correlated variables. In the last lesson, you found the "best-fitting" linear model, called the least squares regression line. This line minimizes the sum of the squared errors (residuals). The three activities that follow give you an opportunity to pull together the important ideas and methods of this unit.

1. The Gallup Poll conducted a survey on how dangerous people thought cities were and then ranked the cities using the results. They also ranked the cities in terms of the actual number of violent crimes per 100,000 residents. The cities and their rankings are listed in the following table. A "1" represents the least safe city.

New York City

City	Perceived Rank	Actual Rank
Miami	1	2
New York	2	3
Los Angeles	3	5
Washington D.C.	4	1
Detroit	5	6
Chicago	6	4
San Francisco	7	10
Philadelphia	8	12
Atlanta	9	9
Houston	10	8
Boston	11	11
Dallas	12	7

Copyright 1993, *USA Today.* Reprinted with permission.

Unit 3

a. Of these cities, which one do people think has the fewest violent crimes per 100,000 residents?

b. Make a scatterplot of the (*perceived rank, actual rank*) data. How do people's beliefs about which cities are most dangerous correlate with the actual rankings?

c. Does it make sense to compute a regression line for the data? Why or why not?

2. The fifteen highest-rated passers in professional football through the 1995 season are given below. (A quarterback is eligible for the list when he makes more than 1,500 attempts.)

Quarterback Passing Statistics

Player	Years	Attempts	Completions	Yards
Steve Young*	11	2876	1845	23069
Joe Montana	15	5391	3409	40551
Dan Marino*	13	6531	3913	48841
Brett Favre*	5	2150	1342	14825
Jim Kelly*	10	4400	2652	32657
Troy Aikman*	7	2713	1704	19607
Roger Staubach	11	2958	1685	22700
Neil Lomax	8	3153	1817	22771
Sonny Jurgensen	18	4262	2433	32224
Len Dawson	19	3741	2136	28711
Dave Krieg*	16	4911	2866	35668
Ken Anderson	16	4475	2654	32838
Jeff Hostetler*	10	1792	1036	12983
Neil O'Donnell*	6	1871	1069	12867
Danny White	13	2950	1761	21959

(An asterisk indicates a player was still active at the end of 1995.)
Source: *1997 World Almanac and Book of Facts.* Mahwah, NJ: World Almanac, 1996.

a. Examine the scatterplot matrix on the following page.

- Which two variables appear to be most strongly correlated?
- Which two variables appear to have the weakest correlation?
- Are any two variables negatively correlated?
- Are there any pairs of variables for which a linear model would not be appropriate?

1. **a.** Dallas was ranked last which means it was perceived as the least dangerous city.

    b. $r = 0.74$

    There is a strong correlation. People rank the cities approximately the same as the statistics indicate they should be.

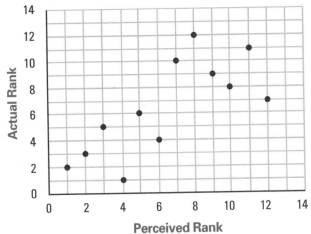

    c. A regression line will not help determine whether people's perception of violent crime in cities is the same as the statistics indicate. A regression line is used to model and predict; there is no reason to make a prediction in this situation. The line $y = x$ is a better model for comparison. The vertical distance to this line from the point can be interpreted as the "error of perception".

2. **a.** ■ *Attempts* and *yards* have the highest correlation. However, *completions* and *attempts,* and *completions* and *yards,* are also very highly correlated. It is difficult to see which of these three correlations is largest from the scatterplot matrix.

    ■ *Years* is weakly correlated with *completions*. However the correlation between *years* and *attempts,* and *years* and *yards,* are almost as weak.

    ■ No.

    ■ Not obviously so. However a linear model would not do well in predicting *attempts, completions*, or *yards* when the number of years is large.

	Years	Atps	Comp	Yards
Years	1.0000	0.6210	0.5823	0.6458
Attempts	0.6210	1.0000	0.9946	0.9972
Completions	0.5823	0.9946	1.0000	0.9929
Yards	0.6458	0.9972	0.9929	1.0000

c. Dan Marino, who had played only 13 years, seems to be most outstanding. Encourage students to find the point for Marino on each scatterplot.

d. The equation of the regression line is $y = 0.604x - 27.165$.
- 0.604
- If a quarterback makes 100 more passing attempts than another quarterback, he would tend to make about 60 more completions.
- The largest residual is 179.167 for Joe Montana. This means Montana completed about 179 more passes than we would expect for a quarterback with 5391 attempts.
- 2389 completions

e. There is a cause-and-effect relationship because an attempt is necessary in order to have a completion. A quarterback can't have a lot of completions without having a lot of attempts. Of course, other variables such as the skill of the players affect the number of completions also.

NOTE: In several scatterplots, such as (*yards, years*), the values of *y* become more spread out as *x* gets larger. This is called *heterogeneity of variance* and is an important feature to note in bivariate data.

Unit 3

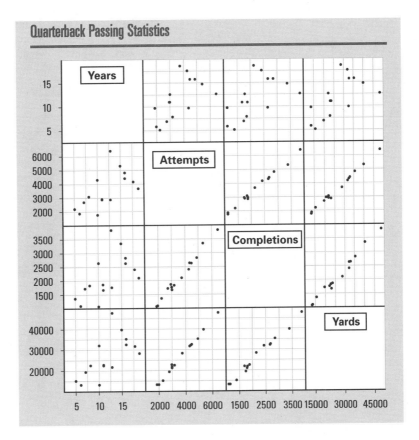

Quarterback Passing Statistics

b. Divide the workload among members of your group and construct the correlation matrix for these data. Check your estimates in part a.

c. From observing the scatterplot matrix, which player appears to be the most outstanding?

d. Find the least squares linear regression line for the (*attempts, completions*) data.

- What is the slope of this line?
- What does this slope mean in the context of these data?
- Which quarterback has the largest residual and what does this fact tell you?
- Use the regression line to predict the number of completions you would expect for a quarterback with 4000 attempts.

e. Comment on the cause-and-effect relationship between number of attempts and number of completions.

Unit 3

3. The Scholastic Assessment Test (SAT) is a test required for admission to many colleges and universities. The average mathematics score for each state along with the percentage of students from each state who took the test are given in the table below.

A scatterplot of the (*% taking SAT, mean math score*) data is shown at the top of the next page.

SAT Statistics by State

State	Percent Taking SAT	Mean SAT Math Score	State	Percent Taking SAT	Mean SAT Math Score
Alabama	8	558	Montana	21	547
Alaska	47	513	Nebraska	9	568
Arizona	28	521	Nevada	31	507
Arkansas	6	550	New Hampshire	70	514
California	45	511	New Jersey	69	505
Colorado	30	538	New Mexico	12	548
Connecticut	79	504	New York	73	499
Delaware	66	495	North Carolina	59	486
D.C.	50	473	North Dakota	5	599
Florida	48	496	Ohio	24	535
Georgia	63	477	Oklahoma	8	557
Hawaii	54	510	Oregon	50	521
Idaho	15	536	Pennsylvania	71	492
Illinois	14	575	Rhode Island	69	491
Indiana	57	494	South Carolina	57	474
Iowa	5	600	South Dakota	5	566
Kansas	9	571	Tennessee	14	552
Kentucky	12	544	Texas	48	500
Louisiana	9	550	Utah	4	575
Maine	68	498	Vermont	48	500
Maryland	64	504	Virginia	68	496
Massachusetts	80	504	Washington	47	519
Michigan	11	565	West Virginia	17	506
Minnesota	9	593	Wisconsin	8	586
Mississippi	4	557	Wyoming	11	544
Missouri	9	569			

Source: *1997 World Almanac and Book of Facts.* Mahwah, NJ : World Almanac, 1996.

Unit 3

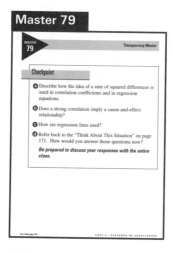

Master 79

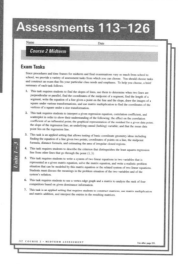

Assessments 94–112

Assessments 113–126

3. **a.** The plot seems to have two clusters. For those states where fewer than 35% take the test, the larger the percentage who take the test, the lower the mean math score. In states where more than 35% take the test, the points seem to cluster around a horizontal line with a mean math score of a little less than 500.

b. As the percent taking the test increases, the mean math score tends to decrease.

c. The correlation will stay the same, -0.86.

d. The data are not linear, so a least squares linear regression line would be misleading. If we wanted to model with a single equation, a curve would be more appropriate. However, since the data seem to fall into two distinct clusters, a single equation wouldn't be the best way to summarize these data.

e. Although students probably won't realize this, the lurking variable is the percentage of students who take the ACT. The states where a small percentage of students take the SAT are in the south and midwest. In those states, most colleges ask for the ACT so students take it rather than the SAT. Most of the students in these states who take the SAT are applying to competitive out-of-state colleges. These are usually the better students who are likely to score high on the SAT.

SHARE AND SUMMARIZE full-class discussion

Checkpoint

See Teaching Master 79.

a A sum of squared differences is used as a measure of distance in statistics, just as it is in Euclidean geometry. Thus it appears in Spearman's correlation coefficient as Σd^2, Pearson's correlation coefficient as $\Sigma(x - \bar{x})^2$ and $\Sigma(y - \bar{y})^2$, in the definition of the least squares regression line (minimize $\Sigma(y - \bar{y})^2$), and in the formula for the slope of the regression line as $\Sigma(x - \bar{x})^2$.

b No. Students have seen many examples of two variables with a strong correlation but with no cause-and-effect relationship. Examples occur when time is a lurking variable; many things tend to increase over time, such as a child's reading level and shoe size.

c There are two important ways. The first is to make an estimate or prediction of y for some particular value of x. An example of this would be to use the regression equation from activity 1 of Investigation 1 in Lesson 3 to predict a ninth-grade GPA if the student had a 2.0 GPA in eighth grade. The second way regression equations are used is as a model of a situation. For example, a scientist might use a regression equation for the (*exposure to radioactive waste, cancer deaths*) data on page 211 of the student text to try to understand the degree to which exposure to radioactivity contributes to cancer deaths. The scientist may not be interested in predicting cancer deaths for some other community, but could be looking for a model of the effect of exposure to radioactivity.

d See possible answers on pages T171 and T231C. Students should now understand that Pearson's correlation coefficient is the best measure of linear association.

JOURNAL ENTRY: You may wish to ask students to search for other contexts in which a regression line is useful. They then can categorize the regression line as helpful for prediction or as a model that helps one understand the underlying relationship between two variables.

See Assessment Resources, pages 94–112, for Unit 3 assessments.
See Assessment Resources, pages 113–126, for Midterm assessments.

SAT Statistics

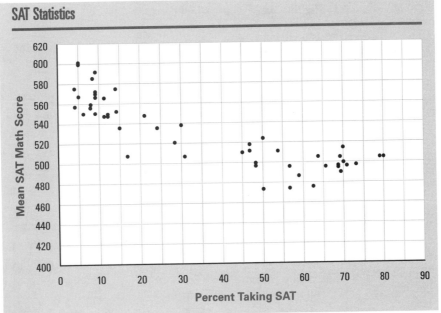

Percent Taking SAT (x-axis), *Mean SAT Math Score* (y-axis)

a. Describe the relation between the percentage of students in each state who take the test and the mean mathematics score.

b. The correlation coefficient is negative. What does that tell you about the association between the two variables?

c. How will the correlation change if you plot (*mean math score, % taking SAT*)?

d. Would the least squares regression line be the "best" model to describe the relationship between the two variables? Why or why not?

e. Comment on a possible cause-and-effect relationship between the two variables.

Checkpoint

ⓐ Describe how the idea of a sum of squared differences is used in correlation coefficients and in regression equations.

ⓑ Does a strong correlation imply a cause-and-effect relationship?

ⓒ How are regression lines used?

ⓓ Refer back to the "Think About This Situation" questions on page 171. How would you answer those questions now?

Be prepared to discuss your responses with the entire class.

Looking Back, Looking Ahead

▶Reflecting on Mathematical Content

The "Patterns of Association" unit builds on the work from several previous units in this curriculum:

- In Unit 1 of Course 1, students learned the first rule of data analysis: look at a plot of the data before making any computations or decisions. This lesson was reinforced in "Patterns of Association" when students learned that properly interpreting the correlation coefficient and the regression equation is impossible without examining the scatterplot for influential points and for a nonlinear pattern.

- In Unit 3 of Course 1, students first learned about linear equations and the idea of a line of best fit to a set of data points. In "Patterns of Association", students learned that the best fit line is the one that minimizes the sum of the squared errors.

- Throughout Course 1 and continuing in Course 2, students learn how to formulate mathematical models. For example, they learned about the types of situations and data patterns that could be modeled well by a linear equation or by an exponential equation. In "Patterns of Association", students more carefully examined methods for assessing how well an equation fits the data. They learned to compute residuals and the sum of the squared errors. They learned that while the correlation coefficient gives some indication of how closely the points cluster about a line, its value by itself does not indicate how appropriate a linear model is for the data.

The major new idea in "Patterns of Association" is the use of a sum of squared differences as a measure of distance in statistics. In fact, every formula that students encountered in this unit involved a sum of squared differences. Much of the mathematical theory of statistics revolves around sums of squared errors and least squares fits (such as the regression formula). Towards the end of Course 3, in the unit "Patterns of Variation", students investigate the meaning and applications of the standard deviation. Just as the mean is the standard measure of center, the standard deviation is the standard measure of spread. It is paired with the mean in much of statistical theory. The standard deviation also involves a sum of squared errors. In the Course 4 unit "Geometry in Space", students again will be reminded that even in Euclidean geometry we use a sum of squared differences as our measure of distance: $\sqrt{(x_2 - x_1)^2 + (y_2 - y_1)^2 + (z_2 - z_1)^2}$.

Finally, in "Patterns of Association", students learned the criterion for fitting (straight) line to data (minimizing the sum of the squared errors). Their calculators or computer software also will fit other types of functions, such as exponential and power functions. This fact is used in the "Exponential Models" unit in Course 1 and in the "Power Models" unit in Course 2. In the Course 4 unit "Function Composition and Inverses", students will learn how such nonlinear models are found. The procedure also uses the theory of least squares by first "linearizing" the data using a suitable transformation, fitting a linear equation using the least squares method, and then transforming the variables back to their original form.

Unit 3 Assessment

Midterm and Cumulative Assessments

Teaching Notes *continued*

Notes continued from page 171

Students may remember the idea of regression and use their calculators or computer software to find a regression line. The least squares regression line is

$$score = 90.9 + 0.000112 \ (expenditure).$$

The slope is positive, indicating a positive association. The slope of 0.000112 indicates that, on the average, when the expenditure goes up $1 per student, the overall score increases by 0.000112. That is, when the expenditure goes up by $1000, the overall score tends to go up by 0.112. Using this equation, the predicted overall score for UCLA would be 93.3. We wouldn't have a lot of confidence in this prediction because we are extrapolating from the top 25 schools to the next 25 schools and the same relationship may not apply. (In fact, UCLA's overall score was 83.2.)

EXPLORE small-group investigation

INVESTIGATION 1 Ranking and Relationships

You might want to introduce this investigation by talking with students about rankings. In what contexts have they seen ranking used? Have them list a number of such contexts (for example, automobiles, football teams, or pop recordings). Even though the text has music types to be ranked, you can substitute another category that generates substantial enthusiasm or replace any of the types of music listed in the text.

You might ask why we would want to assign a numerical value for an association, say between a player's salary and record for the season for some professional sports team. Another issue is the scale of such a value. You could present this issue to your students by saying, "Suppose someone says that the two variables are related and the association measures 100. Someone else looking at the same data has a different way of measuring the association and says that it measures 0.9 on their scale. What would you need to know for either measurement to make sense to you?"

When students begin to work on the activities, individual opinions are important, so students should rank the music or other topic independently without any discussion. You might put your own ranking on the board or overhead, after the students have finished ranking. If someone does not have a partner, then he or she can use your ranking for the plot (and possibly display a negative association). The first two activities are intended to give students an opportunity to interact with and make sense of the problem before any external information is offered.

1. See Teaching Master 57.

   a. Each pair of students probably will have a unique scatterplot. You may want to give them a large piece of paper to use so that when the plots are displayed around the room they are seen easily. Posting the plots around the room allows everyone to compare them easily.

Teaching Notes *continued*

Notes continued
from page 178

a Positive correlation shows up in the list of rankings as small differences between the rankings, in the scatterplot as points that cluster about a line with positive slope, and as positive values of r_s.

b Negative correlation shows up in the list of rankings as large differences between the rankings, in the scatterplot as points that cluster about a line with negative slope, and as negative values of r_s.

c The scatterplot matrix is arranged so that the plots in each row (and each column) all share a single scale. By looking across one row (or down one column) we can see one variable plotted against each of the others with the scales lined up for that variable. We can tell at a glance which variables are positively and negatively correlated with that variable. By highlighting the points for one case, as we did for Riverside, we can see the variables for which that case is higher or lower than the others.

You may wish to have a discussion comparing the methods that students developed in Investigation 1 with Spearman's formula for the rank correlation coefficient.

Your notes here:

Unit 3

Unit 4 ▶ Power Models

UNIT OVERVIEW In the algebra and functions strand of Course 1, students developed an understanding of linear and exponential relationships. The purpose of this unit is to develop student understanding of a much wider range of models including those of the forms $y = ax^2$, $y = ax^3$, $y = \dfrac{a}{x^2}$, $y = \dfrac{a}{x^3}$, and $y = ax^2 + bx + c$. In keeping with the philosophy of the Core-Plus Mathematics Project, these models are introduced to students through the analysis of data.

By the end of the unit, students should have a good understanding of the shapes of the graphs and the numerical patterns in the tables generated by the new models, how these models compare to each other and linear and exponential models, and possible real-world situations that can be represented by each model.

Unit 4 Objectives

- To develop understanding of the types of situations that could be represented by power models, inverse power models, and quadratic models
- To model situations involving direct variation, inverse variation, and quadratic relationships
- To compare patterns found in tables and graphs of models of the forms $y = ax^2$, $y = ax^3$, $y = \frac{a}{x^2}$, $y = \frac{a}{x^3}$, and $y = ax^2 + bx + c$
- To develop understanding of the different rates of change in various models
- To find good estimates of solutions to quadratic equations and to be able to check those solutions
- To simplify expressions by applying properties of exponents and rewriting radical expressions

Power Models

233

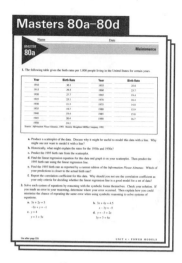

▶Developing Understanding of Power Models Throughout the Unit

In Lesson 1, students explore the relationships between edge lengths, perimeters, surface areas, and volumes of similar figures in order to develop understanding of the basic power models of the form $y = x^2$ and $y = x^3$. Then they explore the shape of the more general form of power models, $y = ax^n$.

In Lesson 2, the notation of inverse variation is introduced in the contexts of the time of a trip and the intensity of sound or light. Here again students develop an understanding of the contexts, shapes of the graphs of the functions, and how these functions compare to power, exponential, and linear functions.

The purpose of Lesson 3 is to explore the properties of quadratic models with rules of the form $y = ax^2 + bx + c$ and to develop ways to solve and check solutions to quadratic equations. (Note that power models $y = ax^n$ are quadratics if the power is 2 and quadratics are power models if both b and c are equal to zero.)

In Lesson 4, power models with exponents of $\frac{1}{2}$ and $\frac{1}{3}$ are introduced through geometric situations involving braces, spirals, and cubes. Students discover how to simplify radical expressions, apply properties of exponents, and solve equations involving radicals and powers.

See Teaching Masters 80a–80d for Maintenance tasks that students can work on after Lesson 1.

Unit 4

Unit 4 Planning Guide

Lesson Objectives	MORE Assignments	Suggested Pacing	Materials
Lesson 1 *Same Shape, Different Size* • To explore simple power models of the forms $y = x^2$ and $y = x^3$ including the relationship of edge lengths, perimeters, surface areas, and volumes of similar figures through tables, graphs, and symbolic rules • To compare power models of the forms $y = ax^2$ and $y = ax^3$ to linear and exponential models • To compare the patterns found in the table and graph of $y = x^2$ to those found in the table and graph of $y = x^3$ • To determine how changes in the coefficients of power models $y = ax^2$ and $y = ax^3$ affect the patterns in corresponding tables of values and graphs	**after page 238** Students can begin Modeling Task 1 or 4; or Reflecting Task 1 or 3 from p. 241. **page 241** **Modeling:** 1 or 2 and 4* **Organizing:** 4 and 5 **Reflecting:** 1 and 3 **Extending:** Choose one*	5 days	• Small cubes • Teaching Resources 81–86 • Assessment Resources 127–132
Lesson 2 *Inverse Variation* • To determine and explore the inverse variation model, $y = \frac{1}{x}$, through tables and graphs • To determine and explore the inverse variation model, $y = \frac{1}{x^2}$, through tables and graphs • To explore the patterns for relations of the forms $y = \frac{a}{x}$ and $y = \frac{a}{x^2}$ through tables and graphs	**after page 252** Students can begin Modeling Task 1 or 2; or Organizing Task 1 from p. 259. **after page 256** Students can begin Modeling Task 3 or Reflecting Task 2 from p. 259. **page 259** **Modeling:** 3 and 1 or 2* **Organizing:** 1 and 2 **Reflecting:** 1 and 2 or 3* **Extending:** 1	6 days	• Flashlight for demonstration • Teaching Resources 80a–80d, 87–92 • Assessment Resources 133–138
Lesson 3 *Quadratic Models* • To determine the patterns that appear in the tables and graphs of a rule in the form $y = ax^2$, $y = ax^2 + c$, or $y = ax^2 + bx + c$ • To estimate the solution of a quadratic equation using a table of values and a graph • To determine if the solution of a quadratic equation is correct • To determine the number of solutions, and to approximate solutions, for various equations related to a quadratic model • To understand the types of situations that could be modeled by quadratic equations	**after page 271** Students can begin Modeling Task 1 or 3 from p. 283. **after page 273** Students can begin Modeling Task 2, 4, or 5; or Reflecting Task 2 or 5 from p. 283. **after page 277** Students can begin Reflecting Task 3, 4, or 5 from p. 283. **after page 280** Students can begin Reflecting Task 1 from p. 283. **page 283** **Modeling:** 1 and choice of one* **Organizing:** 1 and 2 **Reflecting:** Choose two* **Extending:** 2 or 3*	8 days	• Teaching Resources 93–98 • Assessment Resources 139–144
Lesson 4 *Radicals and Fractional Power Models* • To be able to describe the meaning of square and cube roots • To explore properties of square and cube root functions and their role in reasoning about important geometric patterns • To discover and use the basic principle for simplification of radical expressions • To summarize fundamental properties for transforming exponential expressions into alternative equivalent forms	**after page 293** Students can begin Modeling Task 2 or Organizing Task 1 from p. 305. **after page 298** Students can begin Modeling Task 4 from p. 304. **after page 300** Students can begin Modeling Task 5 from p. 305. **page 303** **Modeling:** 2 and 4 or 5* **Organizing:** 1, 2, and 3 **Reflecting:** Choose one* **Extending:** 3 or 4*	5 days	• Teaching Resources 99-104 • Assessment Resources 145–150
Lesson 5 *Looking Back* • To review the major objectives of the unit		3 days (includes testing)	• Teaching Resource 105 • Assessment Resources 151–168

* *When choice is indicated, it is important to leave the choice to the student.*
Note: *It is best if Organizing tasks are discussed as a whole class after they have been assigned as homework.*

Lesson 1 — Same Shape, Different Size

The New York City parade on Thanksgiving Day, sponsored by Macy's Department Store, is famous for its display of very large balloons in the shape of cartoon characters.

Think About This Situation

When a new balloon is designed, the first step is to make a scale model that is smaller than the real balloon will be. Suppose that for a Big Bird balloon, a scale model is made that is $\frac{1}{20}$ of the planned full size.

a If the model is 2 feet tall, how tall would the full-size balloon be?

b If the model has a belt that is 1.5 feet around Big Bird's waist, how long would the belt be on the full-size balloon?

c If the model has a surface area of 6 square feet, how many square feet of material would be required to make the large balloon?

d If the model holds 2.5 cubic feet of air, what would the volume of the full-size balloon be?

e How would your answers to parts a–d change if the full-size balloon were to be only 10 times the size of the scale model?

234 UNIT 4 • POWER MODELS

Same Shape, Different Size

Master 81

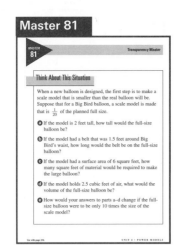

LESSON OVERVIEW   The purpose of this lesson is to develop student understanding of the basic power functions that have rules of the form $y = ax^2$ and $y = ax^3$. By the end of the lesson, most students should have a good idea about what shape of graph to expect from any particular example of this family. They also should be able to describe the shapes of those graphs and the patterns of change in related tables of (x, y) values.

The basic power models are introduced to students through analysis of data. One of the most powerful general principles of quantitative analysis is the fact that when linear dimensions of some object increase by a factor of k, the surface area of the transformed object increases by a factor of k^2 and the volume by a factor of k^3. In this lesson, students will encounter both the shape of basic power rules and examples of situations in geometry and the sciences where those power models are useful.

In the first investigation, students build physical models and discover that length, area, and volume are related by power rules. In the second investigation, students generalize the patterns observed in those particular contexts to the general power rule forms $y = ax^2$ and $y = ax^3$. The MORE tasks give students opportunities to see power models in other contexts and to explore variations on the basic power model rule forms. They also help students to make connections by comparing the power models to linear and exponential models studied in Course 1.

For some other patterns of growth, the appropriate power model is of the form $y = x^r$, where r is some rational number and not necessarily an integer. In fact, using a calculator or computer to find the power model that best fits some data most likely will result in an exponent that is *not* an integer. This introductory lesson concentrates on analyzing and applying the basic power models where r is an integer, but it also introduces the Power Regression feature of graphics calculators and computer software (in Organizing task 5).

Lesson Objectives

- To explore simple power models of the forms $y = x^2$ and $y = x^3$ including the relationship of edge lengths, perimeters, surface areas, and volumes of similar figures through tables, graphs, and symbolic rules
- To compare power models of the forms $y = ax^2$ and $y = ax^3$ to linear and exponential models
- To compare the patterns found in the table and graph of $y = x^2$ to those found in the table and graph of $y = x^3$
- To determine how changes in the coefficients of power models $y = ax^2$ and $y = ax^3$ affect the patterns in corresponding tables of values and graphs

See additional Teaching Notes on page T317C.

INVESTIGATION 1   Starting from Cube One

Students deepen their understanding of the fundamental theorem of proportionality in this investigation. That principle of proportionality states that if two objects are geometrically similar and the scale factor is k, then the ratio of their lengths is k, the ratio of their areas is k^2, and the ratio of their volumes is k^3. Since students explored this concept in Unit 2, "Patterns of Location, Shape, and Size", the investigation should go smoothly. Students need to connect the geometric ideas of dimensions to concrete items such as the perimeter of a face of the cube or the belt of the balloon. The main focus of this investigation is on patterns of change that lead to quadratic and cubic models.

NOTE: Activity Master 82 will help students organize their data from this investigation.

Experiment 1

Before students begin working on Experiment 1, you may wish to spend a few minutes discussing the illustration of cubes in the student text. Here are some suggested discussion questions:

How did the height change from the first to the second drawing? From the first to the third? From the first to the fourth? How does this change relate to the balloon measurements in the "Think About This Situation" on page 234? How did the height of the balloon change?

What does "perimeter" mean? What is the perimeter of the face of the first cube? How does the perimeter of the face change from the first to the second drawing? From the first to the third? From the first to the fourth? What measurement on the balloon is like a perimeter?

How do we calculate the area of a face? How does the area of a face change from the first to the second drawing?

This discussion need go only as far as it takes to remind students of the measurement concepts involved, and to have them focus on change. Students need to build the models to internalize how many cubes are used and to see how quickly the volume changes with an increase of one unit in the length of a side.

As you observe the students at work collecting data, you may need to keep the conversation focused on how the variables change by asking questions such as the following: "Which grows faster with every one unit increase in the length: perimeter, area of a face, or surface area? What does it mean to say that one variable grows faster than another?"

See additional Teaching Notes on page T317D.

INVESTIGATION 1 ▶ Starting from Cube One

The questions about size of scale models and full-size parade balloons involve some very important general relations between length, area, and volume of similar figures. Clues to those relations can be found in data from experiments with cubes of different sizes.

Experiment 1

1. Obtain a set of small cubes and start building a series of larger cubes as shown. Divide the workload among the members of your group.

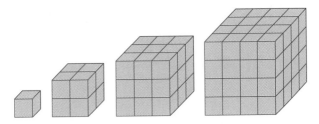

   For each cube you build, and for several more that you may only sketch or imagine, record the following pieces of information in a table like the one below. Be sure to identify what units of measure you use.

   ■ Length of one edge of the cube (like the "height" of the balloon body)

   ■ Perimeter of one face of the cube (like the "waist" or "head" size of the balloon body

   ■ Surface area of the cube (like the "surface covering" of the balloon body)

Cube Measurements

Edge Length (in units)	Perimeter of One Face (in units)	Area of One Face (in square units)	Total Surface Area of Cube (in square units)
1	4	1	6
2			
⋮			

2. To help you search for patterns in these data, make a plot of the (*edge length, perimeter of a face*) data pairs. Then use the data and graph to answer these questions.

   a. If the edge length increases by 1 unit, how does the perimeter of a face change?

   b. Write a rule relating edge length E and perimeter P of a face.

   c. Find the perimeter of one face of a cube with edge length 20 units. Compare it to that of a cube with edge length 1 unit.

   d. What does your answer suggest about the ways that height, waist, chest, and head size of a Big Bird parade balloon would be related to those measurements of a scale model $\frac{1}{20}$ of the full size?

3. Use the data on edge length and area to answer these questions.

   a. As the edge length increases, how does the area of each face of the cube change? How is this pattern displayed in an (*edge length, face area*) plot?

   b. Write a rule relating the face area FA and the edge length E of a cube.

   c. As edge length increases, how does the total surface area change? How is this pattern displayed in an (*edge length, total surface area*) plot?

   d. Write a rule relating the total surface area SA and the edge length E of a cube.

4. Compare the face area and total surface area of a cube with edge length 20 cm to the corresponding areas of a cube with edge length 1 cm. What does that comparison suggest about the way that the surface area of a $\frac{1}{20}$ size scale model would be related to the surface area of a similar full-size balloon?

Experiment 2

1. Consider again the cubes in Experiment 1. This time record data about their edge length and volume. Complete a table like the one at the right.

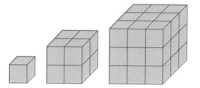

Cube Volumes

Edge Length (in units)	Volume of Cube (in cubic units)
1	1
2	
3	
4	
5	
6	
7	
8	

2.

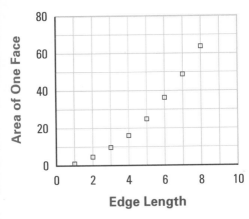

```
WINDOW FORMAT
Xmin =0
Xmax=9
Xscl =1
Ymin =0
Ymax=36
Yscl =4
```

   a. The perimeter increases by 4 centimeters with each 1 centimeter increase of edge length.

   b. $P = 4E$ or $E = \frac{1}{4}P$

   c. The perimeter of one face of a cube with edge length 20 units is 80 units. This is 20 times the perimeter of a cube with edge length 1 unit.

   d. The perimeter of one face of a cube with edge length 20 will be twenty times the face perimeter of a cube with edge length 1. This suggests that the height, waist, chest, and head size of the Big Bird balloon will be 20 times those of the scale model.

3. **a.** As edge length increases by 1, the area increases by larger and larger amounts. The area does not increase at a constant rate, but rather at a rate that continually increases. This pattern can be seen in the plot below at the left, since the plot is a curve and the vertical distance between consecutive points is continually increasing.

   b. $FA = E^2$

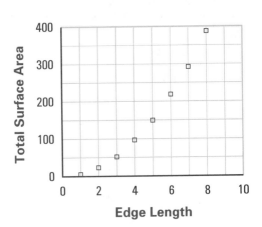

   c. The surface area does not increase at a constant rate, but at an increasing rate. This pattern is revealed in the plot above at the right by the fact that the shape of the plot is a curve that is getting continually steeper.

   d. $SA = 6E^2$

4. For a cube of edge length 20 cm, the face area is 400 square cm or 400 times the face of a 1-cm cube. The total surface area is 2400 square cm or 400 times as great as that of the 1-cm cube. This might suggest that the $\frac{1}{20}$ size scale model will have $\frac{1}{400}$ the surface area of the full-size balloon. Equivalently, the full-size balloon will have a surface area 400 times that of the $\frac{1}{20}$ size scale model.

See additional Teaching Notes on page T317D.

Unit 4

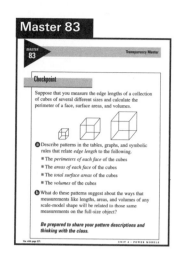

2. a. As edge length changes, the volume of the cube increases at an increasing rate. For example, as the edge length changes from 4 to 5, a change of 1, the volume changes from 64 to 125, or a change of 61. As the edge length changes from 5 to 6, again a change of 1, the volume goes from 125 to 216, a change of 91. The graph of this relation is not linear. It curves upward even more quickly than the surface area plots.

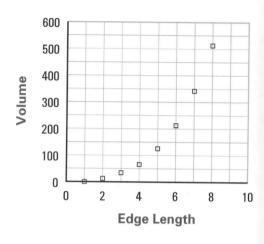

b. $V = E^3$

3. The volume of the larger cube will be 8000 cubic centimeters or 8000 times the volume of the cube with edge length 1 cm. The volume of the full-size balloon would be 8000 times the volume of the scale model.

SHARE AND SUMMARIZE   **full-class discussion**

Checkpoint

CONSTRUCTING A MATH TOOLKIT: Students should summarize the principle of proportionality (the response to checkpoint part b) in their Math Toolkits.

See Teaching Master 83.

While discussing the "Checkpoint" questions you may wish to refer back to the "Think About This Situation" at the beginning of the lesson and provide any closure that is necessary.

See additional Teaching Notes on page T317E.

Unit 4

2. Use the data on edge length and volume to answer the following questions.

   a. As edge length increases, how does the volume of the cube change? How is this pattern displayed in a plot of (*edge length, volume*) data?

   b. Write a rule relating the volume *V* and the edge length *E* of a cube.

3. Compare the volume of a cube with edge length 20 cm to the volume of a cube with edge length 1 cm. What does that comparison suggest about the way that the volume of a $\frac{1}{20}$ size scale model would be related to the volume of a similar full-size balloon?

Checkpoint

Suppose that you measure the edge lengths of a collection of cubes of several different sizes and calculate the perimeters of faces, surface areas, and volumes.

 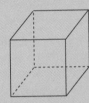 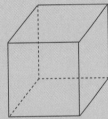

a Describe patterns in the tables, graphs, and symbolic rules which relate *edge length* to the following.

   ■ The perimeters of each face of the cubes

   ■ The areas of each face of the cubes

   ■ The total surface areas of the cubes

   ■ The volumes of the cubes

b What do these patterns suggest about the ways that measurements like lengths, areas, and volumes of any scale-model shape will be related to those same measurements on the full-size object?

Be prepared to share your pattern descriptions and thinking with the class.

Unit 4

On Your Own

The diagram below shows two circles. One has diameter of 1 inch and the other has diameter of 2 inches.

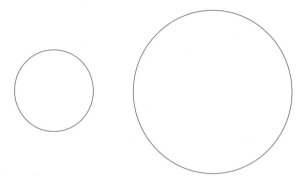

a. Find and compare the circumferences of the two circles.

b. Find and compare the areas of the two circles.

c. How will the circumference and area of a circle with diameter 20 inches compare to those of the circle with diameter 1 inch? How can those comparisons be made without further use of the formulas?

d. How do your answers in parts a–c relate to the results from comparing face perimeters and face areas of cubes in Experiment 1?

e. Make a conjecture about how the volume of a sphere of diameter 2 inches compares to the volume of a sphere of diameter 1 inch. Check your conjecture by using the formula $V = \frac{4}{3}\pi r^3$.

INVESTIGATION 2 The Shape of $y = ax^2$ and $y = ax^3$

In your investigation of cubes, you found that edge length is related to face area by the equation *Face Area* = *(Edge Length)*^{2}. Edge length is also related to total surface area by the equation *Surface Area* = 6*(Edge Length)*^{2} and to volume by the equation *Volume* = *(Edge Length)*^{3}.

In algebraic expressions like x^2 and x^3, the numbers 2 and 3 are called exponents or powers. Equations in the form $y = ax^2$ and $y = ax^3$ are called **power models**. To use these and other power models, it helps to know the shapes of their graphs and the patterns in their tables of values.

▶On Your Own

You may need to help students recall how to calculate the circumference and area of a circle and volume of a sphere.

($C = 2\pi r$, $A = \pi r^2$, and $V = \frac{4}{3}\pi r^3$)

a. The circumferences are π and 2π inches. The larger is double the smaller.

b. The areas are 0.25π and π square inches. The larger is 4 times the smaller.

c. The circumference is 20π square inches and the area is 100π square inches. From the formula, one can see that the circumference of the large circle will be 20 times the circumference of a circle with diameter 1 inch, and the area will be 400 times the area of the circle with diameter 1 inch.

d. Linear dimensions increase by the scale factor of similarity and areas increase by the square of the scale factor.

e. The volume of a sphere with diameter 2 inches will be eight times the volume of a sphere with diameter 1 inch. The volume of a 1-inch sphere is $\frac{4}{3}\pi$ and the volume of a 2 inch sphere is $\frac{32}{3}\pi$.

ASSIGNMENT *pp. 241–249*

Students now can begin Modeling tasks 1 or 4 or Reflecting tasks 1 or 3 from the MORE assignment following Investigation 2.

INVESTIGATION 2 ▶ The Shape of $y = ax^2$ and $y = ax^3$

In algebraic expressions like x^2 and x^3 the numbers 2 and 3 can be called powers, and so equations in the form $y = ax^2$ and $y = ax^3$ are called power models. To use these and other power models, it helps to know the shapes of their graphs and the patterns in their tables of values. The purpose of these experiments is to develop student knowledge and understanding of the way that these basic power models behave; that is, students should see the connection between the symbolic rule form of a relation and the patterns in tables and graphs of that relation. The patterns are generalizations of the specific examples students explored in the preceding cube-building activity. The general challenge is: If you are given an algebraic rule like $y = ax^2$ or $y = ax^3$, what table and graph patterns can you expect and why?

For many students, expressing themselves orally or in written form is difficult when they are referring to mathematical graphs or concepts. In this unit, students are asked to describe and compare numerous graphs and tables. The following activity is suggested to pull together students' ideas about the shapes of graphs.

See additional Teaching Notes on page T317F.

Unit 4

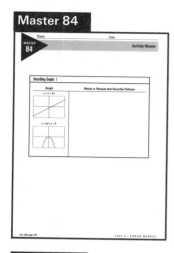

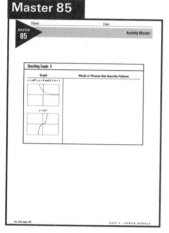

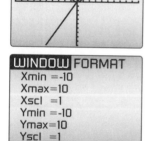

WINDOW FORMAT
Xmin =-10
Xmax=10
Xscl =1
Ymin =-10
Ymax=10
Yscl =1

Experiment 1

1. **As you observe groups, be sure to question students in a way that brings out the fact that the power model is defined for all x, not only the integer values that are convenient to use in a table.**

A table of values and graph of $y = x^2$ are shown below.

x	−10	−9	−8	−7	−6	−5	−4	−3	−2	−1	0	1	2	3	4	5	6	7	8	9	10
y	100	81	64	49	36	25	16	9	4	1	0	1	4	9	16	25	36	49	64	81	100

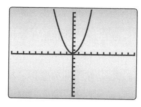

WINDOW FORMAT
Xmin =-10
Xmax=10
Xscl =1
Ymin =-10
Ymax=10
Yscl =1

As x increases from −10 to 10, y starts at 100 then decreases at a decreasing rate to 81, then 64, and so on, until it reaches 0 when x equals 0. As x continues to increase, the y values start increasing at an increasing rate until, when x equals 10, y equals 100. This pattern is illustrated in the graph by a curve that decreases as x changes from −10 to 0, and then increases as x changes from 0 to 10. Note the symmetry in both the table and the graph over $x = 0$.

2. **a.** The graph of $y = x^2$ shows y decreasing as x approaches zero through negative values (from below) and then increasing as x increases from 0. It is a curve that is symmetric about the y-axis. In contrast, the graph of $y = 2x$ is a straight line.

   In the table, as x increases from −10 to 10, the values for x^2 start large and decrease until $x^2 = 0$ when $x = 0$. Then, as x continues to increase, the values for x^2 also increase. The table values for $2x$ increase at a constant rate as x goes from −10 to 10.

x	x^2	2x	2^x
−10	100	−20	0.00098
−8	64	−16	0.00391
−6	36	−12	0.01563
−4	16	−8	0.0625
−2	4	−4	0.25
−1	1	−2	0.5
0	0	0	1

x	x^2	2x	2^x
1	1	2	2
2	4	4	4
4	16	8	16
6	36	12	64
8	64	16	256
10	100	20	1024

   b. The graph of $y = 2^x$ starts close to the x-axis and rises as x increases, while $y = x^2$ decreases and then increases. In the table of values for $y = 2^x$, the values are close to 0 for the negative values of x, but they increase at a rapid rate as x increases from 0 to 10.

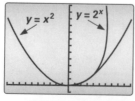

$y = x^2$ $y = 2^x$

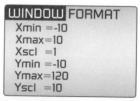

WINDOW FORMAT
Xmin =-10
Xmax=10
Xscl =1
Ymin =-10
Ymax=120
Yscl =10

See additional Teaching Notes on pages T317G–T317I.

Experiment 1

Use your graphing calculator or computer software to produce tables and graphs of linear, exponential, and power models that help you to answer the following questions.

1. In the relation $y = x^2$, how does y change as x varies from -10 to 10? Make a sketch of the graph of this relation. Explain how this pattern of change is illustrated in your graph of the relation.

2. **a.** How is the pattern of change in the relation $y = x^2$ different from that of $y = 2x$? Explain how those differences are shown in graphs and tables of the two relations.

   b. How is the pattern of change in the relation $y = x^2$ different from that of $y = 2^x$? Explain how those differences are shown in graphs and tables of the two relations.

Experiment 2

Now use your calculator or computer software to study the patterns that can be modeled by $y = x^3$, and to compare those patterns with linear and exponential models.

1. In the relation $y = x^3$, how does y change as x varies from -10 to 10? Make a sketch of the graph of this relation. Explain how this pattern of change is illustrated in your graph of the relation.

2. How are the tables and graphs of $y = x^3$ similar to and different from those of $y = x^2$? Explain the difference between *cubing* and *squaring* that causes the differences in the tables and in the graphs.

3. How is the pattern of change in the relation $y = x^3$ different from those of $y = 3x$ and $y = 3^x$? Explain how those differences are shown in the tables and graphs of the three relations.

Experiment 3

1. Suppose a plastic shipping container is in the shape of a cube with edges of length x feet.

   a. Explain why the surface area of the container is $6x^2$ square feet.

   b. Water weighs 62.4 pounds per cubic foot. Explain why the weight of the container filled with water will be $62.4x^3$ pounds more than when it is empty.

Unit 4

2. There are many situations that can be modeled by relations of the form $y = ax^2$ and $y = ax^3$. Use your graphing calculator or computer software to study relations of the form $y = ax^2$ and $y = ax^3$ for various choices of a. Cooperate with group members to share the workload.

a. How does the choice of a in the relation $y = ax^2$ affect the pattern in a table of values and the matching graph, for x varying from -10 to 10? Try different values of a; for example, $a = 1, 2, 3, 5, \frac{1}{2}, -1$, and -2.

b. How does the choice of a in the relation $y = ax^3$ affect the pattern in a table of values and the matching graph, for x varying from -10 to 10? Try different values of a; for example, $a = 1, 2, 3, 5, \frac{1}{2}, -1$, and -2.

Experiment 4

1. The equations $y = ax^2$ and $y = ax^3$ are not the only power models. Use your calculator to investigate patterns in the tables and graphs of the power models $y = x^4$, $y = x^5$, $y = x^6$, and $y = x^7$.

a. How are the patterns in tables and graphs of these relations similar to those of $y = x^2$ and $y = x^3$? How are they different from those of the square and cube models?

b. What patterns do you see that would allow you to predict the shape of the graphs for other power models like $y = x^8$ and $y = x^9$?

Checkpoint

Look back over your discoveries in the experiments with various power models.

ⓐ What patterns do you expect to find in tables and graphs of relations with equations of the form $y = ax^2$ when a is some positive number? When a is some negative number?

ⓑ What patterns do you expect to find in tables and graphs of relations with equations of the form $y = ax^3$ when a is some positive number? When a is some negative number?

ⓒ What patterns do you expect to find in tables and graphs of power models $y = x^n$ when n is a positive even integer? When n is a positive odd integer?

ⓓ How are the patterns in tables and graphs of power models different from those of linear and exponential models?

Be prepared to share your group's conclusions with the entire class.

2. a. A partial table of values is shown below.

x	$y = 2x^2$	$y = 3x^2$	$y = 5x^2$	$y = \frac{1}{2}x^2$	$y = -1x^2$	$y = -2x^2$
-4	32	48	80	8	-16	-32
-2	8	12	20	2	-4	-8
-1	2	3	5	$\frac{1}{2}$	-1	-2
0	0	0	0	0	0	0
1	2	3	5	$\frac{1}{2}$	-1	-2
2	8	12	20	2	-4	-8
4	32	48	80	8	-16	-32

Master 86

MASTER 86   Transparency Master

Checkpoint

Look back over your discoveries in the experiments with various power models.

ⓐ What patterns do you expect to find in tables and graphs of relations with equations of the form $y = ax^2$:
- when a is some positive number?
- when a is some negative number?

ⓑ What patterns do you expect to find in tables and graphs of relations with equations of the form $y = ax^3$:
- when a is some positive number?
- when a is some negative number?

ⓒ What patterns do you expect to find in tables and graphs of power models $y = x^n$:
- when n is a positive even integer?
- when n is a positive odd integer?

ⓓ How are the patterns in tables and graphs of power models different from those of linear and exponential models?

Be prepared to share your group's conclusions with the entire class.

Use with page 586.   UNIT 4 · POWER MODELS

The windows for the following graphs are $-3 \le x \le 3$ and $-10 \le y \le 10$.

$y = 2x^2$

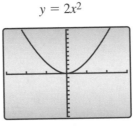

$y = 3x^2$

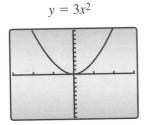

$y = 5x^2$

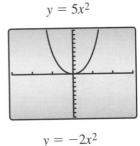

$y = \frac{1}{2}x^2$

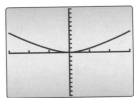

$y = -1x^2$

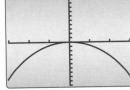

$y = -2x^2$

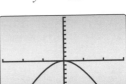

If $|a|$ is large, then the curve rises and falls more rapidly than if $|a|$ is very small. For $a > 0$ the curve opens upward, and for $a < 0$ the curve opens downward. Notice that for $a > 0$ the table values are all positive, and for $a < 0$ the table values are all negative. The graphs are all symmetric about the y-axis and all pass through the origin of the coordinate system.

b. A partial table of values is shown below.

x	$y = 2x^3$	$y = 3x^3$	$y = 5x^3$	$y = \frac{1}{2}x^3$	$y = -1x^3$	$y = -2x^3$
-4	-128	-192	-320	-32	64	128
-2	-16	-24	-40	-4	8	16
-1	-2	-3	-5	-0.5	1	2
0	0	0	0	0	0	0
1	2	3	5	0.5	-1	-2
2	16	24	40	4	-8	-16
4	128	192	320	32	-64	-128

See additional Teaching Notes on pages T317J–T317K.

▶**On Your Own**

a. Graph 2. The graph is decreasing and then increasing, therefore, it is an even power. This is also true of graph 4, but graph 2 rises more slowly than graph 4. Since the only other even-powered rule, in part c, has a coefficient (2) greater than the coefficient for this rule (1), this rule matches graph 2.

b. Graph 1. The graph is always increasing so it is an odd power. Because it rises more quickly than graph 3, and because the only other odd-powered rule has a coefficient less than this rule's coefficient, it must be graph 1.

c. Graph 4. It is an even power that rises more quickly than graph 2.

d. Graph 3. It is an odd power and the curve rises less quickly than graph 1.

MORE
ASSIGNMENT *pp. 241–249*

Modeling: 1 or 2 and 4*
Organizing: 4 and 5
Reflecting: 1 and 3
Extending: Choose one*

When choice is indicated, it is important to leave the choice to the student.
NOTE: *It is best if Organizing tasks are discussed as a whole class after they have been assigned as homework.*

MORE **independent assignment**

Modeling

1. **a.** $P = 4E$
   $SA = 6E^2$
   $V = E^3$

   b.

E	0	0.5	1	1.5	2	2.5	3	3.5	4	4.5	5	5.5	6
P	0	2	4	6	8	10	12	14	16	18	20	22	24
SA	0	1.5	6	13.5	24	37.5	54	73.5	96	121.5	150	181.5	216
V	0	0.125	1	3.375	8	15.625	27	42.875	64	91.125	125	166.38	216

Unit 4

▶ **On Your Own**

Shown below are the graphs of four power models. The scales are the same on all four graphs. Match the graphs to these rules and explain your reasoning in each case.

a. $y = x^2$ **b.** $y = x^3$

c. $y = 2x^2$ **d.** $y = 0.5x^3$

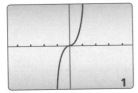

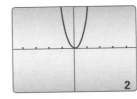

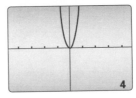

MORE
Modeling • Organizing • Reflecting • Extending

Modeling

1. One way to store dangerous radioactive waste materials is to seal them in containers that are then buried in mine shafts far under the earth's surface. The cube is a shape sometimes used for such containers.

   DANGER

   RADIOACTIVE MATERIALS

   a. Write equations showing how perimeter P of each face, total surface area SA, and volume V of the storage cube are related to edge length E.

   b. Make tables showing the face perimeter, total surface area, and volume of storage cubes for edge lengths from 0 to 6 feet, in steps of 0.5 feet.

c. Sketch graphs of the face perimeter, total surface area, and volume of storage cubes as functions of edge length from 0 to 6 feet.

d. What edge lengths will give cubes with the following measurements?

■ Face perimeter: 12 feet; 23 feet

■ Total surface area: 54 square feet; 105.8 square feet

■ Volume: 64 cubic feet; 132.7 cubic feet

Explain how the answers to these questions can be found using tables and graphs.

e. Which cube measurement—face perimeter, surface area, or volume—is best for predicting each of these properties of the storage cubes?

■ Cost of materials for the cube

■ Amount of material that can be stored in the cube

■ Cost of a metal band around the cube for holding it closed

2. Shown below are some sample braking distances required to bring a car to a complete stop on dry concrete when traveling at various speeds.

Stopping a Car

Speed (mph)	20	30	40	50	60	70
Braking Distance (ft)	16	36	64	100	144	196

a. Make a scatterplot of the (*speed, braking distance*) data.

b. Experiment with different expressions in the functions list of your calculator or computer software to find a power model that is a good fit for this data.

c. Use your power model to estimate braking distances for speeds of 65 mph and for 80 mph.

d. Use your power model to estimate, to the nearest mile per hour, the speed of the car when its braking distance was measured to be 51 feet.

e. A beginning driver might think that if you double your speed, you should double the expected braking distance. What does your model suggest about this point of view?

f. Suppose (*speed, braking distance*) data collected from the same car driven on wet concrete was modeled by a rule of the form $y = ax^2$. Write a paragraph describing how you think the table, rule, and graph for this data would compare with those for the dry concrete surface. Be as specific as possible and include reasons for your conclusions.

c. NOTE: The vertical axes for these graphs represent different units—feet, square feet, and cubic feet—and have different scales.

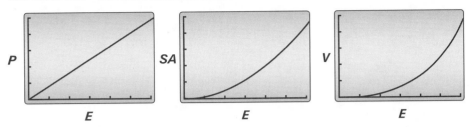

d. ■ When $P = 12$ feet, $E = 3$ feet.
   When $P = 23$ feet, $E = 5.75$ feet.
   ■ When $SA = 54$ square feet, $E = 3$ feet.
   When $SA = 105.8$ square feet, $E \approx 4.2$ feet.
   ■ When $V = 64$ cubic feet, $E = 4$ feet.
   When $V = 132.7$ cubic feet, $E \approx 5.1$ feet.
   The answers to these questions can be found in the table by finding the given value of the perimeter, surface area, or volume and then locating the corresponding edge length. With a technology-generated graph one could use the trace function to find the point with the given perimeter, surface area, or volume as the y-coordinate; the x-coordinate gives the corresponding edge length.

e. ■ Surface area is best for predicting the cost of materials for the cube.
   ■ Volume is best for predicting the amount of material that can be stored in the cube.
   ■ Face perimeter is best for predicting the cost of the metal band.

2. a.

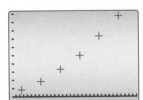 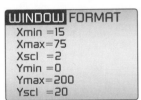

b. Responses may vary but should be close to the equation $y = 0.04x^2$, which fits the data exactly.

c. A speed of 65 mph gives a braking distance of 169 feet. A speed of 80 mph gives a braking distance of 256 feet.

d. A speed of approximately 36 mph gives a braking distance of 51 feet.

e. Doubling your speed more than doubles your braking distance. In fact, doubling your speed quadruples your braking distance.

f. In the rule for a wet surface, a would be a larger number than 0.04. The table values for braking distance would be larger and the graph would rise more steeply. This is because it takes longer to stop on wet pavement than it does on dry pavement.

Unit 4

3. a. Tables may vary, depending on how many entries and what step size students choose.

t	0	1	2	3	4	5	6	7	8	9	10	11
$d = 4.9t^2$	0	4.9	19.6	44.1	78.4	122.5	176.4	240.1	313.6	396.9	490	592.9
$d = 0.83t^2$	0	0.83	3.32	7.47	13.28	20.75	29.88	40.67	53.12	67.23	83	100.43

b. The graphs are similar, because they both open upwards and pass through the origin. This can be seen in the equations because the variables are squared, the coefficients are positive, and there are no constant terms added to the squared terms. The graph of distance on the earth rises faster than distance on the moon. This can be seen in the equations by the smaller coefficient (0.83) for the distance on the moon.

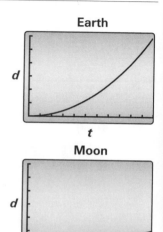

c. It will take longer to fall on the moon. This can be seen in the rule by the lower number multiplied by t^2 for the moon, in the table by noticing lower values in the moon's column, and on the graph by noticing that the moon's graph rises more slowly than the earth's graph.

d. Earth: $300 = 4.9t^2$, $t = \sqrt{\dfrac{300}{4.9}} \approx 7.8$ seconds

Moon: $300 = 0.83t^2$, $t = \sqrt{\dfrac{300}{0.83}} \approx 19$ seconds

These values can be found on a table or a graph by zooming in on y values of 300 and finding the corresponding x values.

4. a. Circumference (linear units): $y = 2\pi r$
Area (square units): $y = 4\pi r^2$
Volume (cubic units): $y = \frac{4}{3}\pi r^3$

3. If you drop a baseball from the top of a tall building, gravity pulls it toward the earth. The distance the ball falls increases as time passes with the approximate rule $d = 4.9t^2$, where time t is measured in seconds and distance d is measured in meters. There is gravity on the moon too, but if you dropped a baseball out of a tower on the moon, the approximate rule relating time and distance would be $d = 0.83t^2$.

 a. Make tables of values of the rules for earth and moon gravity.

 b. Produce graphs of the rules for earth and moon gravity. Compare similarities and differences in the graphs with similarities and differences in the rules.

 c. Will it take longer for a baseball to fall 300 meters on the earth or on the moon? How can you tell by looking at the rules? At the tables? At the graphs?

 d. Find, to the nearest 0.1 second, the time it takes a baseball to fall 300 meters on earth and on the moon. Explain how these estimates can be found using tables and graphs of the rules for earth and moon gravity.

4. The Earth and other planets in our solar system are approximately spherical in shape. The circumferences, surface areas, and volumes of spheres are related to their radii by fairly simple formulas. All spheres are *similar* to each other.

 a. Based on what you've learned about the relations between edge length, surface area, and volume of a cube and their units of measure, which of the following formulas would give the circumference of a sphere as a function of its radius r? Which would give the surface area? Which would give the volume?

 i. $y = 4\pi r^2$ **ii.** $y = \frac{4}{3}\pi r^3$ **iii.** $y = 2\pi r$

Unit 4

b. Use your choices from part a to find the approximate circumference, surface area, and volume of the Earth, which has a radius of about 4000 miles.

c. The planet Jupiter is the largest in the solar system, with radius about 11 times that of our Earth. Use your results from part b to estimate Jupiter's circumference, surface area, and volume.

d. Make tables and graphs showing how the circumference, surface area, and volume of spheres increase as radii increase from 0 to 10. Compare the patterns in those tables and graphs to the patterns for perimeter, surface area, and volume of the cubes you built in Investigation 1.

Organizing

1. Use your graphing calculator or computer software to explore tables and graphs showing the patterns of change for the power models $y = 3x^2$, $y = x^2$, $y = \frac{1}{3}x^2$, and $y = -3x^2$ for $x = -5$ to 5 in steps of 0.5.

   a. For each equation, describe any symmetries you see in its graph. Can these symmetries also be seen in the equation's table? Explain.

   b. How can you use the form of a symbolic rule like $y = ax^2$ to predict symmetries of its graph?

2. Use your graphing calculator or computer software to explore tables and graphs showing the patterns of change for the power models $y = 2x^3$, $y = x^3$, $y = \frac{1}{2}x^3$, and $y = -2x^3$ for $x = -5$ to 5 in steps of 0.5.

   a. For each equation, describe any symmetries you see in its graph. Can these symmetries also be seen in the equation's table? Explain.

   b. How can you use the form of a symbolic rule like $y = ax^3$ to predict symmetries of its graph?

3. The linear models you have worked with usually have been written with rules of the form $y = a + bx$. The exponential models have been written with rules of the form $y = a(b^x)$. In this task, you will compare the patterns that can be described by these two types of models to those of the power models $y = ax^2$ and $y = ax^3$.

   a. Sketch a typical graph for each of the four rules. Assume a and b are both positive numbers.

   b. Briefly describe the shape of each graph in part a.

   c. What symmetries can be found in the tables and graphs of the four different models?

   d. How do the values of a and b affect the rate of change in tables and graphs of the four types of models?

4. b. Circumference = $2\pi(4000) \approx 25{,}133$ miles
Area = $4\pi(4000)^2 \approx 201{,}061{,}930$ square miles
Volume = $\frac{4}{3}\pi(4000)^3 \approx 2.68 \times 1011$ cubic miles

c. Circumference = $25{,}133 \times 11 \approx 276{,}463$ miles
Area = $201{,}061{,}930 \times 112 \approx 2.43 \times 1010$ square miles
Volume = $2.68 \times 1011 \times 113 \approx 3.57 \times 1014$ cubic miles

d.

r	0	1	2	3	4	5	6	7	8	9	10
C (m)	0	6.28	12.57	18.85	25.13	31.42	37.70	43.98	50.27	56.55	62.83
SA (m²)	0	12.57	50.27	113.10	201.06	314.16	452.39	615.75	804.25	1017.88	1256.64
V (m³)	0	4.19	33.51	113.10	268.08	523.60	904.78	1436.76	2144.66	3053.63	4188.79

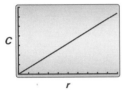 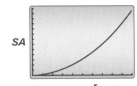 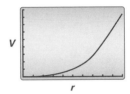

The patterns are similar to the perimeter, surface area, and volume of cubes from the investigation.

Organizing

1.

x	$3x^2$	x^2	$\frac{1}{3}x^2$	$-3x^2$	x	$3x^2$	x^2	$\frac{1}{3}x^2$	$-3x^2$
−5	75	25	8.33	−75	0.5	0.75	0.25	0.08	−0.75
−4.5	60.75	20.25	6.75	−60.75	1	3	1	0.33	−3
−4	48	16	5.33	−48	1.5	6.75	2.25	0.75	−6.75
−3.5	36.75	12.25	4.08	−36.75	2	12	4	1.33	−12
−3	27	9	3	−27	2.5	18.75	6.25	2.08	−18.75
−2.5	18.75	6.25	2.08	−18.75	3	27	9	3	−27
−2	12	4	1.33	−12	3.5	36.75	12.25	4.08	−36.75
−1.5	6.75	2.25	0.75	−6.75	4	48	16	5.33	−48
−1	3	1	0.33	−3	4.5	60.75	20.25	6.75	−60.75
−0.5	0.75	0.25	0.08	−0.75	5	75	25	8.33	−75
0	0	0	0	0					

a. The graphs are symmetric about the *y*-axis. This can be seen in the table because the *y* values for *x* and −*x* are equal.

b. There is symmetry about the *y*-axis. The *y* values will be the same for *x* values with the same absolute value because x^2 is the same for those *x* values. For any point (x, y), the point $(-x, y)$ is also on the graph.

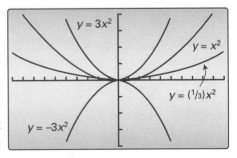

See additional Teaching Notes on pages T317L–317M.

Unit 4

4. This is a good problem to do with the entire class at the beginning or end of a period.

   a. Model A: Exponential

   Model B: Power model

   Model C: Linear model

   b. Model A: *NEXT* = 2*NOW*

   Model B: There is no simple *NOW-NEXT* equation for this model. It is easy to see why from the table if you notice that for almost all *NOW* values, there are two possibilities for *NEXT*. However, if students use the x value associated with *NOW* they might get the equation *NEXT* = *NOW* + (2x + 1).

   Model C: *NEXT* = *NOW* + 2

   c. Model A: $y = 2^x$

   Model B: $y = x^2$

   Model C: $y = -3 + 2x$

   d. Model A: *NEXT* = 2*NOW* is reflected in $y = 2^x$ because if *NOW* = 2^x, then *NEXT* = $2 \cdot 2^x$, which is the same as $2^{(x+1)}$.

   Model C: *NEXT* = *NOW* + 2 is related to $y = -3 + 2x$ because *NEXT* = $-3 + 2x + 2$, which is the same as $-3 + 2(x + 1)$.

5. a.

   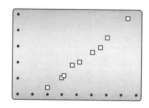

   b. $y = 1.60x^{2.75}$

   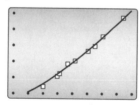

   c. It seems to fit well.

   d. The exponent of a number close to 3 is sensible because as we have seen in earlier problems, volume (and thus weight) is proportional to the cube of the height. We can expect the exponent to be somewhat different from 3 because the data set is small, and also human beings are more similar to an upright rectangular solid than to a cube.

   e. The model predicts a weight of approximately 189 lbs. for a 5'8" or 5.67 foot male. Of course, people vary widely in height and weight, so this prediction may not be accurate for very many men.

4. Given below is a table of (x, y) data from three models—one linear, one exponential, and one power model.

x	–5	–4	–3	–2	–1	0	1	2	3	4	5
Model A: y	0.03125	0.0625	0.125	0.25	0.5	1	2	4	8	16	32
Model B: y	25	16	9	4	1	0	1	4	9	16	25
Model C: y	–13	–11	–9	–7	–5	–3	–1	1	3	5	7

a. Identify the type of model that would describe the pattern of data in each row of the table.

b. For each row, try to find a *NOW-NEXT* equation that describes how values of y change as values of x increase in steps of 1.

c. For each row, try to find an equation in the form "$y = \ldots$" showing how to calculate values of y for any given value of x.

d. Explain how the form of the *NOW-NEXT* equation relates to the "$y = \ldots$" equation for the same model.

5. Here are some data giving height and weight for nine males of different ages.

Height (ft)	4.0	4.5	5.5	5.0	6.0	4.4	5.75	6.5	4.8
Weight (lbs)	72	100	175	135	225	95	190	280	125

a. Enter these data in your calculator or computer software and make a scatterplot.

b. You can find a power model that fits the data well using the power regression command in the statistics menu. Paste or record the appropriate equation in the functions list and then produce its graph.

c. How well does the power model fit the data?

d. Why do you think that the exponent in this power model turns out to be a number close to, but somewhat different from, 3?

e. Using your power model, what do you think the weight of a male 5 feet 8 inches tall might be?

Unit 4

Reflecting

1. In an advertisement for Bigger Burgers, a diagram showed how their regular hamburger was larger than a competitor's. How could Bigger Burgers' claim be accurate?

Our Burger is Twice as Large!

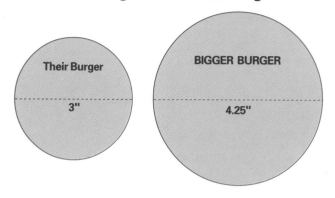

2. Simple linear models, with rules in the form $y = ax$, also can be considered power models if you remember that $ax = ax^1$. Make a sketch showing some of the possible graphs for the simplest power models $y = ax^1$. Consider examples with both positive and negative values of a.

3. Think back to examples of linear and exponential growth you have studied.

 a. What patterns or clues in a problem situation lead you to expect a linear model will fit the situation? What patterns or clues suggest an exponential model?

 b. How does the experiment in which you built similar cubes suggest that power models will be the most appropriate models of growth in human skin surface area and weight of a person?

4. Refer to the data given in Organizing task 5 on page 245.

 a. Use the linear regression command in the statistics menu to find a linear model for the data pattern. Compare the fit of that model to the power model you found.

 b. Use the exponential regression command in the statistics menu to find an exponential model for the data pattern. Compare the fit of that model to the power model.

 c. Which model seems to fit the data best? Why does this make sense?

Reflecting

1. The area of the smaller burger is $1.5^2\pi$ or 2.25π square inches, while the area of the larger burger is $(2.125)^2\pi$ or approximately 4.5π square inches, which is twice the area of the smaller burger. The scale factor is $\frac{4.25}{3}$ or approximately 1.417. Earlier, students should have seen that the ratio of the areas is the square of the scale factor, so in this case the ratio of the areas is $(1.417)^2$ to 1 or approximately 2 to 1.

2. One sample set of graphs might look like the following.

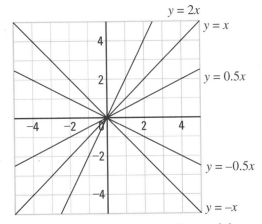

3. **a.** Problem situations in which growth is constant (at a constant rate) are linear. Problem situations in which growth occurs by a factor (such as interest and decay) typically are modeled by exponential equations.

   b. The edge of the cube corresponds to its height. As the edge increased we examined the surface area and volume. The surface area relates to our pattern of skin growth, and the change in volume corresponds to our change in weight. The cube experiment gave us data that was modeled well by power models.

4. **a.** $y = -264.8 + 81.4x$

   There is actually very little difference in the fit of the linear model and the power model. Both models seem to fit the data well. However, when we add the graph of this model to the plot, we see that for smaller and larger heights the line falls below the data points and for the middle heights the line falls above the points. That pattern suggests that there is probably a curve to the true pattern of the relationship.

   b. $y = 9.12(1.70)^x$

   This model differs only slightly from the power model. They both fit the data well.

   c. If all three models are graphed on the scatterplot at the same time it seems that the power model is the best fit. This seems reasonable since weight is related to volume and we know that the best model for volume is a power model.

Unit 4

Extending

1. **a.** ■ 9 squares of each color
   ■ 54 outside squares (6 colors $\times$ 9 squares)

   b. There are $3 \times 3 \times 3$ or 27 small cubes in the large cube. (Actually, there is no cube in the middle so there are 26 cubes.)

   c. ■ 25 squares of each color
   ■ 150 outside squares (6 colors $\times$ 25 squares)
   ■ 5^3 or 125 small cubes would make up the larger cube.

   d. ■ n^2 squares of each color
   ■ $6n^2$ outside squares
   ■ n^3 small cubes make up the larger cube

2. Responses will vary but should include comments about the varying rate of change for power models of the form $y = ax^2$. As the x value increases in increments of 10, the difference between two consecutive y value entries is 1,000 more than the previous difference. That is, for increments of 10, *NEXT* difference = *NOW* difference + 1000.

Extending

1. Rubik's Cube is a fascinating, but difficult puzzle. It is a large cube made up of small, colored cubes (as indicated) that can be rotated into different patterns. When the puzzle is solved, each face will show squares of only one color—orange, blue, green, white, yellow, or red.

   a. Suppose you have solved the Rubik's Cube.
   - How many small squares of each color would there be?
   - How many small squares would appear on the entire surface?

   b. How many small cubes make up such a cube?

   c. Suppose you have a cube, similar to a Rubik's Cube but with 5 small cubes along each edge.
   - How many squares of each color will appear on the faces?
   - How many small squares will be needed to cover the cube?
   - How many small cubes will make up the large cube?

   d. Answer the questions in part c for the general case of a Rubik's cube with *n* small cubes along each edge.

2. Linear models show a constant rate of change. Use the data list capabilities of your calculator or computer software to investigate and prepare a report on the rate of change of power models like $y = 5x^2$. Begin by entering the rule in the function list, say Y_1. Next enter the *x* values from 0 to 90 in increments of 10 into List 1 and the corresponding Y_1 values into List 2. Then create a list whose entries are the differences: $Y_1(20) - Y_1(10)$, $Y_1(30) - Y_1(20)$, and so on.

3. In algebra, the word *model* is used to talk about graphs or symbolic expressions that match patterns in numerical data. In engineering and architecture, the phrase *scale model* often means a copy of some car, truck, train, airplane, rocket, or building that is the same shape, but smaller than the real thing. The *scale factor* is a number that tells the relation between the model and the real thing.

   For example, one model of a truck is $\frac{1}{20}$ the size of the real truck. What relations would you expect between the length, volume, and surface area of the model and the real thing? What if the scale factor were $\frac{1}{15}$ instead of $\frac{1}{20}$? You can get some clues to the answers of these questions by building some models and looking for patterns.

   Start with a model of a truck that is 1 inch wide, 2 inches high, and 4 inches long. Use some small blocks and sketches to study truck models that would be similar to the original model, but larger by scale factors of 2, 3, 4, 5, and 6.

Unit 4

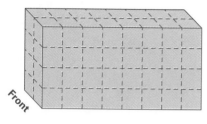

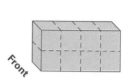

Original Model, Side View   **Scale Factor of 2**

For each "truck" you build or sketch, record the following data in a table: scale factor, length, width, height, front face perimeter (see figure above), and base (bottom face) perimeter. Use your data to complete parts a–d (see figure above).

a. As the scale factor changes at a constant rate, how do the length, width, and height of the "truck" change?

b. As the scale factor changes at a constant rate,

- how does the perimeter of the front of the "truck" change?
- how does the perimeter of the base of the "truck" change?

c. Write rules that show how to use the scale factor k to calculate each of the following measurements on a "truck" that is larger (or smaller) than the original.

- The length L, width W, and height H
- The perimeter of the front PF
- The perimeter of the bottom PB

d. Sketch graphs of the rules in part c and explain the patterns in those graphs.

Refer to the table of data for the "trucks" you built or sketched. Record data about the areas of the front face AF, side face AS, and top face AT of each truck. Use these data to complete parts e and f.

e. As the scale factor changes at a constant rate,

- how does the area of each face of the "truck" change?
- how does this pattern show up in scatterplots of (*scale factor, face area*) data?

f. Write rules that show how to use the scale factor k to calculate each of the following areas on a "truck" that is larger (or smaller) than the original.

- The area of the front AF of each "truck"
- The area of the side AS of each "truck"
- The area of the top AT of each "truck"

Refer again to the table of data for the "trucks" you built or sketched. This time record data about scale factors and volume. Use these data on edge lengths and volume to complete parts g and h.

3. For this table, the front of the truck is represented by the left or right side of the model.

Scale Factor	Length	Width	Height	Front Perimeter	Base Perimeter
1	4	1	2	6	10
2	8	2	4	12	20
3	12	3	6	18	30
4	16	4	8	24	40
5	20	5	10	30	50
6	24	6	12	36	60

a. As the scale factor changes at a constant rate, the length, width, and height also increase at a constant rate.

b. ■ As the factor increases at a constant rate, the front perimeter increases at a constant rate; for each increase of 1 in the scale factor the perimeter increases by 6.

■ As the scale factor increases at a constant rate, the perimeter of the base increases at a constant rate; for each increase of 1 in the scale factor the perimeter of the base increases by 10.

c. ■ $L = 4k$, $W = k$, $H = 2k$

■ $PF = 6k$

■ $PB = 10k$

d. For the following graphs, the scale on the *x*-axis is 1 and the scale on the *y*-axis is 10.

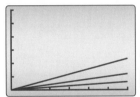
$L = 4k$
$H = 2k$
$W = k$

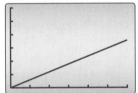
$PF = 6k$

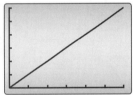
$PB = 10k$

These graphs indicate that the rate of change is constant for each different measurement, but that these measurements are not all changing at the same rate. For example, the perimeter of the bottom is changing faster than the perimeter of the front.

e. Again, the front of the truck is represented by the left side of the original illustration. The side of the truck is represented by the front face of the original illustration.

Scale Factor	Length	Width	Height	AF	AS	AT
1	4	1	2	2	8	4
2	8	2	4	8	32	16
3	12	3	6	18	72	36
4	16	4	8	32	128	64
5	20	5	10	50	200	100
6	24	6	12	72	288	144

■ The area of each face changes by the square of the scale factor.

■ Each scatterplot curves upward at an increasing rate.

f. ■ $AF = 2k^2$

■ $AS = 8k^2$

■ $AT = 4k^2$

Unit 4

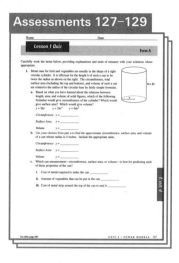

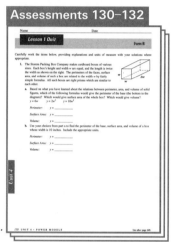

3. g.

Scale Factor	Length	Width	Height	Volume
1	4	1	2	8
2	8	2	4	64
3	12	3	6	216
4	16	4	8	512
5	20	5	10	1000
6	24	6	12	1728

■ As the scale factor increases, the volume increases by a factor of the cube of the scale factor.

■ The scatterplot shows that the points curve upward at an ever-increasing rate, even faster than the plot from part e.

h. $V = 8k^3$

4. a. For this problem you may wish to assign different model gauges to each group so the calculations don't become tedious. See the table below.

For the S-gauge model railroad, the track is 22.22 mm wide and the scale ratio is 64 to 1. This means 22.22 mm is $\frac{1}{64}$ of the actual track size or the actual track is (64)(22.22 mm). This is 1422 mm or approximately 4.7 ft.

b. See the table below.

L = real length SA = real surface area V = real volume
l = model length sa = model surface area v = model volume

Railroad Models

Gauge Name	Track Gauge	Scale Ratio	Width of Real Train Tracks	Length (units)	Surface Area (units²)	Volume (units³)
1	45 mm (1.75 in)	32:1	1440 mm ≈ 4.7 ft	$L = 32l$	$SA = 32^2\,sa$	$V = 32^3v$
O	32 mm (1.26 in)	48:1	1536 mm ≈ 5.0 ft	$L = 48l$	$SA = 48^2\,sa$	$V = 48^3v$
S	22.22 mm (0.875 in)	64:1	1422 mm ≈ 4.7 ft	$L = 64l$	$SA = 64^2\,sa$	$V = 64^3v$
OO	16.5 mm (0.648 in)	76:1	1254 mm ≈ 4.1 ft	$L = 76l$	$SA = 76^2\,sa$	$V = 76^3v$
EM	18 mm (0.707 in)	76:1	1368 mm ≈ 4.5 ft	$L = 76l$	$SA = 76^2\,sa$	$V = 76^3v$
EEM	18.83 mm (0.740 in)	76:1	1431 mm ≈ 4.7 ft	$L = 76l$	$SA = 76^2\,sa$	$V = 76^3v$
HO	16.5 mm (0.648 in)	87:1	1436 mm ≈ 4.7 ft	$L = 87l$	$SA = 87^2\,sa$	$V = 87^3v$
TT (EU)	12 mm (0.471 in)	101:1	1212 mm ≈ 4.0 ft	$L = 101l$	$SA = 101^2\,sa$	$V = 101^3v$
TT (US)	12 mm (0.471 in)	120:1	1440 mm ≈ 4.7 ft	$L = 120l$	$SA = 120^2\,sa$	$V = 120^3v$
N	9 mm (0.353 in)	160:1	1440 mm ≈ 4.7 ft	$L = 160l$	$SA = 160^2\,sa$	$V = 160^3v$
OOO	9.5 mm (0.373 in)	152:1	1444 mm ≈ 4.7 ft	$L = 152l$	$SA = 152^2\,sa$	$V = 152^3v$
Z	6.5 mm (0.255 in)	220:1	1430 mm ≈ 4.7 ft	$L = 220l$	$SA = 220^2\,sa$	$V = 220^3v$

See Assessment Resources pages 127–132.

Unit 4

g. As scale factor changes at a constant rate,

- how does the volume of the "truck" change?

- how does this pattern show up in a scatterplot of (*scale factor*, *volume*) data?

h. Write a rule showing how the scale factor *k* can be used to calculate the volume *V* of any "truck" that is larger (or smaller) than the original.

4. Model railroading is a popular hobby. The following table gives data on twelve kinds of model railroad scales. *Track gauge* is the distance between the two rails of the track (the width of the track).

Railroad Models

Gauge Name	Track Gauge	Scale Ratio
1	45 mm (1.75 in)	32:1
O	32 mm (1.26 in)	48:1
S	22.22 mm (0.875 in)	64:1
OO	16.5 mm (0.648 in)	76:1
EM	18 mm (0.707 in)	76:1
EEM	18.83 mm (0.740 in)	76:1
HO	16.5 mm (0.648 in)	87:1
TT (EU)	12 mm (0.471 in)	101:1
TT (US)	12 mm (0.471 in)	120:1
N	9 mm (0.353 in)	160:1
OOO	9.5 mm (0.373 in)	152:1
Z	6.5 mm (0.255 in)	220:1

a. For each model gauge, calculate the width of the full-size track being modeled. For example, on an S-gauge model railroad, the track is 22.22 mm wide and the ratio of real-to-model train size is 64 to 1. What does that imply about the width of the tracks being modeled?

b. For each model gauge, find rules that can be used to calculate the length, surface area, and volume of a real train car from the length, surface area, and volume of the model train car.

Unit 4

Lesson 2

Inverse Variation

For positive values of x, the power models $y = x^2$ and $y = x^3$ match situations where y increases rapidly as x increases, but eventually not as fast as with exponential growth. In some other situations where x increases, y decreases in a pattern that is similar to exponential decay, but different in some important respects. For example, the following graph shows the typical relation between intensity of an earthquake and distance from the center of that quake.

Earthquakes

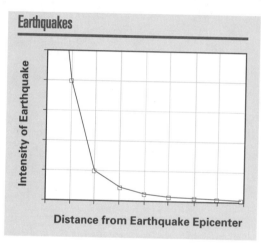

Intensity of Earthquake

Distance from Earthquake Epicenter

Think About This Situation

a How would you describe the pattern of change in earthquake intensity as distance from the epicenter increases?

b How well do you think each of the following suggestions will model the pattern relating distance and earthquake intensity?

- $y = a + bx$, with a positive and b negative.
- $y = a(b^x)$, with a large and b positive but less than 1.
- $y = \dfrac{a}{x^2}$ with a positive.

250   UNIT 4 • POWER MODELS

Lesson 2 *Inverse Variation*

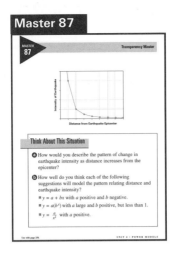

LESSON OVERVIEW   In conventional approaches to algebra, study of the basic quadratic relation $y = x^2$ is followed by extension to the general quadratic $y = ax^2 + bx + c$. In this curriculum, that generalization is developed in Lesson 3 of this unit. We have chosen to focus this second lesson on the very important "inverse and inverse square" models of variation. The rules $y = \frac{1}{x}$ and $y = \frac{1}{x^2}$ are power models, when viewed as $y = x^{-1}$ and $y = x^{-2}$. The goal of this lesson is to develop student ability to recognize tables and graphs where one variable is changing inversely to the other and to predict patterns of change and shapes of graphs from symbolic rules. At this point, student understanding of inverse variation patterns will be informal.

As in the first lesson, the notion of inverse variation is introduced using two real-world contexts in the first two investigations. In Investigation 1, students explore the fact that time of a trip varies inversely with average speed. Investigation 2 introduces the fact that intensity of sound or light varies with distance from its source according to an inverse square law. The third investigation looks at the numerical patterns and graph shapes that one could expect from any inverse variation rule.

The first of the contexts for inverse variation is quite familiar to most students, drawing on fairly familiar variables and relations as well as on the basic time-rate-distance relation that they have worked on in several earlier units. The examples of inverse square variation are probably new to most students, although the fact that intensity of sound or light diminishes with distance from its source should seem extremely plausible. Another example of an inverse square law is gravitation. In all cases, the general idea of decreasing intensity proportional to the inverse square of distance is based on a simple physical model. For example, if you think of a balloon being inflated, as the radius (distance from center to the balloon) increases, the surface area of the balloon increases according to the square of the radius (for a sphere, the surface area is $4\pi r^2$). Thus the balloon material is stretched thinner and thinner. If you think of light or sound energy as being spread over a circle emanating from the source, you can see that the energy density diminishes as the square of the radius increases. While the purpose of this lesson is to introduce the basic pattern that can be expected from a symbolic rule of the form $y = \frac{a}{x}$ or $y = \frac{a}{x^2}$, it will be helpful for students to spend some time thinking about the physical models of those phenomena, giving them valuable physical knowledge and concrete embodiments of the variation pattern.

Lesson Objectives

■ To determine and explore the inverse variation model, $y = \frac{1}{x}$, through tables and graphs

■ To determine and explore the inverse variation model, $y = \frac{1}{x^2}$, through tables and graphs

■ To explore the patterns for relations of the forms $y = \frac{a}{x}$ and $y = \frac{a}{x^2}$ through tables and graphs

See additional Teaching Notes on page T317N.

INVESTIGATION 1 ▸ Travel Times

This situation is familiar to students. After a brief discussion of the context, they should have no trouble answering that the time that the trip takes will decrease as average speed increases. You may need to remind students that the "Think About This Situation" for this lesson asked them to find a model for a situation similar to this, where increasing one variable (in this case *speed*) has the effect of decreasing another (in this case *time*). You may want to tell them that, as in other investigations, they will need to look for patterns in the tables and graphs and relate these patterns to the form of the corresponding equations.

As groups of students work through activities 1 to 4, you might want to ask how their equation relating *time* and *speed* is different from familiar linear models and from the power models they explored in Lesson 1. For example, you might ask, "How is the pattern in the table different from the patterns for linear models and power models?"

1. **a.** 12.5 hours

   b. 6.25 hours

   c. 4.17 hours (approximately)

2. One rule relating time of the trip and average driving speed is $t = \frac{250}{s}$.

   a.

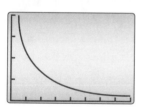

   b. Students should notice that as the speed increases, the time will decrease. Increases of 5 miles per hour in speed produce greater decreases in time at lower speeds than at higher speeds. This is shown in the graph by the downward trend of the curve, which is steeper for small *x*. It also is shown in the table by the pattern of decrease in values for time *y* as values for speed *x* increase in 5 miles per hour steps.

3. **a.** The total time of the trip is reduced by 12.5 hours, from 25 to 12.5 hours.

   b. The total time of the trip is reduced by 1.58 hours or 1 hour 35 minutes, from 7.14 to 5.56 hours.

   c. The total time of the trip is reduced by about 0.83 hour or 50 minutes, from 5 to 4.17 hours.

   d. As the average speed increases the total time decreases, but not at a constant rate. The change in time slows down as the speed increases. This is shown in the graph by the way the curve "levels off." It is demonstrated in the table by observing the differences in consecutive *y* values. These differences get smaller and smaller, yet the values of *x* differ by a constant, 5.

INVESTIGATION 1 Travel Times

Many Americans take long automobile trips for business, vacations, and some-times just commuting to work. While driving at slower speeds can save gaso-line, driving at faster speeds can save time. For example, a 300-mile trip takes 6 hours at 50 miles per hour, but only 5 hours at 60 miles per hour. Think about how driving time would change if the average speed of 50 miles per hour decreased to 40 miles per hour.

Suppose that your family is planning a 250-mile trip by car to visit relatives. Your average speed could vary from as little as 10 miles per hour to 60 miles per hour or more. Your average speed depends on what roads you take, traffic, weather, speed limits, and the driver's preferred pace.

1. How long will that 250-mile trip take if you average

   a. 20 miles per hour?

   b. 40 miles per hour?

   c. 60 miles per hour?

2. Write a rule that gives time of the trip *t* as a function of the average driving speed *s*.

   a. Use your calculator or computer software to make a table showing (*speed, time*) data for the 250-mile trip. Show speeds from 10 to 65 miles per hour, in steps of 5 miles per hour. Then graph that same relation. What window on your calculator or computer gives a good view of this graph?

   b. Describe, as accurately as possible, the pattern relating average speed and time of your 250-mile trip. Explain how that pattern is shown in the table and the graph.

3. How does each of the following increases in average speed affect the time for the 250-mile trip?

   a. Increase from 10 miles per hour to 20 miles per hour

   b. Increase from 35 miles per hour to 45 miles per hour

   c. Increase from 50 miles per hour to 60 miles per hour

   d. How is the pattern of your answers in parts a–c shown by the data in the table and the shape of the (*speed, time*) graph?

4. Estimate the average speed necessary to complete the trip in $4\frac{1}{2}$ hours. Describe the method you used to find your estimate.

5. Now think again about the relation between speed and time for a 300-mile trip.

a. What equation relates driving time t and average speed s for such a trip?

b. Which will produce the greater *change* in driving time: an increase from 40 to 60 miles per hour or a decrease from 40 to 20 miles per hour?

c. How is your answer to part b shown in a graph of the relation in part a?

d. Estimate the average speed necessary to complete this trip in $4\frac{1}{2}$ hours. Use a method different from the one you used in activity 4.

Checkpoint

ⓐ What equation will relate distance d, average speed s, and driving time t for a trip?

ⓑ How does an increase in average speed change the expected driving time for a fixed distance?

ⓒ How is your answer to part b shown in graphs of (*speed, time*) relations for any fixed distance?

ⓓ How is your answer to part b related to the form of speed-time modeling equations for any fixed distance?

Be prepared to share your equation and interpretations with the class.

▶ On Your Own

The distance between New York and Los Angeles is approximately 3000 miles.

a. How long will a trip from New York to Los Angeles take

- by airplane, averaging 450 miles per hour?
- by car, averaging 60 miles per hour?
- by bicycle, averaging 15 miles per hour?

b. What equation gives time t for the trip as a function of average speed s?

c. Make a table showing the relation between speed and time for speeds from 50 to 500 miles per hour, in steps of 50 miles per hour. Then sketch a graph of the (*speed, time*) relation.

d. Which change in speed causes the greater change in time for the trip: an increase from 50 to 100 miles per hour or an increase from 450 to 500 miles per hour?

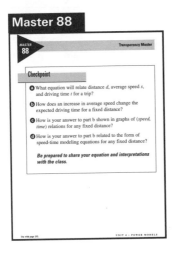

Master 88

4. An average speed of approximately 55.6 miles per hour will allow one to complete the trip in $4\frac{1}{2}$ hours. Students might trace the graph to find the x value corresponding to a y value of 4.5, look in the table of values to find the x value corresponding to the y value of 4.5, or use symbolic reasoning.

5. **a.** $t = \frac{300}{s}$

   b. A decrease in speed from 40 to 20 miles per hour increases trip time by 7.5 hours, while an increase from 40 to 60 miles per hour decreases the trip by only 2.5 hours. The decrease from 40 to 20 miles per hour produces the greater change.

   c. The graph falls more steeply for smaller values of s (speed), showing that a 20 mile per hour change in speed at lower speeds will have a greater effect on change in trip time than the same speed change at a higher speed.

   d. An average speed of 66.7 mph will allow one to complete the trip in $4\frac{1}{2}$ hours.

SHARE AND SUMMARIZE   full-class discussion

Checkpoint

See Teaching Master 88.

ⓐ Equations could be $d = st$, $s = \frac{d}{t}$, or $t = \frac{d}{s}$. While $t = \frac{d}{s}$ is the most natural form to calculate time for different speeds on a trip of fixed distance, this is a good opportunity to press students for alternative formulations of the same conditions.

ⓑ An increase in speed decreases the expected driving time, but the time decreases more at lower speeds.

ⓒ The (*speed, time*) graphs are all monotonic decreasing functions, which fall rather quickly for small speeds and then level out for higher speeds.

ⓓ When you divide a fixed number by a larger number you get a smaller result.

The crucial idea here is that the two variables are inversely related. When students have had an opportunity to complete the Checkpoint and have discussed their answers, you might want to check that they have grasped which characteristic of the symbolic representation is responsible for the inverse nature of the relationship. As part d indicates, dividing by the variable is the key characteristic.

NOTE: Depending on the level of your students, you may wish to introduce more formal language like *concave up, concave down, approaching positive or negative infinity*, and *asymptotes*.

See additional Teaching Notes on page T317N.

MORE
ASSIGNMENT   *pp. 259–264*

Students now can begin Modeling task 1 or 2, or Organizing task 1 from the MORE assignment following Investigation 3.

Unit 4

INVESTIGATION 2   Sound and Light

It should be reasonably natural for students to believe that as distance from a light source increases, the intensity or brightness of the light diminishes. However, the exact pattern of that decrease in brightness is probably not at all obvious. An excellent way to launch this investigation is to let students express their ideas about which of the three proposed (*distance, intensity*) graphs seems most likely to be correct. Let students interpret the shape of each graph and then express their opinions about which is likely to be the best model. It is best not to close that discussion with a report of the correct answer, which would remove the anticipation from the investigation. Rather, promise students that the investigation ahead will suggest an answer.

All three graphs on the introductory page indicate that as the distance from the source increases the intensity of the light decreases. The three graphs differ in the rate of change of the intensity as the distance decreases at a constant rate.

1. This activity can be used for class discussion after groups have completed their discussions.

    a. i.   The intensity decreases rapidly at first but levels off to small decreases for greater distances. The intensity then approaches 0 very slowly. It turns out that of the three given patterns, this is the best model of the (*distance, intensity*) relation.

    ii. The intensity decreases at a constant rate.

    iii. The intensity decreases slowly at first and then more rapidly as the distance increases.

    b. Responses may vary. During the investigation students will discover that graph i best models the relationship between distance and intensity.

2. **An alternate method of collecting data with the entire class is to use the overhead projector. Begin with it inches from the blackboard and gradually move it further away.**

    a. As the penlight is moved away from the desk at a near constant speed, the diameter of the light circle increases, also at a constant speed, while the intensity of the light decreases at a varying rate.

    b. Because students don't yet know how to measure light intensity numerically, they won't discover a rule in this activity. However, most of them should see from the experiment that light intensity decreases rapidly at first, then gradually the rate of decrease slows. This pattern suggests graph i from activity 1.

If students aren't understanding the idea of intensity you might try the following: Place an overhead projector or slide projector very close (10 cm or so) to a white surface. The light will be very bright, perhaps painfully so. How far away does it need to be before it is comfortable? How far away can the projector be and still give a clear image?

INVESTIGATION 2 Sound and Light

Both hearing and sight—whether in humans, animals, or robots—depend on the ability to find patterns in sound and light energy. The intensity of that energy must be in a certain range, however. When a light or sound source is too faint, we can't see or hear it. If the light is too bright or the sound is too loud, a person's eyes or ears could be damaged.

1. The intensity of sound from a radio or light from a lamp is related to the distance from the source—the more distant the source, the lower the sound or light intensity. The graphs below show possible patterns for the relations between distance and sound or light intensity (with distance on the horizontal axis).

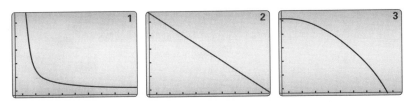

   a. What relation between distance and intensity is shown in each graph?

   b. Which do you believe is the graph that best models the relationship between distance and sound or light intensity? Explain your thinking.

2. You can get a more precise idea of the way that light and sound intensities decrease by doing a simple experiment. Point a small penlight directly at a flat surface like a desk top. It will make a circle of light.

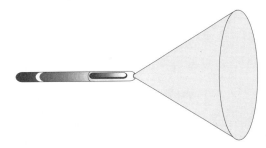

   a. As the penlight is moved away from the surface, what happens to the diameter of the light circle? What happens to the intensity of the light?

   b. Sketch a graph of what appears to be the relation between distance and light intensity. Does your graph match the one you chose in part b activity 1?

In the next activities you will explore, more carefully, the numerical patterns of change that can be expected as a light source moves away from its target. The data and equations are based on measurements from an experiment with a flashlight.

3. The following table shows how the diameter of one flashlight's circle of light is related to distance from the light source. Distance from the light source and diameter are in meters.

Light Circle Measurements

Distance from Light (D)	1	2	3	4	5
Diameter of Light Circle (d)	2	4	6	8	10
Radius of Light Circle (r)					

a. Write an equation relating diameter of the light circle d to its distance from the light source D. Find the radius and write a second equation relating radius r of the light circle to distance D.

b. Compare the pattern in the table above with your results from the experiment in activity 2.

4. Using the (*distance, diameter*) data in the table of activity 3, complete the following table showing how area of the light circle changes as distance from the light source increases.

Light Circle Area

Distance from Light (D)	1	2	3	4	5
Area of Light Circle (A)					

a. Write an equation relating light circle area A to distance from source D.

b. Describe the pattern shown in a graph of the relation in part a.

5. As the light from the flashlight spreads over circles of larger and larger area, its intensity decreases. Light energy is measured in a unit called *lumens*. The intensity of light is measured in lumens per unit of area. The flashlight used for the experiment in activities 3 and 4 produces 160 lumens of light energy.

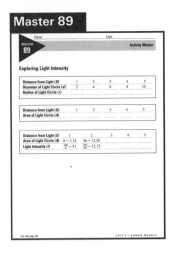

Master 89

3. **See Teaching Master 89.**
   a. $d = 2D$ or $D = \frac{d}{2}$

Distance from Light (D)	1	2	3	4	5
Diameter of Light Circle (d)	2	4	6	8	10
Radius of Light Circle (r)	1	2	3	4	5

   $D = r$

   b. Activity 2 did not require actual measurements, but the general pattern of change in the diameter of the circle should be similar to the one given by the table.

   You can do this sort of experiment with a flashlight in your classroom. If you measure fairly carefully, you should get generally linear (*distance, diameter*) data. However, unless you are using a flashlight that is very much like a point light source, the equation will not be as simple as $y = 2x$. You are more likely to get an equation with a nonzero y-intercept. Nonetheless, this experience creates a nice opportunity to make a connection with linear models.

   Note that the distance from the light is the same as the radius of the circle for this particular data; that fact will be useful in the next activity.

4. The light circle areas can be calculated from $A = \pi r^2$ to get the following table.

Distance From Light (D)	1	2	3	4	5
Light Circle Area (A)	π	4π	9π	16π	25π

   a. $A = \pi D^2$, where D is the distance from the light (*not* the diameter of the circle). Thinking symbolically, $A = \pi r^2$ and $D = r$, so $A = \pi D^2$.

   b. If you consider negative values of D, the graph will be a parabola, like the power models in the form $y = ax^2$. Students may state that the area of the light circle is increasing at an increasing rate.

Unit 4

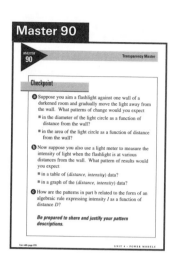

EXPLORE *continued*

5. **See Teaching Master 89.**

    a. You may need to explain to students that the symbol $\approx$ means *is approximately equal to.*

Distance From Light (D)	1	2	3	4	5
Area of Light Circle (A)	3.14	12.57	28.27	50.27	78.54
Light Intensity (I)	50.93	12.73	5.66	3.18	2.04

   b. $I = \dfrac{160}{\pi D^2}$

   c. The intensity of the light decreases but at a slower rate as one moves away from the source. This is shown in the graph by an initial sharp drop in the curve, followed by a leveling off as x becomes very large.

SHARE AND SUMMARIZE   full-class discussion

Checkpoint

See Teaching Master 90.

ⓐ ■ The diameter increases at a constant rate as the distance from the wall increases.

   ■ The area increases as the square of the distance from the wall. The area increases at an increasing rate as the distance from the wall increases.

ⓑ ■ The intensity would decrease rapidly at first and then level off.

   ■ The graph would drop rapidly at first and then level off.

ⓒ The rule has the variable in the denominator and is similar to the rule studied in Investigation 1 of this lesson, so we would expect similar patterns.

a. Use the data on distance and area from activity 4 to complete the following table, showing light intensity as a function of distance from the light source. Light intensity is given here in lumens per square meter.

Light Circle Intensity

Distance from Light (D)	1	2	3	4	5
Area of Light Circle (A)	$\pi \approx 3.14$	$4\pi \approx 12.56$			
Light Intensity (I)	$\dfrac{160}{\pi} \approx 50.93$	$\dfrac{160}{4\pi} \approx 12.73$			

b. Write an equation relating light intensity I to distance from light source D.

c. Describe the pattern in a graph showing light intensity as a function of distance from the light source.

Checkpoint

a Suppose you aim a flashlight against one wall of a darkened room and gradually move the light away from the wall. What patterns of change would you expect

- in the diameter of the light circle as a function of distance from the wall?
- in the area of the light circle as a function of distance from the wall?

b Now suppose you also use a light meter to measure the intensity of light when the flashlight is at various distances from the wall. What pattern of results would you expect

- in a table of the (*distance, intensity*) data?
- in a graph of the (*distance, intensity*) data?

c How are the patterns in part b related to the form of an algebraic rule expressing intensity I as a function of distance D?

Be prepared to share and justify your pattern descriptions.

Unit 4

On Your Own

The intensity of sound can be measured by several different scales. One that uses units of power is *watts per square meter*. It is a measure of the pressure that a sound forces on your ear.

The intensity of sound from a stereo system is a function of the listener's distance from the speakers. Displayed in the table below are some measurements taken at various distances from speakers of a particular stereo system.

Sound Intensity

Distance (m)	0.5	1.0	1.5	2.0	2.5	3.0	3.5	4.0	4.5	5.0
Intensity ($\frac{W}{m^2}$)	80	20	8.9	5.0	3.2	2.2	1.6	1.25	1.0	0.8

a. Describe the overall pattern relating distance D and intensity I in these data.

b. Make a scatterplot of the (D, I) data pairs, and explain how the shape of the graph matches the pattern in the table data.

c. Which of the following movements will cause the greater decrease in sound intensity?

- Moving from 1 meter to 2 meters away from the speakers.

- Moving from 4 meters to 5 meters away from the speakers.

d. Experiment with various rules in the functions list of your graphing calculator or computer software to find a good model of the relation between I and D. Express intensity as a function of distance. If necessary, look back at activity 5 about light intensity for some clues.

INVESTIGATION 3 The Shape of Inverse Variation Models

The activities in which you explored relations between average speed and time for a trip led to relations in the form $y = \frac{a}{x}$. The activities in which you explored relations between light or sound intensity and distance from the source of that energy led to relations in the form $y = \frac{a}{x^2}$.

Because $\frac{1}{x}$ is the *reciprocal* or *multiplicative inverse* of x and $\frac{1}{x^2}$ is the reciprocal or multiplicative inverse of x^2, the equations $y = \frac{a}{x}$ and $y = \frac{a}{x^2}$ are called **models of inverse variation**. Equations such as $y = ax$, $y = ax^2$, and $y = ax^3$ are called **models of direct variation**.

Both inverse and direct variation are examples of power models. The standard form of symbolic rules for all power models is $y = ax^b$. When b is greater than zero, as in $y = 2x^3$ or $y = -3x^2$, the power model represents direct variation and sometimes is called a direct power model. Inverse power models (describing inverse variation) are represented in the standard power model form by use of negative exponents. For example, $y = 2x^{-1}$ represents $y = \frac{2}{x^1}$ and $y = 3x^{-2}$ represents $y = \frac{3}{x^2}$.

▶ **On Your Own**

a. The pattern is the same as with the intensity of light. The intensity decreases but not at a constant rate. It decreases quickly at first and then levels off.

b. As in the table, the graph shows a large decrease at first and the decrease becomes smaller as the distance increases.

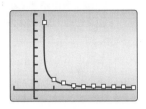
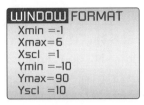

WINDOW FORMAT
Xmin =-1
Xmax=6
Xscl =1
Ymin =-10
Ymax=90
Yscl =10

MORE
ASSIGNMENT   *pp. 259–264*

Students can now begin Modeling task 3 or Reflecting task 2 from the MORE assignment following Investigation 3.

c. The greater decrease is experienced when moving from 1 to 2 meters.
   ■ Moving back from 1 to 2 meters decreases the sound by 15 watts per square meter.
   ■ Moving back from 4 to 5 only decreases the sound by 0.45 watts per square meter.

d. $I = \frac{20}{D^2}$ fits these data precisely.

INVESTIGATION 3   The Shape of Inverse Variation Models

The purpose of this investigation is to generalize the inverse variation patterns that students have observed in several specific contexts. To assist in this generalization, students discuss the differences between inverse variation power models and the linear or exponential models studied previously. The inverse variation MORE tasks again give students opportunities to see that pattern at work in several different contexts (see, for example, M2, M3, and R4).

The introductory paragraphs in the text give some formal vocabulary. It is important to ask your students why "inverse" and "direct" make sense in these situations, as that will help them make the connection between the formal language of the text and the informal observations they have made.

Your students may need some help interpreting negative exponents. In middle school, students may well have seen scientific notation, and certainly calculators use it to display very small numbers. For example, a calculator may display 5E-4, meaning $5(10)^{-4}$. Students should know that this means $5 \div 10^4$. In the "Exponential Models" unit of Course 1, graphs of relations such as $y = 2^x$ were explored, where x took both positive and negative values. Students working through that unit observed that the y values increased by a factor of 2 as the x values increased by 1. Looking at the table of this relation we can also see that the y values decrease by dividing by 2 as x decreases by 1, so we have the following:

x	-2	-1	0	1	2
y	$2^{-2} = \frac{1}{4}$	$2^{-1} = \frac{1}{2}$	$2^0 = 1$	$2^1 = 2$	$2^2 = 4$

See additional Teaching Notes on page T317N.

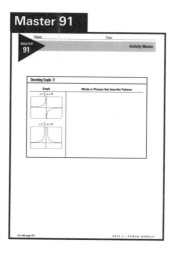

EXPLORE *continued*

Experiment 1

As you observe groups describing the differences between patterns created by $y = x^2$ and $y = \frac{1}{x}$, you may need to push them to explain these differences carefully, and to explain why they occur. Asking the following questions, "What happens in the table if x is a positive number? What if x is a negative number? Why do we see these differences?" forces students to look beyond the obvious. Individual students will not get all of the comparisons, but if you ask probing questions while they experiment, the class discussion following the experiments will be more complete. Of course, you should use your judgment about how formal the language should be.

1. The table and graph are shown below. If students are generating tables using calculators or computer software, an error message should appear for the y value corresponding to $x = 0$. If no one mentions this error draw it to their attention and ask them to think about why it might appear. This is something new. You may wish to ask, "Why have we never seen this error message before?"

x	$y = \frac{1}{x}$	x	$y = \frac{1}{x}$	x	$y = \frac{1}{x}$
-10	-0.1	-2	-0.5	6	0.1667
-8	-0.125	0	not defined	8	0.125
-6	-0.1667	2	0.5	10	0.1
-4	-0.25	4	0.25		

a. The table and graph show y decreasing as x increases, except for a jump at the undefined point $x = 0$. For negative x, the decrease is slow at first and then becomes very rapid as x approaches 0. For positive x the decrease is rapid for x near 0, but then slower as x gets large.

b. The graph has rotational symmetry about the origin and reflection symmetry about the lines $y = x$ and $y = -x$.

2. a. The inverse variation model is similar to a line with negative slope in that the y values decrease as the x values increase. However, the patterns of change in the tables and graphs are very different. The linear model is unbroken with a constant rate of change.

b. The exponential model is never negative. With a base between 0 and 1, the y values decrease as the x values increase, just as happens with the inverse variation function; however, the exponential model increases rapidly for negative values of x.

c. The basic quadratic power model gives a U-shaped graph which is positive for all x. The inverse variation model is similar to the power model $y = x^2$ because if $x > 0$, then $y > 0$, and if $x < 0$, both models have decreasing y values. Students may need prompting by appropriate questions during the development of the class descriptions after Experiment 2 in order to observe these similarities. Differences include the following:

For $x < 0$, the inverse model has negative y values and the power model has positive y values.

In the first quadrant, the power model increases and the inverse model decreases. The power model decreases and then increases while the inverse model always decreases.

The power model has reflection symmetry about the y-axis and no rotational symmetry. The inverse model has reflection symmetry about the lines $y = x$ and $y = -x$ and rotational symmetry about the origin.

See additional Teaching Notes on pages T317O–T317P.

When using inverse power models to solve problems, it helps to know the patterns in tables and graphs that can be predicted from various forms of inverse power equations. You will explore those patterns in the following experiments.

Experiment 1

Use your graphing calculator or computer software for these explorations.

1. Make a table and a graph of $y = \frac{1}{x}$, for x varying from -10 to 10 in steps of 1.

   a. Describe the patterns of change produced.

   b. Make a sketch of the graph and describe any symmetries in the graph.

2. Describe ways that the table and graph patterns for $y = \frac{1}{x}$ are similar to and different from those of the following.

   a. The linear model $y = -x$

   b. The exponential model $y = (0.5)^x$

   c. The power model $y = x^2$

Experiment 2

Use your graphing calculator or computer software for the following explorations. Cooperate with group members to share the workload.

1. Make tables and graphs for relations of the form $y = \frac{a}{x}$ with $a = 2, 3, 0.5$, and -2. You may wish to adjust the y-axis window in order to get a better view of the graphs.

2. Describe ways that the patterns in tables and graphs of these inverse power models are similar to and different from those of the basic form $y = \frac{1}{x}$.

3. Summarize what the value of a allows you to predict about the pattern of the table and shape of the graph of the relation $y = \frac{a}{x}$.

4. How can you use the form of the equation $y = \frac{a}{x}$ to help predict the symmetry of its graph?

Experiment 3

Use your graphing calculator or computer software for the following explorations. Cooperate with group members to share the workload.

1. Make a table and a graph of $y = \frac{1}{x^2}$ for x varying from -10 to 10.

   a. Describe the way y changes as x increases.

   b. Make a sketch of the graph and describe any symmetries in the graph.

2. Describe ways that the table and graph patterns for $y = \frac{1}{x^2}$ are similar to and different from those of the following.

  a. The linear model $y = 2x$

  b. The exponential model $y = 2^x$

  c. The inverse variation model $y = \frac{1}{x}$

3. a. Explore tables and graphs for relations of the form $y = \frac{a}{x^2}$ for various choices of a.

  b. Describe ways that the tables and graphs are similar to and different from those of the basic model $y = \frac{1}{x^2}$.

  c. Describe how the symmetry of the graph of $y = \frac{1}{x^2}$ can be predicted from the form of the rule.

Checkpoint

ⓐ Given below are rules and graphs of four inverse power models. The scales are the same on each graph. Match each graph with the rule it fits best and explain your reasoning.

  i. $y = \frac{1}{x^2}$ **ii.** $y = \frac{2}{x}$

  iii. $y = \frac{1}{x}$ **iv.** $y = \frac{0.2}{x^2}$

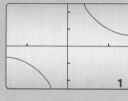

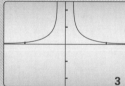

ⓑ What patterns can be expected in tables of (x, y) values for each rule?

ⓒ What patterns of symmetry appear in graphs of the basic types of inverse power models $y = \frac{1}{x}$ and $y = \frac{1}{x^2}$?

Be prepared to share your group's conclusions with the entire class.

2. **a.** The graph for $y = \frac{1}{x^2}$ is not a straight line, it lies only in quadrants I and II, it does not change at a constant rate, and it increases for negative and increasing x but decreases for x positive and increasing. The model $y = \frac{1}{x^2}$ has no y-intercept and is asymptotic to both axes. The graph for $y = 2x$ is a straight line in quadrants I and III, it increases at a constant rate for increasing x, and it has a y-intercept at 0. The two models are similar for values of $x < 0$, since they both increase as x approaches zero.

   b. The model $y = \frac{1}{x^2}$ is similar to the exponential model $y = 2^x$ because the graphs approach the x-axis as x decreases. Also, for negative values of x the inverse square model and the exponential model increase as x increases. The two models are quite different around the origin and in the first quadrant. The exponential model increases rapidly in the first quadrant while $y = \frac{1}{x^2}$ decreases rapidly. Also $y = \frac{1}{x^2}$ is asymptotic to the y-axis while $y = 2^x$ has a y-intercept at 1.

   c. The graph seems to have the same basic shape as $y = \frac{1}{x}$, but it lies only in the first and second quadrants because squaring always leads to positive y values.

3. **a.** Students should use both positive and negative values for a.

   b. If $a > 0$, then the graph lies in quadrants I and II. If $a < 0$, then the graph lies in quadrants III and IV. If $|a|$ is greater than 1, then the curve is farther away from the axes than is the graph of $y = \frac{1}{x^2}$; and if $|a|$ is less than 1, then the curve approaches the axes more quickly than the graph of $y = \frac{1}{x^2}$ does. The tables also have similar patterns. The graphs of $y = \frac{a}{x^2}$ and $y = \frac{1}{x^2}$ have the same basic shape.

   c. For all x, $\frac{a}{x^2} = \frac{a}{(-x)^2}$, so both the points (x, y) and $(-x, y)$ will be on the graph. This implies that the graph will be symmetric about the y-axis.

SHARE AND SUMMARIZE   full-class discussion

Checkpoint

See Teaching Master 92.

a   **i.** $y = \frac{1}{x^2}$; graph 4   **ii.** $y = \frac{2}{x}$; graph 1

   iii. $y = \frac{1}{x}$; graph 2   **iv.** $y = \frac{0.2}{x^2}$; graph 3

b For $y = \frac{1}{x^2}$ and $y = \frac{0.2}{x^2}$, the tables should show all positive values for y. As $|a|$ approaches 0, the y values in the tables will become very large. As $|a|$ becomes very large, the y values in the tables will approach 0.

For $y = \frac{2}{x}$ and for $y = \frac{1}{x}$, the tables will show that if $x > 0$, then $y > 0$. Similarly, if $x < 0$ then $y < 0$. Also, the table will show that as $|a|$ becomes very large, the y values approach 0. As x approaches 0 from the positive side, the y values become very large and positive, and as x approaches 0 from the negative side, the y values are negative and become very large in absolute value.

c The graph of $y = \frac{1}{x}$ has line reflection symmetry about $y = x$ and $y = -x$. The graph also has rotational symmetry about the origin. The graph of $y = \frac{1}{x^2}$ has line reflection symmetry about the y-axis.

> **See additional Teaching Notes on page T317Q.**

CONSTRUCTING A MATH TOOLKIT: Completed Teaching Masters 84 ("Describing Graphs I") and 85 ("Describing Graphs II") could be kept with students' Math Toolkits. If these activity masters have not been completed, students should summarize descriptions for direct and inverse power models in the Algebra and Functions section. They should include examples of contexts, graphs, and equations.

APPLY   individual task

▶On Your Own

a.

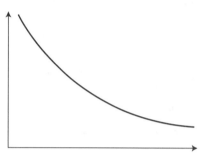

b.   The shape of the graph tells us that as the distance between the two objects increases, the force decreases rapidly at first and then less rapidly.

c.   As you can see from the graph, as the distance between the objects increases, the gravitational force decreases. As this distance increases, the gravitational force approaches 0, and therefore the astronauts gradually become weightless.

MORE
ASSIGNMENT   *pp. 259–264*

Modeling: 3 and 1 or 2*
Organizing: 1 and 2
Reflecting: 1 and 2 or 3*
Extending: 1

When choice is indicated, it is important to leave the choice to the student.
NOTE: *It is best if Organizing tasks are discussed as a whole class after they have been assigned as homework.*

MORE   independent assignment

Modeling

1. **a.** $t = \dfrac{100}{s}$

    b. Using a table for $y = \dfrac{100}{x}$, you can find the differences in average speeds of 40 mph and 45 mph, 40 mph and 50 mph, and 40 mph and 60 mph.

    ■ 0.28 hours or about 17 minutes
    ■ 0.5 hours or about 30 minutes
    ■ 0.83 hours or about 50 minutes

    c. Approximately 57 miles per hour

s	t
40	2.50
45	2.22
50	2.00
55	1.82
60	1.67
65	1.54

▶On Your Own

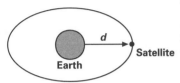

Earth   Satellite

The gravity that pulls flying objects toward the surface of the earth is the same force that holds the moon and NASA satellites in their orbits around the earth. The force of attraction F between any two objects is a function of the distance d separating the centers of those objects. The rule is of the form $F = \frac{a}{d^2}$. The numerical value of a depends on the masses of the objects and the units chosen to measure mass and force.

The form of the rule $F = \frac{a}{d^2}$ can help you predict how gravitational force on astronauts in a space shuttle changes, as that shuttle moves into higher orbits around the earth.

a. Sketch a graph showing the shape of the (*distance*, *force*) relation.

b. Explain in words what the shape of the graph tells about force as a function of distance.

c. How do your responses to parts a and b explain the apparent weightlessness of astronauts in space?

MORE
Modeling • Organizing • Reflecting • Extending

Modeling

1. Many people make very long commutes to work each day, sometimes as much as 100 miles each way! Suppose that one commuter van has a 100 mile trip, and the route taken allows an average speed of 40 miles per hour.

a. Write a rule that will give the time t of the trip as a function of the average driving speed s.

b. How much time will be saved if the van driver finds a route that allows an average speed that is faster by

■ 5 mph?

■ 10 mph?

■ 20 mph?

Explain how you obtained your results.

c. How fast (on average) will the van have to travel in order to make the trip in $1\frac{3}{4}$ hours?

2. At Wolverine Industries, the management has a special company party every year at the Waterworld Amusement Park. For a set fee of $5,000 the company employees can have the entire park to themselves for an evening.

   a. What will this party cost per employee if

   ■ only 20 people attend?

   ■ 100 people attend?

   ■ 500 people attend?

   b. What rule gives the cost per employee C for any number of guests N?

   c. Make a graph of the rule in part b. Explain what the shape of that graph tells about the pattern of change in average cost as the number of guests increases.

   d. Which causes the greater change in average cost per guest: an increase from 10 to 15 guests or an increase from 100 to 105 guests? How is your answer shown on the graph?

3. Many things we buy come in cylindrical containers. Suppose that in planning to market a new brand of anti-dandruff shampoo, Anasazzi Salon Products first considers a cylinder with radius of 2 centimeters and height of 20 centimeters. (Recall that the volume of any such cylinder is given by the formula $V = \pi r^2 h$.)

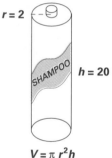

   a. If they then consider a new cylinder with radius 3 cm and the same volume, what will be the height of that cylinder?

   b. If they try another cylinder with radius 5 cm and the same volume, what will be the height of that cylinder?

   c. Write an equation showing how to calculate the height of any new cylinder made to hold the original volume, but having a base of radius r.

   d. Use the equation from part c to produce a table of (*radius, height*) data, for r varying from 0 to 8 cm in steps of 0.5 cm. Then produce a graph of that relation.

   e. Use your table and graph to describe the pattern of change in height as radius changes.

2. a. ■ $250

■ $50

■ $10

b. $C = \dfrac{5000}{N}$

c. As the number of employees increases, the cost per employee decreases at a decreasing rate.

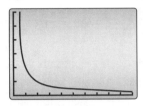 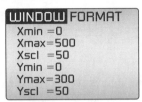

```
WINDOW FORMAT
Xmin =0
Xmax=500
Xscl =50
Ymin =0
Ymax=300
Yscl =50
```

d. The increase from 10 to 15 guests results in a greater change than does an increase from 100 to 105 guests. (The change in cost per employee from 10 to 15 guests is $166.67. The change in cost per employee from 100 to 105 guests is $2.38.) This is shown in the graph by the fact that the graph is steeper for lower values of N than for higher values of N.

3. a. The volume of the original cylinder is $\pi(4)(20)$ or 80π cm^3, so the height of the new cylinder will be $h = \dfrac{V}{\pi r^2} = \dfrac{80\pi}{9\pi} = \dfrac{80}{9} \approx 8.9$ cm.

b. $\dfrac{80\pi}{25\pi} \approx 3.2$ cm

c. $h = \dfrac{80\pi}{\pi r^2}$ or $h = \dfrac{80}{r^2}$

d.

Radius	0	0.5	1	1.5	2	2.5	3	3.5	4	4.5	5	5.5	6	6.5	7	7.5	8
Height	Undefined	320.0	80.0	35.6	20.0	12.8	8.9	6.5	5.0	4.0	3.2	2.6	2.2	1.9	1.6	1.4	1.3

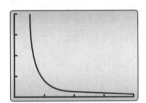

e. As the radius gets bigger the height decreases, but at a decreasing rate.

Unit 4

4. a. As time increases, the number of digits remembered decreases at a decreasing rate.

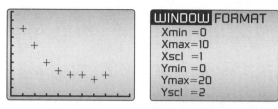

b. **Linear Regression**
$y = 14.43 - 1.51x$

Exponential Regression
$y = 15.39(0.83)^x$

Power Regression
$y = 16.6x^{-0.67}$

c. The power model seems to be the best fit. Plotting each graph with the scatterplot will support that conclusion by showing that the data points are randomly distributed about the graph of the power model. For the other two models the data points are above, then below, and then above the proposed model graphs, which suggests that there is some systematic difference between the pattern in the data and the patterns described by those models.

Organizing

1. Students should be able to write these equations by making sense out of a distance-speed-time context. They do not need to manipulate symbolic expressions to answer parts a–c.

a. $d = st$

b. $s = \dfrac{d}{t}$

c. $t = \dfrac{d}{s}$

To derive	from	perform these operations on each side of the equation.
$d = st$	$s = \dfrac{d}{t}$	multiply by t
	$t = \dfrac{d}{s}$	multiply by s
$s = \dfrac{d}{t}$	$d = st$	divide by t
	$t = \dfrac{d}{s}$	multiply by s and divide by t
$t = \dfrac{d}{s}$	$d = st$	divide by s
	$s = \dfrac{d}{t}$	multiply by t and divide by s

4. As a psychology project to study human memory, two high school students asked their classmates to memorize digits in the number π, which begins

$$3.14159265358979323846264643383...$$

All students practiced until they had memorized 25 digits. Then they were asked to practice no more. They were tested once each week to see how many digits they still remembered. The data in the following table show average results for the group of students.

Memorizing Digits in π

Week	1	2	3	4	5	6	7	8
Number of Digits Remembered	16	12	8	6	5	5	4	5

a. Make a scatterplot of these data and explain what the pattern in the data says about the number of digits remembered.

b. Use your calculator or computer software to find linear, exponential, and power models for the data. Compare the graphs of your models to the data scatterplot.

c. Comment on the fit of each of your rules to the data. Which model seems best and why do you think so?

Organizing

1. In several activities in this lesson, you have explored the relation between distance, speed, and time for travel. Using the variables d, s, and t for distance, speed, and time respectively, write rules giving the following.

a. Distance as a function of speed and time

b. Speed as a function of distance and time

c. Time as a function of distance and speed

Explain how these rules are really different forms of the same relationship by showing how you can derive each rule from each of the other two rules.

2. Given below is a table of (x, y) data from three models—one linear, one exponential, and one inverse power model.

x	−5	−4	−3	−2	−1	0	1	2	3	4	5
Model A: y	32	16	8	4	2	1	0.5	0.25	0.125	0.0625	0.03125
Model B: y	11	9	7	5	3	1	−1	−3	−5	−7	−9
Model C: y	−0.2	−0.25	−0.333	−0.5	−1		1	0.5	0.333	0.25	0.2

a. For each table row, identify the type of model.

b. If possible, find a *NOW-NEXT* equation for each row that describes how values of y change as values of x increase in steps of 1.

c. If possible, find an equation in the form "$y = \ldots$" for each row that gives the value of y for any given value of x.

d. Explain how the forms of the *NOW-NEXT* equations for models A and B relate to the forms of the "$y = \ldots$" equations for the same models.

3. For positive values of x, both inverse power models $y = \dfrac{1}{x}$ and $y = \dfrac{1}{x^2}$ have the property that y decreases as x increases.

a. What sorts of linear models also have that property?

b. What sorts of exponential models also have that property?

4. When examining a table of (x, y) data, what clues would suggest that the relation between x and y is an inverse variation? A direct variation?

Reflecting

1. Why is the point $(0, 0)$ on the graph of every direct variation function, but not on the graph of any inverse variation function?

2. When you take pictures with a flash camera, you generally have to be quite close to the subject of your picture. How does the inverse power model that relates light intensity to distance from the source explain why this is true?

3. Make sketches showing the basic shapes of graphs of inverse power models.

a. What would tables of (x, y) data look like for x values close to 0?

b. What would tables of (x, y) data look like for very large, positive x values?

4. From television and radios to x-rays, microwaves, and radar, the world we live in surrounds us with the energy of electromagnetic fields (EMF). As sources of EMF have become more and more common in our everyday lives, scientists have investigated possible health hazards caused by exposure to EMF.

2. **a.** Model A: exponential

        Model B: linear

        Model C: inverse power

   b. Model A: $NEXT = \frac{1}{2} NOW$

        Model B: $NEXT = NOW - 2$

        Model C: $NEXT = \frac{NOW}{1 + NOW}$ or $NEXT = \frac{1}{\frac{1}{NOW} + 1}$ work, but it is unlikely that most students will discover these. You may wish to give extra credit for Model C to encourage students to spend the time necessary to discover it.

   c. Model A: $y = \left(\frac{1}{2}\right)^x$ Model B: $y = 1 - 2x$ Model C: $y = \frac{1}{x}$

   d. Model A: The coefficient of NOW ($\frac{1}{2}$) in the NOW-$NEXT$ form becomes the base b of the exponential function in the form $y = ab^x$.

        Model B: The number (-2) which is added to NOW to yield $NEXT$ becomes the coefficient of x in the form $y = a + bx$.

3. **a.** Lines with negative slope, that is, models with equations of the form $y = a + bx$, where $b < 0$

   b. $y = b^x$, where b is between 0 and 1

4. Inverse variation models will not have a y value for $x = 0$, and for large positive and large negative values of x, the y values will be close to 0. Direct variation models will be defined for all x values. For very large x values (positive or negative), the y value also will be very large.

Reflecting

1. Every direct variation function is of the form $y = x^a$ for some $a > 0$. Thus if $x = 0$, $y = 0^a = 0$, so the point $(0, 0)$ is on the graph. Every inverse variation function is of the form $y = \frac{1}{x^a}$, so when $x = 0$, $y = \frac{1}{0}$, which is undefined.

2. As you draw further away from your subject, light intensity of your flash on the subject drops quickly, as is seen by the sharp initial decrease in the power model $y = \frac{1}{x^2}$.

3. There are two basic types of inverse power models:

   i.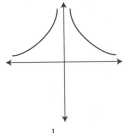

         $y = \frac{1}{x^a}$, a even

   ii.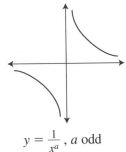

         $y = \frac{1}{x^a}$, a odd

   a. In case i, tables of (x, y) data would have large y values corresponding to x values close to zero (on either side).

        In case ii, negative values of x close to 0 would correspond to large negative numbers, while positive values of x close to 0 would correspond to large positive numbers.

   b. In both cases, for very large x values, y values would get closer to 0.

Unit 4

4. a. As the distance from the source increases the EMF readings decrease—rapidly at first and then more slowly.

b. Possible models fitting the overall pattern of the EMF data are: linear (with negative slope); inverse power; or exponential (0 < base < 1). However, the decrease in EMF readings does not seem to occur at a constant rate, so a linear model is probably not a good choice.

c. The science teacher may not have the acceptable standard at their fingertips, but may be able to direct students to a source.

Unit 4

Intensity of an electromagnetic field will be related to one's distance from the source of that field. To assess the health risks, it is useful to know precisely how intensity of radiation decreases as distance increases. For example, if 2 feet is a moderately safe distance, will 4 feet be twice as safe?

The data in the following table show patterns of EMF measurement (in a unit called the *milligauss*) at various distances from the front and back of a television set and from a VCR.

EMF Measurements

Distance (cm)	2	4	6	8	10	12	14	16	20	24	28	32	36	40	44	48
TV Front	12	10	8	7	6	5	4	3	3							
TV Back		184		126		82		49	30	20	12	8	6	4	3	2
VCR	23	13	6	4	2	2	1	1								

a. What patterns do you see in the relation between these EMF ratings and distance from the TV set, in the two directions given?

b. What sort of algebraic models would you expect to fit the patterns in these data? Explain your reasoning.

c. Check with your science or technology teacher to learn about standards for acceptable exposure to EMF radiation.

Extending

1. Refer to the data on EMF radiation in Reflecting task 4. All three EMF readings decrease as distance increases. Because the patterns of change are not linear or exponential, it is natural to investigate if inverse power models might fit the patterns in the data. However, it is not easy to see exactly what the right model might be. You can use your graphing calculator or computer software to find power models that are best fits for each relation between distance and EMF.

- Enter the (*distance, EMF*) data for each set of distances into data lists.

- For each set of distances, use the power regression command to find a rule of the form $y = ax^b$ for these data. The values of b should be negative. This is just a different notation for inverse power expressions, where $x^{-b} = \frac{1}{x^b}$.

Unit 4

a. Your models probably are not as simple as $y = ax^{-2}$; that is, $y = \frac{a}{x^2}$. What do the values you get tell about the relation between distance and EMF?

b. Compare each of the models to the patterns in the actual data.

- Plot graphs of the models on the data scatterplots.

- Compare tables produced by the modeling rules to the actual data.

c. If you double your distance from the front or back of a television set or from a VCR, will the EMF radiation from that device be cut in half? What evidence supports your conclusion?

d. What other models might fit the scatterplot patterns of (*distance*, *EMF*) data?

e. Which models do you think best fit the data? Explain your reasoning.

2. For an astronaut in a space shuttle orbiting the earth, an increase in distance from the earth reduces the effect of gravity. The astronaut's weight in space is a function of the distance above the earth's surface with rule:

$$W = \frac{W_e}{(1 + 0.00015625h)^2}$$

In that rule, W_e is the astronaut's weight at sea level on the earth's surface (in kilograms) and h is the height of the shuttle above sea level (in kilometers). Suppose the weight, W_e, of one astronaut is 70 kilograms.

a. Use your graphing calculator or computer software and tables or graphs of the weight equation to find the following.

- The astronaut's weight at a height of 1000 kilometers

- The height at which the astronaut weighs only half of his or her weight at sea level on the earth's surface

- The height at which the astronaut weighs only one-tenth of his or her weight at sea level

b. Make a sketch of the graph of the relation between weight and height above the earth's surface. Describe the pattern of change in weight as a function of height as shown on the graph.

MORE *continued*

Extending

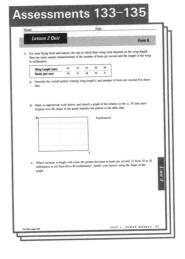
1. a. The exponents are all negative, which indicates that as the distance from the source increases, the EMF reading decreases. The relationships are all inverse variation power models.

b. Each model seems to be a reasonable fit to the data.

TV Front 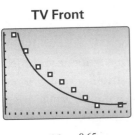   TV Back 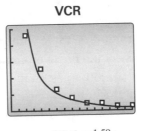   VCR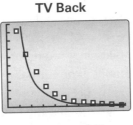

$$y = 23x^{-0.65} \qquad y = 5976x^{-1.91} \qquad y = 90.6x^{-1.59}$$

Distance (cm)	2	4	6	8	10	12	14	16	20	24	28	32	36	40	44	48
TV Front Actual Values	12	10	8	7	6	5	4	3	3							
Power Model Values	14.7	9.3	7.2	6.0	5.1	4.6	4.1	3.8	3.3							
TV Back Actual Values		184		126		82		49	30	20	12	8	6	4	3	2
Power Model Values		423		113		52		30	20	14	10	8	6	5	4	4
VCR Actual Values	23	13	6	4	2	2	1	1								
Power Model Values	30.1	10	5.2	3.3	2.3	1.7	1.4	1.1								

c. Doubling the distance does not halve the EMF reading. This is evident from the table. If distance in centimeters changes from 4 to 8 and then to 16, the decrease in the EMF readings vary.

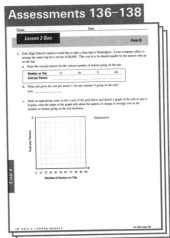
Percent of Reduction in EMF Reading

Distance Change (cm)	TV Front	TV Back	VCR
4 to 8	30%	31.5%	69%
8 to 16	57%	61%	75%

d. Exponential models seem to be a better fit. The points on the scatterplot appear randomly distributed above and below the graph of the exponential models. In the power models, the points appear below then above and then below the graph, suggesting some systematic difference between the data pattern and the power model pattern.

	Power Model	Exponential Model	Linear Model
Dist/TV Front	$y = 23x^{-0.65}$	$y = 13.6(0.92)^x$	$y = -0.5x + 11.7$
Dist/TV Back	$y = 5976x^{-1.91}$	$y = 263.1(0.90)^x$	$y = -3.4x + 133.5$
Dist/VCR	$y = 90.6x^{-1.59}$	$y = 33.2(0.78)^x$	$y = -1.6x + 20.4$

e. Student responses may vary. Look for reasoning that makes use of the properties of linear, power, and exponential equations.

See additional Teaching Notes on page T317Q.

Unit 4

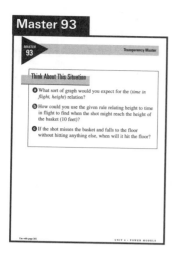

MASTER
93   Transparency Master

Think About This Situation

ⓐ What sort of graph would you expect for the (*time in flight, height*) relation?

ⓑ How could you use the given rule relating height to time in flight to find when the shot might reach the height of the basket (10 feet)?

ⓒ If the shot misses the basket and falls to the floor without hitting anything else, when will it hit the floor?

Use with page 265.   UNIT 4 • POWER MODELS

Lesson 3 *Quadratic Models*

LESSON OVERVIEW The purpose of this lesson is to explore the properties of quadratic models with rules of the form $y = ax^2 + bx + c$. This algebraic form is one of the mainstays of traditional school mathematics curricula and most students spend a great deal of time learning how to solve quadratic equations and to manipulate expressions involving quadratics into equivalent forms, primarily by factoring.

As one rethinks the role of different algebraic forms and procedures in light of emerging calculator and computer technology, it quickly becomes apparent that this traditional topic should be reconsidered. First, if one thinks about curricular priorities on the basis of applicability in genuine problem solving situations, there are other patterns of change (notably exponential and periodic) that are more widely useful than quadratics or higher-degree polynomials. Second, while quadratic polynomials were generally more manageable than exponential or periodic functions in an era of paper-and-pencil calculation, computers and graphing calculators make the more useful models as accessible as the traditional polynomials. The traditional skills of factoring and expanding polynomial expressions are not prerequisites for using algebraic methods to solve important and interesting problems. For these reasons, the *Contemporary Mathematics in Context* algebra strand delays introducing traditional algebraic operations and applications of quadratic polynomials.

Nonetheless, there are useful concepts concerning quadratics that can and should be presented at this stage. Accordingly, this lesson analyzes the variety of patterns (in tables and graphs) that can be modeled by the full quadratic expressions, and the ways that questions corresponding to quadratic equations and inequalities can be solved by numerical and graphic methods. The emphasis here, as in the other algebra units and lessons, is on use of algebraic expressions to represent functional relations among quantitative variables. By the end of the lesson, students should have a good symbol sense about quadratics (the ability to predict the shape of a graph from inspection of the symbolic rule), knowledge of the kinds of solutions that can occur for quadratic equations, and ability to use calculator or computer tools to solve equations and to find maxima or minima of quadratics. The information that can be obtained by manipulating a quadratic into alternative forms (*e.g.* factoring into a product of binomials) is addressed in Course 3, where there is an extensive algebraic reasoning unit.

Lesson Objectives

- ■ To be able to determine the patterns that appear in the tables and graphs of a rule in the form $y = ax^2$, $y = ax^2 + c$, or $y = ax^2 + bx + c$
- ■ To estimate the solution of a quadratic equation using a table of values and a graph
- ■ To determine if the solution of a quadratic equation is correct
- ■ To determine the number of solutions, and to approximate solutions, for various equations related to a quadratic model
- ■ To understand the types of situations that could be modeled by quadratic equations

See additional Teaching Notes on page T317Q.

Quadratic Models

Linear, exponential, and power models match the patterns of change in many important problems. By combining the algebraic expressions for those basic relations, you can build models for many other situations.

Among the most common examples of such combination models are equations in the form $y = ax^2 + bx + c$, the sum of power and linear rules. Those equations are called **quadratic models**. Specific numerical values of a, b, and c give the rules that relate variables in specific situations.

Quadratic models help to describe the paths of many different kinds of flying objects. For example, at many basketball games there is a popular half-time contest to see who in the audience can make a long-distance shot. For a typical shot, the ball's height (in feet) will be a function of time in flight (in seconds), modeled by an equation such as $h = -16t^2 + 40t + 6$.

Think About This Situation

a What sort of graph would you expect for the (*time in flight*, *height*) relation?

b How could you use the given rule relating height to time in flight to find when the shot might reach the height of the basket (10 feet)?

c If the shot misses the basket without hitting anything else, when will it hit the floor?

INVESTIGATION 1 ▸ Going Up…Going Down

Spectator sports provide entertainment for many people, both young and old. One of the most beautiful, but scary, sports in the summer Olympic Games is platform diving. The divers jump from a tower that is 10 meters above the pool and perform twists and flips on their way down to the water. The time from take-off to landing is less than 2 seconds, and the divers are traveling very fast when they hit the water.

Gravity is the force pulling the divers down to the pool. The *distance fallen* is a function of *time in flight*. Assuming the diver's initial jump is not significantly high, distance fallen in meters can be estimated by the power rule $d = 4.9t^2$, where time is in seconds. (If you were to measure distance in feet instead, the power rule would be $d = 16t^2$. Can you figure out why?)

1. Another way to look at the diver's flight is to see how his height above the pool surface changes as time passes.

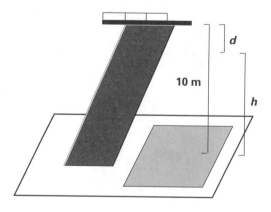

INVESTIGATION 1 Going Up ... Going Down

In this investigation, students will build a general quadratic model, investigating the contextual meaning and the graphical impact of each term. They first explore the constant term and then the linear term. As they investigate a platform diver's height above the water, students probably will use the table function to find specific answers. Ask them to use the graph also, so they can see that the graph does not look like the physical representation of the very tight arc of the dive.

The distance fallen when measuring in feet is $16t^2$ because the force of gravity in feet/second^2 is 16. The conversion from x m/s^2 to y ft/s^2 is the same as from meters to feet: multiply x m/s^2 by 3.28 ft/m. Students may recall that 16 ft/s^2 is one force of gravity constant; you may wish to press them to think about the conversion factor (3.28) for meters to feet.

Unit 4

1. a. The diver's height above the pool can be found by evaluating the expression $10 - 4.9t^2$ for different values of t.

    b.

Time in Flight (t)	Distance Fallen (d)	Height Above Water (h)
0	0	10
0.25	0.306	9.694
0.50	1.225	8.775
0.75	2.756	7.244
1.00	4.900	5.100
1.25	7.656	2.344
1.50	11.025	-1.025
1.75	15.006	-5.006
2.00	19.600	-9.600

    c. Estimating from the table or graph gives a time of approximately 1.4 seconds.

2. Height above water is a function of time in flight with rule $h = 10 - 4.9t^2$. Students may use the table-building capacity of their calculator or computer software, with time increment of 0.25, to match the table from activity 1.

3. a. $h = 20 - 4.9t^2$

    b. The divers would hit the water ($h = 0$) after about 2.02 seconds. Students can use either the table of values or the graph of the equation to find this solution.

    c. The rules are each of the form $h = (height\ of\ platform) - 4.9t^2$. The graphs look the same except that the graph illustrating the 20-meter platform situation is translated upward by 10 units on the y-axis. The heights in the table of values for $h = 20 - 4.9t^2$ are all 10 meters greater than the heights in the table of values for $h = 10 - 4.9t^2$.

a. Using the diagram on the previous page, explain how you would estimate the diver's height above the pool h at any time t. Keep in mind that the divers start at a height of 10 meters above the pool and travel a distance of $4.9t^2$ meters in t seconds.

b. Complete a table like the following one, which shows some sample time, distance, and height estimates.

Diving Estimates

Time in Flight (t)	Distance Fallen (d)	Height Above Water (h)
0	0	10
0.25	0.306	$10.0 - 0.306 = 9.694$
0.50		
0.75		
1.00		
1.25		
1.50		
1.75		
2.00		

c. About how long will it take a diver to reach the water?

2. Write an algebraic rule giving the diver's approximate height above the pool h as a function of time in flight t. Test your idea for the rule by using it in your calculator or computer software to produce a table of (*time in flight*, *height above water*) data. Compare that table with the results in activity 1. Modify your rule if necessary.

3. There are some high-diving competitions in which the tower is higher than 10 meters.

a. What rule would relate time and diver's height above the water if the tower were 20 meters high?

b. Estimate the time it would take a diver to hit the water from a 20-meter tower.

c. Compare the rules, tables, and graphs relating time and height for 10- and 20-meter platform dives. How are they similar and how are they different? What do the similarities and differences tell about the dives?

Unit 4

4. If you were going to make a high dive, you might wonder how fast you would be going when you hit the water. Suppose you jumped from a 20m platform.

a. How far would you fall in the first 0.5 seconds? What would your average speed be in that time interval?

b. How far would you fall in the next 0.5 seconds (from 0.5 to 1.0 seconds)? What would your average speed be in that time interval?

c. How far would you fall in the next 0.5 seconds (from 1.0 to 1.5 seconds)? What would your average speed be in that time interval?

d. When would you hit the water and about how fast would you be falling at that time?

5. The gravity that pulls a platform diver down toward the water acts on all other falling objects near the surface of the earth in the same way—that is, the distance fallen is $d = -4.9t^2$. Find algebraic rules to model the following situations and use those rules to estimate the time when each falling object hits the ground.

a. The relation between height h in meters and time in flight t in seconds of a marble dropped off a tall building from a height of 50 meters

b. The relation between height h in meters and time falling t in seconds of a baseball pop fly beginning at the maximum height of 25 meters

Gravity pulls falling objects toward the earth's surface, but it also acts on things that appear to be flying upward. For example, a springboard diver bounces upward before being pulled back down to the water. In popular sports such as soccer and football, a ball is kicked into the air, only to have gravity pull it back down. In each case, the height at any time t is a function of two things: the initial upward velocity of the flying object and the force of gravity pulling in the opposite direction.

6. Suppose a diver bounces off a 3-meter springboard, moving upward at a speed of 4 meters per second. If there were no gravitational force pulling that diver back toward the pool surface, how would his height above the pool increase as time passed?

a. Complete this table of sample (*time in flight*, *height above water*) data.

Springboard Diving (No Gravity)							
Time in Flight (sec)	0	1	2	3	4	5	6
Height Above Water (m)	3						

b. What algebraic rule would relate height above water h to time in flight t?

c. How would the table in part a and the rule in part b be different if the diver's initial speed was 2.5 meters per second?

d. How would the table in part a and the rule in part b be different if the diver sprung off a 5-meter board instead of a 3-meter board?

4. a. You fall $4.9(0.5)^2$ or 1.225 meters in the first 0.5 seconds. The average speed for the first 0.5 seconds would be $\frac{1.225 \text{ m}}{0.5 \text{ sec}}$ or 2.45 meters per second.

b. In the next 0.5 seconds you would fall $4.9 - 1.225$ or 3.675 meters. This gives an average speed of $\frac{3.675}{0.5}$ or 7.35 meters per second for this time interval.

c. You will fall $11.025 - 4.9$ or 6.125 meters in the next 0.5 seconds. The average speed for this time interval is $\frac{6.125}{0.5}$ or 12.25 meters per second.

d. In activity 3 part b, we found that it would take 2.02 seconds to hit the water when diving off a 20-meter platform. The smaller the time interval used here, the better the approximation for speed will be. Using the distance fallen between 2 and 2.02 seconds we get:

Distance fallen $= 4.9(2.02)^2 - 4.9(2)^2 \approx 0.39$ meters

Average speed $\approx \frac{0.39}{0.02} = 19.5$ meters per second

You may wish to have various groups report their time intervals and average speeds so that all students think about the connection between the time interval and the approximations for average speed.

5. a. $h = 50 - 4.9t^2$
The marble will hit the ground after approximately 3.19 seconds.

b. $h = 25 - 4.9t^2$
The ball will hit the ground after approximately 2.26 seconds.

You may wish to point out that there actually are other factors that influence the flight of the ball, such as air resistance and wind. We have made simplifying assumptions here in order to make the model more manageable.

6. a.

Time in Flight (in sec)	0	1	2	3	4	5	6
Height Above Water (in m)	3	7	11	15	19	23	27

b. $h = 3 + 4t$

c. In the table, for each one second increase, the change in the height above the water would be 2.5 meters instead of 4 meters. The equation would have a linear coefficient of 2.5 instead of 4, that is $h = 3 + 2.5t$.

d. In the table each height entry would be 2 greater. The rule would have a constant term of 5 instead of 3, that is $h = 5 + 4t$.

Unit 4

7. **a.** $h = 3 + 4t - 4.9t^2$

   b. $h = 5 + 2.5t - 4.9t^2$

8. **a.**

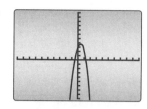 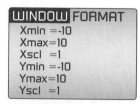

   b.

Responses may vary. Because the initial upward velocity is multiplied by x, one would expect it to have the greater influence. However, for this setting, because of the limitations on both the initial height and upward velocity, a difference is not readily apparent. Students should experiment with different equations and base their conclusions on the results of their experiments. The response will depend some on the actual values that they chose to use.

For the two problem situations from activity 7, the times to perform dives are essentially the same, approximately 1.29 or 1.3 seconds.

9. **a.** $h = 0.8 + 20t - 4.9t^2$

   b. These two equations have the same general form. The coefficient for the squared term (-4.9 or -16) represents the force of gravity; the linear coefficient (20 or 40) represents the initial upward velocity; and the constant (0.8 or 6) represents the initial height of the ball.

Unit 4

7. Now think about how the real flight of the diver in activity 6 results from a combination of three factors: initial height of the springboard, initial upward velocity produced by the spring of the board, and the force of gravity pulling the diver down toward the pool surface.

   a. Suppose the springboard is 3 meters high and the initial velocity of the diver is 4 meters per second upward. What algebraic rule would combine the three factors to give a relation between diver's height above the water h in meters and flight time t in seconds?

   b. How would your answer to part a change if the springboard were 5 meters high and the initial velocity were 2.5 meters per second upward?

8. For each situation given in activity 7, use your calculator or computer software to make tables and graphs showing the expected relation between height above water and time in flight from takeoff to landing in the pool. Which do you think has the greater influence on the time available to perform twists and turns, the height of the springboard or the initial upward velocity of the diver? Explain your reasoning.

The physical forces and relationships that govern flight of a springboard diver apply to many other flying objects as well. Consider, for example, a punt by a football player.

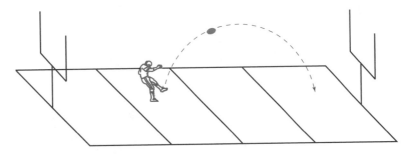

9. The height of a football t seconds after a punt depends upon the initial height and velocity of the ball and on the downward pull of gravity. Suppose a punt leaves the kicker's foot at an initial height of 0.8 meters with initial upward velocity of 20 meters per second.

   a. Write an algebraic rule relating flight time t in seconds and height h in meters for this punt. Compare your rule with that of other groups and resolve any differences.

   b. Compare your rule with the rule on page 265 relating height to time in flight of a basketball shot. In each case, identify the terms that represent force of gravity, initial velocity, and initial height of the ball.

Unit 4

10. Use the rule relating time in flight and height of the football to answer the following questions. In each case, explain how you arrived at your answer.

a. How does the height of the ball change as a function of time?

b. What is the maximum height the ball reaches, and when does that occur?

c. When does the ball return to the ground?

11. How will the rule change if the initial kick gives an upward velocity of only 15 meters per second? Use the new rule to answer the same questions posed in activity 10.

12. Compare the rules and graphs that relate time and height of punts with initial upward velocities of 20 and 15 meters per second. How are they similar? How are they different?

13. How will the rule you formulated in activity 9 change if the kick is a field-goal attempt, where the ball is held on the ground, rather than a punt, where the ball is dropped and kicked in the air?

Checkpoint

The problems about platform divers and football punts involved models that were similar to, but a bit different from, the familiar power models. Compare the diving and punting models to the power model $y = 4.9x^2$.

ⓐ How is the graph of $y = 10 - 4.9x^2$ similar to and different from the graph of $y = 4.9x^2$ or $y = -4.9x^2$?

ⓑ How is the graph of $y = -4.9x^2 + 4x + 3$ similar to and different from the graph of $y = 4.9x^2$ or $y = -4.9x^2$?

ⓒ How are the patterns in tables for the models $y = 10 - 4.9x^2$ and $y = -4.9x^2 + 4x + 3$ similar to and different from those for the power models $y = 4.9x^2$ or $y = -4.9x^2$?

ⓓ How could you predict the patterns in tables and graphs by looking at the ways the symbolic rules for the new relations are built from the basic rule $y = 4.9x^2$?

Be prepared to share your observations and thinking with the class.

Unit 4

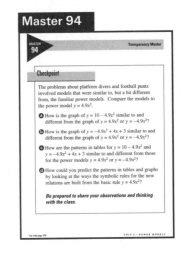

10. a. Initially the height of the ball increases. However, as one would expect, the ball reaches a maximum height and then begins to fall, and then the height of the ball decreases.

b. The maximum height the ball reaches is about 21.2 meters and is reached after about 2.0 seconds. On the table or graph this is the largest h value (or y value), and the corresponding t value (or x value).

c. The ball returns to the ground after about 4.1 seconds. This occurs when h (or y using the tables or graph) equals 0.

11. The new rule will be $h = 0.8 + 15t - 4.9t^2$.

a. The overall behavior of the ball will be just as before, although the actual path the ball takes will be different. It will not achieve as high a maximum height.

b. The maximum height the ball reaches is about 12.3 meters, and this height is reached after about 1.5 seconds.

c. The ball hits the ground ($h = 0$) after about 3.1 seconds.

12. The rules $h = 0.8 + 15t - 4.9t^2$ and $h = 0.8 + 20t - 4.9t^2$ are similar in that each involves a positive linear term, the same negative squared term, and the same constant term. They differ only in the coefficient of the linear term. The graphs for the two rules are both U-shaped curves that open downward. Also, both curves have a y-intercept of 0.8. However, the highest point on the curve of $h = 0.8 + 15t - 4.9t^2$ is lower than the highest point on the curve of $h = 0.8 + 20t - 4.9t^2$. The x-intercept for $h = 0.8 + 20t - 4.9t^2$ is also larger than that for $h = 0.8 + 15t - 4.9t^2$, indicating that its graph crosses the x-axis farther to the right.

13. Some students may not know the difference between a field goal attempt and a punt. For a field goal the ball is held in place on the ground and then kicked. A punt is made by dropping the ball and kicking it as it falls.

The rule will not have a constant term since the initial height will be zero.

SHARE AND SUMMARIZE   full-class discussion

Checkpoint

See Teaching Master 94.

ⓐ All three graphs have the same basic shape. The graph of $y = 10 - 4.9x^2$ and the graph of $y = -4.9x^2$ both open downward, but the graph of $y = 4.9x^2$ opens upward. If you take the graph of $y = -4.9x^2$ and translate it vertically up 10 units, you will get the graph of $y = 10 - 4.9x^2$. The graphs of $y = 10 - 4.9x^2$ and $y = -4.9x^2$ both have maximums, but no minimums.

ⓑ Like the graph of $y = -4.9x^2$, the graph of $y = -4.9x^2 + 4x + 3$ is a curve that has a maximum and opens downward. These two curves are different in that $y = -4.9x^2$ contains the origin and $y = -4.9x^2 + 4x + 3$ does not. The graph of $y = 4.9x^2$ is the same shape as the other two, but opens downward.

See additional Teaching Notes on page T317S.

Unit 4

▶**On Your Own**

a. The coefficient of the squared term would change. The new rule would be $h = 10 - 0.83t^2$.

b. Because the force due to gravity is much weaker on the moon than it is on the earth, you would expect the elapsed time for divers to hit the water to be greater when gravity is the same as on the moon. In fact, $0 = 10 - 0.83t^2$ when $t \approx 3.47$, compared to about 1.43 seconds with earth gravity.

c. Both rules have graphs that are U-shaped and opening downward, with the highest h value achieved when $t = 0$. However, the U-shape in the earth rule is much more narrow than for the moon rule.

The tables also have similar patterns in that both increase as t increases to 0, then decrease as t increases beyond 0. Both tables reach a maximum height value of 10, and this value is reached at the common point where $t = 0$. However, the table for the earth's rule has h values that increase and decrease much more rapidly than those corresponding to the moon's rule.

d. Similarities and differences could be predicted by examining the two rules term by term: constant term for initial height and squared term for force due to gravitational acceleration. The number multiplied times t^2 influences the rate of change for the y values.

MORE
ASSIGNMENT   *pp. 282–288*

Students now can begin Modeling tasks 1 or 3 from the MORE assignment following Investigation 5.

EXPLORE   small-group investigation

INVESTIGATION ▶ 2   Profit Prospects

For a short introduction to set the scene for this investigation, you may want your students to discuss the information given in the graph and the factors that would have to be considered in planning such a concert. Then students can work in groups on this investigation, showing that quadratics can occur in quite different situations than the height situations of Investigation 1. Depending on the strength and confidence of your students, you might want to check on their thinking in activities 1 to 3 before proceeding to activities 4 and 5. A whole-class discussion about how sales, income, and profit are each different functions of price could provide the needed key to what follows. This combination of economic concepts and algebraic thinking might be difficult for some students.

Unit 4

▶On Your Own

a. Refer to the rule your group developed in activity 2. How would the rule change if the diving took place from a 10-meter platform and the gravity were the same as on the moon, where distance fallen (in meters) is given by $d = 0.83t^2$?

b. Would you expect that the elapsed time for divers to hit the water from a 10-meter platform would be greater with earth gravity or with moon gravity? Explain your reasoning. Find what the elapsed time would be with moon gravity.

c. How does the rule for *moon diving* from a 10-meter platform produce table and graph patterns of (*flight time*, *height above water*) data that are similar to and different from the rule for diving from a 10-meter platform with earth gravity?

d. How could the similarities and differences be predicted by studying the two rules?

INVESTIGATION▶2 Profit Prospects

Quadratic relations are also useful models in business situations. For example, if a concert promoter is planning a show by some popular band, research into costs and sales prospects could give a model predicting profit from the show as a function of chosen ticket prices. Suppose the promoter's research provides the data below. (Assume no other expenses or sources of income.)

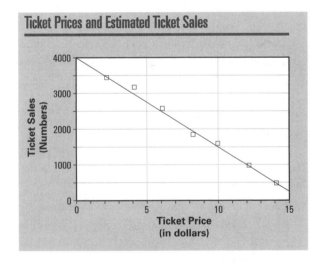

Ticket Prices and Estimated Ticket Sales

Expenses	
Band	$6,000
Theater	$1,500

1. The promoter used the (*ticket price*, *ticket sales*) data and a linear model to come up with the equation *Ticket Sales* = 4000 − 250(*Ticket Price*).

   a. How could the promoter have come up with this equation?

   b. Is the equation a good model of the relation between ticket price and probable ticket sales? Explain your reasoning.

   c. How could the promoter use the equation or graph to predict the number of concert tickets sold?

2. From earlier work on modeling situations involving variables like those in this concert promotion problem, you should recall these basic relations:

   Income = (*Ticket Sales*)(*Ticket Price*)

   Profit = *Income* − *Expenses*

   Using the letter names p for Ticket Price, S for Ticket Sales, I for Income, and P for profit, write equations giving the following.

   a. Ticket sales in terms of ticket price

   b. Income in terms of ticket sales and ticket price

   c. Profit in terms of income and expenses

3. The concert promoter decided that the key variable in planning was the ticket price p and wrote equations showing how ticket sales, income, and profit depended on ticket price. Using your answers to activities 1 and 2, decide whether the equations (shown below) are correct.

   a. $S = 4000 - 250p$　　　　　　　**b.** $I = p(4000 - 250p)$

   c. $I = 4000p - 250p^2$　　　　　　**d.** $P = -250p^2 + 4000p - 7500$

4. Use the relations among ticket price, ticket sales, income, and profit in activity 3 to answer the following questions.

   a. How many tickets probably will be sold if the ticket price is set at $7?

   b. What is the probable income from ticket sales if the ticket price is $7?

   c. What is the probable profit from the concert if ticket price is $7?

5. Use your graphing calculator or computer software to explore the relations among ticket price, ticket income, and concert profit to answer the following questions facing the promoter.

   a. How does the estimate of income from ticket sales change as ticket prices from $1 to $15 are considered?

   b. How does the estimate of profit from the concert change as ticket prices from $1 to $15 are considered?

   c. For what ticket price or prices will the promoter break even on the concert?

   d. What ticket price or prices will lead to maximum profit on the concert?

   e. Look back at your answers to parts a–d and explain why the results are or are not reasonable.

1. **a.** The promoter could have drawn a scatterplot and then drawn a good-fitting line by hand. Using two points on the line, the promoter then could have found an equation of the line. Or the promoter may have entered the data into a calculator and found the linear regression line for the set of data.

   b. Yes, the equation matches the line that is drawn on the scatterplot, and it seems to match the data quite well.

   c. Given a particular ticket price, the promoter could substitute that value into the equation and find the number of concert tickets sold. Using the graph, the promoter could find the appropriate ticket price on the horizontal axis and then move vertically up to the graph then across to the sales axis to find the number of tickets sold.

2. **a.** $S = 4000 - 250p$ **b.** $I = Sp$ **c.** $P = I - 7{,}500$

3. **As groups of students are working on activity 3, you might ask them about the different functions, encouraging them to use appropriate vocabulary. For example, ask: Are these all quadratic relations? How can you tell? (Students probably will pick parts c and d as quadratic, but the equation in part b is equivalent to the equation in part c.) Do you have any mental picture of the shape of the graphs? (The equation in part a should evoke a picture of a line with a negative slope. The ones in parts c and d should bring to mind a U-shape. Some students already will have noticed that the graphs will open downward.) What do you need to know to calculate the number of tickets sold? Income? Profit? (Each of these variables depends on p so only p needs to be known.)**

   All of the relations among variables in this problem are correct equations.

   a. This relation is the equation of the line that fits the (*price, ticket sales*) data.

   b. This relation is based on the notion that income will be the product of ticket sales and ticket price, using the relation between sales and price from part a.

   c. This relation is simply the result of distributing the factor of p.

   d. This function is the result of subtracting costs from income and rearranging terms.

4. These questions are intended to make sure that students are comfortable with the equations in activity 3.

   a. $S = 4000 - 250(7) = 2250$ tickets

   b. $I = 7[4000 - 250(7)] = \$15{,}750$

   c. $P = -250(7^2) + 4000(7) - 7500 = \$8250$

5. **a.** The estimated income increases with increasing ticket price, from $3750 at a ticket price of $1 to a maximum of about $16,000 at a ticket price of $8. As ticket prices continue to rise to $15, the income decreases to only $3750 for a ticket price of $15.

   b. The general patten for profit is the same as the pattern for income. The concert would lose money for any ticket price below about $2.17 or above about $13.83; maximum profit of about $8,500 would occur for ticket price of about $8.

   c. Break-even points are ticket prices of $2.17 and $13.83.

   d. Maximum profit of $8,500 will occur at the $8 ticket price.

   e. This is a classic interaction of price, sales, and income from sales. When the price is too low, there will be low income even though many tickets are sold. As the price rises, the income rises even though lower numbers of tickets are sold, but when the price rises too far, the loss in numbers sold offsets the income from those high prices and the total income decreases. The estimated profit changes in the same pattern, with a downward translation of the graph due to the subtraction of $7500 for operating costs. While we don't expect students to be familiar with all of this, it seems sensible to have them make conjectures about what is going on.

Unit 4

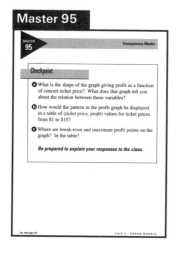

Checkpoint

See Teaching Master 95.

ⓐ The graph is U-shaped and opens downward. The shape tells that profit is negative for low and very high prices, rising to a maximum of $8,500 for a ticket price of $8. If the price is either too high to too low, the concert promoter will lose money.

ⓑ In a table, as ticket prices increase, estimated profits will increase (rapidly at first and then more slowly approaching the maximum) to the maximum of $8,500, and then decrease (slowly at first and then more rapidly) as price rises, until at $13.83 the concert profit estimate slips into negative numbers.

ⓒ The break-even points are the locations where the graph crosses the x-axis and the table values which have y values of 0. The maximum profit point appears on the graph as the highest point and shows up on the table as the largest y value.

APPLY individual task

▶On Your Own

a. ■ $S = 2400 - 300p$ or alternative equivalent form
Students may find this equation using linear regression or by drawing a scatterplot and finding the equation of the line that contains these five points.
■ $I = 2400p - 300p^2$ or alternative equivalent form
■ $P = 2400p - 300p^2 - 3000$ or alternative equivalent form

b. Both estimated income and profit increase as ticket price increases until maximum points are reached, after which both income and profit decrease. This seems reasonable because if ticket prices are too high, sales will drop.

c. ■ Income and profit expected from ticket price of $2 will be $3600 and $600 respectively.
■ Break-even prices are about $1.55 and $6.45.
■ The ticket income hits a maximum of $4800 for a ticket price of $4. Profit hits a maximum of $1800 at this same price.

ASSIGNMENT *pp. 282–288*

Students now can begin Modeling tasks 2, 4, or 5 or Reflecting tasks 2 or 5 from the MORE assignment following Investigation 5.

a What is the shape of the graph giving profit as a function of concert ticket price? What does that graph tell you about the relation between those variables?

b How would the pattern in the profit graph be displayed in a table of (*ticket price*, *profit*) values for ticket prices from $1 to $15?

c Where are break-even and maximum profit points on the graph? In the table?

Be prepared to explain your responses to the class.

▶ **On Your Own**

Suppose that surveys of interest for a different concert produced these data about the relation between ticket price and ticket sales.

Concert Survey

Ticket Price ($)	3	4	5	6	7
Estimated Ticket Sales	1500	1200	900	600	300

The promoter expects costs for this concert to total about $3000. Assume there are no other sources of income.

a. Write algebraic equations that give the following.

- Ticket sales S as a function of ticket price p
- Income I from ticket sales as a function of ticket price p
- Profit P as a function of ticket price p

b. Use your graphing calculator or computer software to explore the pattern of change in estimated ticket income and profit as different ticket prices from $1 to $10 are considered. Describe the patterns you find and explain why those patterns are or are not reasonable.

c. Use the relations from part a to find the following.

- Income and profit expected from a ticket price of $2
- Ticket price or prices that will allow the concert to break even
- Ticket price or prices that will lead to maximum income and to maximum profit. (These maxima may occur at different prices.)

Unit 4

INVESTIGATION 3 The Shape of Quadratic Models

To use quadratic models in solving problems, it helps to know how patterns in such rules are related to patterns in tables and graphs of data from those rules. The starting point for any quadratic model is the basic power model $y = x^2$.

x	$y = x^2$
−5	25
−4	16
−3	9
−2	4
−1	1
0	0
1	1
2	4
3	9
4	16
5	25

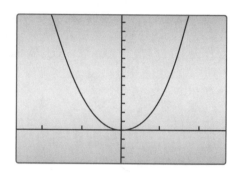

You can build more complex models from the basic rule $y = x^2$ by multiplying, to get $y = ax^2$, and by adding a linear term and a constant, to get $y = ax^2 + (bx + c)$. The experiments of this investigation will help you discover connections between the patterns of change in quadratic models and the symbolic rules for those models.

Experiment 1

1. Use your calculator or computer software to produce tables and graphs for a collection of different quadratic models. Try several combinations of positive and negative values for a, b, and c in the general form $y = ax^2 + bx + c$. Divide the workload among members of your group. As you produce the tables and graphs for those experimental quadratic relations, try to find answers to these questions:

   a. What patterns occur in all the tables and graphs?

   b. What connections are there between the values of a, b, and c and patterns in the tables and graphs?

   c. How are the various tables and graphs similar to, and different from, those for the basic power model $y = x^2$?

INVESTIGATION 3 The Shape of Quadratic Models

The key point of this investigation is to generalize the patterns of quadratic tables and graphs that students quite likely will have observed in earlier investigations. This generalization is encouraged by a series of technology-based explorations, in which many examples are studied to find patterns relating the coefficients in the quadratic equations to the resulting tables and graphs.

The explorations will lead to two basic points, which are (1) a negative leading coefficient makes the graph concave down and a positive leading coefficient makes the graph concave up, and (2) the constant term indicates the y-intercept in any case. Another, more general point that students should see is that the interpretation of the coefficient of the linear term can be interpreted only as it interacts with the sign of the lead coefficient. In general, when the coefficient of x is nonzero the graph will be shifted left or right from its standard position, symmetric about the y-axis. At this point it isn't necessary to stress anything more than that general observation.

One of the risks of doing an open-end exploration of connections between equations and their graphs is that students will note patterns in a few special cases that don't hold in general. Even for the correct generalizations there may be only the observation of a pattern without any underlying explanations of why these patterns occur. For those reasons, it is especially important to follow experiments with careful class discussions in which observations are shared and explanations sought.

Of the basic patterns in quadratics, the easiest to explain is the y-intercept property. In $y = ax^2 + bx + c$ the graph always will include the point with coordinates $(0, c)$, and this can be confirmed by noting that when $x = 0$ the first two terms become 0, leaving $y = c$.

The rationale for effects of positive and negative values of a is not so simple, but very important. One way to think about this is to notice that $y = ax^2$ is always nonnegative for positive values of a and always nonpositive for negative values of a, since x^2 is always nonnegative. Thus, as x gets large (positive or negative), the value of ax^2 also will get large, but the sign of ax^2 depends solely on the sign of a.

The bx term moves the graph left or right and up or down depending on the sign of b in conjunction with the sign of a. Students do not need to make a more specific generalization in this unit.

See additional Teaching Notes on page T317T.

Unit 4

2. In a discussion of whatever results the students have, be sure to press them to explain how they arrived at their ideas and whether they tested many different examples.

Experiment 2

This experiment focuses on the effect of the value of *a*, and it may be a repeat of work in Experiment 1 depending on your students' explorations. You might prefer to discuss these questions orally with the whole class if you have observed that all groups already discovered the pattern in Experiment 1.

1. All tables and graphs have the same symmetric patterns associated with U-shaped graphs centered around the *y*-axis.

2. If *a* is negative, the graph is concave down; if *a* is positive, the graph is concave up. As $|a|$ increases, the table and graph rise (or fall) more and more rapidly for $|x|$ increasing away from 0.

3. **a.** If $a > 0$, the factor *a* produces a size transformation called a *shear transformation* (briefly mentioned in unit 2). The pre-image (x, y) is mapped to the image (x, ay). Visually this is a stretch (if $a > 1$) or compression (if $0 < a < 1$) of *y* values. Students may describe it in terms of a stretch or compression or in terms of the rate of change.

   b. If $a < 0$, the graph stretches or compresses (as described in part a) and also reflects over the *x*-axis.

Experiment 3

The questions of this exploration look at the simplest variation on the basic quadratic power model: translation up or down. The graphs can be misleading in this case, because students tend to focus on the distance from one curve to the other, which appears to change for different *x* values, rather than the vertical difference associated with different *y* values for the same *x* value. When discussing pooled results of explorations, you may need to elicit from students the fact that the graph of $y = ax^2 + c$ is simply a vertical translation of $y = ax^2$, not some sort of slide and expansion.

1. **a.** The table values for $y = x^2 + 8$ are all 8 units larger than the values for $y = x^2$.

x	−10	−9	−8	−7	−6	−5	−4	−3	−2	−1	0	1	2	3	4	5	6
x^2	100	81	64	49	36	25	16	9	4	1	0	1	4	9	16	25	36
$x^2 + 8$	108	89	72	57	44	33	24	17	12	9	8	9	12	17	24	33	44

   b. ■ The top graph is $y = x^2 + 8$.
   ■ For each value of *x* the value of $y = x^2 + 8$ is greater than $y = x^2$ by 8. The graph of $y = x^2 + 8$ is the graph of $y = x^2$ translated up 8 units.

2. Share your experimental results with others in your group. As a group, see if you can explain why things work as they do.

After Experiment 1, you might have some ideas about how the symbolic rule for a quadratic model can be used to predict the shape of its graph and the patterns in tables of values. To find explanations for those observed patterns, it helps to study examples in a systematic order. Experiments 2–4 outline one possible approach.

Experiment 2

Consider the simple quadratic models with rules $y = ax^2$ (values of b and c are both 0). Study the tables and graphs produced by such rules for several positive and negative values of a.

1. What do all the tables and all the graphs have in common?

2. How do different values of a lead to different tables and graphs?

3. Use the ideas of geometric transformations to describe
   a. how the graph of $y = ax^2$, where $a > 0$, is related to the graph of $y = x^2$.
   b. how the graph of $y = ax^2$, where $a < 0$, is related to the graph of $y = x^2$.

Experiment 3

Patterns in tables and graphs of quadratic models like $y = x^2 + c$ and $y = -x^2 + c$ are probably the next easiest cases to figure out.

1. With the help of your graphing calculator or computer software, begin by investigating patterns produced by $y = x^2$ and $y = x^2 + 8$.

   a. Make and compare tables of values for these two models. Build your tables in steps of size 1 starting at $x = -10$. How are the tables related?

   b. Shown to the right are graphs of the relations $y = x^2$ and $y = x^2 + 8$. The graphing window is $-8 \leq x \leq 8$ and $-4 \leq y \leq 40$.

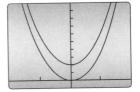

   - Which is the graph of $y = x^2$ and which is the graph of $y = x^2 + 8$?

   - How do the patterns in the graphs match the patterns in the tables of values you produced?

2. Make similar kinds of tables and graphs for each of the following quadratic models. Display all graphs on the same screen or axes. Then look for patterns in the results that allow you to predict and explain the shape of tables and graphs for any model $y = x^2 + c$, or $y = -x^2 + c$ where c is any positive or negative number.

   a. $y = x^2 + 3$

   b. $y = x^2 - 4$

   c. $y = -x^2 + 5$

   d. $y = -x^2 - 4$

3. How are graphs of models with rules $y = x^2 + c$ similar to and different from those of the basic quadratic $y = x^2$? How are the graphs of $y = -x^2 + c$ similar and different?

4. Describe geometrically how the graph of $y = x^2 + c$ is related to the graph of $y = x^2$. Do the same for the graph of $y = -x^2 + c$.

5. How do you think variations like $y = ax^2 + c$ and $y = -ax^2 + c$ behave? Check your conjectures.

Experiment 4

In quadratic models $y = ax^2 + bx + c$, if the value of b is not 0, the patterns of tables and graphs are different from the basic $y = x^2$ model in several ways.

1. Use your graphing calculator or computer software to explore the patterns produced by these models:

   a. $y = x^2 + 6x + 3$

   b. $y = x^2 - 5x + 3$

   c. $y = x^2 - 2x - 4$

   d. $y = -x^2 - x + 3$

   e. $y = -x^2 - 2x - 4$

2. **a.** How are the graphs of all five equations alike and how are they different?

   b. How are the graphs similar to and different from those with rules like $y = x^2$ and $y = x^2 + c$?

3. Test your ideas about the forms of symbolic rules and the shapes of their graphs by experimenting with other quadratic models that show the variety of patterns that can occur in graphs.

2. a–d.

x	−8	−7	−6	−5	−4	−3	−2	−1	0	1	2	3	4	5	6	7	8
x^2	64	49	36	25	16	9	4	1	0	1	4	9	16	25	36	49	64
$x^2 + 3$	67	52	39	28	19	12	7	4	3	4	7	12	19	28	39	52	67
$x^2 − 4$	60	45	32	21	12	5	0	−3	−4	−3	0	5	12	21	32	45	60
$−x^2$	−64	−49	−36	−25	−16	−9	−4	−1	0	−1	−4	−9	−16	−25	−36	−49	−64
$−x^2 + 5$	−59	−44	−31	−20	−11	−4	1	4	5	4	1	−4	−11	−20	−31	−44	−59
$−x^2 − 4$	−68	−53	−40	−29	−20	−13	−8	−5	−4	−5	−8	−13	−20	−29	−40	−53	−68

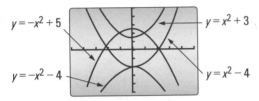
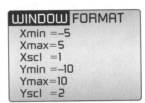

The keys to predicting shapes of $y = \pm x^2 + c$ are that the sign of the coefficient of x^2 tells whether the curve opens upward or downward and the value of c gives the y-intercept. The graph of $y = x^2 + c$ is the graph of $y = x^2$ translated c units. The graph of $y = -x^2 + c$ is the graph of $y = x^2$ reflected across the x-axis and then translated c units.

3. The graph of the model $y = x^2 + c$ has the same shape as the graph of $y = x^2$, but it has different y values (it is a translation c units of the graph of $y = x^2$). The graph of the model $y = -x^2 + c$ also has the same shape, but it opens downward (reflected over the x-axis) and is translated c units.

4. Although the graphs might be a bit misleading (as discussed in the introduction to this experiment), they are actually congruent and translations or reflections over the x-axis of each other.

5. For any specific value of a, the equations corresponding to the examples in activities 1–3 will have the same relations as the examples. The value of a will stretch or compress the graph as was found in Experiment 2.

Experiment 4

1–2. All five graphs have the same U-shape, opening upward or downward based on the sign of the leading coefficient. They are shifted left or right of the y-axis and up or down depending on the coefficient b.

Students should know that the linear term shifts left or right and up or down, but they should not be more specific about the behavior. Again, the value of c moves the graph up or down and is the y-intercept. A complete discussion of the axis of symmetry will take place in Course 3 when students learn to use the quadratic formula. It is not intended that students identify the axis of symmetry at this point in the curriculum.

3. Responses will vary. This question might be used best as a follow-up to a whole-class discussion in which students share their findings from activities 1 and 2.

Unit 4

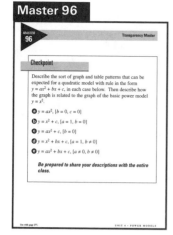

Checkpoint

Describe the sort of graph and table patterns that can be expected for a quadratic model with rule in the form $y = ax^2 + bx + c$, in each case below. Then describe how the graph is related to the graph of the basic power model $y = x^2$.

ⓐ $y = ax^2$, $[b = 0, c = 0]$

ⓑ $y = x^2 + c$, $[a = 1, b = 0]$

ⓒ $y = ax^2 + c$, $[b = 0]$

ⓓ $y = x^2 + bx + c$, $[a = 1, b \neq 0]$

ⓔ $y = ax^2 + bx + c$, $[a \neq 0, b \neq 0]$

Be prepared to share your descriptions with the entire class.

SHARE AND SUMMARIZE full-class discussion

Checkpoint

See Teaching Master 96.

All graphs will be U-shaped and open upward when $a > 0$ and downward when $a < 0$. All tables will show a varying rate of change with the y values obtaining a maximum ($a < 0$) or a minimum ($a > 0$). All tables will have a symmetry and all graphs will be line symmetric.

ⓐ Contains the origin; symmetric about the y-axis; a stretch of $y = x^2$ if $a > 0$ and a compression if $a < 0$.

ⓑ The y-intercept is c; symmetric about the y-axis; a translation of c units and a compression ($a < 0$) or a stretch ($a > 0$) of the graph of $y = x^2$.

ⓒ The y-intercept is c; not symmetric about the y-axis; a translation of the graph of $y = x^2$. (Students are not likely to be able to identify the components of the translation.)

ⓓ The y-intercept is c; not symmetric about the y-axis; a translation and a compression or stretch of the graph of $y = x^2$.

ⓔ The y-intercept is c; not symmetric about the y-axis; a translation and compression or stretch of the graph of $y = x^2$ or $y = -x^2$.

> CONSTRUCTING A MATH TOOLKIT: Following the whole-class discussion, students should summarize their descriptions of patterns in tables and graphs for quadratic models. They can include their descriptions in the algebra and functions section of their Math Toolkits.

APPLY individual task

▶On Your Own

a. **i.** B **ii.** C
    iii. E **iv.** D
    v. A **vi.** F

b. A. $(-2.5, 10.25)$
    B. $(0, -4)$
    C. $(0, 4)$
    D. $(-2.5, -2.25)$
    E. $(0, -4)$
    F. A reasonable estimate from the graph is $(-1, 2)$. If students estimate from the graph, you might ask them how they could find a more accurate estimate. If students use the calculator to draw the graph, they can trace the graph to find the coordinates of the vertex. In this case they should get approximately $(-0.8, 1.9)$.

ASSIGNMENT *pp. 282–288*

Students now can begin Reflecting tasks 3, 4, or 5 from the MORE assignment following Investigation 5.

Unit 4

Checkpoint

Describe the sort of graph and table patterns that can be expected for a quadratic model with rule in the form $y = ax^2 + bx + c$, in each case below. Then describe how the graph is related to the graph of the basic power model $y = x^2$.

a $y = ax^2$, $[b = 0, c = 0]$

b $y = x^2 + c$, $[a = 1, b = 0]$

c $y = ax^2 + c$, $[b = 0]$

d $y = x^2 + bx + c$, $[a = 1, b \neq 0]$

e $y = ax^2 + bx + c$, $[a \neq 0, b \neq 0]$

Be prepared to share your descriptions with the entire class.

The graph of any quadratic model is called a **parabola**. The highest or lowest point of a parabola is called its **vertex**.

▶ On Your Own

Shown below are the graphs of four quadratic models. The graphing windows are the same in each case.

a. Use what you have learned about the connection between quadratic rules and their graphs to match these rules and the graphs. Then check using your calculator or computer software.

i. $y = x^2 - 4$ **ii.** $y = -x^2 + 4$ **iii.** $y = 3x^2 - 4$

iv. $y = x^2 + 5x + 4$ **v.** $y = -x^2 - 5x + 4$ **vi.** $y = 3x^2 + 5x + 4$

b. Estimate the coordinates of the vertex of each parabola.

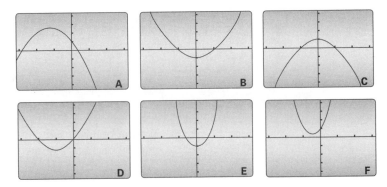

INVESTIGATION 4 Solving Quadratic Equations

Many important questions about quadratic models require solving equations. For example, think again about the concert promoter who estimated profit P as a function of ticket price p with rule $P = -250p^2 + 4000p - 7500$. To find the break-even point, you have to find the value of p that gives a profit P of 0. That is, you have to solve the equation

$$0 = -250p^2 + 4000p - 7500.$$

The values of p that satisfy this equation are called the **roots** of the equation. There are several good ways to solve the break-even equation.

1. The following table shows a sample of values for ticket price and predicted profit for the rule $P = -250p^2 + 4000p - 7500$.

Concert Profits

Ticket Price p ($)	2	4	6	8	10	12	14
Profit P ($)	−500	4500	7500	8500	7500	4500	−500

   a. Use the table to estimate the root or roots of the equation.

   b. Use calculator- or computer-produced tables to find more accurate values of the root or roots.

   c. At what ticket prices will the concert promoter break even?

2. The following graph also shows the pattern of (*ticket price*, *profit*) values.

Concert Profits

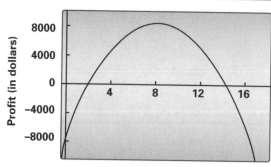

Ticket Price (in dollars)

   a. Use the graph to estimate the roots of the equation.

   b. Use your calculator or computer software to find the roots graphically, as accurately as possible. Compare your answer to part b of activity 1.

INVESTIGATION 4 Solving Quadratic Equations

The use of graphing calculators and computer software in the mathematics classroom allows students to explore alternative methods for solving traditional problems. This is certainly true with the solution of quadratic equations and inequalities. By inspection of tables or graphs of quadratic functions, one can get very good approximations to the real solutions of a quadratic equation, even when that equation is not solvable by the familiar integer factoring routines. Factoring to find roots is replaced in this way by a more powerful, universal method. (At this point, our discussion of roots is limited to real roots.) However, students can not use the table or graph without using important mathematical knowledge and skills. To make the graph, they have to be able to create a reasonable window, which means choosing the range and domain sensibly. To use the table they need to have some idea of the shape of the curve involved, so they can predict how many solutions there might be and can tell from the pattern in the piece of the table initially viewed where to look for other solutions.

Most students will find it fairly easy to generalize earlier solution-by-tables-and-graphs methods to the case of quadratics, but the activities here review that idea and give some guidance. If you see students working with tables, it may be helpful to ask them what shape the graphs would be. Using hand gestures to sketch the graphs in midair keeps students focused on the particular characteristics of the equation under consideration, and that may help them avoid the common error of reporting only one solution when there are two.

1. **a.** Any estimates between 2 and 4 and between 12 and 14 would be reasonable.
   b. More accurate estimates would place the roots at about 2.17 and 13.83.
   c. When tickets cost either $2.17 or $13.83, the concert promoter will break even.
2. **a.** Determine the value of x when $y = 0$ simply by reading the values of x where the graph crosses the x-axis. From the graph the roots appear to be approximately 2 and 14.
   b. Use the calculator or computer software to determine an estimate for the roots by tracing the curve to find x when $y = 0$. Graphing calculators often have an option to allow the calculator to determine the roots, using the graph. On the TI-82 and 83, for example, use the root or zero option from CALC (2nd TRACE); on the Casio CFX-9850G, use G-Solv (SHIFT F5); on the Sharp EL-9300C, use the x-intercept option for JUMP (2nd F EQTN).

EXPLORE *continued*

3. Responses may vary. To test whether or not 3 is a root of the equation, students can substitute 3 into the equation in place of t and see if they get zero. Alternatively, they could go to an x value of 3 in the table of values for $y = -5 + 20x - 6$ and look to see if the y value is 0. They also could trace the graph to determine the y value that corresponds to an x value of 3. Using any of the above methods students should determine that 3 is not a root of the equation. When $t = 3$, the value of the expression is 9.

4. **a.** The area of the billboard is $2h^2$ square feet.

    b. $C = 20h^2 + 300$

    c. $h = \pm 20$ ft

    This means that a billboard with height 20 ft and width 40 ft costs \$8300.

    d. ■ $6080 = 20h^2 + 300$
    $5780 = 20h^2$
    $289 = h^2$
    $\pm 17 = h$

    Only the positive solution, 17 feet, makes sense in this situation.

    ■ This item provides a good opportunity for students to explain to each other what reasoning they used.

5. **a.** $x = 16$

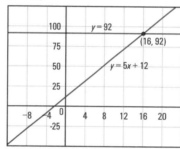

    b. $x = \pm 4$

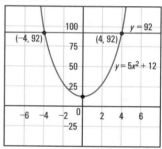

    c. $x = 8$

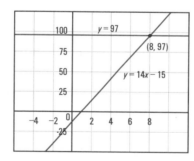

    d. $x = \pm \sqrt{8}$, which is approximately 2.83

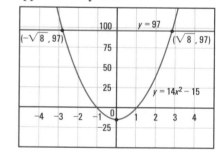

    e. $x = -4$

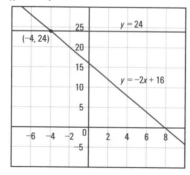

    f. No roots exist.

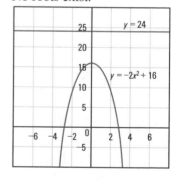

3. If someone claimed that $t = 3$ is a root of the equation $0 = -5t^2 + 20t - 6$, how could you check that claim? Test your method. Is $t = 3$ a root?

Some situations are modeled by simpler quadratic rules than those in activities 1–3. In these situations, it is often helpful to have quick methods for solving corresponding quadratic equations.

4. Billboards often are used to promote events, products, and services. The cost for a billboard advertisement is a function of its size. One company, Great Signs, Inc., uses a standard width-to-height ratio of 2:1 as in the diagram below.

a. What is the area of a Great Signs standard billboard with height h?

b. The cost per square foot is $10 and there is a $300 set-up fee. Write an equation that gives the customer cost C as a function of billboard height h.

c. Solve the equation $8300 = 20h^2 + 300$ and explain what the answer tells about Great Signs billboard costs.

d. Think about how you reasoned without use of tables or graphs to solve linear equations like $76 = 12x + 34$.

- Solve the equation $6080 = 20h^2 + 300$ using similar reasoning and just calculator arithmetic as needed.

- Compare your method to those used by other classmates.

5. Solve each of the following equations by reasoning with the symbols themselves. Then draw sketches illustrating what your solutions mean in terms of graphs of the corresponding models.

a. $92 = 5x + 12$

b. $92 = 5x^2 + 12$

c. $14x - 15 = 97$

d. $14x^2 - 15 = 97$

e. $-2x + 16 = 24$

f. $-2x^2 + 16 = 24$

Unit 4

Checkpoint

Suppose that in modeling some situation, you are required to solve a quadratic equation like:

$$50 = 3.4x^2 + 4.5x + 23.5.$$

ⓐ What is the goal of the process?

ⓑ How can you use a table of values to find the solution or solutions?

ⓒ Describe two ways of using a graph to find the solution or solutions.

ⓓ How can the solution or solutions be checked without using a table or graph?

ⓔ How could you find the solution or solutions by reasoning with the symbolic form if there were no linear term $4.5x$?

Be prepared to explain your solution methods to the class.

▶On Your Own

a. Solve the equation $10 = x^2 + 2x - 5$ using a table of (x, y) values.

- Show the portion or portions of the table that give the solution or solutions.
- Show how the solution or solutions can be checked by substitution in the equation.

b. Solve the equation $-8 = -2x^2 + 6x$ using a graph of (x, y) values.

- Sketch the graph that shows the solution or solutions. On that sketch, show how the solution or solutions can be located.
- Show how the solution or solutions can be checked by substitution in the equation.

c. Solve the equation $56 = 3x^2 + 8$ by reasoning with the symbols themselves. Check your solutions by substitution in the equation.

INVESTIGATION▶5 How Many Solutions Are Possible?

When using a graphing calculator or computer software to solve a quadratic equation, it helps to know what to expect and how to find the solution that you need. Shown at the top of next page is a graph of the quadratic model $y = x^2 - 8x + 12$.

SHARE AND SUMMARIZE full-class discussion

Checkpoint

See Teaching Master 97.

ⓐ The goal is to find a value of x that gives 50 when substituted into the expression on the right side of the equation.

ⓑ Make tables of (x, y) values for $y = 3.4x^2 + 4.5x + 23.5$ then look for $(x, 50)$.

ⓒ Possible responses include the following.

Make a graph of the equation in part b.

Trace the graph and look for the points which have a y-coordinate of 50.

Graph the equation in part b with $y = 50$ and zoom in on the intersection points.

Graph $y = 3.4x^2 + 4.5x + 23.5 - 50$ and find the roots of this equation.

ⓓ Check by substituting a solution into the expression on the right of the equation.

ⓔ First subtract 23.5 from both sides. This gives the equation $26.5 = 3.4x^2$. Next divide both sides by 3.4, resulting in $7.79 \approx x^2$. Finally take the square root of both sides. So $x \approx \pm 2.79$.

APPLY individual task

▶On Your Own

a. The solutions are 3 and -5.

■ Tables used may vary. Here is one possibility for the equation $y = x^2 + 2x - 5$:

x	–6	–5	–4	–3	–2	–1	0	1	2	3	4
y	19	10	3	–2	–5	–6	–5	–2	3	10	19

■ Substitution yields $10 = (-5)^2 + 2(-5) - 5$ and $10 = 3^2 + 2(3) - 5$, both of which are true.

b. The solutions are -1 and 4.

■ Here is one way to look at the problem graphically, with the graphs of $y = -2x^2 + 6x$ and $y = -8$. The solutions are represented by the intersection points of the parabola and the line $y = -8$.

■ Substitution yields $-8 = -2(-1)^2 + 6(-1)$ and $-8 = -2(4)^2 + 6(4)$, both of which are true.

c. $56 = 3x^2 + 8$

$48 = 3x^2$

$16 = x^2$

$\pm 4 = x$

Substituting yields $3(4)^2 + 8 = 56$ and $3(-4)^2 + 8 = 56$, both of which are true.

MORE
ASSIGNMENT *pp. 282–288*

Students now can begin Reflecting task 1 from the MORE assignment following Investigation 5.

JOURNAL ENTRY: Write a letter to your teacher explaining the different methods for solving quadratic equations that you have studied. In your letter be sure to tell your teacher which method you like best and explain why.

See additional Teaching Notes on page T317U.

Unit 4

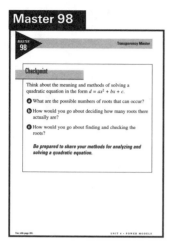

EXPLORE *continued*

1. To help them visualize the two solutions, students may use a ruler or piece of spaghetti to represent the various y values, $y = 12$, $y = 5$, *etc*. If students have entered the function $y = x^2 - 8x + 12$ into their calculator or computer, they also can enter the horizontal lines $y = 12$, $y = 5$, *etc*.

    a. Solutions are $x = 0$ and $x = 8$.

    b. Solutions are $x = 1$ and $x = 7$.

    c. Solutions are $x = 2$ and $x = 6$.

    d. The only solution is $x = 4$.

    e. No (real) solutions exist.

2. Responses may vary. In sharing results and noting patterns, students might comment on the symmetry of solutions that corresponds to the symmetry of the graph. This symmetry gives a strong signal that in many cases there will be two solutions, in a single case there will be one solution, and in the other cases (below the minimum point of the graph) there will be no (real) solutions.

3. Most students will follow the lead given in activities 1 and 2, and choose a y value that the existing graph achieves twice, once, or not at all. A few students may interpret this as a challenge to produce a new relation (*not* using the equation given) that would have two or one or no solutions.

    a. Possible responses are in the form $-x^2 + x + 6 = d$ for any value of $d < 6.25$.

    b. $-x^2 + x + 6 = 6.25$

    c. Possible answers are in the form $-x^2 + x + 6 = d$ for any value of $d > 6.25$.

4. a. The roots of the equation correspond to the x-intercepts of the graph of the equation.

    b. Responses will vary. Most students will build from the quadratic model offered in activities 1 through 3. They could achieve this by translating the existing curve down. Translating $y = -x^2 + x + 6$ down 1 to 6 units would leave a curve that has two x-intercepts; for example, $y = -x^2 + x + 6 - 5$ has two roots. (There are two values of x for which $-x^2 + x + 1 = 0$.) Obviously any translation upwards of the same equation will create a graph with two x-intercepts. A translation down of more than 7 units would definitely place the curve below the axis and produce no x-intercepts; for example, $y = -x^2 + x + 6 - 8$ has no roots.

SHARE AND SUMMARIZE   full-class discussion

Checkpoint

See Teaching Master 98.

Be sure to emphasize when the quadratic equation will have no solutions; this concept seems particularly difficult for many students. Encourage the students to graph the equations to help them visualize the solutions.

ⓐ 0, 1, or 2

ⓑ Find the maximum or minimum y-value; call it k. Then $ax^2 + bx + c = k$ has 1 solution. Values larger or smaller than k will produce equations with 2 or no solutions. Using the graph of the equation $y = ax^2 + bx + c$, students can imagine the line $y = d$ on the graph and count the number of times it intersects the graph of $y = ax^2 + bx + c$.

ⓒ One possible strategy is to graph the two equations $y = d$ and $y = ax^2 + bx + c$ and find any points of intersection. Check by substitution.

CONSTRUCTING A MATH TOOLKIT: Students should record the meaning and methods of solving and checking quadratic equations, with examples, in their Math Toolkits.

1. Use the graph to solve each of the
   following equations.

   a. $12 = x^2 - 8x + 12$

   b. $x^2 - 8x + 12 = 5$

   c. $0 = x^2 - 8x + 12$

   d. $-4 = x^2 - 8x + 12$

   e. $x^2 - 8x + 12 = -6$

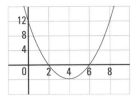

2. What patterns in the graph give clues about both the number of solutions for
   each given equation and how those solutions will be related to each other?

3. Shown at the right is a graph of
   $y = -x^2 + x + 6$. Using the graph
   as a guide, write quadratic equations that have

   a. two solutions.

   b. one solution.

   c. no solutions.

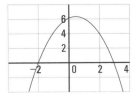

4. Recall that the *roots of a quadratic model* $y = ax^2 + bx + c$ are the values of
   x that satisfy the equation $0 = ax^2 + bx + c$.

   a. How are the roots of a quadratic model related to the graph of that model?

   b. Write a rule for a quadratic model that has

   - two roots.

   - one root.

   - no roots.

Checkpoint

Think about the meaning and methods of solving a quadratic equation in the
form $d = ax^2 + bx + c$.

ⓐ What are the possible numbers of solutions that can occur?

ⓑ How would you go about deciding how many solutions there actually are?

ⓒ How would you go about finding and checking the solutions?

***Be prepared to share your methods for analyzing and
solving a quadratic equation.***

Unit 4

▶ **On Your Own**

Produce a table of values and a graph for the quadratic model $y = x^2 - 4x - 12$. Solve each of the following equations. Explain how the graph gives evidence that you have the correct number of solutions.

a. $0 = x^2 - 4x - 12$

b. $x^2 - 4x - 12 = -16$

c. $-20 = x^2 - 4x - 12$

d. $x^2 - 4x - 12 = 9$

MORE
Modeling • Organizing • Reflecting • Extending

Modeling

1. If a car is traveling 60 miles per hour when the driver must stop as quickly as possible, how far will the car travel before stopping? One formula used by highway safety engineers relates speed s in miles per hour to minimum stopping distance d in feet with the rule $d = 0.05s^2 + 1.1s$.

▶On Your Own

The table will look like this (for integral values of x):

x	-8	-7	-6	-5	-4	-3	-2	-1	0	1	2	3	4	5	6	7	8
y	84	65	48	33	20	9	0	-7	-12	-15	-16	-15	-12	-7	0	9	20

The graph will look like this, with level lines $y = -20$, $y = -16$, $y = 0$, and $y = 9$ also drawn:

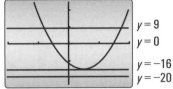

a. The roots are $x = -2$ and $x = 6$. They are shown in the table by the ordered pairs $(-2, 0)$ and $(6, 0)$ and on the graph of $y = x^2 - 4x - 12$ by the points at which it crosses the x-axis.

b. The only solution is $x = 2$. $(2, -16)$ is an ordered pair in the table and the graph is tangent to $y = -16$ when $x = 2$. The symmetry in the table helps us see this is the only solution.

c. There are no solutions since the level line $y = -20$ does not intersect the graph and the value $y = -20$ does not appear in the table. (The pattern suggests that it will not, even if the table is extended).

d. The solutions are $x = -3$ and $x = 7$. They are shown in the table as the ordered pairs $(-3, 9)$ and $(7, 9)$ and on the graph by the intersection points of $y = 9$ and $y = x^2 - 4x - 12$.

Modeling: 1 and choice of one*
Organizing: 1 and 2
Reflecting: Choose two*
Extending: 2 or 3*

*When choice is indicated, it is important to leave the choice to the student.
NOTE: It is best if Organizing tasks are discussed as a whole class after they have been assigned as homework.

Modeling

1. a. The graph indicates that as the speed increases, the stopping distances increase at an increasing rate.

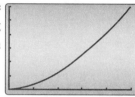

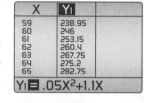

b. ■ By reading the table of values, you can see that the distance is 246 feet.

One way to check the answer is to substitute the values into the equation to determine whether they satisfy the equation: $246 = 0.05(60)^2 + (1.1)60$. This is correct, therefore, the answer is right.

■ Again, the table indicates that the speed was about 39.2 miles per hour.

The answer can be checked by substituting the value into the equation to determine whether it gives a true statement. Since $(0.05)(39.2)^2 + (1.1)(39.2) = 119.95$ this (approximate) value is correct.

c. ■ $180 = 0.05s^2 + 1.1s$
As you can see from the table and the graph, when d is 180, s is 50. This tells us that at a speed of 50 mph, a car will travel 180 feet before stopping.

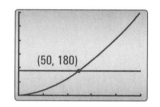

■ $95 = 0.05s^2 + 1.1s$
From both the table and the graph, you can see that when the distance is very close to 95, the speed is close to 34. This means 95 feet are needed to stop when traveling 34 mph.

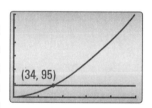

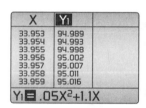

d. This term accounts for distance traveled after the driver sees danger and before the brake is engaged; that is, it accounts for the *reaction time* of the driver.

See additional Teaching Notes on page T317V.

a. Sketch the graph you expect from this rule. Then explain what the shape of the graph tells about the relation between speed and stopping distance—that is, how stopping distance changes as speed increases.

b. Use the stopping distance rule to answer these questions. In each case, explain how you found and checked the answer.

- What is the approximate stopping distance for a car traveling 60 miles per hour?

- If a car stopped in 120 feet, what is the fastest it could have been traveling when the driver first noticed the need to stop?

c. Solve each of the following quadratic equations and explain what each solution tells about speed and stopping distance.

- $180 = 0.05s^2 + 1.1s$

- $95 = 0.05s^2 + 1.1s$

Show how the solutions of these equations can be found on a graph and in a table, and how they can be checked by substitution.

d. In Modeling task 2 on page 242 you may have modeled the *braking* distance b in feet for a car by $b = 0.05s^2$ where s is the speed in miles per hour. Why do you think the linear term $1.1s$ is added when predicting *stopping* distance?

2. The planning committee for a school play at Kennedy High School asked the business class to give them some estimates about income that could be expected at different ticket price levels. The class did some market research to see what students would be willing to pay for tickets. They reported back the following model:

$$I = -75p^2 + 600p,$$

where I stands for income and p for ticket price, both in dollars.

a. Find the predicted income if ticket prices are set at $3.

b. Write equations that can be used to help answer each of the following questions. Then solve those equations, check your solutions, and explain how you found the solutions.

- What ticket price will give income of $1125 dollars?

- What ticket price will give income of $900 dollars?

- What ticket price will give income of $970 dollars?

c. Find the price that will give maximum income, then find the maximum income. Explain your method of finding these values.

3. After studying the model relating height to time in flight for a punt, a group of students proposed the following for the height of a field-goal kick with initial upward velocity of 20 meters per second: $h = 20t - 4.9t^2$.

Unit 4

a. Compare this model to the model $h = 0.8 + 20t - 4.9t^2$ for the height of a punt with the same initial upward velocity.

- How are the two kicking situations different?

- How are the two rules different?

b. According to each model:

- What is the height of the ball when it is kicked?

- What is the maximum height the ball reaches and when does that occur?

- When does the ball hit the ground?

c. What pattern of change in height, as a function of time in flight, is predicted by each model?

d. How could the similarities and differences of results in part b be predicted by comparing the rules for the two models?

e. How are the two models similar to, and different from, basic linear or power models?

4. The drama club from Montclair High School decided to sponsor a fund-raising trip into New York City to see a Broadway play. They arranged for a 60-passenger charter bus costing $420. To help ensure some profit from the trip, they said that the price for transportation would be $10 per person if all seats on the bus were sold, but each empty seat would increase the price by $1 per person. They hoped that people who wanted to go would recruit others in order to keep the price low.

a. Complete a table showing sample data for number of passengers, number of empty seats, price per passenger, and income.

b. Write an algebraic rule giving income I as a function of the number of passengers n. Test your rule by comparing sample data produced by the rule with that in your table from part a. Modify your rule if necessary.

c. What is the minimum number of passengers needed in order for the club not to lose money?

d. What is the maximum income the club can make with this fund raiser? What is the maximum profit, assuming all other expenses are paid by the passengers?

e. Write an algebraic rule giving profit P as a function of the number of passengers n. Explain how you can answer the question in part c using this rule.

3. a. ■ The field goal is kicked from the ground and the punt is dropped to the foot, which is extended above the ground.

■ The rules are only different in their constant terms, which correspond to the initial heights of the ball.

b.

Model	$h = 20t - 4.9t^2$	$h = 0.8 + 20t - 4.9t^2$
Height of ball when kicked	0 meters	0.8 meters
Maximum height reached	20.41 meters	21.21 meters
Time of maximum height	2.04 seconds	2.04 seconds
Time ball reaches ground	4.08 seconds	4.12 seconds

c. Each model predicts that height increases at a decreasing rate as time passes until the football reaches a maximum height. Then the height of the ball decreases at an increasing rate.

d. The height of the ball when kicked is reflected in the constant term of each rule (which is the only difference between these rules). This difference also affects the maximum height reached and the time it takes the ball to reach the ground.

e. The two models are similar to basic linear or power models in that they contain a linear and a squared term. They differ from basic models in general in that they combine two models and also, the second rule includes a constant term.

4. a.

Number of Passengers	Number of Empty Seats	Cost per Passenger	Total Income
60	0	10	600
50	10	20	1000
40	20	30	1200
30	30	40	1200
20	40	50	1000
10	50	60	600

b. $I = n[10 + (60 - n)]$
$I = n(70 - n)$

c. In order not to lose money, the club needs at least 7 people to go on the trip. ($I \geq 420$ when $n \geq 7$.)

d. The maximum income of $1225 is obtained when 35 people go on the trip. In this instance the club's profit is $1225 - $420 or $805.

e. $P = n(70 - n) - 420$

To answer the question in part c, let $P = 0$ and find the corresponding value of n. This can be done using either the table or the graph.

5. In each case the model is linear. Since linear models are either always increasing or always decreasing, only one solution is possible.

    a. $160 = 50 + 5.50N$

          $110 = 5.50N$

            $20 = N$

       20 shirts

       Check:

          $160 = 50 + 5.50(20)$

          $160 = 160$

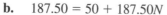

    b. $187.50 = 50 + 187.50N$

          $137.50 = 5.50N$

             $25 = N$

       25 shirts

       Check:

          $187.50 = 50 + 5.50(25)$

          $187.50 = 187.50$

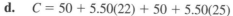

    c. $C = 50 + 5.50(33)$

          $C = 50 + 181.50$

          $C = 231.50$

       $231.50

       Check:

          $231.50 = 50 + 5.50(33)$

          $231.50 = 231.50$

    d. $C = 50 + 5.50(22) + 50 + 5.50(25)$

          $C = 100 + 121 + 137.5$

          $C = 358.5$

       $358.50

       Check:

          $358.50 = 50 + 5.50(22) + 50 + 5.50(25)$

          $358.50 = 358.50$

Organizing

1. **a.** $x = 2$ or $x = 3$

       Check:

          $0 = 2^2 - 5(2) + 6$

          $0 = 0$, therefore 2 is a root.

          $0 = 3^2 - 5(3) + 6$

          $0 = 0$, therefore 3 is a root.

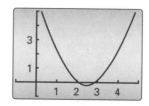

       There are two because $y = x^2 - 5x + 6$ intersects the x-axis twice.

See additional Teaching Notes on page T317W.

5. Production costs at the T-Shirt Factory are given by the rule $C = 50 + 5.50N$, where N is the number of shirts in an order and the design setup cost is 50 dollars. Write and solve equations or make calculations to answer the following questions about T-Shirt Factory costs. In each case, explain how you found the solution, how you know that you have all of them, and how you checked to see that each solution actually works in the given equation.

a. How many shirts can be made if production costs are to be kept at $160?

b. If costs of an order equal $187.50, how many shirts were made?

c. What is the total cost if an order calls for 33 shirts?

d. What is the total cost for an order that has two different designs, with 22 shirts of the first design and 25 shirts of the second design?

Organizing

1. Solve the following equations. In each case, explain how you found the solutions, how you know that you have all of them, and how you checked to see that each solution actually works in the given equation.

a. $0 = x^2 - 5x + 6$

b. $5 = x^2 - 5x + 6$

c. $x^2 - 5x + 6 = -8$

d. $4x^2 + 13 = 45$

e. $0 = 2x^2 - 7x - 4$

f. $2x^2 - 7x - 4 = -25$

2. Use the quadratic model $y = x^2 - 3x + 2$ to write an equation that has the stated number of solutions. In each case, show on a graph of the model how the condition is satisfied.

a. Two solutions

b. One solution

c. No solutions

Unit 4

3. In solving the quadratic equation $1 = x^2 - 3x + 2$, one student produced the following table and concluded that the equation has no solutions. Is the student's conclusion correct? Explain your reasoning.

x	0	1	2	3	4	5	6	7	8
y	2	0	0	2	6	12	20	30	42

4. Remembering the basic shapes of graphs of various algebraic models can provide a quick check on the number of possible solutions for a related equation.

a. How many solutions can there be for a linear equation of the form $c = ax + b$? Explain your response using sketches of linear model graphs.

b. How many solutions can there be for a quadratic equation $c = ax^2 + b$? Explain your response using sketches of quadratic model graphs.

c. How many solutions can there be for an exponential equation $c = a(b^x)$? Explain your response using sketches of exponential model graphs.

5. Refer to Modeling task 4. When confronted with part b, some students preferred to write a rule giving income I as a function of the number of *empty seats s* on the charter bus. The rule they wrote was $I = (60 - s)(10 + s)$.

a. Explain how the students might have figured out this rule.

b. Produce a table and a graph of the relation between income and number of empty seats.

c. How do your table and graph compare to those of quadratic models?

d. Produce a scatterplot of sample (*number of empty seats*, *income*) data. Then use your calculator or computer software to fit a quadratic model to the data.

e. Compare the form of $I = (60 - s)(10 + s)$ with that of the quadratic model in part d. Using number properties, explain why the two forms are equivalent.

Reflecting

1. In your study of linear, exponential, power, and quadratic models, you've learned several methods of solving equations.

a. How do you decide on a method for any particular problem?

b. What are the pros and cons of the various possible methods?

3. No, there are two solutions, one is between 0 and 1 and the other is between 2 and 3. Reducing the step size in the table will show y values closer to 1.

4. **a.** A linear model has exactly one solution. The following is one possible explanation.

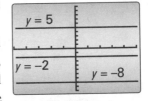

Consider the example $c = 2 + 3x$. This linear model will have exactly one solution. Graph the line $y = 2 + 3x$, and then consider any line $y = c$. These two lines will intersect in just one point. In the graph at the right, three examples are shown. In each case, the horizontal line of the form $y = c$ intersects the linear model exactly once.

b. There can be 0, 1, or 2 solutions to a quadratic equation of the form $c = ax^2 + b$. Examples of each situation are shown in the graph. It is possible to chose c so that the graph of $y = c$ will intersect the graph of $y = ax^2 + b$ either 0, 1, or 2 times.

c. There can be 0 or 1 solution. For any c, the graph of $y = c$ will intersect the graph of $y = a(b^x)$ at most once. Examples of no solutions and of one solution are shown in the graph.

5. **a.** The $60 - s$ represents the number of people on the trip and the $10 + s$ represents the charge for each person. The product $(60 - s)(10 + s)$ represents the total income.

b.

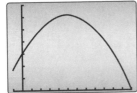

WINDOW	FORMAT
Xmin =–5	
Xmax=60	
Xscl =5	
Ymin =0	
Ymax=1400	
Yscl =200	

X	Y₁
0	600
10	1000
20	1200
30	1200
40	1000
50	600
60	0
X=0	

c. The function is a quadratic model and so both the graph and the table have the same patterns that students have seen in quadratic models.

d.

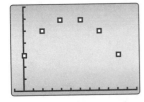

WINDOW	FORMAT
Xmin =-5	
Xmax=60	
Xscl =5	
Ymin =0	
Ymax=1400	
Yscl =200	

The fitted quadratic model has the equation $y = -x^2 + 50x + 600$.

e. If students use the distributive property to simplify $I = (60 - s)(10 + s)$ and then combine like terms, they will get the equation $I = 600 + 50s - s^2$, which is the same equation as the quadratic model.

See additional Teaching Notes on page T317X.

Unit 4

2. **a.** If price is set too low, there will be negative profit. In fact, if price is $0, there will be no income but there will still be expenses. So you will have a loss (negative profit). As the price increases, the profit increases up to a maximum point. After that point the profit declines.

   b. If the price is very low many people will participate, but as the price increases fewer people will participate.

3. **a.** A quadratic cannot have both a minimum and a maximum value because its graph is U-shaped.

   b. If the value for a in the general form $y = ax^2 + bx + c$ is positive, the curve will open upward and the quadratic model will have a minimum value. If the value for a is negative, then the curve will open downward and the function will have a maximum value.

4. The graph of every quadratic model has a y-intercept. You can find the y-intercept from the rule by letting $x = 0$ or by setting the table to start at 0. The y-intercept will always be c if the rule is written in the form $y = ax^2 + bx + c$.

5. **a.** Responses will vary. One possible explanation is that words of a story provide clues to the outcome of the story, just as the symbolic rules of an algebra model provide clues about the shape of its graph, the maximum or minimum value, the number of roots, and the y-intercept.

   b. Algebraic models differ from stories written with words and sentences in that they use abbreviated concise symbols and encode information that may be expressed succinctly.

Extending

1. **a.** Since the diver fell 0.2 meters in 0.2 seconds, a reasonable estimate of speed would be 1 meter per second (0.02 meters/0.02 seconds).

2. In several problems about the relation between prices and profits for a business venture, you worked with quadratic models that have graphs like the one shown here.

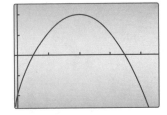

   a. How would you describe the pattern of change in predicted profit for different possible prices?

   b. Why is that general pattern reasonable in a wide variety of business situations?

3. Think about the basic shape and symbolic form of quadratic models.

   a. Can a quadratic model have both a maximum and minimum point? Why or why not?

   b. How can you tell, from the rule of a quadratic model, whether it has a maximum or minimum point on its graph?

4. Does the graph of every quadratic model have a *y*-intercept? How can you determine the *y*-intercept by looking at the rule?

5. Variables and constants can be combined to form a quadratic term ax^2, a linear term bx, and a constant term c. These terms can be combined with other symbols to form the general quadratic model $y = ax^2 + bx + c$. Think about the similarity between English letters, words, sentences, and stories and the language of algebra.

   a. How is reading the words of a story like reading the symbolic rules of an algebraic model?

   b. How are algebraic models different from stories written with letters, words, and sentences?

Extending

1. For anything that moves, **average speed** can be calculated by dividing distance traveled by the time it takes to cover that distance. For example, a diver who falls 10 meters from a high platform in about 1.5 seconds has an average speed of $\frac{10}{1.5}$ or approximately 6.7 meters per second. That same diver will not be falling at that average speed throughout the dive.

   a. If that diver falls from 10 meters to approximately 9.8 meters in the first 0.2 seconds of a dive, what estimate of speed would seem reasonable for the diver midway through that time interval—that is, how fast might the diver be moving at 0.1 seconds?

Unit 4

LESSON 3 • QUADRATIC MODELS   287

b. The relation between the diver's time in flight and height above the water can be modeled well by the equation $h = 10 - 4.9t^2$. Use that rule to make a table of (*time*, *height*) data and then estimate the diver's speed at a series of points using your data. Make a table and a graph of the (*time in flight*, *speed*) estimates.

c. What do the patterns in (*time in flight*, *speed*) data and the graph tell you about the diver's speed on the way to the water?

d. About how fast is the diver traveling when she hits the water?

e. Find an equation relating time t and speed s that seems to fit the data in your table and graph. Use your graphing calculator or computer software to check the rule against the data in part b.

2. Consider the quadratic model of a punted football $h = -4.9t^2 + 20t + 1$, where the height is given in meters and the time in seconds.

a. What question can be answered by solving the following inequality?
$$15 < -4.9t + 20t + 1$$

b. Solve the inequality in part a and answer the question you posed.

c. Write an inequality that can be used to answer this question: "At what times in its flight is the ball within 5 meters of the ground?"

d. Answer the question in part c by solving the inequality you wrote.

3. Important questions about quadratic models sometimes involve solving inequalities like $10 > x^2 + 2x - 5$ or $-8 < -2x^2 + 6x$.

a. What is the goal of the process in each case?

b. How can you use tables of values to solve the inequalities?

c. How can you use graphs to solve the inequalities?

4. Study the equations, tables, and graphs in the flying basketball and football situations in this lesson.

a. Find a pattern in the equations that helps you to predict

- the initial height of the ball (when it is shot or kicked).
- the initial upwards speed of the ball (when it is shot or kicked).

b. Suppose a baseball player hits a high pop-up with an initial upwards velocity of 32 meters per second. Suppose also that the ball was hit at 1.5 meters above the ground.

- Write a quadratic rule that would model this situation well.
- How much time would a player on the opposing team have to get under the ball to catch it before it hits the ground?

1. b. The speeds in the following table are average speeds in the time interval from $t - 0.1$ to $t + 0.1$. There are several efficient ways to get these results using a graphing calculator or computer software, with Y_1 defined to be $10 - 4.9x$. A table can be created calculating $(Y_1(t - 0.1) - Y_1(t + 0.1))/0.2$, using values beginning at 0.1 in steps of 0.2. On the TI-82 or 83, individual values can be found using the YVars menu to access Y_1 on the home screen and calculating the speed for a particular time interval, for example, $(Y_1(0.2) - Y_1(0.4))/0.2$ for the speed at time 0.3 seconds.

Time (s)	Speed (m/s)		Time (s)	Speed (m/s)
0.1	1		0.9	8.8
0.3	2.9		1.1	10.8
0.5	4.9		1.3	12.7
0.7	6.9			

c. The diver's speed increases as she approaches the water. The speed is increasing at a constant rate of approximately 1.96 meters per second for every 0.2 seconds.

d. The diver is traveling approximately -14.7 m/s when she hits the water.

e. $s = -9.8t$ will fit well.

2. a. For what time period will the height of the football be greater than 15 meters?

b.

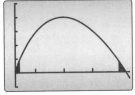

As you can see from the table and from the graph, the approximate solution is $0.8972 < t < 3.1844$.

c. $5 \geq -4.9t^2 + 20t + 1$

d. From the table and graph, you can see the approximate solution is $t < 0.2108$ or $t > 3.8708$; that is, the ball is within five meters of the ground for the first 0.21 seconds of its flight, and again after 3.87 seconds have passed.

3. a. For the first model you want to know what values of x give a value for the quadratic model that is less than 10. For the second model you want to know what values of x give a value for the quadratic model that is greater than -8.

b. By inspecting the tables below, you can determine the values for x which satisfy the inequality. You can see in the first table that for $-5 < x < 3$ the value of the quadratic model $y = x^2 + 2x - 5$ will be less than 10. In the second table you can see that the value of the quadratic model $y = -2x^2 + 6x$ will be greater than -8 when $-1 < x < 4$.

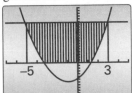

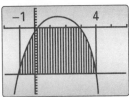

c. By inspecting the graphs above, you can determine which x satisfy the inequality.

See additional Teaching Notes on page T317X.

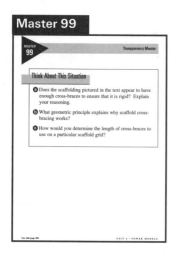

Lesson 4 Radicals and Fractional Power Models

LESSON OVERVIEW In earlier sections of this unit students will have seen how the family of power models includes quite a variety of patterns of direct and inverse variation. Relations between variables that appear quite different turn out to be representable with simple variations of the rule with form $y = ax^b$. Those basic power models can be combined by addition to produce polynomial models like the general quadratic studied in Lesson 3.

The umbrella of power models also includes inverses of the familiar quadratic and cubic functions: the square root and cube root relations. The goal of this fourth power models lesson is to acquaint students with those important algebraic relations and the fractional power and radical expressions used to represent them. By the end of this lesson students should be able to describe the meaning of square and cube roots, to simplify radical expressions, to sketch graphs of square root and cube root functions, and to explain and use basic properties of exponents.

In the first investigation, students are reminded of square roots and radical notation from prior work in geometry as they work on some questions about diagonal bracing in rectangular structures. They inspect the graph of the square root equation $y = \sqrt{x}$ and they also encounter the fact that several different radical expressions can represent the same numerical value. They are led to discover the basic principle for simplification of radicals, $\sqrt{ab} = \sqrt{a}\,\sqrt{b}$. The second investigation applies simplification of radical expressions to study some very interesting spiral patterns. It also connects to the iterative *NOW-NEXT* form of pattern generation that has been so helpful in earlier work with linear and exponential functions. Investigation 3 reaches one step further to cube roots, without any particular emphasis on the principle for simplifying those radicals. Then Investigation 4 summarizes a variety of basic facts of exponents as they occur in various algebraic expressions.

Lesson Objectives

- To be able to describe the meaning of square and cube roots
- To explore properties of square and cube root functions and their role in reasoning about important geometric patterns
- To discover and use the basic principle for simplification of radical expressions
- To summarize fundamental properties for transforming exponential expressions into alternative equivalent forms

See additional Teaching Notes on page T317Y.

Radicals and Fractional Power Models

Construction workers, window washers, and painters use scaffolding on all kinds of building and maintenance projects. Some scaffolds reach as high as three or four stories. The scaffolds usually are made of pipes connected in a rectangular grid. If you have seen such scaffolds, you may have noticed cross-braces used to keep the grid from shifting or collapsing altogether.

Think About This Situation

a Does the scaffolding pictured above appear to have enough cross-braces to ensure that it is rigid? Explain your reasoning.

b What geometric principle explains why scaffold cross-bracing works?

c How would you determine the length of cross-braces to use on a particular scaffold grid?

LESSON 4 • RADICALS AND FRACTIONAL POWER MODELS   **289**

INVESTIGATION 1 The Power of a Brace

Each cross-brace in a scaffold is the diagonal of a rectangle and the hypotenuse of two congruent right triangles. That means that the Pythagorean Theorem can be used to calculate the length of any required cross-brace.

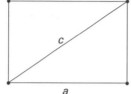

$$c^2 = a^2 + b^2$$

or

$$c = \sqrt{a^2 + b^2}$$

The **radical symbol** $\sqrt{}$ is used to indicate the positive square root of a number. For example, $\sqrt{25} = 5$ because $5 \cdot 5 = 25$.

In general, $y = \sqrt{x}$ if and only if $y \geq 0$ and $y^2 = x$. The positive square root of x also can be represented by use of fractional power notation: $\sqrt{x} = x^{\frac{1}{2}}$ or $\sqrt{x} = x^{0.5}$.

1. In some cases, square roots are easy to calculate with mental arithmetic; in other cases, you might need the $\sqrt{}$ function on a calculator. Using a calculator, explore the relation $y = \sqrt{x}$ and find answers to the following questions.

   a. For which values of x can you find $\sqrt{x}$? Why?

   b. What is the shape of the graph of $y = \sqrt{x}$? What does that shape tell about the rate at which $\sqrt{x}$ changes as x increases?

   c. How are tables and graphs of $y = \sqrt{x}$ similar to and different from those of $y = x^2$?

2. The Tuf-Bilt Equipment Company manufactures and sells industrial-strength scaffolding. To help their sales representatives, they decided to build some scale models of the basic 5 foot by 10 foot by 5 foot scaffold units.

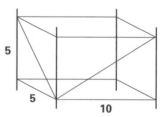

INVESTIGATION 1 The Power of a Brace

From previous work with the Pythagorean Theorem, students have encountered and evaluated square roots of numbers. And in previous chapters students have used tables and graphs to check if two expressions are equivalent. As a brief introduction to this investigation, you might remind students about these ideas and set the stage for further exploration by providing a list of possible equivalencies, such as those below. Then you might ask: What does it mean to say that two expressions are equivalent? How can we check for equivalence? What are some rules for working with symbolic expressions that might be useful in checking equivalence? What does the symbol "$\sqrt{}$" tell you to do?

Is $(2 + x)^2$ equivalent to $2^2 + x^2$?　　Is $3(2 + x)$ equivalent to $6 + 3x$?

Is $(2x)^2$ equivalent to $2x^2$?　　Is $(2x)^2$ equivalent to $4x^2$?

Is $\sqrt{3} \cdot \sqrt{3}$ equivalent to 3?　　Is $(\sqrt{x})^2$ equivalent to x?

Is $(x^{0.5})(x^{0.5})$ equivalent to $x^{0.25}$?　　Is $x^{0.5} \cdot x^{0.5}$ equivalent to x?

Is $\sqrt{1000}$ equivalent to 100?　　Is $\sqrt{100}$ equivalent to 50?

Is $100^{\frac{1}{2}}$ equivalent to 50?

This discussion will allow you to check that all students understand "square root" and "equivalence" and which of them have seen the fractional form, $x^{\frac{1}{2}}$, a new idea for most students.

1. **a.** Only when $x \geq 0$, because when you square any number you get a positive number.
   b. The graph might be described as half of a sideways U. This shape indicates that as x increases, $\sqrt{x}$ increases but at a decreasing rate.

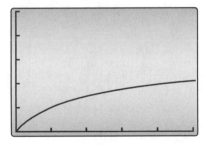

   c. In the tables, the first coordinates and second coordinates are interchanged for all positive values of x and y. The graphs of these functions are reflections of each across the line $y = x$ for all positive values of x and y.

Unit 4

2. a. Scale Model

Model	Base	Height	Crossbrace
#SM1	1	1	$\sqrt{2}$
#SM2	2	1	$\sqrt{5}$

Full-Size Model

Model	Base	Height	Crossbrace
#FS1	5	5	$\sqrt{50}$
#FS2	10	5	$\sqrt{125}$

b. Since the scale model is similar to the full size model and in similar figures, corresponding sides are proportional, the length of the cross brace in the full-size model will always be 5 times the corresponding length in the scale model.

c. There are at least two ways in which students might approach this activity. Some students may use scale factors and multiplication. Others may choose to draw right triangles and use the Pythagorean Theorem. We have provided complete solutions using both methods for part i and only the lengths for parts ii and iii.

i. If the length of the cross brace is 10, then, when the base and height are the same length, the scale factor is $\frac{10}{\sqrt{2}}$ or approximately 7.07. So the length of the base and height will be 1(7.07) = 7.07 feet. In the case where the ratio of the base to height is 2:1, the scale factor is $\frac{10}{\sqrt{5}}$ or approximately 4.47. So the length of the base is 2(4.47) or 8.94 feet and the height is 4.47 feet.

Using the Pythagorean Theorem, we arrive at the same solutions as follows.

Base and height the same length

$2x^2 = 100$
$x^2 = 50$
$x = \sqrt{50} \approx 7.07$ feet

Ratio of base to height 2:1

$5x^2 = 100$
$x^2 = 20$
$x = \sqrt{20} \approx 4.47$ fe

height: 4.47 feet   *base:* 8.94 feet

ii. If the base and the height are the same length, each will be approximately 2.24 feet long. If the ratio of base to height is 2:1, then the base will have length 2.83 feet and the height will be 1.41 feet.

iii. If the base and the height are the same length, each will be approximately 4.74 feet long. If the ratio of base to height is 2:1, then the base will have length 6 feet and the height will be 3 feet.

d. $x = \sqrt{89}$

$y = \sqrt{356} = 2\sqrt{89}$

The ratio of x to y is 1:2. The shortcut is to double x in order to find y. We multiply by 2 since the triangles are similar with scale factor 2.

e. It is important that students spend some time trying to figure this out, but you probably don't want it to go on for too long. Activity 3 provides another opportunity for students to find the property that $\sqrt{a^2b} = a\sqrt{b}$.

Unit 4

a. Calculate the missing numbers in this table of specifications for the components used in scale model and full-size scaffolds. All lengths are in feet. Report cross-brace lengths in *radical form*. (Do not give decimal approximations.)

Scale Model

	base	height	cross-brace
#SM1	1	1	
#SM2	2	1	

Full Size Model

	base	height	cross-brace
#FS1	5	5	
#FS2	10	5	

b. One class that worked on the cross-brace specifications thought that they had a shortcut. Once they calculated the cross-brace lengths for the scale model, they simply multiplied those by 5 to get the cross-brace lengths for the corresponding full-size model. Will their idea always work? If so, explain their method using geometric principles. If not, provide a counterexample.

c. Determine the base and height specifications for a section of scaffolding that requires cross-braces with the following lengths. Consider cases where base and height are the same length and where the ratio of base to height is 2:1.

i. 10 feet   **ii.** $\sqrt{10}$ feet   **iii.** $\sqrt{45}$ feet

d. Now check if the shortcut you investigated in part b works with lengths of this pair of right triangles. Examine the given lengths and decide what the shortcut should be. Then, use the Pythagorean Theorem to calculate x and y. Is there a shortcut to finding y once you know x? If so, explain how the shortcut is related to the two triangles.

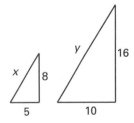

e. In testing the proposed shortcut calculations for diagonal and hypotenuse lengths, you may have noted that different radical expressions can have the same numerical value. For example, $\sqrt{50}$ is equivalent to $5\sqrt{2}$ and $\sqrt{356}$ equals $2\sqrt{89}$. Brainstorm in your group about ways you might rewrite radical expressions in equivalent and possibly simpler forms.

Unit 4

3. When another class did some brainstorming about possible ways to rewrite radical expressions, they proposed four procedures that they thought might produce smaller numbers under the radical sign. Test each idea given below for at least four specific cases like $\sqrt{6}$, $\sqrt{50}$, $\sqrt{75}$, $\sqrt{164}$, $\sqrt{300}$, or $\sqrt{360}$. You may want to try more than four cases. Share the testing among members of your group. If you find a procedure that seems to work, test it with other specific cases. Which of the proposed methods for rewriting radical expressions seem to work always? Compare your findings with those of other groups.

a. Is $\sqrt{a + b} = \sqrt{a} + \sqrt{b}$ for all positive numbers a and b?

b. Is $\sqrt{a - b} = \sqrt{a} - \sqrt{b}$ for all positive numbers a and b?

c. Is $\sqrt{ab} = \sqrt{a} \cdot \sqrt{b}$ for all positive numbers a and b?

d. Is $\sqrt{ab} = a\sqrt{b}$ for all positive numbers a and b?

As you completed activity 3, you may have discovered one key method of writing radical expressions in simpler equivalent forms. Among those equivalent forms, the one that has the smallest positive integer under the radical sign is called **simplest radical form**. For example,

$$
\begin{aligned}
\sqrt{180} &= \sqrt{4 \cdot 45} \\
&= \sqrt{4}\,\sqrt{45} \\
&= 2\sqrt{9 \cdot 5} \\
&= 2\sqrt{9}\,\sqrt{5} \\
&= 2(3)\sqrt{5} \\
&= 6\sqrt{5}
\end{aligned}
$$

which is simplest radical form. Can you find another path to this same radical form?

If you recognized that $180 = 36 \cdot 5$, you could arrive at the simplest radical form quickly by writing

$$
\begin{aligned}
\sqrt{180} &= \sqrt{36}\,\sqrt{5} \\
&= 6\sqrt{5}
\end{aligned}
$$

This result can be checked with your calculator (but be cautious about possible decimal approximation errors) or by squaring: $(6\sqrt{5})^2 = (6\sqrt{5})\,(6\sqrt{5}) = 36\,(\sqrt{5}\,\sqrt{5}) = 36(5) = 180$.

4. Use the general principle you discovered in activity 3 to rewrite each of the following in simplest radical form. In each case, see if you can find several different paths to the final result. Be sure to check that the simplest form you come up with is equivalent to the original radical expression.

a. $\sqrt{54}$ **b.** $\sqrt{48}$

c. $\sqrt{240}$ **d.** $\sqrt{75}$

3. Only $\sqrt{ab} = \sqrt{a} \cdot \sqrt{b}$ is always true.

   a. No, $\sqrt{a+b} \neq \sqrt{a} + \sqrt{b}$ unless a or b is zero.

   b. No, this is only true if $a = b$ (or either is zero).

   c. Yes, $\sqrt{ab} = \sqrt{a} \cdot \sqrt{b}$ for all positive numbers a and b.

   d. No, this rule only works when $a = 1$ (and when a or b is zero).

4. a. $\sqrt{54} = \sqrt{(9)(6)} = 3\sqrt{6}$

   b. $\sqrt{48} = \sqrt{(3)(16)} = 4\sqrt{3}$

   c. $\sqrt{240} = \sqrt{(4)(60)} = 2\sqrt{60} = 2\sqrt{(15)(4)} = 4\sqrt{15}$

   d. $\sqrt{75} = \sqrt{(3)(25)} = 5\sqrt{3}$

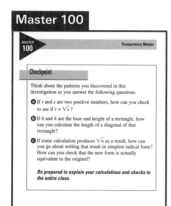
CONSTRUCTING A MATH
TOOLKIT: Students should
record the process of writing
a radical in simplest form,
with a few examples, in the
algebra and functions section
of their math toolkits.

SHARE AND SUMMARIZE full-class discussion

Checkpoint

See Teaching Master 100.

ⓐ $r = \sqrt{s}$ if $r^2 = s$.

ⓑ Using the Pythagorean Theorem, the length of the diagonal is $\sqrt{b^2 + h^2}$.

ⓒ Write n as the product of numbers. For any of those numbers that are perfect squares (the square root is an integer), take the square root and remove it from underneath the radical sign. Check your work by squaring your answer. NOTE: To make sure students understand, it might be helpful to try a difficult example such as $\sqrt{490}$ or $\sqrt{2025}$.

APPLY individual task

▶On Your Own

a. $\sqrt{1^2 + 1^2} = \sqrt{2}$
$\sqrt{2^2 + 2^2} = \sqrt{8} = \sqrt{(4)(2)} = 2\sqrt{2}$
$\sqrt{3^2 + 3^2} = \sqrt{18} = \sqrt{(9)(2)} = 3\sqrt{2}$
$\sqrt{4^2 + 4^2} = \sqrt{32} = \sqrt{(16)(2)} = 4\sqrt{2}$

b. $30\sqrt{2}, \ 50\sqrt{2}, \ 100\sqrt{2}$

c. The length of the diagonal of a square with side length s is $s\sqrt{2}$.

d. Student examples may vary.

   i. $5 = \sqrt{25} = \sqrt{9 + 16} \neq \sqrt{9} + \sqrt{16} = 3 + 4 = 7$

   ii. $5 = \sqrt{25} = \sqrt{169 - 144} \neq \sqrt{169} - \sqrt{144} = 13 - 12 = 1$

   iii. $20 = \sqrt{400} = \sqrt{(100)(4)} \neq 100\sqrt{4} = 200$

e. **i.** $2\sqrt{5}$

   ii. $8\sqrt{2}$

   iii. $\sqrt{210}$

MORE

ASSIGNMENT *pp. 303–310*

Students now can begin
Modeling task 2 or Organizing
task 1 from the MORE assignment following Investigation 4.

Unit 4

▶ On Your Own

The following sketches show four squares, each with one diagonal drawn.

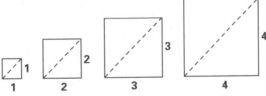

a. Calculate the length of each diagonal in radical form. Then write each result in simplest radical form and check to see that the two forms are equivalent.

b. Study your results in part a and look for a pattern that will allow you to write easily the diagonal lengths of squares with side lengths 30, 50, and 100.

c. Suppose a square has side length s. Write an expression for the lengths of its diagonals in simplest radical form.

d. Give counterexamples showing the following:

  i. $\sqrt{a + b}$ is *not* always equal to $\sqrt{a} + \sqrt{b}$.

  ii. $\sqrt{a - b}$ is *not* always equal to $\sqrt{a} - \sqrt{b}$.

  iii. $\sqrt{ab}$ is *not* always equal to $a\sqrt{b}$.

e. Write each of the following in simplest radical form.

  i. $\sqrt{20}$ **ii.** $\sqrt{128}$ **iii.** $\sqrt{210}$

Unit 4

INVESTIGATION 2 Powerful Radicals

The following photographs show similar visual patterns in familiar objects. Can you recognize all six objects pictured? How would you describe the similar pattern in all the objects?

Can you think of other objects that have the same type of pattern? How would you describe the pattern in mathematical language?

INVESTIGATION 2 ▸ Powerful Radicals

Students need to be able to use the Pythagorean Theorem to access the intriguing spiral in this investigation. They also need to know that $\sqrt{2} \cdot \sqrt{2} = \sqrt{4}$ (or more generally, $\sqrt{a}\,\sqrt{b} = \sqrt{ab}$ which should have come out of Investigation 1) and that $\sqrt{2} + \sqrt{2} = 2\sqrt{2}$. If they are able to work with these tools they will see an interesting pattern. Students probably will want to use decimal approximations in the table in activity 2, because these are familiar and meaningful to them. Tell students that their work will be made a lot easier and more interesting if they use the radical notation, especially if they can write their answers in a "simpler" form. If you observe a student write $\sqrt{8}$, for example, you might ask if $\sqrt{8}$ can be written in another way. ($\sqrt{8} = \sqrt{4}\,\sqrt{2} = 2\sqrt{2}$. It can be argued that $2\sqrt{2}$ is not "simpler" than $\sqrt{8}$, but you can call it an equivalent or alternative form.) In "simpler" form the pattern *NEXT* = *NOW* $\cdot \sqrt{2}$ emerges.

As students work on calculating the lengths and searching for a pattern, it might be helpful to ask how these lengths are changing. In a linear fashion? In an exponential fashion? Connecting this to previous work with exponential models might help them construct a rule for the length of the *n*th segment.

Unit 4

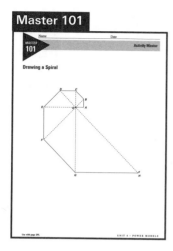

EXPLORE *continued*

1. **See Teaching Master 101.**

    a. To produce this spiral, first draw a right isosceles triangle. Then construct another right isosceles triangle, using the hypotenuse of the first triangle as the base of the second with the right angle towards the outside of the figure. Continue in this manner for as long as you wish.

    b. The segment *HI* will have length equal to *OH* and ∠*OHI* should be a right angle.

    c. These triangles are all similar so the sides are proportional and the angles are congruent.

The DNA model, pasta, spider web, decorative woodwork, pineapples, and galaxy all share a geometric feature called *spiral design*. A **spiral** is a curve traced by a point that rotates around and away from a fixed center point. There are many different types of spirals, and there are many intriguing mathematical ways of generating spirals. This investigation explores spiral-like designs that will help you learn more about square roots and radical expressions.

1. **Drawing a Spiral** The following figure shows the beginning of a spiral made up of connected line segments.

   a. Using a copy of this figure, measure the various segments and angles in the design and see if you can describe geometrically the steps required to produce the drawing.

   b. Draw *HI,* the next segment in the spiral.

   c. What patterns do you see relating sides and angles in the various outlined triangles ($\triangle OAB$, $\triangle OBC$, $\triangle OCD$, ...)?

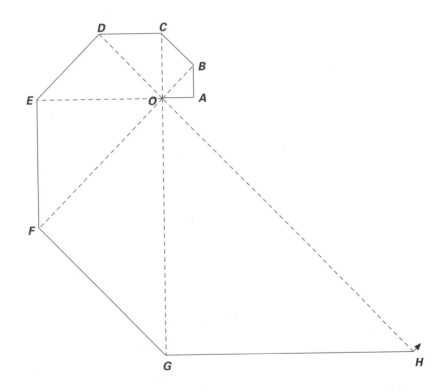

2. **Spiral Edge Length** The first two segments of the spiral (*OA* and *AB*) are each 1 centimeter long. But then, as the spiral path turns, the segments get longer. Each triangle outlined in the figure is an isosceles right triangle.

Unit 4

a. Make a table showing the growth of spiral edge lengths. Report lengths in radical form. Include predictions of the next two lengths that are not shown on the sketch itself. Compare your predictions with those of other groups and resolve any differences.

Spiral Edges

Line Segment	Length (cm)
OA	1
AB	1
BC	
CD	
DE	
EF	
FG	
GH	
HI	
IJ	

b. Study the table of increasing spiral edge lengths. Write an equation using *NOW* and *NEXT* that expresses the growth pattern at any stage after the second. (**Hint:** Remember that for any positive numbers *a* and *b* you know that $\sqrt{ab} = \sqrt{a}\,\sqrt{b}$.)

c. In the given drawing there are just eight segments shown. You have added a ninth segment on your copy. Suppose this pattern were continued to create a design with *n* segments. What rule would give the length of the *n*th segment?

3. **Total Spiral Length** You can sum the entries in the table of edge lengths to get the total length of the spiral at various stages in its growth. With decimal approximations for the various square roots involved, you can get decimal approximations for the total length. But there are some patterns in the way spiral length increases that are easier to detect if you leave the calculations in radical form.

a. Rewrite the spiral edge lengths in your table, if necessary, showing each length in simplest radical form.

b. Combine the ten edge lengths to get a total length of the spiral described and find a way to write that sum in simplest form. (**Hint:** What simpler form do you think is equivalent to $3 + 5\sqrt{2} + 3\sqrt{2}$?)

2. **a.** Students should use the Pythagorean Theorem to find the lengths. Encourage your students to record the lengths in simplest radical form as this will make the rest of the investigation go more smoothly.

Spiral Segment Lengths

Line Segment	Length (cm)
OA	1
AB	1
BC	$\sqrt{2}$
CD	$\sqrt{4} = 2$
DE	$\sqrt{8} = 2\sqrt{2}$
EF	$\sqrt{16} = 4$
FG	$\sqrt{32} = 4\sqrt{2}$
GH	$\sqrt{64} = 8$
HI	$\sqrt{128} = 8\sqrt{2}$
IJ	$\sqrt{256} = 16$

   b. $NEXT = NOW \cdot \sqrt{2}$

   c. The length of the *n*th segment is $(\sqrt{2})^{n-2}$.

      To help students see the pattern, you may wish to suggest that they number the segments in the table from part a.

3. **a.** If students did not put lengths in simplest radical form in activity 2, they should do so now.

   b. $32 + 15\sqrt{2}$

      Although students are not expected to create a table of cumulative sums, they might find it helpful if they make an error.

Spiral Cumulative Lengths

Line Segment	Sum (cm)
OA	1
AB	2
BC	$2 + \sqrt{2}$
CD	$4 + \sqrt{2}$
DE	$4 + 3\sqrt{2}$
EF	$8 + 3\sqrt{2}$
FG	$8 + 7\sqrt{2}$
GH	$16 + 7\sqrt{2}$
HI	$16 + 15\sqrt{2}$
IJ	$32 + 15\sqrt{2}$

Unit 4

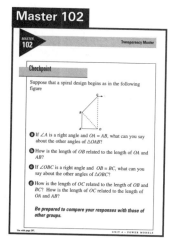

Checkpoint

See Teaching Master 102.

a The other two angles are each 45°.

b $OB = OA\sqrt{2} = AB\sqrt{2}$

c The other two angles are each 45°.

d $OC = OB\sqrt{2} = BC\sqrt{2}$
$$OC = OA(\sqrt{2})(\sqrt{2}) = 2OA = 2AB$$

APPLY individual task

▶On Your Own

Spiral Segment Lengths

Line Segment	Length (in radical form)	Length (in simplest form)
OA	$\sqrt{2}$	$\sqrt{2}$
AB	$\sqrt{6}$	$\sqrt{6}$
BC	$\sqrt{18}$	$3\sqrt{2}$
CD	$\sqrt{54}$	$3\sqrt{6}$
DE	$\sqrt{162}$	$9\sqrt{2}$
EF	$\sqrt{486}$	$9\sqrt{6}$
FG	$\sqrt{1458}$	$27\sqrt{2}$

Checkpoint

Suppose that a spiral design begins as in the following figure:

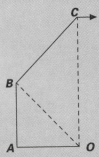

a If ∠*A* is a right angle and *OA* = *AB*, what can you say about the other angles of △*OAB*?

b How is the length of *OB* related to the length of *OA* and *AB*?

c If ∠*OBC* is a right angle and *OB* = *BC*, what can you say about the other angles of △*OBC*?

d How is the length of *OC* related to the length of *OB* and *BC*? How is the length of *OC* related to the length of *OA* and *AB*?

Be prepared to compare your responses with those of other groups.

▶On Your Own

The table below shows the lengths of the edges of a different spiral design.

Spiral Edges

Line Segment	Length (in radical form)	Length (in simplest form)
OA	$\sqrt{2}$	
AB	$\sqrt{6}$	
BC	$\sqrt{18}$	
CD	$\sqrt{54}$	
DE	$\sqrt{162}$	
EF	$\sqrt{486}$	
FG	$\sqrt{1458}$	

Complete the table by expressing each edge length in simplest radical form. Then use the table to help complete the tasks that follow.

a. Write an equation using *NOW* and *NEXT* that expresses the relationship between the lengths of any two successive edges of the spiral.

b. Write a rule that gives the length of the *n*th segment.

c. Calculate the sum of the given edge lengths and express the result in simplest equivalent form.

INVESTIGATION 3 Cube Roots

By now you have seen that if a square has side length x, then its area is x^2. If a square has area y, then its side length must be $\sqrt{y}$. On most calculators, you can calculate square roots by using the $\sqrt{\ }$ function or by entering $y^{\wedge}(1/2)$ or $y^{\wedge}0.5$.

You also have seen that if a cube has side length x, then its volume is x^3. But how would you calculate the edge length for a cube of given volume y?

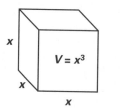 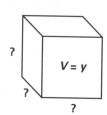

In some cases, you can use trial and error to find the unknown edge length. For example, if $x^3 = 216$, then you need a number whose cube is equal to 216. You can discover quickly that $x = 6$ is a solution of that equation. But what if the equation is $x^3 = 100$?

Mathematicians use several ways of expressing this question in radical and exponential form. They write

> $x = \sqrt[3]{100}$, which is read "x equals the cube root of 100," or
> $x = 100^{\frac{1}{3}}$, which is read "x equals 100 to the one-third power."

Here, the fractional power signifies "one of three equal factors for 100". For instance, 2 is one of the three equal factors that yield 8; so $2 = 8^{\frac{1}{3}}$.

1. Study the power model with rule $y = \sqrt[3]{x}$ or $y = x^{\frac{1}{3}}$.

   a. For which values of x does this rule produce a value of y?

   b. Make a table and a graph of this rule for $-10 \le x \le 10$. Describe the pattern of change in cube-root values as x increases.

   c. Compare the table and graph patterns of $y = \sqrt[3]{x}$ to those of $y = x^3$, $y = x^2$, and $y = \sqrt{x}$. Describe striking similarities and differences, and try to explain why they occur.

APPLY *continued*

a. $NEXT = NOW \cdot \sqrt{3}$
b. The *n*th segment has length $(\sqrt{2})(\sqrt{3})^{n-1}$.
c. $40\sqrt{2} + 13\sqrt{6}$

ASSIGNMENT   *pp. 303–310*

Students now can begin
Modeling task 4 from the
MORE assignment following
Investigation 4.

EXPLORE   small-group investigation

INVESTIGATION 3 Cube Roots

It is important for students to understand the relationship between squares and square roots. This investigation extends those ideas to cubes and cube roots, from a geometric perspective. You might help students to focus on the upcoming ideas by drawing some squares on the board and giving a side or an area for each and asking students to find the other.

Just a few minutes of work here will ensure that students are thinking about finding squares and square roots as processes that connect to geometric ideas. (You might ask some students to use "^ .5" with their calculators or computers as an alternative to "$\sqrt{}$ ", and have them compare results with students still using the radical.) Continue with the geometric connection, in three dimensions, by drawing some cubes on the board and giving a side or a volume for each and asking students to find the other.

Be sure to use the new and unfamiliar notation that $8^{\frac{1}{3}}$ is the same as $\sqrt[3]{8}$. When all students have made sense of cubing edges to find a volume, and calculating the cube root of a volume to find an edge, they can begin the investigation.

1. a. $\sqrt[3]{x}$ is defined for all real values of x.

   b.

WINDOW	FORMAT
Xmin	=-10
Xmax	=10
Xscl	=1
Ymin	=-10
Ymax	=10
Yscl	=1

x	−10	−9	−8	−7	−6	−5	−4	−3	−2	−1	0
$\sqrt[3]{x}$	−2.154	−2.080	−2	−1.913	−1.817	−1.710	−1.587	−1.442	−1.260	−1	0

x	1	2	3	4	5	6	7	8	9	10
$\sqrt[3]{x}$	1	1.260	1.442	1.587	1.710	1.817	1.913	2	2.080	2.154

   As x increases, the cube-root values are increasing, though not at a constant rate. For negative x values, the y values are increasing at an increasing rate; for positive x values, they are increasing at a decreasing rate. The graph is symmetric about the origin.

   c. The graph of $y = x^3$ is a reflection across the line $y = x$ of the graph of $y = \sqrt[3]{x}$. The graphs and tables of both $y = x^3$ and $y = \sqrt[3]{x}$ show that these equations are defined for all values of x and that the y values take on both positive and negative values. However, the graph and table of $y = x^2$ show that the y values for this equation are always positive. Also, the graph of this equation is not always increasing, unlike $y = \sqrt[3]{x}$. One important difference between the graphs and tables of $y = \sqrt[3]{x}$ and $y = \sqrt{x}$ is that $y = \sqrt[3]{x}$ can be evaluated for all real numbers while $y = \sqrt{x}$ is only defined when x is a positive number.

Unit 4

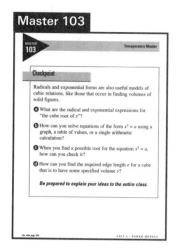

EXPLORE *continued*

2. **a.** $x = 2$ **b.** $x = 4$ **c.** $x = 6$ **d.** $x = 3$

    e. $x = -4$ **f.** $x = 1000$ **g.** $x = -27$ **h.** $x = -3$

3. **a.** $x = \sqrt[3]{100} = 100^{1/3} \approx 4.64$ **b.** $x = \sqrt[3]{-50} = (-50)^{1/3} \approx -3.68$

    c. $x = \sqrt[3]{15} = 15^{1/3} \approx 2.47$ **d.** $x = \sqrt[3]{15.7} = 15.7^{1/3} \approx 2.50$

4. **a.** $w = 0.5x^3$

    b. $0.5x^3 = 32$

    c. $0.5x^3 = 32$

       $x^3 = 64$

       $x = 4$

This tells us that the package should be a cube with edge length 4 inches if the weight is to be 32 ounces.

    d. $w = 0.5(8)^3$

       $w = 256$ ounces

This could be done with a single calculation by remembering that if the edge length is doubled, the volume is eight times as great, so you could simply multiply 32 times 8 to get 256 ounces.

CONSTRUCTING A MATH TOOLKIT: Students should summarize methods for solving and checking equations of the forms $x^3 = a$ and $b = \sqrt[3]{x}$ in their Math Toolkits.

SHARE AND SUMMARIZE   **full-class discussion**

Checkpoint

See Teaching Master 103.

ⓐ The radical form is $\sqrt[3]{x}$. The exponential form is $x^{\frac{1}{3}}$.

ⓑ Using a graph, you would plot $y = x^3$ and $y = a$ and find the intersection. You also could examine the table of values of $y = x^3$, find when $y = a$ and read off the corresponding value of x. The single arithmetic calculation of determining $a^{1/3}$ also provides the solution.

ⓒ Raise your root to the third power to determine whether it equals a.

ⓓ If you are given the volume of a cube, you need to take the cube root of that volume to determine the edge length.

JOURNAL ENTRY: Students need time to reflect on the new ideas, especially on the new notation they have been using, and to find ways to make sense of this notation. Have them respond to such questions as:

Why is "squaring" a good word for raising a value to the power 2?

Why is "cubing" a good word for raising a value to the power 3?

Why is $(\sqrt{2})^2 = 2$?   Why is $(\sqrt{5})^2 = 5$?

Why is $(\sqrt[3]{64})^3 = 64$?   Why is $(\sqrt[3]{4})^3 = 4$?

If $\sqrt{x}$ is the same as $x^{\frac{1}{2}}$, and $\sqrt[3]{x} = x^{\frac{1}{3}}$, how do you think you would write $\sqrt[4]{24}$ and what would it mean? How could you check the answer you gave?

Unit 4

2. Solve the following equations without use of a calculator. Express your answers as both integers and radicals (where appropriate).

   a. $x^3 = 8$ **b.** $x^3 = 64$ **c.** $x^3 = 216$ **d.** $x^3 + 10 = 37$

   e. $x^3 - 12 = -76$ **f.** $10 = \sqrt[3]{x}$ **g.** $-3 = \sqrt[3]{x}$ **h.** $x = \sqrt[3]{-27}$

3. Find solutions for these equations, using a calculator where necessary. Express answers in radical or exponential form and as decimal approximations.

   a. $x^3 = 100$ **b.** $x^3 = -50$ **c.** $5x^3 = 75$ **d.** $x^3 + 20 = 35.7$

4. The makers of Super Gro plant fertilizer package their product in cubical boxes. The fertilizer weighs 0.5 ounces per cubic inch.

   a. Write an equation that relates the weight w of a Super Gro package to the length x of each edge of the cubical box.

   b. What equation could be used to answer the question: "How long should the edges of a Super Gro box be if it is to hold 32 ounces of fertilizer?"

   c. Solve the equation in part b and explain what it tells about Super Gro packaging.

   d. What weight of Super Gro could be contained in a package whose edges are twice as long as those for the 32 ounce package? Explain how you could find the answer to this question using a single calculation and your answer to part c.

Checkpoint

Radicals and exponential forms are also useful models of cubic relations, like those that occur in finding volumes of solid figures.

a What are the radical and exponential expressions for "the cube root of x"?

b How can you solve equations of the form $x^3 = a$ using a graph, a table of values, or a single arithmetic calculation?

c When you find a possible solution for the equation $x^3 = a$, how can you check it?

d How can you find the required edge length e for a cube that is to have some specified volume v?

Be prepared to explain your ideas to the entire class.

Unit 4

On Your Own

a. Write the whole number or decimal equivalent for the following.

i. $49^{\frac{1}{2}}$ **ii.** $\sqrt{169}$ **iii.** $2\sqrt[3]{8}$

iv. $\sqrt[3]{512}$ **v.** $\sqrt{4096}$ **vi.** $3\sqrt[3]{27}$

b. Solve each of the following equations. Explain your reasoning and how you checked your answers.

i. $x^3 = 500$ **ii.** $4x^3 = 200$ **iii.** $43 = 16 + x^3$

INVESTIGATION 4 Operating with Powers

Throughout this unit and in earlier work with exponential models, you've seen many ways to use exponential expressions for calculations. In the same way that $3x$ is algebraic shorthand for $x + x + x$, the exponential expression x^3 is shorthand for $x \cdot x \cdot x$. When you need combinations of exponential expressions, there are some properties of exponents that help in simplifying those expressions.

1. **Product of Powers** For parts a–c, find the value that should replace the question mark.

a. $5^2 \cdot 5^4 = (5 \cdot 5)(5 \cdot 5 \cdot 5 \cdot 5) = 5^?$

b. $2 \cdot 2^6 = (2)(2 \cdot 2 \cdot 2 \cdot 2 \cdot 2 \cdot 2) = 2^?$

c. $b^4 \cdot b^8 = (b \cdot b \cdot b \cdot b)(b \cdot b \cdot b \cdot b \cdot b \cdot b \cdot b \cdot b) = b^?$

d. Look for a general property of exponents illustrated by the examples in parts a–c. Then find the expression to replace the question mark in the following: $b^r \cdot b^s = b^?$

e. Describe the general pattern summarized in part d using your own words.

2. **Quotient of Powers** Similarly, use the first three calculations that follow to find a property of exponential expressions involving fractions and division.

a. $\dfrac{3^4}{3^2} = \dfrac{3 \cdot 3 \cdot 3 \cdot 3}{3 \cdot 3} = 3^?$

b. $\dfrac{10^7}{10^4} = \dfrac{10 \cdot 10 \cdot 10 \cdot 10 \cdot 10 \cdot 10 \cdot 10}{10 \cdot 10 \cdot 10 \cdot 10} = 10^?$

c. $\dfrac{t^4}{t} = \dfrac{t \cdot t \cdot t \cdot t}{t} = t^?$

d. $\dfrac{t^r}{t^s} = t^?$

e. Describe the general pattern summarized in part d using your own words.

On Your Own

a. **i.** 7   **ii.** 13   **iii.** 4

      iv. 8   **v.** 64   **vi.** 9

b. **i.** $x = \sqrt[3]{500}$ or $x \approx 7.94$ Check: $(7.94)^3 \approx 500$

      ii. $x = \sqrt[3]{50}$ or $x \approx 3.68$ Check: $(3.68)^3 \approx 50$

      iii. $x = 27^{\frac{1}{3}}$ or $x = 3$ Check: $3^3 = 27$

MORE

ASSIGNMENT   *pp. 303–310*

Students now can begin
Modeling task 5 from the
MORE assignment following
Investigation 4.

EXPLORE   small-group investigation

INVESTIGATION 4   Operating with Powers

1. **a.** 5^6

     b. 2^7

     c. b^{12}

     d. $b^{(r + s)}$

     e. Add exponents when multiplying using the same base.

2. **a.** 3^2

     b. 10^3

     c. t^3

     d. $t^{(r - s)}$

     e. When dividing using the same base, subtract the exponent of the denominator from the exponent of the numerator.

3. a. 5^8

    b. 2^{15}

    c. m^8

    d. m^{ab}

    e. When raising an exponential expression to a power, multiply the exponents.

4. a. $6^3 5^3$

    b. $2^5 x^5$

    c. $\pi^7 d^7$

    d. $a^n b^n$

    e. When raising a product to a power, raise each factor to that power.

5. a. $\dfrac{2^4}{7^4}$
    b. $\dfrac{c^6}{9^6}$

    c. $\dfrac{4^5}{r^5}$
    d. $\dfrac{c^a}{r^a}$

    e. When raising a fraction to a power, raise the numerator to that power and the denominator to that power.

6. a. $\dfrac{1}{4}$
    b. $\dfrac{1}{5}$

    c. $\dfrac{1}{10}$
    d. $\dfrac{1}{10^2} = \dfrac{1}{100}$

    e. $\dfrac{1}{10^3} = \dfrac{1}{1000}$
    f. $\dfrac{1}{2^2} = \dfrac{1}{4}$

    g. $\dfrac{1}{\left(\frac{1}{2}\right)^3} = \dfrac{1}{\frac{1}{8}} = 8$
    h. $\dfrac{1}{\frac{2}{5}} = \dfrac{5}{2}$

    i. $\dfrac{1}{a^b}$

    j. To simplify an expression involving a negative exponent, write the base expression as 1 divided by the expression to the positive exponent. Apply the positive exponent. If a fraction remains on the denominator you may simplify by using the reciprocal of this fraction.

Unit 4

3. **Power of a Power** Now search for a property of exponential expressions involving powers raised to powers.

   a. $(5^4)^2 = (5 \cdot 5 \cdot 5 \cdot 5)(5 \cdot 5 \cdot 5 \cdot 5) = 5^?$

   b. $(2^3)^5 = (2 \cdot 2 \cdot 2)(2 \cdot 2 \cdot 2)(2 \cdot 2 \cdot 2)(2 \cdot 2 \cdot 2)(2 \cdot 2 \cdot 2) = 2^?$

   c. $(m^2)^4 = (m \cdot m)(m \cdot m)(m \cdot m)(m \cdot m) = m^?$

   d. $(m^a)^b = m^?$

   e. Describe the general pattern summarized in part d using your own words.

4. **Power of a Product** Next search for exponential expressions involving powers of products.

   a. $(6 \cdot 5)^3 = (6 \cdot 5)(6 \cdot 5)(6 \cdot 5) = (6 \cdot 6 \cdot 6)(5 \cdot 5 \cdot 5) = 6^?5^?$

   b. $(2x)^5 = (2x)(2x)(2x)(2x)(2x) = 2^?x^?$

   c. $(\pi d)^7 = (\pi d)(\pi d)(\pi d)(\pi d)(\pi d)(\pi d)(\pi d) = \pi^? d^?$

   d. $(ab)^n = (a^?)(b^?)$

   e. Describe the general pattern summarized in part d using your own words.

5. **Power of a Quotient** Again, search for a property of exponential expressions, this time involving powers of quotients.

   a. $\left(\dfrac{2}{7}\right)^4 = \left(\dfrac{2}{7}\right)\left(\dfrac{2}{7}\right)\left(\dfrac{2}{7}\right)\left(\dfrac{2}{7}\right) = \left(\dfrac{2 \cdot 2 \cdot 2 \cdot 2}{7 \cdot 7 \cdot 7 \cdot 7}\right) = \dfrac{2^?}{7^?}$

   b. $\left(\dfrac{c}{9}\right)^6 = \left(\dfrac{c}{9}\right)\left(\dfrac{c}{9}\right)\left(\dfrac{c}{9}\right)\left(\dfrac{c}{9}\right)\left(\dfrac{c}{9}\right)\left(\dfrac{c}{9}\right) = \left(\dfrac{c \cdot c \cdot c \cdot c \cdot c \cdot c}{9 \cdot 9 \cdot 9 \cdot 9 \cdot 9 \cdot 9}\right) = \dfrac{c^?}{9^?}$

   c. $\left(\dfrac{4}{r}\right)^5 = \left(\dfrac{4}{r}\right)\left(\dfrac{4}{r}\right)\left(\dfrac{4}{r}\right)\left(\dfrac{4}{r}\right)\left(\dfrac{4}{r}\right) = \dfrac{4 \cdot 4 \cdot 4 \cdot 4 \cdot 4}{r \cdot r \cdot r \cdot r \cdot r} = \dfrac{4^?}{r^?}$

   d. $\left(\dfrac{c}{r}\right)^a = \dfrac{c^?}{r^?}$

   e. Describe the pattern summarized in part d using your own words.

6. **Negative Exponents** Recall that $a^{-1} = \dfrac{1}{a}$. Use this fact and exploration with a calculator to rewrite the following exponential expressions in fractional form. Then look for a more general definition of negative exponents.

   a. 4^{-1} **b.** 5^{-1} **c.** 10^{-1}

   d. 10^{-2} **e.** 10^{-3} **f.** 2^{-2}

   g. $\left(\dfrac{1}{2}\right)^{-3}$ **h.** $\left(\dfrac{2}{5}\right)^{-1}$ **i.** a^{-b}

   j. Describe the pattern in part i using your own words.

Unit 4

7. Previously in this lesson you used fractional exponents to denote square roots and cube roots. For example, $8^{\frac{1}{2}} = \sqrt{8}$ and $54^{\frac{1}{3}} = \sqrt[3]{54}$. Investigate whether the rules you formulated in activities 1–6 also seem to hold for exponents that are fractions. Write a report summarizing your findings.

Checkpoint

Rewrite each of the following exponential expressions in an equivalent form. For each, also state the general rule that applies.

a $b^r \cdot b^s$ **b** $(m^a)^b$

c $\left(\dfrac{c}{r}\right)^a$ **d** $b^{\frac{1}{a}}$

e $\dfrac{t^r}{t^s}$ **f** $(ab)^n$

g a^{-b}

Be prepared to share your ideas with the rest of the class.

On Your Own

a. Use the properties of exponents and the relationship between exponential and radical expressions to determine whether the following statements are true or false. If a statement is false, rewrite the right side of the equation to make a true statement.

i. $5^{-1} = -5$ **ii.** $16^{-2} = 8$ **iii.** $3^2 \cdot 3^5 = 3^{10}$

iv. $\dfrac{2^7}{2^3} = 2^4$ **v.** $(5^3)^4 = 5^7$ **vi.** $(5x)^2 = 5x^2$

vii. $\left(\dfrac{2}{t}\right)^3 = \dfrac{6}{t^3}$ **viii.** $\left(\dfrac{4}{x^2}\right)^{-1} = \dfrac{1}{4x^2}$

b. Write each of these exponential expressions in another equivalent form.

i. $r^x \cdot r^y$ **ii.** $\dfrac{x^m}{x^n}$ **iii.** p^{-t}

c. Rewrite these exponential expressions in equivalent radical form.

i. $(s^2 t)^{\frac{1}{3}}$ **ii.** $(5r)^{\frac{1}{3}}$

7. All the rules developed in activities 1–6 will hold for exponents that are fractions.

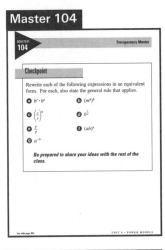

SHARE AND SUMMARIZE   full-class discussion

Checkpoint

See Teaching Master 104.

ⓐ b^{r+s} **ⓑ** t^{r-s}

ⓒ m^{ab} **ⓓ** $a^n b^n$

ⓔ $\dfrac{c^a}{r^a}$ **ⓕ** $\dfrac{1}{a^b}$

ⓖ $\sqrt[a]{b}$

CONSTRUCTING A MATH
TOOLKIT: The properties of
exponents along with examples should be recorded under
algebra properties in students' Math Toolkits.

APPLY   individual task

▶On Your Own

a. **i.** False; $5^{-1} = \frac{1}{5}$ **ii.** False; $16^{-2} = \frac{1}{256}$

   iii. False; $3^2 \cdot 3^5 = 3^7$ **iv.** True

   v. False; $(5^3)^4 = 5^{12}$ **vi.** False; $(5x)^2 = 25x^2$

   vii. False; $\left(\frac{2}{t}\right)^3 = \frac{8}{t^3}$ **viii.** False; $\left(\frac{4}{x^2}\right)^{-1} = \frac{x^2}{4}$

b. **i.** r^{x+y} **ii.** x^{m-n} **iii.** $\dfrac{1}{p^t}$

c. **i.** $\sqrt[3]{s^2 t}$ **ii.** $\sqrt[3]{5r}$

Modeling: 2 and 4 or 5*
Organizing: 1, 2 and 3
Reflecting: Choose one*
Extending: 3 or 4*

*When choice is indicated, it is important
to leave the choice to the student.
NOTE: It is best if Organizing tasks are discussed as a whole class after they have
been assigned as homework.

MORE   independent assignment

Modeling

1. Each small brace will be $\sqrt{12^2 + 24^2}$ or approximately 26.83 inches long. The long brace in back will be $\sqrt{32^2 + 72^2}$ or approximately 78.79 inches long. There are a total of 12 small braces, so about 401 inches of metal brace material would be needed.

2. **a.**

Edge Length	1	2	3	4	5	6	7	8	9	10
Diagonal of Face	$\sqrt{2}$	$2\sqrt{2}$	$3\sqrt{2}$	$4\sqrt{2}$	$5\sqrt{2}$	$6\sqrt{2}$	$7\sqrt{2}$	$8\sqrt{2}$	$9\sqrt{2}$	$10\sqrt{2}$

   b. $20\sqrt{2}$

Unit 4

MORE

Modeling • Organizing • Reflecting • Extending

Modeling

1. Metal storage shelves are designed with braces to add support and rigidity. If the shelves pictured here have dimensions 12 inches by 32 inches by 72 inches, how much metal brace material would you need for the diagonal supports shown?

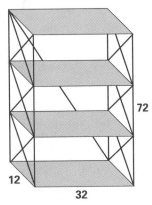

2. Investigate the relationship between the length of each edge of a cube and the length of its diagonals.

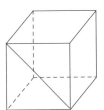

a. First complete a chart of lengths of face diagonals for cubes of edge lengths from 1 to 10. Write the diagonal lengths in simplest radical form.

Cube Face Diagonals						
Edge Length	1	2	3	4	⋯	10
Diagonal of Face					⋯	

b. How long is each face diagonal on a cube with edge length 20?

LESSON 4 • RADICALS AND FRACTIONAL POWER MODELS   303

There is also a relationship between the edge length of a cube and the length of the diagonals that join opposite corners of that cube. In the figure at the right, segment *AC* is such a diagonal.

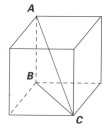

c. Complete a chart like the one below, showing the relation between length of opposite-corner diagonals of a cube and the length of the edges of that cube. Remember that patterns in such a chart will be easier to identify if you enter lengths in simplest radical form.

Cube Diagonals

Edge Length $\overline{AB}$	1	2	3	4	⋯	10
Length of $\overline{BC}$					⋯	
Length of $\overline{AC}$					⋯	

d. If the length of the diagonal of a cube is $8\sqrt{3}$ what is the length of the edge of that cube?

e. If the length of the edge is a, what is the length of the diagonal of the cube?

3. Efficient packing of shipments is important to many companies. Moving companies that make overseas shipments often use standard crates that are nearly cubical in shape. Household goods being shipped often include long thin objects like pole lamps, brooms, or skis. What is the smallest cubical shipping crate that will hold a pair of skis that are 6 feet long?

4. In Unit 2, "Patterns of Location, Shape, and Size", you began to build a two-dimensional coordinate model of geometry. Your model included coordinate descriptions of points, distance, parallel lines, and various transformations of the plane. In this task you will extend your table of coordinate models (see pages 91 and 120) to include a circle. A **circle** is the set of all points in a plane at a given distance from a given point in the plane (called the *center*).

a. Shown at the right is a circle with radius 4 and center at the origin of a coordinate plane. What are the *x*- and *y*-intercepts of the circle?

b. Explain why the point $(3, \sqrt{7})$ is on the circle.

c. Use the symmetry of the circle and the fact that $(3, \sqrt{7})$ is on the circle to name three other related points on the circle.

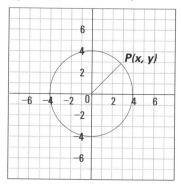

c.

Edge Length $\overline{AB}$	1	2	3	4	5	6	7	8	9	10
Length of $\overline{BC}$	$\sqrt{2}$	$2\sqrt{2}$	$3\sqrt{2}$	$4\sqrt{2}$	$5\sqrt{2}$	$6\sqrt{2}$	$7\sqrt{2}$	$8\sqrt{2}$	$9\sqrt{2}$	$10\sqrt{2}$
Length of $\overline{AC}$	$\sqrt{3}$	$2\sqrt{3}$	$3\sqrt{3}$	$4\sqrt{3}$	$5\sqrt{3}$	$6\sqrt{3}$	$7\sqrt{3}$	$8\sqrt{3}$	$9\sqrt{3}$	$10\sqrt{3}$

d. 8

e. $a\sqrt{3}$

3. Using the pattern developed in task 2 above, we have the equation $a\sqrt{3} = 6$. Thus $a = \frac{6}{\sqrt{3}}$ or approximately 3.46. So the smallest cubical shipping crate that will hold a pair of skis 6 feet long is one that is approximately 3.5 feet per side.

4. **a.** The x-intercepts of the circle are 4 and -4.

   The y-intercepts of the circle are 4 and -4.

   b. The length of the segment that joins the origin to the point $(3, \sqrt{7})$ is $\sqrt{(3-0)^2 + (7-0)^2}$ or $\sqrt{16}$ or 4. Since this circle is the set of all points that are 4 units from the origin, $(3\sqrt{7})$ must be on the circle.

   c. Three other related points on the circle are $(3, -\sqrt{7})$, $(-3, \sqrt{7})$, and $(-3, -\sqrt{7})$.

Unit 4

4. **d.** The points $(\sqrt{7}, 3)$, $(\sqrt{7}, -3)$, $(-\sqrt{7}, -3)$, and $(-\sqrt{7}, 3)$ will also be on the circle since $(\sqrt{7}, 3)$ is also 4 units from the origin. Students may choose 4 different related points also.

e. $x^2 + y^2 = 16$

Students may write this equation in a variety of ways. You may wish to encourage them to write it in what is often considered standard form for a circle centered at the origin with radius r: $x^2 + y^2 = r^2$.

f. $x^2 + y^2 = 100$

$x^2 + y^2 = r^2$

g. Many calculators allow different ways to graph a circle.

On all graphing calculators, you can use the functions list. However, you have to enter two equations, one for the top half of the circle and one for the bottom half. Let $Y_1 = \sqrt{16 - x^2}$ and $Y_2 = -\sqrt{16 - x^2}$. (Because of the pixels on the calculator screen you may see a bit of a gap on either side of the x-axis.)

If you have a TI-82 or 83, another method uses the DRAW menu. From the DRAW menu select the "Circle(" option. Then enter the coordinates of the center and the radius. In this case, the command would be **Circle(0, 0, 4)**. (When drawing a circle in this manner you cannot trace the graph. The circle is considered to be a picture and not a graph of an equation.)

If you have a Casio CFX-9850G, another method uses the Conics mode. From the menu, select 9: Conics then use the arrow keys to find and highlight the first circle equation. Press execute and enter the coordinates of the center and the radius, then press F6 (Draw).

Using any correct method your students may see a graph that looks more like an ellipse than a circle. This can be remedied by graphing using a "true perspective" window such as ZSQUARE on the TI calculators.

5. **a.** No this yacht does not meet the IACC requirements.

$22 + 1.25\sqrt{315} - 9.8\sqrt[3]{21.5} \approx 16.9$ which is not less than 16.296.

b. ■ If the displacement is 15.61 the formula becomes

$$L + 1.25\sqrt{S} - 9.8\sqrt[3]{15.61} \le 16.296$$
$$L + 1.25\sqrt{S} - 24.492 \le 16.296$$
$$L + 1.25\sqrt{S} \le 40.788$$

■ The maximum sail area allowable is found by solving the inequality

$$20.8 + 1.25\sqrt{S} \le 40.788$$
$$1.25\sqrt{S} \le 19.988$$
$$\sqrt{S} \le 15.9904$$
$$S \le 255.69$$

So the maximum sail area that can be used on this yacht is 255.69 square meters.

■ The maximum length can be found by solving the inequality

$L + 1.25\sqrt{185} \le 40.788$ to obtain $L \le 23.786$. So the maximum length for this yacht is approximately 23.78 meters.

Organizing

1. **a.** $4\sqrt{2}$ **b.** $7\sqrt{2}$ **c.** $10\sqrt{3}$
d. $8\sqrt{2}$ **e.** $5\sqrt{10}$ **f.** $4\sqrt[3]{2}$
g. $15\sqrt{3}$ **h.** $28\sqrt{5}$ **i.** $\sqrt{10}$

d. Name four additional points on the circle that are related to each other. How do you know they are on the circle?

e. Let $P(x, y)$ be any point on the circle. Write an equation showing the relationship between x, y, and 4.

f. Write an equation for a circle with radius 10 and center at the origin. Write a general equation for a circle with radius r and center at the origin.

g. Experiment to find a way to produce a calculator or computer graph of the equation of the circle in part e.

5. America's Cup is an international sailing competition. In order to compete in the America's Cup competition, yachts must comply with the International America's Cup Class (IACC) yacht design rules. In 1995, the rules included the formula

$$L + 1.25 \sqrt{S} - 9.8\sqrt[3]{D} \leq 16.296$$

where L is the length of the yacht in meters, S is the sail area in square meters, and D is the volume of water in cubic meters that the yacht displaces.

a. Suppose that a yacht is designed with length 22 meters and sail area 315 square meters. It displaces 21.5 cubic meters of water. Does this yacht meet the IACC requirements? Explain your reasoning.

b. In order to avoid a penalty, the displacement of the yacht must be between 15.61 and 24.39 cubic meters. Suppose a designer decides to minimize the displacement of a new yacht.

- Show that under this condition, the above formula can be simplified to
$$L + 1.25 \sqrt{S} \leq 40.788$$

- If the yacht is designed to be 20.8 meters long, what is the maximum sail area that can be used on the yacht?

- If the yacht has sails with area 185 square meters, what is the maximum length that it can be?

Organizing

1. Use the properties you found in this unit to write the following in whole number or simplest radical form.

a. $\sqrt{32}$ **b.** $\sqrt{98}$ **c.** $\sqrt{300}$

d. $\sqrt{128}$ **e.** $\sqrt{250}$ **f.** $\sqrt[3]{128}$

g. $5\sqrt{27}$ **h.** $7\sqrt{80}$ **i.** $\frac{1}{2}\sqrt{40}$

LESSON 4 • RADICALS AND FRACTIONAL POWER MODELS   **305**

Unit 4

2. Use the laws of exponents and the relationship between exponential and radical expressions to rewrite the following expressions in other equivalent forms, including one that you consider "simplest form."

a. 4^0 **b.** $25^{\frac{1}{2}}$ **c.** $2^5 \cdot 2^8$

d. $\dfrac{5^6}{5^\pi}$ **e.** $(7^3)^5$ **f.** $(3ab)^3$

g. $\left(\dfrac{7}{x}\right)^3$ **h.** $4^{\frac{1}{2}}$ **i.** $(7)^{\frac{1}{3}}$

3. The following statements support the reasoning behind the definitions of a^0 and $a^{\frac{1}{2}}$ for positive values of a. For each step shown, supply a general property of number operations to support that step.

a.
$$1 = \frac{a^x}{a^x}$$
$$= a^{x-x}$$
$$= a^0$$
So $1 = a^0$

b.
$$(a^{\frac{1}{2}})^2 = a^1$$
$$= a$$
So $a^{\frac{1}{2}} = \sqrt{a}$

4. Supply reasons justifying each step given below to prove the basic property for simplifying radical expressions: $\sqrt{ab} = \sqrt{a}\sqrt{b}$ for positive numbers a and b.

$$[\sqrt{a}\sqrt{b}]^2 = [\sqrt{a}\sqrt{b}][\sqrt{a}\sqrt{b}]$$
$$= [\sqrt{a}\sqrt{a}][\sqrt{b}\sqrt{b}]$$
$$= ab$$

Therefore, $\sqrt{a}\sqrt{b} = \sqrt{ab}$

5. By now, you should be familiar with three types of special triangles: right, isosceles, and equilateral. The relationships between the legs and hypotenuse of the isosceles right triangle and the 30°-60°-90° triangle (which is half of an equilateral triangle) are particularly useful in a variety of situations.

a. $\triangle ABC$ is an isosceles right triangle with legs of length a.

- Write a formula for the length of the hypotenuse in simplest radical form.

- Check your formula by finding the length of the hypotenuse of an isosceles right triangle with legs 8 cm in length. Use your formula and the Pythagorean Theorem.

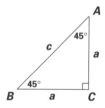

2. a. 1   **b.** 5   **c.** 2^{13}

    d. $5^{6-\pi}$ **e.** 7^{15} **f.** $27a^3b^3$

    g. $\dfrac{343}{x^3}$ **h.** 2   **i.** $\sqrt[3]{7}$

3. Note: This problem may be difficult for some students.

    a. $1 = \dfrac{a^x}{a^x}$ Any nonzero expression divided by itself is one

          $= a^{x-x}$ Quotients of powers rule

          $= a^0$ $x - x = 0$

     so, $1 = a^0$

    b. $(a^{1/2})^2 = a^1$ Power of a power rule

             $= a$ Any expression to the first power equals itself

     so, $a^{1/2} = \sqrt{a}$ Definition of square root

4. $[\sqrt{a}\,\sqrt{b}]^2 = [\sqrt{a}\,\sqrt{b}][\sqrt{a}\,\sqrt{b}]$ Power of a product

            $= [\sqrt{a}\,\sqrt{a}][\sqrt{b}\,\sqrt{b}]$ Commutative and associative properties

            $= ab$ Definition of square root

    Therefore, $\sqrt{a}\,\sqrt{b} = \sqrt{ab}$ Definition of square root

5. a. ■ $c = a\sqrt{2}$

     ■ Using the Pythagorean Theorem:

       $8^2 + 8^2 = c^2$

          $128 = c^2$

      $\sqrt{128} = c$

       $8\sqrt{2} = c$

     which agrees with the formula above.

Unit 4

5. b. ■ $\triangle BAB'$ is an equilateral triangle since each angle has measure $60°$.

   ■ The length of segment BC is half as long as the length of segment BB'. Since $\triangle BAB'$ is equilateral, $AB = 2BC$ as well.

   ■ Using the Pythagorean Theorem and the fact that $c = 2a$ we get:

   $$a^2 + b^2 = (2a)^2$$
   $$a^2 + b^2 = 4a^2$$
   $$b^2 = 3a^2$$
   $$b = \sqrt{3a^2} = a\sqrt{3}$$

   ■ The hypotenuse of the triangle is twice as long as the shortest side and the length of the other side is the length of the shortest side multiplied by $\sqrt{3}$.

Reflecting

1. You could use the definition of what it means to cube an expression, then expand and simplify from that.

   $$(3ab)^3 = (3ab)(3ab)(3ab) = (3)(3)(3)(a)(a)(a)(b)(b)(b) = 27a^3b^3$$
   $$\left(\frac{7}{x}\right)^3 = \left(\frac{7}{x}\right)\left(\frac{7}{x}\right)\left(\frac{7}{x}\right) = \frac{(7)(7)(7)}{(x)(x)(x)} = \frac{7^3}{x^3}$$

2. In order to examine the patterns in some of the sequences such as the edges of the spirals, you really needed to see the numbers in radical form. When you looked at the decimal equivalents, the patterns were not evident.

3. It makes sense to learn about radical and fractional exponent models in the same unit as direct and inverse variation power models because they are a subset of direct and inverse power models. In general, you have a power model when $y = kx^n$. When n is positive you have a direct variation power model, and when n is negative you have an inverse variation power model. By including radical and fractional exponent models, you include all real numbers for n rather than restricting n to only integer values. It is also nice to be able to examine such model pairs as $y = x^2$ and $y = \sqrt{x}$, and $y = x^3$ and $y = \sqrt[3]{x}$. These pairs are inverses of each other. For positive values of x and y, the graphs of the curves are reflections of each across the line $y = x$. Also, the values in the tables are simply reversed for both pairs.

4. Responses will vary and might include such things as building structures, towers, backs of signs, and reinforcements on crates or boxes.

5. You can calculate the population estimates for $t = 0.5$, 1.5, or 2.5 by substituting the appropriate value for t in the equation $P = 50(2^t)$. When substituting for t, the right-hand expression could be rewritten as shown below.

When $t = 0.5$,
$$P = 50(2^{0.5})$$
$$= 50\sqrt{2}$$

When $t = 1.5$,
$$P = 50(2^{1.5}) \quad \text{or} \quad P = 50(2^{1.5})$$
$$= 50(2^{0.5})^3 \qquad = 50(2^{0.5})2$$
$$= 50(\sqrt{2})^3 \qquad = 100\sqrt{2}$$
$$= 100\sqrt{2}$$

When $t = 2.5$,
$$P = 50(2^{2.5}) \quad \text{or} \quad P = 50(2^{2.5})$$
$$= 50(2^{0.5})^5 \qquad = 50(2^{0.5})2^2$$
$$= 50(\sqrt{2})^5 \qquad = 200\sqrt{2}$$
$$= 50(\sqrt{2})^4 \sqrt{2}$$
$$= 200\sqrt{2}$$

Students should explain their work by specifying either the property of Product of Powers or Power of a Power.

Unit 4

b. Now consider the 30°-60°-90° triangle shown at the right. △*AB′C* is the reflection image of △*ABC* across line *AC*.

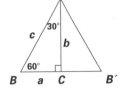

- What kind of triangle is △*BAB′*?

- How is the length of segment *BC* related to the length of segment *BB′*? To the length of segment *AB*?

- Explain why $b = a\sqrt{3}$.

- Write in words how the lengths of the sides of a 30°-60°-90° triangle are related.

Reflecting

1. You have studied several special properties of exponents. If you do not remember the special properties that apply, how can you use the basic definition of exponents to rewrite expressions like $(3ab)^3$ or $\left(\dfrac{7}{x}\right)^3$ in equivalent forms?

2. With a $\sqrt{}$ function on every scientific and graphing calculator it's natural to ask why one worries about procedures for rewriting radical expressions in equivalent forms. What examples have you seen in the preceding investigations that show the value of reasoning with exact numbers, rather than decimal approximations?

3. Why does it make sense to learn about radical and fractional exponent models in the same unit as direct and inverse variation power models? What connections are there between the (*input, output*) assignments of direct variation models and square root or cube root models?

4. In your study of geometry, you have worked with rigid structures. You may have seen metal storage shelves in a basement, garage, or storage shed. This is just one example of a rectangular structure that needs to be reinforced. Where else do you see cross-braces used to increase strength and stability in structures?

5. If bacteria in a cut reproduce with doubling time 1 hour, an initial population of 50 cells might reproduce according to the rule $P = 50(2^t)$ where *t* is time in hours. How would you calculate the population estimate for $t = 0.5$, 1.5, or 2.5? What connection is there in those calculations to properties of exponents and radicals developed in this lesson of the "Power Models" unit?

Unit 4

Extending

1. You have worked with square and cube roots in this lesson's investigations. Use what you know about these roots to predict simpler equivalent forms for the following radical expressions. Then test your ideas by writing each radical expression in fractional exponent form and then using a calculator to find the whole number equivalents for each.

   a. $\sqrt[4]{16}$ **b.** $\sqrt[5]{32}$ **c.** $\sqrt[4]{81}$ **d.** $\sqrt[7]{128}$

2. In about 200 B.C. the Greek astronomer and mathematician, Hipparchus, cataloged all of the stars he could see and classified each star according to its brightness. He gave the brightest star in the sky a magnitude of 1 and the dimmest star a magnitude of 6. Modern scientists still use this system as the basis of ranking stars according to their brightness. They have established a brightness scale in which a star with magnitude 1 is about 100 times brighter than a star with magnitude 6. The relation between magnitude and brightness is illustrated in the following table. Notice that brightness is an exponential function of magnitude.

   a. Complete the following chart that gives magnitude and brightness data.

   ### Star Magnitude Scale

Magnitude	1	2	3	4	5	6
Brightness	$(2.5)^5$	$(2.5)^4$	$(2.5)^3$	$(2.5)^2$	$(2.5)^1$	$(2.5)^0$
	or	or	or	or	or	or
	___	___	___	___	2.5	1

   b. Give the brightness of Vega, which has magnitude 0.03, and Arcturus, which has magnitude –0.06. Use the exponentiation key on your calculator for these calculations.

   c. How many times brighter is a star with magnitude 3 than a star with magnitude 5?

   d. Proxima Centauri is the closest star to us, next to the sun. It has a magnitude of 10.75. Sirius, another star, has a magnitude of –1.47. Which star is brighter and how much brighter?

   e. Sirius is the brightest star after the sun, which has a magnitude of about –27. How much brighter is the sun than Sirius?

Extending

1. a. $16^{\frac{1}{4}} = 2$ **b.** $32^{\frac{1}{5}} = 2$ **c.** $81^{\frac{1}{4}} = 3$ **d.** $128^{\frac{1}{7}} = 2$

2. a.

Magnitude	1	2	3	4	5	6
Brightness	$(2.5)^5$	$(2.5)^4$	$(2.5)^3$	$(2.5)^2$	$(2.5)^1$	$(2.5)^0$
	or	or	or	or	or	or
	97.7	39.1	15.6	6.25	2.5	1

b. Vega   237.5
Arcturus   257.9

c. A star of magnitude 3 is 2.5^{5-3} or 6.25 times brighter than a star of magnitude 5.

d. Proxima Centari has brightness of $2.5^{6-10.75}$ and Sirius has brightness of $2.5^{6-1.47}$. So Sirius is almost 73 thousand times brighter than Proxima Centari.

e. The ratio of the brightness of the sun to the brightness of Sirius is
$$\frac{2.5^{[6-(-27)]}}{2.5^{[6-(-12)]}}$$

or approximately 1.44×10^{10}. So the sun is over 14 billion times brighter than Sirius.

3. **a.** $(\sqrt[3]{8})^2$ or $\sqrt[3]{8^2}$, respectively

   b. 4

   c. The second way is probably easier without a calculator since the numbers are smaller.

   d.

Exponential Form	Radical Form	Whole Number or Decimal Form
$125^{\frac{2}{3}}$	$(\sqrt[3]{125})^2$	25
$1000^{\frac{4}{3}}$	$(\sqrt[3]{1000})^4$	10,000
$9^{\frac{5}{2}}$	$(\sqrt{9})^5$	243
$81^{\frac{3}{4}}$	$(\sqrt[4]{81})^3$	27
$16^{\frac{3}{2}}$	$(\sqrt{16})^3$	64

   e. When the calculator is used, you must place parentheses around the exponent so it calculates the exponent before trying to do the exponentiation.

3. In this unit you have dealt only with fractional exponents with a numerator of 1. Think about the rules for simplifying radicals and the definition $b^{\frac{1}{a}} = \sqrt[a]{b}$, as you complete these problems that involve more general fractional exponents. Use your calculator to verify your answers.

   a. The expression $8^{\frac{2}{3}}$ also can be written as $\left(8^{\frac{1}{3}}\right)^2$ or as $\left(8^2\right)^{\frac{1}{3}}$. Write these expressions in forms that involve radicals.

   b. Simplify your answers from part a confirming that both give the same result.

   c. In working with fractional exponent expressions, one translation to radical form sometimes will be easier than the other, for example:

   $$16^{\frac{3}{4}} = \sqrt[4]{16^3} \qquad \text{or} \qquad 16^{\frac{3}{4}} = (\sqrt[4]{16})^3$$
   $$= \sqrt[4]{4096} \qquad\qquad\qquad = 2^3$$
   $$= 8 \qquad\qquad\qquad\qquad = 8$$

   Which method would you use if you did not have a calculator or computer available?

   d. Copy and complete the following table.

   ### Equivalent Forms

Exponential Form	Radical Form	Whole Number or Decimal Form
$125^{\frac{2}{3}}$		
	$(\sqrt[3]{1000})^4$	
$9^{\frac{5}{2}}$		
$81^{\frac{3}{4}}$		
	$(\sqrt{16})^3$	

   e. When given the expression $(\sqrt{9})^3$ to simplify, one group wrote the fractional form $9^{\frac{3}{2}}$ and entered 9^3/2 into the calculator. Another group said since $\sqrt{9} = 3$ and 3^3 is 27, $(\sqrt{9})^3 = 27$. Neither group could figure out why the calculator gave a different answer. Try this on your calculator. Can your group explain what is wrong with what was entered into the calculator by the first group?

Unit 4

4. The following diagram shows graphs of $y = x^2$ and $y = \sqrt{x}$ in the viewing window $0 \le x \le 5$ and $0 \le y \le 5$.

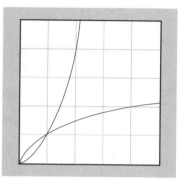

a. Match the graphs with the equations.

b. What are the coordinates of the point where the two graphs cross?

c. There is a geometric transformation that will map one graph onto the other. What type of transformation is it, and what coordinate rule matches points of one graph to the corresponding points of the other?

d. What does your answer to part c tell about the relation between the two relations of squaring and taking the square root?

e. Is there a similar relation between the graphs and equations of $y = x^3$ and $y = \sqrt[3]{x}$ or $y = x^{\frac{1}{3}}$? Give tables, graphs, and reasoning that support your conclusion.

MORE *continued*

4. **a.**

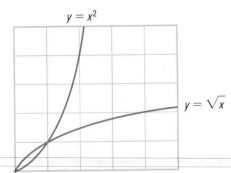

$y = x^2$

$y = \sqrt{x}$

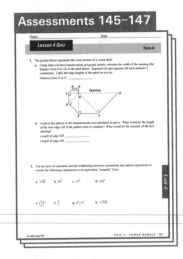
b. (1, 1)

c. The transformation is a reflection. The coordinate rule is $(x, y) \rightarrow (y, x)$.

d. They are opposite or inverse relations.

e. Yes, the curves are reflections of each other across the line $y = x$, and if (x, y) is a point on one curve, then (y, x) is on the other curve. It seems logical that cubing something and taking the cube root of something are opposite or inverse operations in the same way that addition and subtraction, and multiplication and division are opposite or inverse operations.

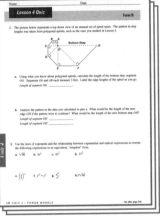
x	$\sqrt[3]{x}$	x^3
1	1	1
2	$\sqrt[3]{2}$	8
3	$\sqrt[3]{3}$	27
4	$\sqrt[3]{4}$	64
8	2	512
27	3	19,683
64	4	262,144

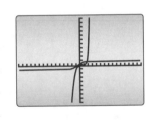

See Assessment Resources pages 145–150.

Unit 4

Lesson 5 *Looking Back*

1. A 5 m/sec change in velocity will influence damage more than a 5 kg change in weight. This should become evident from the work done in this activity.

   a. ■ $KE = 32M$

   ■ *KE* increases at a constant rate of 32 Joules per kilogram.

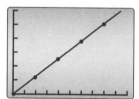

   ```
   WINDOW FORMAT
   Xmin = 0
   Xmax = 1000
   Xscl = 100
   Ymin = 0
   Ymax = 30000
   Yscl = 5000
   ```

Looking Back

In this unit you've learned about several new kinds of algebraic models for relations between variables—power models with direct variation rules like $y = ax^n$, inverse variation power models with rules like $y = \frac{a}{x^n}$, and quadratic models with rules like $y = ax^2 + bx + c$. See how well you can apply what you've learned to the following problems.

1. Carpenters hit nails with hammers; soccer players move the ball with their feet; musicians hit drums with sticks and their hands; speeding cars spin out of control and hit light poles or other cars. Collisions of many kinds occur frequently in everyday life—some are useful and others cause trouble.

   When a moving object collides with a stationary object, the desired work or undesirable damage is caused by a transfer of energy. Principles of physics say that the *kinetic energy* (*KE*) involved is a function of the mass *M* and velocity *v* of the object in motion. Those variables are related by an equation in the form $KE = \frac{1}{2} Mv^2$, where *KE* is measured in joules, *M* is measured in kilograms, and *v* is measured in meters per second. For example, if a car with mass 1000 kilograms and moving at a velocity of 8 meters per second hits a parked car, the collision packs energy of 32,000 joules. Which do you think would influence damage more: if the car were 5 kg lighter, or if it were moving 5 m/sec slower?

   a. Study the pattern of kinetic energy of cars with different masses—all moving at a velocity of 8 meters per second (about 18 miles per hour).

   - What rule can be used to calculate the energy for any mass *M*?

   - How does kinetic energy change as mass increases?

b. Study the pattern of kinetic energy in a car with mass of 1000 kilograms as it moves at different speeds.

- What rule can be used to calculate the energy for any velocity v?
- How does kinetic energy change as velocity increases?

c. Based on your responses to parts a and b, how would you answer the following questions? In each case, explain how the patterns that justify your answers are shown in tables or graphs of the relations between kinetic energy, mass, and velocity.

- If you want to put more power in your soccer kick, would you increase the mass of your cleats by 25% (and lose 25% of your foot speed) or decrease your cleat mass by 25% (and increase your foot speed by 25%)?
- If you want to get more power into the swings of a baseball bat, would you increase the mass of the bat by 20% (and decrease your bat speed by 20%) or decrease the mass of the bat by 20% (and increase bat speed by 20%)?
- If you want to decrease damage in automobile accidents, which change would have the greater effect: decreasing average mass of cars by 10% or decreasing average speed by 10%?

d. How are differences in the patterns of change in linear and power models related to your answers to the questions in part c?

2. In parts of Florida, the weather is always warm. One city's plans for a new high school building include an additional dining area, outdoors. Tables and benches will be placed on two large patios—one is a square measuring 24 feet on each side, the other is an equilateral triangle measuring 36 feet on each edge.

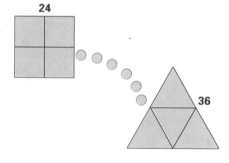

The school art classes are planning designs for those patios. They've agreed that the square should be covered with identical square tiles and the triangle should be covered with identical equilateral triangle tiles.

a. Sketch the tile patterns that would be produced in the following cases:

- The square patio is covered with square tiles measuring 6 feet on each side.
- The triangular patio is covered with triangles measuring 12 feet on a side.

1. b. ■ $KE = 500v^2$

■ *KE* increases rapidly as velocity increases at a steady rate. *KE* increases at an increasing rate.

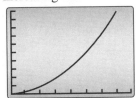

WINDOW FORMAT
Xmin =0
Xmax =16
Xscl =2
Ymin =0
Ymax =100000
Yscl =10000

c. Displayed at the left below is a sample table showing linear change when velocity is constant. Displayed at the right is a sample table when mass is constant.

Mass	$KE = 32M$	Velocity	$KE = 500v^2$
600	19200	2	2000
700	22400	4	8000
800	25600	5	12500
900	28800	8	32000
1000	32000	12	72000
		14	98000

■ Increasing speed and decreasing weight, each by 25%, will cause a 17% increase (multiply by $1.25^2 \times 0.75$) in kinetic energy. Decreasing speed and increasing weight will cause a 30% decrease (multiply by 1.25×0.75^2). You should wear the lighter cleat.

■ If you can use a bat 20% lighter and get 20% more speed into your swing, you will multiply kinetic energy by $1.2^2 \times 0.8$ for an increase of 15%. The heavier bat will decrease kinetic energy by 23%.

■ Decreasing the average speed by 10% will have a greater effect than decreasing the average mass by 10%.

d. The answers all indicate that increasing the velocity will cause the kinetic energy to change more rapidly than the same proportional increase of the mass. By comparing the graphs you can see that the relationship between the mass and kinetic energy is linear, while the relationship between the velocity and kinetic energy is a power model. Linear models increase at a constant rate, while power models increase at an increasing rate.

2. a.

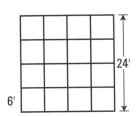

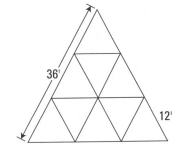

Unit 4

2. b. Most tables students have used had increasing x values. These tables have the first column decreasing in value. In this case, there is a maximum possible edge length but no minimum, thus the decreasing values.

Edge Length in Feet	Number of Tiles Needed	Edge Length in Feet	Number of Tiles Needed
24	1	36	1
12	4	18	4
8	9	12	9
6	16	9	16
4	36	6	36
3	64	4	81
2	144	3	144
1	576	2	324
0.5	2304	1	1296

c. **Square Data**   **Triangle Data**

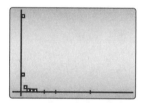 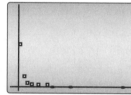 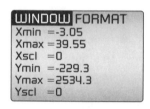

The graphs are of similar shape, however as size of each tile increased the number of tiles needed for the square decreased more rapidly.

d. ■ Inverse power model

■ Inverse power model

e. Square: $y = \frac{576}{x^2}$ Triangle: $y = \frac{1296}{x^2}$

f. Students should realize that you cannot simply use the equation without thinking about the situation.

■ 25

■ You would need to cut 8 of the tiles down to 4×5 and make one of the tiles 4×4.

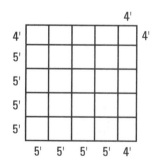

Unit 4

b. Make two tables showing the number of tiles that would be needed to cover each patio as a function of the size of each tile.

Square Patio

Edge Length (in feet)	Number of Tiles Needed
24	
12	
8	
6	
4	
3	
2	
1	
0.5	

Equilateral Triangle Patio

Edge Length (in feet)	Number of Tiles Needed
36	
18	
12	
9	
6	
4	
3	
2	
1	

c. Make scatterplots for the data in the two tables and compare the patterns you see in those plots.

d. What type of algebraic model is suggested for the relation between edge length and number of tiles in the case

- of the square patio?
- of the equilateral triangle patio?

e. Use your calculator or computer software to find models of the types you think will be good fits to the data patterns.

f. Suppose the tile company supplied square tiles that were 5 feet on each side.

- How many of those tiles would cover the square patio?
- What cutting of tiles would be needed and why?

3. One important feature of any engine is its fuel economy. For cars, this is usually measured in miles per gallon (mpg) of gasoline. The scatterplot on the next page shows typical results from tests of the relation between fuel economy and speed of cars. In such a test, the car is driven at some constant speed for a period of time, and fuel use is measured very accurately to get a miles-per-gallon reading at that speed. Then the experiment is repeated for other speeds.

Unit 4

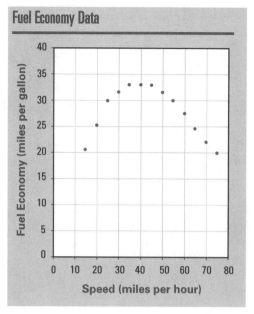

Fuel Economy Data

Source: US Dept of Transportation, Federal Highway Administration, *Fuel Consumption and Emission Values for Traffic Models*, Washington DC, May 1985.

a. What pattern relating driving speed and fuel economy (in mpg) is shown in the scatterplot?

b. Which of the following types of algebraic models would be likely to give a good fit for the pattern of (*speed, mpg*) data? For each possible choice, explain why it would or would not be reasonable.

- Linear
- Exponential
- Direct Power
- Inverse power
- Quadratic

c. Use your graphing calculator or computer software to find a model that fits the data pairs. Compare a table of (*speed, mpg*) data for that model to the actual data.

d. Write two questions that would be reasonable to ask about driving speed and fuel economy for the particular car tested. Explain how you would use your model to help answer them.

e. Fuel economy is influenced by factors other than just speed. List at least two factors that you think might be significant.

f. Try using your calculator or computer software to see what you get when you ask for model rules of types other than what you think is most reasonable. Compare the graphs of those models to the pattern in the data.

3. **a.** As speed increases up to 35 or 40 miles per hour, fuel economy in miles per gallon increases but at a decreasing rate; when speed increases from 40 to 45 miles per hour, fuel economy decreases fairly steadily.

b. The shape of the data is not that of a line, so the pattern isn't linear. It does not have a horizontal asymptote like the exponential models. The curve seems to increase and then decrease unlike the inverse power models. The power model of the form $y = x^2$ seems a likely choice because the curve is nearly parabolic. But because the vertex is on a line other than the y-axis, the most promising model from among those the students have studied so far, is the more general quadratic $y = ax^2 + bx + c$.

c. The numerical results here come from the source data as indicated in this table. The values in L_2 are the actual data from the graph, and the values in L_3 were produced by the rule. You can see that they are fairly close.

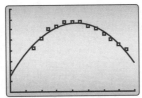

L1	L2	L3	1
15	21.1	22.399	
20	25.5	25.979	
25	30	28.846	
30	31.8	30.998	
35	33.6	32.437	
40	33.6	33.162	
45	33.5	33.173	

L1(1) = 15

L1	L2	L3	1
50	31.9	32.471	
55	30.3	31.055	
60	27.6	28.925	
65	24.9	26.081	
70	22.5	22.523	
75	20	18.252	
	-----	-----	

L1(14) =

QuadReg
y=ax²+bx+c
a=-.0142757243
b=1.215694306
c=7.375524476

d. Responses will vary. Some samples are:

What speed gives the best gas mileage?

What speed gives 0 miles per gallon? Does it make sense?

If you are running out of gas in a speed limit zone of 35 miles per hour, what speed would you drive?

e. Responses may vary. Some examples are:

Weight of the car

Engine efficiency

Construction of the car or the aerodynamics of the car

Direction and speed of the wind

Type of terrain

f. The linear, power, and exponential models do not seem to fit the pattern in the data. The cubic regression does seem to fit the data well for the values on the graph.

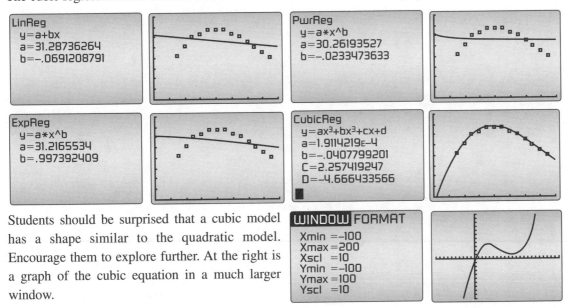

LinReg
y=a+bx
a=31.28736264
b=-.0691208791

PwrReg
y=a*x^b
a=30.26193527
b=-.0233473633

ExpReg
y=a*x^b
a=31.2165534
b=.997392409

CubicReg
y=ax³+bx³+cx+d
a=1.9114219ᴇ-4
b=-.0407799201
C=2.257419247
D=-4.666433566

Students should be surprised that a cubic model has a shape similar to the quadratic model. Encourage them to explore further. At the right is a graph of the cubic equation in a much larger window.

WINDOW FORMAT
Xmin =-100
Xmax =200
Xscl =10
Ymin =-100
Ymax =100
Yscl =10

Unit 4

4. **a.** ■ $23 = -0.014s^2 + 1.22s + 7.38$

     At approximately 16 and 71 miles per hour, fuel usage is 23 miles per gallon.

     ■ $36 = -0.014s^2 + 1.22s + 7.38$

     The car never got 36 miles per gallon.

     ■ $mpg = -0.014(48)^2 + 1.22(48) + 7.38$

     At 48 miles per hour the fuel usage is approximately 34 miles per gallon.

     ■ $20 \le -0.014s^2 + 1.22s + 7.38$

     Between 12 miles per hour and 75 miles per hour fuel usage will be 20 miles per gallon or more.

     Students may find these values using the table of values or the graph along with the trace and zoom functions.

   b. ■ Speeds of approximately 8 miles per hour and 78 miles per hour produce fuel usage of about 17 miles per gallon.

     ■ There is no root for this equation. This means that the car will never get 35 miles per gallon.

     ■ A speed of approximately 92 miles per hour will produce fuel usage of about 0 miles per gallon. **Note:** This may be a good time to discuss limitations of models. According to this model, a speed of 0 mph will produce 7.38 miles per gallon.

     ■ The car will get about 10 miles per gallon when it travels at approximately 2 miles per hour or 85 miles per hour.

   c. The maximum miles per gallon is approximately 34 miles per gallon. This is obtained when traveling at a speed of 44 miles per hour.

Unit 4

4. When one group of students studied the fuel economy data from activity 3, they came up with the quadratic model $mpg = -0.014s^2 + 1.22s - 7.38$, where s stands for speed in miles per hour.

a. Use the given model to answer each of the following questions about the relation between driving speed and fuel economy. In each case, write the equation or inequality that can be used to answer the question, and explain how you found the solution.

- At what average speeds will the tested car get 23 miles per gallon?
- At what average speeds will the tested car get 36 miles per gallon?
- How many miles per gallon will the tested car get at an average speed of 48 miles per hour?
- For what average speeds will the tested car get at least 20 miles per gallon?

b. Solve each of the following equations, which use the students' quadratic model, and explain what the solution tells about fuel economy for the tested car. In each case, explain how you found the solution and then describe another method that could have been used.

i. $17 = -0.014s^2 + 1.22s + 7.38$

ii. $-0.014s^2 + 1.22s + 7.38 = 35$

iii. $0 = -0.014s^2 + 1.22s + 7.38$

iv. $-0.014s^2 + 1.22s + 7.38 = 10$

c. Using the quadratic model $mpg = -0.014s^2 + 1.22s + 7.38$, estimate the maximum miles per gallon that can be expected for the tested car and the corresponding speed.

5. The connections between mathematics and science are well-known. But there are also many important mathematical patterns in art and music. For example, the sounds made by vibrating strings of instruments like the violin and the guitar are related to the lengths of the strings being bowed or plucked. A guitarist or violinist can make many different notes on a single string by pressing the string against the neck of the instrument. Shortening the active length of the string changes the rate of vibration and the pitch of that string.

The chart below shows data on the E-string of a violin. If you shorten the active length to the fractions of full length listed in the table, the corresponding vibration rates of the string will be as shown.

Strings on a cello such as this one are played in the same way as on a violin.

Length and Vibration Rate of a Violin String

Note	Active Length of String	Vibrations per Second
E	$\frac{1}{2}$	659.3
D$^\sharp$	$\frac{8}{15}$	622.3
C$^\sharp$	$\frac{3}{5}$	554.4
B	$\frac{2}{3}$	493.9
A	$\frac{3}{4}$	440.0
G$^\sharp$	$\frac{4}{5}$	415.3
F$^\sharp$	$\frac{8}{9}$	370.0
E	1	329.6

a. Make a scatterplot of the (*length*, *vibrations*) data and describe the pattern in that plot. Include in your description some conjectures about the type of model that will fit the data.

b. Use your calculator or computer software to find a model that fits the data well.

c. How does the context of this situation help you decide on the best model?

6. One of the more beautiful designs in nature is the shell of the chambered nautilus, a sea creature that lives in the South Pacific. As the nautilus grows, it builds and moves through a spiral sequence of chambers increasing in size. The spiral to the right is similar to the chambered nautilus shell. Each outside segment is about 1 centimeter long. The individual "chambers" are right triangles.

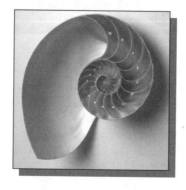

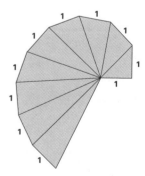

5 **a.** As x increases, y decreases (approaching 0). This pattern suggests an inverse power model or an exponential model with base less than 1.

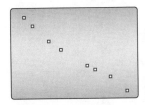

```
WINDOW FORMAT
Xmin =.45
Xmax =1.05
Xscl =0
Ymin =288
Ymax =672
Yscl =0
```

b.
```
PwrReg
y=a*x^b
a=329.7782067
b=-1.006265596
```

Inverse power model: $y = \dfrac{330}{x}$

```
ExpReg
y=a*b^x
a=1292.485614
b=0.2462467449
```

Exponential model: $y = 1292(0.25)^x$

c. The power model seems best because a string length of zero should not have a large number of vibrations per second. The exponential model implies that a string of length zero will vibrate at 1292 vibrations per second. This clearly does not make sense.

Unit 4

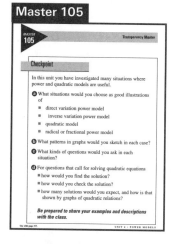

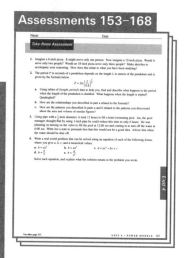

6. a.

Chamber Number	Outside Leg Length	Inside Leg Length	Hypotenuse	Hypotenuse in Simplest Radical Form
1	1	1	$\sqrt{2}$	$\sqrt{2}$
2	1	$\sqrt{2}$	$\sqrt{5}$	$\sqrt{5}$
3	1	$\sqrt{5}$	$\sqrt{6}$	$\sqrt{6}$
4	1	$\sqrt{6}$	$\sqrt{7}$	$\sqrt{7}$
5	1	$\sqrt{7}$	$\sqrt{8}$	$2\sqrt{2}$
6	1	$\sqrt{8}$	$\sqrt{9}$	3
7	1	$\sqrt{9}$	$\sqrt{10}$	$\sqrt{10}$
8	1	$\sqrt{10}$	$\sqrt{11}$	$\sqrt{11}$
9	1	$\sqrt{11}$	$\sqrt{12}$	$2\sqrt{3}$

b. The length of the hypotenuse will be $\sqrt{n+3}$ for $n > 1$.

SHARE AND SUMMARIZE   full-class discussion

Checkpoint

See Teaching Master 105.

Responses may vary based on student illustrations. Examples are given.

ⓐ ■ (*edge length*, *volume*) of a cube or (*edge length*, *area*) of a face of a cube

■ Time as a function of rate for a trip of given length, intensity of light or sound as a function of distance from the source, gravitational force between two objects as a function of the distance between the two objects, number of vibrations per time period as a function of the length of the string

■ Height of a ball as a function of its time in flight, profit as a function of ticket price, stopping distance as a function of speed, miles per gallon as a function of speed

■ Length of the diagonals of a rectangle or rectangular solid as a function of its dimensions

ⓑ ■ Passes through the origin, for even powers the end behavior is in the same direction and the curve is symmetric to the *y*-axis, for odd powers end behavior is in opposite directions and the curve is symmetric about the origin

■ Does not cross the axes, *x*- and *y*-axes are asymptotes, has two branches, even powers are symmetrical to the *y*-axis, odd powers are symmetrical about the origin and across the lines $y = \pm x$

■ Has a minimum or maximum value, is symmetrical about a vertical line, and the rate of change is not constant

■ Contains the origin, has nonconstant rate of change

See additional Teaching Notes on page T317Y.

a. Make a table showing the pattern of lengths for the segments dividing "chambers" of the "shell". Add a column showing those results in simplest radical form as well.

b. What is the length of the hypotenuse in the nth "chamber"?

Checkpoint

In this unit you have investigated many situations where power and quadratic models are useful.

a What situations would you choose as good illustrations of the following?

- A direct variation power model
- An inverse variation power model
- A quadratic model
- A radical or fractional power model

b What patterns in graphs would you sketch in each case?

c What kinds of questions would you ask in each situation?

d For questions that call for solving quadratic equations,

- how would you find the solution?
- how would you check the solution?
- how many solutions would you expect, and how is that shown by graphs of quadratic relations?

Be prepared to share your examples and descriptions with the class.

Unit 4

Looking Back, Looking Ahead

▶Reflecting on Mathematical Content

One of the most important roles of mathematical reasoning is describing and predicting patterns of change in quantitative variables. The concept of function is the unifying thread for finding and exploiting such patterns, and the symbols and operations of algebra are powerful tools for representing and reasoning about functions. After the Course 1 introductory exploration of variables and relations and their representation with tables, graphs, words, and symbols, the algebra and functions strand of the *Contemporary Mathematics in Context* curriculum has focused on three broad but very common families of functions: linear, exponential, and now power models.

The underlying goal of the study of these function families and their algebraic representations and manipulations is to help students develop the ability to recognize important patterns of variations and to use the tools of algebra to represent and reason about those patterns. In this unit on power models, students have analyzed patterns illustrating direct and inverse variation relationships that can be modeled by rules of the form $y = ax^b$. When b is 2, 3, or 4, the resulting relationships are familiar quadratic, cubic, and quartic functions. When b is a negative integer, the resulting relationships are basic forms of inverse variation. When b is the fraction $\frac{1}{2}$ or $\frac{1}{3}$, the models are the square root and cube root functions. Later in the "Geometric Form and Its Function" unit, students are introduced to basic trigonometric (circular) functions in the context of acute angles of triangular models and of circular motion.

With basic linear, exponential, power, and circular variation patterns available, more complex models can be constructed to match other situations. The present unit included one familiar example of such a combination, the general quadratic polynomial $y = ax^2 + bx + c$, which is a sum of basic power and linear models.

In Course 3, students will revisit and extend their understanding of various function families with special attention to connections among their symbolic, tabular, and graphical forms. They also will extend their repertoire of modeling techniques in several ways. First, they will look at situations in which more than two variables are related in combined variation relationships like the familiar formulas for area and volume of solid figures, simple and compound interest, or scientific concepts like pressure-volume-temperature dependence. Second, they will learn how to model systems of linear equations and inequalities with several variables, including use of linear programming. Third, they will study the algebra of polynomials, focusing on rules for algebraic transformations like factoring, expanding, and simplifying expressions that arise in modeling multi-variable situations. Fourth, they will learn how to combine basic function types to build models for situations that have aspects of exponential or power variation but somewhat different symmetries or limits. For example, they'll use the basic exponential decay model to construct models for heating or cooling of solids and liquids or for speed of a skydiver approaching terminal velocity.

In Course 3, students will continue to develop their ability to find algebraic models for data patterns and variation conditions and to interpret given algebraic expressions. They will use increasingly formal reasoning about algebraic forms to derive new insights into given relationships. Course 3 includes more of the formal symbolic work that traditionally has been part of school algebra programs. In this curriculum, students will come to that work with strong symbol sense about patterns of variation and representation, and this background will provide a sound foundation for the powerful but abstract symbolic reasoning that is an important goal of mathematical development.

▶Reflecting on Instruction

If your experience teaching *Contemporary Mathematics in Context* Course 2 is similar to that of teachers who have tested this curriculum, you will probably have observed (with amazement) the amount of mathematics that your students have retained from Course 1. Many features of the curriculum as well as the mode of instruction have contributed to this retention. By concentrating on important mathematical concepts, developing concepts across units, and connecting ideas throughout the strands, students develop rich mathematical understandings which they can apply to new problem situations.

Students who consistently discuss their ideas, investigate multiple ways of approaching problems, raise extenuating questions, and summarize their mathematical learning do seem to retain more. As your students mature physically and mathematically, they will be able to take on additional responsibility for their own learning. You may wish to use the Habits of Mind transparency (from the final checkpoint of Course 1) with your students, to help them understand how far they have come in developing good thinking skills and how you plan to continue helping them develop these Habits of Mind as they study mathematics.

Unit 4 Assessment

Lesson Quizzes	Assessment Resources
Lesson 1 *Same Shape, Different Size*	pp. 127–132
Lesson 2 *Inverse Variation*	pp. 133–138
Lesson 3 *Quadratic Models*	pp. 139–144
Lesson 4 *Radicals and Fractional Power Models*	pp. 145–150
In-Class Exams	
Form A	pp. 151–156
Form B	pp. 157–162
Take-Home Assessment	pp. 163–164
Unit 4 Projects	
The Quadratic Formula	pp. 165–166
Applying Algebraic Models	pp. 167–168

Teaching Notes continued

Notes continued
from page T234

LAUNCH full-class discussion

Think About This Situation

See Teaching Master 81.

It is likely that students will have some ideas from studying similarity in Unit 2, "Patterns of Location, Shape, and Size", that will allow them to deduce answers to the questions about proportional growth. However, some students still may say that the same linear proportionality will apply to areas and volumes since this seems to be a misconception that is difficult for some people to overcome. In the class discussion of the questions, try to solicit all student hunches without indicating the correctness, incorrectness, or incompleteness of ideas. If some students have the correct guess, try not to make a positive or negative comment, since any reaction may discourage or sway other students. Leave the discussion with the challenge to figure out the correct answers as they move ahead in the investigations of this unit. You might make a note of all the comments and guesses so you can return to them as the lesson develops and ideas become clearer.

a The natural and correct guess is 40 feet.

b The natural and correct guess is 30 feet.

c One natural guess is $6 \cdot 20$ or 120 square feet. However, students have observed that area grows as the square of the scale factor in a similarity transformation. The correct answer is 2400 square feet.

d Again, one guess might be $20 \cdot 2.5$ or 50 cubic feet. If students recall their work in Lesson 1 of Unit 2, "Patterns in Location, Shape, and Size", they will know that volume grows as the cube of the scale factor in similarity. The correct answer is 20,000 cubic feet.

e Students may suggest that all the results will be half the responses of parts a–d, or ten times the corresponding measures of the scale model. The correct responses are:

a. The figurine would be 10 times as tall as the scale model or 20 feet.

b. The belt would be 10 times as long as the belt on the scale model or 15 feet.

c. The surface area would be 100 times the surface area of the scale model or 600 square feet.

d. The volume would be 1000 times the volume of the scale model or 2500 cubic feet.

The generalizations are that lengths are multiplied by the scale factor, areas by the square of the scale factor, and volumes by the cube of the scale factor.

Teaching Notes *continued*

Notes continued
from page T235

Many students will not see a multiplication pattern connecting change in length and change in area; that is, they may not see that as the length is increased by a factor of two, the area is increased by a factor of four. They are much more likely to concentrate on change in perimeter in isolation, and say that the perimeter is growing by adding 4 each time (or that the area grows by adding an odd number every time). They also may calculate the perimeter or area correctly, without seeing a pattern. You can help them to connect the patterns of change by asking, "If the length grows by a scale factor of 2 or 20, what happens to the perimeter? To the area?" (Recall that students used the term scale factor in Unit 2.)

If students have thought hard about change in Experiment 1 they will be primed to ask themselves similar questions in Experiment 2. However, the misconception that if length doubles then area and volume also double is hard to overcome. If students present their answers for activity 4 of Experiment 1 and activity 3 of Experiment 2, and they have time to argue about the conclusions, they will be more successful in the "Checkpoint" on page 237.

1.

Edge Length (in units)	Perimeter of One Face (in units)	Area of One Face (in square units)	Total Surface Area of Cube (in square units)
1	4	1	6
2	8	4	24
3	12	9	54
4	16	16	96
5	20	25	150
6	24	36	216
7	28	49	294
8	32	64	384

Experiment 2

Notes continued
from page T236

1.

Edge Length (in units)	Volume of Cube (in cubic units)
1	1
2	8
3	27
4	64
5	125
6	216
7	343
8	512

Unit 4

**Notes continued
from page T237**

ⓐ Patterns Relating Edge Length to Other Measurements

Measurement	Patterns in Table	Patterns in Graph	Symbolic Rule
Perimeter of a Face	As the edge length increases, the perimeter increases at a constant rate.	The graph is a straight line.	$P = 4E$
Area of a Face	As the edge length increases, the area of the face increases at an increasing rate.	The graph curves upward.	$A = E^2$
Surface Area	As the edge length increases, the total surface area increases at 6 times the rate of increase of the area of a face.	The graph curves upward.	$SA = 6E^2$
Volume	As the edge length increases, the volume increases (more rapidly than area does).	The graph curves upward very quickly.	$V = E^3$

ⓑ These patterns suggest that lengths like waist size will increase by the constant scale factor, that areas like the surface of the skin will increase as the square of the scale factor, and that the volume will increase as the cube of the scale factor.

Students may find it hard to articulate their answers. They are likely to revert to the balloon example or the cubes: "If the height of the balloon grows by a factor of 2 (or 10 or 20), then the area grows by a factor of 4 (or 100 or 400)." At this point, however, they should try to generalize their answers.

Teaching Notes *continued*

Notes continued from page T238

After students complete Experiments 1 or 2 on page 239 in the student text, you may wish to use the teaching masters "Describing Graphs I" (Master 84) and "Describing Graphs II" (Master 85) to help develop a common class vocabulary for describing graphs.

- Have students work in pairs or groups to list as many words or phrases as they can to describe the patterns they see in the graphs on the handouts.
- Lead a discussion allowing the students to react to each other's words and come up with a class list. It is important to ask questions that lead students to include important items if students have overlooked them. Words and expressions such as *asymptote* and *positive infinity* are not included in the student text but would be very appropriate for many students.

The following sample questions will help students think about characteristics that they might not have considered. Use the questions only as needed, after the pairs and groups have shared their words and phrases.

Are the values of y increasing or decreasing as the values of x increase?

Is a maximum (or minimum) value shown?

Does the graph seem to be defined for all values of x?

What is the shape of the graph?

Why do you get only negative values for y on one graph, but both positive and negative values for y on the other graph? (This question applies to "Describing Graphs I". An analogous question for "Describing Graphs II" could point out only positive values on one graph.)

What is the rate of change? Is it constant? Increasing? Decreasing?

Which graph is changing faster? Why is this?

Are there x-intercepts?

Are there y-intercepts?

As x becomes very, very large (or small), what happens to y?

Does the graph pass through the origin?

Does the graph exhibit any symmetry? Over a line? Over the y-axis? About a point?

Does the graph open upward or open downward?

It would be helpful to display the class-generated descriptions in the classroom, or provide a copy of the class-generated descriptions for the students to keep in their notebooks and refer to when they are asked to describe graphs.

You may wish to repeat this activity after Experiment 2 of Lesson 2, Investigation 3 (page 257) using the teaching master "Describing Graphs III" (Master 91).

Unit 4

Teaching Notes *continued*

Notes continued
from page T239

Experiment 2

1. In the relation $y = x^3$, y increases at a decreasing rate as x increases from -10 to 0. Then y begins increasing at an increasing rate as x increases from 0 to 10. This pattern can be seen in the graph by noticing that as x increases from -10 to 10, the graph rises rapidly, flattens out near $x = 0$, and then curves upward more and more steeply for greater positive values of x.

x	−10	−8	−6	−4	−2	0	2	4	6	8	10
y	−1000	−512	−216	−64	−8	0	8	64	216	512	1000

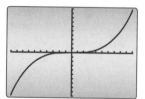

```
WINDOW FORMAT
Xmin =−10
Xmax =10
Xscl =1
Ymin =−1000
Ymax =1000
Yscl =100
```

2. **Using a standard window and integer table values, students will not see what happens between 0 and 1. You may want to suggest they zoom in on that area until they can see which graph is above the other.**

The tables and graphs are similar in that both graphs curve upward quickly for positive values of x. They are different in several ways. For values of x between 0 and 1, $x^2 > x^3$, while for values of $x > 1$, $x^3 > x^2$. Also, for negative values of x, the values for x^2 are positive and decreasing as x increases, while the values for x^3 are negative but increasing as x increases. Any number squared is positive, while negative numbers raised to an odd power will be negative.

Page T239 Teaching Notes continued on next page

Teaching Notes continued

> Notes continued
> from page T239

Sample descriptions

Graph	Words or Phrases that Describe Patterns
$y = a + bx$	Line
	Linear model
	Constant rate of change
	The x-intercept is positive.
	The y-intercept is negative.
	As x becomes very large, y becomes very large.
	As x becomes very small, y becomes very small.
	Defined for all x
	Reflection symmetry over any line perpendicular to the line
	End behavior: the graph goes down on the left and up on the right.
$y = ax^2, a < 0$	Passes through the orgin
	Maximum y value of 0
	For $x > 0$, as x increases, y decreases.
	For $x < 0$, as x decreases, y decreases.
	$y \leq 0$
	Symmetric about the y-axis.
	Rate of change is not constant.
	Defined for all x
	End behavior: the graph goes down on both ends.

3.

x	x^3	$3x$	3^x
-10	-1000	-30	0.00002
-8	-512	-24	0.00015
-6	-216	-18	0.00137
-4	-64	-12	0.01235
-2	-8	-6	0.11111
0	0	0	1
2	8	6	9
4	64	12	81
6	216	18	729
8	512	24	6561
10	1000	30	59049

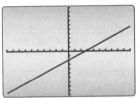

```
WINDOW FORMAT
Xmin =-10
Xmax=10
Xscl =1
Ymin =-1000
Ymax=1000
Yscl =100
```

In the first quadrant, $y = x^3$ increases at an increasing rate and in the third quadrant $y = x^3$ increases at a decreasing rate. The graph of $y = 3x$ is a straight line. The values in its table show a constant rate of increase. The graph of $y = 3^x$ is very similar to $y = x^3$ in the first quadrant, but $y = 3^x$ is never negative and its values approach 0 when x is negative and decreasing. You also can see in the table and graphs that in the first quadrant $y = 3^x$ grows much faster than $y = x^3$, which grows much faster than $y = 3x$ (for $x > 1$).

Unit 4

Teaching Notes continued

Notes continued from page T239

Sample descriptions

Graph	Words or Phrases that Describe Patterns
$y = a(b)^x$, $a > 0$ and $b > 0$	$y > 0$ The y-intercept is positive For $x > 0$, as x becomes very large, y gets closer to 0. For $x < 0$, as x becomes very large, y becomes very large. Rate of change is not constant. Exponential Defined for all x The graph opens upward. No symmetry End behavior: the graph goes up on the left and approaches the x-axis on the right.
$y = ax^3$	Passes through the orgin Rotational symmetry around the origin As x becomes large in absolute value, y also becomes very large in absolute value. Defined for all x Rate of change is not constant. The graph opens downward for $x < 0$. The graph opens upward for $x > 0$. End behavior: the graph goes down on the left and up on the right.

Experiment 3

1. **a.** The surface area is $6x^2$ square feet because each face has an area of x^2 square feet. There are six faces, so the total surface area is $6x^2$ square feet.
   b. The volume of the cube is x^3 cubic feet. Each cubic foot of water weighs 62.4 pounds, so the weight of the filled container is 62.4 pounds per cubic foot times x^3 cubic feet or $62.4x^3$ pounds more than the empty container.

Teaching Notes *continued*

Notes continued
from page T240

The windows for the following graphs are $-3 \le x \le 3$ and $-10 \le y \le 10$.

$y = 2x^3$ 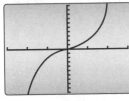

$y = 3x^3$ 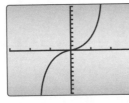

$y = 5x^3$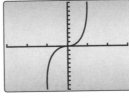

$y = \frac{1}{2}x^3$ 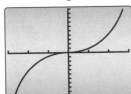

$y = -1x^3$ 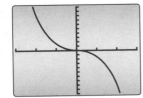

$y = -2x^3$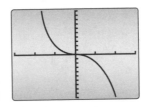

Experiment 4

The greater $|a|$ is, the more sharply the curve rises and falls. For $a > 0$, the curve is in quadrants I and III and for $a < 0$, the curve is in quadrants II and IV. Notice in the table that if $a > 0$, then the value of the function is positive for $x > 0$ and negative for $x < 0$. In contrast, if $a < 0$, the value of the function is negative for $x > 0$ and positive for $x < 0$. The graphs are all symmetric about the origin and all pass through the point $(0, 0)$.

1. a. The patterns in the tables and graphs of $y = x^4$ and $y = x^6$ are similar to the patterns for $y = x^2$. The patterns in the tables and graphs of $y = x^5$ and $y = x^7$ are similar to the patterns for $y = x^3$. For $|x| > 1$, the higher the power, the more rapidly the values of y will rise and fall as x changes. For $|x| < 1$, higher powers lead to values of $|y|$ closer to 0; for example, $0.5^3 > 0.5^4$. This appears in the flatter shapes of the graphs for higher powers when x is between -1 and 1.

x	$y = x^4$	$y = x^5$	$y = x^6$	$y = x^7$
2	16	32	64	128
1	1	1	1	1
$\frac{1}{2}$	0.0625	0.03125	0.015625	0.0078125
0	0	0	0	0
$-\frac{1}{2}$	0.0625	-0.03125	0.015625	-0.0078125
-1	1	-1	1	-1
-2	16	-32	64	-128

Page T240 Teaching Notes continued on next page

Unit 4

Teaching Notes *continued*

| Notes continued
from page T240 |

The windows for the following graphs are $-3 \le x \le 3$ and $-10 \le y \le 10$.

$y = x^4$ $y = x^5$ $y = x^6$ $y = x^7$

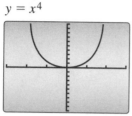 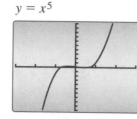 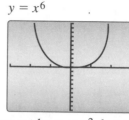 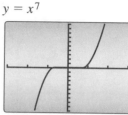

b. Even exponents follow the pattern set by $y = x^2$, but as the value of the exponent increases the curves generally fall and rise more rapidly (except for the interval between –1 and 1, where higher power graphs flatten out more). Odd exponents follow the same basic pattern as $y = x^3$, but as the value of the exponent increases, the curves generally rise more rapidly (again with the exception of the flattening between –1 and 1).

SHARE AND SUMMARIZE   full-class discussion

Checkpoint

See Teaching Master 86.

Before discussing these questions, it might be helpful to have students sketch on the board the curves from Experiment 3, activity 2.

ⓐ The graphs will all be U-shaped parabolas, symmetric about the y-axis.

For positive a, the graphs open upward. The tables of values will show a pattern of decreasing y values as x increases to 0 and increasing y values as x increases from 0. The minimum y value is 0, when $x = 0$.

For negative a, the graphs open downward. The tables show the opposite pattern to the one for positive a. The values of y increase to 0 and then decrease. The maximum y value is 0 when $x = 0$.

ⓑ For positive a, the graphs will open downward for negative x and open upward for positive x. The tables of values will show increasing values of y as x increases, but the rate of increase will not be constant.

For negative a, the graphs will open upward and be decreasing for $x < 0$. For $x > 0$, they will open downward but still be decreasing. The tables will show decreasing values of y as x increases, but the rate of decrease will not be constant.

ⓒ When n is a positive even integer, the patterns of change are similar to those for $y = x^2$ (described in part a).

When n is a positive odd integer, the patterns of change are similar to those for $y = x^3$ (described in part b).

ⓓ Power models do not have straight-line graphs or constant rates of change as do linear models. For even powers, power models are not monotone (only increasing or only decreasing patterns) as exponential models are. When $|x|$ is large, $|y|$ increases without bound in power models (but exponential models approach the y-axis in one direction or the other). We do not expect students to use this technical language to describe what they've observed, but rather to use some informal language for the same ideas.

Teaching Notes *continued*

> **Notes continued from page T244**

2.

x	2x³	x³	½x³	−2x³
−5	−250	−125	−62.5	250
−4.5	−182.25	−91.13	−45.56	182.25
−4	−128	−64	−32	128
−3.5	−85.75	−42.88	−21.44	85.75
−3	−54	−27	−13.5	54
−2.5	−31.25	−15.63	−7.81	31.25
−2	−16	−8	−4	16
−1.5	−6.75	−3.38	−1.69	6.75
−1	−2	−1	−0.5	2
−0.5	−0.25	−0.13	−0.06	0.25
0	0	0	0	0

x	2x³	x³	½x³	−2x³
0.5	0.25	0.13	0.06	−0.25
1	2	1	0.5	−2
1.5	6.75	3.38	1.69	−6.75
2	16	8	4	−16
2.5	31.25	15.63	7.81	−31.25
3	54	27	13.5	−54
3.5	85.75	42.88	21.44	−85.75
4	128	64	32	−128
4.5	182.25	91.13	45.56	−182.25
5	250	125	62.5	−250

a. These graphs have rotational symmetry around the origin. The symmetry can be seen in the table because the y value for x is the opposite of the y value for $-x$.

b. The values of ax^3 will be opposites for opposite values of x. This means that there is rotational symmetry around the origin. For any point (x, y), the point $(-x, -y)$ is also on the graph.

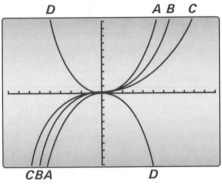

A. $y = 2x^3$ B. $y = x^3$

C. $y = \frac{1}{2}x^3$ D. $y = -2x^3$

3. a–b.

Rule	Graph	Description
$y = a + bx$		The shape of this graph is a straight line which intersects the y-axis at a and has constant slope b.
$y = a(b^x)$		The shape of this graph is a curve crossing the y-axis at a. Note that as x is negative and decreasing the value for y approaches 0.
$y = ax^2$		The shape of this graph is a U-shaped curve passing through the origin. The tails both go upward.
$y = ax^3$		The shape of this graph is a curve passing through the origin. The values for y increase as x increases. The tails go in opposite directions.

Page T244 Teaching Notes continued on next page

Notes continued
from page T244

c. Symmetries

$y = a + bx$	This line has symmetry about any line perpendicular to it.
$y = a(b^x)$	This line has no symmetry.
$y = ax^2$	The curve has symmetry about the y-axis.
$y = ax^3$	The curve has rotational symmetry about the origin.

d. Changing the Values of a and b

Rule	Effect of a	Effect of b
$y = a + bx$	No effect on rate of change.	In the table, each increase of 1 in x leads to a change of b in y. In the graph, b is the slope of the line.
$y = a(b^x)$	A larger a causes greater rate of change.	If x increases by 1, then y is multiplied by b. If $b > 1$, the graph of the model represents exponential growth. If $0 < b < 1$, the model represents exponential decay.
$y = ax^2$	The value of a multiplies the rate of change in tables of the basic $y = x^2$ by the factor a. In the graph, as $|a|$ increases, the curve generally falls and rises more quickly.	
$y = ax^3$	The value of a multiplies the rate of change in tables of the basic $y = x^3$ by the factor a.	

Teaching Notes *continued*

Notes continued
from page T250

LAUNCH   full-class discussion

Think About This Situation

See Teaching Master 87.

ⓐ The intensity of the earthquake diminishes as the distance from the epicenter increases. The rate of change is not constant. The intensity decreases quickly near the epicenter, but as you move farther away the intensity decreases more slowly.

ⓑ ■ A line, even one with negative slope, does not do well to fit the data.

■ An exponential model where a is large and $0 < b < 1$ gives a graph that resembles the pattern of data.

■ An inverse power model also resembles the pattern of data.

Notes continued
from page T252

APPLY   individual task

▶On Your Own

a. Airplane: $6\frac{2}{3}$ hours; car: 50 hours; bicycle: 200 hours

b. $t = \dfrac{3000}{s}$

c.

s	50	100	150	200	250	300	350	400	450	500
t	60	30	20	15	12	10	8.6	7.5	6.7	6

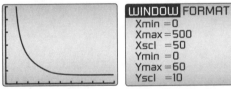

```
WINDOW FORMAT
Xmin =0
Xmax=500
Xscl =50
Ymin =0
Ymax=60
Yscl =10
```

d. An increase from 50 to 100 miles per hour changes the time the trip takes from 60 hours to 30 hours, a 30-hour decrease. An increase from 450 to 500 miles per hour reduces the time of the trip from 6.7 hours to 6 hours, a decrease of $\frac{2}{3}$ of an hour or only 40 minutes. The greater change occurs with an increase from 50 to 100 miles per hour.

Notes continued
from page T256

This previous experience should help students make sense of the negative exponents in inverse relationships. A discussion takes class time but is helpful in the long run.

You also may wish to have students use their calculators or computer software to make tables for several equations. For example, they could try $y_1 = \frac{2}{x}$ and $y_2 = 2x^{-1}$. Ask them to compare the tables, then they could try $y_3 = \frac{3}{x^2}$ and $y_4 = 3x^{-2}$ and again compare the tables.

Student descriptions for experiments should use the class vocabulary that they developed in Investigation 2 of Lesson 1. After they complete Experiment 2, you may wish to distribute the "Describing Graphs III" Activity Master (Master 91). After students have a chance to complete their descriptions with their groups, the whole class can discuss the results.

Unit 4

Notes continued from page T257

Experiment 2

1. Tables and graphs of the examples are shown below:

x	$y = \dfrac{2}{x}$	$y = \dfrac{3}{x}$	$y = \dfrac{0.5}{x}$	$y = -\dfrac{2}{x}$
-10	-0.2	-0.3	-0.05	0.2
-8	-0.25	-0.38	-0.06	0.25
-6	-0.33	-0.5	-0.08	0.33
-4	-0.5	-0.75	-0.13	0.5
-2	-1	-1.5	-0.25	1
0	not defined	not defined	not defined	not defined
2	1	1.5	0.25	-1
4	0.5	0.75	0.13	-0.5
6	0.33	0.5	0.08	-0.33
8	0.25	0.38	0.06	-0.25
10	0.2	0.3	0.05	-0.2

$y = \dfrac{2}{x}$

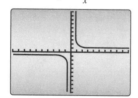

$y = \dfrac{3}{x}$

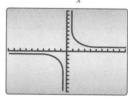

$y = \dfrac{0.5}{x}$

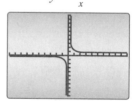

$y = \dfrac{-2}{x}$

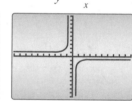

2. The tables and graphs are similar to $y = \frac{1}{x}$ because as x moves closer and closer to 0, the y values move further and further away from zero. All of these graphs approach the x-axis as x becomes very large or very small. All of the graphs approach the y-axis for x values near 0. The greater $|a|$ is, the further away from the origin the graph is. When a is positive the graph is in quadrants I and III, and when a is negative the graph is in quadrants II and IV.

3. For smaller values of a, the graph is closer to the origin and approaches the axes more quickly. For larger values of a, the opposite is true. When a is positive, the curve appears in quadrants I and III, and when a is negative, the curve appears in quadrants II and IV.

4. The fact that $\frac{a}{x}$ and $\frac{a}{-x}$ have the same absolute value for all x tells us that $y = \frac{a}{x}$ will have rotational symmetry about the origin as well as symmetry about the line $y = x$.

Page T257 Teaching Notes continued on next page

Unit 4

Teaching Notes *continued*

Sample Descriptions

Notes continued
from page T257

Graph	Words or Phrases that Describe Patterns
$y = \frac{a}{x}$, $a < 0$ (graph)	As x becomes very large or very small, y approaches 0. As x approaches 0 from the positive side, y becomes very small. As x approaches 0 from the negative side, y becomes very large. The curve has two branches. Reflection symmetry about the lines $y = \pm x$ Rotational symmetry about the origin Rate of change is not constant. The graph opens upwards for $x < 0$; opens downwards for $x > 0$; not defined $x = 0$ End behavior: the graph approaches the x-axis from above the x-axis on the left and below the x-axis on the right.
$y = \frac{a}{x^2}$, $a > 0$ (graph)	As x becomes very large, or very small, y approaches 0 As x approaches 0 from the positive or negative side, y becomes very large. The curve has two branches. $y > 0$ Reflection symmetry about the y-axis Rate of change is not constant. Opens upwards Defined for all $x \neq 0$ End behavior: the graph approaches the x-axis (from above the x-axis) on both ends.

Experiment 3

1.

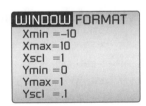
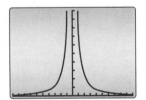

X	Y₁
-10	.01
-8	.01563
-6	.02778
-4	.0625
-2	.25
0	ERROR
2	.25

Y₁ ⊟ 1/X²

X	Y₁
4	.0625
6	.02778
8	.01563
10	.01
12	.00694
14	.0051
16	.00391

Y₁ ⊟ 1/X²

```
WINDOW FORMAT
Xmin =-10
Xmax=10
Xscl =1
Ymin =0
Ymax=1
Yscl =.1
```

a. The y values are all positive and they move closer to 0 as x moves away from 0.

b. The graph is symmetric about the y-axis.

Unit 4

> **Notes continued from page T258**

To focus students on the differences in symbolic forms for the linear, exponential, and power models which have variables that are inversely related, you might ask students to identify the type of model for each equation below.

$$y = 10 - x \qquad y = \frac{10}{x} \qquad y = \frac{x}{10} \qquad y = -10x$$

$$y = 10 \cdot \frac{1}{x} \qquad y = 10^{-x} \qquad y = (\frac{1}{10})^x \qquad y = \frac{1}{x^{10}}$$

Now you may wish to return to the initial "Think About This Situation" questions for Lesson 2. Students should recognize that an inverse power model best represents the situation since there seems to be no *y*-intercept. Challenge students to find an equation to fit this graph. (There is no scale on the graph, and we only see one quadrant, so students should ask about these missing pieces of information. They will have to make some assumptions. There can be no definitely correct answer, just some appropriate suggestions.)

> **Notes continued from page T264**

2. a. ■ The astronaut's weight is about 52.4 kg.
   ■ The height at which an astronaut would weigh half of his or her earth weight is about 2651 km.
   ■ The height at which an astronaut would weigh one-tenth of his or her earth weight is about 13,839 km.
   b. As the height increases the astronaut's weight decreases at a decreasing rate.

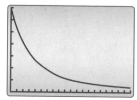
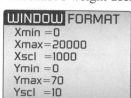

```
WINDOW FORMAT
Xmin =0
Xmax=20000
Xscl =1000
Ymin =0
Ymax=70
Yscl =10
```

> **Notes continued from page T265**

LAUNCH full-class discussion

The classic example of using quadratic functions is to describe projectile motion subject to initial velocity and acceleration due to gravity. Students will have seen several other examples of this kind of function in earlier work. The basketball example used in the lesson introduction is intended primarily as a reminder and an opportunity to check on prior knowledge that may or may not have been retained.

Before assigning the "Think About This Situation" questions for small-group discussion, you might want to discuss the lesson in the "Patterns of Change" unit in Course 1 where students investigated how the velocity of a baseball changed over time, and how the height changed over time. (See Investigation 1 of Lesson 4 in that unit). A softball is a good prop for getting attention in this discussion, and for focusing students on ideas they already have investigated in math class, and are very familiar with outside of math class. The conversation might go like this:

Page T265 Teaching Notes continued on next page

Teaching Notes *continued*

Notes continued
from page T265

When I throw the ball up does the velocity increase or decrease? (Some students will say that it decreases until it becomes zero, and then increases again. Others will remember that the velocity on the way down is negative, so the velocity decreases continuously.) If the velocity does not stay the same, what does that mean about how the height is changing? (The height increases quickly to start with and then less quickly, and then decreases.) Would the graph of height vs. time be linear? (No, height does not grow at a constant rate.)

Next you are going to investigate quadratic models, like $h = -16t^2 + 40t + 6$. How do you know that this is not linear? Not exponential? So what part of the equation do you think makes this "quadratic"? As you investigate this kind of relation you are going to find out about the shape of the graph, the pattern in the table, and where some important points occur.

Think About This Situation

See Teaching Master 93.

As with previous "Think About This Situation" items, the goal of the first example is to launch the lesson, to raise issues, and to stimulate student thinking—not to examine carefully all ramifications of the question. We suggest that after presenting the situation and asking students for their initial ideas about the shape of the (*time, height*) graph, you let groups work for at most 10 minutes on questions b and c to see what instincts they have on how to answer those questions with their graphing calculators or computer software. If many are able to answer the questions, then the transition to subsequent work simply would be that the goal is exploring further situations with the same type of mathematics; if many are stumped, the goal is to explore this new kind of relation so that they will learn how to deal with it.

a You would expect a U-shaped graph that opens downward; the *y*-intercept will be 6 (height of release). It is common for students to get a correct answer by incorrectly thinking about the shape of the ball's path, rather than the (*time, height*) graph. It would be helpful to ask questions of students to determine, for yourself, whether they are thinking about the path of the ball or the (*time, height*) graph. While discussing the "Checkpoint" questions for Investigation 1, you may wish to come back to clarify this common misconception for closure on this idea.

b You could use the table or graph to find *t* when *h* is 10. The ball will be at a height of 10 feet on two occasions: $t \approx 0.104$ seconds and $t \approx 2.396$ seconds.

c The ball will hit the floor approximately 2.64 seconds after release. On the table or graph, this is when the height *h* is 0.

Unit 4

Teaching Notes *continued*

**Notes continued
from page T270**

c The differences between consecutive y values are the same in the tables of values for the three models. Each value in the table for $y = 4.9x^2$ is exactly 10 less than that for $y = 10 - 4.9x^2$. None of the four tables of values show a constant rate of change.

   The tables of values for $y = -4.9x^2$ and $y = -4.9x^2 + 4x + 3$ are similar in that they both show varying rates of change. However, the differences between consecutive y values are not the same for the two models.

d ■ If the coefficient on the squared term is negative, the values increase then decrease rather than decrease then increase.

   ■ If the equation is of the form $y = -4.9x^2 + c$ the constant term $c > 0$ raises the graph of $y = -4.9x^2$ by c units and also raises the table values c units.

   ■ The linear term bx, when $b > 0$, changes the tables and graph of $y = -4.9x^2$ by lowering the y values when $x < 0$ and raising the y values when $x > 0$. The original rule $y = -4.9x^2$ and any variations of the form $y = bx - 4.9x^2$ all contain the origin. Generally, the new graph seems raised and moved to the right. The y-intercept is the origin for all variations. (If students decide to investigate the case when $b < 0$, they should find that the new graph generally seems raised and moved to the left.)

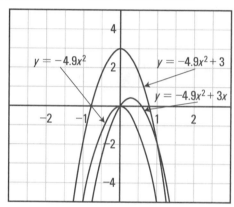

   ■ When both a constant term and linear term are added to $y = -4.9x^2$, all the effects described above occur.

Teaching Notes *continued*

Notes continued from page T274

Another way to think about the full quadratic model is to look at it as the sum of a power model and a linear model. The graph of $(ax^2) + (bx + c)$ will always lie above the line $y = bx + c$ when a is positive and below that line when a is negative (except for the point of tangency which always turns out to be the y-intercept). For example, consider $y = 2x^2 + 3x + 1$ and $y = -2x^2 + 3x + 1$. Including the component power and linear models, the graphs look like this:

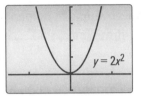
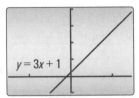
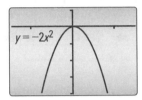
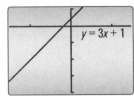

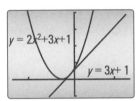
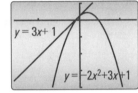

You probably will need to help students talk about the situation in simple and informal language, but it seems useful to press for some intuition about the cause for graphs turning up or down. Students may not need to record all the graphs and tables in these experiments in order to understand the concepts. Tables and graphs are provided here for your information, however.

Experiment 1

You probably will need to press students in their groups to try a wide variety of examples (they will be inclined to try only a few special cases) and then to try to organize their observations. This first exploration is intentionally quite open (to be followed by other, more guided work). If students do not notice patterns because of their methods of searching, encourage them to move on to Experiments 2 and 3. At the "Checkpoint" for this investigation you could come back to Experiment 1 and ask them to think again about ways to organize a search for patterns.

1. **a.** Students might have quite a variety of observations. They should discover at least that all graphs are U-shaped symmetric curves, opening up or down depending on the sign of a. The tables will have similar up and down symmetric patterns.

    b. Patterns that students might observe would relate
    - the sign of a to upward or downward opening of the graph
    - the value of a to the steepness (rate of change) of the curve
    - c to the y-intercept
    - b to a left or right shift of the symmetry of the y-axis.

    c. The graphs and tables of the full quadratics will have the same basic symmetric up then down (or down then up) shape of the power models $y = ax^2$.

Unit 4

Notes continued
from page T280

EXPLORE small-group investigation

INVESTIGATION 5 How Many Solutions Are Possible?

As the student text suggests, it is useful to have some knowledge of what answers might be reasonable before beginning a technology-based search for solutions of any equation or inequality. In the case of quadratics, for example, it helps to know that one can get 0, 1, or 2 distinct solutions for any quadratic equation. The actual result in any specific case

$$ax^2 + bx + c = d$$

depends on the number of intersections of the graphs of $y = ax^2 + bx + c$ and $y = d$. The goal of this investigation is to have students discover this important property of quadratic equations and make the connection to graphs of quadratic relations.

Teaching Notes *continued*

Notes continued
from page T283

2. a. $-75(3)^2 + 600(3) = \$1125$

b. ■ $1125 = -75p^2 + 600p$

The table and the graph both indicate that ticket prices of \$3 or \$5 will give a profit of \$1125. Check this by substituting these values into the quadratic model.

$-75(3)^2 + 600(3) = 1125$, therefore 3 is a solution.

$-75(5)^2 + 600(5) = 1125$, therefore 5 is a solution.

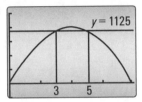

■ $900 = -75p^2 + 600p$

As you can see in both the table and the graph, the roots are \$2 and \$6. This is easy to check by simply replacing p with 2 and 6 to verify that the equation is satisfied.

$-75(2)^2 + 600(2) = 900$, therefore 2 is a solution.

$-75(6)^2 + 600(6) = 900$, therefore 6 is a solution.

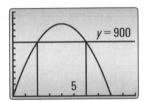

■ $970 = -75p^2 + 600p$

The table and the graph both show that prices of approximately \$2.25 and \$5.75 will yield a profit of \$970. You can verify this by substituting these values into the original equation.

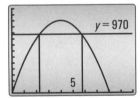

$-75(2.25)^2 + 600(2.25) \approx 970$

$-75(5.75)^2 + 600(5.75) \approx 970$

The right-hand side of both equations is actually equal to 970.3125, but this is close enough since we must determine the price to only two decimal places.

c. The maximum income of \$1200 is obtained when the price is \$4.00. You can answer this question using just the graph or just the table. Here, a combination was used. First, the graph was used to determine x values that are close to giving the maximum profit, and then the table was used to determine a more accurate figure.

Unit 4

Teaching Notes continued

Notes continued
from page T285 ▶

1. **b.** $x = 4.791$ or $x = 0.209$

There are two solutions because the line $y = 5$ intersects the curve twice.

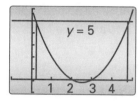

X	Y₁	
4.79	4.9941	
4.791	4.9987	
4.792	5.0033	
4.793	5.0078	
4.794	5.0124	
4.795	5.017	
4.796	5.0216	

Y₁ ◼ X²−5X+6

X	Y₁	
.207	5.0078	
.208	5.0033	
.209	4.9987	
.21	4.9941	
.211	4.9895	
.212	4.9849	
.213	4.9804	

Y₁ ◼ X²−5X+6

c. No (real) solutions

There are no solutions, as we can see by looking at the graph or the table.

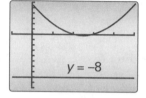

X	Y₁	
0	6	
1	2	
2	0	
3	0	
4	2	
5	6	
6	12	

Y₁ ◼ X²−5X+6

d. $x = \pm\sqrt{8} \approx \pm 2.83$

Students may look at the graph to see that there are two solutions and then choose to solve this equation symbolically:

$$4x^2 + 13 = 45$$
$$4x^2 = 32$$
$$x^2 = 8$$
$$x = \pm\sqrt{8}$$

They also could solve using either the graph or table of values.

e. $x = 4$ or $x = -0.5$

The two solutions can be seen in the graph and in the table of values.

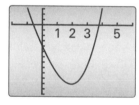

X	Y₁	
-1	5	
0	-4	
1	-9	
2	-10	
3	-2	
4	0	
5	11	

Y₁ ◼ 2X²−7X−4

X	Y₁	
-1	5	
-.5	0	
0	-4	
.5	-7	
1	-9	
1.5	-10	
2	-10	

Y₁ ◼ 2X²−7X−4

f. $2x^2 - 7x - 4 = -25$

There are no (real) solutions as we can see by looking at the graph. The curve $y = 2x^2 - 7x - 4$ never intersects the line $y = -25$.

2. **a.** Any equation where $y > -0.25$. Sample: $1 = x^2 - 3x + 2$

b. $-0.25 = x^2 - 3x + 2$

c. Any equation where $y < -0.25$. Sample: $-1 = x^2 - 3x + 2$

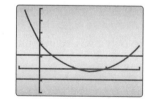

X	Y₁	
0	2	
.5	.75	
1	0	
1.5	-.25	
2	0	
2.5	.75	
3	2	

Y₁ ◼ X²−3X+2

Unit 4

Teaching Notes *continued*

Notes continued
from page T286

Reflecting

1. **a.** Responses will vary.

   For example: First, decide what type of equation it is. If the equation is linear, it might be easy to solve by simple reasoning and symbol manipulation. For the other models, using a graph or a table, or a combination of the graph and the table, might work well.

   b. Responses will vary.

Method	Pros	Cons
Algebraic	If the equation is simple, this is an easy way to solve the problem. You can get an exact answer even if it is a difficult fraction or a radical.	For equations that are not first degree (linear), this method can be difficult, if not impossible.
Graphical	With the calculator or computer, this gives a quick picture of the situation. Cases where there are no roots are easy to see using a graph.	Sometimes it is difficult to set an appropriate window. Also, it is difficult to get an exact answer sometimes because of the way the pixels are read. And finally, zooming in repeatedly sometimes takes more time than using a table.
Using a Table	You know how accurate your answer is because you determine the increment size. The calculator or computer makes this solution method an extremely easy one to use.	You have to have some idea of where a root will be in order to use the table. As with the graphical method, answers are often only approximations.

Notes continued
from page T288

4. **a.** ■ The initial height is always the constant term in the quadratic model.
   ■ The initial speed is the coefficient of the linear term x in the quadratic model.

   b. ■ $h = -4.9t^2 + 32t + 1.5$
   ■ The height will be zero after about 6.6 seconds. Realistically, the catcher will have less time than 6.6 seconds to catch the ball. As the question is stated, the height of the catcher (which isn't given) really should be considered as well. A catcher 1.8 meters tall would have about 6.5 seconds to get under the ball.

Unit 4

Teaching Notes continued

Notes continued from page T289

LAUNCH full-class discussion

Think About This Situation

See Teaching Master 99.

These questions revive connections to geometric ideas that students first met in the Course 1 unit, "Patterns in Space and Visualization". If you have access to some of the models that students made, or have the time to construct a simple prism from straws and pipe cleaners, it would help students to recall their exploration of rigid figures and diagonals. The discussion of the "Think About This Situation" questions should be done very briefly in a large group setting, to set the stage for a more elaborate connection between the Pythagorean Theorem and an exploration of radical expressions.

ⓐ Essentially, every set of parallel bars must have a diagonal brace to stabilize the structure. You might ask the students why the cross braces are needed if the students do not mention stabilizing the structure.

ⓑ In "Patterns in Space and Visualization" students studied rigidity of space-shapes and discovered that the triangle is a rigid plane figure. The shape of a triangle cannot be altered because it is determined by the lengths of the three sides. In order to make a space-shape rigid, the faces need to be triangulated. The geometric principle that models rigidity of any triangular structure is the fact that lengths of three sides uniquely determine the shape of a triangle. In the language of congruence, if three sides of one triangle are congruent respectively to three sides of another triangle, the two figures must be congruent; that is, the corresponding angles must be congruent also.

ⓒ Students should suggest using the Pythagorean Theorem. If the students need prompting, you might ask them what type of angles they see.

Notes continued from page T317

ⓒ ■ For a cube with a specific edge length, what is the volume? For a given face area, what is the edge length?

■ If you travel at x miles per hour, how long will the trip take? If you are x distance from a light source, what is the intensity? For a string of length x, how many vibrations per second are there?

■ What is the maximum ball height? When will the ball hit the ground? What is the maximum profit? What is the break-even-point? If you are traveling at 60 miles per hour, what is your stopping distance? At what speed will you get optimal miles per gallon?

■ What is the length of the diagonal of a given rectangle?

ⓓ ■ By using the table or the graph to find the x value for the particular y value requested

■ By substituting the solution back into the equation

■ Quadratic models have at most two solutions. This is shown in the graph by the intersection of a horizontal line and the quadratic: there are at most two intersection points. At the maximum or minimum point there is one solution. Above or below the graph, there are no (real) solutions.

Unit 4

Index of Mathematical Topics

Index of Mathematical Topics

Index of Contexts

Photo Credits for the Pupil Edition

Unit Opener, 1, Bill Hogan/*Chicago Tribune*; 2, Bob Fila/*Chicago Tribune*; 5, Special thanks to Leslie Grasa and DeWayne Carver; 6, Richard A. Cooke III/Tony Stone Images; 7, AP/Wide World Photos; 9, AP/Wide World Photos; 11, Mark Preston; 13, UPI/Corbis-Bettmann; 16, David Young-Wolff/Tony Stone Images; 17, DM Tech America, 12850 Moore St., Cerritos, CA 90703, (800) 260-2522; 18, Steven Peters/Tony Stone Images; 22, Jack Demuth; 24, Zoological Society of San Diego; 26, Michael LeRoy/Tony Stone Images; 30, ETHS Yearbook Staff; 31, Lori Adamski Peek/Tony Stone Images; 35, Jack Demuth; 36 (left top), UPI/Corbis-Bettmann; 36 (left middle), H.S. Barsam; 36 (left bottom), Chicago Natural History Museum; 38, Philip H. Condit II/Tony Stone Images; 40, Frank Herholdt/Tony Stone Images; 44, Texas Instruments Incorporated, Dallas, Texas; 46, Lee Olsen/*Chicago Tribune*; 47, David R. Frazier/Tony Stone Images; 48, Luigi Mendocino/*Chicago Tribune*; 53, Texas Instruments Incorporated, Dallas, Texas; 54, Chris Walker/*Chicago Tribune*; 56, Walter Kale/*Chicago Tribune*; 57, Luigi Mendocino/*Chicago Tribune*; 59, Jack Demuth; 60, Jack Demuth; 63, Robert Frerck/Tony Stone Images; 67, David Young-Wolff/Tony Stone Images; 71, *Chicago Tribune*; 75, Caroline Wood/Tony Stone Images; Unit Opener, 79, Kevin Horan/Tony Stone Images; 89, Texas Instruments Incorporated, Dallas, Texas; 92, Keith Wood/Tony Stone Images; 95, Natural Ocean Survey; 96, Courtesy of Texas Instruments; 99, Texas Instruments Incorporated, Dallas, Texas; 103, Gerald West/*Chicago Tribune*; 111, Walter Neal/*Chicago Tribune*; 130, Chelsea Brown; 132, © Eastman Kodak Company. Reprinted by permission.; 133, Ken Walczak/Jack Demuth; 142, Dan Casper/*Chicago Tribune*; 145 (left top), Charles Osgood/*Chicago Tribune*; 145 (middle), John Bartley/*Chicago Tribune*; 159, Ovie Carter/*Chicago Tribune*; 165, Pieter Tans; Unit Opener, 169, Val Mazzenga/*Chicago Tribune*; 171 (left bottom), Lawrence Migdale/Tony Stone Images; 172, UPI/Corbis-Bettmann; 173, Keystone Press Agency Inc.; 182, Robert E. Daemmrich/Tony Stone Images; 183, Jack Demuth; 186, Carl Wagner/*Chicago Tribune*; 188, Brown Brothers; 193, Jack Demuth; 195, Jack Demuth; 198, Dan Casper/*Chicago Tribune*; 200, Stuart Westmorland/Tony Stone Images; 203, Hiroyuki Matsumoto/Tony Stone Images; 206, Jack Demuth; 207, Edward Contreras/*Chicago Tribune*; 209, Reuters/Corbis-Bettmann; 215, Michael Budrys/*Chicago Tribune*; 217, Don Smerzer/Tony Stone Images; 219, Andy Sacks/Tony Stone Images; 222, Mike Fisher/*Chicago Tribune*; 224, Christine Longcore; 228, Nancy Stone/*Chicago Tribune*; 231, Jack Demuth; Unit Opener, 233, Peter Pearson/Tony Stone Images; 234, Ed Burke; 242, UPI/Corbis-Bettmann; 243, Science Photo Library; 247, Chuck Osgood/*Chicago Tribune*; 249, © Mark E. Gibson; 250, Michael Fryer/*Chicago Tribune*; 252, Chuck Osgood/*Chicago Tribune*; 256, Anthony Meshkinyar/Tony Stone Images; 259, Steve Weber/Tony Stone Images; 264, NASA; 266, Ed Feeney/*Chicago Tribune*; 270, Ed Wagner/*Chicago Tribune*; 272, Marc PoKempner/Tony Stone Images; 279, *Chicago Tribune*; 282, John Bartley/*Chicago Tribune*; 283, ETHS Yearbook Staff; 284, © Carol Rosegg; 285, Ron Bailey/*Chicago Tribune*; 288, AP/Wide World Photos; 289, Rene Sheret/Tony Stone Images; 294 (left top), M. Freeman/West Stock; (right top), Dean Berry/ West Stock; (left middle), Mellott/West Stock; (right middle), Phil Schermeister/Tony Stone Images; (left bottom), Jean-Paul Manceau/Tony Stone Images; (right bottom), Chris Butler/Science Photo Library; 299, Mike Budrys/*Chicago Tribune*; 305, Erwan Quemere/Tony Stone Images; 307, A.B. Dowsett/Science Photo Library; 308, John Sanford/Science Photo Library; 311, B. Drake/West Stock; 313, Hung T. Vu/*Chicago Tribune*; 315, Honda North America, Inc.; 316, John Bartley/*Chicago Tribune*